Politics, Society and Christianity in Vichy France

Berg French Studies

General Editor: John E. Flower

Politics, Society and Christianity in Vichy France

W. D. Halls

BERG
Oxford/Providence, USA

First published in 1995 by
Berg Publishers
Editorial offices:
150 Cowley Road, Oxford, OX4 1JJ, UK
221 Waterman Street, Providence, RI 02906, USA

© W. D. Halls 1995

Library of Congress Cataloging-in-Publication Data
A catalogue record for this book is available from the Library of Congress.

British Library Cataloguing in Publication Data
A catalogue record for this book is available from the British Library.

ISBN 1 85973 071 X (Cloth)
ISBN 1 85973 081 7 (Paper)

Printed in the United Kingdom by W B C Bookbinders, Mid-Glamorgan

Contents

Preface

Fifty years after the ending of the German occupation of France the years 1940–44 continue to absorb the attention not only of historians, but also of the French public as a whole. What has been termed the 'Vichy syndrome' has been reflected in the many thousands of books and articles to which this black period in the history of France has given rise. It has been fuelled by a series of fresh revelations that have come to light, as archives have gradually yielded up their secrets and criminals and suspects such as Klaus Barbie, 'the butcher of Lyons', and Touvier (who, it is alleged, was at one stage protected by high-ranking ecclesiastics), have been caught and arraigned.

The reasons for this continuing interest in the period are many and varied. Perhaps one of the most signficant is the fact that it was the time when France, under a leader once lauded as the saviour of the Republic, Marshal Pétain, came nearest to lapsing into fascism. Indeed, one of the central themes of this book is that Christians, sometimes at odds with their Church, sometimes remaining steadfastly within the fold, were, perhaps unwittingly, one of the most important interest groups in combatting totalitarian tendencies, either in their daily dealings with the regime, in their writings, both clandestine and public, or, in the last resort, with their spiritual or armed resistance. The Churches, both Catholic and Protestant, were the sole institutions that emerged after the French collapse in 1940 if not unscathed, at least still able to function. The Germans feared they might become a bastion of resistance — the 'soutanes noires' were after all part of a world-wide organisation much more venerable and potentially even more numerous and powerful than the Third Reich. They were guilty of a conspiracy – not, however, as were the Nazis, to conquer the world, but to convert it, beginning with France. The Vichy regime, for its part, pinned its hopes on the Church in order to assist in bringing about 'national revival'. Neither fears nor hopes became reality.

There is no one up-to-date work, in French or English, devoted exclusively to an overall conspectus of French Christians during this period. This book essentially traces the stormy history of Catholics and Protestants from about 1938 onwards, first setting Christianity in its pre-war context, and then dealing with the immediate collapse of France in

1940. The Church's backing of Pétain, followed by a withdrawal from overcommitment to the new regime, is described, whilst indicating nevertheless the tangible advantages it derived from it. The trauma of the treatment of the Jews, which acted upon the Church as a catalyst, is then assessed in detail, as representing a turning-point in Christian attitudes. A section on 'friends and foes', showing how Christians related to the Allies, the Germans, the Resistance and the Vatican, leads on to a discussion of social matters of perennial concern to the Church: the world of work, the family, the destiny of young people, and youth movements. [Education has been omitted from this work; it was studied in my *The Youth of Vichy France*, (Oxford, 1981)]. A final section on the Liberation outlines the fate of those few Christians who actively collaborated with the enemy, and the indictment drawn up against the episcopacy, not for collaborating , but for the aid and comfort the Church gave, as did the majority of the French people initially, to a regime that was fatally flawed from the outset.

Some of the material used in this book has appeared in different and abridged form in short papers contributed to the following books: R. Kedward and R. Austin (eds), *Vichy France and the Resistance. Culture and Ideology*, London, 1985; G. Hirschfeld and P. Marsh (eds), *Collaboration in France. Politics and Culture during the Nazi Occupation, 1940–1944*, Oxford, 1989 (German translation: *Kollaboration in Frankreich*, Frankfurt, 1991).

I should perhaps declare my own religious allegiance: I am a Christian and a Protestant. This may or may not be an advantage in dealing with what is primarily a history concerning Catholics.

It is a source of regret that, despite the wealth of information that has come to light over the past decade, it was not yet possible to consult fully French diocesan archives, which remain closed to most historians.

However, I would like to acknowledge the great debt that I owe to many people, priests, pastors and laity, people of all faiths and of none, as well as to numerous institutions. Madame Chantal Tourtier-Bonazzi, Director of the Section Contemporaine of the Archives Nationales, Paris, was kindness itself: she was instrumental in throwing open to me many 'closed' archives. Monsieur le Chanoine Desreumaux, Chancellor and Archivist of the Diocese of Lille, where are deposited the archives of the Assembly of Cardinals and Archbishops, as well as many other files of more than local interest, performed a similar function with never-failing courtesy. Through the intervention of André Louf, Père Abbé de Sainte-Marie-du-Mont, Bailleul, I was able to interview Abbé Maurice Liénart, the nephew of Cardinal Liénart, probably the greatest French churchman of the period. Père Liénart kindly provided valuable background information. I am grateful to Dr Anne-Marie Duquesne of Lille, a lifelong family friend, for feeding me up-to-date information, and to the stalwarts of the Club-Compagnons, the 'anciens' of the Compagnons de France, whose hospitality I enjoyed and for whose firsthand knowledge of the period I am greatly indebted.

I also owe much to the staffs of the Archives de France, not only in Paris, but also in various 'départements'; the Centre de Documentation Juive Contemporaine; the Centre Protestant d'Etudes et de Documentation; the Public Record Office; the Bibliothèque Nationale; the Foreign and Commonwealth Office Library, to whose archives I had partial access; the library of St Antony's College, as well as the Bodleian and the Taylorian Institution libraries, in Oxford; and many municipal libraries in France (an invaluable source for local newspapers of the period). I am particularly grateful to those numerous Frenchmen, many of whom lived through the period, who generously gave of their time to assist me. I owe a special debt to my son Michael, who helped in the technical production of the book.

Above all, however, I would like to thank Pamela, my wife, for her constant encouragement and never-ending patience.

Many people and institutions have thus helped to improve this work; its errors, however, remain my own.

Oxford
1995   W. D. Halls

List of Abbreviations

ACA	Assemblée des Cardinaux et Archevêques
ACJF	Action Catholique de la Jeunesse française
Actes: Biviers	*Actes du Colloque de Biviers, 1987* (Grenoble, 1987)
*Actes:*Grenoble	*Actes du Colloque de Grenoble,1976* (Lyons, 1978)
Actes: Lille	*Actes du Colloque de Lille,1977* (Lille, 1978)
Actes: Lyons	*Actes du Colloque de Lyon, 1978* (Lyons, 1982)
AD	Archives départementales
A Dio	Archives diocésaines
AJ	Auberges de Jeunesse
AN	Archives nationales, Paris
APEL	Association des Parents de l'Enseignement Libre
BCRA	Bureau Central de Renseignements et d'Action
BSHPF	Bulletin de la Société d'Histoire du Protestantisme français
Cahiers	*Cahiers et Courriers du Témoignage Chrétien, 1941-1944* (Paris, 1980)
CDJC	Centre de Documentation juive contemporaine
CFTC	Confédération Française des Travailleurs chrétiens
CGQJ	Commissariat/Commisssaire général aux Questions juives
CGT	Confédération générale du Travail
CGTU	Confédération générale du Travail unifiée
CIMADE	Comité Inter-Mouvements auprès d'Evacués
CNEL	Comité National de l'Enseignement libre
COIC	Comité d'Organisation de l'Industrie cinématographique
Comte,	*Thesis:* B. Comte 'L'Ecole nationale des cadres d'Uriage (1940-1942)', doctoral thesis, University of Lyons II, 1990.
Courriers	See *Cahiers*
DRAC	Droits des Religieux Anciens Combattants
FCO	Foreign and Commonwealth Office, London
FFACE	Fédération française des associations chrétiennes d'étudiants
FFI	Forces françaises de l'Intérieur

FTP	Francs-Tireurs et Partisans
FNC	Fédération nationale catholique
FUJP	Forces unies de la Jeunesse patriote
IHTP	Institut d'Histoire du Temps Présent, Paris
JAC	Jeunesse agricole chrétienne
JCC	Jeunes Chrétiens Combattants
JEC	Jeunesse étudiante chrétienne (female branch: JECF)
JIC	Jeunesse indépendante chrétienne
JMC	Jeunesse maritime chrétienne
JOC	Jeunesse ouvrière chrétienne
LAC	Ligue agricole chrétienne
LFC	Légion française des Combattants
LOC	Ligue ouvrière chrétienne
LVF	Légion des Volontaires français
MPF	Mouvement populaire des Familles
MRP	Mouvement Républicain Populaire
MUR	Mouvements unis de la Résistance
NEF	Nouvelles Equipes françaises
OCM	Organisation civile et militaire
PDP	Parti démocrate populaire
PPF	Parti populaire français
PQJ	Police des Questions juives
PSF	Parti social français
PRO	Public Records Office, London
RHDGM	Revue d'histoire de la deuxième Guerre mondiale
RNP	Rassemblement National Populaire
SD	Sicherheitspolizei
SGJ	Secrétariat Général à la Jeunesse
SiPo	Sicherheitspolizei
SS	Schutzstaffel
STO	Service du Travail obligatoire
UGIF	Union Générale des Israélites de France
ZO	Zone occupée
ZNO	Zone non-occupée

PART I

CHRISTIANITY IN CRISIS

–1–

Introductory

In the hot, early summer of 1940, within six weeks the German armies had overrun most of France. On 17 June the new head of the French government, Marshal Pétain, the hero of Verdun, asked for an armistice. By 25 June this had come into force. France was divided into two main zones, the one occupied by the Germans and centred on Paris, and the other, unoccupied, where nominally the French writ still ran freely, and which eventually centred on Vichy. On 10 July, meeting in the gaming casinos of the spa, the National Assembly entrusted the aged soldier with full powers to govern until he had drawn up a new constitution. The Third Republic was presumed dead, and only some eighty deputies mourned its passing.

Yet when Philippe Pétain, using the royal plural in a grandiloquent gesture and exercising prerogatives surpassing even those of Louis XIV, proclaimed on 11 July his supremacy as Head of the French State, nothing immediately changed. Many of the same personalities as before continued in public life, although others advocating more authoritarian policies were already waiting in the wings. What is remarkable is just how much of the old order was initially carried over into the new. Faces, priorities and attitudes changed only imperceptibly. Of no aspect of national life was this more true than in the religious domain.

In view of the prominent role to be played by both Catholics and, to a lesser extent, Protestants under the new regime, how strong in 1940 was Christian culture? Where was the Christian faith geographically concentrated? How intensely was religion practised? What charisma did Christian leaders possess? Which ecclesiastical structures regulated the Church? What was its mission? These are key questions in determining the influence that the Church was able to exert upon the Vichy regime and the Germans.

Where lay the bastions of Christianity in 1940? Detailed statistics are lacking but according to Boulard, a pioneer in the sociology of religion, studying religious 'density' slightly later, in the 1950s,[1] geographically the Catholics were most solidly implanted in Alsace-Lorraine, Franche-

Comté and Savoy, the area to the south-east of the Massif Central, the Breton peninsula and French Flanders. Lyons and its hinterland were particularly areas of piety, as befitted the historical capital of French catholicism — this despite the fact that the city was also a hotbed of freemasonry. Vallat, the Catholic politician, delineated an area where at least 30 per cent, and in the majority of cases, 50, per cent, of parents sent their children to the Catholic primary school,[2] identifying especially twelve rural departments: Vendée, Maine-et-Loire, Loire-Atlantique (then Loire-Inférieure), Morbihan, Ille-et-Vilaine, Finistère, Côtes du Nord, Mayenne, Ardèche, Haute-Loire, Lozère, and Aveyron — all areas, incidentally, that had opposed the French Revolution.

Protestantism, although numerically very inferior to catholicism, was strongest in Alsace-Lorraine, and in a broad swathe of territory extending from the Haute-Loire to the Hautes-Alpes, particularly in Drôme and Ardèche, where it included 20 per cent of Calvinists.[3] Whether one was Catholic or Protestant frequently determined political leanings, which meant, as will be seen, that, with the exception of a section of the upper bourgeoisie, most members of the Reformed Church cooled more rapidly in their ardour for the Vichy regime. In a few localities such as Le Chambon-sur-Lignon Protestants numbered nine-tenths of the population, although in Brittany, the centre, and parts of eastern France they comprised less than two in 1,000.[4] Followers of the Augsburg Confession, concentrated in the three departments of Alsace-Lorraine, represented 30 per cent of all French Protestants. Strasbourg, with 50,000 members, was the most Protestant city of France.[5] But Alsace and much of Lorraine were annexed to the Reich after the armistice. Protestants in the unoccupied zone felt intense interest in the fate of their co-religionists, evacuated from Eastern France to Clermont-Ferrand or sprinkled about the Limousin and Périgord, as well as the majority, who had not fled, but were now ruled as part of the Reich.

However, the inhabitants of most of France were indifferent to religion, and certain districts, designated as 'pagan' or 'semi-pagan', were even described during the war as 'missionary territory' ('pays de mission'). These were: Champagne, the areas round Sens (Le Senonais), Limoges (Le Limousin), Chartres [sic] (Le Chartrain), Dreux (Le Drouais), and Aunis.

Another index of Christianity, religious observance, was very variable. In cities such as Paris, Lyons, Lille, and Nîmes (for Protestantism), where the principal religious authorities were located, Christianity outwardly maintained a high profile. Gabriel Le Bras, another early researcher of the sociology of religion, in a work published during the war, nevertheless noted, 'None of our important cities contains a majority of the faithful.'[6] Densely populated areas such as the Paris 'cités ouvrières' of Belleville, Ménilmontant and Montrouge, which housed the poorer workers, estimated in 1943 to number eight millions,[7] even fell into the 'near-pagan' category. In Montreuil, another poor district of Paris, whose population comprised some 78,000 souls, only 2,112 (under 3 per cent) regularly attended Sunday mass. In the Faubourg St-Antoine, 304 youngsters, out of a parish of 35,000 souls, joined in the church's youth activities.[8] The popular working-class view was that church attendance was for the bourgeoisie — although the poor living in the Nord department remained moderately religious. Despite the rise of 'social catholicism' to champion their cause, the industrial proletariat did not forget that the Church had once urged them to accept long working hours and harsh conditions, whereas the revolutionary Left had postulated the alternative of the class struggle in order to achieve a better future. If 80 per cent of Frenchmen in 1940 were still nominally Catholic, perhaps only 30 per cent practised their religion.

That lip-service was still paid to the Christian faith is, however, clear from various statistics. In Paris between 1930 and 1943 80 per cent of infants were baptised, and between 1937 and 1941 43 per cent of all marriages took place in church. Figures for such 'rites de passage' are even more impressive for Marseilles: by 1945, 90 per cent of infants were baptised, and 72 per cent of couples were wed in church.[9] However, contradictory figures can also be cited. In the spring of 1944 a survey of sixty-three parishes, spread out over twenty-five departments, revealed that only thirty-seven could be classified as Christian; of the rest, nineteen fell into the 'indifferent' and seven into the 'near-pagan' category. Indeed in one rural community of 900 inhabitants it was found that 40 per cent of children were not baptised, two-thirds did not attend catechism classes, and among adults, only one-third contracted a Christian marriage.[10] In fact, France in 1940 was a country where perhaps only one in four regularly attended Sunday mass and less than one in three still made their Easter communion. For example, in the Arras diocese the proportion of those attending church at Easter (32 per cent) remained fairly static from 1930 up to the early 1960s,[11] although numbers of both yearly and weekly communicants did rise during the war. By contrast, in the irreligious Limousin area, figures for Easter communicants were much lower:

Limoges and surrounding districts:	13 per cent
Haute-Vienne:	15 per cent
Fifteen towns:	18 per cent
Forty-one rural communes:	11 per cent.[12]

It was this state of affairs that the Church sought to remedy; the new regime, it believed, would help to fulfil its dream of re-Christianising France. The indications are that it had a little, limited success. For example, in the country as a whole one rather sombre criterion, the percentage of religious, in contrast to civil, burials, rose significantly:

Religious and civil burials 1940 and 1945 (per cent)

Year	Civil	Catholic	Protestant	Jewish	Total religious
1940	32	64	0.7	2.7	67.40
1945	20	76	1.2	1.50	78.70

(The virtual halving of the number of Jewish burials is clearly the consequence of the wholesale deportations of Jews.[13])

Nevertheless after the war, according to 1947 figures, it was estimated that, although 91 per cent of the population had been baptised (Paris and suburbs: 70 per cent), only 26 per cent attended Sunday mass regularly and only 31 per cent made their Easter communion. Thus any gains made since 1940 as regards religious practice appear quickly to have evaporated.[14]

For Protestants, figures are imprecise: according to one source, in 1928 they numbered about 633,000.[15] In 1953 the same source gives a total of 800,000. Another authority quotes a larger figure of about 900,000 for 1933. Whether numbers grew in the war is doubtful.[16]

From such isolated statistics, the exact status of religious belief before the war and in the early 1940s is clearly difficult to ascertain. Between the wars religion had certainly declined. Even in supposedly Christian parishes moral standards were not very high. In one such village in Savoy, from 1920 to 1944 the average number of 'forced' marriages (that is, those where a child was already expected) was 18 per cent; between 1934 and 1938 it rose to 28 per cent. Before the war 10.7 per cent of village children were born out of wedlock, a proportion that between 1939 and 1944 soared to 38 per cent.[17]

Such a decline in Christian-based morality, as well as in what might be termed religious observance and culture, was clearly a matter of concern to the Church. The necessary quality for a 'homogeneous' religious culture had been partly destroyed by the influx of foreigners — recent immigrants who had established themselves largely in the principal cities — by the depopulation of the countryside, and the inroads of industrial development, not to speak of such imponderables as the fierceness of the class struggle, the quarrel between clericals and anticlericals, or the far-reaching effects of population redistribution brought about by the First

World War.[18] The flight from the countryside had disoriented people: whereas their homes had once been clustered round the village church, when transplanted to the Paris suburbs they did not even know where their local place of worship was. Moreover, even in rural areas religious observance had become largely the affair of women and the young. The peasant might accompany his family as far as the church porch on Sunday mornings, but he then slipped away to drink in the village 'cabaret', itself a kind of 'counter-Church'. Indeed the cafe, the dance hall (a constant thorn in the side of the parish priest, requiring close surveillance of young people) and the smithy (until this began to decline in importance, as the use of horses became less common) were the three venues where male villagers, young and old, foregathered on the sabbath in a purely secular celebration.[19]

The seeping away of religious culture and morality in rural areas, where almost half the French still lived, was a sign of the times that traditionalists regretted. By 1938 the Jeunesse Agricole Chrétienne (JAC), the Catholic agricultural youth organisation, was struggling to maintain time-honoured 'Christian' customs such as the Yule log, the 'galette des rois' at Epiphany, or pancake-eating at Candlemas ('Mange des crêpes à la Chandeleur/ Si point ne veux tes blés charbonneux'). The 'return of the bells' from Rome at Easter, the midsummer bonfire on St John's day, the decorating of the graves of relatives (in northern France) at All Saints — all such commemorations were on the wane. At Corpus Christi the village maidens might still turn up for vespers but afterwards would bicycle off to keep some secret rendezvous.[20] In parishes characterised as indifferent to Christianity, the priest categorised them in two groups: the 'forward' ones that used make-up, and a minority that remained unadorned[21] and assiduous in Church attendance! As for the young men, they left the village for military service, proverbial for stimulating loose living, and were lost to religion for ever. The Church had also its natural enemies. The local primary school teacher, in cahoots with the local doctor and the chemist, would be at daggers drawn with the priest, who found an ally in the notary. In one Corrèze village in 1936 the 'instituteur' had even succeeded in persuading no less than thirty-six families to take out a subscription to *L'Humanité!*[22] As secretary to the mayor the schoolmaster was a force for 'laïcisme', a militant brand of secularism. The Church fought against his influence in small ways, even to the extent of encouraging the local patois, a move later backed by the Vichy regime: French was, after all, the language of the Revolution, which had brought the secular school to the village.

The professed breakdown of morality was of grave concern to the Church.[23] It pointed to the growth of 'unhealthy pleasures': 'nudisme intégral' [*sic*] on the beach; the dance hall, from where couples could repair to a private room; the cinema; pornographic literature; and periodicals that pandered to the worst taste (as exemplified allegedly in *Marie Claire* and *Notre Coeur*), despite exhortation from the pulpit to read 'la bonne presse'. There was also some truth in the charge that a clergy, old and enfeebled, unable to cope with the pace of modern life, ran a Church that was no longer 'up to it' — 'n'était plus dans le coup', as the saying went.

The exodus from the countryside greatly affected religious practice, and was linked with the breakup of a once stable society. The rural artisans — the basketmaker of the plain, the clogmaker in the mountainous areas, the weaver of the Lyonnais countryside, the cooper in the wine-growing areas — had all migrated to the town,[24] leaving only the peasant. The flight to an urban environment particularly affected the young. Sometimes, as in Brittany and Vendée, because of a surplus of peasant labour, the young men merely used their village as a dormitory, working and spending their leisure time in the nearby town.[25] Young women preferred the temptations of urban life to the trials of unremitting toil from dawn to dusk in the stable or the fields, with its meagre rewards.[26] The influx of foreigners — Poles in the North and West, Italians and Spaniards in the South — had contributed to the breaking of any national religious mould. In the late 1930s the bishops had noted with alarm these signs of disintegration, which impacted unfavourably upon religious life and practice. Only where the rural economy retained its traditional pattern, in remote, inaccessible areas, were the clergy still thick enough on the ground for the Church to retain its hold.

In town and country, therefore, the least well-off members of society were often alienated from Christianity. The urban lower middle classes were frequently religiously indifferent. Only the 'haute bourgeoisie' remained staunch supporters of the Church. 'Black France', as it was known, the France of believers, typically comprised the landowners of the West and the large-scale industrialists of the North.

This was the situation the Church faced in 1940. Who was to deal with it? In 1940 the Hierarchy was an ageing body of ecclesiastics. Of the four cardinals, Baudrillart, rector of the Paris Institut Catholique, was eighty-one, Suhard, archbishop of Paris, sixty-six, Gerlier, archbishop of Lyons, sixty, and Liénart, bishop of Lille, fifty-six. Among the archbishops Mgr Feltin of Bordeaux was fifty-seven, Mgr Roques, then of Aix-en-Provence, was sixty-one. Mgr Saliège had been Archbishop of Toulouse since 1928. In 1942 eighty-two out of eighty-seven metropolitan bishops were born between 1858 and 1896, and all had been elevated to a see (not necessarily the one they occupied in 1940) between 1910 and 1942. The oldest bishop, Mgr Lecœur of St-Flour, was ninety-two and the majority were over sixty. Assuming an age of about twenty-four at ordination, just under half had become priests by the turn of the century and had thus lived through the bitterness of the Separation of Church and State. This was not an ecclesiastical gerontocracy, but was nearer the age of Marshal Pétain, who was in his eighties when he assumed power. The generations almost coincided in age and in experience.

In 1940 many of the lower clergy were also past their prime. In twenty-four dioceses at least 40 per cent of priests were over sixty. In forty-seven rural dioceses priests over that age ranged from 22 per cent of the total (Besançon) to 62 per cent (Auch).[27] Since 1901, moreover, when 1,733 were ordained in one year, there had been a marked decline in the number of vocations; by 1937 the figure had dropped to some 1,400; by 1940, largely because of the war, it had fallen to below 500. Under the Vichy regime, however, there was a resurgence in numbers, although again statistics are unreliable. According to one source,[28] in 1942 some 500 diocesan clergy were ordained, as against 1,300 a year later. Another source reports 1058 ordinations in 1944, and 1160 in 1945, although by 1963 the number had dropped back to 573.[29] Nevertheless, both sets of figures show that the war temporarily stimulated the call to the priesthood. The age disparity between the younger priest and his superiors partly explains their different reactions to the events of the Vichy years, when parish clergy showed themselves to be more *'résistant'* than their bishops, who were bound by their loyalty to Pétain.

The diocesan cardinals personified that loyalty. Mgr Suhard, Archbishop of Paris, was the last to be elevated to the purple. In 1935 he had been consecrated Bishop of Bayeux; a year later he was promoted to be Archbishop of Rheims. He had succeeded Cardinal Verdier in Paris in 1940 and had to cope immediately with a difficult situation. It presented great evangelising opportunities but also great complexity because of the German presence. Suhard was to show himself a discreet and flexible negotiator. His principal preoccupation, however, remained the re-Christianisation of France. He showed a tendency to compromise in small matters whilst standing firm on those of principle.

Cardinal Gerlier of Lyons was a prelate of a different stamp. Born in 1880, he was not ordained until 1921, after qualifying before the First World War as a lawyer and serving from 1909 to 1913 as president of the Action Catholique de la Jeunesse Française (ACJF), the umbrella organisation for Catholic youth movements. His seminary training had been interrupted by the war, in which he had served with distinction. He became Bishop of Tarbes and Lourdes in 1929 and in 1937 was elevated to the archbishopric of Lyons and became a cardinal. His experience and inclinations tended to make him sympathetic to social catholicism. Since his see lay in the unoccupied zone, he was freer than was his Paris confrère to speak his mind.

However, by far the most interesting character of the three cardinals was Bishop Liénart of Lille, who had occupied his see since 1928 and was made Cardinal in 1930. During the First World War he had served as a volunteer chaplain with an infantry regiment, and had been personally decorated for bravery by Marshal Pétain at Verdun. During the strikes of textile operatives in northern France in 1929 he had championed the workers. His sympathy with the Christian trade union movement was well known. His mistrust of communism impelled him to strive for reconciliation between the big industrialists and their employees. He was nevertheless a prelate in the grand manner: a veritable prince of the Church and a natural aristocrat, understanding the aspirations of the working class. Isolated in 1940 in a 'forbidden zone' that the Germans (who ruled it from Brussels) threatened to detach from France, he clung to the Marshal not only out of personal esteem but also as a symbol of 'la patrie', both national and local — was not Pétain himself 'un homme du Nord'? He regarded de Gaulle, a fellow-Lillois, as disloyal but stopped short of dubbing him a traitor. He was genuinely shocked at the British failure to accept Pétain's word that the fleet would not he handed over to the Germans, but had attacked it at Mers-el-Kébir. In every respect his loyalty to the Marshal was absolute.

These, then, were the leaders of the Church in 1940. Their attitudes evolved only slowly during the war years, and they were perhaps never as outspoken as they might have been. Indeed, among the archbishops, only one, Mgr Saliège of Toulouse, whilst still professing loyalty to the Marshal, spoke out frankly on those aspects of current events he conceived to be morally wrong.

One important category of ecclesiastics remains: those in the religious orders. The smaller communities had declined in numbers, but the Jesuits and Dominicans were to play a substantial role under Vichy, to which most of their number were at best lukewarm and sometimes resolutely hostile. The Jesuits, in particular, never lacked recruits.

However, many Frenchmen still viewed both secular and regular clergy with deep suspicion: their enemies held them to be grasping and narrow-minded, putting on false airs of superiority, yet regarded with fear, because through the confessional, where the penitents were mostly women, they exercised power over men's sexuality.[30] Politically anti-Republican, too many were identified with the Right. Some covertly supported *Action Française* even when the movement was banned by the Pope in 1926 — the prohibition was lifted in 1939. It was alleged that

Maurras's newspaper nevertheless continued to be delivered to some episcopal palaces. The clergy had traditionally always been vigorously opposed by the secularising forces of the radical Left, backed by the Masonic lodges.[31]

If the inter-war years had seen an ever-widening gulf between the working class, particularly the industrialised proletariat, and the petty bourgeoisie — save in certain areas such as northern France — by contrast the 'haute bourgeoisie', the estate-owners and industrialists, remained the mainstay of the clergy in western and northern France.

Little information is available concerning the age and social composition of Protestants. Their pastors were generally younger than their Catholic brethren. Pastor Boegner, the head of the Fédération Protestante de France, who also supported Pétain (but only reluctantly at the end), was fifty-nine in 1940, hardly younger than his Catholic counterparts. By 1933 it was estimated that there were some 1,100 pastors, of whom about a fifth ministered in Alsace. With a few exceptions such as Paris, Strasbourg and Lyons, protestantism had been a predominantly rural phenomenon. Even such Reform strongholds as Nîmes and Valence were still comparatively small towns in the 1930s. But after 1918 the flight from the countryside had signalled a decline in churchgoing by labouring-class Protestants, so that by 1940 two-thirds of Protestants consisted of the bourgeoisie and the middle classes.[32] Paris Protestants especially constituted an elite made up of the 'grande bourgeoisie', particularly bankers and financiers, top businessmen and officials, ministered to by theology professors and notably powerful preachers. Their comparatively high socio-economic status may be one reason why Protestants played such a significant part, quite disproportionate to their number, under the Vichy regime.

A few smaller Protestant denominations continued to exist: Baptists (particularly in northern France, although in 1938, according to the World Baptist Alliance, there were only 1,600 baptised members of the church, together with twenty-four pastors), and Darbyists (Plymouth Brethren), the Salvation Army (later disbanded on German orders), Quakers (who functioned throughout the war) and even Jehovah's Witnesses, who were officially already banned in 1939 because of their conscientious objection to military service. However, the mainstream of Protestantism looked towards Geneva where, the outbreak of war brought the beginnings of ecumenicism, led by a Dutchman, Visser 't Hooft. While, as will be seen, the Reformed Church of France maintained secret links with German Protestants and derived its theological beliefs from Germany and from Calvin, there was also a strong British connection. This, coupled with the presence of the dissenting sects of largely English origin, was to feed the suspicions of the occupying authorities. One should also mention the presence of some 80,000 Orthodox Christians, mainly in Paris, made up of a large number of 'White' Russians. The Germans were at a loss to know how to deal with these.

How was the Catholic Church governed? Archbishops and bishops ruled over ninety-four dioceses (including those in Algeria and the colonies) with a large degree of autonomy. Despite a certain independent-mindedness, springing from the Gallicanism of Louis XIV and the old Napoleonic Concordat, ever since Papal Infallibility had been proclaimed at the First Vatican Council the Catholic hierarchy had sustained close links with Rome. The bishops recognised, and during the Vichy regime were grateful for, the authority of a papal nunciature in Paris, with which they maintained close contacts. The experience of Cardinal Maglione, Nuncio from 1926 until 1936, was later to stand him in good stead when he succeeded to the post of Secretary of State in the Vatican. He was followed in Paris by Mgr Valerio Valeri, whose presence at Vichy was another factor in lending credibility to the regime until the very end.

The Assembly of Cardinals and Archbishops (ACA), established in 1918, from time to time published statements on matters of concern, often topical. However, it lacked almost all formal organisation. It at first met only annually, and then twice yearly, but during the war more frequently. After the Armistice, and until the total occupation of France, it was split into two halves: the main assembly, consisting of members from the northern zone, met in Paris; those in the southern zone, who usually endorsed the decisions of their northern confrères, in Lyons, although there was close contact between the two groups. Sometimes Cardinal Gerlier travelled from Lyons to the meetings in the capital. Cardinal Liénart, as the senior cardinal, presided. The ACA possessed no permanent secretariat, but Mgr Guerry, assistant bishop of Cambrai, who was later to become the chief apologist for the Hierarchy's comportment during the war, acted as its Secretary-General. The titular Secretary-General was his superior, Mgr Chollet, Archbishop of Cambrai. Although the ACA possessed no formal mechanism for ascertaining the views of all bishops, it had acquired a certain spiritual authority. Thus from time to time the cardinals issued declarations that represented quasi-officially the views of French catholicism. At diocesan level the bishops publicised these views and added to them in the local *Semaines religieuses*. However, the pronouncements of the higher clergy were hardly known to a wider public.

Whereas the Catholic Church was authoritarian in its structures, with information and instructions filtering down from above, the Protestant churches had no such hierarchical chain of command. In 1938 a synod had set up the Reformed Church of France. This brought together 90 per cent of the two principal existing groups of churches, together with a number of other free churches, and included Lutherans, a small Reformed Church of Alsace-Lorraine, and the main Protestant movement in those two provinces, with allegiance to the Augsburg Confession, as well as Methodists. A tiny minority, however, refused to join the new union and set up the Union des Eglises réformées évangéliques indépendantes, with a tiny theological faculty at Aix.[33] The new national union, formally entitled 'L'Union nationale des associations cultuelles de l'Eglise réformée de France', was based on a common Declaration of Faith dating from 1936.

A Fédération Protestante de France was formally created, led by Pastor Boegner, who was also the head of the Union itself. The latter was governed by a Conseil National. This had under it Conseils Régionaux, which in turn had the oversight of local Conseils Presbytéraux. The effect of this system was that often initiatives came from the parish level and were transmitted upwards.

Such then, were the dispositions of Christianity in France in 1940. How Catholics and Protestants viewed the national and international scene before the collapse has now to be considered.

Notes

Unless otherwise stated the place of publication is Paris.

1. F. Boulard, *Premiers itinéraires en sociologie religieuse*, 1954.
2. X. Vallat, *Le Grain de Sable de Cromwell. Souvenirs d'un homme de droite*, 1972.
3. C. Lévy, 'Compte rendu du colloque Rhône-Alpes', *RHDGM*, July 1979, pp. 124–7; P. Bolle, 'Les Protestants français et leurs églises durant la Deuxième Guerre mondiale', *Revue d'histoire moderne et contemporaine*, April–June 1979, p. 286.
4. P. Lestringant, *Visage du Protestantisme français*, Tournon (Ardèche), 1959, p. 12.
5. Lestringant, *Visage*, p. 13.
6. G. Le Bras, *Introduction à l'histoire de la pratique religieuse en France*, 1942, p. 121.
7. H. Godin and Y. Daniel, *La France: Pays de mission*, 1950, pp. 81ff. (originally published 1943).
8. Godin and Daniel, *La France*, p. 8.
9. J. Chelini, *La Ville et l'Eglise*, 1958, p. 230.
10. F. Boulard, A. Achard, H. J. Emérard, *Problèmes missionnaires de la France rurale*, 1945, vol. 2, p. 276.
11. S. Laury, 'La vie religieuse dans le diocèse d'Arras, 1930–1962', *Revue du Nord*, no. 237, April–June 1978, p. 357. This issue of the review, together with the next one, no. 238 (July–September 1978), contains the 'Actes du colloque de Lille', held in 1977.
12. A. Corbin, 'Prélude au Front Populaire: une étude de l'opinion publique, 1932–1936',

Poitiers, 1968, Doctorat du 3e Cycle. The Limoges diocese shows typically how lip-service was paid to Christianity. In Limoges itself, a town of 100,000 inhabitants, 83 per cent were baptised, 77 per cent had contracted a religious marriage, and 85 per cent were buried by the Church. But only 18 per cent attended Sunday mass and 5 per cent vespers. In the rest of the diocese baptisms stood at 97 per cent, religious marriages at 92 per cent, and religious burials also at 92 per cent, although attendance at Sunday mass was below 13 per cent. Yet the crucifix was to be found in most homes. They were 'Catholiques des quatre saisons', according to L. de Perouse (in 'Les Activités catholiques', *Demain*, 28 March 1943).

13. Extracted from the table in *Archives de Sociologie des Religions*, 9:1960.
14. E. Poulat, *Une Eglise ébranlée*, 1980, pp. 31.
15. E. Léonard, *Le Protestant français*, 1953, p. 80.
16. Lestringant, *Visage*, p. 35. The present writer came across a leaflet in the church of St Martin, Barr (Alsace), which gave the figure as over a million about 1975.
17. Boulard *et al.*, *Problèmes missionnaires*, p. 59.
18. Le Bras, *Introduction*, p. 10.
19. G. Le Bras, *L'Eglise et le Village*, 1976, pp. 41f; see also: 'Une enquête: la forge de village', *Annales d'histoire économique et sociale*, 1935, pp. 603–14.
20. Boulard *et al.*, *Problèmes missionnaires*, vol. 1, p. 20.
21. Ibid. p. 28.
22. Ibid. p. 164.
23. Ibid. p. 168.
24. Report of the yearly Congrès Jaciste: *JAC: I. La Joie au village. II. Fêtes à la campagne,* 1938, p. 5 ff.
25. Congrès Jaciste, I, p. 5.
26. Yann Roulet, 'Découverte d'une paroisse', in: M. Boegner and A. Siegfried (eds), *Le Protestantisme français*, 1945, pp. 125–126.
26. Congrès Jaciste. II, p. 61.
27. Boulard *et al*, *Problèmes missionnaires*, vol. 1, p. 282f.
28. P. Vigneron, *Histoire des crises du clergé français contemporain*, 1976, p. 465, quoting F. Lebrun, *Histoire des Catholiques en France du XVe siècle à nos jours*, Toulouse, 1980, p. 446.
29. L. Pérouas, *Refus d'une religion, Religion d'un refus en Limousin rural, 1880–1940*, 1985, *passim*.
30. Lestringant, *Visage*, pp. 35f.
31. Poulat, *Une Eglise ébranlée*, pp. 31f.
32. S. Mours, *Les Eglises réformées en France (tableaux et cartes)*, Strasbourg, 1958, p. 24.
33. X. de Montclos, 'Les Eglises face à la montée des périls, 1933–1939', X. de Montclos *et al.* (eds), *Eglises et Chrétiens dans la Deuxième Guerre Mondiale. La France, Actes*: Lyons, 27–30 January 1978, Lyons, 1982, pp. 3–9.

–2–

Christians and Pre-War Politics

Since Christianity asserts the total sovereignty of God, Christians have difficulty in maintaining political neutrality where policies contradict their faith. Although the Church has always claimed to stand aside from politics, in reality its involvement in them has been perennial. Throughout the Third Republic and the Vichy years remaining aloof was impossible. Before the war, apart from two brief periods — the Ralliement of the 1890s and a 'second Ralliement' just after the First World War — the hostility between Republican secularists and many Catholics continued unabated.

The conflict, which went back to 1789, was reinforced in the 1880s by the secular education laws, and in the early twentieth century by harsh anticlerical measures. By then the State school had to some extent supplanted the Catholic primary school. Hospitals and even cemeteries had been removed from ecclesiastical control. The clergy became liable to conscription. Without state approval religious orders were banned and the 1901 law on associations allowed the sequestration of their property; appropriation was extended in 1908 to other Church possessions. In 1904 religious orders were forbidden to teach, and their schools were nominally closed, although many continued to function illegally. The formal Separation of Church and State in 1905 abrogated the Napoleonic Concordat; religious affairs were entrusted to the Interior ministry, clerical salaries were no longer paid by the State; episcopal appointments were made by the Vatican alone, although the Third Republic always claimed a 'droit de regard' over them. Diplomatic relations with the Holy See were broken off.

With the advent of the Bloc National government after the First World War, on 18 May 1921 links with the Vatican were restored when Charles Jonnart presented his letters of credence to Benedict XV. A further conciliatory step had been taken when 'associations cultuelles', which had been set up at parish level as a device to administer Church property at one remove, and over which the State had greater control than the bishops, were replaced by 'associations diocésaines', whose members, although subject to ratification by the associations' general assemblies, were appointed by the bishops. The Vatican now appeared reluctantly to accept the status quo.

A new situation was created with the accession to power of the Cartel des Gauches. In 1924 Herriot threatened to abolish the Vatican embassy once more, replacing it with a mission to deal solely with Alsace-Lorraine affairs, still subject to the Concordat. Radicals welcomed the proposal. Their leader, they said, disliked making 'diplomatic genuflexions', since he held 'a very lofty conception of secularism... and wanted to break the links with a spiritual power that claims to be all-powerful'.[1] The move provoked the Right to anger. Canon Desgranges, the deputy for Morbihan, declared that on 17 June 1924, when this proposal was first announced, a decade of peace in Church–State relations had been shattered.[2] Such a move, he declared, would be absurd, when a Protestant country like Britain had its representative at the Holy See.[3]

Herriot's programme also included a more rigorous enforcement of the laws regarding the Congregations: an enquiry revealed just how many members of religious orders were still openly teaching in Catholic schools. The Cartel sought to deprive the churches of the special privileges that religious education enjoyed in Alsace-Lorraine because of the survival of the Concordat regime in the former German province. Bérard, when Education minister in the Bloc National government (he was later Vichy's ambassador to the Vatican), had made Greek and Latin compulsory in State secondary schools; the new administration opted to rescind this measure, a step that Catholics viewed as tending towards a single school, an 'école unique', threatening the existence of their own numerous secondary schools.

Thus between June 1924, when Herriot assumed power, and April 1925, when his government was toppled by the Senate, relations between Church and State became increasingly tense.[4] In Alsace Mgr Ruch, Bishop of Strasbourg, supported by fellow bishops in western France, campaigned against the government's religious policy for the province. (Ironically, in 1940 he, by then expelled from his diocese, was to see the Germans disregard the Concordat in the region, now re-annexed to the Reich.) Right-wing Catholics, led by General de Castelnau, set up the Fédération Nationale Catholique (FNC) initially to combat what they saw as an unjust religious policy. The FNC's best orator, Philippe Henriot (who under Vichy was to become the propagandist of collaboration with Germany), stumped the country on behalf of the Catholic cause. There remained unresolved the State's interest in Christian missions overseas. (The French, like the British, had always regarded missionaries as colonial pioneers, not only for

Christianity but also for French culture and commerce, on the principle that 'trade follows the flag', even if it were men of God who acted as its standard-bearers.)

By January 1925 Herriot had abandoned his more extreme measures. Catholic opinion had prevailed against a government that was not even Socialist, but merely radical. However, the FNC did not stand down its forces, but continued as the watchdog of the Catholic Right. The legal situation nevertheless remained confused. It was this that the Vichy regime was to attempt to remedy.

Meanwhile the ACA pressed home its attack on the secularising state. Its declaration of 11 March 1925 is redolent of similar statements it made, although in more sombre but nevertheless somewhat triumphalist tones, in 1940:

> In every field, in every region of the country, war is openly and unanimously declared on secularism and its principles, down to the very abolition of the iniquitous laws that proceed from it. The school law deceives the intelligence of children... the law of Separation officially involves the public, as well as entailing the scandalous splitting of society from the Church, from religion, and from God. The divorce law legalises adultery.[5]

Unlike Germany, France had developed no large, specifically Catholic political party. The Dreyfus affair (1894–99) had stirred up in the traditionalist wing of the Church monarchist, nationalist and anti-Semitic sentiments. The launching of the Action Française movement in 1898 had attracted a number of these traditional Catholics, who often favoured a 'catholicisme intégral' that chimed well with Maurras's 'nationalisme intégral', as well as with his anti-German views. They remained opposed to any parliamentary regime. Indeed many, as Catholic writers of the time attest — poets such as Péguy, Francis Jammes and Claudel, the neo-Thomist philosopher Maritain, and the novelist and polemicist Bernanos — bore no love for democracy as such. They were therefore dismayed when, despite the trauma of the Cartel des Gauches, Pius XI in 1926 forbade Catholics membership of Action Française. At the same time the appointment of Mgr Maglione as Nuncio showed a papal preference for a brand of catholicism that expressed itself more in the various social movements of Action Catholique. Clearly the Vatican's intention was also to turn the faithful away from Maurrassian politicking — 'politique d'abord'— to social concerns and the more fitting task of religious proselytising.

Two small parties, broadly opposed to extremist catholicism, had already begun to emerge. Both derived from the Le Sillon movement, whose founder, Marc Sangnier, can lay some claim to be the renewer of social catholicism. His movement had been condemned as too political by the Vatican in 1910, but two years later he set up a small party known as the Ligue de la Jeune République which underwent a revival after 1918. The party split, however, about 1932 when a minority, led by Sangnier, wanted to concentrate efforts on the achievement of a lasting peace. Others, such as Philippe Serre and Valabrègues, wished the main thrust to be towards social reform. Their policies were ambitious: more power for the labour force; an end to all hierarchies, save those deriving from the exercise of responsibility; proportional representation; votes for women (a goal not achieved until 1945); and national referendums on all important issues. La Jeune République, whilst still retaining some of its Christian tincture, eventually supported the Front Populaire.[6] On the other hand, the splinter group sought to create a 'social Catholic' party, politically more centrist.

This developed into the Parti Démocrate Populaire (PDP), formally founded in 1924 by André Chatelyn, an ex-Sillonniste.[7] It hoped to attract the less anticlerical Radicals as well as moderates drawn from more enlightened conservative elements. The goal was social harmony, 'la concertation sociale'. After 1931 its leaders drew their inspiration from the encyclical *Quadragesimo Anno*, which had condemned the concentration of wealth in the hands of the few, who were accused of manipulating to their advantage capital they did not own. The party followed in the steps of the 'abbés démocrates', Lemire, Six, Desgranges.[8] Its programme, as elaborated by Marcel Prélot, affirmed its allegiance to the Republican regime, and a commitment to political freedom (including 'la liberté d'enseignement', the right of Catholics to have their own schools). Citizenship, based on moral and religious values, should promote the interests of the workers and the family. The national goal would be the creation of a truly democratic economic and social framework; internationally it sought co-operation between nations, although not at the expense of patriotism. However, the party had little success: it never exceeded eighteen parliamentarians. Their most eminent pre-war representative was Senator Champetier de Ribes, who, together with two other members of the PDP, Paul Simon and Trémentin, was to vote against the granting of full powers to Pétain in 1940. Other party members that were to figure prominently in the history of Vichy were Georges Bidault, who was to head the Conseil de la Résistance, and two other anti-Vichyites, Mendès-France and the writer Jean Guéhenno, as well as Lucien Romier, who became one of Pétain's ministers of state, and Maurice Martin du Gard, the entertaining chronicler of life at the Vichy 'court'. The question of support for Vichy, initially faced with the prospect of a German victory, was to split this small party, which nevertheless represents a key political tendency in social catholicism until the creation of the Mouvement Républicain Populaire (MRP) in January 1944.

Although most Catholics were not political die-hards, they tended to vote for the Right, among whose extremists were some devout Christians. Two such deputies, belonging to the Fédération Républicaine, were Xavier Vallat, who had earlier supported Valois's Faisceau movement and who was to become Vichy's first commissioner for Jewish questions, and Henriot, who banked on a German victory. Another Catholic who had been associated with the Faisceau was Bucard, who in 1933 set up his own Fascist movement, the Francistes, in imitation of Mussolini. Bucard advocated the adoption of the 'Führerprinzip' as opposed to parliamentary democracy, and the uprooting of 'foreign' elements ('les métèques') in French life, including Jews and Freemasons. He favoured corporatism and the promotion of the family. His movement was allowed to continue under Vichy and did attract some young Catholics.

The impending triumph of the Front Populaire deepened further the gulf between secularisers and Catholics. Before the elections in May 1936 the bishops set out guidelines as to how their flock should vote. It should be for the 'best' candidate, but Socialists and Communists were automatically excluded. Mgr Maurin, then Archbishop of Lyons, proscribed the Left in these terms: 'Il n'y a pas et il ne saurait y avoir de socialisme chrétien.'[9] Mgr Du Bois de Villerabel, then Bishop of Annecy, reminded the faithful they could not support any political movement condemned by the Church, and this included not only the Left, but also Action Française. Mgr Caillot, the aged Bishop of Grenoble, pronounced in similar vein.[10] In November 1935 Cardinal Baudrillart, Rector of the Paris Institut Catholique, issued the same warning to his students.[11] On this question the Hierarchy were of one voice.

Nevertheless, a few weeks earlier, broadcasting on Radio Paris (17 April 1936), Maurice Thorez, the Communist leader, had made his sweeping gesture of reconciliation: 'Nous te tendons la main, catholique... parce que tu es notre frère'. His appeal was repeated also after the Left's victory at the polls, but went largely unheeded except for the Christians of La Jeune République and a few intellectuals grouped around Mounier's Catholic review *Esprit*.

Sporadic co-operation between Christians and Communists already existed. Priests in areas of high unemployment sat with Communists on committees to alleviate hardship. An enquiry by the Jesuits of Action Populaire in Vanves in 1937 among 1,000 militant Catholics commended Communist municipal administrations where they were efficient, particularly in operating welfare schemes such as the Secours

Rouge or the charity for conscripts, the Sou du Soldat. At Bobigny, in the working class 'red belt' north of Paris, the priest would even allow the children to leave before the end of mass to attend music classes run by Communists — lessons that would naturally end with the singing of the Internationale or La Jeune Garde.[12] Such clergy were often backed by members of the Jeunesse Ouvrière Chrétienne (JOC) and the Confédération Française des Travailleurs Chrétiens (CFTC). The latter, a Catholic trade union, founded in 1918 on the principles of the papal encyclical of 1890, *Rerum Novarum,* was small in comparison with the Confédération Générale du Travail (CGT) but was disproportionately influential. There even existed a tiny movement, Terre Nouvelle, Anarchist and Communist, that attempted to reconcile Christianity and communism. Founded in 1935 by Laudrain, a former secretary to an auxiliary bishop of Paris, its emblem was a white hammer and sickle superimposed on a cross coloured red. It enjoyed for a while the support of Paul Ricœur, the eminent Protestant philosopher. Dubbed by Mounier as 'Catholic Communists' and 'Christian revolutionaries', its members declared that they would not shrink from violence to achieve a Christian society. Their monthly, *Terre Nouvelle,* was eventually condemned by the ACA and placed on the Index in July 1936.[13] Little wonder, therefore, that the bishops, seeing communism penetrate the Church itself, regarded the Party as its most serious rival.

Against the 'poissons rouges' of the stoup were ranged those who nurtured 'a vigorous and sacred hatred of communism' — the expression is that of Mgr Ruch of Strasbourg[14] — led by Cardinal Baudrillart and General Castelnau. Assiduous readers of *Le Pèlerin* and the *Echo de Paris*[15] feared above all else a Red revolution that would signal the demise of Christian civilisation. However, other Christians, such as Francisque Gay, Etienne Borne and Pierre-Henri Simon, campaigned for the discovery of a 'third way' that would steer a course between Right and Left. Catholics, they wrote, had tolerated social injustices for too long, and they quoted Cardinals Verdier and Liénart in justification.

However, Pius XI, no less than his Secretary of State, Cardinal Pacelli, (who in 1939 became Pius XII), had become 'obsessed' by the fear of bolshevism.[16] Before the 1936 elections the Holy Father reiterated that no reconciliation was possible between catholicism and communism. The French bishops followed his lead: speaking in the Parc des Princes stadium on the fiftieth anniversary of the ACJF, Cardinal Liénart rejected Thorez's overtures. Blum's electoral victory, despite the fact that his new administration included no Communists, caused consternation among the Hierarchy. Canon Lallemant was commissioned to write a work expounding the errors of communism. This project received obliquely the papal blessing when (19 March 1937) Pius XI published his encyclical, *Divini Redemptoris*, condemning 'atheistic communism' in no uncertain terms: 'Communism is intrinsically perverted and in no domain can anyone who wishes to save Christian civilisation allow any collaboration with it.'

The encyclical put an end to what Gaetan Bernoville termed 'la farce de la main tendue' in his book of the same title. Meanwhile on 31 October 1936 the cardinals had published a pastoral letter giving solemn warning of what they considered was happening to France. The country was in a grave crisis, a prey to class struggle and hatred; the 'natural rights' of property and liberty, the sanctity of promises pledged, the observance of duty — these had flown out of the window. The causes were patent: atheism and secularisation, the exclusion of God from society. The need was for the restoration of Christian goals, Latin culture and French traditions. This required the rejection of both nazism and communism. In international relations justice, charity and peace were, somewhat lamely in view of the situation, cited as other prerequisites. In labour relations the social doctrines of the Church should prevail; in the home there should be a renewal of the marriage vows. State schools were particularly targeted: there 'revolutionary viruses' should be extirpated, because 'they were making France one of the countries in the civilised world where most of the generations that arrive at adulthood have been systematically poisoned'.[17] But, as one left-wing critic of the cardinals put it, were they criticising the gesture of the clenched fist 'sans chercher à approfondir le sens?' For example, had not the workers rights that should be respected? The tenor of their declaration matched that of the initial reformist zeal of the Vichy regime: the tone was not far from 'Travail, Famille, Patrie'.

Most Catholics saw little chance of compromise with the Left. There was, for instance, the question of freemasonry, condemned by the Church. But twenty-five out of thirty-five ministers of the Front Populaire were either lodge members or were linked to them. With some Catholics, anti-Semitism surfaced. Vallat, in an infamous speech, pointed at Blum in the Chamber of Deputies and declared that for the first time in its history France would be governed by a Jew. Others, however, saw the events of 1936 differently. Another deputy, Fernand-Laurent, an Independent Republican, asserted that now it was the turn of the rich to pay, this in accordance with the sentiments of the Magnificat; it was, he told Blum, his singular destiny to have been chosen to establish the Kingdom of the Gospel![18]

The sit-in strikes that coincided with the formation of the new government were condemned by most Catholics, although some such as Cardinal Verdier did acknowledge they were symptomatic of the need for a new social dispensation. But for Catholics, even Social Catholics such as the Jesuits of Action Populaire and those who ran the Society's influential journal, *Etudes*, occupation of the factories violated the sacred right to property. The FNC, whose membership in 1936 numbered three millions, mainly drawn from the ranks of the conservative and nationalist Right, became even more strident in support of the traditional social order. (Nevertheless its vice-president, another Catholic parliamentarian, Jean Le Cour Grandmaison, also wanted a more humane way of life that 'would harness money to the service of man'.)

However, those few Catholics who had thrown in their lot with the Front Populaire had created a precedent. Four successful candidates of the Jeune République (out of twenty that had been put up) supported the new government, the first time that Catholics had broken ranks in this way. Despite the views of Marc Sangnier, their fellow Catholics in the PDP joined the opposition. The Christian Anarchist and Communist party, Terre Nouvelle, likewise supported the Front — in February 1936 Cardinal Verdier had judged it necessary particularly to warn Catholics against this faction. Another Catholic, Francisque Gay, the director of the Social Catholic newspaper, *L'Aube*, had cherished hopes of creating a single party of unity to uphold Christian values, although he had failed to be elected. Members of the CFTC, like the members of JOC — the Jocistes — were torn in their allegiance. Although regarding the occupation of the workplace as illegal, they had felt their duty was to be with their non-Christian comrades, just as some years later under Vichy some departed voluntarily to join their fellow-workers for forced labour in Germany. Mounier's journal *Esprit*, rejecting both capitalism and marxism and, somewhat vaguely, substituting for them the realisation of spiritual values in society, gave the Front its critical support. On the other hand the Dominican journal *Sept,* which attracted as contributors such philosophers and theologians, politicians and writers as Etienne Gilson, Etienne Borne, Maritain, P.-H. Simon, Mauriac, Bernanos, Joseph Folliet and Maurice Schumann, most of whom later rejected the Vichy regime, refused 'la main tendue', whilst adopting a position that dismissed both economic liberalism and marxism.

Despite these differing views, an almost universal chorus of Christian approval greeted the social laws that signalled a temporary end to the social unrest. These gave the workers improved wages, the right to collective bargaining, the forty-hour week, and paid holidays. Cardinals Verdier and Liénart even waxed enthusiastic. Mgr Choquet, then Bishop of Langres — 'une girouette', in view of his later support for Vichy? — speculated optimistically about the new world that was dawning. (Even Colonel de la Rocque, the leader of the Croix de Feu, which, as the PSF, became a very significant party in France by 1939, attracting many middle-class Catholics, had avowed in *Sept* [1935] his affinities with social catholicism and now boldly stated: 'Nos idées sont au pouvoir!').[19]

Meanwhile, Mgr Saliège, Archbishop of Toulouse, later one of Vichy's frankest critics, had condemned capitalism outright: 'The present social state cannot last. Founded upon the supremacy of money, bereft of any Christian spirit, tainted by injustice and egoism, it represents a disorder. Christianity has no solidarity with capitalism.'

However, this fleeting sympathy quickly faded and reaction set in. The spectre of a Communist take-over of France that was to haunt the bishops until 1944, and afterwards, loomed once more. There were fears of a *coup d'état*; the Bishops of Versailles and Montpellier even warned priests to have ready civilian clothes and a valid passport in order to flee abroad if the situation worsened.[20] Valerio Valeri, the Nuncio, requested (October 1936) the ACA to pronounce an even sterner condemnation of communism: the Pope required, he said, 'a clear plan of action'.[21] Accordingly, in December the ACA, in a declaration mainly dealing with the Spanish Çivil War, warned the country to end social strife and to return to spiritual values; only so could it withstand Soviet communism and other 'forms of government less in tune with our national temperament'. By the New Year Cardinal Suhard, then Archbishop of Rheims, was again denouncing the violation of property rights, and Mgr Chollet, Archbishop of Cambrai, was asserting that a Marxist France was in the making.[22] Only Mgr Saliège tried to redress the balance in a letter to his flock: 'Que craignez-vous? La Révolution? Faites-la en vous-même et vous ne la redouterez plus' (What do you fear? Revolution? Carry out one in yourself and you will no longer dread it).

From the other side of the fence, Blum, in an interview given to Maurice Schumann and published in *Sept* (19 February 1937), asserted that effective co-operation between the Church and the Front Populaire was still feasible. This roused the hackles of some. Although both Cardinals Verdier and Liénart conceded that the Dominicans had the right to publish this explosive message, it infuriated some Catholics, particularly the FNC. The review persisted, however, in its independent line until its support for the Spanish Republicans incurred papal wrath and it was forced to cease publication in August 1937. (It later reappeared as a weekly, *Temps Présent,* but independent of Dominican control). *L'Aube* was also condemned by Cardinal Baudrillart for expressing similar opinions. Mgr Calvet, the latter's subordinate at the Institut Catholique in Paris, was moved to speak scathingly of 'social priests' ('le clergé social') and rebuked Catholic youth movements such as the JOC for siding with the workers.

One incident, however, showed the higher clergy was not bereft of generosity of spirit, even to its opponents. In November 1936 Roger

Salengro, Interior minister in the Blum Government and Socialist mayor of Lille, committed suicide. This act of despair was brought on by ignominious attacks on him in the scurrilous weekly *Gringoire*, which alleged that when captured by the Germans during the First World War, he had given away military secrets. Insults such as 'Roger-la-Honte' and 'Salengro, sale en gros et en détail' had been heaped upon him. Both Cardinal Liénart, as bishop of Lille, and Cardinal Gerlier expressed revulsion that he had been driven to take his own life. Two Deputies who were also priests, Abbé Desgranges and Canon Polimann (who later collaborated with the Germans), also showed their solidarity by attending the funeral.

Attention, however, was now increasingly diverted to the Spanish Civil War, which fuelled anti-Communist hysteria. Franco's insurrection, which began in Morocco in July 1936, initially evoked a cautious response from Catholics. *Sept* at first condemned both sides. Mauriac, writing in the *Figaro* (25 July 1936), warned Blum against assisting the Republicans. Bidault also came out against intervention. The fear was that the war might spread north over the Pyrenees. Leading Catholics spoke in the same vein, some hypocritically only when they realised Franco was winning. For the FNC, however, General Castelnau, doubtless also with the Front Populaire in mind, characterised the Spanish Frente Popular, the victors in the February 1936 Spanish elections, as the 'frente crapular'. The French bishops were impressed that their Spanish confrères, with the exception of the Basque and Catalan prelates, solidly backed the rebellion. By and large they accepted Bernoville's justification of Francoist cruelty: 'Even if we should admit a few excesses have been committed by Franco's troops, the fact remains that Franco and his supporters are defending Christian civilisation against Marxist barbarism.'[23]

The anti-Communist image of crusaders and defenders of Christian civilisation that the Spanish Nationalists presented — the Republicans indeed killed ecclesiastics almost indiscriminately — was largely accepted by the French bishops, particularly after the Pope had condemned (14 September 1936) the persecution of Spanish Catholics: a figure was given of 16,500 priests, including eleven bishops, murdered,[24] not to mention the raping of nuns and the destruction of churches. Against this should be set the indiscriminate shooting of 'Reds' by the Phalange. *La Croix* reported what it called the 'slaughter' carried out by the 'Moors' — hardly 'Christian crusaders' — after the capture of Badajoz (14 August 1936).

However, there were many more Catholics sceptical of the righteousness of Franco's cause than is generally realised. After the bombing of Guernica (26 April 1937), the cultural and spiritual capital of the Basque people, in May 1937 a group of eminent Christian intellectuals that included Mauriac, Marcel and Mounier, issued a manifesto in favour of the Basques. *L'Aube* came out for the Republic and, with *Sept,* declared that Franco was in no way waging a holy war. Bidault commented sardonically (*L'Aube*, 30 April 1937) that 'a crusader is not a killer of children'. Christian Democrats likewise rejected the future Caudillo, highlighting his use of Spanish North African troops, his Freemason generals and the feudal nature of the system he sought to restore. Even among Catholic supporters of the Republic, however, there was not always unanimity. Mounier was urged at one point by Maritain, joined by Mounier's old professor, Jacques Chevalier (who was pro-Franco, a devout Catholic, and a future Vichy Education minister), to make a 'double refusal' by rejecting both protagonists. Bernanos, whose *Grands Cimetières sous la lune* (1938) signalled a profound change in his political attitudes, could not stomach the 'Reds'[25] but jibbed at the rebel atrocities and the martyrdom of Basque Catholics; he urged international mediation to end the conflict.

There were also divisions among Protestants. On the Right, those who read *La Vie Nouvelle* believed that nazism represented a lesser danger than communism and anarchism, whereas 'Social Christians' supported the Republicans. Those who followed Karl Barth, who always maintained that his quarrel with totalitarian regimes was theological and not political, were cool towards Franco but deprecated the adoption of overtly political attitudes.[26]

However, by March 1939 the white flag had been hoisted over Madrid and Franco emerged as the victor. In February the beaten army of Catalonia had crossed the French frontier to safety — a legacy of refugees that later, under Vichy, was to evoke the practical sympathy of French Christians. By 16 April 1939, the war over, the Pope summed up the situation as he saw it: 'the healthy elements' of the Spanish people had fought 'to defend the ideal of the Christian faith and civilisation'. He went on to compare, somewhat extravagantly, the 'crusade' by Franco to the Spanish conquest and conversion of the New World in the sixteenth century.

In rural and semi-rural France, where almost half the population still lived, the 'Catholic in the pew' certainly saw communism as the enemy. All anti-clericals and Socialists were automatically branded as Communists. The picture abroad was often painted in black and white terms: Stalin was the Satan of this world; Franco had saved Christianity just as had Le Cid. The Communist Party 'parle tricolore, mais pense rouge'. Nevertheless, for the average peasant its members could be divided up into those who carried out 'Agitprop' and were rogues; and those who were 'all right' ('bons garçons') but misguided — although, giving way to their wives' wishes, they might even let their daughter attend catechism classes![27]

It was with relief that the bishops saw the collapse of the Front Populaire. Under the successor regime of Daladier relations with the State became less strained, although one should not forget that Blum had received the papal legate, Cardinal Pacelli, right royally when he had made a tour of French dioceses. The cardinals noted with satisfaction that Daladier spoke of a 'redressement' of France — a term not far removed from that of 'rénovation' favoured by Pétain later for his Révolution Nationale. Cardinal Verdier, for the ACA, wrote to the prime minister in March 1939 pledging full support in this task and also, presumably with Munich in mind, praising his 'defence of freedom'. Later, in May, perhaps incidentally realising the numerical disparity in potential soldiers between France and Germany the cardinals issued an 'appeal concerning the depopulation of France', backing their previous message, and calling for a new moral climate. Thus they came out against divorce and abortion, and in favour of religious teaching for all children. Measures to this effect, they said, would help solve the problem of the steeply declining birth rate.

Soon, however, the shadows of the impending European conflict deepened, overclouding all other considerations. Catholic Democrats remained strongly anti-Hitler. The FNC, fiercely anti-German, advocated a well-equipped army able to defend the national borders. But the average Catholic, like most Frenchmen — and many of their British allies — welcomed almost any move to avoid war. Some Catholics approved the abortive attempt to form an alliance with Italy. The hope persisted that the Nazis would achieve their territorial ambitions through 'Drang nach Osten' — expansion eastwards. Although this would entail the sacrifice of Poland, at least, so Catholics reasoned, the Nazis would be fighting the USSR, the home of communism, which, despite the immediate peril, many still considered the principal adversary. Consequently, the Munich agreement in 1938 was received with enthusiasm. Among Catholics, only the PDP waxed ironical over it, dubbing it 'la glorieuse paix..., où tout fut compromis, même l'honneur'.[28] Few French Catholics, with the exception of a handful of priests who had seen Germany at close quarters, were sufficiently alive to the fact that nazism was the bitter enemy of Christianity. Those Christians who contemplated with dismay the 'paganism' of France failed to realise what inroads that creed had already made into their immediate neighbour. Vatican pronouncements were sometimes ambiguous. In 1936, when the Pope had condemned the Spanish Republicans, he had spoken of 'idéologies absurdes et désastreuses'. *Sept* interpreted this to mean that his strictures also embraced nazism, since they had been made at the very time of the Nuremberg Nazi Party congress.[29] But this Dominican view found little echo. Bidault, however, then writing leaders for *L'Aube*,[30] had also come out against Munich,[31] which the ACJF, supporting one of its former prominent members, also characterised as 'une défaite sans guerre'. When war finally came some traditionalist Catholics attempted to blame the Social Catholics, lumping them together with the Left, by claiming they had encouraged workers to be lazy by their support for the social laws of 1936. Louis Bertrand, the Catholic Maurrassian writer, sided with Cardinal Baudrillart, and against Cardinal Gerlier, in declaring that such reforms had contributed directly to the state of military unpreparedness: at a time when Germans employed in the armaments industries were working flat out, their French counterparts were insisting on the forty-hour week and paid holidays.[32]

Protestant reaction to the political situation in pre-war France was mixed. Barthian theology, predominant in the Reformed Church in the 1930s, posed, as did social catholicism, the question of involvement *qua* Christians in the life of society. For Protestants this 'engagement' did not run counter to their traditional radical republicanism, although a small minority of Royalists also existed among their number. Nazism was presented in journals such as *Le Semeur* and *Foi et Vie* (directed by Pastor Maury from 1930 to 1940) as a great danger. In May 1937 the Conseil de la Fédération Protestante warned against 'toute philosophie matérialiste' and 'toute conception d'origine païenne', neatly lumping together both communism and nazism. After the arrival in Lyons of Pastor de Pury, who edited another influential Barthian periodical, *Hic et Nunc*, he and a fellow Swiss, Denis de Rougemont, sought by every means to awaken Protestants to the perniciousness of nazism. By 1939 Pastor Boegner, as head of the Fédération Protestante, was vigorous in his condemnation of such gratuitous acts of aggression as the German occupation of Czechoslovakia in March, and the Good Friday invasion of Albania by Italy. Protestants were perhaps more alive to the serious threat posed by the Axis powers than were their fellow Christians.

By 1939 those who wielded authority in the Catholic Church continued to be more fearful of communism than nazism. They had feared the Front Populaire heralded the installation of 'bolshevism' in France. They had doubted the patriotism of those who ruled the nation during the mid-1930s. Democracy was not a political creed they favoured; their instincts were for a paternal authoritarianism, such as characterised ecclesiastical structures. Above all, they hankered for what they termed the 'restoration' of moral and Christian values in public life and institutions. They condemned the jungle of the free market, but also a class struggle that sought the hegemony of the proletariat. Co-operation between employer and worker was seen as the way forward — in other words, a form of corporatism. But in reality the immediate enemy was neither Stalin nor the Communist 'fifth column' within the gates, but Hitler.

Notes

Unless otherwise stated the place of publication is Paris.

1. AN F7.13193. *Le Bulletin du Jour* (correspondance de presse du parti radical et radical-socialiste), 3 February 1925.
2. AD du Nord, Lille, M154/116A FNC. Speech at a meeting of the FNC at Dunkirk, 21 May 1925, reported by the Commissariat Central, Lille, to the prefect, 22 May 1925.
3. AD du Nord, M154/118. Speech at a meeting of the ACJF at Roubaix, 23 July 1924, reported by the Commissariat de Police, 4e arrondissement, to the Commissariat Central, Roubaix, 24 July 1924.
4. S. Berstein, *Edouard Herriot ou la République en personne*, 1985, p. 114 and p. 125.
5. Quoted in G. Combes, 'L'Esprit public en Haute-Loire de 1940 à 1942', *RHDGM*, 1972, pp. 56ff.
6. M. Winock, *Histoire politique de la revue 'Esprit', 1930–1950*, 1975, p. 36.
7. For an account of the PDP, particularly in the Nord department, where it was especially strong, see: B. Béthouart, 'Histoire du MRP dans l'arrondissement de Lille' Mémoire de maîtrise, Université de Lille III, 1972.
8. R. Raymond-Laurent,, *Le Parti démocrate populaire, 1924–1944*, 1960, pp. 114ff.
9. Quoted in P. Christophe, *Les Catholiques et le Front Populaire*, 1986, p. 43. For much in the following pages I am indebted to this lucid monograph.
10. Ibid., p. 36.
11. Ibid., p. 34.
12. Y. Tranvouez, 'Les Catholiques: séparer le bon grain de l'ivraie", in: J.-P. Azéma, A. Prost and J.-P. Rioux (eds), *Le Parti communiste français des années sombres, 1938–1941*, 1986, pp. 76f.
13. Azéma, *et al.* (eds), *Le Parti communiste*, p. 73; see also: J. Hellman, *Emmanuel Mounier and the New Catholic Left, 1930–1950*, Toronto, 1981, pp. 104f.
14. Mgr Ruch, writing in the *Bulletin ecclésiastique de Strasbourg*, 1 October 1936.
15. The Catholic monthly, *Le Pèlerin* (established 1873), had a circulation of some 550,000 copies before the war, and was second only to the scurrilous *Gringoire* (650,000 copies), and accountied for some 25 per cent of the circulation of the main weekly or monthly periodicals published in Paris. The two Catholic dailies, *Le Jour* and *L'Echo de Paris*, had a combined circulation of 325,000, representing a market share of some 21 per cent. The Communist *L'Humanité*, with a circulation of some 343,000, was easily the most widely read daily. Nevertheless the figures show the strength of the Catholic non-specialized press. A breakdown of the figures is given in H. Dubief, *Le déclin de la Troisième République, 1929–1938*, 1976.
16. Christophe, *Les Catholiques*. Letter of Cardinal Baudrillart to Mgr Chollet, archbishop of Cambrai, in 1936, quoted on p. 35.
17. Quoted in H. Noguères, *Front Populaire, 1935–1938*, 1977, p. 236.
18. Christophe, *Les Catholiques*, p. 82.

19. See R. Rémond, *Les Droites en France*, 1982, pp. 213f.
20. Christophe, *Les Catholiques*, p.141.
21. Ibid., p .148.
22. Ibid., p. 172.
23. 'Le pays basque à la dérive', *La France catholique*, 31 March 1937.
24. Christophe, *Les Catholiques*, p. 21.
25. Rémond, *Les Droites*, p. 227.
26. *Actes*: Lyons, pp. 69f.
27. Tranvouez, 'Les Catholiques', p. 78–81. Report on a study made in 1939 of the 'Bulletin paroissial', which had 1,500 subscribers, of Saint-Laurent de Lambezellec, near Brest.
28. R. Vandenbussche, 'Opinions et attitudes de chrétiens pendant la Seconde Guerre Mondiale', *Actes*: Lille, pp. 506ff.
29. Christophe, *Les Catholiques*, p. 126.
30. *L'Aube*, founded in 1932 by Francisque Gay, was viewed with deep suspicion by the Catholic authorities. Pius XI, very Italianate in his preferences, was cool towards it ever since it had condemned Mussolini's attack on Abyssinia in October 1935. In May 1936 he was told that it had been penetrated by Communists. Mgr Chollet, Secretary of the ACA, in 1937–38 submitted two adverse reports on it to the Vatican. It was accused of guilt by association, because its contributors included Duhamel, agnostic, Benda, Jew, and Laudrain, Christian Communist. For further details see Christophe, *Les Catholiques,* pp.21–26.
31. Rémond, *Les Droites*, p. 227.
32. Christophe, *Les Catholiques*, p. 16.

–3–

Prelude to Vichy

The French bishops looked to the Vatican for a lead regarding nazism. How that perverted ideology viewed Christianity should have served as a warning to French Catholics and Protestants alike. Closer consideration of events in the Third Reich might have proved instructive.

In *Mein Kampf* Hitler, a lapsed Catholic, had expressed his admiration for the organisation of the Catholic Church. His attitude to the two-thirds majority of German Protestants was, by contrast, contemptuous. His ultimate aim was to close all churches, or convert them to worship of a peculiarly Nazi version of the Deity. Meanwhile, Christian institutions had to be controlled because their culture ran counter to the Nazi *Weltanschauung*. Catholicism was particularly to be feared because of its world-wide ramifications and the power it had exerted throughout history.

Thus after the *Machtübernahme* in Germany itself the Nazis had first sought an accommodation with Rome. On 20 July 1933 the Catholic von Papen signed a Concordat guaranteeing the existence of Catholic schools and freedom of worship. In return, all ancillary Catholic organisations, including those for young people, were to be wound up. The fact that the compact was disregarded almost after being signed should have been a salutary warning to Catholics elsewhere. In Germany already in December 1933 Cardinal Faulhaber of Munich was denouncing the continuing spread of Nazi paganism.

French Christians could also have profited from the experience of German Protestants. Some of their clergy welcomed the advent of Hitler. Pastor Otto Dibelius, Superintendent of Brandenburg, even attended the Führer's installation as Chancellor. The federation of the German Evangelical Church admitted a new movement to its ranks, the 'Deutsche Christen', which soon dominated the synods and elected Müller, a dyed-in-the wool Nazi, as Reich Bishop and effectively the leader of the Reformed Churches. At the same time the shameful 'Aryan paragraph' expelled all Jewish converts from the Church.

The 'Deutsche Christen' movement was opposed by Pastor Niemöller, a hero of the First World War, and by Karl Barth, the Swiss theologian, then a professor at Bonn, who was later to urge French Protestants to resist nazism. A breakaway Confessional Church was founded which, prescribed bounds to Christian obedience to secular authority, a matter of conscience that later also much exercised French Christians. Niemöller was arrested and sent to a concentration camp, where he maintained clandestine contacts with Christians in France throughout the war, as did his fellow Christian, Gustav Heinemann, a future president of the Federal Republic.

The Vatican viewed developments in Germany with growing concern. On 14 March 1937, the encyclical *Mit brennender Sorge*, addressed to the German Catholic bishops, obliquely condemned Nazi doctrines. It would seem that the guiding hand behind this document was not the Pope himself, but Cardinal Pacelli, his successor as Pius XII, who had been Nuncio in Germany for many years.[1] Pacelli, however, still regarded Germany as the main bulwark against communism, and this tempered his views. The repercussions of the encyclical were, as will be seen, felt also in France, but with not much immediate effect. The papal pronouncement also failed to deter some Catholics in the enlarged Third Reich: at the Anschluss with Austria Cardinal Innitzer gave the Nazi salute and shouted 'Heil Hitler' with the rest. It remained for men like the courageous Count von Galen, Bishop of Münster, later to condemn publicly Nazi persecution of Christians in occupied territories and in 1942 to attack from the pulpit such outrages as the murder of the physically and mentally handicapped.

Nazi measures aimed at the subjugation and eventual suppression of Christianity were certainly known to the French bishops. Rank and file priests such as Abbé Naurois and Père Chaillet had seen the Nazis at close quarters, and were not shy of expressing their views. Numerous articles on nazism and religion appeared in the Catholic press. Why then was the Hierarchy not more sensitive to the dangers that nazism presented?

One reason was the Church's obsession with communism, a menace seen as more immediate. Indeed Pius XI, only five days after the encyclical addressed to the Germans, issued another, this time couched in Latin and thus intended for the Church at large. *Divini Redemptoris* pronounced an anathema on atheistic communism. The Catholic press seized upon the second encyclical, to the detriment of the first. Ten leading French Catholic periodicals displayed details of both on their front page, but devoted two-thirds more column-inches to the condemnation of communism. *Le Pèlerin*, the most popular periodical, and representative of traditional catholicism, hardly mentioned *Mit brennender Sorge* at all. Only *L'Aube*, Christian Democrat in tendency, devoted slightly more space to the document intended for Germans.[2]

Père Chaillet, who in 1941 became one of the prime movers behind the Catholic clandestine Resistance periodical, *Témoignage Chrétien*, had travelled in Eastern Europe and Germany and during a stay in Tübingen — more renowned for its Protestant faculty than its Catholic scholars — had studied the works of Möhler, the nineteenth-century theologian who had emphasised the absolute freedom of the Church from the secular power. The German had cited St Anselm of Canterbury, who had held obedience to God to be supreme, above any earthly allegiance. Chaillet, in *L'Autriche souffrante* (1939), drew the obvious parallel, deploring the alacrity with which the Austrian bishops, ignoring Nazi efforts to de-Christianise the Reich, had accepted the new regime.[3] The Jesuit theologian, Père Fessard, had drawn similar conclusions from the Munich crisis of 1938. In his *Epreuve de Force* (1939) he asserted that no understanding with Germany under Nazi domination was possible.[4] It is perhaps significant that members of the various Catholic youth organisations, using such texts as well as the papal encyclical, were more sensitive to the menace of nazism than their elders.

Elected Pope in March 1939, Pius XII gave no indication of siding with the democracies. When Italy struck at Albania he remained silent. On April 16 in a message to Spanish Catholics he had praised 'the very noble Christian sentiments of Franco'; there was no word of comfort for the Basque priests who had remained loyal to their religion and to the Republican cause to the bitter end. On August 23 Charles-Roux, the French Ambassador to the Vatican, handed to Mgr Tardini a note that requested papal condemnation of Germany. The *démarche* was fruitless. It is true that the Pope, using his diplomatic skills somewhat ineffectually, was trying behind the scenes to save the peace, but even after war was declared he did not break his silence. (It could be argued, however, that another encyclical published in October 1939, *Summi Pontificatus*, did indirectly condemn Germany: it not only blamed the outbreak of hostilities upon the lack of solidarity between peoples, ascribed to the deification of the State, but referred in veiled terms to the rape of Catholic Poland.)

Yet, as will be seen, Pius XII remained mute to the very end. By refusing to condemn nazism he may have thought to mitigate the effects of aggression and safeguard the interests of the Church, which for him were paramount. Did not regimes come and go, was not the Church eternal? It is more likely that he held back because he hoped to act as a '*deus ex machina*' serving as the honest broker when the moment was ripe to make peace. To this end he regarded absolute Vatican neutrality as indispensable. This went to extremes: the recall of the Nuncio from

Paris had even been contemplated because on one occasion Valerio Valeri had declared that in any war France would be defeated.[5] In May 1940 Cardinal Suhard, newly promoted to the see of Paris, backed by Paul Reynaud, the Prime Minister, had pleaded with Pius XII to intercede to prevent Mussolini from stabbing France in the back. The Pope refused to intervene.[6]

Little wonder, therefore, that the French bishops, charged with the *magisterium* of the Church, and resenting any interference from less inhibited theologians, were at first disoriented. Lacking clear Vatican guidance, they fell back on their patriotism, which was unquestionable. Bishop Pic of Valence spoke of the war as a crusade, the greatest in all history.[7] In his Lenten letter (2 February 1940) to his diocese he castigated the errors and the racial crimes of Germany. His reaction was typical: the general consensus was that France had embarked upon what was, in the Aquinan sense, a 'just war'.

The history of Protestant theology foreshadowed how Protestants would eventually react to the events leading up to the debacle of 1940.

Nineteenth century French Protestantism consisted of four main movements. Two were predominant, although theologically very different. The Union nationale des Eglises réformées took a liberal view, subjecting the Bible to such rigorous historical criticism that in the end its authority was undermined. The Christian was therefore thrown back upon himself to determine his faith. It was the quality of his inner religious life and how this manifested itself in his moral behaviour that were important. By contrast, the more orthodox approach of the Union des Eglises réformées évangeliques sought its inspiration in the Scriptures, which it often interpreted literally.[8] It was this second strand of Protestantism which came to dominate in the 1930s, constituting the basis for the strongest theological condemnations of totalitarianism. This was reinforced by the ultimate union in 1938 of the majority of French Protestants in the Eglise Réformée de France, headed by Pastor Boegner. The unified structure of this, the principal organisation, signified a return to a more church- and scriptural-centred religion around which the hitherto semi-autonomous Protestant lay movements, including those for young people, rallied.

The writings of the Swiss theologian Karl Barth directly affected the resurgence of French Protestantism during the 1930s. Barthism derived largely from its interpretation of St Paul's Epistle to the Romans, forming the basis of a new 'dialectical' theology, which relied on the Bible as the word of God.[9] Its propositions were simple: since God is all-sovereign, his absolute dominion therefore prevails over all temporal powers. It followed that the State was relativised, being a temporary and subordinate expedient eventually to be supplanted by the advent of

God's kingdom on earth. Meanwhile the State had a duty to ensure the Church's freedom to spread the gospel and administer the sacraments. It was incumbent upon the Church, in its turn, to prevent the State from lapsing into a totalitarianism that required the absolute submission of its citizens.[10]

Barth had experienced nazism at first hand; forced out of his professorship at Bonn, he had returned to his native Switzerland, where he took up a chair at Basle. From this pivotal position both geographically and theologically, he was able to make his views widely known. In 1934 a work castigating nazism had appeared in French under the title, *Le Culte raisonnable*, but had attracted little attention. Before 1939 he also made several visits to Paris and the Midi, where Protestantism was strong. In Lyons he found a gifted propagator of his ideas in his fellow-countryman, Pastor de Pury. Already in *Foi et Vie*, the review he directed, Pury had criticised the Deutsche Christen movement for lauding Hitler, exalting nazism, and rejecting the Jews as social pariahs. He continued by publishing excerpts from a review that Barth had co-founded with another theologian, Thurneysen, *Theologische Existenz Heute*, which had also censured the exclusion of Jewish Christians from the German Church: church membership should be determined not by race but by baptism and the Holy Spirit. At the same time *Foi et Vie* made known the declaration of faith proclaimed by the Confessional Church in Germany. *Hic et Nunc*, another journal with which Pury and Denis de Rougemont were associated, and which enjoyed an ephemeral existence between 1932 and 1936, also printed a crushing indictment of the 'German Christians' and anti-Semitism , pronounced on Maundy Thursday, 1933, by a German, Pastor Heinrich Vogel, and which had achieved wide publicity through the Swiss *Tägliche Rundschau*. Barth's own writings, and particularly his seminal work, *Parole de Dieu et parole humaine* (1933), became known in France through his translators, Pastor Maury and A. Lavenchy. Those who took their religion seriously were left in no doubt as to where the Barthian interpretation of Protestant belief stood in relation to nazism and all its works.

Young Protestant students were particularly well-informed. The 'Fédé' (Fédération française des Associations chrétiennes d'étudiants: FFACE) and former students — the 'post-Fédés' — published in their journal, *Le Semeur*, the proceedings of their national congress held in Montpellier in February 1939, which included extensive extracts of speeches by Pastor Boegner on 'Liberté du Chrétien dans l'Etat' and by Pastor Maury on the 'Service du Chrétien à l'Etat'. Citing Barth, they characterised the only acceptable Christian action in a totalitarian State as collective, organised disobedience. Maury warned prophetically: 'If the days come when the requirements of the French State are unacceptable, remember that it is better to obey God rather than men.'[11] A similar note of foreboding was struck in the Protestant regional press.[12] In addition a non-Barthian review, *Christianisme social*, published no less than thirty-two articles and documents on nazism.[13] Leading theologians' views on the true nature of nazism in this way penetrated Protestant youth.

Nevertheless, when war came, the Christian in the pew did not feel directly affected. Conservative Protestants, like many Catholics, were inclined to view the impending struggle as one that would eventually turn out to be between 'German and Soviet atheism', in which hopefully the two adversaries might eventually destroy each other. Some, mindful of the extravagant language used in condemning Germany in 1914, refrained from speaking of it as a 'holy war'. A few adopted a Quietist position, which easily degenerated into indifference.[14]

It was to jolt them out of these somewhat negative attitudes that Karl Barth despatched to Charles Westphal, a young Grenoble pastor, a first 'Letter to the Protestants of France'. Considerably cut by the censorship, this statement was published in *Foi et Vie* in December 1939. Barth insisted that the Church must proclaim its resistance to the Nazi evil, although he warned that the outcome of the conflict was as yet uncertain. Responsibility was firmly laid upon Britain and France: since their weakness had provoked the Nazi phenomenon, it was they who should eradicate it. It would be better, for example, for his native Switzerland to remain out of the struggle. He did not advocate a personal crusade against Hitler — it should be remembered that 'le Crucifié est mort aussi pour lui' — but the Church must not remain neutralist or pacifist. It should urge Germans to resist. The Third Reich was sick, its people suffering under nazism, which was 'the bad dream of the German pagan who had turned late to Christianity, and then only in its Lutheran form'. Nor must the desired victors of the conflict — the Allies — treat the vanquished as badly as they had done in the Treaty of Versailles. He also warned that if by chance the victory fell to Germany, the Christian must still remain faithful to the cause. There can be no doubt that the rank and file Protestant, although he may have paid little heed to warnings of impending doom, was better informed in 1940 than his Catholic counterpart of the issues at stake.

Yet in July 1940, with the 'Blitzkrieg' as catalyst, France passed at a stroke from a democratic to an authoritarian regime.

How did French Christians react to this unexpected reversal of fortune? Catholics and Protestants alike had been unwavering in support of the war since 1939. In April 1940 the ACA had written to the Prime Minister, Daladier, in very supportive terms.[15]

How had the defeat come about, and how did the Church react? That the Germans had technical superiority there was no doubt. Joseph Barthélemy, a future Vichy Justice minister, a Catholic and close friend of Cardinal Gerlier, commented on the absurdity of using a horse-drawn antitank gun moving at 8 kilometres an hour to attack fast German tanks. But he added that it was intellectual failure that lay behind French inferiority, which was not only industrial and military, but *moral*.[16] Before the war Cardinal Verdier had pointed, as did all the bishops, to the 'corrosive' influence of secularism, which, he asserted, was as much to be feared as German racism.[17] In 1936 all the cardinals had warned France against 'The practical atheism to which our country seems to have resigned itself in its national life. For God, officially expelled from everywhere, has become for the masses the "unknown god" and thus the moral and social order of which He is the necessary foundation was bound to totter.'[18]

Their hope was for a new regime in which, 'under the threefold influence of Christian aspirations, Latin culture, and our French traditions, there will flourish a wise and joyous liberty'. It was a theme taken up in 1940 by *La Gerbe*, the collaborationist newspaper started almost immediately after the collapse by the Catholic writer Alphonse de Chateaubriant. An article (19 September 1940) by Gonzague Truc blamed secularism for the defeat.

Blame was also laid upon individualism. De Tocqueville's definition seems appropriate: 'a deliberate and peaceful sentiment which disposes each citizen to isolate himself from the mass of his fellows which at first saps only the virtues of public life, but in the long run, attacks and destroys all other virtues and is eventually absorbed into pure egoism'.[19] Nor was it only linked to secularism. To some degree bishops, clergy and laity alike had withdrawn into a kind of isolation, an 'inner migration'. Not only Catholics, but many other Frenchmen would have agreed that individualism had contributed to the national collapse. Some social Catholics, not least Mgr Saliège of Toulouse, would even have concurred with those left-wing theorists who asserted that individualism occurred in a state of laissez-faire, anarchy, social atomisation and the exploitation of the poor under a system of individual capitalism.[20] After the debacle some ecclesiastics alleged that France had been punished for its Godlessness and lack of positive godliness, and had to do penance. Luckily, all was not lost, they declared, because a second Joan of Arc, in the shape of Marshal Pétain, had risen to save the country.

Even before the Armistice was signed Suhard had urged Catholics to remember French honour was intact, despite the 'hard blows' France had suffered.[21] One Catholic writer, Claudel, saw the defeat as a deliverance. He wrote in his diary: 'France has been delivered after sixty years from the yoke of the anti-Catholic Radical party (teachers, lawyers, Jews, Freemasons). The new government invokes God... There is hope of being delivered from universal suffrage and parliamentarianism.'[22]

There can be no doubt that the Catholic authorities, like Frenchmen in general, pinned their hopes upon the aged leader who now assumed regalian powers.

Protestants were more reticent regarding the new regime. In 1940, on Bastille Day, Pastor Roland de Pury, preaching in Lyons, and Pastor Charles Westphal, in Grenoble, reserved judgement. Pury chose as his text Exodus 20:15, and entitled his sermon 'Tu ne déroberas point' ('Thou shalt not steal'). France would be better dead than to have sold out to the enemy. The war was just: 'as if the defeat could take away from the conflict its character of justice; as if success was the measure of truth'. It was a theme that was to recur. Westphal insisted that the regime of the Third Republic had not been wholly bad. In Bourdeaux (Drôme) Pastor Gidéon Sablet called for vigilance, because institutions were only of the same value as the men who directed them.[23] In occupied Paris Pastor Bertrand, speaking at the Oratory, had to be more circumspect, but also insisted against any idolising of success without regarding the merits of the cause. These attitudes were typical of their fellow-pastors elsewhere. The history of Protestant persecution had made them wary of any changes in the status quo.

In October 1940 Barth therefore again addressed himself to France. His 'A Question and a Request to the Protestants of France', which circulated in duplicated form, was a call not to assume the burden of guilt or obey the exhortations to repentance urged upon Christians. The 'question' which he posed was: will France continue to participate in the struggle and assume its responsibility? The 'request' was similar; it was to continue to resist nazism: 'You will do so inwardly by your faith and prayer and, as a consequence, externally by your speech and action, according to the extent of your knowledge and power.'[24] Defeat had changed nothing for France, 'although for the time being this struggle is no longer yours, but may be taken up by others, in the Channel, over London, or in Egypt (and who knows where else tomorrow?). Absolutely nothing has changed for French Protestants, neither the motive, nor the necessity, nor the right to make war on Hitler.'[25] For Barth Hitler represented the Apocalypse. Any thought of neutrality or collaboration with the Germans should be banished. The evil of nazism remained undiminished.

By contrast, the Catholic Hierarchy gave the impression that a mood of repentance — ridiculed by secularists as 'bondieusard' ('pious') and 'pleurnicheur' ('whining') — was more appropriate.[26] Cardinal Gerlier went so far as to say that if France had been victorious it would have remained the prisoner of its errors: through having been secularised, France had been in danger of dying.[27] For Archbishop Feltin of Bordeaux 'a miraculous victory would not... have put an end to our sins, it would not have made us resolve determinedly to undertake the task of inner regeneration, which is the prime condition for our revival'.[28] Even Mgr Saliège, the independent-minded Archbishop of Toulouse, later to embody the defiance of Catholic resistance, formulated a prayer of penitence, asking forgiveness for France: it had expelled God from the school and the law courts, had put up with a corrupt press and literature, tolerated the white slave traffic, and allowed a degrading promiscuity of the sexes in workshops, offices and factories. He asked what use France had made of the victory of 1918, and what use it would have made of victory in 1940?[29] Perhaps most reactionary was the attitude of Mgr Caillot of Grenoble. Even before Pétain had assumed absolute power the bishop had pledged complete loyalty to the Marshal, as 'l'homme providentiel'. If previously he had been outspoken in his condemnation of Hitler and nazism, after the defeat he had drawn a veil over his previous utterances. The humiliation of France, in his view, presented it with a heaven-sent opportunity to effect a moral and religious transformation. Harking back to his own early days, he indicted those who had voted for the Separation and the expulsion of religious as the ones ultimately responsible for the catastrophe. He also arraigned the Freemasons and Jews — the latter 'non au sens religieux, mais au sens cosmopolite'. In his view, the fortunes of France since the Revolution and 1940 constituted an 'evil parenthesis' in its history.[30] 'Turn back the clock' could surely go no farther. As Mgr Choquet expressed it in his diocese of Lourdes, 'The misfortunes of France are the consequence of its errors',[31] and Mgr Durieux, Archbishop of Chambéry, *(Quinzaine religieuse*, Chambéry, 15 July 1940), even prematurely rejoiced in the 'unexpected consolations' arising from the defeat.

Nor was this attitude of contrition confined to Church leaders. The organisers of a pilgrimage to the Black Virgin of Rocamdour (Lot) wrote: 'The gentle Madonna will see us at her feet *gementes et flentes.*, for our prayers and hymns will this year be prayers and hymns of repentance and sorrow.'

The posture of penitence continued for a long time afterwards. Mgr Maisonobe, Bishop of Belley, in his Lenten letter for 1942, still spoke of the war as 'the punishment for the disorderly conduct of men who have denied God'[32] — although by then he may have subsumed the Germans in his indictment. As late as 31 January 1943 Père Forestier, chaplain of the Chantiers de la Jeunesse, the compulsory youth organisation set up under the new regime, in a sermon given in Clermont cathedral ascribed the causes of the fall of France to a rebellion against God that dated back to the eighteenth century. This had given rise to insubordination, to lack of authority, whereas 'l'univers entier est une grande hiérarchie'.[33] That a reasonable deduction from all such breast-beating might be that God had sided with nazism escaped the perception of most.

It is true, however, that other Catholic voices spoke differently from the very beginning. The Bishop of Annecy denounced 'the mechanical victory of chunks of ironmongery organised in the service of barbarous cupidity'.[34] There were reminders that France had entered the war to protect civilisation against barbarism. In the *Figaro* Mauriac, the Catholic writer, wrote: 'We have no need to blush for having cherished liberty, but only for having defended it so badly.'[35] Where the German presence was most oppressive, as in northern France, the mood of repentance soon passed, and rallying to the Pétain regime was even seen by some as an act of defiance against the occupier.

Thus Catholics, left without a lead from the Vatican, were forced back on remorse for alleged past misdeeds. It was almost as if they regarded the Nazis — surely far more corrupt than any leaders of France under the Third Republic — as God's avenging angels. The Protestant minority, on the other hand, had an alternative: they could embrace Barth's counsel of defiance. What united all Christians in 1940, however, was a sentiment of patriotism embodied in Marshal Pétain, although from the outset there was a certain ambiguity in expectations of how he and the regime he established would act. What did Vichy represent for Christians, and above all, what could Marshal Pétain do for them?

Notes

Unless otherwise stated the place of publication is Paris

1. X. de Montclos *et al.* (eds), *Eglises et Chrétiens dans la Deuxième Guerre mondiale. La région Rhône-Alpes, Actes*: Grenoble, p. 56. Intervention of André Latreille in the discussion.
2. *Actes*: Lyons, diagram on p. 31. For a note on *L'Aube* and the pre-war Catholic press see Appendix I.
3. R. Bédarida, 'Le Père Pierre Chaillet: de la théologie de Möhler à la Résistance', in: P. Bolle and J. Godel (eds), *Spiritualité, théologie et résistance, Actes*: Biviers, pp. 56f.
4. G. Fessard, *Epreuve de Force*, 1939, pp. 70f.
5. M. Martin du Gard, *La Chronique de Vichy, 1940–1944*, 1948, p. 87.
6. P. Duclos, *Le Vatican et la seconde guerre mondiale. Action doctrinale et diplomatique en faveur de la paix*, 1955, p. 123.
7. G. Cholvy and Y.-M. Hilaire, *Histoire religieuse de la France contemporaine, 1930–1988,*

1988, pp. 69f.

8. A. Dumas, 'Courants théologiques dans le Protestantisme français entre 1930–1939', *Actes*: Biviers, p. 73.

9. L. Boisset, 'Paysage théologique et montée du Nazisme (1930–1939)', *Actes*: Biviers, p. 33.

10. P. Bolle, 'Les Protestants et leurs Eglises devant la persécution des Juifs en France', paper given at the colloquium *L'Etat, les Eglises et les mouvements de Résistance devant la persécution des Juifs en France pendant la Seconde Guerre mondiale*, Paris, 1979, Centre de Documentation Juive contemporaine, p. 1.

11. This was the theological point of departure for many Protestants.

12. For example, *Le Nord Protestant*; *L'Ami chrétien des Familles*; *Nouvel Echo de la Drôme et de l'Ardèche*, (circulation 20,000).

13. Bolle, 'Les Protestants', p. 3. Contributors to the review included François Wendel, Edmond Vermeil, Elie Grenelle, Wilfred Monod and Jean Cavaillès, who was shot by the Germans in February 1944.

14. Cholvy and Hilaire, *Histoire religieuse*, pp. 69f.

15. Verdier spoke on the radio, 20 January 1939; letter to Daladier reported in *Le Temps*, 1 April 1939: see J.-L. Crémieux-Brilhac, *Les Français de l'An 40. I: La Guerre, Oui ou Non?* 1990, p. 64.

16. AN 2 AG 75. Typescript of speech given at the prize-giving to pupils of the Canton of L'Isle Jourdain, n.d.

17. Verdier's article, written for the *Semaine religieuse* of his diocese, was censored on 9 February 1939 by Daladier, but was published the following week after protests from Catholic deputies. See Crémieux-Brilhac, *Les Français*, p. 325.

18. Quoted in J. Delperrié de Bayac, *Histoire du Front Populaire*, 1972, p. 317.

19. A. de Tocqueville, *De la démocratie en Amérique*, ii, 2, ch. 11, in *Œuvres complètes*, edited by J.M. Mayer, 1951, vol. 1, pt. 2, p. 10.

20. See Mary Douglas, foreword to Marcel Mauss, *The Gift*, translated by W.D. Halls, London, 1990. It is interesting that Durkheim and his school likewise condemned capitalism, as did many 'Social Catholics'. See S. Lukes, *E. Durkheim. His Life and Work*, London, 1973, pp. 197f.

21. A Dio, Lille. Document in file ACA 2 B 1.

22. P. Claudel, *Journal intime*, 10 July 1940, quoted in R. Griffiths, *Marshal Pétain*, London, 1970, p. 251.

23. R. Nodot, 'Le pasteur Roland de Pury et les protestants de la région lyonnaise', *Réforme* (Lyons), 15 May 1992; see also P. Bolle, *RHDGM*, 1979, p. 288.

24. The text of Barth's letter of October 1940 and that of December 1939, are given in *Actes*: Biviers, pp. 155–70.

25. Barth's mimeograph letter of December 1940.

26. J. Cornec, *Laïcité*, 1965, p. 157.

27. Quoted in Cholvy and Hilaire, *Histoire religieuse*, p. 73.

28. Quoted in H. Amouroux, *Quarante millions de Pétainistes*, 1977, p. 269.

29. *Mandement* ('Charge') published in *La Croix*, 28 June 1940, quoted in G. Miller, *Les Pousse-au-jouir du Maréchal Pétain*, 1975, p. 44.

30. J. Godel, 'Monseigneur Caillot, évêque de Grenoble (1917–1957) et le régime de Vichy', *Actes*: Grenoble. pp. 77f.

31. Quoted in a brochure: J. Cotereau, 'La France a-t-elle collaboré?', series *Problèmes actuels*, May 1946, no. 6, p. 5.

32. L. and G. Trenard, *Histoire des diocèses de France*, vol. 7, *Le diocèse de Belley*, p. 252.

33. Quoted in *La Semaine des Chantiers*, Clermont-Ferrand, January 1943, p. 24.

34. Cholvy and Hilaire, *Histoire religieuse*, p. 73.

35. F. Mauriac, 'Ne pas se renier', *Le Figaro*, 23 July 1940.

PART II

ASPIRATIONS, REALISATIONS AND DISAPPOINTMENTS

—4—

The Man of Destiny

The shock experienced by Church and State as, like a flood tide, the invaders rolled across France, had had a mobilising effect. Baudouin, Pétain's first Foreign Minister and a practising Catholic, had recently reread Renan's essay, written after the debacle of 1870, *La réforme intellectuelle et morale de la France*. For him its condemnation of materialist doctrines and demand for 'intelligent' public institutions were just as applicable to the defeat of 1940.[1] General Weygand, a like-minded Catholic and perhaps one of those closest to Pétain at the time, shared Baudouin's concern. He had been a sympathiser with Colonel de la Rocque's Croix de Feu, drawn originally from ex-soldiers of the First World War, whose 1936 programme had proclaimed a mystique based on 'Travail, famille, patrie'.[2] The desire for a spiritual and moral renewal of the nation was strong among prominent Catholics.

As well as the belief that Marshal Pétain could prove the saviour of France, the Church wished to press home the material advantage it could derive from the new situation. In the face of the advancing German armies Cardinal Liénart in Lille and Cardinal Suhard in Paris, like most of their priests, had not fled. They expected their steadfastness to be rewarded. Thus the bishops welcomed Pétain's assumption of power. Already on 27 June Cardinal Suhard had dubbed him 'the unimpeachable Frenchman'.[3]

There was no mourning the death of the Third Republic: parliamentary democracy had not favoured the devout; the left-wing dogmas so often associated with it were held to be anti-Christian. Now, in the aftermath of defeat, which many Catholics believed France had merited by turning its back on God, the hour of repentance would prelude a national renaissance. From a negative, or at best a neutral, stance towards secular authority, the Church at last felt it could adopt a more positive attitude.

At first, however, prudence was the watchword. The 'internal migration' of the Church under the Popular Front had bred caution. Meanwhile, the presence of numerous Catholics at Vichy, where the new regime was finally constituted, was moderately reassuring. On 9 July Cardinals Gerlier and Suhard met in Paris to discuss how to remedy the disorganisation caused by the invasion and physical division of France, which sometimes cut dioceses in two. Both cardinals were wary not only of the Germans but also of others, particularly Laval and the Maurrassians, that had foregathered in the spa.[4] Those Catholics who had loyally upheld the papal ban on Action Française in 1926 harboured misgivings. Gerlier, however, expressed confidence that Catholics could eventually derive substantial benefits from the new regime.[5]

The first meeting of the ACA took place in Paris on 28 August 1940. Cardinal Liénart, as its president, managed to travel from Lille, despite difficulties arising from the administrative amputation of the Nord department from the rest of France — it was attached to the German High Command in Brussels. (When Liénart had met Suhard in Paris at the end of July, he had secured a temporary travel permit from the Germans. Before permission was granted to go to Paris for a second time the Germans had insisted on his reporting on the 'course and outcome' of his first trip.[6] They continued to subject the cardinal to great harassment on such matters, at first requiring a permit for travel within his diocese, even on Sundays.)

The Assembly exhorted clergy: to adopt a 'practice of loyalty to the legitimate authority' ('la pratique du loyalisme envers le Pouvoir légitime'); to observe order and discipline as regards the Occupation troops; and to exercise discretion in public utterances. This early insistence on Vichy's 'legitimacy' may, paradoxically, indicate that its validity for some Catholics was already questionable.

The bishops seized upon Pétain as the symbol of French salvation. The moral sanction they now gave to the new regime was one of the decisive factors in its obtaining national acceptance.[7]

The hope was that the new era would signal, *mutatis mutandis*, a fresh alliance between 'throne and altar', and, in MacMahon's phrase, the 're-establishment of the Moral Order'. More recently, the papal encyclical *Summi Pontificatus* (20 October 1939), had deplored the decline in ethical values, on which public and private actions had once been judged.

'Travail, famille, patrie', elevated to the status of the new national motto, gratified Cardinal Gerlier, who declared that these three words were those of the Church also. Liberty, equality and fraternity had held no great appeal for traditionalist Catholics, which extremists even considered inimical to true religion, had not prevailed. For over forty years the cultural climate had been hostile to Christian teaching. Hence the defeat: 'pour nos péchés, cette infortune', as *La France catholique*, the organ of the FNC succinctly summed it up.[8]

The portents for concerted action between Church and State were favourable. Pétain sought a 'Révolution nationale', or, as he preferred to call it, a 'redressement intellectuel et moral'. This required above all loyalty, but what did the concept mean? An effort was made to spell this out.[9] Submission to civil authority, it was argued, required absolute obedience to its edicts unless they were 'manifestly' contrary to divine law; it demanded 'sincere' support for government legislation aiming at the common good and moral rehabilitation of France. Hasty judgements were to be avoided. The sole reservations of the Church might relate to matters of detail of direct concern to it, such as educational and social measures, and 'certain spiritual dangers that might arise from collaboration with Germany on the economic and political planes' ('certain dangers spirituels qui pourraient venir d'une collaboration sur les plans économique and politique avec l'Allemagne'). The phrase 'the common good', as will be seen, was to come back to haunt the bishops. Meanwhile one notes a reluctance to favour too close co-operation with the Germans.

Loyalty was already being put to the test. The promulgation of the first Statute of the Jews and, following almost immediately, the internment of foreign Jews, coupled with Pétain's meeting with Hitler at Montoire on 24 October, upset many Christians, as indeed many other Frenchmen. On the other hand, it provoked one bishop, Mgr Dutoit of Arras, to come out openly in favour of collaboration.

In 1940 there was in fact little choice save to rally behind Pétain. Some Christians, such as Mounier, the editor of *Esprit*, clung to the hope that they could temper authoritarian rule from within the system. Another option open — hardly realistic in the circumstances — was to throw in one's lot with the 'dissidents', then represented only by the shadowy presence of de Gaulle in London. An almost unthinkable alternative was to join the vociferous few in Paris, who now banked on a German victory. They were as antidemocratic as the Vichyites and pro-Nazi into the bargain. To the average Frenchman, no less than the ordinary Christian, there was no doubt that the Pétainist regime had to be the preferred option.

The Hierarchy took the lead in backing the Marshal, insisting that he could save France as he had in 1916. By the autumn of 1940 messages of support flowed in from all sections of the Church. Despite the overt Anglophilia of his flock, Liénart wrote to Pétain, 'I am conscious of fulfilling a duty of my episcopal charge in declaring my loyalty to the Head of State.'[10]

For Cardinal Gerlier also, loyalty was no mere show, but the expression of an inner conviction. His public statements reflected this. For him the apogee was reached when Pétain paid a two-day visit to Lyons, and was received at the Cathédrale Saint-Jean. The Cardinal recalled that this was the traditional place for welcoming the Kings of France, and asserted that God was responsible for the Marshal's presence there.[11] Later, as cheers rang out from the crowd, Gerlier spoke words that he must later have bitterly regretted: 'Have you noticed, Marshal, that the resounding cries of the crowd, at first many different ones, have been reduced to two: "Long live Pétain!" and "Long live France!" Not even this — they have now dissolved into one single shout. *For Pétain is France, and France, today, is Pétain!* [emphasis added].'[12]

This apostrophe, sometimes quoted omitting the word 'today', has been used to condemn Gerlier, but by inserting such a qualification, the cardinal perhaps showed the caution of the onetime lawyer.

To Mgr Martin, Bishop of Le Puy, Cardinal Gerlier wrote (14 October 1940):

> I have always esteemed, and I believe it more firmly than ever, that we must, in the present circumstances, lend our support to any co-operation that is not ruled out by the principles of which we are the guardians. We have suffered too much from the opposing attitude, and the duty of backing the Marshal is too plain for us possibly to hesitate.[13]

By putting in the phrase 'in the present circumstances', he again exhibited prudence.

Nevertheless, the bishops, no less than the cardinals, were enthusiastic. Pétain's military record weighed with them. Some fifty of the ninety-six prelates had served in the First World War. Archbishop Feltin and Cardinals Gerlier and Liénart had won the Médaille Militaire. On 25 June the Marshal broadcast the first of his celebrated 'messages' to the nation, in which he declared that the spirit of pleasure had destroyed the spirit of sacrifice, interpreted by the bishop of Aire-Dax to mean that 'the pagan spirit had destroyed the Christian spirit'.[14] Mgr Rastouil, Bishop of Limoges, who was to alter his tune radically as the war progressed, urged his flock: 'Listen to the French radio from morning to night: all the principles that the French people are being reminded of concerning human dignity, morality, conscience and the family [...] are those that spring forth abundantly from the pages of the Gospel, the catechism, and the papal encyclicals.'[15] A pastoral letter of Mgr Mesguen, Bishop of Poitiers, entitled 'The Social Virtues of the Present Hour', looking forward to 1941, spoke of the duty for Catholics 'to set an example of sincere deference to the established authority' since 'submission to a legitimate authority is one of our first social duties'.[16] The Lenten letters of the bishops in 1941 were replete with terms such as 'Révolution nationale', 'révolution spirituelle', 'renouveau français', 'servir' and 'discipline'.[17]

The messages of the Head of State continued to give great satisfaction to the Church. They caused Gerlier to remark, 'What an impressive coincidence between the teaching of the Church and the words of the Marshal'.[18] Innumerable sermons and talks commented on Pétain's every word. Typical, for example, was a series given in Aix by Père Coulet, entitled, 'Confiance en Dieu', 'Dignité dans le malheur', 'Devoir du travail', 'Restauration de l'autorité et de la discipline', 'Retour à la terre', and 'Restauration de la famille'.[19] Other Christian groups echoed such sentiments. Thus Pastor Boegner, speaking for the Reformed Church — but not for all its members — asserted categorically, 'There is only one duty: to follow the Marshal.' Nevertheless prudence occasionally crept in. Thus Mgr Valeri, the Nuncio in Paris, warned against too overt a commitment to the regime.[20]

Reciprocally, it was also evident that the attitude of the State to the Church had changed profoundly. Already on 25 June Pétain's ministers had attended a solemn mass at Bordeaux Cathedral, and the Marshal, Head of Government but not yet Head of State, had knelt at the Elevation, an official act of symbolism unknown for many a decade. Much later, at his trial, Pétain asserted that he had aspired to represent a tradition, that of French and Christian civilisation. Baudouin, in the limbo between two regimes, wrote in his diary for 26 July 1940: 'We wish to remain faithful to Christian morality; and we want man, as a human being, to remain free to believe in God and serve God as he understands him.' The years would show how difficult this was to become.

Other clergy, who were veterans of the First World War or who had known the upheavals between Church and State at the beginning of the century, followed their superiors' line. Younger clergy were less fervent in their support. Cardinal Suhard, meeting his diocesan priests on 13 December 1940, noted already one dissentient: Mgr Chevrot, the priest of Saint-François-Xavier in Paris.

Of the various religious orders, the Jesuits and Dominicans were more restrained in their support. Indeed Père Dillard, who was later to speak out forcibly, termed the Vichy enterprise 'a magnificent adventure to be resisted'. Another Jesuit, looking back in 1944 on the heady early days of the Marshal's rule, reflected that 'the Head of State, the totem of the secularisers of Action Française, had been presented in the churches as a kind of prophet.'[21] Père Desbuquois, head of the Catholic social welfare organisation, Action Populaire, signified his approval because he hoped that at long last his programme of social reform would be realised. Contrary to many others in their order, religious such as Pères Forestier and Doncœur, who were prominent in the Catholic youth organisations, were even more enthusiastic in their protestations of absolute loyalty.

Meanwhile lesser fry in the Church hastened to pledge their backing. After a visit by Pétain to the Carmelite convent at Agen, where his niece, Sœur Geneviève de Jésus, was a nun, the Mother Superior wrote to the Marshal: 'From the very first day, we have been for you, and profoundly for you... We are "your" Carmel of Agen, just as you are "our" Marshal.'[22]

Catholic educational circles added their meed of praise and loyalty, although the Institut Catholique at Toulouse was far less enamoured than its sister institutions in Paris and Angers. Cardinal Baudrillart, as rector of the Paris Institut Catholique, later the most notorious Christian collaborator of all, sent a message on behalf of the bishops responsible for his institution, expressing 'admiration, gratitude, confidence and attachment'.[23] Mgr Costes, Bishop of Angers, signing himself 'Chancellor of the Catholic University' located there [*sic*] (the Third Republic had removed the right of Catholic institutions of higher education to call themselves universities), pledged the support of the bishops of the Catholic West — and incidentally slipped in a request for subsidies for Catholic education.[24]

Thus ecclesiastical opinion was clearly in favour of the new order. What of other Catholic politicians who had functioned under the Third Republic? It was perhaps symptomatic that the majority of the two Christian parties in the National Assembly, the PDP and the less committed Jeune République, had voted for the installation of the new absolutism.

What, in particular, was the attitude of the PDP, which was closest to the Church? Its leader, Champetier de Ribes, had opposed the granting of full powers to Pétain. A different tendency in the party was represented by his colleague, L.-A. Pagès, who was connected with the Pau newspaper, *Le Patriote des Pyrénées*, influential in the South-West, and like many in the PDP therefore at first broadly favoured the new regime. However, one incident showed how fluid the situation was. On 29 October 1940 the newspaper published an article by R. Berriot entitled 'Loyalisme conditionnel'. This set out what became finally recognised as Catholic doctrine: no government could exact obedience if it contravened God's law and the individual's rights. A follow-up article by Pagès, 'Comment il faut servir' (1–2 November 1940), stipulated that the new constitution that Pétain had promised had to meet with general approval and guarantee freedom of expression to all political groupings. This smacked too much of old-style democracy for Vichy extremists, who accused the PDP of 'sulking' in its attitude to the regime. They, on the contrary, favoured a constitution that would not only punish acts of disloyalty but also 'crimes of opinion' ('délits d'opinion'). The affair was duly reported to the Marshal's entourage.[25]

Pagès, worried by this denunciation, became eager to distance himself from his leader, Champetier de Ribes, and sought now to reconcile himself with the regime. He informed Lucien Romier, who had been instructed by Pétain to mount an enquiry, that, although he had no recent contact with Ribes, he knew his leader 'would never agree to support the government' ('qu'il ne consentirait jamais à appuyer ce gouvernement'). He volunteered to enlist other PDP deputies in active support of the regime, and promised the backing in the future of *Le Patriote des Pyrénées*, and of two other newspapers with which he was associated, *Le Mémorial de la Loire* and *Le Journal du Tarn*. He believed that most of the members of the PDP, like other Catholic organisations such as the 'Semaines sociales' of the Action Populaire, to which the party was closely linked, and, in his view, the Christian trade unions, stood solidly behind the government's reform programme. As one on the party's right-wing, he belatedly regretted that in the past the PDP had followed 'des méthodes un peu trop parlementaires' and had co-operated unduly with the Centre and the Left. He now acknowledged the need to rally to a regime free of 'politiciens', one which sought to restore spiritual values, promote specialists and elites, and condemned the excesses of capitalism, while fighting collectivism and reinstating the principle of authority — a not inaccurate summary of what the regime allegedly intended. After what was in effect a *mea culpa* and a profession of loyalty Pagès discreetly advanced his qualifications for some post under the new dispensation.[26] This proclamation of loyalty cut no ice with his original accuser, Loustaunau-Navarre, who dubbed him a 'red Christian'. Meanwhile Champetier de Ribes's loyalty to the regime was indeed doubtful. Still opposed to the Armistice, he was soon to contact the incipient Resistance movement 'Liberté'. Georges Bidault, also a PDP member, after his release from a prisoner of war camp, adopted a similar course of action. Such wavering between refusal and acceptance of the new regime was typical of the more politically-minded Catholic.

With strong ties to the PDP, the CFTC, the Christian trade union, was also divided. A majority was unwilling to embrace wholeheartedly the regime if only because Jules Zirnheld, its leader, would not concede that the pro-union legislation passed under the Third Republic was bad. Interest centred on the possibility of Pétain promulgating a new constitution in which the role of labour would figure prominently. On the other hand a not unjustified apprehension was that other plans for the organisation of the work-force by the regime might signal the demise of the CFTC.

Ecclesiastical adulation of the Head of State reached a climax in 1941. *La Revue Moderne* published a 'Crédo de la France' dedicated to the

'Prestigieux Pilote' (the Marshal, none other) which, parodying the Lord's Prayer, ran:

> Notre Père, qui êtes/ A notre tête / Que votre nom soit glorifié/ Que votre règne arrive/ Que votre volonté soit faite/ Sur la terre pour qu'on vive/ Demeurez sans retour/ Notre pain de chaque jour/ Redonnez l'existence/ A la France;/ Ne nous laissez pas retomber/ Dans le vain songe/ Et le mensonge;/ Et délivrez-nous du Mal/ O Maréchal.

Pétain, flattered by this invocation, conveyed his 'congratulations' and 'satisfaction' to its authors.[27] In similar vein Mgr Martin, of Le Puy, was told by Pétain during a visit that the couplets of the *Marseillaise* required alteration. Some of the bishop's diocesan priests therefore submitted a new version, entitled 'Travail, Famille, Patrie: La Marseillaise des temps nouveaux':

> Dans la FAMILLE il faut que chante
> Ta (France) sainte flamme, amour vainqueur.
> Dieu le veut: notre race ardente
> Sèmera la vie à plein cœur.(bis)

and continued,

> Chef glorieux de la PATRIE,
> Père au grand cœur, va, nous t'aimons,
> Tes enfants ont l'âme meurtrie,
> Mais, commande, et nous te suivrons (bis).[28]

It was also proposed that, in the mass, for the versicle 'Domine, salvam fac Rempublicam' ('O Lord, Save the Republic'), which, instituted after the 1801 Concordat, had survived the Law of Separation of Church and State, and had been chanted in a few dioceses right up to the Armistice, there should be substituted 'Domine, salve fac Philippum, ducem nostrum' ('O Lord, save Philip our Leader'). The Conseil d'Etat, however, advised that such an invocation would not meet with Vatican favour because the Marshal was not a hereditary ruler. To accept 'ducem', moreover, might constitute an awkward precedent, with demands from elsewhere for the insertion of such titles as 'Duce' or 'Führer'. The suggestion was dropped.[29] Alternatively it was proposed that 'Domine, salvam fac Rempublicam' should become 'Domine, salvam fac patriam (Galliam) nostram', to keep up with the times.[30]

In many ways the Church carried flattery to an extreme. The feast of Saint-Philippe, in honour of the Marshal, was celebrated conveniently on May Day, the former Labour Day. Curiously. the Church officially made less of Joan of Arc Day (May 11) than did, for mutually opposing reasons, the collaborationists and Gaullists. Nevertheless, such patriotic manifestations as Claudel's oratorio, *Jeanne d'Arc au bûcher*, set to Honegger's music, which toured France in the summer of 1941, were commended to Catholics; Péguy's poetry, both for its religious and its patriotic content, remained popular with them. Inevitably Pétain, dubbed 'le miracle de Dieu pour la France', was compared to the saint whom the English had burnt at the stake.[31] Mgr Mennechet, Bishop of Soissons, informed the Marshal that on Saint Quentin's Day prayers had been offered for 'the wonderful leader that Providence has given to France'; at the pontifical mass the choir had sung an anthem, 'Fortissima Galliae duci Philippo valetudo et fides intrepida' ('Boundless health and intrepid faith [be given] to Philip, leader of France').[32]

Some Catholics were plainly upset that Pétain failed to demonstrate more publicly his adherence to the Church. One correspondent, an officer, signing his letter in full, asked, not only whether France was on God's side, but 'you, Marshal, are you on God's side? For — and this is terrifying — there is no half-way house. Are you on God's side? I have already listened to many discussions on this: no one dares to affirm it is so.'[33]

It was a Catholic trade unionist and PDP member, Marcel Poimbœuf, who first raised the question of the Marshal's marriage. According to an informer, he had queried at a meeting in Lyons whether Pétain, married in a civil ceremony to a divorcee, could in all sincerity uphold the family and Christian moral standards.[34] The question exercised a number of Catholics: how could a new State professing Christian principles be headed by a personage, however distinguished, whose past conduct belied those very principles? It was admirable that as a boy the Marshal had regularly attended the village church in his native Cauchy-à-la-Tour (Artois). Folk memory had it that his humble posture at mass contrasted with his natural leadership in children's games.[35] At eleven he had been packed off to the Collège Saint-Bertin at Saint-Omer, a military-style school run by priests, and then at fifteen to the Dominican college at Arcueil, in order to prepare for entrance to Saint-Cyr. Such an exemplary Catholic upbringing was naturally gratifying to the Church, now seeking State aid for its schools.

His later comportment was not so acceptable. His liaison with Eugénie Hardon, a married woman, began even before she had divorced in 1914. He had eventually married her in a civil ceremony in Paris in 1920. In 1929 'Madame la Maréchale' had obtained an ecclesiastical annulment of her first marriage. Pétain was therefore free to go through the religious ceremony his wife desired. This, Catholics considered, was long overdue; in 1940 both Cardinal Suhard and the Pope were anxious to obtain a 'regularisation' of the situation. Pétain delayed taking action, however, until March 1941 when he was married secretly by proxy at a ceremony in the archbishop's chapel.[36] No publicity was given to the event, although of course Pius XII had been informed by Suhard. To the public Pétain had been presented as a saint — 'le Maréchal-Christ'.[37] In fact, Pétain was not very religiously-minded, although he once jovially remarked, 'Une bonne messe n'a jamais fait de mal à personne.'[38] In his youth he had been much influenced by two priests who were related to his mother.[39] He was fairly regular in his attendance at mass at the Saint-Louis church in Vichy, where children gathered outside would sing 'the Marshal's song', 'Maréchal nous voilà', as he left. He was nevertheless convinced that French 'regeneration' could only be based on Christian foundations. To this extent, therefore, his beliefs were important.

His seeming lack of a firm religious faith was the subject of gossip. Once an obscure village priest in Uchard (Gard) spoke out from the pulpit: the Head of State — and his government —should set a better example if they wished to discourage secularism: Pétain had not even taken communion on Easter Day. Such outspokenness earned the humble cleric a stinging rebuke from his diocesan, the Bishop of Nîmes.[40]

At the first ACA meeting in August 1940 an agenda of concrete desiderata had been discussed, as well as the questions of loyalty and of behaviour towards the Germans. A number of matters were to be raised with Vichy. Thus, for example, educational demand for subsidies for Catholic schools would be put forward; school time should be set apart for the teaching of the catechism; a traditional morality based on religion should be instilled, as no less than the secularist Jules Ferry himself had advocated; textbooks should be reviewed to remove anticlerical bias; segregation of the sexes in school should be strictly enforced; above all, teachers should be 'moral, religious and patriotic'. To deal with the immediate situation, additional chaplains should be appointed to minister to the 1.5 million prisoners of war. Although a law promulgated ten days previously had banned employers' and workers' confederations, including the CFTC, Christian trade union leaders should be allowed to continue their activities among the workers, as should Jocistes (the members of JOC) and the Ligue Ouvrière Chrétienne (LOC), a family organisation. The Church wanted the religious orders to be more involved in social work, as well as to foster apostolic vocations among the laity, both tasks considered more urgent than ever before. Clearly the ACA had great expectations of the new order. It has, however, been reproached with first seeking only to profit from the catastrophe.[41]

The Révolution Nationale comprised a series of measures largely promulgated between July 1940 and November 1942, which were the core of the programme of 'national renewal'. Some — particularly those affecting the Jews, education, youth, and social matters — touched the Church more closely and are dealt with separately. But there were other issues affecting Christians.

As the goodwill messages to the Marshal flowed in at the turn of the year, the Church declared itself satisfied with the new dispensation. It gave its positive blessing to most of the innovations: the creation of the Légion Française des Combattants (LFC), composed of ex-servicemen; measures favouring the family and the corporative organisation of occupations, including the peasantry, together with an eventual Labour Charter; the breakup of Freemasonry; the regimentation of young people; educational reform; the suppression of alcoholism and vice. The views of 'integrist Catholics' were particularly well served. Some Christians felt uncomfortable at moves against foreigners and Jews, but as yet the conscience of the majority was not awakened. It was as if the Church, looking inward, had forgotten the battles still raging around France.

Attachment to the new dispensation also manifested itself in other ways. The Church, like the regime itself, became a lover of 'passéisme' and pious symbolism. The style of Vichy, with its somewhat Ruritanian pomp and circumstance and pre-Revolutionary echoes, met with episcopal approval. The resurrection of the medieval provinces, the projected appointment of governors for them (on the Franco model?); a certain 'patriotisme du clocher' that showed itself in the revival of folkloric traditions of dance, music and the arts and crafts; nationally, the spectacle of 'elites' parading in colourful uniforms, under banners among which the Tricolour might eventually even be supplanted by the fleurs-de-lis: these phenomena of 'Vieille France' underwent a revival welcomed by Catholics and Maurrassians alike. Old customs were restored. In 1941 for the first time for many a year, the procession on Corpus Christi emerged from Notre Dame and moved along the Paris streets.[42] (Before the Separation such a procession would have been flanked by soldiers, obeying the military order, 'Genou terre!' for genuflexion at the appropriate moment.) Time-honoured practices were revived in 'la Royale': at sunset in some naval vessels the officer of the watch recited the Lord's Prayer before the colours were ceremonially lowered.

On every kind of official occasion the Church was now represented. When in the late summer of 1941 a contingent of Vichy troops returned to Privas from their unsuccessful Syrian campaign, Mgr Couderc, the diocesan bishop, stood with the civil authorities to greet them.[43] It was this mixture of parades, politics and pious manifestations that eventually caused at least one priest, initially pro-Vichy — Père Dillard — to protest, seeing it as a hollow sham.

From 1941 onwards Catholics were petitioning Pétain to allow France to be dedicated to the Sacred Heart; its image should be placed on the national flag, because 'c'est un cœur, le symbole de l'amour'. One lady from Nantes even submitted a miniature flag adorned in this way, and asked that the feast-day become France's National Day.[44] Others favoured the national holiday being moved to Joan of Arc Day. Why should the festivities merely celebrate the destruction of a prison? One might just as well commemorate the building of the Eiffel Tower, remarked one correspondent.[45]

Solidarity between Church and State did not go unquestioned. One matter that rumbled on throughout the Occupation concerned the display of religious emblems. The Separation theoretically entailed the banning of these from all State institutions, particularly schools and the town halls. However, in practice there was great geographical variation. In devoutly Catholic areas such as western France, the crucifix had continued to occupy a place of honour in state schools. Under Vichy this practice became widespread, especially arousing the protests of the largely secularist Paris collaborationists, supported by the Germans. (In the Reich itself, a dispute about the crucifix in schools had lasted from 1937 to 1941, and Hitler's portrait had finally supplanted it. But in Catholic Bavaria the ban was quietly lifted in 1941 because it was so deeply resented.) Darlan ruled that the crucifix in schools and elsewhere offended the principle of 'neutrality' and in April 1941 ordered its removal[46] — this at a time when Pétain's portrait was beginning to appear in every classroom. A storm of indignation from the Church forced him to back down. In July he alleged that he had been misinterpreted: where the emblem had traditionally held pride of place in a school, or it had local approval, it could remain.[47]

This did not settle the matter entirely to ecclesiastical satisfaction. The Bishop of Nancy claimed that no law forbade religious emblems *inside* a public building: Article 28 of the law of 9 December 1905 merely prohibited their placing on the *exterior* of public monuments (*Journal des Parquets*, 1907, p. 46, was cited as authority). Nor did the law passed in 1882, establishing the principle of 'neutrality', *necessarily* imply the removal of emblems.[48] Any ruling to the contrary would signal 'a return to the times of masonic persecution'. At a meeting with Gerlier on 22 July 1941 the Marshal nevertheless informed the cardinal: 'To give the order to reinstate it [the crucifix] everywhere would be premature. I must avoid arousing the protests of the Occupation authorities; above all I am anxious to avoid any profanation of the image of Christ.' Once the

Révolution Nationale had been accomplished the desired result would automatically be achieved.[49] It was one of several occasions when, pressed by the Church to act, the Marshal temporised, declaring the time was not ripe.

Nevertheless uncertainty still reigned. Rouilleaux-Dugage, a former deputy for the Orne, asked Pétain to give clear instructions to the prefects.[50] Agence France-Presse reported how three mayors of villages in the Franche-Comté had attended a religious ceremony at which the crucifix had been restored to their public buildings, from which they had been removed 'sur l'ordre des francs-maçons'.[51] Official functions of this kind proliferated. On Christmas Day 1941 the mayor of the village of Ecot, where the crucifix was solemnly reinstated, spoke of it as 'un geste de réparation envers Notre Seigneur Jésus-Christ'. The act was accompanied by a reading from the 'Paroles du Maréchal' and of the 'Principes de la Communauté' — the official statement of the regime's general aims, — which were then solemnly affixed to the walls of the 'mairie'.[52] *L'Œuvre* reported tongue in cheek on the restoration of the crucifix in Lleuran-Gabriès, a village in the Hérault:

> Facing the 'mairie', on whose facade fluttered the old flag [the Tricolour] that saw the departure of Christ, the crowd intoned the Parce Domine. The deputy-mayor [...] recalled the history of the years 1880–1907, and in the name of the whole population greeted the return of the One who had never wished to leave. Then the Credo burst forth from the crowd, which was visibly very moved, whilst a little girl, after having kissed the crucifix, handed it to the Mayor, who in turn kissed it and installed it in the 'mairie'. 'Speak, command, reign.' [53]

By November 1942, in the Verdun diocese alone, the crucifix had been replaced in 500 schools.[54]

Darlan had meanwhile reminded prefects that on the outside of public buildings only religious symbols legally authorised could be displayed. Lavagne, of Pétain's Private Office and responsible for religious matters, received guidance as to how to reply to the many enquiries as to what was permitted,[55] although the overall legal position remained unclear. The Conseil d'Etat had given a number of individual rulings: a local council had no right to remove a large cross from a public cemetery; there was no law against placing a cross in the vicinity of a war memorial. On the other hand, no religious monument could be erected on a public highway, and no cross placed on private property if it abutted a road. In certain circumstances prefects could require the removal of the crucifix from a school, but councils had the right to repair existing calvaries, etc.

Eventually the controversy died away, although this comparatively trivial issue held great symbolic significance. At a local level many school teachers fought tooth and nail against the restoration of the crucifix in their classrooms, being continually at daggers drawn with the parish priest on the issue. At a national level, such quarrels demonstrated that Republican secularism survived among such very diverse groups as teachers and Paris collaborationists, and was now directed against the regime as well as the Church. Nevertheless the upshot of the disputes indicated that Pétain wished to give religion a more privileged position, such as he had seen the Church enjoying under Franco when he was ambassador to Madrid.

A major measure of immediate concern to the Church was the abolition of 'secret societies'. On 13 August the Masonic lodges had been closed down. Public officials and army officers had to declare whether they had ever been Freemasons. Lists of Masonic dignitaries were painstakingly compiled and made public. Sanctions were taken against those who had held office or who failed to acknowledge their masonic allegiance. This witch-hunt — for such it was — may be characterised as an official act of revenge against the Third Republic.

The Church played very little direct part in this purge, although the conflict between catholicism and Freemasonry dated back almost to 1789 and had continued ever since. Of the two main 'obédiences', the Grande Loge and the more numerous Grand Orient, the latter had a fiercely pro-Republican reputation and had been a hotbed of free-thinkers and progressive liberals. Such politicians as Jean Macé, the founder of the anticlerical Ligue de l'Enseignement, and Jules Ferry and Paul Bert, who had instituted the secular school in the teeth of Catholic opposition, or Jean Zay, the penultimate Education minister of the Third Republic, had been lodge members. Indeed Freemasons, who had made peculiarly their own Gambetta's telling phrase 'le cléricalisme, voilà l'ennemi', had been dubbed 'the Jesuits of the Republic'. From 1877 onwards the lodges had become atheistic and antireligious, or at best anticlerical. A Masonic network functioned all over France, comprising members from occupations such as teachers, doctors and small businessmen, all opposing the parish priest and the country landowner. Throughout the twentieth century they had been attacked by the political Right — and, as Simone de Beauvoir once remarked, 'La religion *est* la Droite' — and by Action Française, which, despite its long period of interdiction, continued to influence clerical opinion. For its part, the Church had long forbidden Catholics to become Freemasons.

It was therefore in character for the new regime to lump Freemasons with other 'undesirable' elements such as Jews and foreigners (on July

30, a law 'cleansing' the civil service of the latter had been promulgated). The idea of a purge of Freemasons may have been in imitation of the special court, the Tribunal de Masonería y Comunismo, that Franco had instituted in Spain. But it was Raphaël Alibert, the regime's first Justice Minister and an over-zealous Catholic convert, who was responsible for the law of 13 August 1940 outlawing the lodges. Their office-holders were particularly targeted because Masonic politicians had freely promoted their 'brothers' in the public service.[56] Another practising Catholic, Bernard Fay, who in December 1940 succeeded Julien Caïn, dismissed because he was Jewish, as head of the Bibliothèque Nationale, set up a 'service des sociétés secrètes'. Aided by a fellow Catholic, Vallery-Radot, just as fanatical as he was, he set about exposing former Masonic dignitaries. According to *La Croix* (16 October 1941) some 12,000, out of a total of 50,000 Freemasons in all, fell into this category. The two 'purgistes' installed their office in the Paris premises of the Grand Orient lodge, and as a result of their activities, many public servants, including 328 teachers, were dismissed.[57] Denunciatory lists were published in *Les Documents maçonniques*, edited by Vallery-Radot, a publication that appeared from October 1941 and ran for almost a year.

As the war continued efforts were made in other ways to discredit Freemasonry. The film *Forces occultes* (1943) even accused the Grand Orient of being the hand behind the French declaration of war.[58] But there were counter-attacks: one Resistance source claimed that Fay's 'service' had as its purpose to create vacancies in key posts, to be filled by 'certain Catholic traitors to their country'.[59]

Fay saw the linked hands of Freemasonry everywhere. He was particularly wary of Protestants. Pastor Boegner complained to Pétain in late 1941 that in lectures up and down the country Fay, not content with condemning the Reformation, had accused Protestantism of having provided the text for at least part of the Masonic ritual. He was, declared Boegner, 'organising, under cover of an anti-Masonic campaign, a movement hostile to French Protestantism' ('était en train d'organiser, sous le couvert d'une campagne anti-maçonnique, un mouvement hostile au protestantisme français'). Invited by the Marshal to answer Boegner's specific charges directly, Fay denied them, but informed the Protestant leader that there were nevertheless good historical precedents for suspicion, and 'at the present time... it would be extremely serious for French Protestantism if it appeared to serve as a support and cover for Freemasonry on the decline', adding hypocritically, 'I shall fight against this tendency.' Moreover, he added, many Catholics thought that this was precisely the path that Protestants were pursuing.[60]

To Pétain Fay was more specific. Harking back to 1877, he asked whether it was not a certain Pastor Desmonds of Nîmes, in the heartland of French Protestantism, who had been instrumental in eliminating from French Freemasonry all deistic references to 'the Great Architect of the Universe'. 'In all the lodges of the Midi', he went on, 'the Protestant element is considerable: it is they who have caused Boegner's imprudent intervention.' This is why Boegner had not been able to rally his flock to the Marshal. At a meeting of eminent pastors and bankers in Paris in November 1941 — 'the dispensers of funds to Protestant churches' ('bailleurs de fonds des églises protestantes') — General Brécard, a Protestant member of Pétain's entourage, had failed to win them over to the regime. One banker, Mirabaud, had even dared to speak against the Marshal. Moreover, had not another leading Protestant, André Siegfried, ostentatiously renounced his appointment to the Conseil National, Pétain's new consultative body; and 'need one recall that recently one of Boegner's sons has gone off to England?'[61] But the Marshal, who considered Boegner 'one of his best friends', was unlikely to have been impressed by Fay's remarks.

Fay probably got short shrift from Catholic leaders as well, for the anti-Masonic 'service' he ran did not hesitate to impugn Cardinal Gerlier and certain religious. Between the wars two Jesuits, Père Bertheloot — an expert on the lodges —and Père Riquet had studied the possibility of a rapprochement between the Church and Freemasonry. Fay had met with a refusal when he had approached Gerlier to ask whether Bertheloot could now be released to help him in his 'purge'. He thereupon accused Gerlier's entourage of opposing his campaign; Catholics had even been badgered to assist dismissed Freemasons, and Christian Democrats were, he declared, spreading far and wide the dreaded 'esprit démocratique et maçonnisant'.[62] Plainly no love was lost between Fay and Gerlier. To Lavagne, of Pétain's Private Office, he declared that the cardinal was too powerful, and saw the Marshal too frequently; his influence should be replaced by that of Suhard, and he added ominously, 'les Allemands, en outre sont très mécontents.'[63] Fay's opinion of Gerlier would not, however, have been given credence, because Pétain considered the cardinal's loyalty as unquestionable as Boegner's. The evidence for Jesuit collusion with freemasonry is likewise slim. However, a Fighting French document reported a meeting at Montauban just before Whitsun 1943 attended by sixty Jesuits, ostensibly to discuss post-war developments, and noted that, surprisingly, two members of the Supreme Council of the Scottish Rite of freemasonry were present; hence, 'guilt' must have been by association.[64] Later in the same year Vallery-Radot claimed that Christian Democrats were allying themselves with Freemasons.[65]

At local level hostility between Catholics and Freemasons undoubtedly still smouldered. There were many examples of this. A nun in charge of an orphanage at Belleney-Tournus complained that the mayor and the chairman of the local hospice committee, both Freemasons like other leading lights in the commune, were withholding a legacy bequeathed to her institution.[66] Nationally, however, it is plain that, although the Church had no love for the square and compass, apart from one or two zealots it gave no special support to the campaign against it. Indeed the evidence is that other Christians were already realising that after the war Catholics and Freemasons would have to co-exist in greater harmony. This indeed occurred, at least until the Sacred Congregation in 1981 reasserted the incompatibility between Christianity and freemasonry.

On communism, on the other hand, the Church could be more decisive. The papal condemnation of it was crystalclear. In September 1939 the Daladier government had outlawed the Communist party. The Church's fears of a Communist take-over, with Moscow aiding and abetting, strong in the days of the Front Populaire, had been at first allayed by the installation of the new regime. But it was scandalised and alarmed by the rumours of covert Nazi-Communist collaboration in the months following the defeat. These were put to rest by the German invasion of the USSR in June 1941. Acts of Communist resistance to the Germans then multiplied and special tribunals were established to try these latest 'dissidents'. Barthélémy, then Justice minister and a friend of Cardinal Gerlier, urged that appeal courts should choose judges of absolute loyalty, with the suppression of the Third International high on their list of priorities.[67] Henceforth the Church lumped Communists with other 'terrorists' and 'rebels', although individual priests were prompt to offer assistance to those fleeing from justice or sentenced to death, whether Communists or not.

The most eminent Catholic anti-Communist, which went with his pro-Nazi stance, was undoubtedly Cardinal Baudrillart. In August 1941, shortly after the German onslaught on the Soviet Union, in an interview with Mallet (the future biographer of Laval) published in *Toute la Vie*, the cardinal set out his position:[68] Christianity and marxism were irreconcilable. The latter viewed human society as mere matter operating according to its own laws, and a perpetual conflict — a dialectic — based on social position, was being waged with the aim of bringing about a classless State. The concept of God and the soul were excluded. In such a system man had no free-will: the 'spiritual principle of his moral behaviour' and the sole hierarchy possible were determined by the economic system. Thus the cardinal supported this extension of the war: 'As a priest and a Frenchman... should I refuse to approve this noble common enterprise, in which Germany is taking the lead?'[69] Accordingly he backed the formation of the Légion des Volontaires Français (LVF) to fight on the German side: 'These legionaries are the crusaders of the twentieth century. May their arms be blessed! The tomb of Christ shall be delivered!'[70]

However, it was Moscow rather than Jerusalem that the aged cardinal had in mind. *Tempus iracundiae* for him had come, that time of wrath that Péguy had predicted, when the forces of good and evil would be locked in a definitive struggle. The inhuman Soviet system had to be destroyed. Mercifully (for Baudrillart) he died in 1942 and did not live to see the outcome of the conflict.

As the Allied victory eventually became more likely, the Church's apprehension of a Communist coup increased once more, as will be seen. In this first phase of the Révolution Nationale, however, it did not dominate the bishops' thoughts. But the situation bothered Resistance Catholics from the very beginning: Edmond Michelet wrote later: 'Catholic members of the Resistance wanted to *hope* that the Communists would not mean communism.'[71]

In 1940–41 the Church was hand in glove with the regime, dazzled by the glory in which Pétain basked and convinced of the need for national reform. It viewed uncritically controversial measures such as the anti-Masonic, anti-Communist and xenophobic legislation, including the first Statute of the Jews, and some churchmen even regarded them with benevolence. By midsummer 1941 it pronounced its verdict: although there was still confusion as to whether the regime was merely 'established' ('établi') rather than legitimate ('légitime'), it pledged 'loyalty without enthralment'. This formula was first used by the ACA at its meeting of 24 July 1941 in the occupied zone and affirmed for the unoccupied zone on 5 September 1941. The text ran: 'Nous voulons que sans inféodation soit pratiqué un loyalisme sincère et complet envers le pouvoir établi.' It went on to say, 'Nous vénérons le Chef de l'Etat' [...] nous encourageons nos fidèles à se placer à ses côtes dans [son] œuvre de redressement.'[72] It did, however, make one caveat in the declaration that is often forgotten: 'As the Church we stand solely on a religious plane, outside any party politics... we intend to foster actively the national interest, to which we are never indifferent.' This was held to be the Church's formal support for 'national renewal', a policy that was essentially political, and as such was unprecedented in the history of the Assembly's existence since 1918. Already, however, some were saying that the Church had acted too hastily in committing itself.

That the declaration applied more to the Marshal than his government was self-evident. The Church had not mourned the departure of Laval in December 1940. He was too closely identified with the old regime to favour what the Church desired. Yet he was feared. The devout Alibert, then Justice minister, had first gone on his knees in anxiety and trepidation in Vichy's Saint-Louis Church to entreat the Almighty's help before having Laval arrested.[73] But the Church had not warmed especially to the appointment of first Flandin, and then Darlan as his successor — the latter was reputed to be indifferent or even hostile to religion. According to Barthélémey, until 1943 Justice minister after Alibert's departure, the admiral's anticlericalism stemmed from the number of religious services he had been forced to attend in his early years![74] With Carcopino, his minister of Education, Darlan had effectively, if unwittingly, brought about the disappearance of 'God' from the state schools' moral curricula, a topic that Chevalier, Carcopino's predecessor, had previously been at pains to reinstate in the syllabus.

Meanwhile the bishops continued to laud the Marshal to the skies. For many a year such an atmosphere of sweetness and light between Church and State had not been so apparent.

Thus even the defeat of 1940 could, from the religious (and ecclesiastical) viewpoint, be turned to national advantage. Cardinal Gerlier even went so far as to proclaim, 'Victorious, we would probably have remained the prisoners of our mistakes. Through having been secularised, France was in danger of dying' ('Victorieux nous serions probablement restés emprisonnés dans nos erreurs. A force d'être laïcisée, la France risquait de mourir'). Mgr Brunhes, Bishop of Montpellier, even thought it fitting to compare the misery of France at that time to the despair felt by the disciples after the body of Jesus had been laid to rest! Little wonder that disloyalty to Pétain was equated with want of patriotism.

The bishops expatiated on the themes of duty and service in their Lenten messages to the faithful. Their use of these messages as propaganda for the regime was criticised. However, some three-quarters dealt with purely religious and ecclesiastical matters, ranging from pious exhortations to appeals to increase the number of vocations. The rest were almost equally divided between topics relating to politics, war and peace and, to lesser extent, social matters. In 1940 war and peace was in fact the predominant theme; in 1941, French 'renewal'. By 1943 references to this renaissance were few, as they were also to peace. As the Liberation approached social themes also became more numerous. Occasionally an intriguing symmetry is apparent. In 1941, Mgr Rodié of Agen discussed the Christian significance of 'Travail, Famille, Patrie' — one wonders whether the Revolutionary motto ever received such treatment. In 1945 his Lenten letter dealt with the meaning of 'Resistance, Liberation and Reconstruction'.[75]

The local *Semaines Religieuses* were more topical. Thus Mgr Pic of Valence enthusiastically reprinted regularly Pétain's 'Messages' to the French people. These diocesan bulletins of religious news and comment also castigated the tares of the Third Republic: liberalism, democracy, parliamentarianism, and elections; divorce and sexual promiscuity; sloth and the love of such worldly pleasures as dancing and strong liquor. Xenophobia occasionally went hand in hand with blatant anti-Semitism. Jean Zay, the Education minister in 1939, and a Jew, was accused by Mgr Caillot, Bishop of Grenoble, of having changed his name because it was too foreign-sounding.[76] In June 1941 Mgr Delay (Marseilles), could write, concerning the law depriving the recently naturalised, among them many Jews, of French nationality, 'Already there are appearing the outlines of a more attractive France, cured of the wounds that were often... the work of foreigners.'[77] Surprisingly, however, the disbandment of the Masonic lodges, the repression of communism and, above all, the outbreak of war with the Soviet Union received scant attention in these local publications.[78]

Although the bishops were able to use these channels to impose their *magisterium*, their monopoly in teaching did not go unchallenged. In particular, priests and pastors were sometimes able to use their sermons to good effect. Their pronouncements were often attacked in the collaborationist press. In June 1941 *Gringoire* expostulated at 'the evil-minded [Catholic] shepherds' who attacked from the pulpit any Vichy policies that were pro-German, and Protestant pastors who delivered 'strange Anglophile and Gaullist homilies'.[79]

All was not entirely plain sailing in Church-State relations. In a confidential pastoral letter to clergy Cardinal Liénart laid down the parameters of compliance. The Church, he declared, was no vassal of the civil power; even whilst submitting to it, 'one has also the right to express reservations about this or that governmental measure'. At this time (October 1941) one might, for example, have misgivings about economic and political collaboration with Germany but one would be ill-advised to express these 'except in cases of necessity'.[80] Likewise an anonymous Provincial wrote to his brethren in the Toulouse area that, although loyalty was imperative because the regime was 'legitimate', 'I do not pretend to claim that everything in the government's actions is perfect.'[81] As time wore on matters of contention and conscience between Church and regime became more numerous.

Notes

Unless otherwise stated the place of publication is Paris

1. P. Baudouin, *Neuf mois au gouvernement, avril–décembre 1940*, 1948, p. 214f. Diary entry for 25 June 1940. English edition: *The Private Diaries of Paul Baudouin*, translated by Sir Charles Petrie, London, 1948.
2. AD du Nord, Lille, M154/253A. Brochure.
3. A Dio, Lille, ACA 2 B1. Document, 'Le mot du cardinal', Paris, 27 June 1940: 'le Français sans reproche'..
4. J. Duquesne, *Les Catholiques français sous l'Occupation*, 1966, p. 40. (a new, slightly enlarged edition was published in 1986).
5. C. Paillat, *L'Occupation. Le pillage de la France, juin 1940–novembre 1942*, 1957, pp. 159f.
6. A Dio, Lille. Guerre 1939–1945. 8 M 7. Relations avec les Allemands.
7. H. Rousso, 'Pouvoir et société. L'impact du régime sur la société: ses dimensions et ses limites', in: J-P. Azéma and F. Bédarida (eds.), *Vichy et les Français*, 1992, p. 573; see also: J.-M. Guillon, 'La nature du régime: la philosophie politique de la Révolution Nationale: des principes à la pratique', ibid., p. 167.
8. Quoted in F. Lebrun, *Histoire des catholiques en France du XVe siècle à nos jours*, Toulouse, 1980, p. 465.
9. A Dio, Lille. Guerre 1939–1945. De '39 à '42. Annales 8 M 1. *Le loyalisme envers le gouvernement*.
10. AN 2 AG 493. Letter from Cardinal Liénart to Pétain, Lille, 21 November 1940.
11. J.-P. Azéma, *1940: L'année terrible*, 1992, pp..237f.
12. Quoted in Y. Tranvouez, 'Entre Rome et le peuple, 1920–1960', in: Lebrun, *Histoire des catholiques*, p. 465.
13. Quoted in A. Rivet, 'Les chrétiens de la Haute-Loire dans la Révolution Nationale et sous l'occupation allemande, 1940–1944', *Revue d'Auvergne*, Clermont-Ferrand, 1982, p. 391, n. 3.
14. Diocesan *Semaine religieuse*, 28 February 1941, quoted in: C. Langlois, 'Le régime de Vichy et le clergé d'après les "Semaines religieuses" des diocèses de la zone libre', *Revue française de Science politique*, 22:4, August 1972, p. 765.
15. *Semaine religieuse* (Limoges), 6 September 1940, quoted in: G. Miller, *Les pousse-au-jouir du Maréchal Pétain*, 1975, p. 46.
16. AN 2 AG 74 SP.1. Pastoral letter, Poitiers, 8 December 1940.
17. Langlois, 'Le régime de Vichy', pp. 753f.
18. Cardinal Gerlier, in a lecture on 'Eglise et Patrie', reported in the *Semaine religieuse* of Marseilles, 13 April 1941.
19. Quoted in *Histoire des diocèses de France* (edited by J. R. Palanque). *No. 3: Le diocèse d'Aix en Provence*, 1975, p. 230ff.
20. R. Bédarida, 'La hiérarchie catholique', in: J.-P. Azéma and R. Bédarida (eds), *Vichy et les Français*, 1992, p. 445.
21. AN F1a. 3784. Fighting French file. Report to the Commissaire à l'Intérieur, received in May 1944, ref. CDD/DH.
22. AN 2 AG 74. Letter to Pétain dated 3 September 1941.
23. AN 2 AG 493. Letter of Baudrillart to General Laure, of Pétain's Private Office, Paris, 27 November 1940.
24. AN 2 AG 493, Letter of Mgr Costes to Pétain, Angers, 20 November 1940.
25. AN 2 AG 449. Letter of Commandant Loustaunau-Navarre to Du Moulin de Labarthète, Vichy, 8 November 1940.
26. AN 2 AG 499. CCXVIIB. Parti démocrate populaire. Intercept dated 2 May 1941 of a letter from L.-A. Pagès, *Mémorial de la Loire et de la Haute-Loire,* to Lucien Romier, Nebrouze par Soual, Tarn.
27. See J. Lacroix, J. Vialatoux, 'Chroniques: le mythe Pétain', *Esprit*, September 1951.

28. AN 2 AG 76. Letter from Mgr Martin, Le Puy, to Dr Ménétrel, Pétain's private secretary, 21 March 1941.
29. AN 2 AG 492. Letter of Lavagne, as head of Pétain's Private Office, to Louis Canet, Vichy, October [?] 1941.
30. A Dio, Lille, ACA 2B1. 'Mémoire à consulter pour une politique religieuse de l'état', signed by Sauret, 'sous-directeur des cultes', Interior ministry, and marked 'sans doute de 1941'.
31. AN 72 AJ 257. Talk given by Abbé Sorel, Conseiller National, in Foix Cathedral, 11 May 1941.
32. AN 2 AG 493. Letter to Pétain, Soissons, 24 October 1941.
33. AN 2 AG 493. Letter of J— C,— 'chef d'escadron, Commandant le Parc'. 'Sous contrôle' [censored?], Périgueux, 26 October 1941.
34. AN 2 AG 449 CCXVIIB.
35. AN 2 AG 74. 'Causerie aux gars du Pas-de-Calais, au Stalag IIIA, par M. Combezou-Tahon', primary teacher at Cauchy.
36. G. Blond, *Pétain, 1856–1951*, 1966, pp. 371f.
37. M. Ferro, *Pétain*, 1987, p. 227.
38. Duquesne, *Les Catholiques français*, p. 17.
39. H. Lottman, *Pétain. Hero or Traitor?* London, 1985, p. 20
40. AN 2 AG 493. Report on Abbé Astruc, ref: Ministère de l'Intérieur (Sec. Gén. de la Police), no. 2448, Vichy, 21 August 1941, to Lavagne, head of Pétain's Private Office.
41. A. Latreille, *et al.*, *Histoire du catholicisme en France*, vol. 3. *La période contemporaine*, edited by R. Rémond, p. 613.
42. AN 72 AJ 1863. Report from Radio Vichy, 19.00, 3 June 1941,
43. Paillat, *Le Pillage de la France*, p. 525.
44. AN 2 AG 609. Letters to Pétain from G—— B——, Lyons, 22 March 1941 and 6 June 1941; letter from Thérèse M——, Nantes, 2 April 1941.
45. Ibid. Letter of A—— A—— to Pétain, Gap, 1 May 1941.
46. Circular of Interior ministry, 15 May 1941.
47. Circular of Interior ministry, 18 July 1941. Copy in AN 72 AJ 1863.
48. AN 72 AJ 1863. 'Note juridique sur les emblèmes religieux à l'intérieur des écoles publiques et les mairies', *Semaine religieuse* (Nancy), 6 July 1941.
49. AN 2 AG 492. 'Entretien du Maréchal avec le Cardinal Gerlier, 22 juillet 1941'.
50. *Le Publicateur de l'Orne*, 21 September 1941.
51. AN 72 AJ 1863. Report from Besançon, 9 October 1941.
52. 'Le Christ est repris à l'école', *Le Petit Champenois*, 3–4 January 1942.
53. *L'Œuvre*, 'Liberté de conscience pas morte', 13 April 1942 The article was based on an account in the *Bulletin paroissial* of the Basilica of Nîmes.
54. Duquesne, *Les Catholiques français*, pp. 84f.
55. AN 2 AG 492. Secretary-General, Interior ministry, to Lavagne, 8 January 1943, *Jurisprudence relative à l'application de l'article 28 de la loi du 9.décembre 1905*.
56. R. Paxton, *Vichy France. Old Guard and New Order, 1940–1944*, London, 1972, p. 17.
57. Ibid., p. 151.
58. Ibid., p. 170.
59. AN F17.13346. Pamphlet entitled, *France de demain*, no. 1, bound for concealment in what appeared to be an Education ministry journal, *Revue de l'enseignement supérieur*.
60. AN 2 AG 75. Letter of Fay to Pastor Boegner, Paris, 14 January 1942.
61. AN 2 AG 495. Letter of Fay to Pétain, Paris, 6 January 1942.
62. AN 2 AG 492. 'Mémorandum sur la situation actuelle des relations de l'Eglise catholique avec la maçonnerie', n.d. [1942?].
63. AN 2 AG 492. Handwritten note by Lavagne headed 'Visite Bernard Fay, 12 août 1941'.
64. AN F60.1674. Service Doc. CNAI, no. 2844, July 1943.
65. AN F60.1674. Broadcast on Radio Paris, 20.00, 30 October 1943: 'Un pacte entre l'Eglise et la franc-maçonnerie'.

66. AN 2 AG 493. Letter of Sœur Thérèse Ravat to the head of Pétain's Private Office, 27 July 1942.
67. A. Paxton, *Vichy France*, pp. 224f.
68. A. Mallet, *Pierre Laval*, 1955, vol. 2, pp.164f.
69. Quoted in: R. Bédarida, (ed.), [Facsmiles of] *Cahiers et Courriers du Témoignage Chrétien, 1941–1944, Cahiers II et III,* 1980, pp. 78f. This reproduction of the clandestine Resistance publication is an invaluable source.
70. Declaration of 4 December 1941, quoted in: H. Amouroux, *Les beaux jours des collabos, juin 1941–juin 1942,* 1978, p. 253.
71. E. Michelet, *De la fidélité en politique,* 1949, p. 16.
72. The text is given in AN 2 AG 494.
73. M. Martin du Gard, *La Chronique de Vichy, 1940–1944,* 1948, p. 152.
74. J. Barthélémy, *Ministre de la Justice, Vichy 1941–1943. Mémoires,* 1989, p. 82.
75. An analysis of an opportunity sample of the Lenten letters was made in conjunction with a complete list of their titles given in J.-M. Mayeur, *Lenten Letters of the French Bishops (Repertory, 1861–1959),* Strasbourg, 1981. None was issued from Strasbourg during the Occupation. In Metz Mgr Louis, the successor to the banished Mgr Heintz, issued three Lenten letters in German.
76. *Semaine religieuse* (Grenoble), 4 September 1941. For a study of the *Semaines religieuses* of five bishoprics in the unoccupied zone (Annecy, Grenoble, Valence, Lyons, Chambéry), see J. Boisson *et al.,* 'Les réactions des Chrétiens d'après les *Semaines religieuses* de cinq diocèses de zone libre', in: *Actes*: Grenoble.
77. *Semaine religieuse,* Marseilles, 29 June 1941.
78. C. Langlois, 'Le régime de Vichy et le clergé d'après les "Semaines religieuses" des diocèses de la zone libre', *Revue française de science politique,* no. 4, August 1972, pp. 755f.
79. *Gringoire,* 17 June 1941, quoted in F. and R. Bédarida, 'Une résistance spirituelle. Aux origines du "Témoignage Chrétien", 1941–1942', *RHDGM,* 61:1966, pp. 1–31.
80. AN AJ 40.563. Pastoral letter of October 1941.
81. AN 2 AG 609. Toulouse, 18 July 1941.

–5–

Christians in Disarray

The sense of unease felt by Catholics with the realisation that there would be no early end to the war and as the State became more authoritarian, continued to grow. Already strictures coming from the regular orders and minor clergy were not unusual. To a student audience the Abbé Marc Lallier, although insisting the regime was legitimate and must command loyalty, claimed that in 1939 France's war had been just; however, one might well be estranged from one's former allies without denying past friendship.[1] Moreover, personal comments on Pétain were sometimes made from the pulpit, as we have seen.

Protestants were alarmed by the turn of events. It is true that Pastor Boegner, as head of the Reformed Church, wrote thanking Pétain for the 'great work of moral renewal that you have undertaken in our country', and for his 'solicitude' for the family and young people.[2] This did not deter him a few weeks later from making public his anxiety about the treatment of the Jews. Indeed by October 1941 some of his pastors had been interrogated by the Sûreté about their loyalty.[3]

Even such a spirited supporter of the Marshal as Mgr Piguet, Bishop of Clermont-Ferrand, voiced his unease when his clergy were invited to take an active part in the departmental propaganda organisation established by the Information ministry. In an intercepted letter to his neighbour, the Bishop of Tulle, he expressed no doubt as to where the line between politics and the Church should be drawn: 'Our position of utter loyalty to the Marshal's government and our spiritual role proscribing enthralment to any political regime prevails, and resolves the question of Propaganda delegates. This means of serving the government cannot and must not be ours.'[4]

A vague sentiment that the Church might have gone too far initially in identifying itself with the political aims of the regime thus surfaced. An ACA meeting on 4 and 5 September 1941 now asserted that certain activities, perfectly respectable in themselves, bordered on the political, and clerical participation in them was inappropriate. Priests involved in them should discreetly withdraw. Lay leaders of Catholic movements should do likewise, 'in order to forestall equivocal situations that could harm both sides'.[5]

The Légion Française des Combattants (LFC), which functioned only in the unoccupied zone, was clearly one such organisation. Created in August 1940, this amalgamation of unions of ex-servicemen from both world wars was seen by the Marshal as a surrogate for the discredited political parties. It grew rapidly: by 1941 it had 1.6 million members, including some bishops. From the beginning Catholics had assumed a prominent role in it. The first secretary-general was Xavier Vallat, the prominent Catholic, former deputy, and Jew-hater; its first deputy director-general was François Valentin, a former ACJF leader in Lorraine; Jacques Péricard, a vice-president, had also founded the Droits des Religieux Anciens Combattants (DRAC), a militant organisation of ex-servicemen priests. Canon Polimann, the pro-German former deputy, was a member of the Légion's governing body. The political links of some such Catholics caused the Hierarchy concern. Moreover, ten priests were members of the departmental committees of the Légion, and 192 others held local office.[6] On the other hand, it was perhaps inevitable that bishops — a majority of them veterans of the First World War — were called upon to celebrate masses for the Légion and were invited to other ceremonial occasions.

However, after Darlan's assumption of power in January 1941 the Légion began to take a more authoritarian stance, which increased during the summer after Pucheu became Interior minister. Backed by his henchman Marion, he favoured turning it into a monolithic national movement, totalitarian and tied to a new 'European order'. This the Church was unable to accept. An immediate cause of friction was the Légion's move to create youth sections, strongly opposed by Gerlier.[7] He saw it as a threat to the Church's own youth movements. Pucheu, who had also an alternative plan to convert the State movement Compagnons de France into the sole national youth movement, thus became doubly suspect to the Church, since any concept of a 'jeunesse unique' was unacceptable. When in September 1941 the ACA specifically forbade priests and leaders of Catholic movements to hold office in the Légion, whilst allowing them to remain members, the pretext given was that the movement fulfilled a civic role difficult to divorce from politics. On 4 June 1942 Valentin finally resigned from the Légion, escaping to London to join de Gaulle. His departure was significant: he had been the sole leading light who belonged to the younger generation of veterans.

Further misgivings soon began to creep in. The Church's unease over any participation in LFC activities grew after Laval returned to power in April 1942. According to Ambassador Abetz, the new Head of

Government had confided to him that he intended to reform the Légion because it had become a prey to chauvinist and clerical elements. He wished to purge the movement at the top, while reinforcing the position of those local leaders who were anti-British. The implication clearly was that the Church had been playing too political a role.

The evolution of the LFC from January 1943 onwards indeed justified the Church's worst fears. From it emerged the dreaded Milice, whom the Germans were to use as an instrument of terror. Bishop Rastouil of Limoges, who had increasing doubts about the movement, had already in the summer of 1942 forbidden his clergy to take part in demonstrations or sport the Légion badge.[8] This was held against him. A report on him conceded — a point in his favour! — that he had not protested immediately to the Légion against the treatment of the Jews. The clergy did not all support their bishop: indeed two priests who taught in the local school had taken part in a demonstration on 30 August 1942 to oppose the ban. Rastouil thereupon formally submitted his resignation from the LFC and directed his clergy to do likewise, because, as he put it mildly: 'Inspired by the Marshal and by the initiatives of its leaders, the Légion has over the months become more an action group entrusted with very diverse missions that are not always compatible with the absolute reserve that the clergy must exercise as regards political action, and which people demand of it.'

Dussart, head of the Légion's Limoges section, commented to the Légion headquarters in Vichy that the resignation 'reflects very clearly the attitude that had already long been adopted by Mgr Rastouil towards the Légion and the regime itself'.[9] In fact, the bishop's disenchantment and increasingly rebellious posture were eventually to lead to his arrest by the Germans.

The ACA was more diplomatic. Even when it voiced its disapproval of a special meeting of clerical members called by the Légion it hastened to add that this was not a 'témoignage d'un sentiment hostile'.[10] Perhaps it hedged too much. In any case, the diminishing warmth of the Church for Pétain's favourite movement mirrored the waning enthusiasm for certain aspects of the Révolution Nationale. Catholics felt their cosy relationship with the regime was now fast disappearing. At the beginning the new, hierarchical order, badly needing leaders, had freely drawn them from existing Catholic cadres. Now new elites, not necessarily Christian, were emerging to assume power.

Another cause of unease for Christians was the oath of allegiance to Pétain that top civil servants and the armed forces were obliged to take. Loyalty oaths were usually sworn to monarchs or dictators — it did not go unnoticed that the Nazis and the Wehrmacht had to pledge personal allegiance to Hitler in this way. In particular, Protestant susceptibilities were aroused, because, as Pastor Boegner, speaking for the National Council of the Reformed Church, argued, oaths could be made only to God. At a meeting of young pastors and students at Tarascon-sur-Rhône in September 1941, from which emerged the *Thèses de Pomeyrol,* a set of principles to govern Protestants' attitude to secular affairs, a modified form of the oath was drawn up. It stipulated that loyalty could indeed be sworn to the Head of State but only 'as regards everything that he might order to be done for the good of the service'.[11] Boegner enlisted the support of Gerlier for this alternative formulation, which the cardinal submitted for advice to Barthélemy as Justice minister. He counselled delay,[12] but through the intervention of René Gillouin, Pétain's Protestant adviser, the revised oath was approved by the Marshal. Since faithfulness to God stood paramount in its new form, this was a convenient escape route for the conscience of many Christians, including officers of the Armistice army, who had sworn it but who later joined the Resistance.

Already in July 1940 the Marshal had announced his intention of drawing up a new constitution. There were few regrets among the bishops about the one that had been voted out of existence, and with it the parliamentary regime. (They doubtless shared the sentiments of the obscure country priest who in May 1941 wrote in his parish magazine: 'Elections are "out of work". Is this such a great evil? Universal suffrage, which had been called "universal stupidity" — as it was conceived and practised — did irreparable harm to our country.'[13])

A Conseil National was set up in January 1941 to help in framing the constitution promised in July 1940. This never met as a unitary body, but only in commissions whose task was to advise the Marshal on the form the constitution might take. The initial 188 appointed to the Conseil included several Church notables, among them Cardinal Suhard, Canon Polimann, and Jean Le Cour Grandmaison, Vice-President of the FNC; to represent Protestant interests, an invitation was extended to Pastor Boegner. Pétain, despite his mistrust of Parliamentarians, now felt sufficiently sure of their loyalty to appoint to it seventy-eight members drawn from the former Senate and Chamber of Deputies. The rest of the body consisted either of experts in a particular field or members of local councils.[14]

Having provisionally signified his acceptance of membership, Cardinal Suhard then decided to withdraw, and proposed Mgr Beaussart, his auxiliary bishop, in his place. The cardinal would in any case have had difficulty in attending meetings in the unoccupied zone.[15] To Pétain the cardinal explained his scruples. His devotion to the Marshal remained 'total', but he wished to maintain an apolitical position. He could not in any case accept the (not inconsiderable) emoluments offered. Pétain reluctantly concurred, declaring that he understood the cardinal's desire to devote himself entirely to spiritual and ecclesiastical matters. He therefore would allow him to resign as soon as possible and meanwhile would not summon him to any meetings. In a delicate touch, he enclosed a cheque for 100,000 francs — the amount of the emoluments in question — to be used for charitable works.[16] Police reports confirmed that prominent Catholics felt the appointment of religious leaders to the Conseil should be referred to the Pope, who surely would disapprove of his bishops dabbling in politics. Even if one or two were allowed to accept they would not be permitted to attend regularly.[17]

In the event Mgr Beaussart attended the meetings of the Conseil youth commission in March 1941, as did Pastor Boegner.[18] Pétain's personal secretary at the time, Du Moulin de Labarthète, a keen observer of the political scene, remarked that in any case 'the purple of a prince of the Church would not fit in'.[19] Suhard's refusal marks a considerable step towards the withdrawal of the Church from its initial overcommitment to the Vichy regime.

Within the Conseil National a constitutional commission eventually proposed bicameral State organs, not based on direct elections. The suggested constitution was never made publicly known, but when a draft was 'leaked' to Abetz, the German ambassador in Paris, he reported to Berlin that it was 'clerico-bourgeois-reactionary' and not at all compatible with a future 'Socialist' Europe.[20] According to the Catholic writer Henry Bordeaux, to whom Pétain showed the draft constitution in July 1943, it envisaged a president with strong powers; Pétain claimed that it had been approved by the Nuncio and the bulk of the clergy, except the Christian Democrats.[21] Meanwhile the ecclesiastical authorities asserted they had no wish to influence the Marshal in his choice of structures for a new State, although in 1940 they had come out against a monarchy.[22] The precise role that the Church would play in a new constitutional regime is not known, although it is likely that its functions would be much greater than under the Third Republic but less than in Franco's Spain.

Despite the Church's reluctance to become more politically involved, at the end of 1941 the prefects reported that on the whole their relationships with the clergy were excellent, although there were occasional discordant notes. Carles, the Prefect of the Nord department, noted that some clerics feared the advantages given to Catholic schools would provoke an anticlerical reaction. In Ille-et-Vilaine chaplains of JOC, the Catholic young workers' movement, criticised government labour policy as tending towards a new form of socialism and statism. In the Héricourt area (Haute-Saône) Protestants were uneasy because they believed efforts were being made to establish catholicism as the official religion. The police reported that 'a group of clergy', allegedly in the interests of national reconciliation, criticised the government for ostracising as dangerous deputies elected under the Front Populaire.[23] In an oblique warning (August 1941) to his religious the Dominican Provincial Prior of Lyons summed up the situation: 'Let us therefore be loyally subject to the Marshal and work with him for the revival of our country... so as to dispel the illusion that the orders in general, and the Dominicans and Jesuits in particular, are Gaullists. Let us retain our spiritual role.'[24] Despite this exhortation, a spirit of dissent increased in both religious orders. Nevertheless, in expressing to Pétain his good wishes for 1942 Cardinal Suhard could aver: 'I have become convinced that one single concern inspires all your actions: to fashion a new France'.[25]

By 1942, however, a mood of disillusionment was fast setting in. The inability of the Germans to break the Allies — despite victories on the Russian steppes, in Africa and in the Atlantic, the *Endsieg* was as far distant as ever; the entry of the United States into the war; the impending failure of the Révolution Nationale; the stirrings of internal Resistance — all this made Christians, like the rest of the 40 million Pétainists of 1941, lose confidence in the regime. But the events of the new year at first did little to shake episcopal devotion to Pétain.

However, at least half a dozen prelates (Fleuret, Nancy; Blanchet, St Dié; Dubourg, Besançon; Feltin, Bordeaux; Grente, Le Mans; Duparc, Quimper) deemed it imperative to re-emphasise the duty of their flock to obey the 'legitimate government'.[26] For Mgr Marmottin (Rheims), not to do so was a sin: 'A Catholic has in all conscience the duty to obey him [Pétain], to serve and uphold him; in fact, he is guilty of a sin if he does not do so.'[27] When a journalist in Nevers accused the clergy of 'gaullisme chronique' there was an indignant episcopal reaction: 'Le clergé français n'a rien de commun avec l'étrange aventure de Gaulle — d'ailleurs il ne le peut pas, parce que la morale catholique le défend.'[28] Another report, this time from a Gaullist source, drew a distinction between the higher and the lower clergy: 'The former... raise no official protest against the inhuman and anti-Christian attitude of the Germans.' Others claimed that the clergy as a body 'saw only the person of the Marshal'.[29] Indeed Cardinal Suhard, who never missed an occasion to demonstrate his loyalty, wrote to Pétain on May Day, celebrated as the feast-day of St Philip, just when the persecution of the Jews was about to be unleashed in earnest, declaring his undying attachment.[30]

Meanwhile in April Laval had returned to power. How would the Church now fare? Darlan, although cool towards religion, had granted subsidies to Catholic schools. Laval also held no brief for the Church. Not only had he no time for doctrine, but he abhorred any manifestations of clericalism. Mgr Chappoulie, as the Church's representative at Vichy, counselled prudence and reserve towards the new head of government.[31] But Catholics sensed that their once cosy relationship with the regime would now disappear for ever. There was also a feeling of let-down: the new dispensation had promised much, but had not given enough.

Above all, the treatment being meted out to the Jews was beginning to fill Christians with consternation and abhorrence. The somewhat belated protests by the Hierarchy during the summer and autumn left the lower clergy, in particular, bewildered at the turn of events. Cardinal Gerlier, for example, was asked by his diocesan priests what guidance on current affairs they should give to their parishioners. If they gave none, 'they would say that the clergy of France did not even possess the same courage as those of Germany or Belgium... these did not hesitate to speak out when they considered the Church had something to say'.Gerlier replied that the moment would come, but for the time being, at the Marshal's specific request, they should remain silent. This was deemed unsatisfactory, and provoked the retort that the Head of State was not the head of the Church.[32]

In the occupied zone the clergy were similarly restless. In the Cambrai diocese, for example, they were put firmly in their place. Archbishop Chollet, banned from his see since 1940, was allowed by the Germans to return in August 1942. The returnee immediately published a letter to his priests[33] asserting that Pétain alone was capable of resolving political problems and that 'la dissidence serait un péché grave contre la Patrie'. The Marshal's power was 'absolument authentique'. (Somewhat bewilderingly, the prelate threw in for good measure a warning against 'indecent practices' bordering on nudism, which, in his eyes, were becoming more frequent because of the increased mixing of the sexes; there was no word of other more horrendous 'practices' being perpetrated that summer.) A few weeks later Chollet found himself in hot water on another matter. A curate openly deplored the fact that communications from the bishop to him had to pass government censorship, a usage that had died out with Napoleon. He alleged that the archbishop had also criticised the procedure. Called to account, Chollet said he had been misinterpreted: on the contrary, he had *praised* Laval for his 'broad-mindedness' ('largeur de vues') in permitting him to publish a pastoral letter on Pius XII and peace.[34]

However, as 1942 wore on, the Marshal's influence was plainly waning. The bishops, as if to atone for their disloyalty in criticising the regime for the deportation of the Jews, were again anxious to show their support for him. After another visit to Pétain just before the North African landings, Cardinal Suhard reaffirmed the position of the Church:

nothing had changed since the ACA declaration of 24 July 1941 asserting Vichy's legitimacy. Hence, 'We intend to forebear in regard to him from any attitude of opposition and denigration... All in all, we intend to help him in his work.'[35] Suhard remarked that the exercise of religious functions of course did not depend on the government, but sometimes interests coincided, and this he saw as all to the good. Even Mgr Saliège protested against the use made abroad of his strictures on the persecution of the Jews, and reaffirmed his loyalty to Pétain.[36] In the Grotto of Miracles at Lourdes Gerlier again proclaimed that Pétain was the God-given leader around whom Catholics were 'happy and proud' to rally, and to serve.[37]

Yet what critics of the regime called exaggeratedly the 'grand offensive' against the anti-Jewish measures made by certain bishops in the late summer had in particular alarmed Action Française. Maurras saw his enemies on the 'Catholic Left' as troublemakers. In a series of articles in *Action Française* (from 24/25 to 30 October 1942) he was at pains to reiterate that no less than forty bishops had publicly and individually pledged their loyalty to Pétain since July 1940, that the ACA had given him its blessing, and the Nuncio, on 1 January 1942, had again dubbed him 'l'homme providentiel'. The bishops' statements, culled in the main from the various *Semaines religieuses*, were reprinted in a pamphlet, *Français, vos évêques vous parlent*. The list of 'loyalist' bishops did not include those whom the Royalist leader particularly disliked: Gerlier, Liénart, Saliège, Théas and Ruch — perhaps a kind of accolade for them.[38]

The Allied invasion of North Africa appeared to have little perceptible effect upon the bishops' support of Pétain. However, after the Armistice Day occupation of the 'free zone', the threat of the Marshal to withdraw entirely from public life immediately provoked declarations of continuing loyalty from worried prelates. They doubtless feared that the total occupation of France heralded a process of 'Polandisation' by the Germans as well as inaugurating religious persecution.

What a Third Republic politician thought of this unswerving loyalty about this juncture can be seen in a caustic letter from Paul Reynaud, interned at Le Portalet, to Cardinal Gerlier on 24 October, some while after the Dieppe raid in the summer, when Pétain and Laval had even thanked the Germans for repulsing the Allies. He accused both leaders of betraying France and detailed their 'crimes'. First, they had capitulated and thus broken their word to the British not to make a separate peace. Pétain had stated that the selfsame principles that had ensured German victory in 1940 were those of Frenchmen now. Next, he had removed France from the ranks of the democracies and after Montoire had announced a policy of collaboration. One practical consequence had been to allow the Germans to use French air bases in Syria. In the name of 'civilisation' the Marshal had wished for the defeat of the Soviet Union. He had agreed to send young people for forced labour in Germany (Service du Travail Obligatoire: STO). To this indictment, Reynaud asked, what had been Gerlier's response? At Lourdes he had not only proclaimed Pétain as sent by Providence but had asked God's blessing upon him and his government. The ex-prime minister went on to apostrophise the cardinal: 'In no time at all you will realise that by making common cause with Pétain and Laval, you have worked mightily towards the divorce of the Church from all the healthy elements in the nation.' Gerlier had proved himself to be on the side of the 'Nazis décivilisés' enthroned at Vichy; he was also something of a turncoat, like the archbishop who, after crowning Louis XVI, had also assisted at Napoleon's coronation. Gerlier should learn that: 'It is not through ceremonies, incense, organ music and Latin words, it is through the soul that you could win back those whom you have lost. Why have you not opted for the soul?[39] In this denunciation there is a hint of the note struck in the first *Cahier* of the clandestine publication, *Témoignage Chrétien* (November 1941).

Such recriminations fell on deaf ears. From the North Africa landings to the end of the year bishop after bishop renewed his conviction that the regime was legitimate. This may have been provoked by tracts by anonymous theologians, such as 'Le Prince esclave', that challenged this legitimacy and were circulating about this time. Some prelates, such as Mgr Béguin, Archbishop of Auch, and Mgr Brunhes, Bishop of Montpellier, even went so far as to urge submission to the Germans; their conquerors were worthy of respect and merited correct behaviour calculated not to 'provoke' them.[40] Particularly poignant was a telegram of loyalty from Mgr Gounot, Bishop of Carthage and Primate of Africa, despatched on the very day of the total occupation of France.[41]

As an Allied victory became more probable, Church leaders decided to withdraw still further from political involvement. However, other clergy favourable to political collaboration pointed menacingly to North Africa, where Liberation had meant the freeing of political prisoners and Jews, according to them a signal warning against the installation of a Communist regime in mainland France.[42]

The additional powers conceded by Pétain to Laval in November aroused apprehension, although Suhard, for his part, did not believe the head of government would openly attack the Church. The Fighting French reported that Nice Catholics now feared equally a German or an Allied victory; the first, for obvious reasons, the latter, because it 'consacrerait la politique du Front Populaire'.[43] From Vichy a police report, almost contemporaneous, noted the continuing loyalty of rank and file clergy, but also their desire for a German defeat, because Nazi ideology represented a greater danger for the Church than the 'democratic idea' of the United Nations.[44] There was clearly much concern by now about the outcome of the war. The bishops pinned their hopes on a compromise peace, with the Pope, Pétain, or even, ironically, Laval, acting as 'honest broker'. Hence the decision to continue to support the Marshal. In his Christmas wishes to Pétain Gerlier waxed lyrical over the Head of State's 'grandeur sereine dans la tempête actuelle'.[45] The Hierarchy still failed to realise that he had now lost practically all power to influence events.

Typical of this misapprehension was the attitude of one newly consecrated bishop. Received by Pétain in January 1943, Mgr Jaquin, recently appointed Bishop of Moulins, wrote thanking the Marshal for the audience and added: 'I shall not fail [...] to stimulate my diocesans to repose the greatest confidence in the one who holds in his hands the destiny of our country.'[46]

Alas, neither parish priests nor their congregations believed any longer that the fate of France lay in the Marshal's hands. Purblind, the bishops continued to think otherwise because of their dread of communism and the faint hope that France might 'sauver les meubles' in a stalemate peace. In public they concealed any misgivings.

The attitude of Mgr Serrand, Bishop of St-Brieuc, highlights indirectly the thinking about this time of those Catholics whose heads were buried in the sand. In a pastoral letter, whose contents were later widely publicised by the Information ministry and commended in the collaborationist *Le Franciste* (23 October 1943) the good bishop wrote:

> I was surprised to learn that the directives I gave the diocese in November 1940 concerning the attitude for Catholics to observe towards the government of Marshal Pétain are regarded by some as no longer valid. It is seemingly stated with assurance that, if I had to speak out today, I would express myself differently. This is a distortion of the reality about which I must not keep silent.[47]

He rejected such an interpretation of his views. The voting of full powers to Pétain in 1940 by a huge majority was still as valid as ever (the 1878 Constitution, he added incidentally, had only been approved by a majority of one). He reminded the faithful that the Pope continued his support. Moreover, no one could take the Marshal's place. It was rumoured he was playing a double game and was really working hand in glove with the 'dissidents'. If this were true, the bishop concluded, 'Je serais incapable d'accorder plus longtemps mon estime au chef de l'Etat', because this would be to elevate duplicity to a virtue.

The very need for such a statement demonstrates the disarray of the laity in 1943. The clandestine *Front National* commented that when a government's authority is waning, citizens, Catholics or no, have the right to replace it. Furthermore, 'When de Gaulle lands no bishop will ask that he be resisted in the name of loyalty to the legitimate government'.[48] It reminded readers that in North Africa and Corsica (a part of metropolitan France) the bishops had accepted de Gaulle and Giraud despite the presence of the Nuncio at Vichy.

Another straw in the wind was the clergy's attitude to the creation of the Milice, whose brutal co-operation with the Germans in suppressing the Resistance was to become notorious. In January 1943 the Nice clergy refused to attend the constituent assembly of this organisation presided over by Darnand. A Jesuit, claiming to be a Vatican envoy, had advised the clergy to boycott the occasion.[49]

Another Jesuit became involved in severe criticism of the regime. Père Dillard, who was to end his days in Dachau (died 12 January 1945), was a frequent preacher at St-Louis in Vichy, the fashionable church of the establishment, but also spoke out against nazism. His sermons were often sharply critical of the regime's 'paper reforms'.[50] The Vichy police characterised him as a 'nationalist Catholic',[51] but the London radio described him as 'le seul homme courageux du régime'. In January 1943 he published an article in the Catholic review, *Cité Nouvelle*, that was to send out shock waves within and outside France. In 1940, he wrote, the government had settled in Vichy, with its debilitating atmosphere, where:

> Everything counsels calm, everything inclines to a certain restful relaxation, a beneficent, resigned apathy. Refreshing summer showers of rain, the petty bourgeois ravages of the Allier river... landscapes devoid of rocks or mountains, winterless villas... everything is antirevolutionary to perfection, everything cries out with every step you take, that 'things are not so serious'.

But, he went on, alas, the 'operette' had given way to tragedy: 'When, on the morning of 11 November 1942, the townsfolk of Vichy saw the German uniforms, they began to realise that the adventure was growing worse, that the drama was moving towards its climax... They perceived that the house was still in ruins.'

This mental set, concluded Dillard, arose from a morbid taste for 'doctored' news — including stories emanating from foreign radio retailing that the Marshal was having fainting fits and receiving injections! In the end, in spite of all efforts to the contrary, individualism prevailed and there was a lack of that community spirit so extolled by the Révolution Nationale.

Such torpor, Dillard emphasised, was not the Marshal's fault. Frenchmen had wished to forget the defeat of 1940. Pétain had shocked Lamirand, the Secretary-General for Youth, when he had told young people that their country had been beaten. The Marshal had wished to re-Christianise France without setting off a new wave of clericalism. The 'cohorte chamarrée des bien pensants' — 'the gold-lace-embroidered crew of smug thinkers' — had interpreted this to mean resounding open-air masses and military parades with clerics dancing in attendance. Dillard stigmatised the protagonists of a 'cléricalisme politicailleur' ('politicking clericalism') who paid due regard to the Church and its outward ceremonies, but were more concerned with political than spiritual matters. Pétain, on the other hand, the victim of a personality cult, was the true representative of the continuity of France. His aim of re-christianising the country was failing because his administration was incompetent and lacked real leaders.

The article had many repercussions. The collaborationist press in the main commended it for its assault upon the failings of Vichy. Luchaire's *Les Nouveaux Temps* (7–8 March 1943) published an editorial entitled 'Les jugements d'un Jésuite', but regretted that Laval had not been mentioned. In Brussels Degrelle's Fascist paper *Le Pays Réel* (12 March 1943) praised the 'impartiality' of the observations, which were 'justes, fines, voire même audacieuses'. The Swiss press ensured that the article received wide coverage among the Allies and the neutrals.

Before publication Dillard had consulted Dr Ménétrel, Pétain's private secretary, whose view was that besides overemphasising the Marshal's age, the article did him a disservice.[52] Dillard retorted that at that time what was needed was to 'explain' Pétain to the people, because they were becoming disaffected.[53] Eventually pressure was exerted upon the turbulent priest to leave Vichy as being no longer 'persona grata'.

By 1943 the bishops were coming under fire from all sides. Laval's cronies remarked how often, in pastoral letters exhorting their flocks to gather in the crops or comply with the laws on obligatory labour service in Germany, they referred only to Pétain and never to the Head of Government.[54] Paris collaborationists disapproved of all the diocesan bishops save one, the luckless Mgr Dutoit of Arras, whose message still ordered absolute obedience: 'We have a double duty: that of carrying out the order we are given, and that of not refusing our share of the sacrifice demanded of our country.'[55]

Rumours that the French Church was in a state of upheaval, supposedly emanating from London, reached Bérard, the French envoy to the Vatican. Mgr Chappoulie reported these to Cardinal Suhard, who wrote reassuring the ambassador that his confrères' faith in Pétain was unshaken, and they remained loyal to the government.[56] Despite the attacks mounted in various clandestine theological tracts, they had no wish to intervene in politics, although, he added mildly, they had certain reservations regarding the STO. Prefects reported that on the whole the clergy still believed in the government's right to govern but noted its authority and prestige had diminished. The rank and file Catholic believed there should be no collaboration with the Germans, only any essential material co-operation, because their promises had proved worthless. There were few openly Gaullist and Anglophile priests, despite the fear of Nazi paganism.[57]

Subtle changes in the thinking of the higher clergy were becoming apparent in late 1943. Writing in his diocesan *Semaine religieuse* (5 October 1943), Mgr Rastouil of Limoges conceded that 'le gouvernement de notre pays battu et occupé est le gouvernement légal', but went on to state 'l'histoire est témoin que les régimes passent, mais que la France demeure. L'Eglise aussi demeure.' Three influential voices in the Church — Valeri, the Nuncio, Cardinal Suhard, and Mgr Chappoulie – now saw Pétain as the sole Frenchman — perhaps the only statesman anywhere — able to strike a deal with the Americans, on whom they now pinned their hopes of peace.[58] Valeri also judged it opportune to bolster up the Marshal's reputation by reiterating (20 November.1943) in flowery language papal support for the internal programme of reform (which by now had almost disintegrated): 'The programme of the Holy Father is close to that of that wonderful Head of the French State: Family, Work and Country.'[59]

The year of Liberation dawned with the traditional presentation to Pétain of their good wishes by the various bishops. Mgr Delay, of Marseilles, added emphatically, 'Je souhaite passionément que tous les Français lui obéissent.' The Catholic laity, like other French, in the main now disregarded this pious sentiment. However, a key to the thinking of certain bourgeois 'bien-pensants' about this time is given in a document entitled 'Opinion d'un père jésuite de Grenoble, 27 January 1944' that reached the Fighting French in Algiers.[60] This affirmed that Pétain's government had been legitimated by circumstances, as had de Gaulle's rule over North Africa, Corsica and the colonies. But, the Jesuit continued, Cardinal Gerlier believed that the dissident French leader was only the springboard for the Communists to take over power. Pétain was now a virtual prisoner. After November 1942 the Catholic laity had not rated the Gaullists very highly. They had been disappointed by the easing out of Giraud, and by the increasing power of the Jews in the Algiers Committee — 'ces gens-là sont puants', [*sic*] said the priest. Catholics in Algiers such as de Menthon and Tietgen were powerless in the face of atheistic Communists. If the Allies won, the fear was of Soviet domination. After a recent visit to the USSR the Archbishop of

York had allegedly said that the papacy would be the real loser in the war, and had promoted the idea of an alliance between Anglicans and the Russian Orthodox Church. In any case bourgeois Catholics held that the British were merely self-seeking; as for the Americans, they knew nothing of European problems. The bourgeoisie even had difficulty in believing that an invasion was coming; they looked to Laval, who had in the past been able to manipulate the Germans and maintain contacts with the Allies, to broker a compromise peace. However, this would be followed in France by a Red revolution, which would inevitably lead to religious persecution. Such was the pessimistic scenario sketched out for France and the Church.

In another document[61] it was reported that Abbé Maury, Gerlier's secretary, had sounded out the cardinal's views on the future. Gerlier also believed in a Communist take-over. He now perceived that Pétain, as the shield and buckler against communism and stimulator of national revival, had not been equal to the task, partly because he had lacked the effective means. It was time therefore to reconsider the position of the Head of State. He (Gerlier) knew nothing of the activities of the Algiers Committee but was not in principle opposed to it. On the other hand, he had family reasons for disliking de Gaulle, whose distant cousin ('cousin issu de germain') he was. He had heard that both the Germans and the Milice were planning to kill him (Gerlier). Angéli, the Regional Prefect, had confronted the Germans with this rumour, which had been denied, although it was admitted that at one time the Gestapo had contemplated his arrest.

The ACA Declaration of 17 February 1944 marked a watershed in the Hierarchy's relationship with the Laval Government. Those parts of the message relating to the Allied bombing and 'terrorism' naturally met with the regime's approval. Other strictures were less palatable: disapproval of the general wartime disregard of morality; the condemnation of total warfare; the threat to call up women for the STO; the state of disorder reigning in France, which it was the authorities' duty to remedy. The message spelled out the essential principles on which civilisation should be based: 'le respect de la personne humaine [a clear reference to the Jews and to the deportations], la sauvegarde du foyer familial, la fidélité à une règle de droit'. At this point the censor intervened, cutting out what followed: 'supérieure à l'autorité de l'Etat et aux intérêts immédiats de chaque nation'. *La Croix* was ordered to publish the message as censored, but Cardinal Gerlier forbade it to print anything save the full text. The ACA approached Laval to attempt to avoid the inevitable suspension of this, the semi-official organ of catholicism, that would follow refusal. Other newspapers did publish the bowdlerised version, although the complete message quickly became known through the Swiss French-language media.[62] The *Journal de Genève* reported that the bishops interpreted the censoring of the declaration as a politically motivated move to curb not only the Church but Christianity itself. In Paris *L'Œuvre* (9 March 1941: 'Réticence inutile') took a different view: the declaration merely provided arguments for 'réfractaires' from the STO and a justification for the Maquis; it rebuked the Hierarchy for daring to criticise government decisions.

The break with Laval and his government was almost complete. Pétain, completely sidetracked, now received only the rare expression of loyalty. One exception came from Rome, where the R.-P. Gillet, the French head of the Dominicans, in May 1944 coupled a message of 'devotion and fidelity' with a disavowal of the activities in the Algiers Consultative Assembly of a fellow Dominican, Père Carrière.[63] Xavier Vallat, who took over Philippe Henriot's radio broadcasts after the latter's assassination, on 9 July 1944 made a desperate plea for loyalty, citing a long list of bishops who, he alleged, continued actively to support the regime. By now, however, Catholics were largely case-hardened to such appeals.[64]

On 16 August Mgr Chappoulie sent a note to Dr Ménétrel from Paris in which he noted that the city was calm, and that on the previous day, the Feast of the Assumption, the churches had been full and prayers had been offered for the Marshal. But Chappoulie had finally acknowledged in May that the Marshal was powerless, although he thought it desirable for the Church to maintain close contact with him to the very end.[65]

However, by 26 August Pétain had been bundled off to Germany, Paris had been liberated, and Cardinal Suhard had been snubbed, having suffered the indignity of being shut out from his own cathedral when de Gaulle attended a service of thanksgiving in Notre Dame. The almost boundless commitment that the Church had officially made to Pétain and the Etat Français since 10 July 1940 was finally shattered. What had motivated such devotion? There was fear of the Germans, fear of a Communist victory, fear of an extremist Gaullist government; there was dislike of the Allies; there had been the desire to back a Révolution Nationale from which the bishops expected much; there was Pétain's potential role in the likelihood of a compromise peace. In the event, hopes were dupes and fears were liars. Would the Church therefore not have done better to retreat into a dignified silence for four years, if it felt itself too weak to speak out against persecution and oppression?

Notes

Unless otherwise stated the place of publication is Paris.

1. AN 2 AG 292 Talk given to the students of St Etienne-du-Mont, 16 June 1941.
2. AN 2 AG 495 CC.77C. Protestantisme. Letter to Pétain, Nîmes, 10 January 1941.
3. AN 2 AG 495. Letter from Boegner, Nîmes, 24 October 1941, to Lavagne, of Pétain's Private Office.
4. AN 2 AG 493. Intercept of letter from Mgr Piguet, Clermont, 29 October 1941, to Mgr Chassaigne, Bishop of Tulle.
5. *Semaine religieuse* (Rodez), quoted in *La Croix*, 5 November 1941.
6. J.-P. Cointet, 'L'Eglise catholique et le gouvernement de Vichy. Eglise et Légion', *Actes*: Lyons, p. 437.
7. AN 2 AG 492. Report of Renseignements Généraux, Vichy, 3 November 1941.
8. AN 2 AG 492 Report of Renseignements Généraux, ref: DJ/10 (secret) Note de renseignement No. 37623/16B (Source: 'sure'), Vichy, 23 September 1942.
9. AN 2 AG 493. Letter of Bishop Rastouil to Dussart, the Director of the Légion, Limoges, 3 June 1943, and letter of Dussart to the Légion headquarters, Limoges, 5 June 1943.
10. A Dio, Lille, 2 B1 ACA 1942-1945. Meeting of ACA, 20–21 October 1943.
11. R. Mehl, *Le Pasteur Marc Boegner. Une humble grandeur*, 1987, p. 151.
12. AN 2 AG 493. Intercept No. 2633. Letter from Gerlier to Boegner, Nîmes, 6 November 1941.
13. *Bulletin paroissial,* May 1941, Questambert (Morbihan), quoted in: R. Lambert, *Carnet d'un Témoin*, 1985, p. 187.
14. AN 72 AJ 249 gives the composition of the *experts* appointed to the Conseil National as follows: thirty-two agriculturalists, twenty-one members of the professions, eighteen from the armed forces and the administration, sixteen syndicalists, seven artisans or workmen, six from the Légion des Combattants.
15. AN 2 AG 492. Report dated 28–30 January 1941 by Peretti della Rocca.
16. AN 2 AG 493 'Note pour Monsieur le Maréchal', n.d; letter from Pétain to Suhard, Vichy, 10 March 1941.
17. AN 2 AG 492. 'Note de police (secret)', 24 February 1941.
18. For an account of the commission's proceedings see W.D. Halls, *The Youth of Vichy France*, Oxford, 1981, p. 145 and pp. 149ff. See also: M. Cointet, *Le Conseil National de Vichy: vie politique et réforme de l'Etat en régime autoritaire*, 1989.
19. H. Du Moulin de Labarthète, *Le Temps des illusions*, Geneva, 1946, p. 272.
20. Telegram 3022, Paris, 6 October 1941, despatched to Berlin; quoted in R. Paxton, *Vichy France. Old Guard and New Order, 1940–1944* , London, 1972, p. 195, n. 119.
21. H. Lottman, *Pétain, Hero or Traitor?* London, 1985, p. 309.
22. Pertinax, *Les Fossoyeurs*, New York, 1953, vol. 2, p. 271.
23. AN 2 AG 492. 'Note', Vichy, 9 April 1941, by the Inspecteur Général des services de la Police administrative, ref: Pol. Rens. No. 2404/1.
24. AN 2 AG 492. Postal intercept 23 August 1941 of letter from Emmanuel Cathelinau, Provincial Prior, Lyons, to Père Férand, Prior of the Dominicans at St-Alban-en-Leysse (Savoie).
25. AN 2 AG 74. Letter to Pétain, 27 December 1941.
26. AN F6O.1674. Report of broadcast, n.d., n.p., by Xavier Vallat.
27. *Bulletin diocésain* (Rheims), 25 January 1942.
28. AN 72 AJ 1863. 'Le Loyalisme du clergé français', *Semaine religieuse* (Nevers), 7 February 1942.
29. AN F60.1674, ref: CNAIFL B8725.
30. AN 2 AG 493.
31. A. Mallet, *Pierre Laval*, vol. 2, 1945, pp 166ff.

32. AN 2 AG 492. Ref. dj 10. Rens. Gen. Note de renseignement No. 3757/16B. Vichy, 25 September 1942.
33. AD du Nord, Lille, 1 W 2187. Circulaire diocésaine No. 7.
34. AD du Nord, Lille, 1W 2187.
35. AN F60.1758 Reported by Radio Montpellier, 18.00, 3 November 1942. The context does not make clear whether, in the quotation, Suhard was referring to Pétain or the government.
36. AN F60.1758 and AN.72 AJ 1863. Message published in *La Semaine catholique*, quoted by Agence Havas (O.F.I.), 4 October 1942.
37. AN 72 AJ 1863. Agence Havas, 6 October 1942.
38. C. Maurras, 'La Voix de l'Eglise de France', a series of six articles appearing in *Action Française* between 24 and 30 October 1942.
39. P. Reynaud, *La France a sauvé l'Europe*, vol. 2, 1947, pp. 542ff.
40. AN 2 AG 494. *Semaine religieuse* (Auch), 21 November 1942; Pastoral letter (Montpellier), 14 November 1942.
41. AN F60.1674. Telegram from Mgr Gounot, 11 November 1942. Similar protestations of loyalty (see AN 2 AG 494) came from Mgr Delay (Marseilles), Mgr Du Bois de la Villerabel (Aix), Mgr Choquet (Lourdes), Mgr Rastouil (Limoges) and other bishops.
42. AN 2 AG 492 (Secret) Rapport de police, Vichy, 5 December 1942.
43. AN F60.1674. C.N.I. No. 1060. Orientation, 25 November 1942.
44. AN 2 AG 492. Rapport de police, Vichy, 5 December 1942.
45. AN 2 AG 493.
46. AN 2 AG 493. Moulins, 15 January 1943.
47. Quoted in *Le Franciste*, 23 October 1943. See AN F60.1674 and AN 2 AG 82, folder P 10 E, *Esprit catholique*.
48. *Front National*, Nouvelle série, no. 2, November 1943.
49. AN 2 AG 492. 'Note [de police].(Secret)', 5 March 1943..
50. See *Weltwoche* (Zurich), 25 June 1943.
51. AN 2 AG 75 Note [de police] (Secret), 6 March 1943.
52. AN 2 AG 120. 'Note'.
53. AN 2 AG 120. Letter of Dillard to Ménétrel, Vichy, 2 rue de l'Eglise, 19 December 1942.
54. AN 2 AG 75. Note (Secret), 6 March 1943.
55. *Semaine religieuse* (Arras), 1 April 1943.
56. AN 2 AG 492. Letter, ref: 972/886, Vichy, 15 May 1943.
57. AN F60.1674a. 'L'opinion des préfets sur le clergé français', Bureau de la Presse de la France Combattante, BCRA No. 3197, 2 September 1943.
58. AN F60 1674 C.N.I. marked: 'Service courrier. Fin 1943'.
59. AN 2 AG 494. At an official reception at the prefecture of the Tarn, 20 November 1943.
60. AN F1a 3784.
61. AN F1a 3784. Service Comm. Int. Ref. XCG/1/35700. 'Très secret. A ne pas diffuser'.
62. AN 2 AG 494. Document: (Secret) 'Dissidence: télégramme d'information'. Report of broadcast by Radio Geneva, 21.30, 31 March 1944, . See also: AN F1a 3784. Doc. MTB/2/35001.
63. AN F60.1674 Radio Paris, 20.00, 18 May 1944.
64. AN F60.1674. Radio Vichy, 9.July 1944.
65. AN 2 AG 75. Letter to Ménétrel, Vichy, 6 May 1944.

–6–

The Church: New Laws

Despite the friction that ultimately developed between Church and State the regime was ready to promulgate legislation that lifted restrictions on its activities as well as giving it considerable advantages. The Third Republic had seriously limited the Church's freedom of action with regard to education, the status of the religious orders, and the management of Church property. New Vichy laws set out to remedy this state of affairs. The main thrust of the flurry of laws and decrees that emerged concerned education, which lies outside the scope of this volume. These were the work principally of Chevalier and Carcopino as Education ministers. However, and not only in education, for its part the Church hoped for a definitive statute regulating relationships with the State. This did not come about.

The question of the recognition of the religious orders, which was a key issue, loomed large. Almost one of the last acts of the Third Republic had been to allow the Carthusian monks to return to their old home, Grande Chartreuse, near Grenoble. But since their order was legally 'unauthorised', the return of an advance party of very old monks later in September 1940 to the buildings they had left thirty-seven years earlier was theoretically illegal. It was not until a decree of 21 February 1941 that the situation was regularised by recognition being given, so that the remainder returned.[1] Other orders demanded recognition: in March the Salesians, a teaching order, applied, and its application was favourably received.[2] The more amenable attitude of the regime gave rise to expectations that other oppressive laws would eventually be repealed.

The demand for recognition was taken up by a militant, extremist pressure group, the Ligue des Droits des Religieux Anciens Combattants (DRACS). Founded in 1924 by a Benedictine, Dom Morau, and Abbé Bergey, a priest from St-Emilion who was later accused of collaborationism, the movement had originally been started in order to counter Herriot's policy of secularisation. In 1940 the DRACS put out a pamphlet attacking the law of 1901, which denied religious orders the right of association.[3] Unless explicitly authorised by the State they therefore had no right to exist. Thus, argued the DRACS, religious orders were still outlaws, either because they had not requested authorisation or had been rejected. (It will be recalled that since the First World War, when they had rallied round the Republic in the cause of the 'Union sacrée', and served their country well, authorised or not, the religious orders had been 'tolerated'.) The DRACS's pamphlet set out the legal situation. Thus if three nuns met together to pray, they were committing an illegal act and could be prosecuted for a crime that was vague in the extreme. Even authorised orders could be dissolved by a simple decree. The State could exercise a tight hold over their membership and accounts. They were disqualified from benefiting directly from any legacy, and could not own any kind of immovable property. If expelled from their convent, they had no right to establish themselves elsewhere. Although the missions they had started in French possessions overseas were considered a national asset, they remained pariahs in their own country. The situation, the DRACS concluded, was intolerable.

Although Waldeck-Rousseau, by the law of 1901, had sought merely to regulate the order, his successor, the 'petit père' Combes who was a former seminarist, had intended to abolish them. In 1903 orders that were not recognised or had not made a demand for recognition had theoretically been disbanded. The principle of recognition was in practice simply set aside.

In 1940 confusion reigned as to the true situation, particularly after a law of 3 September 1940 legalised what was already accepted practice, the right of the religious orders to teach. This right still meant, however, that they had to seek authorisation to exist. Cardinal Gerlier, himself a lawyer, raised the matter with Pétain in an interview (22 July 1941). Since it was one that involved papal authority he thought the Nuncio should be brought into the discussion. The Marshal, subjected to pressure in the opposite direction from Darlan, his chief minister, temporised, contenting himself with vague generalities. A future constitution, he said, 'conçue dans un esprit véritablement chrétien', would regulate matters, and went on: 'I will help the French clergy, but at the present time I need its unrestricted backing, with no reservations, in order to carry out the Révolution Nationale.'[4]

The DRACS kept up their campaign, although Du Moulin de Labarthète, of Pétain's Private Office, informed the organisation that public opinion was ill-prepared for the sort of blanket legislation they sought.[5] The Marshal required more time to study the question. Meanwhile André Lavagne, as a 'Maître des requêtes' at the Conseil d'Etat with considerable legal expertise, who had by then joined Pétain's staff with particular responsibility for religious affairs, applied himself to the problem. He was warned by Sauret, his counterpart in the Interior ministry, that the DRACS had been warmly praised in the autumn of 1940 by the *Frankfurter Allgemeine Zeitung,* which was hardly a recommendation.[6] He quickly decided that the DRACS were 'noisy agitators' not qualified to speak for the religious orders: 'ce sont des francs-tireurs', he declared. They intimidated the superiors of the religious orders — and did not even deign to consult the female orders. Many bishops hoped that they would be put in their place. Their demands were exorbitant: they did not even wish to be subject to the law on associations, but claimed rights under common law. They characterised four orders that wished to submit to the State — Lazaristes, Sulpiciens, Pères du Saint-Esprit and Missions Etrangères — as the 'quatre plaies de l'Eglise'.[7]

Nevertheless, the text of a new law giving greater freedom to the Congregations was drafted in early 1942, despite the orders not having been directly consulted. The Superior of one of them bitterly remarked that the legislation could only be flawed since it would have been elaborated 'sans nous, en dehors de nous, et cela délibérément', because the loyalty of the congregations was considered to be suspect[8] — incidentally, a not unjustified allegation. Barthélémy, the Justice minister, although Cardinal Gerlier's friend, and very opposed to Title III of the 1901 law which the new legislation would replace, raised legal objections to the draft text. There was the prospect that with the imminent return of Laval to power the project would fall through, given his secular views. Working with Sauret, and Moysset, one of Pétain's advisers, Lavagne persevered in his efforts. The final law bore the date 8 April 1942 but was not in fact signed until 16 April, and then by ministers of the outgoing government, and not by Laval and his incoming ministers.[9]

The new law did not make applications for recognition mandatory, but, subject to the approval of the Conseil d'Etat, any religious order could apply. More importantly, any religious order that had previously been dissolved under earlier legislation and whose property had not already been sold off by the State could recover it. This meant that monasteries and convents that had remained in State ownership could be restituted.

The Church as a whole hoped that the legislation would presage a definitive statute regulating all aspects of Church-State relationships. The religious orders failed to take immediate advantage of the law. But it pleased the Secretary-General of the powerful Christian Brothers, Frère François de Sales, who stated he would now seek recognition, trusting that this might well bring about not only the return of the seat of his order to France — they had moved first to Belgium and then to Rome after 1905 — but also the appointment of a Frenchman to head it and the restitution of property confiscated in 1904.

For this very reason reaction in some Vatican circles to the practical effect of the law was not entirely favourable, as Canon Monulle, a legal counsellor at the French Embassy to the Vatican, reported. The Holy See had progressively tightened its grip on those orders of French origin that had moved their headquarters to Rome to escape the 'penal laws'. Cardinal Maglione, who as Vatican Secretary of State had been instrumental in their move, was reluctant to see them reacquire a national ethos and relative autonomy. Appointments to posts such as superior of an order had by now become a Vatican prerogative, as had the appointment of a director-general for each Province. (In the nineteenth century such appointments had been made by the members of orders themselves.) The system thus concentrated power in Rome. Maglione would only go as far as conceding that a council should be appointed to 'advise' each provincial director. The fact remained that those congregations originally French now often consisted of two-thirds of foreigners, and this robbed France of much influence in the Catholic world. Lavagne would appear to have been Gallican in his thinking, a charge that was also levelled against the Conseil d'Etat (some even considered it still Republican!), which was to play a key role in recognition of the orders. The French Church had not existed as a distinct entity since 1905, and the French bishops hardly constituted a corporate national body. A French State allied with a Church based on the old Gallican liberties would obviously be stronger in a 'new European order', if such an outcome of the war had to come to pass.

Laval, despite his religious indifference, might well also have adopted a similar posture. As it was, he did not react to this law brought in almost literally behind his back. In fact, few orders applied for recognition, perhaps for fear that any decision of the Conseil d'Etat might go against them. The Christian Brothers, for example, were eventually refused recognition — their application had dragged on to August 1944 — precisely because their headquarters remained in Rome. The turbulent DRACS were also not happy, because orders applying for recognition were left in limbo as to their status. As late as January 1943 the movement were still hounding Sauret, the 'sous-directeur des cultes' in the Interior ministry, for his part in drawing up the law, with its reference to the approval of the Conseil d'Etat, and even wrote to the collaborationist Admiral Platon, a member of Pétain's entourage — and a Protestant! — demanding that the luckless official be dismissed.

In the press the law had a mixed reception. In Catholic Brittany *Le Nouvelliste de Bretagne* headlined an article: 'Après 40 ans d'un injuste ostracisme, la France va reconnaître tous ses fils.' The Paris collaborationist newspapers were less enthusiastic. The reaction of *La France socialiste* was typical. The fact that the 'Rapport' which preceded the text of the law alluded to a 'solution d'ensemble' was taken to mean that steps were being taken towards a new Concordat. It was seen as the climax of a long campaign of clericalism, which had been played out 'to the end' — the writer doubtless meant that the return of Laval had written 'finis' to it.[10]

At the turn of the year Lavagne was instrumental in pushing through further measures giving greater freedom to the religious orders. On New Year's Day, 1943 he informed the Nuncio that Pétain had just signed a law allowing religious orders to own property in their own right, and not through the mediation of a third party, and granting exemption from any legal charges due.[11]

This settlement, unsatisfactory as it was — after the Liberation there was a reversion to the *status quo ante bellum* — is further proof that the quarrel between clericalism and anticlericalism continued as fiercely as ever under Vichy, as did the struggle for Gallican rights, although not so overtly. Pétain moved cautiously in the matter, anxious not to revive openly the religious battles that had scarred the history of the Third Republic.

Two further laws relating to the Church were also promulgated on 31 December 1942. The law on the Separation voted on 3 July 1905 by the Rouvier government had decreed that all ecclesiastical buildings would pass to the local communes, which would allow specially formed religious associations (in practice the bishops and clergy) to continue to use them. This was felt by the Church to be particularly humiliating. Thus as early as September 1940 Mgr Choquet, then Bishop of Tarbes, had appealed to Pétain for the return from the local town council of the Grotto of Lourdes.[12] Buildings of outstanding historical interest had passed directly into the ownership of the State, and up to now it would only repair this particular category of ecclesiastical property. Under a new law it now contracted to assume financial responsibility for the repair of all churches. A further law allowed diocesan associations, like the religious orders, to receive directly gifts and legacies. (Another law of 15 November 1943 reduced the tax on such benefits to 12 per cent.)

Cardinal Suhard, on his visit to the Pope in January 1943, was thus able to carry copies of some of the new measures with him as tangible proof that the regime was favourable to the Church. Lavagne was justly pleased with his legislative achievements. Writing to the editor of a Marseilles newspaper, the *Eveil Provincial,* he commented: 'Je dirais que par la faute de l'anticléricalisme, l'Eglise a "pris le maquis" [*sic*]; il est temps qu'elle revienne dans la vie de la Cité.' The innovations introduced would allow it to participate fully in national life. But Pétain, he declared, wished to move forward gradually and had not annulled 'les grandes lois de 1901 et de 1905'. He believed the reforms he had now been instrumental in bringing about were irreversible.[13]

Incidentally, the State subsidised considerably the building of new churches in the Paris area, and the repair of others, continuing the work begun in 1931 by Cardinal Verdier, 'le cardinal aux 100 églises'. From 1941 to 1943 56 million francs of public money were used by Mgr Touze, the diocesan Vicar-General, in collaboration with the Finance ministry and the Prefect of the Seine, to complete building or initiate repairs on seventeen churches, including the Sacré Cœur. Pétain took a personal interest in this project.[14] Léon Noël, Laval's 'directeur de cabinet', a 'closet Gaullist', warned Cardinal Suhard that this would stop if the regime collapsed. In point of fact it continued, although at a much slower pace.

Nevertheless no definitive statute for Church–State relations in France was ever realised, not even in Catholic education.

Notes

Unless otherwise stated the place of publication is Paris.

1. AN 72 AJ 1863; see also *The Times*, 7 March 1941.
2. AN 2 AG 493. Letter from P. Sauret, 'sous-directeur des Cultes', Interior ministry, to Lavagne, 'chef de cabinet' in Pétain's Private Office, Vichy, 11 March 1942, stating that he saw no objection to recognition.
3. A copy of the pamphlet is to be found in AN 2 AG 493.
4. AN 2 AG 492. Memorandum prepared for a discussion between Pétain and Cardinal Gerlier, 22 July 1941.
5. AN 2 AG 609. Letter of Labarthète, Vichy, 2 August 1941,
6. AN 2 AG 493. Letter of Sauret to Lavagne, 12 August 1941.
7. AN 2 AG 609. 'Note à propos des revendications de la DRAC', ref: ML/GC. Vichy, 8 August 1941.
8. AN 2 AG 493. Letter to General Laure, a member of Pétain's staff, from Père Rieu, the Superior of the Marist Fathers, La Neylière, by Sainte-Foy l'Argentière, Rhône, 27 February 1942.
9. For a detailed discussion of the new laws affecting the religious orders, see N. Atkin, *Church and Schools in Vichy France,* New York and London, 1991, pp. 114–30.
10. *Le Nouvelliste de Bretagne*, 30 April 1942. Article by Pierre Lessageon, quoting René Chateau, 'Le retour des congrégations', *La France socialiste*, 19 April 1942.
11. AN 2 AG 492. Letter from Lavagne to Valerio Valeri, Vichy, 1 January 1943.
12. AN 2 AG 616. Letter of Mgr Choquet to Pétain, Lourdes, 18 July 1940.
13. AN 2 AG 492. Letter to E. Marret, 31 boul. Chave, Marseilles, Vichy, 4 January 1943.
14. M. Brisacier, 'L'implantation des lieux de culte dans le diocèse de Paris (1871–1980)', *Les Cahiers de l'IHTP*, no. 12, October 1989, pp. 79f.

PART III

THE SCAPEGOATS

–7–

Christians and Jews — I

A waning enthusiasm for the Révolution Nationale had refocused Christians' attention on disquieting earlier innovations in Vichy policy. Chief among these was the treatment of the Jews, which was eventually to prove the major stumbling-block to the Church's acquiescence in the course the regime was pursuing. However, having in the past disregarded the Augustinian doctrine of the common humanity of all men, it had itself by no means an unblemished record concerning the Jews.

Constitutionally a secular state, the Third Republic kept no tally of the number of Jews living in France: for it, Judaism was a religion like any other. Statistics are therefore unreliable. However, it is estimated that, whereas in 1919 they numbered some 150,000, by 1939 this had increased to 300,000, representing 0.7 per cent of the population.[1] The 1919 figures included Jewish families established in France before the Revolution, nineteenth and early twentieth century immigrants, and those living in Alsace-Lorraine, by then restored to France. During the 1920s some 50,000 more arrived from Eastern Europe, and between 1930 and the outbreak of war a wave of refugees from Germany and Austria swelled the numbers by another 100,000. Of the total number in 1939, some 110,000 lived in Algeria, officially a part of metropolitan France; of the rest, it is estimated that perhaps as many as 150,000 were technically foreigners or recently naturalised. The most recent arrivals did not integrate easily into a French environment, and xenophobia and anti-Semitism went hand in hand.

Anti-Semitism was episodic in French political life. Drumont's extremist, fanatically anti-Jewish newspaper, *La Libre Parole*, had reached a peak circulation of half a million in the 1890s. Action Française, with its policy of 'la France seule', a movement founded at the height of the Dreyfus Affair, remained a permanent focus for anti-Semitism in the inter-war period. When the Protocols of the Elders of Zion were shown in *The Times* (August 1921) to be a forgery, Bainville wrote: 'What does that prove about the Bolsheviks and the Jews? Absolutely nothing!'

Maurras lumped Jews with Freemasons and foreigners as 'the enemy'. Writing in *Action Française* (9 June 1925) about Schrameck, the then Interior minister, he declared: 'No one knows, no one could say, whence you come... but you are the foreigner... you come from... your name seems to point to it, from the Rhineland ghettos... We will kill you like a dog... It would be without hatred or fear that I would give the order to shed your blood.'

This onslaught appeared in a newspaper that, until it was banned by the Pope in 1926, was read by bishops and was preferred reading among a section of the 'bonne bourgeoisie', members of the FNC. The Stavisky affair (1934) exacerbated anti-Semitic feeling. When the Catholic deputy Xavier Vallat insulted Blum in the Chamber of Deputies he conveniently forgot that Blum's mother was a Christian.[2] Meanwhile from 1933–39, supported by activists funded by the Nazi *Weltdienst* in Erfurt, Action Française kept up its anti-Jewish campaign.[3] The Fascist leagues of the 1930s were also anti-Semite, although de la Rocque's Croix de Feu, which, as the Parti Social Français (PSF), in 1939 attracted many Catholics, was not. It is true that Darquier de Pellepoix, who later succeeded Vallat as Commissioner for Jewish Questions, was for a while a member of the PSF, but de la Rocque also welcomed into his movement Jews such as Jakob Kaplan, who had fought at Verdun. Cardinal Liénart had deplored the slur on Salengro, another eminent Jew, hounded to suicide by *Gringoire*.[4] This periodical rivalled in venom the Nazi anti-Jewish *Der Stürmer*, although it shared this dubious accolade with another, more intellectual publication, *Je Suis Partout*..[5]

A few intellectuals and a section of the press had always been prone to racist attitudes. Even Péguy, a devout Catholic who had been a Dreyfusard and, like Jacques Chevalier, his philosophy professor, had remained a disciple of the Jewish philosopher Bergson, had extolled 'la race française' in almost Kiplingesque terms. The very Catholic Chevalier, when briefly Vichy's Education minister, blew hot and cold regarding the Jews, whilst never wavering in his allegiance to Bergson. Contemporary Catholic writers such as La Varende, Chateaubriant, Béraud and Beauplan were anti-Jewish. Bernanos, fiercely anti-Jewish until his conversion to Gaullism in 1940, had written, glorifying Drumont, his *La Grande Peur des Bien-pensants*. Minor publications such as the anti-Masonic journal, *Revue internationale des sociétés secrètes*, run by two priests, Mgr Jouin and Abbé Boulin, rounded on the Jews as being responsible for capitalism, communism and (for good measure)... nudism. It attacked Catholics such as the Jesuits Pères Bonsirven and Merklen, since 1927 respectively directors of the influential Catholic journals, *Etudes* and *La Croix*, whose attitudes were more liberal. Bonsirven, a specialist in Jewish studies, had discerned in France just before the war a revival of a principled, latent and widespread anti-Semitism.[6] Another strong Catholic, Claudel, although professing a liking for Jews, complained that too often they were to be found leading 'the parties of subversion'.[7] Thus in 1940 there was fertile ground for anti-Jewish measures.

Christians (and others) often confused the distinction between being anti-Semitic and anti-Jewish. Whereas anti-Semitism, strictly speaking, was a racial concept, the label 'anti-Jewish' served as a term of opprobrium referring to secular as well as religious matters. The papacy had not condoned anti-Semitism in the pre-war period. Indeed Pius XI had come out against it in a decree of 21 March 1928 issued by the Holy Office: 'The Holy See condemns most categorically ["maxime damnat"] hatred of the people who were once the people of God, that hatred which today generally goes under the name of anti-Semitism.'[8]

A decade later, addressing a group of Belgian pilgrims, he had spoken out again: 'Anti-Semitism is inadmissible. Spiritually we are Semites', although he added that others had the right to defend their interests (presumably meaning against the Jews). Meanwhile Nazi Germany had promulgated the Nuremberg racial laws, and in 1938 'Kristallnacht' (November 9–10) marked a new peak of anti-Semitism. The papal encyclical *Mit brennender Sorge* (1937), directed to the Germans, but whose content was known in France, had condemned the 'idolatrous cult of race'.

After the death of 'der Judenpapst', as the Nazis described him, his successor, Pius XII, in the first encyclical of his reign, *Summi Pontificatus* (27 October 1939), had in his turn inveighed against 'an exacerbated nationalism, the idolising of the State, totalitarianism, *racism*, and the cult of brute force'.[9]

Church leaders in France had followed the papal lead. Archbishop Saliège of Toulouse had spoken out shortly after the Nazi take-over in Germany: 'I feel as if I myself am struck down by the blows rained on the persecuted... I cannot forget that the tree of Jesse blossomed in Israel and it was there that it yielded fruit... catholicism proclaims the essential equality of all races.'[10] Cardinals Verdier, Liénart and Gerlier — the last emulating his predecessor, Archbishop Maurin of Lyons — had conveyed their sympathy and expressed solidarity with the Jewish community both in 1933 and 1938. Mgr Ruch, Bishop of Strasbourg, had joined in the chorus of condemnation; his support was significant because anti-Semitism in Alsace flourished, although more especially among the Protestant nobility. Not only the Jesuits of *Etudes*, but also the missionary priests of Notre-Dame-de-Sion, who published a *Bulletin catholique de la Question d'Israël*, expressed their opposition to anti-Semitism.

Lay Catholics also voiced their indignation — politicians such as Bidault and Marc Sangnier, philosophers such as Maritain, the author of *L'impossible antisémitisme*, and Vialatoux, academics such as Père de Lubac and Abbé Richard of the Catholic faculties of Lyons, writers such as Mauriac and Mounier, and journalists such as Francisque Gay and Robert d'Harcourt.

The Protestants Wilfred Monod, and André Philip, the Socialist deputy who later defected to de Gaulle, condemned the Nazi persecution — had not they also suffered as a minority sect for their beliefs, between 1680 and 1760? Barthism had stimulated Protestants' interest in the Bible, and study of the Old Testament had sensitised them to the links of Christianity with Judaism: the Bible called the Jews 'God's chosen people'. Protestants were better informed concerning conditions in Germany, and were aware of the split among their German co-religionists concerning the so-called 'Aryan paragraph' and the 'Theses of Barmen'. After 'Kristallnacht' the Fédération Protestante de France had denounced the pogroms (29 November 1938) and racial doctrines 'contrary to Christ's teaching and that of the Apostles'.[11] Pastor Boegner, as head of the Reformed Church had preached in Lent 1939 on 'the tragic situation of the Jews in totalitarian States'.[12]

French anti-Semitism was of course welcome to the Germans. Their brainwashing of French politicians had even penetrated Radical circles: on 6 December 1938 Georges Bonnet fawningly avowed to Ribbentrop that France was seeking a 'solution' to the 'Jewish problem'. After the occupation of Paris in June 1940 the SS leader Knochen had installed a detachment especially to study this French 'problem'.

On 26 July, backed by the Reformed Church, Pastor Boegner went to Vichy to protest against the Armistice clause that stipulated that German political refugees — some of whom were of course Jewish — should be handed over to the Nazis. His impression was not only that clericalism was rife there but also that the 'passionate anti-Semitism of several ministers was being given free rein, quite apart from any German pressure'.[13] He also discussed with Lucien Romier, then responsible for broadcasting, the content of Protestant religious programmes, which had aroused adverse comment because they 'exalted' the people of Israel. If pastors had to talk of a chosen people, he was informed, could they not select a people other than the Jews?

Intervention in favour of the Jews cut no ice with the new regime. At Vichy Maurrassian influence ensured that an 'antisémitisme de peau, antisémitisme de religion, antisémitisme d'Etat'[14] would prevail. André Siegfried offered a slightly different explanation for such prejudice: anti-Semitism was attributable more to nationalism than to racism, particularly in Pétain's case, and Laval's stance was taken not on principle, but more to curry favour with the Germans. Nevertheless discriminatory measures began. The law of 22 July 1940 removed French nationality from any foreigner naturalised after 1927. This deprived 15,514 of citizenship, of whom 6,307 were Jews.[15] These went to swell the number of foreign Jews — 150,000 — that by then had taken refuge in France.[16] Incitement to racial hatred, forbidden by the Marchandeau law passed at the outbreak of war, which was now repealed, was again permitted: scapegoats were needed, and the Jews were readily available.

Many Christian leaders, despite their sympathy, believed there was a 'Jewish problem' caused by the large number of foreign immigrants and by 'hasty or unjustified naturalisations', at a time when, in the aftermath of the debacle, unemployment was still high.[17] However, when the ACA met in the occupied zone in August 1940, the Jewish question was not even discussed. But on 31 August when their counterparts in the unoccupied zone convened, the matter was raised because it was anticipated that 'grave' but 'justifiable' measures were imminent. They therefore sought to define the Christian attitude. They believed there existed an international community consisting of Jews from every nation, who differed from foreigners yet remained unassimilated to the host communities. This obliged the State to take measures for the 'common good'. But it should not expel Jews without distinguishing between their activities that were licit, and those that were not, nor deny them their natural rights:

> To conclude, it may appear legitimate for a State to envisage a special legal statute for Jews (as the papacy in Rome had once done). But this statute [must]... be based upon the rules of charity and justice, not be inspired by a spirit of hatred or political revenge, but strive towards the double objective of safeguarding the rights of the human person, whilst preventing any kind of activity that might harm the national common good.[18]

One notes again the argument of the 'common good', the definition of which was later to be hotly disputed by dissentient theologians. The idea of a statute chimed with Vichy views. It may have been formulated by Mgr Guerry, as secretary of the ACA, who had leanings towards Action Française, or — less likely — by Cardinal Gerlier.[19] It was alleged that the cardinal had an instinctive dislike of Jews: in his childhood the family fortunes had suffered when the Union Générale bank collapsed and Jewish financiers were blamed. On the other hand, there is no doubt that he enjoyed good relations with the Jewish authorities in Lyons, and was well esteemed by them.

Nevertheless, according to Vallat, who claimed to have studied the question, the Church had consistently shunned the Jews as pariahs. He cited three Church Councils, beginning with that of Vannes in 405, which had forbidden fraternisation with them. The second Council of Orléans had banned intermarriage; that of Clermont (535) had debarred them from the magistrature; that of Macon (581) had declared they should not become taxcollectors; the Council of Paris, finally, had prohibited them from holding any public office. In the ninth century St Agobard, Archbishop of Lyons, had written an episcopal letter entitled, 'De insolentia Judaeorum'. These were measures taken within France itself. Outside France, between 1217 and 1755, twenty-nine popes, according to Vallat, had published fifty-seven bulls regulating economic and social relations with the Jews, even approving the creation of ghettos. St Thomas Aquinas, while advocating in the *Summa Theologica* tolerance of Judaism, had favoured a general curbing of Jewish influence in Christendom. It was Pope Honorius III who had introduced the rowel, the yellow star of David worn by the Jews in the Middle Ages. Finally Vallat appealed to the New Testament: had not St Paul written (I Thess. 2:13): 'The Jews... are heedless of God's will and enemies of their fellow men', and was it not they 'who killed the Lord Jesus'?[20] (One recalls that right up to 1945 prayers were often offered on Good Friday 'pro perfidis Judaeis'.)

Such arguments from tradition were not uncommon among Christians and non-Christians alike. The anonymous author of an undated (but probably of 1941) memorandum found among the files of Pétain,[21] put the case strongly for Jews to wear the yellow star, not to hold any post in the public service or belong to any non-Jewish association. He even quoted a converted Jew, Abbé Joseph Lemann, who in *L'entrée des Israélites dans la société française* had asserted that the Church's teaching laid down that no Jew should teach Christian children, sit upon the judicial bench (above which had hung the crucifix), or participate in the law-making process of a Christian State. A Protestant theologian, Pierre Lestringant, at the time took a different view: if Israel had been great because it had been chosen by God, it was also guilty because it had rejected Christ. However, since all peoples disobeyed God, what distinguished Jews from the rest was merely that they had done so first. For Christians, therefore, the 'Jewish problem' boiled down to making the necessary conversions — this, after all, had been the mission of the apostles. Even if all the descendants of Israel were killed, it would be to no avail, because God raises up the dead.[22]

The first Statute of the Jews, promulgated on 3 October 1940 by Alibert, defined a Jew even more rigorously than did the Nuremberg laws. A Jew was any person with three grandparents of the Jewish race, or with two grandparents, and a spouse who was Jewish or of the Jewish religion before 25 June 1940. Jews could no longer be top-ranking civil servants — and only remain minor ones if they had served in the First World War or had had a distinguished record in the 1940 campaign; they were excluded from being officers and NCOs in the armed forces, or active in teaching, the media and the arts. For the liberal professions quotas were to be set. The law, coming on the heels of the repeal of the Marchandeau Law, effectively made French Jews second-class citizens and worsened the plight of foreign Jews. The Hierarchy nevertheless at first remained silent, and the general public were somewhat indifferent, largely because of more immediate concerns. Moreover, some eminent Jews were exempted from the law, and neither the property nor the person of Jews yet came under attack.

Pétain was clearly a stern believer in severe measures against the Jews. The Chief Rabbi wrote to him almost immediately protesting against the Statute, whilst declaring that Jews would obey the law. The Marshal, evading the main point, sent a harsh reply, merely stating that obedience to the law was essential in any State and indispensable for French revival. He noted stiffly with satisfaction that the Chief Rabbi felt the same way.[23]

The sole Catholic voice raised swiftly and publicly in protest against these first anti-Jewish measures was that of the Jesuit priest, Père Fessard, who on 15 December 1940, at the invitation of Père Dillard, gave a lecture obliquely referring to the Statute under the innocuous title, 'Le sens de l'histoire', in the St Louis church at Vichy.[24]

However, when Bergson died in January 1941, Chevalier, the philosopher's disciple, then Education minister, sent condolences to his widow, and the government was officially represented at the funeral. At his death Bergson was near to conversion: in a statement published posthumously he declared: 'My thinking has brought me ever closer to catholicism. I would have become a convert if over the years I had not seen the build-up of a mighty wave of anti-Semitism.' He would not now abandon his co-religionists. He had even risen from his sick-bed to register as a Jew. A close confidant, Père Sertillanges, said after his death, 'God has this soul.' The Church deemed him to have received the baptism of desire and Cardinal Suhard authorised prayers to be said at the funeral.[25]

Chevalier's ambivalence concerning Jews was such that he intervened to prevent the dismissal of Halphern, a Jewish professor, but approved that of another, one of his own colleagues at Grenoble University, even against the wishes of his own students. (The departure of the fanatical Alibert from the Justice ministry, had signified that exceptions were more easily granted.) Nevertheless Mounier, the editor of the Catholic review *Esprit*, which had just been given permission to reappear, confided to his diary (19 October 1940) his abhorrence of what to him was the 'shameful statute of the Jews', and later (9 January 1941) wrote how greatly he despised Chevalier whose pupil and friend he had been, for implementing such laws. When he heard of dismissals he wrote in his diary: 'From today onwards a final stop is put to my relationship with this peculiar Christian', and, 'If the law on the Jews had existed forty years ago Chevalier would not exist, since Bergson would have been eliminated from the French university.'[26] He began to voice his disapproval by oblique references to Péguy in the January 1941 issue of *Esprit*. In June he published a review of the scurrilous Nazi film, *Jew Süss*, by Marc Beigbeder, who described it as 'not aiming to face up seriously to the Jewish problem, which nobody dreams of denying [*sic*], but to embroil individuals and attack them in their very condition of human beings'.[27] The critic went on to applaud students who had booed the film. This hostility was one factor in the closing down of the review by Vichy two months later. Other Catholic publications, such as *Temps Nouveaux*, edited by Stanislas Fumet, eventually suffered the same fate for having denounced the film.

From his American exile, Jacques Maritain, another, but more eminent Christian philosopher than Chevalier, castigated anti-Semitism as anti-Christian, a conspiracy to nullify the effects of Christ's Passion, since Israel's suffering was that of Christ himself.[28]

Meanwhile the Vichy regime in October 1940 had ordered the internment of 40,000 foreign Jews in four camps located in the unoccupied zone, the largest of which was Gurs. It was Protestants who first organised help for this camp, as well as those at Rivesaltes, Noë and Récébédou, through CIMADE (Comité Inter-Mouvements Auprès d'Evacués), an organisation started in late 1939 to help evacuees, principally from eastern France. This joint venture, presided over by Boegner, was made up of five Protestant youth movements: the French equivalents of the YMCA and the YWCA, the French branch of the World Student Council and the Scouts and Guides. A key figure in it was Madeleine Barot, who eventually became its Secretary-General. After the defeat the relief organisation concentrated its efforts on the plight of all remaining refugees, the bulk of whom were Jews, including those from the occupied zone and from the Reich itself. These latter the Germans dumped without warning in Vichy's lap. Thus on 24 October 1940, 7,200 Jews, many enfeebled and ill, arrived unexpectedly from Baden and the Palatinate and were consigned to Gurs. By then the camp housed some 13,000–17,000 'undesirables',[29] including incidentally some 650 Protestants. It comprised, among others, a very mixed bag of doctors, lawyers, world-class musicians and small businessmen. By stealth Madeleine Barot and Jeanne Merle d'Aubigné had managed to install relief workers in the camp itself. Later they were joined, in a gesture of solidarity, by some Catholics, such as Abbé Glasberg, a Jewish convert. Glasberg was so appalled at the conditions in the camps that he asked Cardinal Gerlier to intervene. Gerlier delegated the mission to Mgr Guerry who saw Peyrouton, then the Interior minister, but the authorities washed their hands of the task, whilst letting outside help continue. Relief work did indeed spread to the other camps, and CIMADE obtained permission for a representative of the International Red Cross to visit them. From January 1941 until September 1942 a co-ordinating committee chaired by Dr Donald Lowrie, an American official of the International YMCA, organised assistance.[30] Funds came from the International YMCA and the Comité pour l'Aide aux Réfugiés, set up by the budding World Council of Churches from Geneva. For a while centres were established outside the camps for the very old and for young mothers and their children, although these were closed after a few months when a policy of deportation was decreed.

If Christians in general had been embarrassed by the anti-Jewish measures, some had nevertheless exulted. In a Lenten sermon the aged Mgr Caillot, Bishop of Grenoble, dwelt on the fact that punishment had descended not only upon the Freemasons, but also on 'that other no less pernicious power, the dagos, whose most distinctive specimen was the Jews'.[31] The Bishop of Chambéry was of like mind, as were certain collaborationist priests in the Bordeaux area. Tongue in cheek, the *Croix de Savoie* (22 June 1941), which also had pro-German sympathies, even averred that Vichy's sole aim had been to put a stop to the Jews' obnoxious political activities.

By contrast, the Protestant conscience was now fully aroused. Pastor Boegner was the first religious leader to take up the cudgels on behalf of the Jews. He did so after sending two circular letters to the eight presidents of the Church's regional councils in the unoccupied zone, inviting comments on the position the Church should adopt. The circular letter of 23 December 1940 put forward a number of propositions for consideration: (1) for the Church there was no Jewish problem; (2) for certain States there was a 'Jewish problem', and the Church had no right to dictate to the civil authority what measures it should take to deal with it; (3) nonetheless, the Church was in duty bound to remind the State that the demands of justice and respect of the person be observed. If the Synod was to speak on behalf of the Church, every Christian should have the right to express an opinion. He therefore wished pastors to write to him on these points. Many did so. Several complained of the apparent silence of the Church and wanted it to speak out.[32]

By the spring of 1941 Protestants had made up their collective mind.

On 23 March, on the authority of the Protestant Conseil National, Boegner wrote to the Chief Rabbi expressing sympathy for the 'countless trials and injustices' to which Jews had been subjected, and which Protestants had also once undergone. Between Protestants and Jews, he declared, there existed indissoluble links. He was in no doubt that the Statute of the Jews required revision, although he conceded that 'a grave problem had been posed for the State by the recent massive immigration of foreigners, Jews and others, and by hasty and unjustified naturalisations'. The letter achieved wide publicity, and Boegner's action was endorsed by the Synod held at Alès in May, although some felt that he should have been even firmer, as the Dutch Protestants had been.

Boegner had an ally at Vichy in a fellow Protestant, René Gillouin, who had written some of Pétain's speeches and was not afraid to plead the cause of the Jews with the Marshal. In fact, Gillouin, very anti-German, wrote no less than a dozen letters to Pétain on the subject before escaping to Switzerland in 1943. Nor did he mince his words. In one letter (August 1941) he declared that the revocation of the Edict of Nantes was 'une bergerie à côté de vos lois juives, Monsieur le Maréchal'.[33]

Boegner also approached Darlan as Head of Government; he had known the admiral since boyhood, when they had both been in the same lycée preparatory class for entry into the Ecole Navale.[34] His letter of 26 March criticised Darlan's intention to set up a Commissariat Général aux Questions Juives (CGQJ). Whilst conceding there was a Jewish problem and allowing for the pressures to which the regime was subjected, he could not accept racism as the basis for a law. (It was a common misapprehension at the time that Vichy's measures were dictated by German pressure.) He asked why in certain localities the Jews had been forbidden to meet for worship. If the object of the CGQJ was merely to shield Jews from further discrimination, this would be accepted by Christians. He requested at least a reform of the statute, whose impact had been disastrous outside France.[35] Although Darlan agreed to meet Boegner in May, the admiral then evinced little interest in the questions he had raised. Darlan assured him that his sole purpose was to save French Jews; he also warned Boegner that a second statute was imminent. This was disconcerting news, if only because Boegner realised that it would jeopardise support for the Révolution Nationale (in which he still firmly believed at the time) among 'Bible Protestants' — Barthists, liberals and Lutherans. They would, he believed, be even more opposed to the Vichy measures, which they regarded as the rejection of the 'chosen people' of the Old Covenant in the name of a pagan ideology.[36]

Despite Boegner's careful assertion that he was pleading the cause of

French Jews only, his intervention was not even acceptable to all his co-religionists. A Protestant sect, the Eglise Réformée Evangélique, which comprised some 10 per cent of the total and had remained independent of the Fédération Protestante de France, alleged to Pétain that Boegner had falsely claimed his letter to the Chief Rabbi had been written with the full approval of the Marshal and Darlan, and they, as Protestants, dissociated themselves from his action.[37] Boegner hastened to deny this, and in fact Lavagne, now dealing with religious affairs for Pétain, wrote a letter of support to the pastor disclaiming all knowledge of the affair.[38] In another letter, this time to Gillouin,[39] Boegner reiterated he had made clear that there was 'a problem' regarding foreign and recently naturalised Jews. The Evangelical Protestants had merely wished to discredit him because they were appealing to the Conseil d'Etat on the disputed ownership of certain Church property in Marseilles. However, the matter did not end there. Boegner was accused by some high-placed laity in Montpellier and Lot-et-Garonne of largely acting on his own initiative. Moreover, on 12 January 1942 General Brécart's son, a prisoner of war, informed the Marshal that he and his Protestant brother-officers had been 'stupefied' to hear of Boegner's message to the Chief Rabbi.[40]

On 29 March 1941 Vallat's appointment as head of the newly created CGQJ confirmed that State anti-Semitism was no passing phenomenon. On 2 June the second Statute on the Jews was published. It defined a Jew even more narrowly. To the previous classification was added a further restriction: a person with two Jewish grandparents, if he or she were of the Jewish religion, even if the spouse was not Jewish, was considered to be a Jew. As before, there were certain exceptions. A further step was the taking of a census of Jews in the unoccupied zone; one had already been carried out in the northern zone, where the Germans were busy seizing Jewish property; in July Vichy ordered a similar sequestration for the whole of France. By now Jews were excluded absolutely from all forms of state employment. The proportion of Jewish doctors and lawyers could not exceed 3 per cent; other liberal professions were limited to 2 per cent. A *numerus clausus* of 2 per cent was applied to Jewish students. (Later Jewish schoolchildren were similarly penalised.) Jewish POWs and their families were exempted from the effects of the law, but only until their release. Vallat's ultimate aim was to assign Jews a very diminished role in national life. He sent Cazagne, the son of the Mayor of Lourdes, to do the rounds of all the bishops in the unoccupied zone and sound them out regarding the measures. They were all in agreement with them, Cazagne reported, although Cardinal Gerlier was somewhat reticent. Vallat shrugged this off, saying that the archbishop, whom he professed to know well, had at least expressed no reservations about his appointment. Later, at his trial Vallat was to allege that the Church had not admonished him for the legislation; if such a warning had been given he would either have sought to withdraw the laws or resigned.[41]

On 1 July Heilbronner, the President of the Consistoire Israélite de France, and a friend of Gerlier — they had studied law together — made his own appeal, based on religious grounds, to Pétain. He wrote:

> The Bible is the sole holy book of the Jews: is, then, its teaching pernicious when they follow it, since it is considered by Christians to be the expression of the divine Word and, under the name of the 'Old Testament' is one of the sacred books of the Catholic and Protestant churches? We are all the children of Abraham, the 'sons of the Bible', declared his Eminence Cardinal Verdier... Why need those who today practise the faith of Israel be outcasts in their own country?[42]

However, in their July declaration in which they pledged 'loyalisme sans inféodation', the ACA did plead for 'a sense of respect for the human person', and warned against 'all injustices'. This may well have been framed with the Jews in mind, because rumblings of discontent by Catholics had now been heard. Père de Lubac, in lectures at the Catholic faculty of Lyons the previous January, had affirmed Nazi racism was a doctrine no good Catholic could accept, since catholicism signified universality. On May 22 Mgr Bruno Solages, the head of the Toulouse Institut Catholique, had given a lecture on 'Bergson, témoin spirituel', which ended with an implicit indictment of the persecution. Abbé Chaine and Canon Richard, of the Catholic faculty at Lyons had drawn up a draft declaration dated 17 June condemning the new statute as 'unjust', whilst also acknowledging there was a 'Jewish problem'. They were supported by two of their Jesuit colleagues, Père de Lubac and Père Bonsirven.[43] The aim was to secure the signatures of all the faculty. However, the ecclesiastical authorities intervened, on the grounds that the document was too 'chimerical' and might harm the institution. With Cardinal Gerlier's sanction copies of the draft were made and circulated privately. The statement may have provoked the ACA allusion to 'respect for the human person', because, exceptionally, Gerlier attended its Paris meeting.

Since the attempt misfired, Père de Lubac and his colleagues published *Israël et la Foi chrétienne* in Fribourg (Switzerland) in 1942. Copies of the book were smuggled into France. Interestingly, it was published with the *nihil obstat* of the vicar-general, Mgr Rouche, of the Lyons diocese, and thus presumably with Gerlier's consent.[44] The work appeared just after two pro-Jewish *Cahiers* of the clandestine *Témoignage Chrétien*

(*Cahiers* VI and VII, April–May 1942) had been circulated. In it the authors reproached Christians for not recognising the value of the Old Testament: the writings of Moses, on the authority of St Irenius, were also those of Christ. Another attempt to influence Catholic opinion was made by Père Riquet, who as a trained biologist attacked Nazi race theorists relentlessly, and just before the ACA meeting had submitted a note to it condemning the new statute as 'a scandal for the Christian conscience as well as a challenge to French intelligence'.[45] Claudel — whose repeated defence at Vichy of a Jewish friend, Paul-Louis Weiller, a relative by marriage, and co-director with the Catholic writer of an aeronautical firm, caused him to be placed under police surveillance — in late 1941 wrote a letter of sympathy to the Chief Rabbi somewhat reversing his previous position. He expressed the 'disgust, horror and indignation felt by all good Frenchmen, and particularly Catholics, at the iniquities, the plundering and ill-treatment of all kinds to which our Jewish fellow countrymen have fallen victim at the present time'.[46] This letter was taken up and circulated as a clandestine tract.

Claudel was not alone in his feeling of revulsion. Commenting on the blowing up on 2 and 3 October by Doriotistes of seven Paris synagogues, the *Journal des Débats* wrote: 'Among the great truths of Christian morality, one of the noblest and the most deeply rooted in the soul of our people is the principle of religious tolerance.' However, attacks on synagogues were not infrequent: on 18 August thirteen Doriotist members of the Compagnons de France were arrested for having blown up the synagogue at Vichy.[47]

Meanwhile, in the northern zone, the Germans had begun further round-ups of Jews. In mid-May they had arrested in Paris some 5,000; a further raid occurred in Belleville, in the suburbs, on 19 and 20 August. The collaborationist Déat, referring to the May round-up and the efforts of priests to shield Jews by issuing them with false baptism certificates, wrote in his diary: 'The Church is clearly supporting the Jews, because it finds in them a new and abundant clientele.'[48]

Among most Protestants the second Statute on the Jews was considered an outrage. On August 23 Boegner wrote a letter of protest to Pétain. On 16 and 17 September a meeting of Protestant youth leaders, inspired by Jacques Monod, drew up a first version of the *Thèses de Pomeyrol* (a second version followed in September 1942) condemning the statutes outright. Indeed by the autumn the protests of some pastors were so vociferous that they attracted the attention of the Sûreté.

All this aroused disquiet at Vichy, so much so that on 7 August Bérard, the Ambassador to the Holy See, was ordered by Pétain to sound out the Vatican's views as to whether the statutes were compatible with Church doctrine. Why the papacy should have been asked to pronounce at this stage, when the legislation was already in place, is not clear. Was the Marshal himself uneasy at the severity of the measures? A different explanation has been given. De Lubac considers[49] the request may have emanated from Darlan, who gambled that Bérard would report that the Vatican had given the regime a clean bill. Since the draft statement by Abbé Chaine of the Lyons Catholic faculty had received Gerlier's blessing and the ACA had cautiously expressed reservations about the law, clearance from the Vatican would enable Darlan, who bore no love for the bishops, to reassert his political authority.

Bérard's own political position was plain. He favoured a liberal interpretation of the 'collaboration' agreed at Montoire. In presenting his letters of credence to the Pope (2 September 1940) he had spoken of French 'duties towards Europe', thus aligning France with Germany in a new German-led continent. It was almost certain therefore that at first he personally approved of the laws.

The ambassador sent back two reports in 1941, the last dated 2 September. He prefaced his reply with an historical exposition before saying that he had spoken with 'highly authorised' representatives of the Church — these turned out to be Cardinals Tardini and Montini of the Vatican's State Department — and they had seen nothing intrinsically wrong with the anti-Jewish legislation. The Church, whilst condemning racism, acknowledged a 'Jewish problem' had existed for centuries and in the Middle Ages popes themselves had taken steps to debar or regulate Jewish activity in certain occupations. The sole caveats put forward by the Vatican related to the concept of race: since marriage was a sacrament, mixed marriages between Jew and Gentile were to be respected; converts from Judaism were to be considered as fully Christian. Moreover, in the application of the statutes the precepts of law and justice were to be respected.[50] It was plain that Bérard had not mentioned the violent arrests and splitting up of families that were taking place.[51] Moreover, having left France for Rome in 1940 he may have been unaware of the increased sympathy for the Jews that was becoming evident.

The tenor of Bérard's report gives rise to questions. How far were his respondents authorised to reply on behalf of the Vatican? Was the Pope ever consulted personally? Certainly Valerio Valeri, the Nuncio, criticised Bérard's interpretation of the Vatican's opinion on the subject as being simplistic. Backed by the Vatican Secretary of State, Cardinal Maglione, who considered that Bérard's report, although 'balanced', had been misinterpreted by Vichy, the Nuncio sent a note of clarification to Pétain. Maglione hoped that the steps taken to discover what the Vatican was thinking 'would serve at least to mitigate in practice the interpretation and rigorous application of the harshest provisions of this disturbing law'.[52]

Valeri declared that he saw in Bérard's report the hand of Père Gillet, the head of the Dominicans, who resided in Rome. So far as the Vatican was concerned, however, there the matter rested. Xavier Vallat made capital out of the reply: a press release from the CGQJ (11 October 1941) stated categorically that 'there was nothing in the laws passed to protect France from Jewish influence in opposition to Catholic doctrine'.[53]

Cardinal Gerlier gave further signs of the malaise he felt at the anti-Semitic policy. In September 1941 he met the regional director of the CGQJ, and merely stated that he understood the *economic* case against the Jews. In October he came face to face with Vallat, who prided himself that the cardinal considered him 'an excellent Christian'. Gerlier told Vallat the measures were not unjust but lacked 'justice and clarity' in their enforcement.[54] This was to confuse legality with morality. In October 1941, at a mass for lawyers killed in the 1940 campaign, he alluded also to hostages recently shot by the Germans, many of whom were Jews: 'I know not whether they were of our religious faith, but I acknowledge in them my brothers in Christ, who died to expiate crimes of which they were innocent.'[55] When Pétain visited Lyons, in the same month, he handed the Marshal a joint note from Boegner and himself warning of 'certain disadvantages that might result from too harsh anti-semitic measures'.[56] At the opening of the 1941/1942 academic year of the Lyons Catholic faculty he instructed the students to 'proscribe all hatreds of class, rank and race'.[57] It was probably his unconditional loyalty to Pétain that inhibited him from speaking out more openly at this stage.

By November 1941 the noose around the Jews was being drawn ever tighter. Jewish members of Parliament were formally dismissed. All Jewish organisations save the central Consistoire were dissolved. A law created the Union Générale des Israélites de France (UGIF), a new body that eventually was responsible to the government and the Germans for seeing that Jews became virtually their own executioners. In the same month appeared in Lyons the first number of *Témoignage Chrétien*. Its challenging slogan, 'France, prends garde de perdre ton âme!' seemed singularly apt. Although it contained only a passing reference to the plight of the Jews, it gave a foretaste of what was to come. In December a further round-up of Jews occurred in the occupied zone. The Jews, apprehensive that worse was to follow, were desperate to demonstrate their loyalty to the regime. The Chief Rabbi even wrote to the Marshal associating his congregation and himself with the condemnation of attacks against Occupation troops, whilst denying any Jewish involvement.[58]

Fear of giving offence, a general ineffectiveness and even indifference, and a desire not to rock the boat: these were the motives that determined many Christian reactions to the anti-Jewish measures in 1940–41. In 1942, and right up to the last deportations from France in August 1944, the consequences of this initial 'laissez-aller' were to be horrendous.

Notes

Unless otherwise stated the place of publication is Paris.

1. R. Schor, *L'opinion française et les étrangers, 1919–1939*, 1985, p. 182.
2. X. Vallat, Chamber of Deputies, May 1936: 'Pour la première fois ce vieux pays gallo-romain sera gouverné... par un Juif.'
3. L. Landau, review article in: *Revue d'Histoire et de Philosophie religieuses*, 1973, pp. 246–64.
4. P. Pierrard, *Juifs et Catholiques français. De Drumont à Jules Isaac*, 1970, p. 29.
5. *Je Suis Partout*, whose most eminent contributor was the nominally Catholic Brasillach, may be described as 'culturally Christian', although other contributors such as Drieu la Rochelle and Rebatet were anti-Christian, and another, the scatalogical Céline, was scornful of catholicism.
6. J. Bonsirven, 'Y a-t-il un réveil de l'antisémitisme?' *Etudes*, 20 January 1935.
7. Schor, *L'opinion française*, p. 186.
8. Quoted in H. de Lubac, *Résistance chrétienne à l'antisémitisme. Souvenirs 1940–1944*, 1988, p. 25.
9. See F. Delpech, 'Les Eglises et la persécution raciale', *Actes*: Lyons, pp. 257ff.
10. 12 April 1933. Quoted in: de Lubac, *Résistance chrétienne*, p. 11.
11. P. Bolle, 'Les Protestants et leurs Eglises devant la persécution des Juifs en France', paper given at a colloquium, *L'Etat, les Eglises et les mouvements de Résistance devant la persécution des Juifs en France pendant la seconde guerre mondiale*, 10–12 March 1979, (Centre de Documentation Juive contemporaine [CDJC] Paris).
12. Published in *L'Evangile et le racisme*, June 1939: 'La situation tragique des Juifs dans les Etats totalitaires', cited in Bolle, 'Les Protestants'.
13. P. Bourdrel, *Histoire des Juifs de France*, 1974, p. 349.
14. J.-P. Azéma, *De Munich à la Libération*, quoted in: R. Tournoux, *Le Royaume d'Otto. France 1939–1945*, 1982, pp. 179f.
15. R. Paxton, *La France de Vichy*, 1973, pp. 168f.
16. Delpech, *Actes*: Grenoble, p. 146, quotes a figure of 340,000 Jews, two-thirds of whom were foreigners.
17. R. Bédarida (ed.), *Cahiers et Courriers*, vol. 1, p. 146.
18. Procès-verbal de l'ACA, ZNO, 31 August 1940.
19. Mgr Guerry's *L'Eglise catholique en France sous l'Occupation* (1946), a tendentious pleading *pro domo* for the Church, when published was much criticised, not least by Catholics.
20. Bourdrel, *Histoire des Juifs*, p. 352.
21. AN 2 AG 495. 'Note sur le problème juif'.
22. P. Lestringant, 'La Correspondance fédérative de la zone non-occupée', Supplément of the *Semeur*, no. 1, November 1940, pp. 16f; see also: A. Michel, *La JEC face au nazisme et à Vichy*, Lille, 1988, pp. 148ff.
23. AN 2 AJ 257. Letter from Chief Rabbi, Paris, 23 October 1940, and reply from Pétain dated Vichy, 25 October 1940.

24. J. Chelini, *La Ville et L'Eglise*, 1958, p. 198.
25. A. Fabre-Luce, *Journal de la France, 1939–1944*, 1946, vol. 2, p. 374.
26. E. Mounier, *Œuvres*, vol. 4. *Recueils posthumes: Entretiens XI, 9 January 1941*, 1963.
27. Quoted in M. Winock, *Histoire politique de la revue 'Esprit', 1930–1950*, 1975, p. 228.
28. J. Maritain, article in: *Christianity and Crisis*, 6 October 1941, quoted in the clandestine *Témoignage Chrétien*, nos. VI and VII.
29. *Actes*: Lyons, p. 295.
30. A number of organisations participated with CIMADE in the work, including a Quaker relief organisation, the Secours suisse aux Enfants, the US Unitarian Service Committee, and two Jewish charitable agencies, the Œuvre de Secours à L'Enfance and Organisation, Reconstruction, Travail.
31. *Semaine religieuse* (Grenoble), 17 April 1941, quoted in F. Delpech, 'La persécution des Juifs et "L'Amitié Chrétienne"', *Actes*: Grenoble, p. 158.
32. Bolle, 'Les Protestants.'
33. M. Marrus and R. Paxton, *Vichy France and the Jews*, London, 1981, p. 192, and p. 204f.
34. Darlan and Boegner had been 'camarades de promotion' in the 'classe préparatoire' for the Ecole Navale at the Lycée Lakanal in Paris. Boegner had been obliged to give up the idea of a naval career because of bad eyesight.
35. M. Boegner, *L'Exigence œcuménique. Souvenirs et perspectives*, 1968, p. 344.
36. P. Bolle, 'Les Protestants français et leurs Eglises durant la Deuxième Guerre mondiale', *Revue d'histoire moderne et contemporaine*, April–June 1979, p. 293.
37. AN 2 AG 495. Letter to Pétain, Montpellier, 19 November 1941.
38. AN 2 AG 495. Letter to Boegner, Vichy, 30 October 1941.
39. AN 2 AG 495. Letter to Gillouin, Nîmes, 29 November 1941.
40. AN 2 AG 495. File: Protestantisme.
41. Bourdrel, *Histoire des Juifs*, p. 449.
42. Ibid., p. 583.
43. Mgr Guerry, in: *L'Eglise catholique sous l'occupation*, 1947, makes it appear that the motion was a full-blown, public statement, which it certainly was not. See *Actes*: Grenoble, pp. 195ff; *Actes*: Lyons, p. 285; *Actes*: Biviers, p. 111, n. 88.
44. G. Marcel and G. Fessard, *Correspondance*, 1985, p. 221, n. 6.
45. R. Lambert, *Carnet d'un témoin, 1940-1943*, 1985, p. 129, n. 47.
46. *Cahiers du Témoignage Chrétien*, nos. VI and VII; Marrus and Paxton. *Vichy France*, p. 206; C. Flood, 'Theatrical Triumph and Political Ambiguity', *French Cultural Studies*, Chalfont St Giles, 3:1, February 1992, p. 22 and p. 47, n.19.
47. P. Limagne, *Ephémérides de quatre années tragiques (1940–1944)*, 1987, vol. 1, p. 227.
48. Quoted in: R. Tournoux, *Le Royaume d'Otto, France 1939–1945*, 1982, p. 98.
49. De Lubac, *Résistance chrétienne*, pp. 80ff.
50. J. Duquesne, *Les Catholiques sous l'Occupation*, 1966, p. 20.
51. J. Vanino, *De Réthondes à l'Ile d'Yeu*, 1952, p. 280ff.
52. Quoted in F. Delpech, 'Les Eglises et la persécution raciale', *Actes*: Lyons, p. 267. The present writer is much indebted to M. Delpech's account.
53. Quoted in Marrus and Paxton, *Vichy France*, p. 202.
54. Ibid., p. 200.
55. AN F60.1674. Fighting French file, reporting *Le Temps*, 31 October 1941.
56. Ibid., reporting *Chicago Daily News*, 30 October 1941.
57. *Le Temps*, 14 November 1941.
58. 2 AG 495. CC77D. Letter to Pétain signed Schwartz, Paris, 11 December 1941.

–8–

Christians and Jews — II

The year 1942 saw an acceleration of anti-Jewish activity. By then it was plain the Germans intended to clear Western Europe of all Jews, and eventually make the whole continent 'Judenfrei'. The suggestion to create the CGQJ had come from them, although the statement by Barthélémy, the Justice minister, writing long after the event, that 'the so-called anti-Jewish legislation of Vichy' was entirely of German origin is palpably inaccurate.[1] By now, however, the Germans had completed their own arrangements to deal with the Jews in France. For the Wehrmacht, Dr Michel, of the German military administration, ran a Jewish section to deal with economic matters under Dr Blanke, whose main aim was to promote the German war machine. For Wilhelmstrasse, a section of the Consul-General's office in the charge of the malevolently anti-Jewish diplomat, Zeitschel, handled Jewish questions. But the most significant German agency for dealing with the Jews was the SS, particularly after the arrival in Paris in June 1942 of SS Brigadeführer Oberg, whose *Judenreferat* was staffed until July by the notorious Dannecker, and then by Rothke. None of this complex organisation could, however, function without the active support of French officials, particularly Bousquet, appointed Secretary-General for the Police Nationale in May 1942. It was, for example, the French police that were responsible for rounding up the Jews; in any case Pucheu, then Interior minister, had set up the special police for Jewish Affairs (Police des Questions Juives) in the previous autumn. By 1942 the co-operation between occupiers and occupied had become much closer. Vichy's own initiatives against the Jews and their complicity in German ones rendered the position of Christians even more uncomfortable. In early 1942 Vallat was reported as saying that he did not know whether he was Commissaire aux Questions juives or Commissaire aux Questions des prêtres, so persistent had become their interventions on behalf of individual Jews.[2] On New Year's Day Gerlier, held to be the most flexible and prudent member of the episcopal bench,[3] admonished Catholics: 'No Christian should add to this pitiful situation by words or deeds that stir up hatred and vengeance.'⁴ Later, on 21 January, he wrote to the Chief Rabbi expressing his sorrow as a Catholic at 'the hideous persecutions to which our brothers of Israel are victims in our land'.⁵ The cardinal was naturally unaware of the meeting convened by the infamous Heydrich, the head of the Reichssicherheitshauptamt (the Reich Security Office), at Wannsee, near Berlin, on 20 January, at which the SS leaders decided upon the extermination of the Jews as the 'final solution'.

In January also, Pastor Boegner saw Pétain once more and pleaded in vain the Jewish cause. He still impugned no blame to the Marshal, confiding to his diary: 'He [Pétain] clearly saw great injustices were being committed. But he felt powerless to prevent these injustices or to redress them.'⁶ Any final resolution of the 'Jewish question', according to the Marshal, must await the end of hostilities.

In late March the tempo of the impending tragedy quickened. The first convoy to Auschwitz of 1,112 foreign Jews (but including some French nationals) from the occupied zone left Drancy for Germany — the gas chambers had been made ready in Central Europe the previous December; other Jews were to follow in May. Meanwhile, on 26 April the return to power of Laval inaugurated the period of greatest persecution. His appointment of the fanatical anti-Semite Darquier de Pellepoix as Commissioner for Jewish Questions on 5 May was a concession to the Germans, to whom Vallat had never been *persona grata* — he was, in fact, virulently anti-German. Laval's policy, as it evolved, was clear. He put the saving of French Jews above all else, but was ready to give way when pressed, if there were some material advantage to be gained: for this horse-trading politician Jews — any Jews — represented a bargaining counter.

That spring also, *Témoignage Chrétien* published nos. 6 and 7 (April–May 1942) of its clandestine *Cahiers*, entitled 'Antisémites'. The number, with a print run of 2,000 copies (four times that of its first issue), was a collective effort by Pères Chaillet, Ganne, de Lubac and J. Hours. The moment had come, its anonymous authors said, for Christians to break the silence about the fate of the Jews: They had now to speak out. Vallat was attacked. Although, in a rather gruesome metaphor, he had declared himself to be a 'surgeon' rather than a 'butcher' or an 'executioner', the fifty-seven laws, decrees and regulations he had promulgated during a year of office showed him in a different light, as really serving the cause of Hitler. The *Cahiers* reported approvingly the Protestant *'thèses de Pomeyrol'*,⁷ one of which began: 'Founded on the Bible, the Church recognises in Israel the people that God has chosen to give a Saviour to the world.'⁸ Père de Lubac, in an important section headed 'Antisémitisme et conscience chrétienne', stressed that anti–Semitism, totally incompatible with Christianity, meant the abolition of the Old Testament and eclecticism regarding the New Testament, producing a distorted picture of Christ.

All such declarations had little direct effect, but the Jewish authorities were grateful for them, no less than for any action undertaken on their behalf: on May 13 Heilbronner, the president of the Jewish Consistoire, addressing the general assembly of French rabbis, thanked Christians, Catholics and Protestants alike, for their assistance,[9] and especially Gerlier: 'My gratitude goes out particularly to that Prince of the Church, compassionate and charitable in all misfortunes, who today exercises, both in reality and as titular head, with so much greatness, the Primacy of the Gauls.'[10]

On 29 May a German ordinance decreed that all Jews in the occupied zone over the age of six should wear the yellow Star of David. The Conseil de la Fédération Protestante, meeting on 5 June, decided on yet another appeal to Pétain, this time drawn up by Pastor A.-N. Bertrand, Boegner's deputy in Paris. It protested against 'a measure [the wearing of the rowel] that can in no way contribute to the solution of the Jewish problem' but was a humiliation for all Jews, including war veterans, young children and even those baptised as Christians. Other pastors were also exhorted to write to Vichy, but to do so in terms of 'Christian thought and action'.[11] Boegner handed the letter to the Marshal in person on 27 June. But the tone was too deferential to make an impression. Notably, Cardinal Suhard, as Archbishop of Paris, did not join in the protest. After the war Bertrand complained that on this and other occasions when he had asked for the support of the Catholic authorities he had been rebuffed.[12] However, the wearing of the yellow star was not extended to the unoccupied zone. Suhard contented himself with a weak but futile appeal to Brinon, Vichy's representative in Paris, to intercede with the Germans for exemptions for converts.[13] From Catholic Brittany the Prefect of Morbihan reported (3 August 1942) that almost unanimously the imposition of this badge of shame was criticised. The Prefect of Seine-et-Oise reported that its wearers were more the object of sympathy than repulsion.[14]

The Germans had attempted to stir up as much ill-feeling as possible against the Jews. In May 1941 they had sponsored an Institut pour l'Etude des Questions juives, headed by a Captain Sézille, a drinking companion of Darquier de Pellepoix, who had assembled by September a travelling exhibition, 'Les Juifs et la France', which was even promoted as a class outing for schoolchildren. Indeed by 1942 the Jewish refugees arriving from the North had attracted adverse comment in the unoccupied zone, where they were accused of buying up food on the black market and living a life of luxury on the Riviera. There were fears of local pogroms after a band of some twenty-five youths armed with clubs and iron bars on 16 June attacked Jews worshipping in the synagogue at Nice, with only minimal intervention by the police. Only three were arrested but later released without charge.

The executant of mass extermination, the indefatigable Eichmann, had agreed with Dannecker that France should deliver up 100,000 Jews. Accordingly, on 27 June the Germans demanded the deportation of the first 50,000, eventually to include those from the unoccupied zone. As an initial step Laval agreed to hand over all foreign and stateless Jews, including young children. On 16 and 17 July there occurred the mass arrest of 12,884, including 4,051 children, in Paris, their herding into the Vel' d'Hiver, and their subsequent concentration at Drancy prior to deportation. This at last acted as the catalyst for more widespread Christian condemnation.

The ACA may well have discussed the Jewish 'question' at its four meetings in 1941, but the upshot of its deliberations was not made public. It did, however, deal with aid to 'interned foreigners'. Likewise in January 1942 the agenda contained a reference to the Jews, but there is no indication as to how it was treated. In June it expressed regret at the sacking of the Nice synagogue. But the Paris raid marked a watershed, and after a meeting in Paris on 22 July it issued a solemn protest. Cardinal Suhard had already made his views known privately to Laval. Now, on behalf of the ACA he wrote to Pétain: it was, he said, 'an anguished cry for pity at this immense suffering; above all, for that which strikes so hard at mothers and children'.[15] Mgr Valerio, the Nuncio, thought the tone of the protest was 'a little insipid' (*piuttosto platonica*). Nevertheless Suhard's letter quickly became known outside France, and even appeared in a New York publication, the *Contemporary Jewish Record*.

On 8 August, in accordance with Laval's undertaking, the deportation of 11,485 foreign Jews was begun from the Gurs and Rivesaltes camps in the unoccupied zone. CIMADE, the Protestant relief organisation, was allowed to rescue foreign Jews who had fought for France, those with a French spouse, those with children under five, and orphans under eighteen. But children over five had to leave with their parents.

CIMADE itself was evolving. Earlier in the year Beaujolin, a Protestant, and Pierrebourg, despite being a professed anticlerical, proposed that Protestants and Catholics should unite to succour the Jews. Boegner and Gerlier were persuaded to give their blessing to a new organisation, Amitié Chrétienne, in which Catholics such as Père Chaillet, the founder of *Témoignage Chrétien*, and Père Glasberg, who had already collaborated with Protestants in the Gurs camp, together with other Catholics in the Lyons area, worked with CIMADE.

Priorities had to be established. The decision was taken that the main thrust should be on rescuing Jewish children, so that they did not leave with their parents. This agonising course of action eventually brought them into conflict with Laval and forced them into complete clandestinity.

Another organisation, the co-ordinating relief committee for the camps, worked from Nîmes. It consisted of CIMADE itself, the Red Cross, the Quaker relief committee, the Swiss Service Civil International, and the International Fellowship of Reconciliation. It sent a delegation, consisting of McClelland, a Quaker, Lowry, an American working for the International YMCA, and Père Arnoux, who represented Gerlier, to lobby Pétain. They also were anxious to save the children, as well as those foreign Jews who had successfully applied for visas to emigrate and were awaiting final clearance. The Marshal merely referred them to Laval. As for French Jews, their position, Pétain maintained, was protected by their statute, and only foreign Jews were being handed over to the Germans. They too came away under the impression that Pétain was powerless in this matter.

On August 17 the Chief Rabbi of Lyons, Kaplan, saw Gerlier on behalf of the Chief Rabbi of France, Schwartz, and begged him to intervene again, asserting that on their arrival in Germany his co-religionists were being slaughtered.[16] In fact, the argument that only healthy males were being deported for work in Germany was no longer credible: it was plain that the weak and elderly were also being dispatched. On 7 August Valeri, the Nuncio, had written to Cardinal Maglione in Rome that there was much unease as to their true destination.[17]

Gerlier replied to Kaplan that Suhard had already interceded with Pétain; he himself was in bad odour at Vichy where he was reckoned to be 'the official defender of the Jews'. However, he would consult with Boegner and they would both write separately to Pétain.

Thus on August 20 Boegner once again penned a letter to the Marshal. The tone was stronger than before. He wrote, he said, 'to express to you the indescribable sadness that our Churches feel at the news of the decisions taken by the French government, with regard to foreign Jews, whether converted to Christianity or not'. As Vice-President of the Ecumenical Council of Christian churches he also invoked the revulsion felt in Switzerland, Sweden and the USA. The way in which the deportations were being carried out was deplorable: a lack of sanitation, the use of freight cars, and a prohibition against the Quakers and the Jewish Consistory of Lyons feeding the deportees as the trains steamed north. He went on: 'The truth is that there have been handed over to Germany, or about to be handed over, men and women who are refugees in France, of whom several know in advance the terrible fate that awaits them.'[18]

The text of the letter was communicated to the US embassy, where it was cabled to Washington and then broadcast on the Allied radio; it was distributed in Lyons, and even in the flower markets of Marseilles, and read at meetings of priests and charity organisations.[19] But the Protestant leader got nowhere with the Head of State. He thereupon contacted Laval on 27 August, declaring that the Churches could not remain silent in the face of such events; the right of asylum should be respected. Deportations to the unoccupied zone should be halted. But he was addressing a blank wall. Laval said that he could not act otherwise: 'je fais de la prophylaxie', he retorted. Not even the children could remain. By deporting foreign Jews he was attempting to shield French Jews. For his part, he believed the deportees were to be set to work as agricultural labourers in a new Jewish state to be established in southern Poland. Boegner remarked in exasperation: 'I spoke to him of massacre; he answered me with horticulture.'[20] Although such a confrontation may have caused disquiet among the Marshal's entourage, it was not calculated to have much effect on Laval, who by then was the real wielder of power and had committed himself to a German victory.

Gerlier's own letter was, by contrast, in the judgement of one French historian, Delpech, 'of an astonishing moderation', and was characterised as weak and pitiful.[21] He did not repeat what he had learnt from Rabbi Kaplan, that Jews were leaving for 'extermination', but merely said their later treatment was to be 'foreseen'.[22] He of course had no proof that wholesale slaughter was occurring and esteemed Pétain too highly to go against him outright. Père Glasberg, who did so much to alleviate the fate of the deportees, remarked bitterly that Gerlier was gratified that their journey as far as Paris would be in third-class coaches rather than cattle trucks![23] Nevertheless town councillors of Lyons, particularly a certain Drevet, resented what they held to be the Cardinal's interference, and, as a gesture of protest, refused to attend a religious ceremony at which Gerlier officiated. Consequently Gerlier felt impelled to write a letter of justification to Villiers, the mayor appointed by Vichy to replace Herriot, claiming that he had confined himself to the 'strictly moral and spiritual' sphere and had not deviated from the traditional loyalty of the Church to the established regime.[24] In fact Pétain had merely passed on his letter to Laval. Nevertheless, for the first time Christian voices had been raised in defence of foreign as well as French Jews.

It fell to Mgr Saliège, Archbishop of Toulouse, despite his severe physical paralysis, to utter what was the first public disapproval by a bishop, in a message to be read by his diocesan priests at mass on 23 August. His action may have been influenced by a secret letter from de

Gaulle that reached him on 17 May` in which the General feared that some of the episcopacy were too identified with Vichy.[25] Père de Lubac, at the instigation of Père Chaillet, had been despatched to seek the ailing archbishop's intervention.[26] It was secretly agreed that both Saliège and Gerlier would prepare messages to be read in public, which the police would only learn about afterwards.[27] (One source reports that de Lubac's visit had been instituted by Gerlier himself.)[28] Local incidents may also have incited Saliège to intervene. The parish priest of Portet-sur-Garonne had reported to him the anguished scenes when convoys had left the camp at Récébédou, near Toulouse — most of the camps for internees were located in the area. Saliège had likewise seen an account of the deportations drawn up by the Red Cross.[29] In July already he had written sympathetically to the Rabbi of Toulouse: since Catholics, he said, were spiritually Semites they suffered with the misfortunes of Israel.[30] His public message was more forceful than Gerlier's. Despite all precautions, the regional prefect learnt of it the day before; an attempted visit to Saliège, accompanied by the Commissaire de Police, proving abortive, he contacted parish priests via the local mayors instructing them not to read it out, as 'it could be interpreted by certain of the faithful in a way hostile to the government'.[31] In fact, the text was couched on a higher plane: it evoked a common humanity: 'The Jews are men and women. Not every action may be committed against them. Foreigners are men and women. Not every action may be committed against them, against these men and women, against these fathers and mothers of families. They are part of the human race.'[32]

Those priests that had failed to read the message were instructed to do so the following Sunday, August 30. Official attempts to ban it were frustrated by having it read at low mass; by ten o'clock, the time of high mass, mayors had been able to pass on to the parish priests the regional prefect's prohibition.[33]

The protest penetrated as far south as Luchon and Ax-les-Thermes, almost on the Andorran border. According to the Vichy police, the message was distributed by 'a nucleus of Christian Democrats' mobilised by Mgr Bruno de Solages, the head of the Institut Catholique in Toulouse, and Abbé Gèze, the diocesan director of the Œuvres de Jeunesse.[34] The tone of the pronouncement, and the fact that foreign diplomats sent copies of it to their governments, prompted Laval to action. He summoned Mgr Rocco, representing the Nuncio, who was temporarily absent, and bluntly declared such intervention by the Church in State affairs was inadmissible.[35] Saliège's letter, he said, provided fuel for British propaganda, and the Germans would certainly demand an explanation. The archbishop should be invited to retire on grounds of ill-health. When Cardinal Tardini received the Nuncio's report at the Vatican, together with this request, after consulting Pius XII, he merely wrote on it a terse: 'Acknowledged', and took no further action. Laval accused those around the archbishop of being Gaullists; Saliège he said, even tolerated the publication of the clandestine Resistance tract *Combat* from the episcopal palace. He reiterated his determination to pack all Jews off to Germany, including those he knew were hiding in religious institutions.[36]

Meanwhile a massive round-up of Jews occurred in Lyons between 26 and 28 August, whose repercussions, as will be seen, were far-reaching. It was plain that Gerlier's appeal to Pétain had been ineffectual.

On 28 August, in fact, Saliège's example was followed by Mgr Théas, Bishop of Montauban, whose message was couched in accusing tones judged by Valeri, the Nuncio, to be 'even stronger':

> I voice the indignant protest of the Christian conscience and I declare that all men, Aryan or non-Aryan, are brothers because created by the same God; that all men, regardless of race or religion have the right to the respect of individuals and States. Now, the present anti-Semitic measures are contemptuous of human dignity, and a violation of the most sacred rights of the person and of the family.[37]

On 30 August the message was read at low mass in churches of the Montauban diocese. On the same day the bishop himself, together with the prefect, M François Martin, was officiating at a mass for the Légion des Combattants. He had submitted an advance copy of his message to Martin, adding, 'I know that the Prefect of Tarn-et-Garonne cannot approve of my initiative and I ask him simply to disregard it. But I know also that M François Martin [i.e. the prefect, as a private individual] shares my sentiments and reproves that which I reprove.'

It was agreed that the message would not be re-read at the public ceremony. Théas merely informed the prefect of what he had done. Martin replied: 'Monseigneur, in my office I spoke to you as the prefect. Today, in your church, I speak to you as a Christian, I approve, and I congratulate you.' Later the bishop wrote:

> On Sunday, 30 August 1942, during a celebration of the Légion which followed soon after the first [sic] persecutions of the Jews, the prefect took as the theme of his discourse the condemnation of violence and the appeal to Christian charity, saying in particular: 'Among all the heroes of history I give first place, beyond the place of warriors, the learned men, the thinkers, and the statesmen, to Saint Louis and Saint Vincent-de-Paul.' And he ended with an affirmation of his faith in the destiny of those peoples who had loved the most, and not those who killed the most.[38]

A similar message of condemnation by Mgr Delay, of Marseilles, was also read in his diocese, but the bishop added the rider that France had a right to defend itself against those who had done it so much harm in recent years, and to punish those who had abused its hospitality. Prejudice died hard. But the bishop also later rebuked Carbuccia, the editor of *Gringoire*, for publishing a derogatory article entitled 'Simple histoire juive', and for asserting that the Bible was a suitable tract for Hitler's propaganda.

It was not until 6 September that Gerlier joined in the public protest. His message, to which, he stipulated, not a single word should be added, began by insisting that 'we have the categorical and painful duty to voice the protest of our conscience' ('nous avons l'impérieux et pénible devoir d'élever la protestation de notre conscience'), and mentioned particularly the break-up of families that was occurring. However, he then continued, as if halfexcusing the deportations, 'We do not forget that the French authorities have a problem to resolve, and we can judge the difficulties that the government must be facing.' He spoke of 'the inalienable rights of the human person' ('les droits imprescriptibles de la personne humaine'), 'the sacred character of family ties', ('le caractère sacré des liens familiaux'), 'the inviolability of the right to asylum', ('l'inviolabilité du droit d'asile'), but concluded on a different note by invoking the Marshal:

> It is not on violence and hatred that the new order can be built. It will only be constructed, and Peace with it, on the respect of justice, in the beneficent union of hearts and minds, to which we are invited by the Marshal's voice of greatness, and in which will flourish once again the time-honoured prestige of our country.[39]

Like most of his fellow bishops, the cardinal seemed anxious not to offend Pétain. His insistence on the family, whose virtues the Marshal had extolled, must nevertheless have struck a chord.

Meanwhile, other Catholics expressed their concern. The London-based periodical *Volontaire pour la Cité chrétienne* reported that a priest — not named — had delivered a sermon on 23 August at Lourdes before an audience of 30,000 pilgrims that included the exhortation: 'Pray for France, for our prisoners and, very especially for our Jewish brethren, who are the most unfortunate of all.'[40] Mgr Kolb, evacuated from Strasbourg, wrote to the regional prefect at Clermont-Ferrand, in whose area were many refugees from Alsace-Lorraine, protesting against the deportation of Jews from the annexed provinces, whose plight was worse because they were no longer considered French by the Germans. Canon Rocq, of Pau, wrote to the editor of the *Patriote des Pyrénées*, complaining that an article had attempted to justify the deportations by citing St Thomas Aquinas; a Catholic newspaper should not support the violation of Jewish rights: 'It is inexcusable that a newspaper run by priests should treat so lightly the Christian conscience and Church honour.'

On 20 September two other bishops, Mgr Moussaron of Albi, and Mgr Vansteenberghe of Bayonne, added their protests. Mgr Rastouil, Bishop of Limoges, for his part, was disappointed that the Légion des Anciens Combattants, with which he had been so closely associated, failed to protest.[41] Rastouil had been infuriated when a local Jewish doctor, Dr Meyer, a holder of the Croix de Guerre, had been banned from practising; he had also intervened in favour of a young Communist — this time more successfully. To Lavagne, of Pétain's Cabinet Civil, he wrote: 'Les Français ne se réconcilieront pas dans le sang.'[42] Even Mgr Caillot, the reactionary Bishop of Grenoble, now intervened with the prefect on behalf of a group of foreign Jews.[43] On the other hand, a few bishops made only belated protestations. Thus Mgr Piguet, of Clermont-Ferrand, contented himself with publishing a general declaration by the Hierarchy in March 1943.[44]

Public protests from Church leaders in the occupied zone were conspicuously few. They contrasted with Dutch Christians, for example, who had been forthright in their condemnation despite the omnipresence of the Germans. Cardinal Suhard claimed that if he had spoken out publicly it would have been his priests, and not he, that would have been put in prison, although there is no doubt that he made many representations in private.

The public silence of Cardinal Liénart is less explicable. Before the war he had been represented at various meetings held in the Nord to condemn racism and anti-Semitism. It is true that in the department in 1942 there were only some 2,000 Jews, of whom 'only' 234 were killed. In the Pas-de-Calais area there were considerably more, particularly immigrant Poles working in the mines of the Lens area, if the number reported killed (1,647) is any guide.[45] On 11 September there was a round-up of foreign and naturalised Jews in the region, and some 800 were deported to Germany via Belgium. Liénart refused to intervene, despite the entreaties of a well-known local priest, Abbé Catrice, and a clandestine committee for the aid of Jews, which urgently needed to find shelter for forty children. The wife of the regional prefect, Madame Carles, herself Jewish, was a member of this committee. Eventually another priest, Abbé Stahl, found a place of safety for the children. There is, however, evidence that the cardinal, no less than his collaborationist neighbour, Mgr Dutoit, Bishop of Arras, did give much private assistance to Jews. Liénart's earlier attitude, as revealed in an archival note, was that Jews should not be subject to any exceptional laws, but treated like any other foreigners.[46] He had, moreover, signed the ACA letter of protest to Pétain of 20 July. His public silence — for he was not afraid of standing up to the Germans — can only be explained by his unshakeable loyalty to the Marshal.

In the occupied zone the Germans were at pains to justify the measures they were taking. The Propagandastaffel tried to achieve this even by using diocesan bulletins. The Archbishop of Rouen had refused to publish a German note of explanation, and found his bulletin promptly banned. The neighbouring diocese of Evreux thereupon agreed to publication in its own *Semaine religieuse.*

In the unoccupied zone at least two bishops sided with Vichy. The Prefect of the Var department reported (1 October 1942) that Mgr Gaudel, of Fréjus, had declared himself satisfied with the way in which the round-up of Jews had been handled: it had been accomplished with 'all the humanity that as a Christian he could have desired'.[47] The Prefect of Lot reported (30 October 1942) that Mgr Chévrier of Cahors, would take steps to prevent the messages of Gerlier and Saliège becoming known in his diocese.[48] It may be significant that the latter two prelates had been promoted to their dioceses in September 1941, and Vichy by then exercised influence over new episcopal appointments.

Meanwhile the Protestants had not been idle. Early in September, at a meeting of pastors, Boegner advised each one to act according to his conscience. He had visited the United States' chargé d'affaires to see what could be done to save Jewish children. He had also begged Admiral Platon, one of his former parishioners, but who had turned pro-German, to intervene: Platon refused, and charged Boegner with going against government policy. On 22 September the Conseil National de l'Eglise réformée drew up a declaration that was read from the pulpits of Protestant churches on 4 October, because, it declared, it was a matter of conscience for the Church to speak out: 'Divine law does not allow families created at God's wish to be broken up, children separated from their mothers, the right of asylum and divine pity to be brushed aside, the respect for the human person to be violated and defenceless creatures to be delivered up to a tragic fate.'[49] That same month the Protestant journal *Notre Chemin* published an editorial on 'The Two Halves of the People of God' ('Les deux moitiés du peuple de Dieu'): 'They are rejected, persecuted, weighed down with the burden of their errors, and of those that others heap upon them... let us take care that in abandoning them it is not our Lord that we are rejecting.'[50]

Nevertheless one pastor refused to read the letter in public, because 'the Jews had shown themselves to be the worst enemies of God and Christ'.[51]

The much smaller Protestant grouping, the Eglises Réformées Evangéliques, however, adopted a different line. One of its pastors, Bruston, of Saint-Jean-du-Gard (Gard) was rebuked for reading out a protest in September. The sect's own message, disseminated on 12 October, warned against interference in political matters; loyalty and obedience to the civil authority were required; Jews had to recognise their error and turn towards Him whom they [*sic*] had crucified.[52]

Church leaders had reacted slowly to the anti-Jewish measures. So long as steps were being taken only against foreign Jews they did not feel overconcerned. But as those measures became manifestly harsher, then involved French Jews, and gave rise to apprehension as to their fate, they began to have misgivings. As visible proof of the mistreatments meted out became known, their indignation grew. Mgr Saliège and Pastor Boegner were the most outspoken critics. Cardinal Gerlier's attitude was inscrutable: opinions regarding his comportment vary. Germaine Ribière, of Amitié Chrétienne, the organisation that tried to help Jews, considered that he had to be constantly spurred on to action, on at least one occasion because he was afraid.[53] A man of the world, the cardinal sought always to put the best gloss on affairs. Cardinal Suhard, ever discrete, was content to work behind the scenes. Cardinal Liénart's position remains more enigmatic, although loyalty to Pétain probably coloured unduly his thinking. But only five prelates, all in the unoccupied zone, made public protests that became widely known, and of these only Saliège and Théas refused to mention the 'problem' that Vichy allegedly faced. But by now the rank and file of the Church were aroused to solidarity with their less fortunate brethren.

How was this solidarity expressed? What practical measures were undertaken by Christians? What reactions did the Church's evolving position evoke among the Germans and the collaborationists? What was the attitude of the Vatican? These questions must now be examined.

Notes

Unless otherwise stated the place of publication is Paris.

1. J. Barthélémy, *Ministre de la Justice, Vichy 1941–1943. Mémoires*, 1989, p. 311.
2. AN F60.1674. 'Source: service de renseignements (FFL), No. 430', 5 February 1942.
3. N. Gourfinkel, *Aux prises avec mon temps*, vol. 2, *L'autre Patrie*, 1953, p. 264.
4. Delpech, *Actes*: Grenoble, p. 162, quoting the *Semaine religieuse* (Lyons).
5. P. Bourdrel, *Histoire des Juifs de France*, 1974, p. 598.
6. Cited by Delpech, *Actes*: Lyons, pp. 265ff.

7. See Chapter 5, p 66 ..
8. 'Fondée sur la Bible, L'Eglise reconnaît en Israël le peuple que Dieu a élu pour donner un Sauveur au monde.'
9. Bourdrel, *Histoire des Juifs*, p. 45.
10. Cited in Mgr Guerry, *L'Eglise catholique en France sous l'occupation*, 1947, p. 60.
11. AN 2 AG 495. Intercept of a letter from the Reformed Church to Pastor Tirel, Mazamet, Tarn, containing the text of Bertrand's letter, dated Paris, 11 June 1942; pastors had to write 'sur le terrain de la pensée et de l'action chrétiennes'. See also: Louis Noguères, *Le véritable procès du Maréchal Pétain*, 1955, pp. 280ff.
12. Report to 'l'Assemblée Générale du Protestantisme français', Nîmes, 23 October 1945.
13. AN F60.1485.
14. G. Cholvy and Y.-M. Hilaire, *Histoire religieuse de la France contemporaine, 1930–1988*, 1988, p. 95.
15. AN 2 AG 543. Letter to Pétain dated 22 July 1942.
16. J. Kaplan, *Justice pour la foi juive*, 1977, p. 132.
17. M. Marrus and R. Paxton, *Vichy France and the Jews*, New York, 1981, p. 354.
18. AN 2 AG 495. Letter from Boegner to Pétain, Nîmes, 20 August 1942.
19. Interview with Boegner by Marcel Gosselin, *Nouvelles des émissions protestantes*, no. 13, October 1963.
20. Bourdrel, *Histoire des Juifs*, p. 457.
21. Delpech, *Actes*: Grenoble, p. 168.
22. H. de Lubac, *Résistance chrétienne à l'antisémitisme. Souvenirs, 1940-1944*, 1987, p. 161.
23. Père Glasberg, *Actes:* Grenoble, Discussion, p. 204.
24. AN 2 AG 492.
25. De Lubac, *Résistance chrétienne*, p. 160.
26. H. de Lubac, *Mémoire sur l'occasion de mes écrits*, Namur, 1989, p. 50.
27. *Actes*: Biviers, p. 111.
28. Ibid.
29. M. Goubet and P. Debauges, *Histoire de la Résistance dans la Haute-Garonne*, Cahors, 1986, p. 30, n. 22.
30. AN F60.1674. Letter reported in a French publication, *Pour la Victoire*, appearing in New York, 4 July 1942.
31. AN F60.1674.
32. The texts of the various episcopal messages, extracts of which are given here, are to to be found in *Témoignage Chrétien 1941–1944*, vol. I, 1980, pp. 209ff.
33. AN F60.1674.
34. AN 2 AG 493. 'Note (Secret)', 8 March 1943.
35. F & CO archives. Microfilm frame 220323. Telegram 37332 dated 28 August 1942, signed Abetz.
36. L. Papeleux, 'Le Vatican et le problème juif, 1941–1942', *RHDGM*, no. 107, 1974, p. 79.
37. Ibid.
38. Hoover Institution, *France during the German Occupation, 1940–1944*, Stanford, 1958, vol. 1, p. 428. Quoted in English.
39. One notes the use of the phrase 'new order', which by September 1942 was more associated with the new European dispensation of the Germans than that to be accomplished by the Révolution Nationale.
40. Cited in leading article, 'Vichy contre l'Eglise', *Volontaire pour la Cité chrétienne*, London, no. 12, 30 September 1942, p. 1.
41. AN 2 AG 492. Note de renseignement No. 3723/16B, DJ.10 (Rens. Gen) (Secret), Vichy, 23 September 1942.
42. AN 2 AG 493. Letters to Lavagne, of Pétain's Cabinet Civil, dated 6 June, 11 July, 29 August , and 29 October 1942.
43. E. Jarry and J. R. Palanque (eds), *Histoire des diocèses de France: Grenoble*, 1967.
44. Mgr Piguet, an ardent 'maréchaliste', was later arrested by the Germans and deported to Germany.

45. See D. Lemaire and Y.-M. Hilaire, 'Chrétiens et Juifs dans le Nord–Pas-de-Calais pendant la Seconde Guerre Mondiale', *Revue du Nord*, no. 237, April–June 1978, pp. 451–6.

46. A Dio, Lille, ACA 2 B 1. The note is part of the papers relating to the meeting of the ACA of 15 January 1941. It ends: 'statut à établir'.

47. It must be said that this attitude was by no means shared by all the bishops.

48. P. Laborie, *Résistants, Vichyssois et d'autres. L'évolution de l'opinion et des comportements dans le Lot de 1939 à 1944*, 1980, p. 235.

49. *Actes*: Biviers, 1987, p. 178.

50. Cited in *Actes*: Grenoble, p. 236.

51 P. Bolle, 'Les protestants français et leurs Eglises durant la seconde guerre mondiale', *Revue d'histoire moderne et contemporaine*, April–June 1979, pp. 293 ff.

52. *Actes*: Biviers, p. 192, n. 36.

53. *Actes*: Grenoble, p. 205.

–9–

Christians and Jews: The Aftermath

Bérard had reported the alleged papal reaction to the persecutions in 1941. How did the Vatican view a year later the declarations of the bishops and the harsh measures against the Jews, which they now criticised? A German source reported that the Pope had intervened to ask for milder treatment, having seen how the average Catholic reacted. The French had not complained at the deportation of foreign Jews; now their fellow countrymen were being drawn into the net their attitude had changed.[1] On August 12 Vichy denied American radio reports that Laval had rebutted papal intervention. Yet it is certain some remonstrance was made through Valerio Valeri, which Laval had deemed unacceptable. He had in fact instructed Mgr Rocco, the Paris Nuncio's deputy, to inform the Vatican that the Church should keep well out of affairs of State; clergy aiding Jews must expect the police to act against them.[2] However, a story circulated that at a lunch attended by the Nuncio Pétain had mentioned the round-up of the Jews in Paris and had remarked, 'The Pope understands and approves my attitude', which brought a 'respectful' rejoinder from Valerio Valeri: 'The Holy Father neither understands nor approves.'[3] From London, Mgr Godfrey, the Apostolic Delegate, mentioned a rumour that already some time previously the Vatican had denounced the expulsion of foreign Jews,[4] but regarding these unfortunates the Nuncio, had reported to the Vatican that Laval's decision was irrevocable; further intervention would consequently be fruitless. Nevertheless, it was apparent that the regime was disconcerted by the new stance of the Church.

Bérard himself returned to France on a visit at the end of August 1942, and privately conceded that the Vatican was displeased that the bishops had not spoken out earlier and more vigorously.[5]

A war of words also broke out on the air. Radio Vatican, on 14 September, pleaded for the Jews:

Jesus Christ first cared for those sheep that belonged to his chosen people, the Jewish people, for all those of his own race out of which has sprung the salvation of the world... He cared for this Jewish people with an infinite love... Those who in their heart refuse to acknowledge the dignity of all the children of God are committing sacrilege.[6]

It also broadcast Mgr Saliège's denunciation of the persecutions twice and commented on it six days running.[7] At the end of September Vichy radio riposted, attacking the Vatican for ordering the Nuncio to protest.[8] In fact, Valerio Valeri had held a secret meeting on 15 April 1942 with Mgrs Gerlier, Liénart and Piguet (Bishop of Clermont-Ferrand) to discuss the situation. In August he had protested to Pétain and had even gone to Rome to explain what was happening.[9]

For its part, Radio Vatican did not give up. As late as 25 June 1943, when the outcry had abated (although deportations continued), it broadcast a talk beamed at France which again proclaimed, 'There are neither Greeks nor Jews, but only men facing their God. Those who make distinctions between them forsake their God.'[10]

Two substantial cases of unsucccessful intervention by the Vatican may nevertheless be cited as evidence of the extreme caution the Pope exercised in attempts to save Jews. The first concerns the German takeover of the small zone of France occupied by the Italians. The latter, who showed sympathy for the plight of the Jews, had allowed large numbers to take refuge in its zone. The Italian withdrawal meant they were in imminent danger. The Jewish authorities sent 'an heroic Capuchin' monk, Père Marie Benoît, to Rome to ask for Vatican protection for them. After an audience with the Pope on 16 July 1943, Sephardic Jews were to be 'repatriated' to Spain and a plan was drawn up to evacuate others — the majority — to North Africa. The project received the approval of Osborne and Tittman, the British and American ambassadors to the Holy See, and four Italian transport ships were hired. But negotiations were so long drawn-out that no action had been taken before the Allied armistice with Italy on September 8, when the Germans began moving in. Some Jews were caught in the trap; the rest, about 50,000 in all, had to flee south as best they could.[11]

Even after their parents had been deported the Vatican still vacillated over the Jewish children left behind. By now some 3,500 youngsters had been made virtual orphans. Laval's intention was to deport *all* Jewish children, willy-nilly. On August 29 an inter-denominational group in Geneva had asked the Vatican to intervene to procure transit visas through Portugal for them, so they could be settled in Latin America. The Fribourg cleric who passed on this request stressed that the matter was urgent, one perhaps of hours. Yet only nineteen days later did the Vatican check the information with Valerio Valeri. The Nuncio replied that meanwhile these 'orphaned children' had had to be entrusted to

Jewish charities for dispersal within France. All this gave the impression that the Holy See was indifferent to their plight.[12] At about the same time the US State Department offered 1,000 visas for Jewish children, and the possibility of many more. Laval, who had categorically rejected Boegner's plea to save the children on 9 September, nevertheless passed on the offer to the Germans for them to decide. They hesitated, fearing adverse publicity. Negotiations dragged on, and after the invasion of North Africa it was of course too late.

In fact, there appears to be no evidence that the Pope or the Vatican gave any practical support to the saving of French Jews, although they may well have intervened in individual cases concerning converts. This inertia is all the more surprising, because elsewhere in occupied Europe papal intervention was vigorous and effective. Thus the persecution of Jews in Slovenia stopped in autumn 1942 after the Pope made his disapproval known. When, after the German occupation of Rome, the Germans proposed to deport 8,000 Jews from the city, Pius XII was able also to frustrate the move. In France the lack of a positive lead from the head of the Church naturally threw the bishops into confusion.

Meanwhile the Germans had been somewhat taken aback by the vehemence of episcopal dissent. Krug von Nidda, the German Consul at Vichy, had a long interview with Pétain, a report of which Abetz forwarded to Berlin. It appeared that the Marshal had rejected the Church's claim to intervene: 'The Jewish question has recently been hotly discussed, particularly by the Churches, which he [Pétain] will not allow. Reasons of State must prevail over any understandable humanitarian feeling.' Surprisingly, Abetz added a word of commendation — a doubtful accolade in the circumstances — for Cardinal Suhard and others: 'A section of the clergy, particularly Archbishop Suhard of Paris, have shown greater understanding about this matter than other bishops.'[13]

The feebleness of the protests by prelates in the occupied zone was indeed noteworthy. Nevertheless there had been one spectacular action: when the Germans had decreed the registration of all Jews in their zone, Mgr Roeder, bishop of Beauvais, had made a dramatic gesture. Declaring that he had to register because one of his ancestors was a Jew, he had processed to the registration office in full pontificals, preceded by an acolyte bearing the crucifix.[14]

For their part, Darquier de Pellepoix and the Commissariat Général aux Questions Juives went over to the attack on Church leaders. Reports in October 1942 by local representatives of the CGQJ complained that the rank and file clergy, on the whole hostile, were trying to stir up sentiment against the deportations. They cited the declarations by Saliège and Gerlier as the cause of this unrest . The local

CGQJ official in Toulouse even requested that the Nuncio should be asked to take sanctions against the archbishop. Mgr Rémond, Bishop of Nice, was also singled out because he had forbidden any checking of baptismal certificates by the anti-Jewish police; a report from Nice dated 30 September claimed that 'it is of public notoriety that he [the bishop] sets himself up as champion in defence of the Jews'.[15] Among other Protestants, Pastor Boegner was put under surveillance, his telephone tapped, and his mail intercepted. The CGQJ even saw an allusion to the deportations in the Christmas Day sermon of the Bishop of Annecy, who mildly exhorted the faithful to pray for children and mothers who had been separated. One development was that from the autumn of 1942 Darquier de Pellepoix and a certain 'Abbé Jacques' began regular anti-Jewish propaganda broadcasts.[16] Collaborationists mounted attacks on synagogues, to which the local bishops responded by writing letters of sympathy to the rabbis concerned: Mgr Delay to Rabbi Salger of Marseilles; Cardinal Gerlier to the Chief Rabbi; and Mgr Sol of Pau, and Mgr Louis of Périgueux to the local Jewish authorities.[17]

The collaborationist press in Paris saw the clergy as the main stumbling block to the success of the anti-Jewish measures, and exploded in wrath at the episcopal protests. The recalcitrant bishops were branded as anglophile Gaullists deliberately out to wreck the sterling work of the regime. It is true that in certain areas the text of Saliège's declaration had been posted up and used by Commmunists as representing the reassertion of true French patriotism.[18] Fuel was added to the flames when both Gerlier and the Protestants were represented in September at the funeral of the chief Rabbi of Lyons, Edgard Sèches, which was widely interpreted as yet another gesture of public sympathy.[19] Gerlier became a prime target. *Le Pilori* published two articles in October 1942 in which he was dubbed 'le prélat félon' and 'le nouveau Cauchon'. The peroration of the second article ran: 'In the name of France... in the name of the whole of Christendom, I demand the head of Gerlier, cardinal Talmudist, raving lunatic, a traitor to his faith, his country and his race. Gerlier, I hate you.'[20]

L'Œuvre (23 September 1942) commented sardonically: 'There has been recently in the unoccupied zone something like a mobilisation of episcopal croziers concerning the measures taken against the Jews.'[21] On October 22 it went a step further and asserted that a veritable declaration of war on the new European order had been made by 'certain princes of the Church': 'Do not let ourselves be deceived. The alliance of the great johnnies-come-latelies of the Catholic Church with the Jewish community remains total and absolute.'[22] At the same time *Paris-Soir* launched a series of articles under the general title: 'How the Jews of the unoccupied zone abused the credulity of the higher clergy' ('Comment les Juifs de la zone non-occupée abusèrent de la crédulité du haut clergé'). It hinted darkly at Ultramontanism (8 October 1942). Other periodicals referred to an 'unforeseen alliance' between catholicism and democracy.[23] *Aujourd'hui* (26 October 1942) reported the views of the collaborationist Abbé Sorel, a member of the Conseil National, who broadened the argument: speaking at a meeting of the Groupe Collaboration he declared it necessary 'to put a stop to Jewish activities', because this would mean that 'collaborationism would give France its due place in the new Europe'.[24] Alas, he added, few clerical voices had been raised positively favouring the persecutions; even fewer were attracted by collaborationism.

In the unoccupied zone the Information ministry tried to persuade the press to support Vichy's Jewish policy. In a series of articles appearing in *Le Grand Echo du Midi*, under the pen-name of 'Saint-Jean', the Catholic Vallery-Radot, abandoning for the moment his anti-Masonic activities, attacked the bishops.[25] Again, one cleric, possibly the collaborationist Abbé Bergey, was recruited by Simon Arbellot, who was in charge of Vichy propaganda, to write an article, 'La Papauté et les Juifs', to demonstrate that the bishops' attitude ran counter to the allegedly anti-Semitic views of St Thomas Aquinas.[26] Maurice Sarraut, of the *Dépêche de Toulouse*, was invited to publish this comminatory article, but refused, a gesture welcomed by Archbishop Saliège.[27] Vichy pressed other newspapers to print it. It eventually appeared in *Le Grand Echo du Midi* (3 September 1942), which had already accused the bishops of hypocrisy. Vichy was duly grateful to the newspaper for expounding 'the sound doctrine of St Thomas Aquinas and the papacy'.[28] Laval's own newspaper, *Le Moniteur*, also reproduced the original article, as did the Limoges *Courrier du Centre*, on which served Alex Delpeyrau, notorious for having inspired an anti-Jewish campaign launched by the collaborationist Radio-Révolution.[29] Another newspaper, the *Echo de Jurançon*, attacked the attitude of the leader of the Christian Democrats: 'When the Spanish Reds were massacring and hanging their clergy not a single friend of Champetier de Ribes protested... But if on the other hand the finger of a little Hebrew gets caught in the door during transport for deportation, the passive witnesses to atrocities still close in time and space give full vent to their indignant remonstrances.'[30]

A Nice publication, the *Bulletin d'Informations Corporatives*, provoked one bishop, Mgr Rastouil of Limoges, to express his anger at a slur on the episcopacy. The article had spoken of disloyalty, of the 'ludicrous' stances taken by the prelates in the face of the 'severe', but 'just and salutary' measures against foreign Jews, 'who had made our country the dumping ground for all the rubbish of Europe'.[31] There followed a list of the crimes alleged against these unwelcome guests: they thrived on the black market, were mixed up in all kinds of illegal trading and flaunted their luxurious life style. However, despite the disreputable behaviour of its bishops, the article concluded, 'le catholicisme est la moëlle de la France'. Bishop Rastouil did not take up the cudgels directly on behalf of the Jews, but indignantly repudiated the charge of disloyalty: the episcopacy, he declared, had given 'a thousand testimonies' of their fidelity to the regime. He disliked intensely the tone of the article; the bishops had indeed reminded the French of the universality of human rights, although they were conscious that the government had a problem to solve. Rastouil's rejoinder had to be submitted twice to the censor before publication was allowed in his *Semaine religieuse* (13 November 1942).[32] The bishop thereupon wrote to Pétain complaining about the censorship. Lavagne, of Pétain's Cabinet Civil, replied (Vichy, 29 October 1942) that the Marshal had ticked off severely the author of the article, but that the bishop should have been more careful to express specifically 'un mot de fidélité au chef de l'Etat'. The affair is symptomatic of Catholic leaders in late 1942: utter loyalty — but to Pétain, and not necessarily to Laval; and the continued acceptance of the existence of a 'Jewish question'.

It is in fact remarkable that even before the storm raised by their protests had died down bishops were again lavish in their expressions of loyalty to the Marshal. On 20 September, the Archbishop of Aix and the assembled bishops of the South-East thought fit to send a telegram to him pledging continuing support in his task of 'redressement national'.[33] A few days later Suhard, two archbishops and eleven other bishops, all from the occupied zone, met for the consecration of Mgr Petit, a new bishop, and agreed to the despatch of a telegram by Tissier, Bishop of Chalons, informing Pétain of their prayers for the reconstruction of France, 'to which you have so generously devoted yourself'.[34] In the *Semaine Catholique* of his diocese, dated 27 September, even Saliège objected to the way his protest had been misused, and reaffirmed his loyalty to the Marshal.[35]

By October 1942 a police report, based on opinion in Maurrassian circles, deemed that recent declarations made by Suhard and Saliège indicated that the period of tension between the Church and State was over. It was believed that 'the conciliatory attitude adopted by the higher clergy, and especially Mgr Saliège, is due to the efforts made by M Léon Bérard, who has had various contacts with a number of bishops'. Action Française considered Laval should seize the first opportunity to demonstrate that 'an entire identity of views prevails between the French government and the Church'.[36]

Summaries of censorship intercepts demonstrate a similar evolution in opinion. On 12 September they showed that the Jews were attracting considerable sympathy among Christians. On 10 October they noted that the episcopal declarations had not appeared to have shaken the bishops' faith in Pétain; episcopal protests might in fact have had the not unwelcome effect of laying the blame for anti-Jewish measures on the Germans.[37]

By 29 October official reconciliation was perhaps complete. Cardinals Suhard and Gerlier met Pétain and Laval at Vichy, attended a military parade, and then engaged in discussions that resulted in the government giving, for the first time for over half a century, subsidies to Catholic higher education. The hardliners at Vichy saw this détente as a sign of ecclesiastical weakness. The rank and file clergy, who had been hostile to the deportations, were, according to General Bridoux, the Defence minister, now coming round to the view that protests only made the situation of the Jews worse.[38]

A Vichy report of December 1942, after the Allied landings, claimed that clerical opinion in North Africa had undergone a complete turnabout. Although, in Algeria particularly, anti-Semitism had been strong, even before the arrival of the Americans the clergy had campaigned against the anti-Jewish measures. Nevertheless, after the release of political prisoners and the Jews by the Allies the clergy now feared for the fate of the Church 'if the Anglo-Saxons should happen to be victorious'.[39] In fact, after the Allied invasion the anti-Jewish laws had not been immediately repealed: full citizenship rights to North African Jews were not restored until 1943.[40]

Both Gerlier and Suhard continued, however, to make their opposition to persecution known. In January 1943 Gerlier was visited by the Lyons commander of the German garrison, who told him that the Reich would not harm the Church if it did not oppose the anti-Jewish laws or protect Jews. The cardinal abruptly terminated the conversation and informed the German officer that no less a person than the Pope had condemned such legislation.[41] After deportations from France resumed in February 1943 Suhard wrote to Pétain pleading for them to be carried out more humanely, whilst conceding that France had no longer complete control over its own affairs. He complained that arrests of Jewish spouses in Catholic families were taking place without taking into consideration past military service, or in the case of a mother, the number and age of her children. In a memorandum attached to his letter regarding recent arrests of the young, the sick and the aged, he drew attention to some shocking cases. For example, on February 10, French police inspectors arrived at the Orphelinat de la Fondation Rothschild at 6.30 a.m. and took away twelve orphans aged between five and thirteen; at 1 a.m. the following morning they returned and this time removed four girls aged between fifteen and sixteen. There is no doubt that the plight of Jewish children, and particularly the separation from their families, was what most moved the average Frenchman. Tardily, by September 1943, Laval was forced to change tack and arrange with the Germans that children would no longer be separated from their parents.[42] The arrangement was often ignored.

Meanwhile other official means of solving the 'Jewish problem' were desperately sought by sympathetic Catholics such as Lavagne, in charge of religious matters for Pétain. A certain Abbé Catry was introduced to Lavagne by René de Chambrun, Laval's son-in-law. Catry was a long-standing anti-Semite. He had quit the Jesuit order in 1938 because he alleged it was negotiating with Freemasons and was too liberal in its attitude to the Communists; more to the point, he had asserted that the Church was not facing up to the 'Jewish question'.[43] Catry had published a scurrilous anti-Jewish pamphlet entitled 'L'Eglise et les Juifs'. Gerlier particularly resented his lobbying activities at Vichy.

Catry put forward to Lavagne a plan devised by Kadmi Cohen, a naturalised French lawyer of Polish-Jewish origin who had volunteered in August 1914 for the French army and had since settled in France. In December 1941, along with some other Jewish professional men, he had been rounded up by the Germans and sent to the staging camp at Compiègne, but had then unexpectedly been released. The 'Massada plan', named after the last Jewish citadel that had resisted the Romans, envisaged a Jewish state made up of Palestine, Transjordan and the Sinai peninsula.[44] Catry saw the project as adroitly ridding France of the Jews, but one that would forestall Catholic opposition and could be represented as a *Jewish* solution to the Jewish question.[45] Lavagne also favoured the plan as being an 'effective', 'humane' and 'Christian' solution. It would lift a terrible burden of guilt from French shoulders; at the same time it would act as a powerful antidote to communism and the 'bolshevistic messianism' of the Jews of the Diaspora. The plan, however, found no support elsewhere. (The Allies, who then occupied Palestine, were naturally not consulted, although of course the idea of a Jewish homeland was not new.) The Lyons Jewish Consistoire was not impressed because its own policy was one of assimilation. In March 1943 Heilbronner refused even to meet Kadmi Cohen. But the biggest stumbling block was the Germans, who had already turned down the plan in January, this despite the fact that in the spring Goebbels asserted that Germany was not against a more humane solution or even a Jewish state. Hitler, however, had set his face against any such scheme. This led Lavagne to comment despondently: 'Any collaboration with the Germans on the level of racist anti-Semitism simply constitutes criminal complicity. Darquier de Pellepoix has done nothing else.'[46] There the matter rested. Cohen was re-interned, and in March 1944 put on a train for Auschwitz, whence he never returned. The whole incident demonstrates that Vichy — at least those in the Pétain camp, (which also included practising Christians such as Lavagne whose conscience had always been greatly exercised) — seeing the balance of advantage was now tilting towards an Allied victory, or at least a compromise peace, were uneasy as to how the anti-Jewish action would be viewed when the war was over.

In May 1943 the Protestant National Synod discussed the condemnatory message that Pastor Boegner had sent out the previous autumn. A few hostile pastors had refused to read it to their congregations, because, as one put it, 'The Jews have declared themselves to be the worst enemies of God and Christ.' They aligned themselves with the small royalist and nationalist 'Sully group' of Protestants.[47]

From the Catholic bishops as a whole there came no further word. At the October 1942 meeting of the ACA, at its four meetings in 1943, and at the last before the Liberation, held in February 1944, the specific question of the Jews was not raised again. It is true that in February 1944 Brinon was asked to intervene on behalf of all political and racial prisoners in Germany, and Suhard approached Abetz. But nothing came even of this.

Laval, however, pressed on. Falling in with German wishes, he proposed in August 1943 to revoke a further batch of naturalisations, thus depriving of their citizenship many more Jews who had become French even before 1927. This prompted Mgr Chappoulie, possibly acting on behalf of the ACA, to intervene. He declared it to be against natural law, of which the Church was the guardian, to snatch children from their parents and to break up families when the only complaint against them was the fact that they belonged to a particular race. As the official Catholic representative to the regime, he wrote to Jean Jardel, of Pétain's Cabinet Civil, 'Today fresh deportations would provoke among Catholics an increased wave of emotion and sadness and it is probable that the bishops would think themselves once again obliged to make their voice heard.'

Pétain was informed that the Pope grieved at the prospect of further measures, and even feared for the Marshal's salvation. He was plainly shaken by this reaction, and turned down the proposed law. If he gave way to German demands he would, he averred somewhat disingenuously, be defaulting on a solemn promise given by the government of the Third Republic! Henceforth denaturalisations should not treat whole categories of people, but only individual cases.[48]

However, the official government line remained unchanged: whilst the clergy had the right to speak out in favour of the Jews, they must acknowledge that matters of internal and external policy were involved that affected the State's decisions.

How did Catholic Gaullists view Jewish persecution? One curious reaction was that of Blocq-Mascart, a leader of the Resistance movement OCM, and himself of Jewish origin, but who had become a 'spiritualiste catholique'. In June 1942 he proposed to London that measures should be taken to distribute Jews more evenly over France, so as to facilitate assimilation. Simone Weill, on the other hand, writing from London, wanted to speed up the disappearance of the Jewish minority by familiarising it with a 'generalised' form of Christianity.[49] On the other hand the concern of the Catholic writer in exile, Georges Bernanos, previously fiercely anti-Semite, was for the danger that threatened Mandel, the Jewish former politician of the Third Republic, imprisoned by Vichy:

> If your masters do not give Mandel back to us alive, you will have to pay for this Jewish blood in a way that will astound history — do you hear me, you curs? — every drop of this Jewish blood shed in hatred of our former victory is more precious than the purple cloak of a Fascist cardinal — do you quite understand what I mean, you admirals, marshals, excellencies, eminences and reverends?[50]

From the few Catholics in the opposing, collaborationist camp there was no sign of any softening in attitudes. One Milicien wrote ingratiatingly to Pétain recounting how he and his comrades had listened to a talk on anti-Semitism given by 'un grand catholique', M Delpont de Vaux: 'He made us realise how the whole of Israel, which already holds the entire world in its claws, is under the devil... Let us pray for the victory of Christianity over bolshevism.'[51] It is notable how frequently the Jews were identified with the Communists.

There matters connected with policy rested. But Christians — Catholics and Protestants alike — gave great practical help to the deportees. Boegner and Gerlier had both sponsored the new organisation, Amitié Chrétienne, in which had joined the Protestant CIMADE and Catholic groups working in the Lyons area and elsewhere to save the Jews. Catholic participation was led by Père Chaillet.[52] A Jesuit, he knew Germany well. Before the war he had taught philosophy and German theology at the Fourvière, the Lyons scholasticate, to where he had returned in 1941. His associate was Père Glasberg, who had already worked with Protestants saving refugees. The other Catholic who assumed a prominent role was Germaine Ribière of the JECF, who took on the dangerous task of escorting Jews to safety, and maintained contact with those interned. The new rescue group, under a Catholic organiser, J.-M. Soutou, established close relations with Jewish agencies, which sought assistance in concealing Jewish children in various Christian institutions. Among Protestants many pastors gave unstinting assistance, among them Roland de Pury, and his colleagues in Lyons, Rivet and Eberhard, Pastors Westphal, Girard-Clot and Virieu at Grenoble, Trocmé and Theis at Le Chambon-sur-Lignon.

Le Chambon and its surrounding area was in fact the centre of a largely Huguenot enclave in the Haute-Loire. Situated on a high plateau, it was a comparatively isolated region to which access was difficult. A village of 'peasants, ploughmen and cattle breeders', under Pastor Trocmé, backed by Pastors Theis and Charles Guillon, a former mayor who had promptly tendered his resignation in June 1940, it became a veritable centre of the Protestant Resistance, and sheltered many young men fleeing from forced labour in Germany. On a larger scale, the area, with some 40,000 inhabitants, hid permanently some 800–1,000 Jews and aided perhaps 4,000 more being smuggled to Switzerland or Spain. Among these simple countryfolk one oral tradition was strong: the tale of the persecution of their Huguenot ancestors. They did not hesitate to challenge Lamirand, the Secretary-General for Youth, regarding Vichy's treatment of the Jews when he visited the area in August 1942. A close-knit community, they were convinced of the religious justification for their actions, and had spectacular success, outwitting searches by the Vichy police, and again by the German Feldgendarmerie in June 1943.[53]

Special mention must be made of the role played by Pastor Pury in Lyons. As a Swiss he was able to make frequent trips to Geneva, where he liaised with the embryo Ecumenical Council, under its secretary-general, Visser 't Hooft, Alec Cramer of the Swiss branch of the Red Cross, an exiled German pastor, Adolf Freudenberg — the friend of Pastor Niemöller — and others. Geneva provided welcome access to the outside world. Pury also hid many refugees in his own parish. Some feats accomplished were remarkable. Thus the role of Mme André Philip, the wife of the Protestant politician, entailed her crossing the Swiss frontier by train, regularly disguised as a fireman, with her face suitably blackened, riding on the locomotive tender.[54] Nor was Protestant help confined to the south. Carlo Schmid, the prominent post-war German Socialist, at the time a military adviser in the Oberfeldkommandantur of Lille, wrote in his memoirs: 'What some of the pastors risked to help the Jews to flee will remain a glorious page in the history of the Reformed Church.'[55]

The concealment of Jewish children was first carried out in the Toulouse area with help from Mgr Saliège. But in fact, Amitié Chrétienne had rapidly established a semi-clandestine network throughout the southern zone offering assistance of all kinds. Refuges and hiding places had been established in convents and churches. Escape routes were constituted, running from Toulouse to Spain, and from Lyons, Grenoble and Valence to Switzerland. Priests in Haute-Savoie took on the role of 'passeurs', frontier guides who led their charges to safety. The nuns of Notre-Dame-de-Sion in Lyons, under Mère Clothilde, the Mother-Superior, became specialists in forging identity papers and documents. Protestant hostels run by the 'Amies de la Jeune Fille' in Lyons were used as hideouts.[56] The vast enterprise was a remarkable practical example of budding interdenominational co-operation. The disproportionate role played in it by Protestants was because the pastors involved were young – many not above thirty; constituting a small group, they knew each other and their parishioners well and were supported by the youth groups they ran. At a special meeting at Mas Soubeyran on September 6 some sixty of them had been briefed by Pastor Boegner and had laid plans to create what became known as the 'Refuge cévenol'.[57]

The most notable exploit of Amitié Chrétienne was the snatching of Jewish children from deportation at Vénissieux station, in which Madeleine Barot, and Pères Chaillet and Glasberg took a prominent part. After the large-scale round-up of Jews in Lyons on 26 August 1942, Amitié Chrétienne resolved to save the children, whose deportation had been ordered by Laval. A telegram to this effect arrived from Vichy but was intercepted by Glasberg, who did not reveal its contents, so that arrangements to rescue the children continued . The numbers involved have been variously estimated at between 100 and 200 — one contemporary source gave the figure as 160.[58] Their sorrowing parents signed custody forms, realising they would not see their offspring again. The children were then swiftly hidden in seminaries and other religious institutions in the area.[59] At first Cardinal Gerlier knew nothing of this development. The following day the prefect, Angéli, acting on Laval's instructions, enquired the children's whereabouts. Glasberg was summoned to the archbishop's palace and ordered to provide a list of their addresses. It appears that Gerlier had agreed to give this information to Pétain, who had promised not to pass it on to the Germans. Eventually Glasberg provided the cardinal with a list of false addresses.[60] There is some evidence that Pétain, as distinct from Laval, was in any case lukewarm in wanting to trace the children. When Angéli went on trial at Lyons after the Liberation, Gerlier swore an affidavit to the effect that the prefect had been very half-hearted in his efforts, and had 'punished' the Church very lightly after the deceit had been discovered.[61] The prefect's reluctance was shared by General de St Vincent, the military governor of Lyons, who categorically refused to assist the police in their abhorrent task and was dismissed for his pains.[62]

The Germans were furious at such clerical intervention in their plans. They demanded sanctions. Laval informed Abetz, the German Ambassador, that on 1 September Père Chaillet had been arrested for his part in the affair. This may not have been strictly true. It is certain that Chaillet was threatened with internment in Fort Barraux, but the threat may not have been carried out. He was, however banished from Lyons for a month and placed under supervised residence at Privas. According to a report by the BCRA, de Gaulle's intelligence service, Gerlier may have shielded Chaillet. After a long interview with Angéli, and then with the head of the Private Office of Bousquet, Secretary-General of the Police, the cardinal allegedly declared: 'There are limits that a Christian conscience may not exceed. These children will remain under our protection and you will only learn their place of residence if the government gives us its formal promise that they will not be handed over to Germany.'[63] But the children never saw their parents again.

This account of the cardinal's part in the affair appears at odds with that of Abbé Glasberg. However, at Pétain's trial after the Liberation, Pastor Boegner also credited Gerlier as being the prime mover in saving the children. Abetz's telegram to Berlin played down the incident. He spoke of only eighty children being involved. He added, optimistically, that Laval's part in the affair might heighten his popularity with the working classes, who in the unoccupied zone had become very anticlerical. His further comment on the relationship between Chaillet and Gerlier seems exaggerated: 'This is the first time in a long while that so highly-placed a cleric has been arrested in France, and the measure should have an even more lasting effect because Chaillet is the right hand of the very anti-German Primate of the Gauls, Archbishop Gerlier.'[64]

One outcome of the affair was that the main Lyons seminary was thrown open as a refuge for Jews,[65] although aid organisations realised Jews could find no really safe haven in France and made feverish arrangements to evacuate them to safety abroad. After a visit to Berne Pastor Boegner secured Swiss assent to a system whereby Jews sponsored by the organisation would not be refused entry at the frontier provided that they could quote their visa number, which was not stamped in their passport but which they had to commit to memory. Christians who sought to help the Jews were nevertheless faced with a cruel dilemma. The Révolution Nationale, which they had supported, had exalted the family. Their own inclination was to keep families together. Yet when they saw the conditions under which the deportations were being carried out, and surmised the miserable fate that awaited the deportees (even if they did not realize it was death), they deemed it their duty to prevent children from deportation. Indeed a clandestine tract circulated in the unoccupied zone entitled 'Vous n'aurez pas les enfants.' In August 1943 Mgr Chappoulie, declared publicly that the Church as the guardian of the natural law was against the break-up of families, particularly when no charge was made against them save that they belonged to a specific 'race'. Despite this public remonstrance, the deportation of semi-orphaned Jewish children continued almost to the end: in April 1944 forty-one youngsters aged between three and thirteen housed in a home in Izieu (Ain) were taken off to Drancy and later put on an eastbound train.[66]

After the total occupation of France, from November 1942 such organisations as Amitié Chrétienne began to break up. Increasingly CIMADE's activities passed into clandestinity. Abbé Glasberg, who had become ever more deeply involved in the Resistance, was condemned to death in his absence for co-operating with railway workers in acts of sabotage, and fled from Lyons at the end of 1942. Père Chaillet was also forced into permanent hiding. Such active sympathisers as Pastor Pury also feared for their liberty. (He was in fact imprisoned for five months in 1943 before being released to his native Switzerland.) A few helpers, such as Germaine Ribière, continued to aid Jewish escapees to flee, but by the end of 1943 most activity had to cease and she also went into hiding. Sadly, despite all their valiant efforts, only a few thousand Jews had been saved.[67]

Meanwhile a number of bishops had also played their part in assisting Jews. Mgr Rémond, as well as flouting the CGQJ by conniving at the issue of false baptismal certificates, also actively helped Moussa Abadie to hide children. Mgr Théas of Montauban, later to be deported by the Germans, with the connivence of François Martin, the Prefect, threw open the doors of seminaries and Catholic schools to those seeking asylum:[68] when the Germans occupied the whole of France these institutions were not searched.[69] Mgr Pic, Bishop of Valence, notable for his ambiguous attitudes, did likewise; he also provided Jews with false identity papers and new ration cards (by December 1942 all Jewish ration cards had been stamped with a large 'J') and arranged for them to be passed on from one parish house to another on their way to safety. Saliège's auxiliary bishop in Toulouse, Mgr Louis de Courrèges, gave generous assistance to those in flight.[70] Gerlier ordered convents in his diocese to be made available to escapees. At Annecy the Catholic Ligue Féminine, at the request of the bishop, Mgr Cesbron, took in forty Jewish children. But such actions by the bishops were not so frequent as were those of smaller fry, whether clergy or laity.

Indeed it was the minor clergy, particularly in rural areas — in the towns they inclined to be more 'maréchaliste' — who were most sympathetic. In the countryside those who rang the bell of the presbytery in the small hours, whether Jews, fugitives from the Vichy or the German police, or members of the Resistance, were almost sure of assistance. As *Témoignage Chrétien* noted at the time: 'The calm, obscure courage of the humblest priests will make up for other attitudes. It may well be that in the hour of wrath and justice, when all accounts come into the light of day, those of the "green-mould cassocks" will become the lightning-conductors of the Church of France.'[71] This judgement turned out to be not far from the truth.

The distinguished Jewish medical specialist, Robert Debré, relates how in the occupied zone, where helping Jews was much more dangerous, Père Jacques, the head of the college of Avron, near Fontainebleau, hid many children; Pastor Daniel Monod issued them with false baptismal certificates; Debré himself arranged for them to be passed on to a more permanent place of refuge and for false papers to be prepared for them in his laboratory.[72] The Jewish author Georges Wellers describes how his non-Jewish wife hid their two children in a 'colonie de vacances' near Compiègne run by a Protestant pastor, where they were joined by others.[73] At Toulouse Mgr Bruno de Solages, the head of the Institut Catholique, saved young Jews by allowing them to enrol as students or attend Catholic schools.[74] Jews dismissed from their teaching posts in the state system were sometimes taken on in Catholic schools. The Jewish poet Max Jacob was sheltered by a priest at Saint-Benoît-sur-Loire until captured by the Germans and despatched to Drancy, where he died within a few days.[75] He was seemingly acting as sacristan, living in the parish house, and when caught in February 1944 was still wearing the Star of David. At Saint-Etienne the Catholic movement Aide aux Mères, and particularly its head, Mlle Vidal, with various social workers some of whom were themselves Jewish, accomplished all kinds of dangerous missions. Nuns were particularly courageous: the Benedictine convent at Pradines succcessfully hid a number of Jews.[76] In Paris Père Devaux and the nuns of Notre-Dame-de-Sion sheltered many Jewish children, succeeding in placing no less than 444 of them in non-Jewish families in the Paris area and elsewhere — one workman, of Ivry, already the father of five children, adopted two more.[77]

These examples, taken almost at random, show how the role played by Christians in assisting Jews should not be underestimated. Gendarmerie statements revealed their stubborn persistence: one report ran, 'the clergy has openly come out in their [the Jews'] favour' and cited the case of the Jews of Francheville (Rhône), who, pursued by gendarmes, took refuge in the chapel attached to a retreat for missionary priests at Chatelard. The Superior categorically refused the gendarmes access, and only gave way when the Prefect intervened with Cardinal Gerlier.[78]

The complexity of Gerlier's reactions to Jewish persecution is apparent. His role was crucial. He did not hesitate to intervene with Valentin, then Director of the Légion des Combattants, and Vallat, the first Commissioner for Jewish Questions, to plead the cause of Jewish ex-servicemen of the First World War. He protested publicly against the ill-treatment of deportees, but was also compliant on occasion to Vichy's wishes, whilst still aiding Jews on the run. One eminent French historian's judgement on him is mixed: 'The general public and the ordinary people of Lyons in particular knew that he was very pro-Pétain and generally concede there were mitigating circumstances.' His attitude was both prudent and courageous, but for a long time hesitant, a reticence that might be ascribed to his legal training, and his tendency to be diplomatic: 'It would be pointless to hide the black spots, but it would be unfair to present too black a picture.'[79] A Jewish commentator was not so favourably impressed with the conduct of the cardinals in general: 'Is it not possible that the princes of the Church were [...] rather "given a shove" from below in their interventions in favour of the Jews?'[80] The same writer goes on to concede, however, that the actions of the clergy in general went far beyond the public declarations they made. An even more authoritative Jewish view is that of Serge Klarsfeld, the French lawyer and relentless pursuer of many Nazi war criminals: 'We must emphasise that it is to Cardinal Gerlier, a pillar of the Vichy regime, that is owed, more than to any other, the abrupt slow-down of the massive police co-operation given by Vichy to the Gestapo.' For Klarsfeld, the SS recognised in Gerlier its most formidable adversary, so that Laval, seeing the resistance of the Church, eventually shrank from further anti-Jewish measures.[81] Certainly the CGQJ, one of Vichy's main instruments of persecution, reckoned the Church among its foremost enemies. In a report after the main round-ups had taken place, the head of its 'Investigation and Control' section — a euphemism for the anti-Jewish police the commission had set up — this was acknowledged: 'With the upper clergy in the van, a large part of the French population has risen up against the measures taken at the end of last August (1942).'[82] The Nice section of the CGQJ protested against the 'wicked [*sic*] influence' of declarations made by Saliège and Gerlier. Meanwhile Jews themselves had earlier expressed their gratitude to Christians, at the opening of the general assembly of the French Rabbinate by the president of the central Consistoire.[83]

Although there was no clear lead from any ecclesiastical authority, its protests did appear to have had some effect. It was representations by the Church that caused Vichy to refuse, as already mentioned, the request by Rothke, the SS officer in charge of deportations for further denaturalisations.[84]

The conscience of influential lay Catholics had been deeply perturbed at the happenings of 1942. They acknowledged that France had acted more harshly than other occupied nations,[85] and at this stage were seeking any expedient that offered security to the Jews.[86]

Vichy's treatment of the Jews is indeed one of the most inexplicable acts of the regime. Of the 300,000 Jews, French and foreign, in France in 1940, a number (unknown) were deported in 1941; in 1942 a further 42,000 were deported; in 1943–44, a further 33,000. In all perhaps 75,000 were slaughtered, one-third of these being of French nationality.[87] Between 27 March 1942 and 18 August 1944 eighty convoys of trains left France, carrying, according to another authority, about 80,000 deportees; it is stated that one-third of these were French.[88] Only 2,000–3,000 survived the death camps.[89]

If there was hatred of the Jews it was confined to the few, and was often for personal reasons. Few Christians really believed the measures against them were a 'punishment' for the death of Christ. Mgr Guerry's post-war apologia for the measures, that the presence of a Jewish minority impaired national unity, may be dismissed as an inadequate excuse. Nevertheless, for some Frenchmen, including some Christians, the Jews served as a convenient scapegoat for the defeat of 1940. As in Nazi Germany, the real motives for their persecution were in the end economic rather than racial — racialism merely gave a gloss of 'ideology' to the treatment meted out. The government held that they dominated unduly national life, particularly in the commercial and professional fields. Opportunists saw the chance to profit from the misfortune of others by joining in the expropriation of Jewish property. Church leaders, whilst not unkindly disposed to Jews that had been French for generations, believed that the influx of refugees before the war and after the defeat, coupled with an indiscriminate granting of French nationality, posed a 'problem' that threatened national unity and perhaps Christian culture.

Those same leaders, however, did not foresee the terrible consequences that flowed from their attitude. Tardily they protested. They criticised the deportations, although their reproaches seemed too often to bear more upon the manner rather than the act of deportation or its consequences. On humanitarian and religious grounds they opposed the separation of families, until the cruel dilemma was posed: either to allow children to leave with their parents to face an uncertain future, living at best in unbearable conditions, or to attempt to save them. Christian — Catholic and Protestant alike — resorted to clandestine means to rescue them. For the bishops, who believed that salvation for France could only come through the Marshal, this posed an agonising dilemma of loyalty. Some of the Hierarchy, such as Cardinal

Liénart, seemed to evade the choice by maintaining a public silence. For those Christians — and they were many — who opted against condoning persecution it was the catalyst for joining the Resistance. They did so with a good conscience, and thus helped to sustain French honour.

Although deportations continued, the last one taking place as late as August 1944, the Church's attention was diverted as it was confronted with another problem, one that concerned a larger body of people: the STO: the shipping off to Germany of young men as forced labour for the German war machine.

Notes

Unless otherwise stated the place of publication is Paris

1. FCO archives,: Microfilm frame No, 220417. German telegram 2322 of 14 September 1942, sent from Rome and signed Bergen.
2. FCO archives: Microfilm frame No. 220323. German telegram 3732 of 28 August 1942, signed Abetz, and frame No. 220282, German telegram 212 of 18 August 1942, signed Bergen.
3. AN F60.1674.A later document in this Fighting French file, ref: B 2725 'Note d'Orientation', La levée des crosses, August 1942, adds that Pétain retorted in turn to the effect that he relied on information from Bérard, his envoy to the Vatican: 'Je lis les rapports de mon ambassadeur.'
4. L. Papeleux, 'Le Vatican et le problème juif, 1941–1942', RHDGM, 107:1974, pp.79ff.
5. AN F60.1674. 'Note d'orientation', No. B 2725, August 1942.
6. Quoted in R. Bédarida, 'La Voix du Vatican (1940–1942). Bataille des ondes et Resistance spirituelle', Revue d'Histoire de l'Eglise, vol. 64, 1978, p. 224f.
7. H. de Lubac, Résistance chrétienne à l'antisémitisme. Souvenirs, 1940–1944, 1987, p. 171.
8. Papeleux, 'Le Vatican', p. 80.
9. De Lubac, Résistance chrétienne, pp. 169ff.
10. AN F60.1758. File E24, Radio Vatican, 21.00, 25 June 1943. Talk: 'The Church, Mother of Nations'.
11. P. Duclos, Le Vatican et la seconde guerre mondiale. Action doctrinale et diplomatique en faveur de la paix, 1955, pp. 189f.
12. Papeleux, 'Le Vatican', p. 79. Papeleux, who reports this incident, adds: 'Aucun document n'apporte la preuve que le Saint-Siège s'intéressa encore à ce douloureux problème.'
13. FCO archives: Microfilm frame 220498. Telegram 4340 (to Wilhelmstrasse) of 30 September 1942, signed Abetz: 'Die Judenfrage sei in letzter Zeit stark diskutiert werden, vor allem von kirchlicher Seite, was er [Pétain] nicht billige. Die Staatsräson musse vor jeder verständlichen Menschlichkeit walten'; Ein Teil der Klerus, vor allem der Pariser Erzbischof Suhard, haben hierfür grösseres Verständnis gezeigt als andere Bischöfe.'
14. The Tablet (London), 24 October 1942, reported in AN F60. 1758.
15. A. Cohen, 'Le peuple aryen vu par le Commissariat Général aux Questions Juives',

RHDGM, 141, January 1986, p. 50: 'il est de notoriété publique qu'en réalité il se fait champion des Juifs'. The author is much indebted to Cohen's article.

16. M. Marrus and R. Paxton, *Vichy France and the Jews*, New York, 1981, p. 299.
17. P. Bourdrel, *Histoire des Juifs de France*, 1974, p. 451.
18. Papeleux, 'Le Vatican', p. 80.
19. AN 2 AG 492.
20. Cited in de Lubac, *Résistance chrétienne*, p. 189.
21. *L'Œuvre*, 23 September
22. *L'Œuvre*, 22 October 1942, quoted in Bourdrel, *Histoire des Juifs*, p. 495
23. AN F60.1674.
24. AN 2 AG 492.
25. AN F60.1674, Folder B2725: 'La Chrétienté et l'Etat'.
26. AN F60.1674.
27. M. du Gard, *La Chronique de Vichy, 1940–1944*, 1948, pp. 286f.
28. AN F60.1674. 'Note d'orientation' No. 2212, Vichy, 4 September 1942.
29. AN F60.1674. 'Note d'Orientation' No. B2725.
30. Bourdrel, *Histoire des Juifs*, p. 495.
31. A.-M. Giaume, 'Brève contribution à l'étude du problème juif', *Bulletin d'Informations Corporatives*, (Nice), 5 October 1942, p. 1.
32. AN 2 AG 493. 'Réponse à une calomnie'.
33. AN 2 AG 492.
34. AN 2 AG 492.
35. Marrus and Paxton, *Vichy France*, p. 277, citing *La Semaine Catholique* (Toulouse), 82:39, 27 September 1942.
36. 2 AG 492. 'Note de police (Secret)', 6 October 1942.
37. AN 2 AG 461. CCXXXVI G. Synthèses des contrôles 5.5.42–10.11.43. No. 198 of 12 September 1942 and monthly summary covering 10 September–10 October 1942. Incidentally, it is perhaps significant that during the overall period of this batch of reports, covering one year and five months, there were only three references to Christians and the churches.
38. Bridoux, *Cahiers*, 2 October 1942, quoted in R. Tournoux, *Le Royaume d'Otto. France 1939–1945*, 1982, p. 160.
39. AN 2 AG 492. Police report, Vichy, 5 December 1942. 'Réactions du clergé français à la suite des événements d'Afrique du Nord'.
40. Marrus and Paxton, *Vichy France*, p. 197.
41. AN F60.1674. Report from the Franco-Swiss frontier published in *France* (London), 18 January 1943.
42. AN 2 AG 492. Report of Lavagne, of Pétain's Cabinet Civil: 'L'arrestation des juifs en France', ref: IV H.D. Vichy, 29 September 1943.
43. AN 2 AG 495. A letter from Catry to Lavagne dated Vichy, 26 April 1943, explained his background. The archives give a complete account of what became known as the 'Massada affair'.See also: Marrus and Paxton, *Vichy France*, pp. 310–15.
44. AN 2 AG 495. Lavagne, 'Note sur le mouvement "Massada" et son promoteur, M. Kadmi Cohen',Vichy, 2 June 1943.
45. Ibid., 'Note de l'abbé Catry', 12 December 1942.
46. Ibid.
47. P. Bolle, 'Les Protestants et leurs Eglises devant la persécution des juifs en France', mimeograph paper given at a colloquium held in Paris, 10–12 March 1979, CDJC, pp. 10f.
48. AN 2 AG 495. Letter of Chappoulie to Jardel dated 21 August 1943, and communication to Pétain dated 2 September 1943. Cf. also Marrus and Paxton, *Vichy France*, p. 326.
49. *Actes*: Lyons, p. 279.
50. Quoted in the clandestine publication *Libération* (*Sud*), 1 June 1943, which copied it from the London Gaullist paper, *La Marseillaise*.

51. AN 2 AG 609. Letter from Jean Mulson, Béziers, to Pétain, dated 20 June 1943.

52. *Actes*: Grenoble, pp. 162ff.

53. P. Joutard, J. Poujol and P. Cabanel, *Cévennes. Terre de refuge, 1940–1944*, Montpellier, 1987, pp. 17f; see also Philippe Boegner, *Ici on a aimé les Juifs*, 1982. A comprehensive local study of the Le Chambon area was made at a colloquium held there in 1990. The proceedings were published under the direction of P. Bolle by the Société d'Histoire de la Montagne, as *Le plateau Vivarais-Lignon. Accueil et Résistance, 1939–1944*, Le Chambon-sur-Lignon, 1992. Pasteur Trocmé, when told by the Prefect that the authorities were to proceed to the registration of local Jews, replied, 'We do not know who a Jew is, we only know human beings' (p. 12).

54. R. Nodot, 'Le pasteur Roland de Pury et les protestants de la région parisienne', *Réforme* (Paris), 15 May 1982.

55. Carlo Schmid, *Erinnerungen*, Frankfurt, 1979.

56. Nodot, 'Le pasteur Roland de Pury'. See also *Actes*: Grenoble. 'Discussion', in which Abbé Glasberg participated, pp. 204ff.

57. Joutard *et al.*, *Cévennes*, pp. 331f.

58. AN F60.1674.

59. Archives of the CDJC, Paris. File CDXCIV-7-8. This German document, headed, 'Entnommen aus Vorgang 80170/43g. Feindaktenmaterial 7. Akte Laval, 7.Januar 1943', mentions a figure of 200 children and asserts they were saved from deportation on Gerlier's instructions.

60. See *Actes*: Grenoble, Glasberg's intervention on p. 204 and Delpech's account on pp. 165ff.

61. H. Lottman, *The People's Anger. Justice and Revenge in post-Liberation France*, London, 1986, pp. 150f., quoting AN C.J. 171.

62. AN F60.1674.

63. AN F60.1674, p. 12.

64. FCO archives: Microfilm frame No. 2203435. Telegram 3818, dated 2 September 1942, signed Abetz.

65. AN F60.1674.

66. E. Jäckel, *Frankreich in Hitlers Europa*, Stuttgart, 1966, p. 312.

67. *Actes*: Grenoble, p. 178.

68. Bourdrel, *Histoire des Juifs*, p. 494.

69. Pétain, *Le procès du Maréchal Pétain*, vol. 1, 1945, p. 693.

70. Bourdrel, *Histoire des Juifs*, p. 494. Incidentally, after the war Jews put up a plaque in honour of Saliège, and a street in Haifa is named after him.

71. *Témoignage Chrétien*, no. 26–27. 'Exigence de la Libération'.

72. R. Debré, *L'honneur de vivre*, 1974, p. 229.

73. G. Wellers, *L'étoile jaune à l'heure de Vichy*, p. 350.

74. P. Pierrard, *Juifs et catholiques français. De Drumont à Jules Isaac*, 1970, p. 321.

75. M. Martin du Gard, *La Chronique de Vichy, 1940–1944*, 1948, p. 460.

76. *Actes*: Grenoble, Monique Lévi, 'Le destin des juifs et la solidarité chrétienne à Roanne entre 1940 et 1944', pp.181–99.

77. Pierrard, *Juifs et Catholiques*, p. 322.

78. C. Paillat. *L'Occupation. Le pillage de la France, juin 1940–novembre 1942*, 1987, pp. 634f.

79. *Actes*: Grenoble. F. Delpech. Discussion, p. 208, 'Le grand public et le petit peuple lyonnais savent qu'il a été très pétainiste mais lui accordent généralement les circonstances atténuantes.'

80. Cohen, 'Le peuple aryen', p. 57.

81. S. Klarsfeld, 'L'affaire Touvier: une dette immense à l'égard de l'Eglise', *Le Monde*, 3 June 1989.

82. Cohen, 'Le peuple aryen', p. 52, quoting AN AJ 38. 'Rapport du directeur de la section d'enquête et de contrôle en zone non-occupée', Vichy, 6 October 1942.

83. Bourdrel, *Histoire des Juifs*, 1974, p. 452.

84. *Actes*: Grenoble, p. 173.

85. Lavagne, 'Note sur le mouvement Massada'.
86. Ibid.
87. G. Cholvy and Y.-M. Hilaire, *Histoire religieuse de la France contemporaine, 1930–1988,* 1988, p. 98.
88. *Actes*: Lyons, pp. 275f.
89. Marrus and Paxton, *Vichy France,* p. 372.

PART IV

FRIENDS AND FOES

–10–

Christians and the Allies

Had it been a Christian act to open hostilities in September 1939? What attitude should Christians adopt towards France's former allies as they continued to wage war? What should be the Christian position after June 1941, when the Russian bear joined the British bulldog in the struggle? Both their countries, now allies, were fighting for their lives, although in France the one was feared for its ideology and the other mistrusted for its single-minded devotion to its own interests, seemingly at the expense of the French Empire. Then, when in December 1941 the United States entered the war, how did this change the situation? Such were the questions that exercised the minds of Christian theologians and intellectuals. Whereas Protestants perhaps judged events with greater equanimity, Catholics pondered what they might mean for the survival of their Church no less than the survival of France itself. The bishops had made their commitment to Pétain absolute. Did this mean a state of permanent neutrality? Few wanted a German victory, but most dreaded the triumph of communism. They found themselves between Scylla and Charybdis.

The Armistice had left France without allies, faced with the aftermath of a war cruelly lost. The general view was either that the Germans would be in London within a few weeks, or that a compromise peace, perhaps at French expense, would be worked out. French public opinion considered, with hindsight, that it had been foolhardy to declare war in 1939. But the question that agitated some Christians was not one of expediency but of principle: had the Allies been morally justified in beginning the conflict, and was there justification for continuing it?

Not until two years later was a detailed statement on the theological position, based upon Aquinas's doctrine of the just war, worked out. A document dated Christmas 1942 and merely signed 'a theologian', circulated clandestinely about this time. Its conclusion was that although the war had not been well prepared for, it was just. A pastoral letter of Mgr Guerry was even cited in evidence. Likewise, a war against the former allies would be unjust. Despite 'recent events' — an allusion to the North African landings — Catholics had meanwhile a duty to aid the Vichy regime insofar as it sought to promote the common good and to maintain public order.

The present position *vis-à-vis* the Germans required further detailed theological analysis. Were the Allies right to continue the war against them? This moral question had to be decided before France accepted or rejected a policy of collaboration. The occupiers had certainly violated international law in their treatment of the French. Pétain had resisted their demands, but had had to succumb to their pressure by tolerating the LVF and the Falange Africaine, and above all agree to the sending of forced labour to Germany. German conduct outside France had been sacrilegious, even in small matters. Cases of this were cited: in Luxembourg they had converted the abbey church of Clairvaux into a cinema, its crypt into a shower-room, and the Hitler Youth movement had supplanted the monks. But these were mere misdemeanours as compared with the sufferings they had inflicted on the Jews and Poles.

Collaborationism had therefore to be rejected. The Catholic attitude should be to remain faithful solely to France and the Church. The Armistice had submitted the country to temporary obligations. It had not created a state of neutrality and even less one of alliance with the victors. The Germans sought to shape France in accordance with National Socialist ideology, imposing a 'spiritual vassaldom' that imperilled not only national independence but the Christian faith. This was the greatest danger.[1] The theologian author of the document condemned the continuing war as waged by the Germans as unjust, but carefully refrained from pronouncing on the justification for the war that the three main Allies were now fighting.

It is doubtful whether the ordinary Christian bothered himself much with these general questions. Occasionally, however, there are surprising references to them from unexpected sources. Thus *Le Progrès de Finistère* published an article in February 1942,[2] which declared that the defeat had shaken the moral beliefs of Frenchmen, but 'an ideal does not lose its nobility, an idea does not cease to be right ['juste'] because it has been betrayed'.

One searches in vain among the many pronouncements of the higher clergy for such views. The striking exception was Archbishop Saliège, who was not afraid to speak his mind, or to fear his words would be reported. To Catholic Scouts obliged to leave to work in Germany he declared: 'Our cause was just, you can never be told this enough. If through our error, we lost the war, the justice of our cause remains intact.'[3] But wars are 'justified' by force of arms rather than words. How then should Christians react to what by then had become the Fighting French movement?

After the Armistice only a few hundred Frenchmen had rallied immediately to de Gaulle's call from London to continue the struggle. The General was unknown to most French Christians. His appeal of 18 June 1940 had gone unheard or unheeded. The Hierarchy backed the Armistice, and Catholics followed their lead. Protestants, however, were not so sure, as the story of Etienne Boegner, the son of Pastor Boegner, head of the Reformed Church, illustrates.

In the summer of 1940 Etienne Boegner, working for a French optical instrument firm, found himself outside France, where his German-born wife and children still were. By October 1940 he had made contact with the Gaullists and travelled from London to Lisbon, from where he hoped to contact his father and urge him to persuade 'Frenchmen of prominence and the highest moral standing' to come to Britain to give 'quality' to the Free French movement, as it then was — in itself an indictment of its unrepresentative nature. Failing to establish touch with his father, on 14 January 1941 he returned to London, where he was introduced to Lord Halifax, then Foreign Secretary, by no less a person than the Archbishop of Canterbury. By then he had changed his mind as to the wisdom of inducing Frenchmen to flee across the Channel. In view of the increased spirit of resistance (to the Germans) at Vichy, it was now preferable to establish contacts with Pétain and Weygand to apprise them of the mood prevalent in Britain. It was agreed that 'good' Frenchmen should now stay in France. He then returned to Lisbon.

On 12 April 1941 he wrote to his father, addressing him as 'Cher, cher père', and voiced his conviction of ultimate British victory. He urged his father to tell the truth about the war to Pétain and to anybody else who would listen. He believed his attitude was 'perfectly in accordance with that of the Marshal and yourself'.[4] It would seem there was a plan afoot, but which fell through, for American Protestants to invite Pastor Boegner to visit them, where his eyes would be opened to the stubborn resistance and high morale of the British. On 21 May 1941 Etienne Boegner spoke by telephone from Lisbon to his father, who was on a visit to Switzerland. The line was cut before the conversation ended but Pastor Boegner was able to say he had received his son's letter, and that things were going on at Vichy (at the time fresh measures were being taken against the Jews in the occupied zone and Darlan was acquiescing in the transit of German planes to Iraq via Syria) of which he thoroughly disapproved; he wished his friends abroad to know that he was 'absolutely against' the changes taking place.[5] It may be significant that these exchanges, obviously with British connivance, took place when Darlan was in power, on the supposition that Boegner may have had some influence over the Admiral. The Foreign Office[6] was aware, as it expressed it, that the two had been 'boys together' at the same school.

(Etienne Boegner then dropped out of the picture as regards Britain. He left for Canada and the USA. In late 1941 René Pleven proposed him to de Gaulle as head of the Free French delegation in the USA. In the event the General chose the other name put forward, the Socialist Tixier, later to become his first Interior minister. Boegner was, however, invited to act as temporary head of mission until Tixier was free to take up the appointment, and remained a member of the delegation, taking part in political discussions with Sumner Welles.[7] In 1942–43 he must have fallen out with the Gaullists because he was accused of intriguing against them and poisoning the minds of the Americans against de Gaulle.[8])

His son's recommendation against flight may have influenced Pastor Boegner to remain in France, although with his religious contacts in Geneva Churches he had more than one opportunity to leave. (He was of course even more influenced by Pétain's own resolve not to flee.) Nevertheless there is little doubt that most French Protestants believed in the righteousness of the Allied cause. Their problem up to late 1942 was to know how best to serve it. The options were: to escape to London; to contemplate active or passive resistance in France itself; or to moderate extremism at Vichy by participating in public affairs. Many Catholics faced the same dilemma.

In 1940, however, Gaullism as such had had a bad press. The acquiescence in the British attack at Mers-el-Kébir, and in the autumn the defection of part of the Empire to the Free French, had been counterbalanced by the failure at Dakar. These events did, however, succeed in making the name of their leader more widely known, as did BBC broadcasts, particularly in northern France. The belief remained widespread among Catholics, at least until the following spring, that the Marshal and the dissident General were secretly in league, as Canon Maréchal, the 'éminence grise' of the collaborationist Bishop of Arras, reported disapprovingly to the Head of State.[9] On May Day 1941, Pierre Nicolle, the industrialist, noted in his diary: 'The Gaullist movement is making progress, especially among the young, encouraged, it is said, by the clergy.'[10] A few months later the Jocistes, the members of the Catholic young workers movement, particularly in the Lille area, de Gaulle's birthplace, were already turning increasingly to London for a lead.[11]

Meanwhile, by that autumn de Gaulle's name had become anathema at Vichy. Speaking in the church of St Louis on the anniversary of the Dakar expedition (25 September 1941), and after the Vichy troops in Syria had had to surrender to a force that included Free French, Canon Moncelle, a counsellor at the Vatican embassy, dubbed their troops 'a band of rebels lacking any mandate, without brains and without heart, one that I shall not even name, since St Paul forbids us to do so in church'.[12]

The views of Protestants regarding de Gaulle about this time were uncertain. In Andouze (Gard), for example, those who had rallied to the Révolution Nationale professed also to be Gaullist, which gave rise to tension with the local Catholic minority. The Prefect even asked Pastor Boegner to straighten matters out. After the invasion of the Soviet Union Protestants, less convinced of a German victory, had certainly hardened in their attitude to Vichy.[13]

The bishops, by contrast, came out strongly against Gaullist 'dissidence'. The reaction of Mgr Flynn of Nevers is perhaps typical. Writing in the *Semaine religieuse* of Nevers (7 February 1942), he indignantly refuted a claim by Max Dupont, a journalist, that the French clergy seemed smitten by a 'chronic Gaullism'. On the contrary, he asserted, they dissociated themselves from the 'étrange aventure de Gaulle', which ran counter to Catholic morality and the ACA declaration of loyalty to the regime. Indeed strictly conformist Catholics did not hesitate to denounce Gaullist tendencies among their co-religionists. When the name of Abbé Duperray, the head of a seminary at Montbrison (Loire), was canvassed as a candidate for a vacant bishopric, the Marshal was promptly informed that the Abbé, as well as having been a Christian Democrat sympathetic to the Front Populaire, had become 'un gaulliste militant'.[14] No more was heard of his candidacy. Later a Carmelite nun, 'S.G.', from Agen — perhaps Sœur Geneviève, Pétain's niece — complained of 'the real evil that the Carmelite Fathers are doing here by subtly spreading their Gaullist theories in certain twisted minds'.[15]

Gaullism became a matter of concern for the Paris collaborationists. It was noted approvingly in *L'Œuvre* that at a service commemorating the first anniversary of the founding of the LVF, no less than Cardinal Suhard himself had pronounced the absolution for those Frenchmen who had fallen on the Russian front. This 'political gesture' was one on which Catholics would do well to reflect, for 'perhaps it will contribute to putting the brake on the wave of Gaullism that is unremittingly sweeping through the presbyteries and the [Catholic] charitable organisations'.[16]

The brake, however, was not effective. Even before the North African landings the local Vichy propaganda delegate signalled to the Prefect of Nord, Carles, a number of cases of flagrant disloyalty by clergy; the Prefect passed them on to Cardinal Liénart. Thus a school chaplain was accused of offering 'an apologia for the ex-General de Gaulle' and the priest of a Lille parish of 'singing the praises of the criminal General' ('faire l'éloge du général félon').[17] At the other extreme of France it was evident that young Catholics also were enthusiastic for the Fighting French. In February 1943 the police reported seminarists of Rodez as having 'very marked sympathies for their friends the English' ('des tendances bien marquées pour leurs amis les Anglais'), a fact that demonstrated their 'extreme Gaullism' ('du gaullisme à l'outrance').[18] The report went on to say that such sentiments were shared by all the religious orders, with the exception of the Christian Brothers. This was perhaps a little wide of the mark, although by then many young seminarists were in revolt at the threat of being called up for forced labour in Germany.

By 1943 the number of defectors to de Gaulle and the Allies was growing. Mgr Serrand of Saint-Brieuc, as their Bishop, exhorted his priests to have no truck with them, despite the fact that 'a few months ago we saw so many highly placed personages [who], one after another, trampled underfoot their most solemn oaths, before the whole world'.[19] This was a clear reference to Giraud and Darlan but an example good Catholics had not to follow.

In that same summer there had been a neutral assessment of Catholic opinion by a Swiss newspaper,[20] which neatly divided Catholics into three categories. The Catholic elites and the masses were either for Giraud or, with men such as Romier, Massis, Henry Bordeaux and Gustave Thibon, could be categorised as Vichy 'attentistes'. Then came a group of collaborationists, represented in the Catholic press by journals such as *Demain* and *Vaillance*, and by writers such as Chateaubriant and Daniel-Rops, the author, and publisher of the series *Présences*. The last group were the pro–Gaullists within France, either those such as the 'Rouges Chrétiens', with Communist tendencies, or others associated with *Témoignage Chrétien*, or the by now defunct *Esprit* and *Temps Nouveau*, whose protagonists abroad were Maritain and Bernanos. The survey did not mention two national organisations where Catholics were prominent which were also suspected of Gaullist leanings. The Secours National, headed by Garric, was reckoned to be clerical and 'attentiste', but looking towards the General. The French Red Cross was even described by Déat as being 'the aristocracy of Gaullism'.[21]

In fact, by mid-1943 Catholic opinion had begun to crystallise in the ways outlined. Undoubtedly the persecution of the Jews, the Allied successes in North Africa and forced labour in Germany had immeasurably helped the Gaullists. On the other hand, the Allied bombings, about which the bishops had begun to protest loudly earlier in the year, and the increasing activities of the Resistance, which some prelates characterised as 'terrorism', as we shall see, may have had a negative effect. Moreover, the Russians' stubborn resistance undoubtedly did revive the spectre of a Communist France. The question had become: if Germany lost the war, could catholicism win the peace?

Yet it was known that Catholics who had once been close to Pétain had now changed sides. François Valentin, of the very Pétainist Légion des Combattants, and a former ACJF leader, had reached London, and had spoken on the Fighting French radio in support of Gaullism.[22] There were, however, conflicting reports. In the autumn a London source reported the opinion of the prefects that the bulk of the clergy remained loyal to Vichy and only 'some' were Gaullist; the report added cryptically, 'the remainder rely on the traditional virtues of France'.[23]

By 1944 the alarm bells were ringing in some Catholic quarters even more insistently at the prospect of a total Allied victory. The hold of the Jews and Communists on the Algiers government was held to be firm, and damaging to the future of catholicism. De Gaulle had always said that 'la cathédrale (lui) envoie moins de monde que le synagogue'. In February 1944, there were persistent rumours of a negotiated peace. Might not this be the best solution for French Catholics?[24] This had undoubtedly been one reason for the bishops rallying round Pétain once more in 1943, despite the difficult relations between them and Vichy that had arisen by the end of the previous year.

After the Normandy invasion, however, the time for speculation was past. On 18 June 1944 Mgr Picaud, Bishop of liberated Bayeux, had greeted the General and officiated at the first Te Deum in freed French territory. This had upset many Catholics. François Garreau, writing in a newspaper appearing in the occupied zone, declared it ran counter to the relations Vichy enjoyed with the Vatican. However, the luckless bishop could do no right. A British Catholic periodical charged him with having been proud, distant and formal with the General.[25] The reception of de Gaulle by the Pope later threw Catholics into further disarray. Xavier Vallat, a prominent Catholic, waxed sarcastic on Radio Vichy:

De Gaulle is not only the head of the faithful, of all the faithful, he is also one of the new top authorities of the world, and of the free world, thank God... I do not acknowledge his authority, but to refuse him a grace would be to have to refuse advice to a [one word inaudible] soul... An audience with the Pope is a grace he grants, it does not mark any adherence [to de Gaulle]... It would be an exaggeration to say that it constitutes a recognition by the Vatican of a government of France... Rest assured, the Pope has not turned Gaullist.[26]

Nevertheless, there was a perceptible change in the attitude of some bishops after the Bayeux meeting and the papal audience. Abetz, the German Ambassador, noted that Cardinal Suhard had become more cautious and reserved. His utterances after the assassination of Philippe Henriot had been even more guarded.[27] The total liberation of the country, which did not lead to the feared Communist takeover of government, left many Catholics — among them not a few bishops — looking somewhat sheepish and not a little bewildered. Whilst they had not exactly backed the wrong horse, they had certainly not chosen the winner. It was an error for which some Gaullists were determined they would pay dearly.

Attitudes towards Gaullism were of course coloured by French Christians' views of the Allies in general, which also evolved. The events of 1940 had confirmed the traditional French opinion of 'la perfide Albion'. Only a few took a long-term view. The initial question was whether Britain could hold out. Gabriel Marcel, the Catholic philosopher, writing to Mgr Fessard, the theologian, in August 1940, was convinced it could, despite the 'slave dictatorship' the Germans had imposed upon France in order to finish the war quickly.[28] His conviction was shared by some of the rank and file clergy. Thus the Marseilles gendarmerie reported on the parish priest of Berre in the autumn of 1940: 'In every one of his Sunday sermons [he] regularly exalts England and predicts its victory. This priest is becoming popular and never have his sermons had such success.'[29]

Even so close a confidant of the Marshal in 1940 as the Protestant philosopher and literary critic, René Gillouin, who wrote some of Pétain's speeches at the time, was reckoned to be a subversive, an agent of the infamous 'Intelligence Service', who made out Laval was engaged in the black arts, such as table-turning, casting spells and involving himself in Black Masses.[30] Meanwhile Marc Boegner, whose misgivings regarding Vichy have already been mentioned above, as head of the Protestants was accused by his right-wing co-religionist, Noel Vesper (Pastor Noel Nougat) of 'Anglophilie'. Another influential Catholic voice, General Castelnau, the FNC president, wrote to his friend Charles Mellerio in April 1941, after the Battle of Britain, denouncing the Vichy regime — there was no love lost between the Marshal and his fellow general of the First World War: 'Whether we wish it or not, there is patently a divorce between the spirit of Vichy and that of the majority of citizens, even [sic] in the occupied zone. Vichy is fiercely Anglophobic, whereas France pins its hopes on the liberation, on the victory of the Anglo-Saxon world.'[31]

He, for one, had seen through the claim of the regime to represent the people. As the head of the largest Catholic adult movement his opinion carried weight.

Not all 'bien pensants' shared his view of the situation. Another letter, presumably to Cardinal Liénart since it is preserved in the Lille diocesan archives, from the aristocratic-sounding Catholic, Du Plessin de Grenadan, written in May 1941, is proof of how deeply Christians were divided. Since 1870, the writer declared, Britain had continually betrayed France, as it had done in previous centuries by burning Joan of Arc and appropriating parts of the burgeoning French Empire. Colonies had been attacked, raids carried out on French merchant shipping; other more recent events had exposed British perfidy. What were Muselier ('the corrupted admiral' — 'l'amiral taré'), Catroux or de Gaulle worth as compared with Pétain? The leader of the Free French had enticed French youth down the wrong path: 'Nothing can any longer cleanse that man of the French blood on his hands, nor from the division that he has brought about among Frenchmen.'[32] Since Europe would emerge from the conflict ruined, collaboration with all countries (which doubtless included Germany) would be required.

The attack on the USSR reinforced diehard opinion. Typical perhaps was the reaction of Mgr Piguet, Bishop of Clermont-Ferrand. He took his lead from Pius XII, who, the bishop said, saw the onslaught on Russia as a 'crusade' against bolshevism. (He was mistaken: although Cardinal Baudrillart spoke of it in these terms, the Pope never used the word in this context.) The British were allied to the Communists; it was they — Protestants, incidentally! — who were bombing France, not the Germans. His hope lay in a united, Catholic Europe.[33] The concept of a New Order in a Europe without Britain was common talk about this time. Generally, however, whatever their private views, the bishops at first spoke only discreetly regarding the war against the Soviet Union. On the other hand, the behaviour of the British in 1940 continued to rankle.

Mgr Serrand, Bishop of St-Brieuc, whose loquacity generally was to land him in trouble at the Liberation, set out to his clergy his view regarding the British in 1941. He was neither Anglophile nor Germanophile, he declared, but French. While he still retained some remnants of sympathy and even friendship for the British, their rulers had inflicted grievous wounds on France. As for the Germans, he, as a veteran of the First World War, considered the French had obligations towards them as the occupying power; they were not implacable, and, in his view, 'ils dominent leur victoire'.[34]

The events of autumn 1942 kindled fresh hope among Christians, who began to see the Americans as playing the deciding role in the future of France. Some, however, such as the Nice clergy, still feared that this might well lead to a Communist takeover or at the very least a return to the bad old days of the Front Populaire. On the other hand increased collaboration with the Germans, which the new powers assigned to Laval signified, remained unpalatable.[35] By December there were even reports of a resurgence of pro-British sentiment in Catholic circles. The brother of Mgr Bruno de Solages was the subject of a police report for his 'Anglophilie'.[36]

Nevertheless the question of the attitude to be adopted towards the Soviet Union continued to exercise Church authorities. Opinion vacillated. In January 1943, however, it was alleged that in the entourage of Cardinal Suhard — Mgr Chaptal was specifically cited — the belief was that, contrary to Laval's view, the USSR had abandoned its aim of installing communism everywhere in Europe. If this were the case, France's role on the continent would be more secure.[37] The police reported that by 1943 anti-Soviet propaganda in the southern zone had been achieving less success. In February Catholics in Nice had shifted their position: their view now also was that the Soviets were becoming more tolerant of religion. They adduced the better relations existing between Stalin and Metropolitan Sergei of the Orthodox Church, and asserted that agreement would soon be reached with the Pope about Catholics in the Soviet Union.[38] This new attitude towards the USSR was alleged to be unwelcome to Cardinal Gerlier, who was seen as firmly anti-Communist. To another leading Catholic, Le Cour Grandmaison, he had confided his fear that even the higher clergy were weakening in their opposition to communism, although his rural priests still stood firm against the 'Bolshevik peril'.[39]

The cardinal, however, was now being openly attacked by collaborationists. Fantastic rumours went the rounds. Thus in March 1943 a tract circulating in the Lyons area entitled, 'Lyonnais, voici ton maître', reproached him for his 'softness' towards the Jews, and asserted that his record was that of a 'politicien' — the appellation is pejorative — who had been secretary to Paul Boncour and associated before the war with men such as Zay, Sarraut, Mandel and Herriot. Now, 'thirsting for honours and drunk with pride' ('assoiffé d'honneur et ivre d'orgueil') he was after the papacy, which, in a secret agreement approved by the Masonic orders, had been promised him after the war by Britain, which was determined to break the Italian monopoly of the Holy See.

In that spring some religious orders were even reported as being pro-Soviet. From their convents they followed assiduously the progress of the Soviet armies in the Swiss Catholic newspaper, *La Liberté*, published in Neuchâtel, which had consistently lauded Soviet prowess and courage.[40] Meanwhile Cardinal Liénart, all unwittingly, was receiving the plaudits of Moscow, both for his advice regarding the STO and his defence of the trade unions against Vichy's reorganisation policy.

On 21 April 1943 Radio Moscow was reported as saying: 'We must give great praise to Cardinal Liénart. He could not oppose all collaborationist measures. The Communists will be able to help the cardinal to defend the Christian unions at present being attacked by the Boches and the men of Vichy.'[41] In fact, about this time collaborationists were putting round the slogan: 'Crusade of the democracies, Catholic crusade. Should one go further and state openly: Soviet war = Church war?'[42]

Indeed throughout 1942 a polemic regarding the Church's future had been carried on in the collaborationist press. Déat wrote a series of articles in *L'Œuvre* stating that the moment had come for the Church to opt for a 'European revolution'. He rounded off the year by reiterating that the Church had to choose between the old order and 'le nouvel ordre communautaire'. In a new, revolutionary atmosphere the Church could rejuvenate its own 'totalitarianism' by contact with the 'young states'.[43] It should, he warned, beware of the Protestants, who were strongly represented in Algiers. This drew a broadside from Le Cour Grandmaison, as Vice-President of the FNC, in *La France catholique* (3 March 1943), counter-claiming that it was for Déat's 'revolution' to choose, but in favour of a Christian solution. Jacques de Lesdain, of the collaborationist *L'Illustration*, had joined in the argument, charging the Church with fearing Nazi totalitarianism more than bolshevism, because it was apprehensive that the former would destroy its dogmas, whereas — and this on a note of irony — the latter would merely persecute it until it had had its fill of corpses. (Some Catholics, as we have seen, were indeed resigned to a Communist bloodbath in the event of an Allied victory. Others felt that the threat of Russia overrunning France was real. The visit of the Archbishop of York to Moscow was seen as a preliminary to an alliance of Anglicanism and Orthodoxy against the papacy.) Paul Chack, a collaborationist like Déat, berated Catholic leaders for not calling for a ninth crusade: did they not realise that the Germans were the sole remaining bulwark of the Church? The clergy, blinded by Allied propaganda, had naively believed that Moscow and the Vatican had struck a bargain in the summer — but the leopard had not changed its spots.[44]

Protestants continued indeed to be suspected of Allied sympathies. German suspicion fastened upon the Salvation Army, 'une armée anglo-saxonne'. In the northern zone its religious activities had been banned, but its welfare activities had been allowed to continue. However, in 1943 it was finally wound up in both zones (Decree of 1 September 1943), despite two protests from the Secours National, which particularly valued its work in providing soup kitchens, and material aid to refugees and prisoners of war. Pastor Boegner also protested to Laval,[45] claiming that the movement was no more 'anglo-saxon' than the Catholic Church was Italian. The reply came back that a stop had been put to its activities at the Germans' request, because the movement was suspected of spying for the Allies.[46] Some of its welfare activities were eventually taken over by the Protestant organisation, L'Œuvre des Diaconesses. It would seem that at the same time the Germans had also requested the disbanding of the Quakers — presumably also because of their English connections, and despite the high esteem in which the Germans had held them in the First World War — and, for good measure, even of the Frères de la Doctrine Chrétienne (Christian Brothers).[47]

Towards the end of the Occupation the Hierarchy, perhaps like Pétain himself, pinned their hopes increasingly on the Americans rather than the British. They noted how de Gaulle, whom generally they disliked, was ignored by Roosevelt, how Vichy had been able to maintain until comparatively recently diplomatic relations with the US and Canada. They had been gratified in early 1941 when Cardinal Villeneuve, Archbishop of Quebec, had praised Pétain in a speech.[48] The stock of the British had gone down — although their accuracy in bombing military targets was compared favourably with the more indiscriminate pattern bombing of the Americans. Contrary to belief, perhaps even in northern France 'Anglophilie' as such was not so widespread as it had been in 1940. A Catholic, later a priest, from Boulogne, then a young man, has testified that the 487 Allied bombings of his town had been hard to take. Despite his own Resistance activities and the delusion, at least until 1942, that the General and the Marshal were in cahoots, the young Boulonnais had a gut reaction ('réaction épidermique') against the British; any remaining love for them was 'un amour de raison'.[49]

It is to the Church's reaction to these bombings and other acts which some bishops lumped together as 'terrorisme' that we now turn.

Notes

Unless otherwise stated the place of publication is Paris

1. AN 2 AG 492. Document signed 'a theologian'.
2. 'C.G.', 'Catholiques et Français', *Le Progrès de Finistère*, 1 February 1942.
3. Quoted in the *Courrier de Genève*, 10 September 1943,
4. PRO FO. 371 (1941) 28446. File: M Etienne Boegner.
5. Ibid. Report by letter 349/5/41 dated 25 May 1941, British Embassy, Lisbon, to R.R. Makins, Foreign Office, London, signed by Sir Norman Charles.
6. PRO FO.. 371 (1941) 28446.
7. C. de Gaulle, *War Memoirs,* vol. I, *The Call to Honour*, 1940–1942, Documents, London, 1955, p. 225.

8. PRO FO 371 (1944) 42075. File: Religious Matters.
9. AN 2 AG 74. SP1. Letter to Pétain from Canon Maréchal, Vicar-General, archbishopric of Arras, Arras, 6 April 1941.
10. P. Nicolle, *Cinquante mois d'armistice. Vichy 2 juillet 1940–26 août 1944. Journal d'un témoin*, 1947, vol. 1, p.243.
11. L. Berthe, 'La JOC du Pas-de-Calais pendant la guerre', *Actes*: Lille.
12. AN F60.1764. Revue de presse B2725.
13. AN 72 AJ 429. Report of Prefect of Gard to Interior minister, Nîmes, 10 September 1941.
14. AN 2 AG 492. CC. 72 BC. Dossier: 'Divers'. Letter from F——, 14 January 1942.
15. AN 2 AG 609. Letter from 'S-G' [Sœur Geneviève?] of 'S-B', Agen, 1 May 1942, to Cabinet Militaire of Pétain.
16. *L'Œuvre*, 29–30 August 1942.
17. A Dio, Lille. Guerre 1939–1945. 'du '39 à '42': letter of Prefect to Mgr Liénart, Lille, 11 October 1942.
18. AN 2 AG 492. 'Note de Police (Secret): Politique religieuse du PPF'. Vichy, 20 February 1943.
19. AN 2 AG 82. SP 10E *Eglise catholique*. Letter of Mgr Serrand to be communicated to his clergy.
20. *Vaterland* (Zurich), 16 June 1943.
21. M. Déat, 'Les Jeunes dans les ruines', *Le National-Populaire*, 11 September 1943.
22. AN 2 AG 75. Correspondance de Ménétrel.
23. AN F60.1674. 'L'opinion des préfets sur le clergé français'. Bureau de presse de la France Combattante, 2 September 1943.
24. AN Fla.3784.
25. *Echo de France*, 20 June 1944; *The Tablet*, 1 July 1944.
26. Recording made by Fighting French of talk entitled, *La Chrétienté et l'Etat'*, Radio Vichy, 19.30, 9 July 1944.
27. Telegram to Berlin ref: 3410/14.7.44; text given in full in: PRO. FCO Archives No. 6455 GFM2.
28. G. Marcel and G. Fessard, *Correspondance*, 1985. Letter headed Clermont-Ferrand, 24 August 1940.
29. Quoted in C. Paillat, *L'Occupation. Le pillage de la France,* 1987, p. 197.
30. M. Martin du Gard, *La Chronique de Vichy, 1940–1944*, 1948, p. 87.
31. Cited in P. Reynaud, *La France a sauvé l'Europe*, Aix, 1947, vol. 2, p. 541.
32. A Dio, Lille. Dossier: Pétain 8M9: Folder 117/3.
33. J. F. Sweets, *Choices in Vichy France. The French under Nazi Occupation*, New York, 1986, p. 133.
34. AD du Nord, IW 1262. The letter, although written in 1941, was circulating in the Lille area in July 1944.
35. AN F60.1674. Note d'orientation No. 60. Commissariat National à l'Intérieur, London, quoting intelligence report from Vichy dated 25 November 1942.
36. AN 2 AG 492. Rapport des Renseignements Généraux, Vichy, 5 December 1942.
37. AN 2 AG 492 CC72 BC,.'Note (secret)', 30 January 1943.
38. AN 2 AG 492 'Note (secret)', Vichy , 2 March 1943.
39. AN 2 AG 492 'Note (secret)', 25 February 1943.
40. AN F60.1674. 'Résistance du clergé français', NM. 229 (AG). 13 April 1943.
41. A Dio, Lille. Letter signed Kervarec, Commissariat aux Renseignements Généraux, Lille, to Préfet du Nord, 3 May 1943, citing a Radio Moscow broadcast, 22.30, 21 April 1943.
42. Ibid.
43. M. Déat, 'Entre l'Eglise et l'Etat',, *L'Œuvre*, 13 December 1943.
44. P. Chack, 'Troisième Lettre à un prélat', *Aujourd'hui*, 31 August 1943; see also *Aujourd'hui*, 30 September 1943.
45. AN 2 AG 487. Letter from Pastor Boegner to Laval, Nîmes, 4 February 1943.

46. Hoover Institution, *France during the German Occupation, 1940–1944*, Stanford, 1958, vol. 2, p. 86.
47. According to Georges Hilaire, then Secretary-General for Administration in the Interior ministry . See also Hoover Institution, *France,* vol. 1, p. 401.
48. H. Du Moulin de Labarthète, *Le Temps des illusions*, Geneva, 1946, p. 127.
49. Testimony of Canon Danton, *Actes*: Lille.

-11-

Christians, Bombings and 'Terrorism'

Although northern France sustained prolonged bombing throughout the war, it was not until late 1942 that Allied air raids became extensive over the whole country, when to the terror by night was added that of the arrow that flies by day, in the shape of the American Flying Fortresses. Likewise, although active Resistance was apparent almost immediately after the collapse, it was not until 1943 that the Maquis, led by the FFI, Gaullist or Allied agents, spread its net over the national territory. It was these new manifestations of war that caused some ecclesiastics to speak of 'terrorism', a characterisation that some had later cause to regret. Many bombs did indeed rain down indiscriminately and not a few exploits by so-called 'patriots' were carried out by robber bands whose links with the genuine forces of Resistance were often tenuous or non-existent. The clandestine publication *Témoignage Chrétien* drew clear distinctions between what were legitimate acts of war and what were not, but reminded Frenchmen of the sacrifice made in 1914–18, when 1,000 soldiers had been killed every day for four years.[1] To their great credit many civilians accepted stoically and courageously these new trials as harbingers of hope and heralds of ultimate German destruction.

The RAF raid on the Renault works at Boulogne-Billancourt (3–4 March 1942), which killed 623 people, aroused the first significant ecclesiastical reactions. Père Roguet spoke of it on Radio Lyons: 'In the name of law, humanity and France, we condemn these assassins and butchers.'[2] The Hierarchy was, however, more restrained. The clandestine *Voix du Nord* (18 March 1942) acknowledged the dignity shown by Cardinal Suhard at the funeral ceremony held in Notre Dame, when he declared that the victims had died for France, although no one would wish to make a spectacle of their suffering. *Témoignage Chrétien* praised the cardinal, who had characterised the bombings as the 'douleureuse conséquence de l'état de guerre'.[3] But his failure to condemn the 'crime' or name the 'assassins' drew down the wrath of the collaborationist press.[4] A similar reticence observed by the Archbishop of Rouen after the bombing of his see on 5 September was also condemned by Paul Chack, the collaborationist journalist ('Seconde lettre à un prélat', *Aujourd'hui*, 7 October 1942). But then, added Chack for good measure, the priests of the diocese had likewise omitted to mention the name of the murderers of Joan of Arc on her feast day; had not the British, he mendaciously alleged, unloaded leaflets after the raid bearing the message, 'Vous êtes nos ennemis. Nous détruirons la France?'

By 1943, however, the position of the bishops regarding both the bombings and Resistance activities had hardened dramatically. Mgr Duparc was quoted on 2 February 1943 as declaring that the recent bombing of Morlaix was 'a new bloodstain that barbarism has just added to the catalogue of its exploits'. According to one source, in the raid forty-two kindergarten children and forty other civilians had been killed.[5] When Brittany again came under fire in March, this time it was Mgr Roques (Rennes) who spoke out: the 'Anglo-Americans' had committed a crime: 'War, even with all its chance occurrences, does not justify a massacre of the innocents.'[6] It was a sentiment widely shared at the time. Meanwhile, the martyrdom of northern France continued. After a raid on the Lille area in January Cardinal Liénart had declared: 'When it [war] becomes carnage it deserves to be condemned.'[7] After another raid on Lille the following month he returned to the attack, referring to 'these bombs which have once again haphazardly sown the seeds of death, cutting down women and children. In the face of this dreadful war we have the right to protest.'[8]

The renewed bombing of Rouen in March, coupled with the terrible destruction wrought at Amiens, now inspired the same sentiments in Mgr Petit de Julleville: the feeble excuse of the British that it was war would not wash; there were higher realities such as law and justice that had to be observed.[9] Nor was Paris spared a fresh attack. In April another raid occurred on Boulogne-Billancourt, which claimed 220 victims. This time Cardinal Suhard likewise changed his tone; his theme was justice: 'Justice will never admit that such powers of destruction should be unleashed without strict discrimination.'[10] It was notable, however, that the bishops did not always condemn the bombing campaign as such, but insisted more on its indiscriminate nature. However, a similar change of attitude is discernible in May, when it was the turn of Brest. This time, since Lyons had adopted the 'ville sinistrée', it was Cardinal Gerlier himself who went to view the damage and hold a funeral ceremony for the victims. The note of condemnation was more severe. After touring the town, he commented on 'the dreadful sights [he had] seen, in the face of which we cannot restrain the shock to our conscience' and at the requiem mass asserted: 'War has its inexorable necessities but who could say that it justifies everything, particularly when there is such a huge disparity between the sufferings inflicted on the civil population and the results achieved?'[11]

The outskirts of Paris were bombed again in July. Cardinal Suhard now went further and taxed those responsible for the raid as war criminals; his attitude had appreciably hardened: 'Once more we repeat that those responsible for such atrocities must bear the responsibility for their crimes.'[12] Such comments were gratifying to the Germans and the collaborationists. The latter were particularly anxious to stir up hostility towards the former Allies. Thus a Rheims priest was attacked in *L'Appel* (1 July 1943) for a Good Friday homily in which, after having spoken of 'le calvaire que gravit la France', he had failed even to mention the raids.

By then it was generally realised that, so far as France was concerned, the war was entering a new, more violent phase. A majority of Frenchmen acknowledged this, not necessarily approvingly, but at least with a nod towards necessity. If and when the invasion came, it would now be France that would be the battlefield. The bombings therefore might be regarded as an indispensable preliminary. A minority, which included a few articulate bishops, as well as the regime and the collaborationists, now fiercely attacked the Allies. In the summer of 1943 Mgr Piguet (Clermont-Ferrand) declared there were no longer any laws of war: 'Its evils [have] today become cataclysms of extermination.'[13] Paul Chack, in his third 'Lettre à un prélat' (*Aujourd'hui*, 31 August 1943), sarcastically apologised for disturbing again the 'pious meditations' of the Archbishop of his diocese, Rouen, who must, he surmised, be nevertheless secretly filled with horror at the bombings. However, Mgr Petit de Julleville, after another raid on 4 September 1943, wrote to Dr Ménétrel at Vichy revealing his feelings: 'So as not to get too much out of the habit, we were bombed this morning. It is not easy to see what could have been aimed at, but the clearest result has been the demolition of a few more houses and the death of a score of my fine citizens of Rouen.'[14]

By 1943 the activities of the Resistance were also becoming ever more widespread, and arousing episcopal anger. However, when Laval asked the ACA to issue a declaration condemning 'terrorist' attacks, it refused, stating that the Church's position was well known. The rejection was undoubtedly motivated by a mistrust of Laval's motives and a reluctance to appear to be acting at the behest of the civil power.[15] At an Armistice commemoration service Cardinal Liénart nevertheless declared that the 'terrorists' represented a false patriotism[16] and Mgr Béguin, Archbishop of Auch, joined in the condemnation a few days later. The latter spoke of the 'menées terroristes' and for the first time raised a new spectre, that of civil war. Such a fratricidal struggle would, he declared, be horrific[17] In December Mgr Le Bellec (Vannes) used the term 'le banditisme' to describe what was rife in his diocese.[18] The Gestapo intervened to demand that Cardinal Suhard speak out against the 'dissidents'. This he refused to do, although he did hold out a vague hope that the ACA would meet to discuss the situation,[19] and the next day, in a Christmas message, warned against extremism, which would lead to Frenchmen killing more Frenchmen.[20]

The year 1944 brought a further crop of episcopal pronouncements the length and breadth of France. Mgr Dutoit (Arras) tried to pour oil on troubled waters: alien voices wanted to provoke civil war, in their own interests; terrorism was abroad in the land; but, thanks to Marshal Pétain, 'it is indisputable that goodwill and understanding reign between the French and German authorities' — a view that was not to help him a few months later when he was accused of collaborationism.[21] In a pastoral letter Mgr Megnin (Angoulême) also raised the nightmare of fratricidal strife: 'The assassinations, the acts of banditry are terrible... Is it love of country that incites Frenchmen to mete out death and spread the germs of civil war?'[22] Mgr Villeplet (Nantes), in a pastoral letter condemning the 'luttes fratricides', accused certain members of the Catholic bourgeoisie of now looking to Moscow for salvation. 'Maurice Jacques', in a radio commentary on the message, remarked that this was 'far removed from the cosy personal religion that a clique of "bien pensants" had worked out for themselves since the Armistice, [a group] who see salvation for Christianity only in the bloodstained cassocks of priests massacred by the genial "Pope Joseph", otherwise named Stalin'.[23] The reproach was not without substance. After November 1942 some of the Catholic bourgeoisie had indeed retreated into a religious hibernation, from which they hoped they could emerge at an Allied victory. Occasionally specific acts of 'terrorism' were commented on by the bishops. Thus Mgr Choquet (Tarbes), lamenting an attack on a Pau-Toulouse express train, asked: 'Who in France would not grow indignant at such an exploit? Patriotism has no need of such criminal acts.'[24]

In vain did Cardinal Suhard declare that patriotism could not justify anarchy. In vain did the Archbishop of Auch appeal for national unity 'around the flag and him who bears it'. (See: 'France: what the bishops are saying', *The Tablet*, London, 22 January 1944.) By February 1944 matters were approaching a climax, as the run-up to the invasion accelerated bombings and active resistance. Dr Bell, the Anglican Bishop of Chichester, spoke out in the House of Lords: the Allies would incur almost universal hatred if they continued their heavy-handed raids. Almost simultaneously, for the ACA the three cardinals at last issued their own declaration (17 February 1944), which was partly censored. Apart from the bombings, the statement incidentally inveighed against the general misery being experienced by the poor, linked to the requirement for social justice, and the conscription of women for the STO, which was then rumoured to be mooted. These last points, which are dealt with elsewhere, were struck out by the censorship.

The censoring of the text was undertaken on the direct orders of Henriot, the once active propagandist for catholicism. Not only were passages omitted, but words were changed, so that the general effect was to distort the whole tenor of the declaration. Among the uncensored passages was a condemnation of the bombing of open towns and 'terrorism': 'It will be said that these are the laws of war. No! A state of war, however abnormal and inhuman it may be in itself, does not justify all such measures.'[25] War, it went on, indeed had its laws, but primacy must go to those fixed by natural morality and divine law. The essential principles on which civilisation was based were the respect for the person, the safeguarding of the family home, and faithful adherence to the rule of law. (There followed another passage that had been struck out: 'Above the law of the State and the immediate interest of every nation [is] that of peaceful understanding among peoples ('supérieure à l'autorité de l'Etat et aux intérêts immédiats de chaque nation, [est] l'entente pacifique entre les peuples').' The message went on to proclaim that France's mission had always been to defend civilisation. To continue to do so in a future Europe at peace it must constitute one national community. 'This is why we condemn these appeals to violence and these acts of terrorism, which today are tearing the country apart... ' ('C'est pourquoi nous condamnons ces appels à la violence et ces actes de terrorisme, qui déchirent aujourd'hui le pays... '). Another censored passage followed: 'Action must be taken in the way we have indicated... it is the very grave duty of those who bear the heavy responsibility for nations, it is also a categorical duty for each one of us to restore his own conscience.' ('Il faut qu'on agisse dans le sens que nous avons rappelé... c'est le devoir très grave de ceux qui portent la lourde responsabilité des Etats, c'est aussi un devoir impérieux pour chacun d'opérer le redressement de sa propre conscience.')

Altogether about half of the declaration had been censored. The text was, however, published in full, with a commentary, in the *Gazette de Lausanne* (Robert Vaucher, 'En France, la voix de l'Eglise étouffée', 1 April 1944). *La Croix* was ordered to publish the bowdlerised version. Cardinal Gerlier instructed it not to do so but insisted that the message should appear in its entirety. Laval intervened, and would not give way, although he finally accepted the refusal of *La Croix* to publish the censored message — the rest of the press had tamely followed the orders of the censorship and published the amended text — and did not even suspend the newspaper. So the semi-official organ of catholicism was the only publication in which no word of the declaration appeared. However, the uncensored text quickly became known, via the Swiss press. Thus *The Tablet* quoted the full text from another Swiss source, the *Journal de Genève* (31 March 1944). The Paris press naturally expressed its hostility to the declaration. *L'Œuvre* (9 March 1944), under the title 'Réticence inutile', characterised it as verbose and tortuous, providing arguments for the disaffected and the Maquis. The Church had no right to question government decisions. *Le Cri du Peuple* saw the declaration as the definitive breach of the Church with Vichy, a divorce that would end with the clergy siding with the Resistance. However, Paul Chack took a different line: after a routine attack on his local archbishop, he spoke approvingly of the declaration, which 'nails the responsibility on those states which are the accomplices of the Red Tsar, the sovereign of the Godless'.[26] Certainly it does seem, if it can be deduced from one sentence in their message, as if the Church leaders were at the end of their tether: 'It is in no one's power to apply an immediate remedy to the state of disorder denounced in our declaration' ('Il n'est au pouvoir de personne d'apporter un remède immédiat à l'état de désordre dénoncé par notre déclaration'). It was surely a counsel of despair.

The tone of the document aroused the anger of Mgr Saliège (Toulouse), whose health had not permitted him to attend the meeting of the ACA at which the declaration had been drawn up. His letter to Cardinal Liénart was couched in harsh terms:

> This document speaks of only one kind of terrorism. It remains silent concerning the terrorism of denunciation which has brought it about that at present there are now over 300,000 French civilians prisoner in Germany, a number that is increasing daily. It is a one-way condemnation. I am persuaded that this omission was involuntary. The public, even the Christian public, will attribute it, and seemingly not unreasonably, to a different motive... Do you not think that people will find that much time has been spent in lamenting the misdeeds of total war that have, however, occurred since 1940, and that it will not be said that the bishops only protest when their own interests are jeopardised?[27]

He finished prophetically by saying that the document, because of its omissions and timidity, could only portend an unhappy future for the Church; it was a fresh concession to State totalitarianism. The rather lame reply he received from Cardinal Liénart, as president of the ACA, was that the document had not been inspired by fear, and could indeed lend itself to 'malevolent interpretations' ('des interprétations malveillantes').[28] But it had been unanimously approved by the ACA. There the matter rested.

The bombings intensified during the spring of 1944. Mgr Delay (Marseilles), after the devastation of part of the conurbation, characterised it as 'a crime without excuse'.[29] A raid in May on St-Etienne was denounced by its Auxiliary Bishop, Mgr Bornay.[30] The Lille area was still suffering enormously. Again Cardinal Liénart, at yet another funeral for civilian victims, in April, appealed to the Allies to call a halt, 'to spare the lives of our people and to give up methods of combat that attack us so harshly'.[31] This drew Déat's approval in *L'Œuvre*, who otherwise bore no love for the cardinal. A month later, on a similar occasion, Liénart returned to the subject in even more piteous terms: 'If at least [my voice] could reach to the hearts of the British and Americans, I would show them this people of France, whose fate is infinitely worthy of respect.'[32]

Despite the severe tone of his letter to Cardinal Liénart, Mgr Saliège now joined in the chorus of condemnation. After a second bombing of Toulouse, at a funeral service for the victims, he instructed Abbé Sapène to read out a message: 'Total war is inhuman, contrary to natural law, to international law. The Church condemns it as it condemns all injustices, all acts of cruelty, all barbarism.'[33] One notes however that his indictment was not specifically aimed at the Allies, despite the occasion for it, but could be interpreted to include the Germans as well.

On May Day 1944, however, the three cardinals decided to appeal directly to the Catholic bishops of the Allied countries,[34] as Cardinal Liénart had foreshadowed. The original suggestion probably came from Mgr Chappoulie. In a letter to Cardinal Liénart from Paris (3 May 1944), he proposed the message be sent to the Archbishop of Westminster and the Cardinal Archbishops of Quebec and Boston. The appeal, made on the radio by Cardinal Suhard, was simple and direct. The British, he said, knew what bombing raids were like. The bishops were asked to intercede with the Allied governments to spare the civilian population. They were reminded of the Pope's message of Christmas 1942, when a similar plea had been made. Suhard was upset that his recorded broadcast appeared to have been truncated at the behest of the Germans. Abetz, to whom he complained, replied that the whole text had in fact been broadcast, but the Paris press, acting on an erroneous censorship instruction, had omitted to publish parts of it. On 28 May came the reaction from the British Hierarchy. They affirmed that Britain indeed knew at first hand the effects of bombing, and this was a question that had exercised them for a long while. They asserted that pilots had strict instructions to avoid civilian deaths. But Frenchmen could see the link between the raids and future military operations. An Allied victory would allow France once more to assume its rightful role in Europe.

This was an uncompromising reply, although *The Tablet*, which affirmed that the original appeal had not asked the Allies to call a halt to the bombing, but only to spare the population and monuments, commented prophetically: 'It will emerge as one of the truths of this war that bombing is at most a subsidiary weapon' unable to shatter civilian morale (20 May 1944). The American bishops were a shade more sympathetic.[35] The Apostolic Delegate in Washington had passed his reply on to Valerio Valeri, the Nuncio, who communicated it to Cardinal Liénart by a letter dated 24 June 1944, hence after the invasion. The American bishops also deplored indiscriminate bombing and reminded their French confrères that they had urged the US government on several occasions to take precautions and had received assurances. Meanwhile the fate of their French brethren was often in their thoughts.

Lille diocesan files contain a number of interesting reactions to the cardinals' appeal.[36] The view of the man in the street was that it would help the German cause: 'They didn't do as much when the Germans came to bomb Citroën, in Paris itself, on 30 May 1940' ('Ils n'en ont pas fait autant lorsque les Allemands sont venus bombarder Citroën, en plein Paris, le 30 mai 1940'). In intellectual circles the initiative was also condemned, for the same reason. After all, the raids had been going on for two years, but only now, when they were succeeding in paralysing communications used by the Germans, were formal objections being raised. As for the bishops' censure of Resistance 'terrorism' their attitude was consistent with others they had adopted, such as towards the STO, when, despite 'd'hypocrites réserves', certain of their statements may well have facilitated the deportation to Germany of young men. Even earlier, in 1942, when the regime had forced peasants to hand over their grain stocks, some bishops had supported the measure, although one purpose had been to prevent supplies going to the Maquis, which was then steadily expanding. The sad conclusion was reached: 'In certain Catholic circles, and even among practising Catholics, it is reckoned that the French higher clergy is now utterly discredited, by reason of the pro-German attitude it has adopted since the outbreak of war.'[37] Thus after an Allied victory the higher clergy would no longer be able to continue in office; to save catholicism a Gallican Church was required. These somewhat tendentious comments must have profoundly depressed the ACA about the time of the Allied invasion.

Nor could the bishops draw comfort from elsewhere. The *Daily Telegraph* (18 May 1944) claimed that a toll of civilian lives was the price that had to be paid for Liberation. In the First World War French clergy had had no compunction in blessing planes taking off to bomb Germany. General Vallin, commanding the Fighting French air forces in Britain, had insisted (in a 'United Nations' broadcast in English from an American station located 'in Europe', 21.30, 18 May 1944) on the precautions taken, to the extent that if the target could not be located the bombers returned with their payload intact. The remedy lay in the hands of Vichy: it should provide adequate shelters and evacuate civilians located near military targets. Even the Germans proved unsympathetic to the appeal. Radio Berlin (broadcast in English, 14.30, 16 May 1944) declared that the lack of response to it showed that the higher clergy no longer had influence anywhere with national governments. The broadcast added, however, that it highlighted how Churchill now openly admitted the need to kill working people. Besides, the Allies had not spared Monte Cassino. 'They receive their orders from Jewish international finance,' Georges Suarez remarked sardonically in *Aujourd'hui*. At last the ACA had realised that public opinion had hardened against the raids. The last word, however, should go to General Smuts, the distinguished South African member of the British War Cabinet, who was reported (*The Tablet*, 27 May 1944) as saying that northern France and the Low Countries had suffered over the previous few months the most sustained bombing campaign ever carried out: the ordeal of Hamburg had been briefer, the attacks on the Ruhr had not been so concentrated or so continuous. But he too noted that the French cardinals had not asked for the total cessation of bombing.

French Catholic trade unionists had followed up the cardinals' appeal by a similar, but clandestine, one addressed to their American fellow workers. They began by asserting that unionists, including many Catholics, had probably constituted the first organised Resistance movement. Incidentally, they declared themselves dismayed at American opposition to de Gaulle. But above all, they wished the Allies to refuse 'to exploit measures of destruction of civilian populations without precedent in the history of humanity',[38] because in western and northern France, and in the Paris area, the bombings had stirred up nothing but hostility towards the Allies.

After the invasion had begun the Conseil National de la Résistance commented that the cardinals' appeal had been used by collaborationists as pro-German propaganda. In any case, why had they not condemned the 'terrorism' of the barbarous acts committed by Germans against Frenchmen?[39] *Témoignage Chrétien* [40] likewise assured its numerous Catholic readers that 'le terrorisme' and 'le banditisme' were merely words to cause the bourgeoisie to shudder. It was the Nazis who were responsible for the anarchy that now reigned in France. The true 'Maquisard' had strict orders not to attack patriotic Frenchmen. But when he or fellow Resisters were attacked he had the right to strike against traitors. 'Thou shalt not kill' was an imperative normally to be obeyed, but since France was still at war with Germany, to strike one's enemy down in a just war was defensible, because the end, the destruction of nazism, was laudable. On the other hand — and the encyclical *Nova et Vetera* (1943) was cited — reprisals were never justified. As for appropriation of property, the 'requisitioning' of provisions and materials — a sore point with many Frenchmen — this was permissible only in cases of absolute necessity.

There the matter rested. The invasion changed everything: what some had regarded as dubious means of carrying on the struggle became legitimised in the eyes of most Frenchmen. However, the repeated interventions of the Hierarchy, well-meaning as they may have been, betray a certain ineptness; they were singularly mistimed, and gave the appearance of giving succour to the Germans, which the overwhelming majority of the bishops in no way sought to do. Once again their clinging to the Vichy regime, and particularly to Pétain, had led them astray.

Notes

Unless otherwise stated the place of publication is Paris.

1. *Témoignage Chrétien*, 'Exigences de la Libération', 1944. *Cahiers* XXVI–XXVII, vol. 2, p. 153–181.
2. AN F60.1674. Quoted in *News Digest* (Free French) No. 763.
3. *Témoignage Chrétien*, *Cahiers* XXVI–XXVII, vol. 2, p. 158.
4. See Jean Bosc, *Paris Soir*, 2 May 1942.
5. AN 2 AG 494. Articles et documents réservés à la Presse catholique. Information de l'Etat Français; and Radio Brussels, 18.45, 11 March 1943.
6. AN F60.1674. Report on Radio Paris, 14.00, 11 March 1943
7. AN F60.1674. Quoted on Radio Paris, 22.00, 21 January 1943.
8. AN 2 AG 494.
9. AN F60.1674. Transocean News Agency.
10. AN F60. 1674. Reported on Radio Paris, 7 April 1943.
11. Reported in *Ouest-Eclair*, 25 May 1943.
12. AN F60.1674, Reported by Radio Paris, 14,00, 16 July 1943.
13. Reported under the heading 'Liberté de conscience' in *L'Avenir du Plateau central*, 28 July 1943.
14. AN AG 76. Correspondence Ménétrel L–Z. Letter dated Rouen, 4 September 1943.
15. AN F1a.3784. Inf. Nov. '43, ZLZ/1/35500, 6 November 1943.
16. AN F60.1674. Reported on Radio Paris, 08.00, 16 November 1943.
17. AN F60.1674. Reported on Radio Paris, 09.00, 20 November 1943.
18. AN F60.1674. *Semaine religieuse* (Vannes), quoted on Radio Paris, 09.00, 1 December 1943.

19. AN F60.1674. Reported on the Poste National, 12.00, 19.December 1943.
20. AN F60.1674. Reported on Radio Vichy, 19.30, 20 December 1943.
21. AN F60.1674. Reported in English by Transocean News Agency, 6 January 1944.
22. AN F60.1674. Reported on Radio Paris, 14.00, 8 January 1944.
23. AN F60.1674. Radio Berlin, 06.45, 16 January 1944. 'Causerie matinale'.
24. AN F60.1674. Reported on Radio Paris, 13.00, 24 January 1944.
25. A Dio, Lille. 2B1 ACA 1942–1945. Dossier ACA 1944.
26. 'Quatrième lettre à un prélat', *Aujourd'hui*, 25 February 1944,
27. Letter to Cardinal Liénart, president of the ACA, Toulouse, 26 February 1944. The text is reproduced in full in *Actes*: Lyons, pp. 350f.
28. Ibid. For the text of the reply, cf. *Actes*: Lyons, p. 35.
29. AN F60.1674.
30. AN F60.1674. Reported by Radio Paris, 24.00, 29 May 1944.
31. AN F60. 1674. Reported by Radio Paris, 08.00, 15 May 1944:
32. AN F60.1674.
33. AN F1a.3784. Note d'information ref: ACB/9/36801, 4 May 1944, repeating a radio broadcast.
34. A Dio, Lille, 2B1 ACA 1942–1945. File: May 1944. 'Appel des Cardinaux français aux Evêques d'Angleterre et des Etats-Unis'.
35. Ibid.
36. Ibid.
37. Ibid.
38. AN F1a.3784. Service d'Informations du Commissariat à l'Intérieur, No. MUR/18/35501, citing G. Suarez, 'La protestation de l'Eglise', *Aujourd'hui*, 25 May 1944.
39. AN F1a..3784. 'Service Courrier' ref: CDO/FO.
40. *Témoignage Chrétien, Cahiers* XXVI–XXVII, vol. 2, p. 163 and p. 167.

Christians and Germans

In 1940 the institutions of French society had collapsed. The one exception was the Church, whose hierarchical organisation was still intact and whose influence — as is frequently the case in war — had increased. Within Germany itself the Nazis had at first been circumspect in their dealings with Christians. Although they had finally succeeded in sowing division among German Protestants, Catholics had remained united. In 1940 they realised that for France a change of tactics would be necessary: there would be a much smaller Protestant minority but they would have to treat with 'the eldest daughter' of a Catholic church headed by four cardinals, with a strong Gallican tradition of independence. The Occupation troops therefore approached their task with caution.

As a first step close surveillance of the bishops was ordered. When the advance forces entered Lyons Cardinal Gerlier became temporarily a hostage.[1] Eventually, however, General Henrici, the local commander, allowed him to move around freely within his command area. He was permitted to celebrate mass in the primatial cathedral of Saint-Jean on 14 July, turned by Pétain into a day of national mourning.[2] After the German withdrawal from southern France Gerlier enjoyed the greatest liberty of movement of the three diocesan cardinals. On July 16 he made his first visit to Vichy, less than a week after Pétain had been granted full powers, and had been able to meet Cardinal Suhard in Paris a week earlier.

In Lille Cardinal Liénart received more cavalier treatment. After the occupation of the city he had been summoned to Rüdiger, its temporary governor, and exhorted to use his influence to ensure the population obeyed German orders and resumed work. This was to apply a policy of 'using' the bishops adopted elsewhere. The other feature of the policy, one of conciliation, so that the German forces should not be impeded by the civilian population in their continuing struggle against Britain, was less easy to implement.

Liénart received assurances that his person would be respected, that he could exercise his ministry freely, and that nothing would be asked of him incompatible with his honour as a French bishop.[3] The cardinal soon realised the hollowness of these promises. On 27 July his palace was searched, on the flimsy pretext that he had been in touch with German émigrés opposed to the Nazi regime. In a letter to Rüdiger,[4] fired off the same day, he protested that the real motive was to pry into the nature of his ministry. Throughout the five-hour search, carried out by the Geheimfeldpolizei, the field security branch of the Wehrmacht, he was kept under close surveillance. He demanded the return of documents concerning the Holy See and the ACA that had been confiscated. Rüdiger replied (31 July 1940) that as well as contacting émigrés, the cardinal had in his possession letters written by Frenchmen for forwarding, and this was illegal. The search was 'a measure to which everyone must submit' ('Massnahmen denen sich jedermann unterwerfen muss'). Indignantly Liénart took his complaint to General de Laurencie, the French Delegate-General to the occupation forces in Paris (letter of 29 July 1940). He related how one of his guards had declared, when he had protested, 'Nous avons le droit and, tapping his revolver, had added, 'et nous avons aussi les armes', to which he had retorted: 'Les armes allemandes ne me font pas peur, je les ai vues en face à Verdun.' It was, he added, particularly regrettable that a Frenchman had participated in the search.

On July 27, but over a period of three days, Cardinal Suhard was subjected in Paris to the same treatment, in order, so the Germans alleged, to investigate the links that had existed between Suhard's predecessor, Cardinal Verdier, the Jews and Freemasonry.[5] His palace was searched, as was the residence of Cardinal Baudrillart at the Institut Catholique, and he was placed under armed guard. Unlike Liénart, he submitted to this treatment resignedly.[6] and showed himself more forgiving. As he told his diocesans, somewhat apologetically, in a statement read from the pulpit, 'We were pained by this action. We have talked it through with the German authorities. We wish to forget it.'[7] (Incidentally, the statement is noteworthy for its being the first time Suhard spoke of the Vichy regime as 'le gouvernement légitime'.) Later, the seals were removed from the palace offices through the intervention of a certain 'Dr R', a German civilian administrator, who also prevailed on the Gestapo and the military to allow the cardinal to resume publication of the diocesan *Semaines religieuses*, to derequisition partially seminaries and to free Abbé Le Sourd, Suhard's private secretary. It would appear that 'Dr R' was entrusted with the task of working out a *modus vivendi* between the French Church and nazism. He eventually consulted Doriot, Déat, a certain Vignat (a personal friend of Laval's), Abbé Renaud, and Mgrs Beaussart and Baudrillart, as well as others in the unoccupied zone.[8] The identity of this mysterious emissary is not known, nor how satisfactorily he fulfilled his mission.[9] In September Suhard disclosed that the Verdier files the Germans wanted had been removed to the seminary at Issy-les-Moulineaux. A few hours later they were in Gestapo hands.[10]

Initially the Wehrmacht did not intervene in civilian or ecclesiastical matters, unless German military interests were directly involved. The Hague Convention merely enjoined an occupying army to respect religious beliefs, which meant allowing Church services to continue. Its administrative branch, the Militärverwaltung, however, developed an interest in Catholic education, which it dealt with in a special section, 'Kultur und Schule'.[11] More deeply involved in ecclesiastical matters was Abetz, the German Ambassador, responsible to Ribbentrop in Berlin, who sedulously cultivated contacts with Cardinals Suhard and Baudrillart. The third, and most sinister group with its finger in the pie, was the SS, with its two branches, the Sicherheitspolizei (SiPo) and the Sicherheitsdienst (SD), which were, as in Germany itself, extremely hostile to the Church. The SD was formally charged with its surveillance, and for detecting any anti-German activities, particularly among the bishops.[12]

The SS saw its overarching task as to prevent any military revival of French fortunes, whilst subduing the civilian population until the war was over. (For the period after victory Hitler and the Nazis had more sinister plans that would change the face of Christianity.) Meanwhile a certain rivalry existed between these various German authorities, with an occasional difference of views emerging, as, for example, their treatment of Catholic youth organisations illustrates. Ultimately it was the will of the SS that prevailed, as the Vichy regime degenerated into being a puppet of the Nazi State.

Perhaps a harbinger of the fate of the French churches was their treatment of Alsace and part of Lorraine, territories now annexed to the German Reich. There the German Interior ministry showed nazism in its true colours, taking Draconian measures regarding religion, as an integral part of a 're-Germanisation' programme. Two Gauleiters, Wagner in Alsace and Bürckel in Lorraine, were entrusted with the task. A first clash with the Church came when they flatly refused to allow Mgr Ruch, Bishop of Strasbourg, to return to his diocese, from which he had been evacuated. His confrère, Mgr Heintz, Bishop of Metz, was summarily expelled to unoccupied France on August 16, 1940. Despite German demands, the Pope refused to name their successors, on the grounds that neither had resigned their see. Later the two Vicars-General, Kretz and Kolb, were also uprooted, as were hundreds more ecclesiastics and religious, whilst others who had fled were not allowed to return.[13]

Alsace's population of two million was three-quarters Catholic. When the Germans arrived all religious activity apart from church services was forbidden: youth movements, parish meetings, Scouts, and adult groups were closed down. Some Church assets were expropriated: the funds and property of the Strasbourg Fédération catholique de Charité, for example, were seized and handed over to the NS Volkswohlfahrt, the Nazi welfare organisation. In July the Napoleonic Concordat, which had survived previous German rule, was abrogated. For the future financing of all denominations — Catholic, Lutheran or Reformed — the German system of the 'Kirchenbetrag' (Church tax) was introduced, whereby Church members had to pay an annual levy, varying according to income, to support their local church. (In the meantime the Germans advanced a sum taken from the French budget for Alsace-Lorraine in 1940).[14] Those who wished to opt out of the tax had merely to state they were 'Gottgläubig', but of no denomination. The priest himself was responsible for compiling a list of those willing to pay.[15] Strasbourg cathedral was closed for services. Catholics feared it would be handed over to Protestants, but Gauleiter Wagner assured them this would not happen.[16] Rumour had it that Hitler, who had visited Strasbourg in triumph, had indeed offered it to the Reformed churches, who had refused it. Nazi youth organisations supplanted Catholic ones. Any Catholic group wishing to start up again had to obtain government permission. Catholic primary schools lost their exclusively confessional character. Teachers in religious orders were dismissed. Lay teachers were transferred elsewhere in the Reich to be indoctrinated into the workings of the Nazi school system. Other educational institutions run by the Church were abolished, save for institutes for the handicapped. Religious education was fixed in theory at two hours a week, but other events were often deliberately arranged to supervene. Secondary school children over fourteen had the right, even without parental consent, to opt out of religious instruction classes. Any person over that age also could also quit a religious order or junior seminary without further ado. The episcopal seminary was shut, as was the university, including its two theology faculties.[17] The Catholic press was drastically reduced. By the end of 1940 20,000 Catholics had been expelled from the province.[18]

The Germans demanded the return of the Strasbourg Cathedral plate and other treasures — the Armistice had stipulated that public property that had been removed to a place of safety should be handed back. Barthélemy, as minister responsible for the annexed provinces, replied that such objects had to be returned to the local French authorities, but in Alsace these were no longer functioning. Moreover, since the Germans did not recognise the Church as a public service, the disposal of its possessions did not fall within the Armistice terms. Lastly, since the cathedral was closed for worship, 'là où on ne dit pas la messe, il n'y a pas besoin de calice'.[19]

The situation was paralleled in Lorraine. When they entered the province the SA and the SS desecrated the churches, spoliating religious statues and pictures with almost Cromwellian rage. The Nazis despised all clerics: speaking at Hayange in April 1941, Bürckel ridiculed what he called the 'white Jews', as well as the 'black Jews'. Some 300 clergy were expelled from Lorraine, particularly those who ministered to French-speaking parishes. Likewise summarily deported to the unoccupied zone were many monks and nuns, although others fled or were forced to renounce their vows and seek civilian employment. Diocesan property was confiscated: at the bishop's palace in Metz a sum of four million francs was seized. Even choir practices were forbidden. Occasionally the parish priest was allowed to hold a brief weekly prayer or Bible meeting ('Seelsorge'). On Sundays the distribution of ration tickets was often purposely set to coincide with the times of mass. Religious customs, such as the tolling of the Angelus bell, were forbidden. The aim was clear: to tear out the core of religious belief from an area where its roots ran very deep.

Occasionally Nazification was judged, even by its leaders, to be proceeding too quickly. At Château-Salins (Germanicised to Salzburg) the Gestapo closed all ecclesiastical buildings. Archdeacon Goldschmidt broke into his locked church, and, having summoned his flock by bells, preached to an overflowing congregation in German and in French (the use of which was strictly forbidden). Bürckel took no action. Sunday became a working day but, after protest, this practice had to be modified. On the other hand, Church membership was made difficult. The sum demanded as 'Kirchenbetrag' from an industrial worker was exorbitant. For permission to teach the catechism a priest had to demonstrate he was of good character, of pure Aryan descent and ideally embraced nazism.[20] All in all, the situation in the annexed provinces was not an auspicious portent as to what might happen to the rest of France if the Nazis were victorious.

They were under no illusion as to how they would be received by the Church. Arriving in Paris on 14 June 1940, Professor Grimm, attached to the German Embassy to work as a propagandist, declared that, no less than the Jews and the upper bourgeoisie, 'our enemies are the clerics of both denominations.'[21] He advised the military to act accordingly, because the French would understand firmness. Since he was believed to have the ear of Hitler[22] the High Command paid heed to his warning. A fortnight before the meeting of Hitler and Pétain at Montoire, Abetz reported that the Vichy regime found its strongest support among the army and the clergy, the majority of whom opposed Franco-German collaboration, favouring instead a policy of 'attentisme'.[23]

The Germans were conscious of the tortuous course they had to steer between clericalism and anticlericalism. They wished to discourage the regime from paying undue attention to Church opinion, believing it to be shot through with nationalism and 'revanchisme'. They viewed Pétain's Révolution Nationale as essentially antisecular. They even sent packing a German professor teaching in Paris because of his strong Christian views, for, 'with the upsurge of clericalism in France in the field of cultural policy such a basic attitude is palpably inappropriate'.[24] They deplored the strongly confessional character that anti-Masonic propaganda assumed under the Catholics Vallery-Radot and Marques-Rivière. Their journal, *Les Documents Maçonniques*, gave 'anti-freemasonry propaganda a [religious] bias that from a German political viewpoint is not at all to be welcomed.' When Admiral Platon took over from Fay, entrusted by Vichy with rooting out Freemasons, despite the former's Protestantism, the Germans still found the set-up too 'clerical' and antisecularist.[25]

On the other hand, although the Germans had few allies among the clergy, they thought those few who showed themselves as not antipathetic had not to be discouraged — a trickish task because the Germans' main support came from many more collaborationists who were anticlerical. However, on one occasion they even prohibited the publication of a series of violently 'secularising' articles, censoring them on the grounds that they did not wish to provide ammunition for the BBC, which was only too anxious to accuse them of anticlericalism.[26]

For the SS, the Church remained the arch-enemy. At one stage they even accused it of interfering in the field of geopolitics by supporting an alleged Vatican project to create a bloc of Catholic nations in south-west Europe opposed to the Reich. To realise this aim, the SS maintained, the French Church would first seek to forge a unity with the masses and the State.[27] The charge may not be as far-fetched as at first appears. A plan for a 'European Christian Union', drawn up by a certain Charles-Ernest Riche, on LFC notepaper, was circulating at Vichy in mid-1942. Riche was styled as 'délégué permanent du Directoire National [de la LFC?] pour la Suisse [sic]'. Pétain handed Riche's 'Plan de politique chrétienne européenne' to Barthélémy, the Justice minister, who returned it with the pious comment: 'The spiritual future of humanity must be saved. I do not believe we can hope to arrive at it outside Christianity.'[28] The project envisaged a Catholic 'union' of the north European and Mediterranean countries of France, Portugal, Switzerland, the Low Countries, Hungary, the German lands south of the Elbe, including Austria, and perhaps Ireland and the Catholic areas of Prussia, 'in order to save western and southern Europe, and to provide France with a very great outreach in Europe' ('afin de sauver l'Europe occidentale et méridionale et de donner à la France un très grand rayonnement européen'). The question of Protestant and Orthodox participation was left in abeyance. If Germany won, the union would act as a counterbalancing force to nazism, and European co-operation would continue. If it lost the war against Russia (the war against the other Allies was not mentioned) France would back German Catholics against any Slav 'Drang nach Westen'. Such a union, it was rather vaguely stated, would not be political, but should rather be seen as a movement, with Switzerland as its ideal point of departure.

As the Occupation wore on the Germans were better able to size up the leading figures in the Church, despite the obvious reluctance of the pastoral cardinals to become reconciled to their presence.

Liénart, living in the reserved zone, and regarded by Carles, the regional prefect, as an indispensable ally in his dealings with Oberfeldkommandantur 670 (OFK 670) in Lille, could, however, hardly avoid contact. The Occupation authorities considered he was a 'nationalist', and labelled him most probably as anti-German.[29] The initial mistrust of him remained. His motives for applications for permits, whether for visiting Paris or the 'forbidden' coastal zone, or for merely being out after curfew, were questioned. Applications were often held up or 'lost'. In July 1942, for failing to hand in an expired pass for the 'zone interdite' he was threatened with punishment 'according to the laws of war' ('nach den Kriegsgesetzen'). The admonition arrived at the bishop's palace addressed insultingly to 'Herrn Liénart, Achille'.[30] In September 1943 he was summoned to give evidence at a court case in Paris, in which priests of his diocese were accused of currency offences. Wisely seeing this would be construed as guilt by association, he refused to attend and in the event was represented by his secretary.[31] Such petty harassment was aimed at wounding his pride. German officials clearly did not intend to make life easy for him.

In fact, Christians had a staunch ally within OFK 670. Carlo Schmid, the post-war SPD politician, a lawyer, had been appointed to Lille as Militärverwaltungsrat in June 1940, where he remained to the end. Half-French by his mother, and born in Toulouse, he was never a member of the Nazi party. He maintained good personal relations with both Catholics and Protestants, as two Lillois, Canon Detrez and Pastor Pasche, attested after the war.[32] He worked with Pastor Pasche to save Jews from deportation, giving them passes for less dangerous areas — some even escaped to Switzerland. Through Pasche he obtained information on the French Resistance for Moltke, of the German resistance group Kreisauer Kreis. With Pasche and the help of the Swiss Consul he succeeded in freeing most of the political prisoners held by the Germans before their retreat from the city in 1944.[33] Schmid was arrested in Lille in 1944 on suspicion of being involved in the plot against Hitler's life, but was freed after a week. When the German troops retreated from northern France, he saved the public utilities and the coal mines from destruction, in exchange for a promise by the Resistance that the retreating army would not be fired upon. Liénart was well aware of this 'friend' in the enemy camp.

Although avoiding contact as much as possible, Liénart did not hesitate to intervene with General Niehoff, the Lille Commandant, in order to obtain the release of imprisoned Frenchmen, or to gain some or other concession. There were many instances of this, particularly in the early years. Thus he sought the release of priests held as prisoners of war in the local barracks, of a prison chaplain who had posted letters for prisoners, of a priest who had started up a Scout troop, of another who had been caught listening to the BBC. The list is long and varied. Although no lover of 'dissidence', Gaullist or otherwise, he pleaded for the release of teachers of the Institut Commercial Saint-Louis in Lille, arrested after a pupil had been reprimanded by them for wearing a Nazi badge. Niehoff replied that the matter was more serious. On the school walls had been chalked a Croix de Lorraine and the inscription, 'Vive de Gaulle, à bas Hitler. A la mort Laval.' Liénart nevertheless secured the teachers' freedom, although the headmaster continued to languish in jail.[34] He was unsuccessful, however, on a still graver matter: the saving of Abbé Bonpain, curate at Rosendael, condemned to death for Resistance activities in 1943.[35] It was said that the cardinal's intervention might have succeeded if it had not been for the coincidentally ill-timed statement he made regarding the STO in March 1943. This infuriated collaborationists and Germans alike, and the execution of Bonpain may have been intended as a warning to Liénart. The cardinal's disapproval of Resistance activities may explain why he apparently intervened less in the closing months of the Occupation. He was undoubtedly sincere in the assurance he had given to Niehoff, and to Falkenhausen in Brussels, that catholicism in France 'wanted only to occupy itself with religious matters'.[36]

Despite being by no means pro-German, the cardinal allegedly made one statement flattering to the occupying forces that is puzzling and, to say the least, economical with the truth. In January 1944, at the Oberfeldkommandantur in Lille (according to a German source), Liénart is reported to have thanked the Germans 'for the fact that the behaviour of the occupier had always been correct and benevolent towards their persons [the clergy], as it had been towards the Church'.[37] He professed understanding for the fact that occasionally the Germans had to bear down severely; for his part, he would always act to pacify the population and exhort it to act correctly. The clue to this somewhat surprising statement perhaps lies in the reference to his clergy. Liénart had a strongly paternalist attitude towards his diocesan priests, and, aware that some were actively engaged in the Resistance, may have sought to throw a protective smoke-screen round them.

One last incident before the Liberation was to summon up all the cardinal's tact and diplomacy. On the evening of 1 April 1944 a train carrying troops of the armoured Hitlerjugend Division was derailed by the Resistance at Ascq, near Lille. No Germans were killed but as a reprisal for the act of sabotage ninety of the villagers were brutally massacred in the space of two hours, including the local priest and his curate. On 4 April Liénart lodged a strong protest and demanded an interview with the German authorities. Received by General Bertram — incidentally, the brother of Cardinal Bertram, Archbishop of Breslau — Liénart declared that this time it was impossible for him to pacify the population unless the Germans responsible were punished. This did not occur, and he was later reproached by townspeople for not speaking out more frankly in condemnation of the slaughter, when he presided over the funeral mass next day. Instead, he enjoined silence regarding the sentiments that had been so fiercely stirred up. This, for many, contrasted unfavourably with the condemnations he had made of the Allied bombings and Resistance 'terrorist' activities.[38] In the event it was the local population that was to suffer: eight inhabitants of Ascq were found guilty of sabotage. Cardinal Liénart was informed of this judgement, but merely replied that it was unacceptable.

The comportment of Mgr Suhard in Paris is more difficult to fathom, but it was slightly more favourable to the Germans. He was, like Liénart, anxious to depoliticise his clergy, according to German military reports, and genuinely sought a *modus vivendi* with the occupying forces.[39] Abetz even noted approvingly that he had a 'disposition à collaborer'.This was confirmed when, on 12 December 1940, Suhard himself declared to the ambassador that the Church inclined to favour Franco-German collaboration and that one of his dearest wishes was that their two peoples should arrive at an understanding.[40] This was not exactly the kind of collaboration, between equals, that the Nazis desired. Nevertheless Suhard persisted in his belief that every problem that arose was negotiable. His concerns were above all pastoral rather than political, although events forced him to take up positions on the broader issues that arose.

The first attack on a German, that by Colonel Fabien at the Barbès Métro station on 21 August 1941, followed less than a week later by the shots fired by Colette at Laval and Déat — palpable evidence in Suhard's eyes of the 'vent mauvais' that Pétain then detected was sweeping the country — prompted him to warn that reprisals would inevitably follow.[41] However, when the Germans executed hostages in revenge for the attacks on German officers in Nantes and Bordeaux, on October 26 he protested to Otto von Stülpnagel, the German commander.[42] The Bishop of Nantes, Mgr Villeplet, had interceded in vain, as had the local mayor and the prefect.[43]

Suhard, like some of his colleagues, backed the German war against the Soviet Union. However, in contrast to most of them, he maintained this support to the very end. As late as 7 June 1944 he was characterising the conflict in the East as 'a European crusade'. He gave his blessing to the 'relève', Laval's arrangement whereby for every three workers that left to work in Germany a French POW would be released, regarding it as 'a moral obligation' for workers to volunteer. But his attitude towards the STO law was identical to that formulated by Liénart, although its seeming ambiguity aroused the hostility of the Germans so much that, according to one source, they 'advised' the collaborationist press from June 1943 onwards to attack the cardinals and the papacy.[44]

German resentment at the ingratitude of the Church, whose battle they considered they were fighting in the East, as manifested by the Church's attitude to the STO, gave rise to the more serious incidents with which Suhard had to deal. One concerning the legality of Catholic youth movements ended indecisively.[45] However, by now the Germans were occupied with weightier matters, in particular, coping with the Resistance. According to one report, in December 1943 the Gestapo wanted Suhard to issue a declaration condemning 'dissident' activities. The cardinal convened a meeting of bishops, but only two thought a public statement appropriate at that juncture.

On 7 February 1944 Suhard visited Abetz — the visit paralleled that which Liénart had paid to OFK 670 the previous month. According to the ambassador, the cardinal 'was gratified at the good relations it had been possible to establish in France between the Church and the occupying Power'.[46] Suhard, however, put forward a request that all prisoners arrested by the Germans should have access to priests. Abetz's reaction to what might be described as a 'charm offensive' was to brush the request aside. He merely responded that if the attitude of the higher clergy was mainly correct, their subordinates were too often wont to launch anti-German attacks.

Suhard also took up the cudgels generally on behalf of all those oppressed by the Germans. In a letter dated 17 February 1944. he deplored the conditions in which civilian prisoners were kept, without news, parcels or spiritual ministrations; he deprecated the violent methods employed by the German police. His tone was firmer than in previous years: 'We ask for war not to usurp all rights: the end does not justify the means. We ask that the fundamental values of Christian civilisation be respected.'[47] It was the counterpart to the official ACA declaration denouncing total war, the bombing of open cities, and injustices committed by both sides. On 15 March, replying to Suhard's letter, in thinly veiled terms, Abetz countered by voicing his disquiet at statements by Church leaders, which, he said, gave fuel to the Resistance, in which priests were becoming increasingly embroiled.

By now, however, Suhard was preparing for the inevitable German defeat. He redoubled his efforts to coax humanitarian concessions from them. He sent an envoy to Pétain enquiring whether, if the Marshal appealed to the Pope, Paris could be declared an open city. Instead, the Marshal approached Rundstedt directly and was informed that the Wehrmacht would not defend Paris.[48] The cardinal's more noticeable coolness to the Germans did not go unremarked by the collaborationist press. It detected a lacklustre note in his condemnation of the spring air raids (20 and 24 April) on Paris, in contrast to his previous utterances.[49] The change in attitude was also perceived by Abetz. Suhard, in fact, had begun to distance himself from anything that smacked even remotely of 'collaboration'. The German envoy reported that Suhard thought Germany should try to reach an understanding with the Western Allies, if only because of the persistent danger of bolshevism.[50] The suggestion was rejected out of hand by Ribbentrop, who remained as anti-British as ever. A further report from the Paris embassy is perhaps even more revealing, and somewhat contradictory. Suhard allegedly now thought Germany had never intended to come to an accommodation with the Western Allies (which was clearly what he, at one stage at least, would have wished). Now the Allied bombing of German cities had awakened such hatred in the German population that any such entente was impossible.[51] Having for four years steered an uncertain course, Suhard was beginning to move towards the Allied camp, somewhat tardily, as soon became apparent.

The case of Cardinal Baudrillart is considered elsewhere. Here it suffices to note that, perhaps because of his fiercely Germanophobic statements before the war, he was never entirely trusted by the Nazis. It is perhaps significant that, despite his backing of the LVF, there was no official German representation at his funeral in May 1942.

Cardinal Gerlier, in Lyons, had fewer dealings with the occupying forces, who nevertheless characterised him as anti-German and an ambitious intriguer. Until the total occupation of France any interventions on behalf of those in trouble with the Germans he naturally made through Vichy. One of the most notable was the attempt to save the life of Pierre d'Harcourt, son of Robert d'Harcourt, the distinguished Catholic intellectual who had been a professor at the Paris Institut Catholique. Pierre d'Harcourt, working for the French secret service, had been wounded and captured by the Germans with incriminating documents on him which would certainly lead to a death sentence. Gerlier wrote to Pétain asking him to intercede with his captors.[52] The Marshal agreed. It would seem that the Pope also appealed for clemency, and eventually d'Harcourt's life was saved. Gerlier may have made a number of such interventions. Stanislas Fumet, the former director of the Catholic *Temps Nouveaux*, asserted that Gerlier had done much to help political prisoners.[53] On the other hand, Germaine Ribière, of the Amitié Chrétienne group working to save Jews, says the cardinal was unwilling to help personally to secure the freedom of one of her colleagues, Jean-Marie Soutou, arrested in January 1943, although he did support others' efforts: 'The cardinal assisted by giving his endorsement, but he had to be goaded on with a sword at his back... for he was afraid, he didn't want to do so.'[54] His fear was probably that of compromising the Church rather than any lack of personal courage. By then Church leaders had clearly resolved to withdraw even more from any remotely political action.

Certainly Gerlier's reputation among the Germans was one of being hostile to collaboration. Yet on one occasion (October 1943), perhaps to secure the release of prisoners from Fort Montluc, he buttered up the SD by surprisingly declaring that only a few doctrines separated the Church from the Germans, for whom he had warm feelings. This may have been the precursor of the similar remarks made by Liénart and Suhard in the early new year, likewise also to win favours.[55] For the Germans, however, Gerlier remained a prince of a hostile Church living in what one German-controlled newspaper, the *Strassburger Neueste Nachrichten*, described as 'the most Gaullist city in France', Lyons.[56]

From early 1944 the Germans no longer hesitated to take action against the bishops personally. SS Gruppenführer Heinrich Müller — 'Gestapo-Müller' as he was known — received orders from Himmler to act with the utmost severity.[57] The Church and all its clerics, high and low, were declared the enemy. If the occasion arose, even the Pope would not be exempt: had he not been elected in 1939 through the machinations of the American bishops, on the orders of their government? In France the first victim of this iron-fisted policy was Mgr Piguet, of Clermont-Ferrand. Hardly a model of Resistance, he had nevertheless assisted a priest on the run from the Germans. He was arrested by the Gestapo on 28 May, despatched to the notorious Struthof camp in Alsace and eventually ended up in Dachau.

The case of Mgr Théas, of Montauban, was still more flagrant. In the spring of 1944, at Montpezat (Tarn-et-Garonne), the Germans, suspecting Resistance activity, set fire to the church and presbytery, and forbade the priest to attempt to save his possessions. Théas wrote to the

Toulouse Kommandantur: 'I would be failing gravely in my duty if, in the face of such acts of terrorism and barbarism I did not make known the indignant protests of the human, Christian conscience... If the victor indulges in terrorism, he is disqualified from prohibiting it.'[58]

Arrested and sent to the Compiègne transit camp on 9 June, together with Mgr Bruno Solages, rector of the Toulouse Institut Catholique, from there Théas was eventually freed by the Allies and made a triumphal return to his diocese on 9 September. Also interned in Compiègne was Mgr Rodié, of Agen. Mgr Saliège, the ailing Archbishop of Toulouse, the most fearless and outspoken of all the prelates, was visited by two German officers on 9 June with orders to arrest him. But, finding him half-paralysed and unable to speak, they withdrew.[59] Other prelates suffered indignities at German hands. Mgr Moussaron, Archbishop of Albi, was arrested on 15 June and remained in custody for a week. Mgr Heintz, Bishop of Metz, who had taken refuge with Cardinal Gerlier, had undergone a long interrogation in May. In July Mgr Rastouil was arrested at Limoges by the Milice, but freed after a fortnight, thanks to the Nuncio's intervention with Laval.[60]

Among those who, surprisingly, remained at liberty was Mgr Rémond, Bishop of Nice and Monaco. Rémond was a much decorated officer of the First World War who in 1921 had been Chaplain-General to the French occupation forces of the Rhine. After the Liberation Gestapo documents were found that branded him as a 'leader of the liberal Judaeo-Masonic class', one who gave out false baptismal certificates to Jews, maintained contacts with the Allies, made anti-Nazi propaganda in his sermons, possessed a radio transmitter and went in for spying! Despite this litany of offences he was never arrested. On 1 July 1944 he presided over a memorial service for Henriot; in his address he did not mention the assassinated collaborationist once by name, but used the occasion to condemn crimes of all kinds, not forgetting those committed by the Gestapo and their French friends. The next day, whereas the local PPF had demanded his arrest, he was cheered at a religious ceremony by a crowd 30,000 strong. His priests were active in the Resistance and he was even credited with giving permission to his seminarists to take a 'sabbatical year' off in order to serve in the Maquis of Haute-Savoie![61]

The lower clergy and religious orders suffered rougher treatment by the Germans. In September 1940 already German reports alleged that clergy were aiding British propaganda by promoting the idea of revenge in their sermons or by discreet whispers in the confessional. Despite Suhard's efforts to 'depoliticise' his clergy, that autumn arms caches were found in presbyteries. German surveillance was tightened up but in February 1941 ten priests were arrested for helping POWs to escape, and distributing anti-German tracts.[62] The Germans took good note of the fact that in early 1941 a highly-placed Catholic source estimated that among the rank and file clergy only one in four favoured any form of collaboration.[63] They thought they perceived, at least in Catholic schools, after the attack on the USSR, an improvement in attitudes towards them.[64] This, however was not to last. By the end of 1941 the German Embassy was reporting that, no less than the lower clergy, Catholic schoolteachers were among their most dangerous enemies.[65] The collaborationist Rebatet noted bitterly that in the spring of 1942 parish priests were reciting the rosary to invoke a prompt retreat from Russia by the German army, which 'alone could bar the road to bolshevism'.[66] Meanwhile German pursuit of those who helped its enemies continued. One bishop, Mgr Faure, of St-Claude, even wrote to Pétain protesting somewhat naively that one of his clergy in the occupied zone had been imprisoned merely for having given alms to escaping prisoners.[67] In 1942 a Breton priest preached a sermon giving what he termed practical, common sense advice on how the Germans should be treated: No hostile action, no refusal to supply Germans with food; but remember, don't let them have any luxuries: milk, butter, sugar are for French children. Shopkeepers, keep your goods for us. Girls, don't go out with German soldiers. 'The enemy does not require us [...] to forget [...] that he is the enemy.' At the end of the service he told his congregation: 'If it pleases anyone among you to go and denounce me, I can inform you that I shall be at the presbytery, where I shall await the Germans.'[68]

In fact, in an end of year evaluation, the Fighting French esteemed that priests in rural areas were very friendly to 'la dissidence', helping the Jews and others. So were the religious orders, particularly the Jesuits, who were even aiding their former opponents: a Jesuit college, for example, had appointed as a teacher an ex-Freemason dismissed by Vichy.[69] An anonymous Toulouse Provincial — the document does not specify details — circulated instructions to the priors and superiors of his province regarding collaborationism: on the ideological and religious plane this was 'dangerous', because of the German pagan conception of the State, race and blood. Loyalty to the regime was indeed necessary, but the main task was to keep 'Christian Frenchmen uncorrupted by error'.[70]

Little wonder, therefore, that by 1943 the Germans were becoming ever more vigilant and severe. In March the SS officer Kuntze declared that all priests were anti-German resisters who should be 'broken'.[71] Six months later, in September, the Abwehrstelle in Bordeaux stressed 'the very dangerous activities of the clergy'.[72] Such assessments were not without foundation, as examples show. A case in point was the arrest of the Superior General of the Filles de la Charité de Saint-Vincent de Paul. This caused Lavagne, as head of Pétain's Private Office, in February 1943 to ask Brinon in Paris to intercede with the Germans on her behalf. The charge against the Mother Superior, the head of 'the most powerful and the most effective of female religious orders', whose antennae stretched all over the world, was that her nuns had harboured suspects and spies. Later the Germans also arrested the provincial Superior in the unoccupied zone and the head of the order in Montpellier.[73] Brinon merely replied that he would intervene as requested, but had not much hope of success. In March Abbé Morelli, a priest at Cannes, was arrested for asking his parishioners to pray for General Weygand, by then under lock and key in Germany. This prompted his bishop, Mgr Rémond, to warn his clergy discreetly to exercise prudence. To his friends he remarked, 'I myself feel under close surveillance'.[74] Occasionally the Italians took a hand. Thus they arrested at Annecy Abbé Camille Folliet, the local JOC chaplain, on suspicion of subversion. After a spell in Italian gaols, he lived to take part in the Resistance but was killed in fighting in the Alps in 1945.[75] Another priest met a more horrible fate. Mgr Chevrot, vicar of St-François-Xavier in Paris, was one of the leaders in the Front National, the Resistance movement. He escaped arrest by the Germans, but his curate, Abbé Roger Derry, who probably had no knowledge of what was going on, did not. He was tried and beheaded at Cologne on 15 October 1943.

By 1944 German wrath at the clergy had boiled over. Suspicion turned to persecution. The Germans were aware of the scarcely concealed hostility of the rank and file. They knew that in the countryside parish priests were hiding 'réfractaires' escaping the STO. Himmler believed the bishops had deliberately sent their seminarists to Germany to work against nazism, assisting in this task those priests who had already gone clandestinely.[76] From January the SS were operating hand in glove with Darnand's Milice, which now ranged all over France in their hunt for 'terrorists' and were allowed to carry arms even in the former occupied zone. On 15 January Abbé Naudin, vicar of Sept-Deniers, Toulouse, well known for his democratic views, was imprisoned because he had fallen foul of this organisation, now the dreaded French arm of German repression. His crime was he had not officiated at the funeral of Costes, a Milicien who had been assassinated in August 1943; worse still, he had celebrated masses for Edmond Guyaux, shot by the Germans.[77] Brutal repression continued to the very end. On 28 June, the day when Henriot was assassinated by the Resistance, Père Corentin Cloarec, a popular Franciscan, was gunned down in Paris by the Gestapo for no apparent reason; his body was found riddled with bullets.[78] The Germans had now thrown prudence to the winds in their handling of the Church, and, abetted by the Milice, had installed a veritable reign of terror in which no one was spared. The cases cited could be repeated many times over. If the Church had some collaborationists it also had its martyrs.

Prominent Catholic laymen also came under suspicion. That Lamirand survived for so long as Secretary-General for Youth was solely due to Pétain's backing, because he was disliked by the Germans. Another Catholic, Jacques Chevalier, lost the Marshal's support when Darlan came to power. Long after he had ceased to be Education minister adverse comments on him came flooding in to the Germans. From Bordeaux he was reported in July 1941 as 'deutschfeindlich' (hostile to Germans), for having referred in a book published before the war to the 'Boche', whose dream of conquest was to enslave and exploit the world — unlike the Cartesian French, who sought to enlighten and liberate it.[79] Garric, the prominent Catholic head of the Secours National, the national relief organisation, was accused of being anti–German. Laval had a meeting with him, having heard that immediately before the war he had been 'assistant director of the University of London [sic]', but agreed to protect him.[80] Whereas, partly through German insistence, Lamirand and Chevalier were eventually ousted, Garric remained at his post, and continued in it even after the Liberation.

Those who knew Germany well were treated by the Occupation forces with vigilance. From the aged Bishop of Grenoble, Mgr Caillot, who had taught in Germany, they had nothing to fear. But of others, even such as Père Doncœur, a strong Pétainist, Père Chaillet, who turned to the Resistance, and Abbé Naurois, who after the departure of the staff of the 'leadership school' from Uriage at the end of 1942, joined the Maquis, — of men such as these the Germans were deeply suspicious.

They were even more distrustful of the Protestants, whose pre-war contacts with Germany as well as Britain had been frequent. Through the embryo World Council of Churches and the Swiss pastor, Roland de Pury, of Lyons, Protestant links with the outside world were not cut off. In 1940, so anxious were the Germans themselves to keep an eye on the Protestant upper bourgeoisie, whose role in diplomacy, banking and finance, and heavy industry was considerable, that the SS brought from Germany to advise them a Protestant pastor who had once ministered to the German colony in Nice. They were always alive to any hint of resistance, even confiscating a few thousand tracts of the Société des Missions évangéliques de Paris because of the 'incriminating' phrase that appeared, 'The Gospel is not bound to a flag.'[81]

Pastor Boegner, their leader, was regarded with the utmost mistrust. His Anglophile sentiments were notorious. On 11 July 1940 his apartment in Paris was searched. In September he therefore installed himself in Nîmes, leaving the Vice-President of the Fédération Protestante, Pastor A.-N. Bertrand, in charge of the occupied zone. He did not move back to the capital until February 1943 and was consequently for a long while out of the reach of the Germans. After his return to Paris he was kept under strict surveillance. They disliked his interventions in favour of the Jews, but what rankled perhaps even more was his telling Laval he would never be forgiven for publicly expressing his desire for a German victory. In June 1943 his arrest was contemplated, but the Germans thought this would put Catholics at too great an advantage — their policy was to try to play one religious group off against another. If Boegner were taken into custody Cardinal Gerlier, with whom the pastor enjoyed good relations, would have to be arrested also; this would cause too much of an uproar, both internationally and at Vichy, where both enjoyed Pétain's protection. Instead Laval was instructed to ask Boegner to soft-pedal his opinions. The pastor's name was placed on a list of hostages to be rounded up immediately after an Allied invasion, but this too was not carried out.

The situation of Protestant pastors was precarious. Both Boegner and Bertrand tried in vain to persuade the Germans to allow back those pastors who had fled from what became the 'zone réservée' in northern France in order to resume their ministry. As early as October 1941 pastors were suspected of contact with the Resistance and were placed under surveillance. This was progressively intensified — not without cause: a Vichy report from Privas of 14 October 1942 noted that Gaullism and pro-British sentiment were to be found above all in Protestant circles.[82] Obliquely Protestants made their views known. One pastor, for example, preaching on Naboth's vineyard, drew the obvious parallel between Ahab's greed and that of the Germans. At a meeting of the Protestant History Society, on 20 June 1943, Philippe de Felice, its Secretary-General, by alluding to past persecution of generations of Protestants, was able to make his point: 'What did they murmur, then, these people handed over to the executioner? — Songs of joy.' And referring obliquely to the Maquis, he said that the selfsame songs arose, 'Yonder, in those mountain solitudes where those who have been able to escape persecution have taken refuge.'[83]

In July the SS visited the Bibliothèque du Protestantisme français in Paris to demand the surrender of some thirty historical documents concerning Protestants who had fled to Switzerland, England or Germany. The order came from Himmler himself. The papers were required for police files, and would test the 'Aryan' origins of such families. They might also serve, it was argued, as a basis for the Germans to claim estates and property in France abandoned 250 years ago by the families who had fled repression.[84] The Nazis were nothing if not thorough.

Other prominent Protestants had narrow escapes from the Germans. André Philip, onetime economics professor at Lyons and a Socialist deputy since 1936, a Jewish convert to Protestantism, and in frequent contact with Gerlier, made good his escape to London before all France was occupied.[85] Philip was the friend of Edmond Vermeil, a Catholic professor who had taught at Strasbourg and who after the defeat was appointed to Montpellier. In 1943 Vermeil also escaped and arrived in London. Preaching in St Paul's Cathedral on 9 February 1944, Vermeil spoke of how Protestants and Catholics in France were now co-operating; he also told how Roland de Pury had been arrested in Lyons.[86] Pury had been seized on 30 May 1943 at the chapel in the Rue de la Lanterne where he officiated, and interrogated regarding a number of suspect activities. He had half anticipated his own arrest, since a colleague, Pastor Schwendener, had been picked up the day before. He was accused of passing on news of the German Confessional Church and also questioned about his relations with Pastor Niemöller, with whom Hitler had been, according to his captors, 'infinitely patient', and Karl Barth, the Swiss Protestant theologian, whom the Nazis characterised as 'the worst enemy of the Reich'. As a Resistance leader, he was told, he must know the whereabouts of Henri Frenay (of the Resistance movement Combat) and Abbé Glasberg, who had effected the escape from German clutches of many Jews. Since his interrogation was fruitless, and because he was a neutral, Pury was eventually exchanged, with other Swiss nationals, for German prisoners at Bregenz on 28 October.[87]

By now the Germans suspected any and every Protestant. One reason for the raid they made on 25 November at Clermont-Ferrand, where the Université de Strasbourg in exile had been installed, was that not only were students and staff Alsatian, and in Nazi eyes therefore German, but also some were Protestant. During the raid Colomb, a professor in the Faculty of Letters, had been killed, but the one professor wounded, Eppel, belonged to the Protestant theology faculty. Upon his recovery he was deported. Another Protestant faculty member, Hauter, had earlier been shipped off for refusing to reveal where his son was hiding. After the raid several Protestant students were also sent back to Germany.[88]

Protestant pastors continued to be arrested almost to the end: Swiss sources reported in May 1944 that a group of ten had recently been packed off to concentration camps, seven of them to Dachau.[89]

If the Catholic hierarchy had not been firmer in its opposition to the Germans, it was partly because of apprehension that a Communist takeover would follow the Liberation. But one group of French priests, in a last open letter to German Catholics in 1944, painted a different picture. They pointed out that France had suffered terribly in the previous three years, both physically and mentally, Christian patriots had endured all manner of tribulations because of their resistance. Although the Germans had a right to punish them, they should not be branded as terrorists or Communists. Indeed, many genuine Communists had died because they loved their country. 'You cannot expect us to disown them.' The document continued, 'Perhaps we also must learn how you have suffered so that we can forgive each other.'[90] Thus a first gesture of possible reconciliation with German Christians was made.

Reconciliation with nazism was of course impossible for Christians. For Nazis it was a clash of ideologies. Their misconception of the French Church had been total. They sought to play 'clericals' off against 'secularists' in order to neutralise its influence. Their handling of Christians was at first done gingerly — except in Alsace-Lorraine — but soon with increasing fury at what they saw as the Church's ingratitude. Were they not protecting it against bolshevism and 'liberalism'? In return they had met with indifference, 'attentisme', and finally, resistance. For their part, Church leaders attempted unsuccessfully to ignore the German presence. But frictions inevitably arose and clashes were therefore inevitable. In the end the protagonists — the Church and the Germans, not to mention the regime itself — were all defeated in their divergent aims. Nevertheless in the eyes of one (German) historian, ecclesiastical opposition to the Germans could have been greater; he concludes, 'Perhaps the churches did not completely exhaust all the possibilities open to them in relation to the occupation forces.'[91]

Notes

Unless otherwise stated the place of publication is Paris

1. G. Cholvy and Y-M. Hilaire, 1988, *Histoire religieuse de la France contemporaine, 1930–1988*, 1988, p. 71.
2. C. Paillat, *L'Occupation. Le Pillage de la France, juin 1940–novembre 1942*, 1987, p. 93.
3. A Dio, Lille. Guerre 1939–1945. 8 M 7. 'Rapport personnel (de Liénart) de la perquisition'.
4. Ibid. Letter to Rüdiger, Regierungspräsident [his civil service rank], Lille, 27 July 1940.
5. Cardinal Suhard, *Vers une Eglise en état de mission*, 1968, p. 79.
6. Paillat, *L'Occupation*, p. 160.

7. A Dio, Lille, ACA 2 B 1. 'Le Mot du Cardinal', No. 5., 10 August 1940.
8. AN 2 AG 492 CC 72 BC. 'Note', n.d., n.p.
9. The palaces of the bishops of Autun and Nancy were also searched later that autumn.
10. AN F60.1758. Radio France, 20.00, Algiers, 17 April 1943.
11. I am much indebted throughout this chapter to the contribution by Hans Umbreit to the Lille Colloquium. See *Actes*: Lille, H. Umbreit, 'Les services d'occupation allemands et les églises chrétiennes en France', pp. 299ff.
12. Umbreit, 'Les services d'occupation allemands', p. 308, quotes an order to this effect: MBF IC Nr. 410/41G. Abt. Verw. Nr. 460/461, 25 March 1941. Betreff: Einsatz der Sicherheitspolizei und des SD in den besetzten Gebieten, ZdL.
13. See *La Délégation française auprès de la Commission allemande d'Armistice en France*, Recueil de documents, 1948, vol. 2, p. 114, pp. 240f. and p. 302.
14. AN 2 AG 494. Letter of Mgr Ruch to Valerio Valeri, the Nuncio, Périgueux, 11 June 1941.
15. AN 2 AG 494. 'Note sur la situation religieuse en Alsace et en Lorraine', 6 September 1941.
16. AN 2 AG 494. 'Note sur la situation de la cathédrale de Strasbourg', January 1941.
17. AN 2 AG 494. Ordinance of 18 March 1941 by Wagner, the Gauleiter.
18. AN 2 AG 494. Extract from *La Voix du Vatican*, 4 April 1941.
19. J. Barthélémy, *Ministre de la Justice, Vichy 1941–1943. Mémoires*, 1989, p. 299.
20. AN 2 AG 494. 'Renseignements sur la situation religieuse en Lorraine', 14 August 1941.
21. Umbreit, 'Les services d'occupation allemands', p. 301.
22. H. Michel, *Paris Allemand*, 1981, p. 40.
23. O. Abetz, *Pétain et les Allemands*, 1948, p. 17. Report of Abetz, 8 October 1940.
24. FCO archives: German Embassy telegram signed Krüger, July 1942, relating to Professor Conrad.
25. FCO archives: File No. 22010. Telegram 3218 of 27 July 1942, signed Krüger (German Embassy) to Berlin.
26. AN F60.1674.
27. AN 72 AJ 260. Analysis (in translation) of a memorandum, ref: R70/Frankreich 2, 'Hostile influences active in France', probably by a Dr Thomas, and destined for Heydrich himself, but emanating from the 'chief delegate of the SiPo and the SD for France and Belgium'.
28. AN 2 AG 609. The plan was returned to Pétain on 6 June 1942.
29. Simone de Beauvoir maintained he even preached anti-German propaganda from the pulpit. See her *La Force de l'Age*, p. 546.
30. A Dio, Lille, Guerre 1939–1945, 8 M 7. Relations avec les Allemands.
31. A Dio, Lille, Guerre 1939–1945, 8 M 7. Summons from the Devisenschutzkommando, Paris, 29 September 1943.
32. See L. Detrez, *Quand Lille avait faim (1940–1944)*, Lille, 1945, *passim*.
33. See H. Auerbach, 'Die politischen Anfänge Carlo Schmid', *Vierteljahrshefte für Zeitgeschichte*, vol. 36, 1988, p. 595–648. See also C. Schmid, *Erinnerungen*, Munich, 1945.
34. The long list of cases is given in: A Dio, Lille, Guerre 1939–1945. 8 M 7. 'Interventions'.
35. *Actes*: Lille, p. 644.
36. A Dio, Lille, Guerre 1940–1945 8 M 7. 'Relations avec les Allemands'. Message to Falkenhausen, Brussels, 14 October 1941. Mallet asserts that at the ACA meeting in January 1942 he had, for the same reason, condemned the collaborationist position adopted by Cardinal Baudrillart. See A. Mallet, *Pierre Laval*, 1955, vol. 2, p. 163 ff.
37. Lagebericht ('sitrep') of OFK 670 Lille for January 1944, cited in *Actes*: Lille, H. Claude, 'La hiérarchie catholique, le gouvernement de Vichy et l'occupant, dans la zone réservée', p. 270. Claude's article is seminal for a study of relationships with the Germans in northern France.

38. F. Codaccioni, 'Dans la tourmente de la Seconde Guerre mondiale', in Y-M. Hilaire (ed.), *Histoire du Nord-Pas-de-Calais de 1900 à nos jours*, Toulouse, p. 354

39. Paillat, *L'Occupation*, p. 162f., citing German Lageberichte.

40. Umbreit, 'Les services d'occupation allemands', p. 307.

41. *Semaine religieuse*, Paris, 27 September 1941.

42. H. Umbreit, *Der Militärbefehlshaber in Frankreich, 1940–1944*, Boppard, 1968, p. 132.

43. Y. Durand (ed.), *Histoire des diocèses de France: Nantes*, 1985, p. 283.

44. M. Martin du Gard, *La Chronique de Vichy, 1940–1944*, 1948.

45. See Chapter 17.

46. Telegram 610 to Berlin from Abetz, dated 9 February 1944. Quoted in *Actes*: Lyons, p. 394.

47. A Dio, Lille, ACA 1944. ACA meeting of 16–18 February 1944.

48. G. Blond, *Pétain, 1856–1951*, 1966, p. 457.

49. 'Les Nazis attaquent le cardinal Suhard', *France* (London), 4 May 1944, quoting Jean Bosc, writing in *Paris-Soir*, 2 May 1944.

50. FCO archives: Serial No. 6455 GFM 2. Telegram 3410 to Berlin signed by Abetz, 14 July 1944.

51. FCO archives: Serial No. 6455 GFM 2. Telegram 1543 signed by Hilger, 17 July 1944.

52. AN 2 AG 493. Letter from Gerlier to Pétain dated 5 September 1941.

53. AN F60.1674. Letter from Stanislas Fumet to a person whom he addresses as 'cher ami', dated 28 February 1942. He also referred to someone whom Gerlier saved and whose death sentence had been commuted — he may have been referring to Pierre d'Harcourt.

54. *Actes*: Grenoble. Discussion. Intervention of G. Ribière, p. 205.

55. Umbreit, 'Les services d'occupation allemands', p. 306, quoting a German Embassy telegram dated 19 October 1943.

56. *Strassburger Neueste Nachrichten*, 3 October 1942.

57. AN F1a. 3784. Information received December 1943–January 1944. Ref: XCG/1/36000.

58. AN F1a.3784 Information received 4 May 1944. Ref: ACB/9/35.800.

59. C. Falconi, *The Silence of Pius XII*, translated. by B. Wall, London, 1970, p. 77.

60. J. de Launay, *La France de Pétain*, 1972, p.174; *Courrier* no. 11, July 1944, p. 1, mentions other bishops who had allegedly been arrested about this time: Mgr Feltin (Bordeaux), Mgr Martin (Le Puy), Mgr Blanchet (Saint-Dié) and Mgr Chévrier (Cahors). The present writer has been unable to confirm these arrests, which may have been only temporary.

61. F. Hildesheimer (ed.), *Histoire des diocèses de France: Nice et Monaco*, 1984, pp. 318–20.

62. Paillat, *L'Occupation*. p. 162f. Note, quoting from German Lageberichte.

63. AN AJ 40.563. 'Beiakte zu VKult 410, Bd I'.

64. AN AJ 40.563. File: Allgemeine Angelegenheiten: Lagebericht, June–July 1941.

65. Umbreit, 'Les services d'occupation allemands', p. 306, quoting from a German Embassy report, 'Bischofskonferenz des besetzten Gebiets', PA/Botschaft, Paris Nr. 2481. 'Katholische Kirche', 6 November 1941.

66. L. Rebatet, *Les Mémoires d'un fasciste*, vol. 2, *1941–1947*, 1976, pp. 52f.

67. AN 2 AG 75. Letter of Mgr Faure to Pétain, headed Lons-Le-Saunier, 9 July 1941.

68. AN F60.1674. Sermon preached in a Breton parish on 6 April 1942.

69. AN F60.1689. 'Rapport de fin d'année', Ref: CNI Note d'orientation No. 1184.

70. AN 2 AG 609. File: 'Attitude des autorités religieuses à l'égard du gouvernement, des Allemands, juillet 1941–juin 1943'.

71. AN F17.13346. Note by Emile Moreau to Education minister Bonnard, 8 May 1943.

72. AN 2 AG 459.

73. AN 2 AG 493. Letter of Lavagne to Brinon, Vichy, 18 February 1943.

74. AN 2 AG 492. 'Note (Secret)' (police report), 2 March 1943.

75. AN F60.1674 (Fighting French file). Rapport Nilo, 1 July 1943.

76. AN F1a. 3784. Information received December 1943–January 1944. Ref: XCG/1/36000.
77. AN F1a. 3784. Information received 26 January 1944. Ref: XCG/4/36021.
78. AN F60.2674. Information received 12 August 1944. Ref: CNI No. 6431.
79. Letter, ref.:ID 1450, 2 July 1941, from the head of the Militärverwaltungsstab, Bordeaux, to Verwaltungsstab, Militärbefehlshaber in Frankreich, regarding a book on Descartes.
80. Hoover Institution, *France during the German Occupation*, Stanford, 1958, vol. 2, pp. 862f. Testimony of Pilon, Secretary-General of the Secours National.
81. *Actes*: Grenoble, p. 277.
82. Ibid.
83. Rapport du Secrétaire de la Société de l'Histoire du Protestantisme français, 78ᵉ Assemblée Générale, *BSHPP*, Fascicule IV, 1943, pp. 6–7.
84. Rapport du secrétaire, Ph. de Felice, 80ᵉ Assemblée, 13 May 1945, BSHPF, Fascicule VII, 1945, pp. 3ff.
85. FCO archives: ref: no. 220258. German telegram to Berlin 3468, signed Feihl, 11 August 1942. *The Socialist Christian*, London, September–October 1942, vol. XIII, no. 5, reported his arrival.
86. *Catholic Bulletin of Foreign News*, Ministry of Information, London, 4 March 1944, p. 1.
87. R. de Pury, *Journal from my cell* (*Journal de cellule*), translated by B. Mussey, London, 1948, *passim*. Pury gives details of his imprisonment at Fort Montluc in Lyons. He was in solitary confinement for seventy-five days, in a cell measuring 2 by 3 metres. Exercise lasted a quarter of an hour a day, and on it he saw old men of seventy-five and boys aged fifteen, as well as Catholic priests.
88. *BSHPF*, Fascicule VI, 1944, pp. 46f. 'Allocution prononcée le 25 novembre 1944 dans la Cour d'Honneur de la Sorbonne par Ph. de Felice, doyen de la faculté de théologie protestante de Paris, pour commémorer le premier anniversaire des atrocités commises par les Allemands, le 25 novembre 1943, contre l'université de Strasbourg repliée à Clermont-Ferrand.' See also *La Vie Protestante* (Geneva), 24 December 1943.
89. AN F60.1674. Report of Schweizerisch Evangelischer Pressedienst, 10 May 1944.
90. AN F60.1674. File: 'Opinions et résistance des catholiques (clergé et fidèles)', *News Digest* No. 11, London, quoting *Neue Zürcher Nachrichten*, 21 July 1944.
91. Umbreit, 'Les services d'occupation allemands', p. 308.

-13-

Christians and the Resistance

How many Frenchmen belonged to the Resistance? The figures are disputed, but Paxton, perhaps more reliable than French sources, puts the total at 400,000, or about 2 per cent [sic] of the adult population.[1] Even this number, however, must be qualified. From 1940 to November 1942 the total was comparatively small. The events of 1942 — in particular, the persecution of the Jews and the landings in North Africa — caused the numbers to swell. In 1943 the conscription of young men for work in Germany and the growing conviction that Germany would be defeated signalled a considerable increase in those taking to the Maquis. In 1944 came the flood tide of recruitment, and de Gaulle's final call to insurrection was answered by many men and women anxious to help free their own locality.

This progressive increase in numbers among the population as a whole was typical also of practising Christians. Politically, Catholic Resisters were drawn from the traditional Right and from the officer class, as well as from the Christian Democrats: the Centrist PDP and the more left-wing Jeune République, despite its pre-war pacifist leanings. They were to be found more among the lower rather than the higher clergy, and among the members of the ACJF, especially the JEC and JOC, as well as of the CFTC. Also prominent were readers and contributors of such periodicals as *Temps Présent*, the successor to the Jesuit *Etudes*, which appeared from December 1940 to August 1941 as *Temps Nouveau*; *Esprit* (also closed down in August 1941); its more popular version *Le Voltigeur français;* the Dominican *La Vie Spirituelle* or *Sept*, its predecessor, the pre-war *L'Aube* (Francisque Gay, Bidault, Michelet, Schumann) and *La Chronique sociale* (Joseph Vialatoux, Joseph Folliet). In the regular orders Resisters tended to be Jesuits or Dominicans, such as de Lubac, Lebreton, and Montcheuil, whereas female religious belonged to many different congregations. The Resistance also included Christian intellectuals and theologians sensitised to the evils of nazism. Inevitably, because of the weakness of catholicism among industrial workers, at first Christian Resisters sprang from the bourgeoisie and the middle classes.

Protestant Resisters were also drawn from the religious youth movements, strongly backed in the southern zone by their pastors.

Christian activities in the Resistance developed progressively: from the circulation of tracts many passed to the production of full-blown clandestine periodicals, such as *Témoignage Chrétien*. The step from the passive collection of intelligence useful to de Gaulle or the Allies to more sophisticated forms of espionage was small. More deliberate, because it usually entailed leaving home and family behind, was the transition to acts of sabotage and armed attacks upon the Occupation forces. 'Groupes francs', 'hit squads' set up to carry out small-scale direct actions, were quickly formed, but the deployment of larger military detachments did not occur until 1943. The progression was from passive to active Resistance. Christians were represented in all these activities, so much so that by June 1944 they and the Communists, were acknowledged to be the most influential in many Resistance groupings.

The Church authorities did not encourage the Resistance in any way. The bishops' attitude was one of condemnation of what they termed 'terrorism'. The exploits of the Maquis were dismissed as acts of 'banditry'. Such terms were naturally bitterly resented by 'dissident' Catholics. With one or two exceptions, the bishops bore down heavily upon those of their flock who deviated from the official line. Thus, for example, *Témoignage Chrétien* was the butt of their vituperation. Mgr Delay (Marseilles) rebuked publicly those responsible for this clandestine publication. At one point Cardinal Gerlier, after reading a copy, let it be known that he forbade further issues.[2] This did not prevent him, however, from allegedly claiming in Canada after the Liberation that he was its founder. On the other hand Mgr Saliège (Toulouse) gave it his blessing, and others such as Mgrs Théas (Montauban), Terrier (Moutiers) and Vansteenberghe (Bayonne) were sympathetic to it.

The ACA adopted the same condemnatory line as regards the anonymous writings by theologians (of no mean repute) that sought to justify resistance to the regime. These included Jesuits such as de Lubac and Pierre Ganne, of the Fourvière scholasticate at Lyons, or others involved with *Etudes*, such as Gaston Fessard, Yves de Montcheuil and, at a different level, a prominent layman, Robert d'Harcourt. They were branded by the ACA as 'hommes sans mission et inconnus'. Obloquy was heaped upon them: were not their ecclesiastical superiors the sole qualified to pronounce on theological matters?[3] Yet after the war Mgr Guerry, in his 'plaidoyer pro domo' for the Church, spoke of these selfsame theologians as 'having rendered the Church a precious service'.[4]

Christian Resisters reacted indignantly to such treatment. Bishops received anonymous notes on which the single message ran: 'Mercier ou Innitzer?' — a reference to the courageous stand of the Belgian cardinal in the First World War against the Germans, as opposed to the Austrian cardinal who had greeted the Anschluss in 1938 with the Nazi salute.[5] A more reasoned statement came in March 1943 from an anonymous group of Catholics, who addressed an appeal to the ACA. They were, they said, engaged in a struggle not only against the Germans, but also against Vichy; they were determined to participate in the liberation of France and the installation of a new political order. Treated as 'francs-tireurs' and disavowed by the bishops, they warned of a recrudescence of anticlericalism among the industrial and agricultural population, which 'associates the Church with a government that is detested, one considered by everybody as the servant of the enemy', and this at a time when the outcome of the war was no longer in doubt.[6]

Meanwhile Catholics condemned many acts of their bishops, as another anonymous document submitted to the ACA made plain.[7] It was abhorrent that the ACA had pronounced its 'veneration' for Pétain, and certain priests had even dubbed him a saint. One bishop had thought it appropriate to attend the ceremony at which a regional prefect had administered to his functionaries the oath of loyalty to the Marshal. Some *Semaines religieuses* had categorically forbidden Catholics to listen to the BBC. The bishops had condoned many appalling actions of the regime, if only by keeping silent. Had not Peyrouton, when Interior minister, issued a circular (24 December 1940) requesting mayors to draw up regulations for brothels — 'un des fléaux les plus destructeurs des vertus'? Adultery had been encouraged by a law (14 September 1941) that allowed married men to legitimise their bastard offspring. The Charte du Travail had decapitated Christian trade unions. The anti-Semitic legislation was neither humane nor Christian. The messages of the Pope and the broadcasts of Radio Vatican had been jammed on Vichy's orders. Moreover, did the bishops not realise that 'l'hérésie qui constitue le nazisme' would, in the event of a German victory, unleash religious persecution? The document concluded with a personal attack on Pétain on familiar lines:

> Throughout his life this man has distanced himself not only from religious practices, but any kind of asceticism is foreign to him. He is still in an irregular matrimonial situation; his wife is divorced; her first husband being still alive [this was not true] no religious marriage can be celebrated... Let an end be put to these exaggerated and resounding perpetual praises from a Christian pulpit of the person of the Marshal.[8]

The Resistance, Christian or otherwise, was thus particularly incensed against the Church's leaders. In the clandestine publication *Défense de la France* (July 1943) a priest stigmatised the attitude of 'certain bishops serving the enemy', who, blissfully unaware of the sentiments of ordinary people, had adopted a course wounding to Catholics, which could have unpleasant consequences in the near future: 'Once more they have followed the "bien-pensants," instead of leading.' They had even dared to compare the Marshal to Saint Louis.[9] The fear was that after the war the people would blame the Church for the errors of the regime.[10] Anti-Catholic Resisters were even more virulent: 'The Church has found a preponderant place in fascism. It is howling with the wolves. Beware of it. Clericalism is an enemy.'[11] A portent from London was the demand that in a liberated France Rome should appoint bishops that had not been compromised. In vain those associated with *Témoignage Chrétien* in 1944 sought to exonerate the Church as an institution, blaming French misfortunes on 'un cléricalisme d'Etat, dont l'Eglise ne veut pas'.[12]

Incidents involving the highest clergy rankled with the Resistance. For Cardinal Liénart everything hinged, they felt bitterly, on the premise that Pétain could do no wrong. Cardinal Suhard made promises he did not keep: in February 1942 he assured Germaine Tillion, deeply embroiled in the Resistance activities of a group of academics at the Paris Musée de l'Homme, that he would ask for mercy for those who had been caught, ten of whom had been sentenced to death. He failed to keep his word.[13] Resisters resented the fact that Cardinal Gerlier was willing to attend a mass for the assassinated collaborator Henriot (on the grounds that he was a government minister), but refused to participate in the funeral ceremony for the Catholic Resister Gilbert Dru, executed by the Germans on 27 June 1944. Even after the liberation of Bayeux, Coulet, the 'commissaire régional' left behind by de Gaulle to govern the area, had almost to force the bishop to attend a Te Deum of thanksgiving, because at first he had refused, declaring he was no Gaullist.[14] Other bishops, particularly those of Saint-Brieuc, Poitiers and Pamiers, expressed the strongest hostility to the Resistance. One sore point was the refusal by some — the bishops of Dijon, Luçon and Nancy were cited — to appoint chaplains to the Maquis — a matter of utmost gravity for the Church because Catholic Resisters were in danger of death and therefore had an undoubted right to its ministrations.[15] The Bishop of Ardèche, who had previously refused to name a chaplain, when he learnt that Pierre Limagne, the prominent journalist of *La Croix*, had joined the local Maquis, sent a message to him on the eve of the Liberation, informing him he was now willing to do so. The Maquis were so indignant at this tardy conversion that they wanted, a few weeks later, to arrest the luckless prelate.[16] However, the position regarding chaplains changed in June 1944 when the Nuncio learnt that the Pope had authorised such appointments.[17]

On the other side of the coin, when Closon, de Gaulle's emissary, came secretly from London to make contact with Mgr Saliège in Toulouse, and was introduced by Mgr Solages, the ailing archbishop was able to say, 'Dites bien au Général que nous sommes avec lui.'[18] In his Lenten letter for 1944 he made known publicly his views. Citing St Paul and Joan of Arc, he told his flock:

> You are afraid of communism. I do not say you are wrong, but I say that for you Christians communism has special significance — it demonstrates an unfulfilled duty... To suffer injustice without protesting, without struggling against it, to accept disorder, is unworthy of both a man and a Christian. Faith does not make people who are resigned, it makes them bold.[19]

Likewise Saliège's friend and protégé, Mgr Maisonobe, Bishop of Belley, assisted young members of JAC who had joined the Resistance, and supported his priests in their contacts with the Ain Maquis. Mgr Terrier (Bayonne) was also an active helper of Resisters. Other prelates, such as Mgrs Béguin (Auch) and Piguet (Clermont-Ferrand) and on occasion even Cardinal Suhard, did indeed help those on the run from the Germans, even when it involved clashing with the Milice. Their motives, however, were charitable rather than because of any belief in the justice of the Resistance cause.[20] In any case, such examples of episcopal backing were not frequent.

Yet, if Mgr Tisserant, the pro-Gaullist French cardinal who spent the war years at the Vatican, is to be believed, it was the Resisters who were esteemed in Rome, and not the rest. 'How many times have the Holy Father and the cardinal (Cardinal Maglione, Secretary of State) said to me regarding the latter [that is, the non-Resisters]: "We would never have believed that France could stoop to such abjection..." '[21] It is difficult to accept that this Vatican view, if it was accurate, was not known to the bishops.

All in all, therefore, at the Liberation the Resistance, particularly Catholics, had just cause for complaint. As one such, Père Bruckberger, said at the time: 'Catholics of the Resistance, we have not been obedient', a sentiment echoed by another, Joseph Folliet, 'As Resisters', he said, 'we were rebels', and he added significantly, 'Something of this cannot fail to remain with us.'[22]

One authoritative historian has written that Christians in the Resistance were initially a 'minority of a minority'.[23] This is perhaps to discount the numbers of those who professed to be Christians, albeit non-practising, but had no links with the committed Catholics and Protestants in the various networks and movements. Small in number though the latter were, the role they assumed, particularly in the early and closing stages of the Occupation, as well as in the first years of the Fourth Republic, was extremely important.

Whether Christians joined the Resistance because of their faith has been much debated. Like other Frenchmen, they probably acted out of patriotism rather than from religious belief. A few, such as Père Chaillet, were motivated because of their first-hand knowledge of the evils of nazism. Protestants, mindful of their own history, had been alerted to the iniquities of nazism by Karl Barth. Many Christians of course had specific reasons for opposition. Thus Christian Democrats wished the return to a democratic system. In northern France Christian memories of the brutal German occupation from 1914 to 1918 were strong. For Christians of Alsace-Lorraine evacuated to the southern zone there was the horror of becoming German, coupled with a longing to return home. Many Christians were indignant at the persecution of all kinds. Those liable to forced labour in Germany, on practical — and sometimes on idealistic — grounds, resorted to arms. Moreover, as time passed, some joined the Resistance because they realised that otherwise the Communists would predominate, and this would bode ill for the Church in a post-war France. Thus their religion strengthened but did not motivate their decision.

On the other hand, those Christians who submitted to Vichy and the Occupation also had their reasons. Practical motives for acceptance of the regime also abounded. Few, for example, reacted as did Edmond Michelet, the father of eight children, whose immediate instinct was to resist: they believed they were not justified in jeopardising their family. In short, most Christians, like most Frenchmen, whilst remaining anti-German in their heart of hearts, could not, or would not, become actively involved in the Resistance.

However, as the war proceeded, the Christian conscience was increasingly awakened. By 1943 a new generation of young Catholics — but still a minority — did not submit unquestioningly to the yoke their bishops imposed upon them, much less to the timid acquiescence advocated by some ACJF leaders.[24] Nevertheless, the leaders of the first Resistance movements that Christians joined took a long while to repudiate Pétain. Henri Frenay, the career army officer who eventually became the leader of Combat, the first large movement, in fact waited until the summer of 1942 before doing so.

The honour of being the first Catholic to protest against any surrender to the Germans, and perhaps of being the first Resister of all, goes in fact to Edmond Michelet, of Brive-la-Gaillarde. A Royalist turned Christian Democrat, he headed the local group of Nouvelles Equipes Françaises (NEF), the study groups founded in 1938 by the Amis de *l'Aube*, the pre-war Christian Democrat newspaper. He was also a member of the

Equipes Sociales. On 17 June 1940, on the very day that Pétain announced he was suing for an armistice, he distributed typed copies of a tract he had written, in which Péguy was quoted with singular aptness: 'He who does not give in is right, as against the one who does... In time of war, he who does not surrender is my man, no matter who he may be, from where he comes, or whatever his party.'[25] Incidentally, after the war Michelet declared that in the southern zone the NEF groups formed the infrastructure of the Resistance.[26]

Family circumstances militated against Michelet's joining de Gaulle, and he continued to distribute tracts denouncing Vichy concessions to the Germans. In August 1940 he sheltered his first group of refugees: fourteen anti-Nazi Germans and Austrians, among them Dietrich von Hildebrand, the Munich philosophy professor, were passed on to him from Toulouse by Mgr Bruno de Solages. The party eventually reached Spain.[27] From his position as departmental delegate (Corrèze) for the Secours National he was well placed to help those on the run.

In 1941 Michelet joined forces with Frenay in the Combat Resistance movement, where he headed the 'R 5 District', which consisted of nine departments and was centred on Limoges. He seemed oblivious to danger and continued to use his own home as a safe haven, even for his fellow Resisters. This horrified Frenay, who urged him to take to the Maquis. He refused, again on family grounds.[28] Inevitably he was caught. Arrested in Brive on 25 February 1943, he was sent to Fresnes, where he was befriended by the German chaplain, Father Stock, who proved indefatigable in his efforts to help French Resistance prisoners.[29] From Fresnes he was shipped to Neue Bremen, near Saarbrücken, and finally landed up in Dachau.[30] After the Liberation he joined the MRP, eventually becoming Armed Forces minister in de Gaulle's government.

Michelet belonged to the Brive group of NEF. Other future resisters belonged to NEF groups elsewhere: Fréville (Rennes), Charles Aragon (Tarn), Etienne Borne (Haute-Garonne). Maurice Schumann, a former political editor of *L'Aube*, who lectured to NEF groups, joined de Gaulle in London. But perhaps the most eminent member, in view of his later career, was Georges Bidault.[31] A history 'agrégé' who taught at the Lycée du Parc in Lyons and a former leading light in the ACJF, he was perhaps better known as a leading light before the war of *L'Aube*. After returning from captivity in 1940 he devoted himself to clandestine activities.

Michelet had quickly made contact with former members of the PDP and Jeune République. He joined forces with François de Menthon, P.-H. Teitgen and Alfred Coste-Floret to produce a clandestine periodical, *Liberté*, aimed at intellectuals, which first appeared in the unoccupied zone in November 1940. Michelet's job gave him access to transport, which facilitated the distribution of the periodical. Menthon had escaped from being a prisoner of war. A former ACJF leader and economics professor in the Nancy law faculty,[32] he found a new post at the university in Lyons. Teitgen had been his colleague at Nancy, and was a pre-war Christian Democrat and onetime Vice-President of the Assemblée Nationale. He had secured another appointment at Montpellier. The centre of activity moved to Lyons, which quickly became the 'capital' of the Resistance. Links were not only established with Alfred Coste-Floret, also a law professor, in Clermont-Ferrand, but with the latter's brother Paul Coste-Floret, in Algiers. Marcel Prélot joined the group. He had been living in Strasbourg, but had been evacuated to Clermont-Ferrand. Bidault became associated with this group of Catholics in 1941, when he was living in Vichy. Almost all those connected with *Liberté* belonged to the PDP. The party's leader, Champetier de Ribes, was also in touch before he was arrested in 1942 and imprisoned in Evaux-les-Bains, where, incidentally, Blum was held for a while. The group's activities eventually centred on Lyons. Although rejecting the Armistice and the anti-Allied policy of Laval, all were hesitant as to whether to support de Gaulle. They were not opposed to Pétain's ideas for the regeneration of France, although by October 1941 their opinion was fast changing about what their periodical referred to as 'le malheureux gouvernement de Vichy'.[33]

Menthon took the lead in initiating further covert action. In May 1941 groups had been set up to organise demonstrations, to distribute clandestine publications and tracts and denounce the collaborationist press, such as the infamous *Gringoire*. The invasion of the Soviet Union took the group by surprise. Although anti-Communist, they were anxious that the German attack should not succeed.[34] It was nevertheless a long time before they could accept Communist Resisters as allies.

In the autumn of 1941, however, some of the group fell under suspicion. Menthon was arrested, but released after a warning that, although anti-German remarks might just be tolerated, speaking against Pétain was not permissible.[35] After October no further issue of *Liberté* appeared, but this was because by then Menthon and his group had agreed to join with Frenay, who had by chance seen a copy of *Liberté*. On 1 June 1941 their appeared the first issue of Frenay's own clandestine journal, *Les Petites Ailes*, to which, incidentally, Père Chaillet contributed articles on the anti-Christian, pagan nature of nazism. This quickly changed its name to *Vérités*, but as such was short-lived, as will be seen. Frenay had begun his Resistance career by starting in Marseilles a Mouvement de Libération nationale, drawn mainly from the officer and bourgeois classes. In November 1941 Menthon met Frenay and they agreed to merge. Thus in December 1941 a new publication, *Combat*, appeared. Its first issue was a denunciation of collaboration. *Combat* eventually gave its name to the movement that arose from the fusion. It was agreed that a directorate of six — eventually seven, because Bidault joined it later — should constitute the new Resistance grouping: Menthon, Alfred Coste-Floret and Teitgen would link up with Frenay and his two lieutenants, Chevance and Bourdet. The extremely important movement that emerged may have been no longer specifically Catholic, but Catholic input was strong. Lyons Catholics such as Joseph Hours, a teacher colleague of Bidault, Jean Lacroix, and Stanislas Fumet, the editor of the (legal) *Temps Nouveau,* and Plaisantin, the Christian trade unionist, became notable anonymous contributors to its clandestine journal.

Frenay ran the organisation on military lines. In addition to its other activities, Combat would constitute direct action, commando-style squads for small operations, but would also form larger groupings, with which other Resistance organisations could link up, in an 'Armée secrète'. The unoccupied zone was divided into six regions, three of which were placed under the Catholics associated with Menthon: R3 (Montpellier and six departments), under the joint command of Teitgen and René Courtin, a Protestant, who like his colleague, taught at the local university; R5, under Michelet; and R6 (Clermont-Ferrand and five departments), under Coste-Floret. Contact was also established with dissidents in the occupied zone, such as Père Riquet.

Whereas these early Resistance groupings were wary of de Gaulle, in the meantime an isolated group in western Dordogne, started by a country landowner, Louis de la Bardonnie, with a group of friends, was desperately trying to establish contact with the Fighting French in order to pass on military information. In October 1940 they succeeded in sending an ageing priest, Abbé Dartein, to London, with details of the German-occupied harbour of Bordeaux. The following month de Gaulle despatched 'Rémy' to contact them, and the intelligence network Confrérie Notre Dame, was duly formalised as a Gaullist organisation.[36] Nevertheless the view that the dissident general was a 'traitor' still continued to be widely held among Catholics.

One notes other close interconnections between those who were unwilling to accept the defeat of 1940. Frenay was in contact with Segonzac, of the 'leadership school' ('école des cadres') at Uriage. This idealistic cavalry officer, who had been with Frenay at St-Cyr, also refused to accept German hegemony, but had decided to work for the rehabilitation and restoration of France within the framework of the Vichy State. Frenay, despite having 'gone underground' after resigning his commission, visited Uriage on the very day when Darlan was there on an inspection tour, and had even mingled with the admiral's party.

The network also included Louis Terrenoire, the friend of Stanislas Fumet and a Catholic fellow journalist, who was later to become the Secretary-General of the Conseil National de la Résistance. Pères Chaillet and Fessard were also associated with Fumet. The web of relationships between those Catholics who became active Resisters and those Catholics who were anti-German but did not necessarily join them is intricate and complex. There can be no doubt that those who kept within the regime were aware of the former's clandestine activities.

In the northern zone the budding Resistance had not the same freedom of movement as in unoccupied France. Christian Resisters were dispersed among the various movements that arose. Moreover, with the exception of leaders like the industrialist Jean Catrice, whose Resistance group at Roubaix had connections with the PDP, the Christian nature of their commitment to the Resistance was not so apparent. However, Christians were prominent in the initial activities that were undertaken: the escape routes established for British stragglers left behind at Dunkirk, and for escaping POWs and shot-down RAF pilots. From this emerged the Voix du Nord network, which was the joint creation of Natalis Dumez, a former mayor of Bailleul long associated with the Sillon movement, and Jules Noutour, a Socialist, who edited the movement's clandestine periodical – *Voix du Nord* – until his arrest in September 1942. The periodical did not hesitate to condemn collaborationists such as Mgr Dutoit and the separatist Abbé Gantois, or criticise the regime and its legitimacy.[37]

Christian Democrats, particularly of the PDP, were strong in northern France. Men such as the Catrice, Jules Catoire, of the CFTC, a reserve officer, and Louis Blanckaert, the party's local secretary and a professor at the Lille Institut Catholique (known as 'la Catho'), became prominent in the local Resistance. Resisters might well belong to more than one movement. Libération-Nord, the counterpart in the occupied zone of the southern-based movement Libération, included Socialists and CGT members such as Pineau, but also many from the Christian trade unions. Other Resistance movements such as the Organisation Civile et Militaire (OCM), consisting largely of rightist officers, writers and politicians, and Ceux de la Résistance, comprised many Catholics, in particular members of the CFTC, including Gaston Tessier, its Secretary-General and a former Jociste. Christian Democrats, led by René Théry, another professor at 'la Catho', distributed the *Voix du Nord*, and later *Témoignage Chrétien* (for the Nord department), as did Catoire (for the Pas-de-Calais). Catrice specialised in plans for escapees and in obtaining military intelligence,[38] and later liaised closely with Bidault, who appointed him to oversee all information-gathering in the area.

Locally the CFTC were active in the strike that from 26 May to 7 June 1941 paralysed the mines in the two northern departments and affected three-quarters of the workers. Not unsurprisingly, after a meeting at Lens, it declared that it would not participate in the Charte du Travail. In February 1942 its delegates made known their flat refusal at a meeting with Lehideux, the Industrial Production minister, in Lille. This was the signal for some to join the various Resistance movements, including even the Communist-inspired Francs-Tireurs et Partisans (FTP).

In the North, as well as in the unoccupied zone, the Alliance, a national network, flourished, but one which worked exclusively with the British. It had been started by Captain Loustaunau-Lacau in April 1941, after he had contacted a British agent in Lisbon. His successor, Marie-Madeleine Fourcade, was the only woman to lead a Resistance organisation. She was responsible for giving London the first information regarding German plans to make an atomic bomb.[39] The arrest in Dunkirk on a charge of espionage for Alliance, and the subsequent execution, in March 1943 of a young priest, Abbé Bonpain, despite a plea for mercy by Cardinal Liénart, caused a stir locally[40] and stimulated recruitment.

In the occupied zone a number of other clandestine periodicals with Christian Democrat connections flourished, mainly ephemeral. Thus one with the significant title of *Valmy*, and the banner slogan, 'Un seul ennemi, l'envahisseur' was started in Paris in September 1940 by a group of young intellectuals, all supporters of Jeune République. In the Nantes area young Christian Democrats, readers of *Temps Présent*, started *En Captivité*, with the aim of countering German propaganda. In 1941, heralding the New Year, they wrote: 'France can [still] hope in God. In spite of its official atheism in the past, it remains the most Christian of nations.' On 27 April 1941, after the British bombing of Brest, they accused the Germans of having deliberately dive-bombed a hospital and then blaming the British.[41] Thus even in very Catholic western France the bishops' position was undermined.

For Catholic Resisters, however, the Communists still posed a problem. Initially their attitude towards them was one of great mistrust, which for some lingered even after the Liberation. For others, however, during the Occupation years a mutual respect grew up, as it became apparent by 1944 that Communists and Catholics would be key players in shaping post-war France. Nevertheless, what they saw as the manœuvring of the Communist party was for Catholics unfathomable. In 1939 the party had denounced what it dubbed a Capitalist war and had been outlawed for its pains. Immediately after the defeat some Communists had even appealed to the Germans to allow *L'Humanité* to resume publication. Catholics argued that, apart from a clash of ideologies, these were concrete reasons for suspicion of duplicity. If, as has been asserted, Thorez and Duclos had launched a call to resist on 10 July 1940, the day the Third Republic finally died, it was couched in terms that urged the working class to free themselves from the iron hand of capitalism rather than as call for action against the invaders. It is true that that same summer the Communist Rizo, the founder of Francs Tireurs et Partisans, had been imprisoned for handing out anti-Nazi tracts. *L'Humanité*, eventually appearing clandestinely, also opposed Montoire and the new 'European Order'.[42] In May 1941, with the Communist party playing the predominant role, a Front National was formed. Besides attracting such well-known academic sympathisers as Langevin, Wallon and Frédéric Joliot-Curie, contact was also established with Catholics such as Tessier, the Secretary-General of the CFTC, Canon Chevrot, of the Paris church of St-François-Xavier, R.P. Philippe, Provincial of the Carmelites, and Mauriac.[43] The Front's ambition was to operate in all zones, and represent all shades of opinion. It did in fact attract a number of priests, and at one point, even Bidault, who had begun his Resistance career in Combat.

In June the German attack on the Soviet Union marked the real beginning of Communist armed resistance. In a flashback to 1936 *L'Humanité* (no.123 of 7 August 1941) wrote: 'The Communists extend a brotherly hand to the Catholic patriots, who are legion' ('Les Communistes tendent une main fraternelle aux catholiques patriotes qui sont légion'). On 22 May 1942 it returned to the fray in an evocative article entitled, 'La main tendue aux catholiques': 'In their immense majority the Catholics are patriots.' Elsewhere it recalled that priests had been imprisoned; Dominicans had been arrested by the Gestapo; Lieutenant d'Estienne d'Orves, shot for espionage, had been a practising Catholic, and in northern France a priest had offered up a mass for Communists who had died under the rifles of German firing squads.

The FTP became the military arm of the Front National. Although Communist-dominated, it comprised Catholics and Protestants, as well as liberal elements. Under Tillon, the veteran Communist, it became the largest and most effective of all the combat units.

In the field, particularly in the Nord department, young Communists and members of Catholic youth organisations fraternised freely; the party bosses made every effort to convert them to communism.[44] The JOC responded by even copying some of the methods of young Communist resisters.

In the southern zone, however, extreme distrust persisted, until Rémy, for de Gaulle, and Fernand Grenier, for the Communists, in November 1942 signed a formal pact pledging mutual co-operation.

Frenay, and the Catholics who had joined him, nevertheless still shrank from out-and-out collaboration.

The history of the Resistance movements as they developed is tortuous and complicated. Although the Catholic group Liberté had amalgamated in November 1941 with Frenay's Combat, Catholics still retained their influence. But other movements had also grown up. Emmanuel Astier de la Vigerie, an aristocratic naval officer and journalist, had created Libération in December 1940. It comprised many Socialists, including the Protestant André Philip before he departed to London, Jews, intellectuals, Christian Democrats, and members of the CGT and CFTC. A year later Jean-Pierre Lévy had established Franc-Tireur (not to be confused with the FTP of the northern zone), to which former radicals but also members of the Jeune République adhered. These three southern movements therefore represented politically respectively the Right, the Left and the Centre. Frenay and Astier had made contact with each other by the end of 1941, and discussed the possibility of establishing a co-ordinating committee in the South, to include all Resistance movements. These main groupings eventually united in the Mouvements Unis de la Résistance (MUR) on 26 January 1943, under a directorate consisting of their leaders, and headed by Jean Moulin. A similar co-ordinating committee in the former occupied zone was established in March, to include OCM and the Front National, the two largest movements, and Libération-Nord, Ceux de la Libération and Ceux de la Résistance. This last group had been set up after Frenay's Combat, which had already extended operations to the northern zone and had suffered severe losses. In December 1943 MUR incorporated other movements, including Défense de la France and the Voix du Nord, and changed its name to Mouvement de Libération Nationale (MLN).

Already by early 1942 Jean Moulin had been officially appointed de Gaulle's representative to the Resistance. A more formal overarching organisation, with various committees, now became possible. In July 1942 a Comité Général d'Etudes was established in order to work out the economic and social structures of France after the Liberation. Its chairman was Menthon, and Teitgen also served on it; both were future ministers of de Gaulle. In fact, of the committee's eight members a majority were practising Christians.[45] In Paris Bidault set up a Bureau d'Information et de Presse. Its task was to receive and disseminate information from London, as well as to transmit intelligence back. Two Catholics were appointed to it: Teitgen, and Louis Terrenoire, the former journalist on *L'Aube*. The final step in the organisational process was taken on 21 February 1943, when the Conseil National de la Résistance was created with Moulin as its chairman. It was intended to act as the consultative body in France for de Gaulle: eight members were drawn from the Resistance movements, two from the trade unions (including Tessier, of the CFTC) and six from the political parties or 'tendencies' (this included Bidault for the PDP). It first met in Paris in May, but on 21 June, the betrayal of Moulin and his capture by the Gestapo left it leaderless. In September Bidault, who was acceptable both to the Right and the Left (since he had served both in Combat and in the Front National), was appointed in his stead — a signal triumph for the Christian Democrats.[46]

In January 1944 a group of Catholics under Bidault met to draw up plans for a new unitary Christian Democratic party — although both the appellations 'democrat' and 'party' were deemed unacceptable. Instead it was to be styled the Mouvement Républicain Populaire (MRP). It would seek to establish a society based on Christian and democratic principles, the abolition of Capitalist trusts and cartels, the nationalisation of monopoly enterprises, and the participation of workers in management, with security of employment guaranteed. Uniting the strands of reformism and social catholicism, the MRP was to become for a while the largest party in post-war France. It was in this way that Catholics, together with the Communists, emerged as the most influential of all the groupings in the final months of the Resistance and the first months after the Liberation.

Meanwhile, however, victory had still to be won. In February 1944 a military regrouping of Resistance forces took place with the creation of the Forces Françaises de l'Intérieur (FFI). The battle of France was about to begin.

Christian youth had a part to play in that battle. Some members of JOC, like other movements of the ACJF, had accepted the STO; others had decamped to the Resistance. Less markedly, the same parting of the ways occurred among the Catholic Scouts. Many suffered a cruel fate. One Scout, 'Emmanuel' (Jacques Molé) of Grenoble, where a 'maquis d'élite' of young men was formed, was caught and tortured by the Milice before being shot.[47] On a visit to Catholic students of the Vercors Maquis, Père de Montcheuil, who was acting as their chaplain, was captured and shot with some other young Christians on 11 August 1944.[48]

In fact Christian youth was prominent in many Resistance movements. In 1944 Albert Gortais, in 1940 President of the ACJF, for example, was fighting in Brittany in the movement Défense de la France. Co-ordination was deemed necessary. After a clandestine meeting of the ACJF council in November 1943, Bidault and Pierre Corval, both former ACJF leaders, decided to create an 'umbrella' organisation for young Christians, the Jeunes Chrétiens Combattants

(JCC). The intention was, however, that they should continue in their respective movements as hitherto. The eventual leader of the new JCC was Maurice-René Simonnet, a future Secretary-General of the MRP. In the Nord department the JCC comprised no less than 15,000 members, mainly drawn from the JOC. It even sent delegates to sit in the Algiers Consultative Assembly.[49] A similar national organisation for all young people, Christian or otherwise, the Forces Unies de la Jeunesse Patriote (FUJP) was established, in which Catholics, Protestants, and young people in the other Resistance movements were federated.[50]

Throughout the occupation there had come from the world outside encouragement by Christians that stiffened Christian Resistance. Bernanos, in exile in Brazil, broadcast on the BBC in support of de Gaulle. Thierry d'Argenlieu, the Carmelite turned admiral in the Free French navy, attacked Vichy for daring to characterise itself as a symbol of 'return to the Christian tradition'.[51] Maritain's book, *A travers le désastre*, written and published in America, severely critical of Vichy, was commented on by the BBC on several occasions, and other statements by the well-known Christian philosopher were broadcast. That his messages went home can be gauged by the reaction of the collaborationist press. Rebatet, in *Je Suis Partout*, treated him as a 'cur'.[52] Others from France itself who made the perilous journey via Spain or directly across the Channel, such as André Philip, were pressed into service. François Valentin, onetime leader of the LFC, broadcast from London a call to resist on the third anniversary of the Légion's foundation (29 August 1943). The Gaullists had of course their own French-language press, among which figured the Christian periodical, *Volontaires pour la Cité chrétienne*, on which collaborated François Closon (later Commissaire de la République in Lille), Maurice Schumann, Abbé de Naurois, who from being chaplain at Uriage became a commando chaplain, and Mira Benenson, an English lady with connections with *Temps Présent* and Stanislas Fumet.[53] *Volontaires* circulated mainly in Britain and North America, but occasionally information from it filtered through to France from Switzerland.

Within France, there existed what might be termed, somewhat loosely, 'passive' Resistance groups — 'loosely' because belonging to such groups did not exclude participation in more 'active' operations. These groups dispensed anti-German and anti-Vichy 'propaganda', often to good effect. Probably the most important clandestine periodical for Catholics and Protestants alike was *Témoignage Chrétien*, whose role has already been touched upon several times.[54] Its founder, the Jesuit Père Chaillet, had close links with Frenay's Combat movement (*Combat* and *Témoignage Chrétien* were at first printed on the same presses). His colleague, Père Fessard,[55] it will be recalled, wrote the challenging opening article to the first issue – 'France, prends garde de perdre ton âme!' – which had originally been intended for a JIC group in Lyons.[56]

The *Cahiers*, appearing every two months, rose to a circulation of 50,000. (Its offshoot, the more populist *Courrier*, less intellectual in content, was started in 1943 as a monthly and had an eventual circulation of 100,000.) In it, for the first time since the early nineteenth century Christians set out freely positions hostile to Church authority on topics of the day that for them had become matters of conscience. Information was also given as to the comportment of Christian leaders elsewhere in occupied Europe, and unfavourable comparisons drawn with the French bishops. As Maritain remarked in 1943: 'They [the group around *Témoignage Chrétien*] have put themselves outside the ambit of the Hierarchy, outside the ecclesiastical world that was theirs.' ('Ils se sont mis en marge de la hiérarchie, du monde ecclésial qui était le leur.'). They declared their own attitude was orthodox as regards doctrine, their intention humane. They sought to appeal to all Christians — the original title, *Témoignage Catholique*, was changed to *Témoignage Chrétien* at the very last moment to connote an ecumenical approach. Of the 448 pages of the *Cahiers* that appeared over thirty-two months, eight issues represented contributions by Catholic priests, principally Chaillet himself and de Lubac, but also Fessard, Montcheuil and others; one contribution came from Pastor Pury, and nine from laymen such as Mandouze and Hours. The main circulation was in the southern zone, although a quarter of all copies were distributed north of the demarcation line, and even outside Notre Dame. The tone was pitched more to the middle classes. Cardinal Gerlier and his fellow bishops received copies. The former suspected the journal's origin, and its connection with Fourvière, the Lyons scholasticate. It even received (adverse) recognition in *Action Française*.[57] Its printer, Eugène Pons, of Lyons, who had perhaps the most perilous task of all associated with the journal, that of producing it, was a Christian Democrat who also printed other clandestine periodicals. He was eventually caught and died in a concentration camp.

Whether Mounier and his journal *Esprit* should be characterised as belonging to the 'passive' Resistance has been hotly disputed. Chaillet took the philosopher to task for maintaining links with the Vichy youth authorities; Mounier in turn attacked the attitude of Fessard,[58] Chaillet's colleague. However, Mounier's doctrine of personalism influenced other elements which for a while formed part of the Vichy establishment but eventually rebelled against the regime. From November 1940 to July 1941, when it was banned, *Esprit* was increasingly critical of Vichy, and less and less supportive of the Révolution Nationale. Eventually Mounier was arrested because of suspected complicity with Frenay's

Combat, but was freed in June 1942, after three weeks on hunger strike. In fact Mounier also maintained contacts with other elements linked with the Resistance, such as the group Liberté, and André Philip.[59]

Other institutions that, like *Esprit*, were Christian or had strong Christian connections may be classed as having links with the 'passive' and, on occasion, 'active' Resistance. At first they tried to function within the framework imposed by the regime. When this proved impossible they broke up and their members, either individually or as a group, resumed working clandestinely. The activities of CIMADE, the Protestant relief organisation and Amitié Chrétienne, an ecumenical venture, have already been described; another such institution, the 'école des cadres' ('leadership school') at Uriage (see Chapter 17) might also fall in this category. Passions, however, as to which institutions and persons may legitimately be included in the Resistance proper have not yet died down in France.

Whilst there was no large specifically Protestant Resistance as such, pastors and members of its youth movements consistently challenged the regime. They were concerned, as we have seen, mainly with the safety of those fleeing from the German or Vichy police. (The means of rescue were sometimes ingenious: on one occasion, a Protestant pilgrimage from Nîmes to the Musée du Désert included as 'pilgrims' a massive contingent of Jews.[60]) Pastors such as Marcel Heuze (Marseilles), who was caught in February 1943 and died in Ravensbrück, Charles Roux (President of the Protestant regional council), who died in Buchenwald, and Yann Roullet (La Rochelle), who was killed in the Struthof camp, all harboured Resisters. Pastor Yves Crespin (Saint-Brieuc) died in Dora after having hid Alsatian deserters from the Wehrmacht.[61] A Maquis of Germans who had fought on the Republican side in the Spanish Civil War was sustained by a number of pastors in the Cévennes.[62] The part played by Pastor Trocmé at Chambon-sur-Lignon has already been mentioned. Another pastor, Albert Chaudier (Limoges), at first a leading light in Vichy's LFC, later became very active in the Resistance. In 1944 he was made president of the Liberation Committee of Haute-Vienne, and ended up as its acting prefect.[63] Altogether fifty-five Protestant pastors and seminarists were victims of the war, either as soldiers or in the Resistance.[64]

Perhaps deserving special mention is 'Major' Georges Flandre, of the Salvation Army, whose *nom de guerre* was 'Montcalm'. He became one of the most prominent Resistance leaders in the South, first heading a network at Montpellier, then Marseilles. Captured by the Gestapo, he was tortured, cruelly branded with the Croix de Lorraine, and shot on the eve of the Liberation.[65]

Catholic priests, religious of both sexes, particularly women, and ordinary lay people were no less courageous than their Protestant counterparts. At Vierzon, clergy conducting funerals that ended with burials the other side of the demarcation line spirited wanted persons across in the funeral cortège.[66] In the same diocese of Bourges a cathedral canon, several of whose fellow priests had been arrested by the Gestapo, and three shot, eventually sat on the departmental Liberation Committee. Much indeed depended on the attitude of the diocesan bishop. Mgr Lefèbre, who occupied the see of Bourges from 1943 onwards, did not discourage resistance to the Germans. On the contrary, Mgr Cesbron, Bishop of Annecy, held his priests on a tight rein, so much so that his position was in jeopardy at the Liberation. Yet at Ville-la-Grand, on the Swiss border itself, future Salesian monks were responsible for over a thousand successful escapes. According to one source, the 'majority' of Resisters in this key area, particularly on the Glières plateau, where they were annihilated by the Germans in March 1944, were drawn from the various Catholic movements.[67] On another frontier Sister Hélène (Studler), who belonged to the order of the Grande Charité in Metz, was indefatigable in helping escaping prisoners of war, as was Suzanne Tham. Among the escapees was Abbé Maziers, a future Archbishop of Bordeaux.[68]

Nor was it solely in border areas that this kind of resistance was carried on. In Nantes Yolande de Sesmaisons accomplished similar dangerous missions, aided and abetted by Visitandine nuns, by Père Huntziger (the brother of the general who was for a while Pétain's War minister), and even by Mgr Villeplet, Bishop of Nantes.[69] Frère Pascal Bréhault, a former member of the Maquis, protested that his monastery in the Morvan, wrongly accused of harbouring the notorious Touvier, had on the contrary been the hiding-place for 'réfractaires', Jews and Allied airmen.[70] Sometimes Resistance activities led to mass arrests. In July 1944 about one hundred priests arrived at the transit camp at Compiègne. Their monastery of the Pères Oblats de Marie, in Seine-et-Marne, had been an arms depot for the Resistance. When the Germans uncovered it, a score of them had been shot on the spot; eighty-six were eventually deported to Buchenwald.[71]

Dachau, however, was the camp where most priests finally landed up, whether caught for Resistance activities in France or for passing themselves off as French workers in Germany.[72] This was the eventual fate of the Jesuit Père Riquet, director of the Conférence Laënnec in Paris (a group of Christian medical students), who as a biologist had spoken out against the Nazi racial theories,[73] had run escape networks to Spain and had helped Frenay recruit for Combat. First sent to Mauthausen, where he associated with Communists and formed what he termed 'ces amitiés rouges que j'espère bien n'avoir jamais à renier',

Riquet lived to tell the tale.[74] Père Dillard, who had been virtually expelled from Vichy for his explosive article in *Cité Nouvelle* (January 1943) on the 'torpor' of the regime, may also be counted among the Resisters, if only for his outspokeness. He was yet another who at first had tried to reconcile himself to the regime and reform France from within the system. He had not hesitated to praise lavishly the work of Bergson, immediately after the Jewish philosopher's death:[75] 'He it is who has transformed our reason... He it is who has made us correct Descartes.'[76] On 14 June 1942, when the persecution of the Jews was approaching its peak, in the church at Vichy he had invited those present to pray not only for the prisoners of war, but also for the '80,000 Frenchmen who are ridiculed by being made to wear the Star of David'.[77] He finally went as a clandestine priest to Germany, disguised as a workman electrician, but was denounced and sent to Dachau, where he died on 12 January 1945.

Women, religious and laity alike, were particularly remarkable for their bravery not only in hiding wanted persons and weapons, but also for gathering intelligence, and producing forged documents, from identity documents to ration cards. Even more remarkable was their fortitude when caught. Mother Elisabeth de l'Eucharistie, for example, was arrested in Lyons in March 1944 for concealing arms in her convent. Sent to a concentration camp, in order to fortify the courage of women singled out for extermination because unable to work, she voluntarily joined their number. On Good Friday 1945 she mounted with them the lorry that was to take her to the gas chambers of Ravensbrück, saying, 'I am leaving for Heaven' ('Je pars pour le Ciel'), adding almost casually, 'Let them know in Lyons'.[78]

Only a few examples of the part played by Christians in the Resistance have been mentioned here. The roll of honour is long and may make up for the less honourable or mistaken attitudes of other Christians. This was acknowledged at the time. The movement Défense de la France, which functioned mainly in the northern zone and in which two Protestants, G. and R. Monod, played a key role, published an article in its clandestine journal in 1943 in which the contribution of the ordinary clergy was recognised.[79] In May 1944 *Témoignage Chrétien* paid a similar tribute,[80] remarking that their action might serve later to redeem the inaction of the higher clergy. Some parish priests, such as those in Brittany, were reported in London as early as 1941 as 'constituting one of the best elements in the Resistance'.[81] Further numerous reports on the lower clergy's favourable attitude to the Resistance came from other very different regions of France — Franche-Comté, Burgundy, the Vosges, the Limousin, Champagne, and even from areas extremely indifferent to religion such as Saint-Quentin.[82] The historian Latreille, when in charge of religious affairs in the Interior ministry after the Liberation, drew the clear conclusion: the clergy most in contact with the people were for the most part for the Resistance.[83]

Exact figures for all the movements are not obtainable. However, one evaluation made in Algiers in November 1943, when numbers had begun to increase rapidly, showed that Combat could muster a strength of 33,000, Libération 17,000, and Franc-Tireur (not connected with the FTP, but the movement run by Lévy) 14,800. There were 516 local and national leaders for these three movements, of which seven were ecclesiastics (1.36 per cent).[84] Another source quotes the local network of Cahors-Asturies as comprising 756 men, of which nine were ecclesiastics (1.20 per cent).[85] Making allowance for the special nature of their calling, it would seem that the proportion of ecclesiastics in relation to the overall percentage of those involved was about average. Moreover, in the closing days before the Liberation, despite the ACA's declaration of February 1944 against the 'appeals to violence' being made and Pétain's message of 28 April 1944. condemning the Resistance, numbers of Christians may have swelled disproportionately.

Finally, the attitude of the Catholic intellectual community to the Resistance must be mentioned. The two most eminent Catholic writers who spent the Occupation years in France were Claudel and Mauriac. Claudel was notoriously anti-German before the war. However, he approved of the end of the Parliamentary regime and, despite the 'handshake of Montoire', on Christmas Day 1940 wrote an ode to Pétain: 'France, écoute ce vieil homme sur toi qui se penche,/ et qui te parle comme un père,/ Fille de Saint-Louis, écoute-le!' However, as the war progressed his views evolved, although in no sense could he be called a Resister. Nevertheless, he made no secret of his disgust at the treatment of the Jews, and at the Liberation, somewhat incongruously in view of his previous effort, even went so far as to compose an 'Ode' in honour of de Gaulle.

Mauriac, by contrast, was more consistent. In the Spanish Civil War he had been one of the few Catholic writers, with Charles du Bos, Bernanos and Maritain, to oppose Franco. His hostility to Germany was also well known, which meant that he was attacked in the collaborationist press, and in 1941 particularly in the most 'intellectual' journal of the collaborationists, *Je Suis Partout*. He was, however, friendly with the German writer Gerhard Heller, the officer in Paris responsible for liaising with French publishers. Through Heller, to whom he dedicated the book, in 1941 he managed to have published *La Pharisienne*. However, when the clandestine Editions de Minuit was set up — it published Vercors's classic story of the Occupation, *Le silence de la mer* — he published, under the *nom de guerre* of Forez, *Le Cahier noir*;

he also contributed to the clandestine periodical *Les Lettres françaises*, and joined the underground Comité National des Ecrivains, started mainly under Communist aegis to promote the unity of all anti-German French writers. Mauriac was in fact the sole member of the Académie Française who was actively involved in the Resistance. At the Liberation he at first took a stern view of authors that had collaborated, but ended up writing in *Le Figaro* pleading for them to be shown clemency.

Gabriel Marcel, the philosopher, published little during the war. A student of the German phenomenologists, he inaugurated in France what might be described as a Christian existentialism, with the aim of deepening spiritual and religious values. This was probably more influential after the Liberation than during the Occupation. It constituted a countervailing influence to that of the neo-Thomist Jacques Maritain, the first Gaullist Ambassador to the Vatican, who spent the war years in New York. However, Marcel did openly criticise at the time Chevalier's educational measures as inept and dictatorial.[86]

What was the toll exacted from Christians for their opposition? One source estimates that some 500 priests were deported because of Resistance activities, about 100 were killed in the Gestapo prisons, and a further 210 were imprisoned, but freed later.[87] A more conservative estimate states that 153 priests were shot or died in concentration camps, 369 were deported, and 338 were imprisoned, making a total of 860.[88] An even more prudent estimate by historians gives 216 priests and seven pastors as executed or dying in captivity; a figure of 118 dead is quoted for members of JEC, to which must be added a number from JOC and the Catholic scouts.[89]

Adversity — or resistance to oppression — makes strange bedfellows. The mutual esteem that grew up between Christians and Communists during the occupation is one indication of how fellow Resisters viewed each other. Another movement, the OCM, maintained Catholics joined its ranks because they preferred disorder to the kind of order that would otherwise be imposed by the Germans.[90] Catholics felt themselves somewhat isolated, because they lacked official blessing. The more intellectual therefore seized upon the writings of Maritain and 'dissident' theologians to justify their actions. Whereas other Resistance groups containing army officers, members of political parties or trade unionists could usually rely on support from at least some of their pre-war leadership, this was largely denied Catholics as such. The CFTC is perhaps an exception — at the Liberation proportionally fewer of its officials were forced to resign than those in the CGT.[91] Yet Christian Resisters prospered, and their cause yielded political results. Of the 204 MRP deputies elected in 1945–46, 126 had served in the Resistance.[92] Although dispersed over many movements, at the end of the war they were able to come together as a mass party for the first time. Reconciled with de Gaulle, despite the mistrust he had engendered in 1940–41, Christians, largely because of their Resistance credentials and the social orientation they gave to the policies they formulated, played an important role in the Fourth Republic until their star began to wane in the late 1940s.

Notes

Unless otherwise stated the place of publication is Paris

1. R. Paxton, *Vichy France*, London, 1974, p. 295. In note 12 he states that 'other estimates' (unspecified) put the number of active Resisters at only 45,000. D. Schoenbrun, *Maquis. Soldiers of the Night. The Story of the French Resistance*, London, 1981, p. 254, quotes Manuel, Passy's deputy in London, as saying in 1977 that during the war the Resistance comprised 5 per cent of the population.
2. *Actes*: Grenoble, 1978, Intervention in the discussion by Abbé Glasberg, p. 205.
3. R. Bédarida, 'Avant-propos', *Témoignage Chrétien, 1941–1944*, p. 14, quoting an ACA statement published in *La Croix*, 4 October 1943.
4. Mgr Guerry, *L'Eglise catholique en France sous l'Occupation*, 1947, p. 344. Quoted by Bédarida, 'Avant-propos', p. 15, n. 12.
5. J. Rochelle, 'Epreuve du catholicisme français', *France Libre* (London), 17 April 1942,
6. AN 2 AG 492. 'Appel à l'ACA'.
7. AN 2 AG 492. 'Mémoire aux évêques de France', unsigned, dated 30 June 1942.
8. The details of Pétain's religious remarriage in 1941 had not yet leaked out
9. AN F60.1674. ,Radio Algiers, 12.30, 10 December 1943. 'Revue de la presse clandestine', by Jean Rouard. See also H. Michel, *Les Courants de pensée de la Résistance*, 1962, pp. 175ff..
10. Michel, *Les Courants*, p. 176, quoting *Les Cahiers français*, London, September 1943, p. 48.
11. *L'Insurgé*, no. 3, May 1942, quoted in Michel, *Les Courants*, pp.175ff.
12. *Courrier*, '14 juillet', no. 11, March 1944.
13. Schoenbrun, *Maquis*, pp. 121f.
14. Ibid.,p. 392.
15. A. Latreille, *De Gaulle, la Libération et l'Eglise catholique*, 1978, pp. 53f.
16. P. Limagne, *Journaliste sous trois Républiques*, 1983, p. 106.
17. L. Papeleux, 'Le Vatican, Pétain et de Gaulle', *RHDGM*, no. 141, January 1986, p. 84.
18. F. L. Closon, *Le Temps des passions. De Jean Moulin à la Libération, 1943–1944*, 1974, pp. 152ff.
19. Quoted in Closon, *Le Temps des passions*, pp. 152f.
20. Latreille, *De Gaulle*, pp. 56f.
21. Letter from Tisserant to Louis Cruvillier, 4 September 1943, quoted in F. and R. Bédarida, 'Une résistance spirituelle: aux origines du *Témoignage Chrétien*, 1941–1942', *RHDGM*, no. 66, January 1966, p. 30.
22. F. Lebrun, *Histoire des catholiques en France du XVe siècle à nos jours*, Toulouse, 1980, p. 466.
23. P. Bolle, 'Les Chrétiens et la Résistance', *Actes*: Grenoble, p. 222.
24. J.-P. Azéma, *De Munich à la Libération*, 1979, p. 250.

25. G. Cholvy and Y.-M. Hilaire, *Histoire religieuse de la France contemporaine, 1930–1988,* 1988, p. 72; P. Christophe, *1939–1940: Les catholiques devant la guerre,* 1989, pp..27f; H.R. Kedward, *Resistance in Vichy France,* 1978, p. 25; H. Amouroux, *Le peuple réveillé,* 1979, p. 213: 'Celui qui ne se rend pas a raison contre celui qui se rend... En temps de guerre, celui qui ne se rend pas est mon homme quel qu'il soit, d'où qu'il vienne et quel que soit son parti.'

26. F. Mayeur, *Actes:* Lyons, p. 43.

27. G. Marcel and G. Fessard, *Correspondance,* 1985, pp. 204f.

28. Schoenbrun, *Maquis,* p. 146 and pp. 240f.

29. R. Closset, *L'Aumônier de l'Enfer. Franz Stock, aumônier de Fresnes, du Cherche-Midi et de la Santé, 1940–1944,* Mulhouse, 1965.

30. E. Michelet, *Rue de la Liberté, passim.*

31. F. Mayeur, *L'Aube (1932–1940). Etude d'un journal d'opinion,* 1966, p. 215.

32. Diane de Bellescizes, 'Le Comité général d'études de la Résistance', *RHDGM,* no. 99, July 1975, pp. 6f.

33. Delbreil, *Actes:* Lyons, 1982, pp. 124f.

34. Kedward, *Resistance,* pp. 125 ff.

35. Schoenbrun, *Maquis,* p. 146.

36. Kedward, *Resistance,* pp. 66f.

37. M. Sueur, 'Des Chrétiens dans la Résistance: l'exemple de la "Voix du Nord" ', *Actes:* Lille, pp. 629–38.

38. Caudron, *Actes:* Lille, pp. 589ff.

39. M.-M. Fourcade, *L'Arche de Noé,* 1968.

40. See L. Detrez, *Du Sang sur les parvis lillois (1940–1945),* Lille, 1947, pp. 246–57.

41. H. Amouroux, *Le Peuple réveillé,* 1979, pp. 197ff., citing issues of *En Captivité,* 29.December 1940 and 27 April 1941.

42. Schoenbrun, *Maquis,* pp. 88f, citing *L'Humanité,* 30 October 1940.

43. J. Chapsal, *La Vie politique en France depuis 1940,* second edition, 1969, p. 94; J. Thorez, *Mémoires. Dans la bataille clandestine,* Part I, 1940–1942, 1970, pp. 133f.

44. AD du Nord, Lille, 1W 1356. Report of Charlet, 'responsable communiste de la Région du Nord', intercepted by Vichy, copied and sent out by Pucheu, the Interior minister, to the prefects, Vichy, 8 October 1941.

45. Bellescizes, 'Le comité général d'études', pp. 6f.

46. G. Bidault, *D'une Résistance à l'autre,* 1975, *passim.*

47. E. Jarry and J.R. Palanque (eds) *Histoire des diocèses de France: Grenoble,* 1979, p. 279.

48. See P. Bolle and J. Godel (eds), *Spiritualité, théologie et résistance. Yves de Montcheuil, théologien au maquis du Vercors,* 1987; R. Jouve, 'Le Père Yves de Montcheuil (In Memoriam),' *Etudes,* January 1945, pp. 112ff.

49. A. Latreille (ed.), *Histoire du catholicisme en France.* vol. 3, *La période contemporaine,* Book VII, edited by R. Rémond, p. 619.

50. Cholvy and Hilaire, *Histoire religieuse,* p. 109. See also AD du Nord, Lille, IW 1355.

51. Broadcast of 1 September 1940. See *Les Voix de la Liberté. Ici Londres 1940–1944,* vol. 1. *Dans la nuit, 18. juin 1940 – 7 décembre 1941,* 1975.

52. G. and J. Ragache, *La vie quotidienne des écrivains et des artistes sous l'Occupation, 1940–1944,* 1988, p. 233.

53. R. Bédarida, 'Un journal de la France libre: *Volontaires pour la Cité chrétienne',* *Revue Historique,* no. 543, July–September 1985, p. 225–44; Closon, *Le Temps des Passions.* pp. 28f.

54. For the short sketch that follows I am much indebted to R. Bédarida, 'Avant-Propos'; see also F. and R. Bédarida, 'Une résistance spirituelle'.

55. Chaillet had written, from first hand knowledge of the Nazis, *L'Autriche souffrante* (1938); Fessard was a pre-war editor of the Jesuit journal *Etudes.*

56. P. Limagne, *Journaliste sous trois Républiques,* 1983, p. 86.

57. AN F60.1674. Allusion to an article in *Action Française,* 17 April 1944.

58. Marcel and Fessard, *Correspondance,* p. 27.

59. Cf. B. Comte, 'Emmanuel Mounier devant Vichy et la révolution nationale en 1940–1941', *Revue d'Histoire de l'Eglise de France*, LXXI:187, July–December 1985, pp. 253–80. André Philip, the most eminent pre-war Protestant politician — he was a Socialist deputy for Lyons — joined Libération in 1941. Very devout, but afraid of being recognised if he went to a Protestant church, he attended mass instead. It was in the summer of 1942 that he left for London, where he became de Gaulle's Commissaire à l'Intérieur.

60. H. de Lubac, *Résistance chrétienne à l'antisémitisme. Souvenirs, 1940–1944*, 1988, p. 144.

61. R. Nodot, 'La porte qui s'ouvre enfin', *Réforme*, Lyons, 15 May 1982..

62. E. and Y. Brès, *Un maquis d'antifascistes allemands en France (1942–1944)*, Montpellier, 1987, pp.43–68.

63. A. Chaudier, *Paris-Limoges*, 1980, *passim*.

64. H. Clavier, *The Duty and the Right of Resistance*, Oxford, 1946, p. 99.

65. Clavier, *The Duty and the Right*, p. 97.

66. G. Devailly (ed.), *Histoire des Diocèses de France: Bourges*, 1973, p. 232.

67. H. Baud, *Histoire des Diocèses de France:(Genève), Annecy*, 1985, pp. 268ff.

68. C. Paillat, *L'Occupation: Le Pillage de la France, juin 1940– novembre 1942*, 1987 p. 355.

69. Paillat, *L'Occupation*, p. 384.

70. 'Monastère dans le Morvan: Moines patriotes', *Le Monde*, 3 June 1989.

71. Closon, *Le Temps des Passions*, p. 92.

72. For an account of their life in the camps, see P. Durand, *Les armes de l'espoir. Les Français à Buchenwald et à Dora*, 1977, pp. 115ff.

73. G. Benoit–Guyon, *L'Invasion de Paris (1940–1944). Choses vues sous l'Occupation*, 1962, p. 255.

74. See M. Riquet, *Chrétiens de France dans l'Europe enchaînée*, 1972.

75. A. Tasca, *Archives de Guerre, Cahiers XX*, January–August 1942, Paris and Milan, p. 369.

76. Quoted in *La Croix*, 6 January 1942.

77. Marcel and Fessard, *Correspondance*, p. 209, n. 3.

78. H. Amouroux, *Un printemps de mort et d'espoir. Novembre 1943–6 juin 1944*, 1985, p. 347.

79. Article signed 'Un prêtre de France', *Défense de la France*, no. 35, 5 July 1943.

80. *Témoignage Chrétien*, nos. XXVI-XVII, 'Exigences de la Libération,' vol. 2, pp. 157f.

81. AN F60.1689. Opinion publique, 1940–1942. Interrogation dated 3.December 1941: 'The Breton clergy is excellent in every respect and constitutes one of the best elements in the Resistance. In the pulpit they speak out constantly for it.'

82. Latreille, *De Gaulle*, pp. 56ff.

83. Ibid., p. 35.

84. A. Chambon, *Quand la France était occupée 1940–1945*, 1987, pp. 88ff., quoting Veillon, *Le Franc-Tireur*, 1977.

85. M. Granet, *Histoire du réseau de Résistance Cohors-Asturies*, 1971, quoted by Chambon, *Quand la France*, p. 89.

86. See H. Lottman, *The Left Bank: writers in Paris from Popular Front to Cold War*, London, 1982. Other Catholic writers of note, but in the opposing camp, were Massis and Bordeaux, both traditionalist Catholics, and the minor author, the openly collaborationist Alphonse de Chateaubriant.

87. Chambon, *Quand la France*, p. 90.

88. AN 72 AJ 1895, 'Le clergé et la Résistance', quoting figures given in *La Nation*, 28 October 1945.

89. Cholvy and Hilaire, *Histoire religieuse, passim*.

90. Les Catholiques et la Résistance', *Cahiers de l'OCM*, no. 4, September 1943, quoted in Michel, *Les Courants*, p. 176.

91. P. Novick, *The Resistance versus Vichy. The Purge of Collaborators in Liberated France*, London, 1968, p. 134.

92. J.-M. Mayeur, *Catholicisme social et démocratie chrétienne*, 1986, *passim*.

-14-

Vichy, the Church and the Vatican

Since the beginning of the century the relations between the French State and the papacy had hardly been marked by tolerance or cordiality. After the Separation of Church and State and the passage of the secular laws it was not until 1921 that diplomatic relations with the Vatican were renewed. A conciliatory step was taken when the 'associations cultuelles', set up at parish level to administer Church property, were replaced by 'associations diocésaines', over which the bishop had greater control. However, although the Bloc National Government had been more favourably disposed, the Cartel des Gauches was hostile. Herriot, its Radical leader, adopted a secular policy, and as early as 1924 announced his intention of abolishing the Vatican embassy, because, according to his party, he disliked making 'diplomatic genuflexions', held 'a very lofty conception of secularism... [and] wanted to break the links with a spiritual power that claims to be all-powerful'.[1] The move, however, provoked the Right to anger. Canon Desgranges, the deputy for Morbihan, declared that ten years of peace between Church and State had been shattered.[2] The decision was absurd, because Protestant Britain, then ruled by a Socialist government, nevertheless had its diplomatic representative to the Holy See.[3] Eventually diplomatic relations were fully restored.

In 1939, on the eve of war, the state of relations between Paris and Rome, as we have seen, did show small signs of improvement, but the overall position remained unsatisfactory. It was this situation that the Vichy regime sought to improve still further by cultivating closer diplomatic ties, by abolishing the so-called 'penal laws' that inhibited some forms of religious activity, and by seeking a better working arrangement, if not a Concordat, between the State, the French Church and the Vatican.

The Pope, as the Nuncio in Germany at the time, had approved the Concordat with Hitler, regarding that nation, as he still did in 1939, as the main European bulwark against communism. Only as the war dragged on was his opinion modified. One small indication, however, that he had no real sympathy with nazism is the fact that he, and not Pius XI, had been the real instigator of *Mit brennender Sorge*.[4] He was, however, prepared to be flexible.

In matters sacred rather than secular he could, on the other hand, show himself unyielding. Not only did he refuse to appoint Germans permanently to fill the sees of Strasbourg and Metz, incorporated in 1940 into the Reich, but he instructed Valerio Valeri, the Nuncio, to support Barthélémy, the Justice minister, in charge of Alsace-Lorraine affairs, in not handing over the plate and sacred vessels of Strasbourg Cathedral to the Germans. The *Curia* appeared to react more strongly when Church prerogatives, and not human rights, were at stake.

Pius XII saw the silence he maintained as to the rights and wrongs of the war as in conformity with the traditional impartiality of the Holy See. He must have been shocked if, as was reported, he received a request by Myron Taylor, Roosevelt's emissary to Europe in 1941, to declare war on the Axis powers.[5] A diplomat by training and experience, he believed that indirect methods were always preferable to confrontation. This was not pusillanimity, but prudence, perhaps carried to an extreme. In any case, he reasoned that French Catholics were not psychologically ready to face up to the reality of persecution if they defied the Germans. Although early in 1942 some Vatican ecclesiastics actively supported the Allies,[6] until the summer he probably believed, like his representative in Paris, in a German victory; by a diplomatic silence he thought that if this came about he could safeguard the existence of the Church in Germany and in Europe. Anti-Communist and having lived in Germany for many years, he had a strong sympathy for its people, although after the invasion of the Soviet Union, Bérard had already reported that he feared Hitler more than he did Stalin.[7] He waxed indignant at the bombing of German towns in 1942, but failed to condemn the 'Baedeker raids' on English cathedral cities. He and his principal collaborators, Cardinal Maglione, the Secretary of State, and the latter's two deputies, Mgrs Tardini and Montini, were Italian (although it was rumoured that Maglione had pro-Allied sympathies), and were later to favour a separate peace for Italy. A report that he had protested to Roosevelt after the bombing of Rome in July 1943 was denied by Radio Vatican. He had, however, deplored the reluctance of both sides to make it an open city, although forthrightly declaring that 'the neglect of the laws of humanity, morality, and justice and the human person count for more than the destruction of monuments'.[8]

The Vatican as a whole was nevertheless not entirely muted. A redoubtable pro-Allied figure in the *Curia* was the French Cardinal Tisserant. This Lorrainer, who had suffered the rigours of German Occupation during the First World War,[9] on 11 June 1940 warned

Cardinal Suhard as to the fate of Western Europe: 'Germany and Italy will dedicate themselves to destroying the inhabitants of the regions they have occupied, just as they did in Poland.'[10] Later he betrayed himself to be no enthusiast for Darlan.[11] In a letter to his family in France that was intercepted by the censorship, the cardinal made what was described as 'odious and unspeakable attacks' ('des attaques odieuses inouïes') on the Admiral.

Radio Vatican, run by Jesuits, was another independent voice in Rome. It broke to the Allies and the neutrals the news of Nazi persecutions of Catholics and Jews, first in Poland and then elsewhere. Until April 1941, when, after Nazi protests, the Pope urged restraint, it attacked the treatment of Catholics in Germany itself, asserting that Christianity had to confront squarely pagan, totalitarian doctrines. The Jesuits' General, Mgr Ledochowski, was asked to forbid such broadcasts. The collaborationist Catholic journal *Voix Françaises* even thought it necessary to warn readers that the Vatican's control over the programmes was limited.[12] By November 1941 the broadcasts were more confined to religious subjects, although from time to time they contained veiled political allusions.

The programmes of this Jesuit-controlled radio station inspired a group of Avignon school teachers, members of the order, to launch from Marseilles in July 1940 the first clandestine Christian publication, *La Voix du Vatican*. Originally a single typed sheet, it soon attracted the support of former associates of such Catholic periodicals as *Sept* and *Temps Présent*, and ex-members of the ACJF such as Louis Cruvillier.[13] The broadsheet reproduced Radio Vatican broadcasts, usually much later than the date of transmission. Thus issue no. 12 (February 1941) printed a Vatican broadcast of October 1940; which it interpreted as a rejection of the policy of collaboration agreed at Montoire. The bishops' reaction to the clandestine publication was mixed. Mgr de la Villerabel, then Archbishop of Aix and notoriously pro-Action Française, roundly condemned it.[14] On the other hand, his near neighbour, Mgr Delay, of Marseilles, although he must have known of the publication's existence since it originated in his diocese, maintained a discreet silence. When, however, the radio station was forced to moderate its tone, the journal lost its cutting edge. Nevertheless, as Renée Bédarida remarks,[15] *La Voix du Vatican* represents 'the first attempt to shake Catholics out of their inertia and stir them from their quietism.'

The *Curia* took an intense interest in the destinies of France after the collapse. At the very beginning, with a few notable exceptions, its stance was on the whole pro-Vichy. It was a posture which Valerio Valeri in Paris reflected to the very end. In June 1940 he, as doyen of the diplomatic corps, had persuaded his fellow diplomats not to contemplate leaving for North Africa with President Lebrun and certain members of the government, as had then been mooted.[16] Instead, he accompanied Pétain to Vichy, only to find the German authorities at first categorically forbade his return to the capital. For its part, the government valued his presence at Vichy highly. As Dr Ménétrel, the Marshal's private secretary, remarked: 'This little man with the pointed beard is the ambassador of 400 million people. That means something. So long as he remains in Vichy we must stay there.'[17] The Nuncio was nevertheless not always universally esteemed. To the regret, for example, of two Alsace-Lorraine parliamentarians, Senator Canon Müller (Strasbourg) and Heid (Sarreguemines), he failed to intervene with the Pope to secure the release of Schumann, a former junior minister who had fallen foul of the Germans, but had merely contented himself with approaching Laval.[18]

The French Church strove to maintain maximum contact with Rome during the war. After the defeat the Pope had addressed a letter (29 June 1940) of commiseration to the bishops, affirming his belief in a French revival. Bérard, the new Ambassador to the Vatican, presenting his letters of credence, received a sympathetic welcome.[19] On other occasions messages in a similar vein were addressed to French Catholics.[20] There was no lack of cordiality on either side. Collaborationists laboured the point, even claiming that the Pope had stressed that good relations should be maintained between the French Church and the Germans.[21] The bishops reciprocated with messages of loyalty and appreciation, underlining their desire to maintain their religious institutions without political involvement — the Pope's own policy.[22]

The measures taken by the regime, from the granting of subsidies to Catholic schools to the high profile given to Catholics in youth organisations and other fields of national life, could not fail to gratify the Holy See. Radio Vatican, despite its otherwise independent line, backed those messages of Pétain that urged moral reform within the framework of the Révolution Nationale.[23] The Marshal even submitted, through the Nuncio, the draft of his 'Principes de la Communauté' to the Pope, who gave them his blessing but delicately suggested some clarification of individual rights would be helpful.[24] The *Osservatore Romano,* the Vatican's semi-official newspaper, joined in praise for Vichy's appeal to the civic and moral consciousness of Frenchmen. (However, the paper then lapsed into silence as regards France until after the Liberation, when it lauded 'the hour of de Gaulle, which is also the hour of France'.)[25]

Nevertheless, signs that the Pope's views regarding France and the outcome of the conflict were evolving were eagerly looked for. The Allies, for their part, were at pains to demonstrate that he drew a distinction between nazism and communism, maintaining that, if publicly he declared both anti-Christian, in private audiences he was more discriminating: nazism was nothing but hatred and envy, whereas communism had certain redeeming features.[26] Whether this fine distinction was perceived in France or not, many at Vichy believed that if the Pope were eventually to mediate between the belligerents, France would have a special role to play. In ecclesiastical and governmental circles the Pope was accepted to be the best hope for peace, although it was realised that he had to bide his time in order to succeed.[27] ACA archives contain an anonymous draft message to the Pope in which this putative key role in re-establishing peace was acknowledged, particularly when it was clear the United States had thrown in its lot with Britain. It even speculated on the form that peace might take, arguing that at an international conference Churchill could hardly refuse the 'proletarian' [sic] nations access to the natural resources then shared between the British Empire, the USA and the USSR.[28]

Laval's return to power in April 1942, which it was feared would move the United States to break off relations with Vichy, was a setback to any hope of peace. Nevertheless Bérard reported to Laval in May that rumours that Germany and the Soviet Union might conclude a separate peace were persistent, although Cardinal Maglione believed that preliminary negotiations had failed.[29] On 22 June Laval made his infamous declaration in favour of a German victory in order to stave off the spread of 'bolshevism'. The new head of government had difficulty in dealing both with the 'Pastor Angelicus', as the Pope was known in some quarters, and his turbulent priests. On Ascension Day 1942 the Church in France celebrated the twenty-fifth anniversary of the Pope's consecration as a bishop. Archbishop Saliège heralded this 'jubilee' in a message claiming that the Pope had endorsed the French cause as being just, had anathematised cultural and racial repression, and denounced the principle of absolute State sovereignty.[30] The ACA, in its own message, took a pessimistic line. Although asserting that peace could come about through the Pope, the tone was more despairing: 'It is time for the world to return to wisdom, unless it wishes to sink into chaos.'[31]

A slight indication that the papal position was shifting occurred at the end of 1942. The Vatican had proclaimed the consecration of the world to the Immaculate Heart of the Virgin Mary. In his announcement (31 October 1942) the Pope had expressed the hope that the Soviet Union would be 'given peace' and would return to the 'sole fold' ('l'unique bercail'). Not a word did he utter against atheistic communism. By contrast, in a sentence interpreted as applying to Germany he had alluded to neopaganism, invoking the Almighty to 'halt its invading flood' ('arrêter le déluge envahissant'). This text was to be read in all the churches of France on the Feast of the Annunciation (25 March 1943). The Gestapo approached Cardinal Suhard with a strong request that the damning phrase be omitted. This was ignored.[32]

Papal declarations were likewise embarrassing for Laval. The Pope's 1943 New Year message was heavily censored, which gave rise to Catholic discontent.[33] *La Croix* published a speech by the Pope made on the feast of Pope St Eugene, which contained sympathetic references to the fate of Poland and the Jews. Publication in other newspapers was banned.[34]

About this time Mgr Chappoulie began to play a more prominent role in matters that concerned the Vatican, Vichy and the bishops. Originally appointed by the ACA to represent it with the new regime, this outstanding prelate, intelligent and diplomatic, undertook his mission with considerable flair. His work necessitated shuttling between Vichy and Paris, liaising with the Nuncio, consulting with Mgr Chollet, the ACA Secretary-General, and maintaining frequent contacts with Cardinal Suhard and other bishops, as well as the Vichy government. He was excoriated by Germans and collaborationists alike. The Occupation authorities had harassed him in the past by occasionally refusing him permission to cross the demarcation line.

On 5 January 1943 Cardinal Suhard left Paris for Rome, his first visit since the outbreak of war. He was accompanied by Mgrs Chappoulie and Courbe, Secretary-General of Action Catholique. The Germans were highly suspicious of the reasons for the journey — indeed the exact purpose of the visit remains a mystery — and at first held up the *laissez-passer* allowing the party to leave. Upon his return Suhard maintained a discreet silence. The Vatican merely stated that in the course of two lengthy interviews the cardinal and the Pope had discussed the state of the Church in France.[35]

However, the Americans had declared that they were not interested in the future form of the French government, but would pledge themselves not to let the Communists take over the country.[36] Cardinal Suhard may have used the visit to contact Tuck, the American chargé d'affaires, on this matter of prime importance for the Church. Given this guarantee, the Vatican had now switched its focus away from Germany. For Suhard personally it was doubtless gratifying that through the Vatican links had now been re-established between Pétain and the Americans.[37]

Other accounts of the visit said that the Pope had been impressed by the work of moral regeneration that had been accomplished in France, as outlined by Suhard.[38] The Transocean News Agency even reported that the cardinal had characterised his relations with the Occupation authorities as 'excellent'.[39]

In his dealings with the French government, as distinct from Pétain, Pius XII was more reserved. How far he trusted Laval is problematic. According to Mgr Piguet, Bishop of Clermont-Ferrand, Pius XI, his predecessor, had a high opinion of the horse-trading politician. (In conversation the bishop had remarked, 'He is of my diocese.' The Pope had replied: 'So he is. He is a man of true worth.') Later, it seems that Cardinal Verdier had passed on a message from Pius XI to Laval, who had reciprocated by remarking smugly, 'I rely on him, next to God, to save the world from this war.'[40] Pius XII probably did not wholly endorse these views: all his preference was for the Marshal.

The Pope was generous in donations to assist the French, particularly prisoners of war, but Vichy's appeals for help from the Vatican were surprisingly few. However, one curious effort to enlist papal aid arose from the acute food shortage in France during the winter of 1941–42, as the British blockade began to exert its grip on occupied Europe. A proposal was mooted that French merchant ships, manned by French crews but flying the papal flag — a 'neutral' flag — should be used to import supplies. Ships and crews would nominally be 'lent' to the Pope for this purpose. The papal flag had been flown by ships until about 1850. The Vatican already used for its own imports four freighters whose home port was Civitavecchia (declared a free zone for the purpose) and whose neutrality was respected.[41]

The first step was to write a letter from Pétain to the Pope outlining the project. Various drafts were made. One difficulty was to know how the Pope should be addressed: 'Holy Father' sounded odd coming from an octogenarian, as did the ending 'Votre dévot fils'.[42] The text had to be submitted to Admiral Darlan, as responsible for all maritime matters. He said the project was technically viable if the ships nominally became Vatican property and if the belligerents accepted the proposal. Bérard had already been asked to take informal soundings, but had found the Vatican's first reactions rather negative. Even before the letter could be sent Pius XII signalled his rejection of the plan. A *sine qua non* was of course the acceptance by the British of such an arrangement. There had been a precedent. The Greek Orthodox Patriarch had asked the Pope in 1941 to intercede with the Allies in favour of allowing food into Greece, where famine was rife, with people dying on the streets of Athens. Pius XII's intervention had met with a categorical refusal.[43] Thus Valerio Valeri finally communicated the Vatican's rejection of the use of the papal standard as a flag of convenience. An alternative put forward by the Secours National, the national relief organisation, of reviving the medieval fleet of the Order of Malta also foundered: it was doubtful whether the good Knights any longer enjoyed sufficient international credibility to be able to 'own' merchant ships. The project, first aired in

December 1941, was finally abandoned in the summer of 1942.

However, by far the most important part of unfinished business between the Vatican and France remained the question of a definitive religious settlement. The 'Union sacrée' achieved in the First World War had led in 1918 to a plea for a new Concordat, which had been rejected. In April 1939 Champetier de Ribes, the Christian Democrat deputy, had led the French delegation to the coronation of Pius XII, and had held preliminary discussions with the Vatican authorities.[44] Between the 1940 armistice and the ACA meeting of 28 August, someone — who is not known — drew up the outlines of a Concordat.[45] The document comprised seven articles: the continuance of diplomatic relations; the right of Catholics to carry on their activities within the common law (i.e. without special legislation usually being needed); guarantees for the rights of religious: the famous 'circulaire Malvy' of 2 May 1914 suspending the laws of 1901 and 1904 would be maintained until a new law had been elaborated; religious instruction for all children of one hour a week for parents who requested it, to be given by the clergy in premises to be determined — i.e. not necessarily in Church buildings. and perhaps even in the state school; Church property confiscated at the Separation and not otherwise reallocated to be handed over to diocesan associations; churches to be exempt from taxation and presbyteries available rent-free to parish priests; the norms at present applicable for appointment to bishoprics to be extended to include the French Empire. Surprisingly there was no mention of State interests, and in particular, the traditional Gallican liberties enjoyed by the French Church. In the event the document was not used as a starting-point for any discussions, but is noteworthy because of the celerity with which it was drafted immediately after the defeat. However, by the end of the year both Pétain and Laval had instructed Bérard that the moment was not opportune to negotiate any such agreement.[46]

However, a second important document[47] recently discovered is a long memorandum dated 15 January 1941 by Sauret, the Vichy 'sous-directeur des cultes' in the Interior ministry. His paper weighed the requirements of the State against the needs of the Church: the State, for example, would wish for some say in episcopal appointments. Despite the document's length little detail of any proposals is given.

However, Bérard's appointment as envoy to the Holy See did represent a commitment to establish closer relations. When André Lavagne, like the Ambassador also a devout churchman, as well as being a legal specialist. joined Pétain's staff at Vichy serious attempts were made by both to formulate a religious policy, which naturally included the study of how to arrive at a lasting *modus vivendi* with the Vatican.[48] Since Lavagne, as well as being responsible for religious questions, had also the oversight of affairs relating to Alsace-Lorraine, he was therefore familiar with the problems raised by the Concordat still nominally in force there.

On 4 August 1941 Lavagne drew up a policy note which specifically stated that shortly 'it may be hoped to negotiate a Concordat with the Holy See'.[49] It should be based on the principle of reciprocity — *do ut des*. Lavagne considered France had a duty to favour the Catholic Church, as representing the majority religion, but freedom of conscience and prudence had to be observed so as not to offend secularist opinion. He doubtless recalled the hostility aroused by the abortive attempt made by Chevalier, when Education minister, in January 1941 to reintroduce religious instruction into state schools.

For Mgr Chollet, the ACA's Secretary-General, the question of a Concordat was clearly still on the agenda that autumn. Writing to Liénart on another matter, the recognition of Catholic youth movements by the government, he stated that the bishops would wish any negotiations regarding their recognition to be postponed if and when a dialogue was begun between the Holy See leading to 'the preparation of a Concordat like those which have recently been worked out between several States and the Church'.[50]

When the question was raised with Valerio Valeri, however, towards the end of the year, the Nuncio rejected talks on the grounds that the Vichy regime was still a transitional one.[51]

The Spanish example to which Mgr Chollet clearly alluded was keenly studied: in June 1941 a Concordat with Franco was regarded as imminent, although in fact it was not formally signed until 1942, when catholicism was formally recognised as the State religion. The Spaniards had reached a provisional arrangement regarding the thorny problem of episcopal appointments. The Papal Nuncio in Spain, after consulting the government, would submit six names for a bishopric to the Vatican, which would then choose three. From these three the government would make the final appointment.[52] (In France the first procedure for the appointment of bishops dates back to 1107, when Philippe I accepted at Troyes papal authority in such matters.) The Spanish accord would, it was held, provide a useful precedent. Laval may in fact have stipulated that any Concordat had to concede to the State some say in episcopal nominations: the government should at least be allowed to present names to the Pope, although the final choice would lie in the latter's hands.[53] Cardinal Gerlier and Mgr Fontenelle had conferred with the Nuncio and Mgr Chappoulie on this point, but the question by then may well have been academic, since rumours of a Concordat having been arrived at were formally denied the following spring.[54] The press was even more categorical: all rumours of negotiations were completely without foundation.[55]

This did not deter Bérard, who continued a search for precedents. He drew up a detailed comparative study of the Concordats concluded from the papacy of Benedict XV in 1928 to that of Pius XII, of which that with the Spanish Caudillo was the most recent. In forwarding his report to Vichy he emphasised that it had no immediate application; rather was it a guide for those who might eventually negotiate. He warned that previous Concordats had ended up by giving additional powers and prerogatives to the Pope, and in France the policy of secularism pursued under the Third Republic had paradoxically fuelled Ultramontanism.

From his survey Bérard concluded that over the past fourteen years no government had retained an absolute right to nominate bishops, a privilege earlier Popes had accorded more liberally. The ambassador speculated on what might be the Vatican's conditions for an agreement: subsidies for Catholic education on a permanent basis — the law put through by Carcopino, Chevalier's successor as Education minister, only guaranteed them for the duration; religious instruction on the state school's timetable; regarding marriage, canon law to take precedence over civil law; a say in the appointment of bishops, as previously mentioned; perhaps a State contribution to the salary of the clergy.[56]

Bérard's conclusions struck an optimistic note: if and when the question was reopened: 'Our representatives will be able to treat in the name of a renovated State that has proved by its actions its intention to apportion its due share to spiritual values, to religious sentiment and to Catholic influence in the task of renovation that it has undertaken.'[57] By the autumn of 1942 Bérard had come round to the view of others that any Concordat would have to await the peace, although he believed some provisional arrangement was possible and continued to busy himself with details. Thus he envisaged a global sum being given to the Church annually by the State to subsidise the stipends of parish priests: 'We know how greatly, from the human viewpoint, this would be equitable and just, when we realise the unfortunate condition of a large number of priests, particularly in rural areas and certain districts.'[58]

By mid-1942 the Vatican was already reaffirming its conclusion that a Concordat was still inopportune, if only because the war was beginning to turn in the Allies' favour and Vichy could more than ever be considered only a stop-gap regime. The bishops, who had expressed few views publicly on an agreement, the Vatican authorities, and the Germans (who had already disregarded their own 1933 Concordat and were busy dismantling in Alsace-Lorraine the nineteenth century Concordat that had survived since the Wilhelmine Empire) — in fact, all the interested parties — were once again unanimous that the time was not ripe.

In January 1943 Suhard's visit to the Pope nevertheless restimulated interest. However, Mgr Courbe, Secretary-General of Action Catholique, who had accompanied Suhard, explained that although the question of a Concordat had been touched upon, it was agreed that its realisation was a long way off.[59] In February 1943 a new element intervened: Doriot's collaborationist Parti Populaire Français (PPF) began to woo the clergy. It sent out a brochure, 'Vers une politique religieuse', advocating a Concordat to a number of clergy.[60] Ménétrel noted[61] that the PPF propaganda had made little impact on the rank and file clergy and that such an agreement was inappropriate at the present time, although it would improve [their] material conditions'. ('bien qu'il améliorerait [*sic*] la condition matérielle du Bas Clergé'), because the State might contribute to their salaries.

Nevertheless Pétain's staff continued to work on guidelines for the State in its dealings with the Church. In a document dated 9 May 1943,[62] rules for negotiating such agreements were propounded. Thus the negotiation should always be on the diplomatic plane, and conducted as between equals. The Church, 'having eternity on its side', had a long memory both for favours granted and for misdeeds committed against it. It could not be threatened, coerced or bought. It was always ready to sacrifice any debt of gratitude to a higher duty. It had a doctrine, even if the State had none. It tended to move the boundaries between the temporal and the spiritual as it pleased. It was prepared to disown those who negotiated on its behalf at any time, if the situation justified it, especially when subordinates were acting on behalf of their superiors. Having ascribed to Rome precepts not unworthy of Machiavelli, the authors of the document concluded that so long as there was no Concordat only acts of expediency were possible. They remarked, somewhat cryptically, that democratic opinions were as likely to be found within the Church as elsewhere.

By July 1943 different collaborationist elements, alarmed at the independent stance that continued to be taken by some prelates, favoured a Concordat as a means of placing religion more firmly under State authority. Otherwise the Church should simply be banished from public life because, as Drieu la Rochelle insisted in *Révolution Nationale* (10 July 1943), religion and politics did not mix. In *L'Œuvre*[63] Déat sternly declared that the time had come for the Church to opt definitively for the new German-led European order.

There the matter of a Concordat rested. It had not been discussed so intensely for over a century, and its feasibility has not been seriously raised since. The constitutions of the successor republics to Vichy have continued to proclaim that France is a secular State. The Vichy regime therefore marks a phase when relations between Church and State came closest to a consensus.

Throughout, however, the question of the Gallican liberties of the French Church underlay all speculation. Rome was resented as well as admired, even in such a trivial matter as the pronunciation of Latin, where its 'initiatives italianisantes' were criticised. When Cardinal Maglione was Nuncio, he had, against the wishes of Pius XII, then Cardinal Pacelli, imposed the Italian pronunciation upon the French clergy. Other nations did as they pleased. Thus 'German priests celebrate in the occupied zone in the German manner, whereas French priests in the free zone, celebrate in the Italian manner, even in the presence of the Marshal.'[64]

A more serious question was posed by the religious orders. The law of 8 April 1942 regularising their situation had already been promulgated, but the question of individual recognition arose. Bérard raised the case of orders and institutions that were originally established in France but since 1904 had settled in Rome. In some cases a foreigner had even been appointed as their head: thus the Vicar-General for the Sœurs de Saint-Joseph de Cluny was a Portuguese. The situation of the Christian Brothers was particularly anomalous. It was a congregation 'excellemment française' through its founder, Jean-Baptiste de la Salle. In Rome the Brothers were strictly supervised and the (French) Superior-General was even 'mis en résidence canoniquement surveillée'.[65] The matter cropped up again in 1944 when the question of the recognition of the Brothers was formally mooted, at a time when the post of head of the order was vacant. Some feared that this very powerful, international congregation with its centralised organisation located in Rome, might one day force the French branch of the order to submit to strict Vatican control. This would mean that the 4,000 Christian Brothers installed in France, their 75,000 French pupils and 400–500 schools in France and the colonies would pass out of immediate French control. Nevertheless, it was agreed that the Brothers' property, in accordance with the new Vichy laws, should be restored to them, provided that in its spirit and leadership the order remained French. This view was shared by Pétain, Laval and the Interior ministry, but opposed by the Foreign Affairs ministry because the French element in the congregation was now in a minority and the Superior might well not be French. However desirable such a move might be, the Vatican would always be against the return to France of the seat of the order.[66] Recognition was therefore denied. As the archives make plain, the ultimate aim of all the French parties concerned was nevertheless 'la refrancisation des Frères'. Once again, in accordance with Gallican traditions, one notes the desire to safeguard the interests of the nation and its Church.

The part played by the key figures in relations with the Vatican — Valerio Valeri, Chappoulie and Bérard — in the last few months before the Liberation is unclear. By then the position of the Pope himself was insecure: the Germans were believed to want to remove him from Rome to Vienna.[67]

Within France Valerio Valeri continued to play a mediating role to the very end. In 1944, after the arrest by the Germans of three bishops (Montauban, Rodez and Agen) and a number of priests, he intervened with the Germans in an effort to secure their release, with partial success.[68] When Théas, Bishop of Montauban, was set free later, he was warmly received by the Pope. The bishop, despite his Resistance stance, had never quarrelled with Pétain; thus the gesture might be seen as reconciling the old order and the new.

It was to the Vatican also that Pétain turned in 1944 when he realised his regime was crumbling. Mgr Chappoulie was asked to take steps to ensure a smooth transition to the new government, that is, the formal 'passation des pouvoirs' (handing over of power) from the Marshal to de Gaulle. The attempt to achieve this was unsuccessful, largely because the Algiers government had never recognised the legitimacy of Vichy. Also it was the Nuncio, together with the Swiss Ambassador, who was present as a witness when Pétain was forcibly removed from the Hôtel du Parc to Germany. However, after the Liberation, Valerio Valeri's close involvement with Vichy clearly made it inappropriate for him to remain as the papal envoy. After long delays, he was finally recalled to Rome and his place taken by Cardinal Roncalli (the future Pope John XXIII). As a mark of esteem, however, de Gaulle conferred upon him the Grand' Croix of the Légion d'Honneur.

Meanwhile, in July 1944 de Gaulle had been received by the Pope. On 24 August Bérard formally notified the Vatican that his mission was at an end and that French diplomatic relations were now in the hands of M Guérin, the representative of the Algiers government, who had arrived in Rome a few days previously. Later Jacques Maritain, the philosopher, was appointed as Ambassador, despite objections that his Thomist views would make him unacceptable to Vatican theologians.[69]

Faced not only with the Nazi brutalities and exactions in France, but the even worse crimes they committed elsewhere, the silence of Christ's Vicar on earth, who, after all, had been the author of *Mit brennender Sorge*, is baffling. Tisserant, the Gaullist cardinal in the *Curia*, remarked sarcastically that Pius XII would have done well to write a similar encyclical on liberty of conscience.[70] It was alleged he was inhibited from doing so because of his belief that his mission was to save Catholic Europe, in the face of the Allies, who were largely Protestant and had become linked to a godless regime.[71] Certainly only belatedly, and then hardly perceptibly, did he favour the Anglo-American side. And the moment for which he had 'reserved himself' to act as mediator in a compromise peace never came. For France his silence was disastrous. Up to mid-1942, and even beyond, this gave rise to a certain assent to, or at least acceptance by, the Church of State and German measures that profoundly shocked most Frenchmen. The Vatican has its share of responsibility for the fact that the French Church upheld, if only by tacit consent, a regime that was fundamentally flawed because in the end it had lost popular support.

Notes

Unless otherwise stated the place of publication is Paris

1. AN F7.13193. *Le Bulletin du Jour* (Correspondance de Presse) [du Parti Radical et Radical-Socialiste], 3 February 1925.
2. AD du Nord, M.154/116A. FNC. Speech at a meeting of the FNC at Dunkirk, 21 May 1925, reported by the Commissariat Central, Lille, to the Prefect, 22 May 1925.
3. AD du Nord, Lille, M.154/118. Speech at a meeting of the ACJF at Roubaix, 23 July 1924, reported by the Commissariat de Police, 4e arrondissement, to the Commissariat Central, Roubaix, 24 July 1924.
4. *Actes*::Grenoble, 1978, p. 56. Intervention of Latreille in discussion.
5. 'Un non poli', *La Gazette*, 5 February 1941.
6. AN 2 AG 492. Report of Bérard to Pétain, Vatican, 2 February 1942.
7. G. Cholvy and Y.-M. Hilaire, *Histoire religieuse de la France contemporaine, 1930–1988*, 1988, p. 78.
8. *Journal de Genève*, 26 July 1943.
9. Tisserant, born in 1884, was made a cardinal in 1936. He was Secretary of the Congregation of the Eastern Church at Rome.
10. Quoted in C. Falconi, *The Silence of Pius XII*, translated by B. Wall, London, 1970, p. 198.
11. AN 2 AG 493. 'Note', Vichy, 8 July 1941.
12. AN 72 AJ 1863. 'A propos de la Radio du Vatican', *Voix Françaises*, 23 May 1941.
13. P. Christophe, *1939–1940: Les Catholiques devant la guerre*, 1989, p.107.
14. *Semaine Religieuse* (Aix), 23 November 1941, quoted in Renée Bédarida, 'La Voix du Vatican (1940–1942). Bataille des ondes et Résistance spirituelle', *Revue d'Histoire de l'Eglise de France*, vol. 64, 1978, pp. 233f.
15. Ibid.
16. See P. Simonnot, *Le Secret de l'Armistice 1940*, 1989.
17. M. Martin du Gard, *Chronique de Vichy , 1940–1944*, p. 356.
18. AN 2 AG 493. Rens. Gén. L.O.8/G1. 'Renseignement, Vichy, 9 août 1941. Objet: a/s de l'attitude du nonce apostolique'.
19. *Acta Apostolicae Sedis*, Rome, vol. 32, pp. 299f; and pp. 550ff.
20. Letter to ACA in Occupied France, 28 February 1941, published in *Semaine Religieuse* (Paris), 29 March 1941. Letter to ACA in Unoccupied France, 1 March 1941, published in *Semaine Religieuse* (Verdun [sic]), 1 May 1941. Letter to Cardinal Suhard, 10 January 1942, published in *Semaine Religieuse* (Paris), 7 February 1942.
21. AN 72 AJ 1863. Agence Française d'Information de Presse, 'Une lettre-circulaire du Pape', 29 March 1941.

22. A Dio, Lille, 2 B 1. 'Lettre à Pie XII', Paris, 15 January 1941.

23. Bédarida, 'La Voix du Vatican', p. 223.

24. Cholvy and Hilaire, *Histoire religieuse*, p. 78; P. Duclos, *Le Vatican et la seconde guerre mondiale. Action doctrinale et diplomatique en faveur de la paix*, 1955, p. 153, n. 3.

25. Duclos, *Le Vatican*, p. 189.

26. AN 72 AJ 1862. Report of broadcast, Radio-Londres [*sic*], 21 October 1941..

27. AN 2 AG 494. 'Note sur l'attitude du Saint-Siège en matière internationale', n.d.

28. A Dio, Lille, ACA 2 B 1. ACA meeting of 23 April 1941. The message is marked: 'Vœu non transmis au Saint-Père car on semble ignorer tout ce qu'il fait pour la paix.'

29. AN 2 AG 609. Documents divers. Lettres adressées au Commandant Féat. Letter of Bérard to Laval, 1 May 1942.

30. AN 60.1674. Text of message appearing in the *Semaine Religieuse* (Toulouse), 19 April 1942.

31. AN 72 AJ 1862. File: 'Actes de S. S. Pie XII, 1939–1942'. Message dated 25 April 1942.

32. Duclos, *Le Vatican*, pp. 64f.

33. AN 2 AG 492. 'Note (Secret)', 21 January 1943.

34. AN F60. 1674. CNI. Notes d'Orientation nos. 2826 and 2827.

35. AN 2 AG 494. Articles et documents résesrvés à la presse catholique. Informations de l'Etat français. Document dated 22 January 1943.

36. AN F1a 3784. Information received 5 February 1943. Ref: LIBE/9/14.

37. AN F60.1674. CNI. Informations générales. Ref: LO68 B 2725 of 13 February 1943.

38. AN 2 AG 492. Report of Bérard to Laval, as Foreign minister, Vatican, 18 January 1943.

39. AN F60.1674. *News Digest* (London), No. 1035, 16 January 1943.

40. Hoover Institution, *France during the German Occupation, 1940–1944*, Stanford, 1958, vol. 2, p. 1421. Testimony of Maurice Vallet, journalist.

41. See W.D. Halls, *The Youth of Vichy France*, Oxford, 1981, p. 203; also AN 2 AG 494. 'Note pour Monsieur le Maréchal', 18 February 1942; and report in *L'Avenir de la Vienne*, 25 February 1942.

42. AN 2 AG 495. 'Projet de lettres', 7 March 1942.

43. AN 2 AG 495. 'La sous-alimentation en France'. 'Note', Vichy, 6 May 1942; and letter from Darlan, 18 March 1942.

44. Duclos, *Le Vatican*, pp. 155f; Charles-Roux, *Huit Ans au Vatican, 1932–1940*, 1949, p. 286.

45. See *Actes*: Lyons, F. Delpech, 'Le Projet de Concordat de l'été 1940', pp. 185–8; also A Dio, Lille, ACA 2 B 1, 'Convention entre la République française [*sic*] et le Saint-Siège'.

46. AN 2 AG 492. Report of Bérard to Laval, Vatican, 8 June 1942.

47. Delpech, 'Le Projet de Concordat', p. 186.

48. Cholvy and Hilaire, *Histoire religieuse*, p. 78.

49. AN 2 AG 492. Rapports avec le Saint-Siège. 'Note sur une politique religieuse de l'Etat Français', Vichy, 4 August 1941.

50. A Dio, Lille, ACA 2 B 1 ACA of 24 July 1941. The letter, however, is dated Vénissieux, 25 *October* 1941.

51. Delpech, 'Le Projet de Concordat', p . 185.

52. AN 72 AJ 1862. Relations du Vatican avec divers pays, 1941–1942.

53. C. Cianfarra, *La guerre et le Vatican*, 1947, p. 232.

54. AN F60.1674. Information reaching London, 25 April 1942.

55. *Journal des Débats*, 2 May 1942.

56. AN 2 AG 543 Divers. CC142. 'Dépêche de M. Bérard', 8 June 1942.

57. Ibid.

58. AN 2 AG 492. Bérard, 15 October 1942: 'Note sur une négociation éventuelle entre la France et le Saint-Siège'.

59. AN 2 AG 492. 'Note (Secret)', 21 January 1943.

60. AN 2 AG 492. 'Note (Secret)', 10 February 1943.
61. AN 2 AG 75. Correspondance et documents de Ménétrel. 'Note (Secret)', 26 March 1943.
62. AN 2 AG 82. 'Règles à suivre en matière de politique religieuse', Cabinet Civil, Vichy, 19 May 1943.
63. M. Déat, 'L'Eglise et la Révolution', *L'Œuvre*, 15 May 1943.
64. AN 2 AG 492. 'Note de L(ouis) C(anet) Conseiller d'Etat: Note pour M. Lavagne', Royat, 2 October 1941.
65. AN 2 AG 492. Bérard, 15 October 1942. 'Note sur une négociation éventuelle entre la France et le Saint-Siège'.
66. AN 2 AG 493. 'Note sur le problème posé par la reconnaissance des Frères Chrétiennes', 10 February 1944.
67. AN F1a.3784. Document marked 'Très secret'. Information received Algiers, January 1944. Ref: ZAC/7/36800.
68. P. Blet, 'Pie XII et la France en guerre', *Revue d'Histoire de l'Eglise de France*, LXIX,:1183, July–December 1983, p. 226.
69. AN F1a.3351. 'Note' by André Latreille, appointed to head the Direction des Cultes in the Interior ministry, Paris, 15 January 1945.
70. *Actes*: Grenoble, p. 363.
71. The Pope remained anti-Communist to the end. See AN 2 AG 82 Note signed by G. Morancé, 22 February 1944.

PART V

THE CHURCH AND SOCIETY

-15-

The Church and Economic and Social Affairs

Religion before the war was most practised by the bourgeoisie: the Church had largely lost the battle for the working class. As an institution it supported the established order, and under the influence of Action Française, until the Ligue was banned, and even afterwards, was strongly patriotic. Traditionalists within it held up an almost medieval ideal, where the peasant family worked the land — until 1934, it must be recalled, less than half the population lived in towns. Where industry existed, the ideal was of a docile work-force ruled by an elite.

This view of the relationship of the Church to the economy and society was challenged by another trend which may be broadly characterised as social catholicism. This had many different points of emphasis. Mounier's philosophy of personalism, for example, as regards society, sought to discover a rationale based neither on capitalism nor on socialism. Others such as Joseph Folliet, of the review *Chronique sociale*, stressed social justice. Whilst social catholicism held its main purpose ultimately to be evangelisation, it believed the Church had a major role to play in social and even political life.

Social catholicism was based on the encyclical *Rerum Novarum* of Leo XIII, promulgated in 1890, when he was already eighty years old — the same Pope who two years later had urged Catholics to rally to the Republican regime. The encyclical contrasted the wealth of the rich to the misery of the poor, and the easy life of the employer to the hard lot of the worker. It exhorted both social partners to acknowledge their mutual duties. The worker should not be treated as a slave, a mere tool for the production of profit, but his employer had a right to expect him to give of his best.[1] These precepts of the encyclical had been reinforced in another papal pronouncement, *Quadragesimo Anno* (1931). In this Pius XI had likewise shown a distrust of capitalism as well as socialism or communism.

The overarching practical task for Social Catholics was to resolve, in the light of Christian doctrine and the Church's teaching, the social and economic problems arising from the Industrial Revolution and from *laissez-faire* liberalism. For some this meant the rejection of the society that had sprung from the Reformation and the 1789 Revolution, and their twin abuses, individualism and secularisation. For others, to overcome these 'evils', a benevolent paternalism in industry and a hierarchy in society provided the solution. For yet others the repression of both liberalism and capitalism required the shaping of a democratic, non-elitist society. This reformist wing of social catholicism included Christian Democrat politicians, Christian trade unionists, the Church's youth movements, and organisations such as Action Populaire, led by Père Desbuquois. All these, as Social Catholics, struggled to make their voice heard at Vichy on social matters, but were eventually forced either to compromise, to yield, to abandon the struggle, or join the Resistance. The prejudice against them by integrist Catholics and others was great: they were held to have played into the hands of the Left.[2] Louis Bertrand even asserted that social catholicism bordered upon downright materialism.

Action Populaire, presided over by Père Desbuquois since the beginning of the century, had formed ever since an important Christian forum for the discussion of social questions. Its centre at Vanves, staffed by a dozen Jesuits, acted as an information centre and ran conferences and study sessions for seminarians and Church organisations. In 1940 Desbuquois had settled in the unoccupied zone and was thus able to maintain close contact with those at Vichy involved in drawing up new social legislation. This co-operation was later criticised but, like Mounier, he justified it after the event as seeking to influence the regime from within.[3] To Mgr Chollet he once remarked: 'Even if the devil were at Vichy, I think one should remain there.'[4] A 'politique de présence' was needed to counteract the influence of the Maurrassians and the more reactionary strands of catholicism.

Linked to Action Populaire were the Semaines Sociales, which dated back to 1904 and were presided over by Eugène Duthoit, Dean of the Catholic law faculty at Lille. As well as putting on lectures on social matters, once a year it held a week-long rally ('semaine') which assembled academics, economists, philosophers, theologians, industrialists and trade unionists to address a broad social topic in the light of Church teaching. The war interrupted these annual gatherings, but the influential governing committee of the Semaines Sociales, its twenty-strong Commission Générale, continued to meet to discuss policy developments. On it served, for example, Alfred Michelin, influential with both *La Croix* and the Christian trade unions, who was eventually to quarrel with Desbuquois over Vichy's social legislation.

The divisions of opinion that occurred in both Semaines Sociales and Action Populaire were reflected in the post-defeat publications of both organisations. For Action Populaire, *Renouveaux*, appearing in October 1940, urged a return to a spiritual order, demanding 'reflection' on Pétain's broadcast 'messages'. *Cité Nouvelle* in January 1941 favoured a strongly authoritarian State, closely linked to the family and the world of work. Another Jesuit, a friend of Desbuquois, Père Desqueyrat, who later developed ties with André Philip and the Resistance, thereupon accused Desbuquois of turning his back on the democratic values he had previously embraced. At a meeting of the committee of Semaines Sociales in February 1941 Desbuquois also clashed with Poimbœuf, the Christian trade unionist, over Vichy's proposals for the family and youth, the organisation of rural workers, a minimum wage, and co-operation in the workplace. Desbuquois's friend, Joseph Folliet, who returned to Lyons from captivity in 1942 to become Secretary-General of the Semaines Sociales and editor of its *Chronique Sociale*, also tried to work for change within the system, but soon fell foul of the censorship. In its issue of September–October 1942 the periodical asserted that it was the right and duty of Christians to disobey unjust laws: the offending pages were promptly excised. Since many Social Catholics had been appointed by Vichy as local councillors and used the publication to obtain information about their new task, the regime was extremely sensitive to anything that might be construed as subversive. If many associated with the Semaines Sociales, such as Mgr Bruno de Solages, Michelin, and the trade unionists Prélot and Tessier, were hostile to Vichy, others such as the Abbé Tellier de Poncheville, and Gounot, the inspirer of the 'family law' of 29 December 1940, favoured co-operation, as did Desbuquois himself, who was much influenced by Cardinal Gerlier. Moreover, through Lucien Romier, a minister of state, who had long backed Action Populaire, Desbuquois had access to Pétain. However, after the return to power of Laval, whilst remaining loyal to the Marshal to the end, he realised that no purpose was served by prolonging his stay at Vichy and returned to his centre at Vanves. The disagreements that arose over the regime's social policy even in this, considered to be the more democratic strand of social catholicism, illustrate once again Catholic ambiguity towards Vichy.

Mention should also be made of Economie et Humanisme, a movement with similar aims to the Semaines Sociales, but more oriented to the economic aspects of reform. It was established in the unoccupied zone on 24 September 1941 and had its main centre in Marseilles. Its founder was the Dominican Père Lebret, a supporter of the Révolution Nationale who was backed by the academic economist François Perroux. Less populist in its approach, it attacked both liberal individualism and Marxist collectivism,[5] seeking a 'third way' between profit-oriented capitalism and egalitarian socialism, both of which it considered to be fatally flawed. It was 'communautaire', in the sense that the common good was an overriding concern: 'moi pour toi, toi pour moi' was its watchword. With the work force organised in corporations, the ideal was a humane economy in which organisation, efficiency and order should nevertheless prevail. By applying the doctrines of a Christian humanism, and in particular Mounier's philosophy of Personalism, the group believed that a study of the Gospel would yield solutions on which to build this new economic order. However, although it managed to hold two congresses, at La Bourboule (Puy-de-Dôme) and Le Mont-Dore (Puy-de-Dôme), to publicise its views, its main vehicle for the dissemination of its ideas was the then very popular method among Catholics of social enquiry ('enquête'); it was more concerned with teaching than direct action.

A similar movement, Jeunesse de l'Eglise, also influenced by personalism, was launched by another Dominican, Père Montlucard. Using the enquiry method, the group reflected on contemporary social and economic values. One question, which caused a stir at the time, was: 'Has Christianity 'devirilised' men?' By 1945 it found itself in sympathy with the Christian Progressivists who openly espoused Marxist doctrines; eventually the movement was wound up at the Church's request.[6]

How did the bishops stand in relation to social catholicism? The fiftieth anniversary of *Rerum Novarum* in May 1941 was the occasion for a number of pronouncements. Speaking in his cathedral, Cardinal Gerlier, extolled Leo XIII as the 'workers' pope' who had denounced the oppression of the poor and weak and the transformation of the worker into a machine, but had nevertheless held the right to property to be sacred.[7] Other prelates treated the subject differently. Mgr Delay of Marseilles laid stress on Leo XIII's condemnation of the 'fundamental error' ('l'erreur foncière') of socialism. He had predicted the catastrophes that this materialist doctrine would precipitate: the class struggle and 'the inevitable unleashing of the basest desires'.[8] Mgr Blanchet, Bishop of Saint-Dié, was even blunter: 'Socialism is a dead end.'[9]

By contrast, the most anti-Capitalist — and most radical — prelate was undoubtedly Mgr Saliège. He believed that the institution of property should be for the benefit of the community. Private ownership might be a moral necessity, but it was a mere expedient, a consequence of original sin.[10] He attacked the domination of money; according to a police report his sentiments were calculated to shock the bourgeoisie: 'Miserable 1000-franc notes, how many sins, how many crimes they cause to be committed... So long as money remains the master, a country cannot be happy.'[11] The report commented that the half-paralysed archbishop, hardly able to speak, was occasionally carried away by his pen, and astounded even some of his priests. Left-wing circles might claim that he had accepted communism, but his views appeared to command support in Rome. Conveying the Pope's New Year greetings, Cardinal Maglione had assured him that his pastoral concerns ('sollicitudes') were echoed by the Holy Father. In a Lenten letter read from the pulpit on 28 February 1943. Saliège even deplored the fact that the Capitalist regime had not yet disappeared. Opening the academic year on 10 October 1943 of the Ecole Normale Ouvrière, organised by the local Christian trade union in Toulouse, he outlined a far-reaching reform programme. He saw the union as working towards the abolition of the proletariat. The system of liberal capitalism, which glorified output and efficiency, had likewise to disappear. At present the working class was powerless against the domination of the financiers and trusts; these controlled the press, propaganda, and even the nation–state itself, thus making wars inevitable. The scandal was that abundance could bring about poverty and technology could enslave the workers, whereas a machine culture, by freeing men from drudgery, should generate prosperity for everybody. But technology lacking any humanising quality — any 'quality of love' — merely ground down the less fortunate. This quality of love should inspire the work of trade unionists.[12] This was strong meat for the bourgeoisie.

Saliège's perspective of social catholicism was hardly one to appeal to the reactionary paternalists of the Vichy regime, with their elitist concept of society, nor indeed to its 'jeunes cyclistes', the budding technocrats. It did, however, have great attraction for the Left, as well as for the Christian Democrats of the PNP and Jeune République, and for the Resistance in general.[13] As for other democratically-minded social Catholics, they might disagree about the means, but were at one on the overarching goal: 'a return to a moral economy, to a more humane community, freed from the pecuniary selfishness of capitalism'.[14]

For 'Social' Christians a crucial question was how the Vichy regime conceived the internal organisation of the world of work. It professed to share many of the views of social catholicism, particularly emphasising that the antagonism between capital and labour should end. In his message of 11 July 1940 Pétain had extolled honest labour as the chief source of national wealth and had denounced both international capitalism and international socialism.[15] In subsequent messages he decried the power of money — 'la tutelle la plus misérable, celle de l'argent' (12 August 1940) — whose misuse brought misery to many; he wished to restore the dignity of labour and ensure a decent livelihood and working conditions for the workers. But it must be honest toil:

before the war, said one Vichy propagandist, Frenchmen loved neither one another nor their work — a job was merely the means for gratifying ever-increasing wants.[16] Liberal capitalism had led to bitter struggles, with trusts, cartels and employers ranged against employees and trade unions. As a result a chaotic economy had performed lamentably. Modernisers such as Bouthillier, the Finance minister, and Belin, the ex-CGT leader appointed by Pétain as Production and Labour minister, as well as technocrats appointed under Darlan such as Pucheu and Berthelot — all wanted an efficiently planned system.

The Germans were largely indifferent to these aims, merely seeking to exploit French industry and agriculture for their military machine. However, even before the war, conscious of the key role played by labour in the French economy, Abetz had sought a dialogue with the Confédération Française des Travailleurs chrétiens (CFTC), the PDP and other 'social' Christians. Gaston Tessier, the CFTC Secretary-General, was not unwilling to engage in dialogue, but when in 1937 the German had invited a group to see for itself the social and industrial achievements of nazism, the invitation had been refused, and contact was broken off.[17]

The Church in general shared Vichy's views on the demerits of a Capitalist system in which individualism ran riot, and the weakest went to the wall. It particularly wanted an end to class warfare. The disagreement was on how to remedy these ills. Right-wing sympathisers with Maurrassians, such as Mgr Guerry, thought the solution was for the working class to become property-owners and by amassing more material possessions to acquire a vested interest in the economy.[18] For some, a particular target was limited companies, whose abolition Le Cour Grandmaison and other FNC leaders had suggested in March 1938. Pétain's line was not dissimilar: in an important speech (12 October 1940) on social matters, he postulated as the ideal the family business. Like Le Play, the nineteenth-century sociologist, he thought this would overcome individualism. However, one alternative, State ownership of the means of production and distribution was anathema to Vichy and Catholics alike. Nor was Déat's neosocialism, which merely sought to control capitalism and limit its capacity for profit, acceptable.[19] The institution of private property remained sacrosanct, although there was concern that the excesses of capitalism should be eradicated.

What then was the solution to this antinomy between capital and labour? Pétain and the Church favoured corporatism as the basis for reorganising the economy. The Révolution Nationale sought to revive the 'natural' communities of the family, occupation, province and commune which, according to La Tour du Pin, another nineteenth-century sociologist, would counteract revolutionary individualism.[20] The corporative reorganisation of industry would enable the reciprocal duties of industrialist and worker in an occupation to be effectively discharged. Entirely consonant with *Rerum Novarum*, such ideas were appealing to many Catholics.[21] In the 1930s similar views had been current in circles centred round such movements as *Ordre Nouveau* and *Esprit*, which were already seeking to steer a middle course between capitalism and collectivism.

For the Vichy regime this meant essentially the re-establishment of the network of corporations that had subsisted until 1791. Henceforth employers and employed would be grouped in unitary bodies according to occupation. This would, it was believed, eliminate at a stroke the class struggle from the equation and mitigate the evils of competition. However, in practice this corporatism was tinged with statism, and had little room for the more ethical economy favoured by Mgr Saliège. In fact, the system that emerged, as developed by the regime's technocrats, who still wished to exercise a large measure of control, continued to serve more the interests of big business than the workers.

In the new dispensation that was propounded the sticking point for many Social Catholics was the State's decision to abolish all trade unions and employers' associations at national level. It wished to create a 'syndicat unique', obligatory for employers and employees alike. This meant the virtual disappearance of the unions, including the CFTC. Bishops viewed this Christian workers' union, particularly strong in western and eastern France, and in the textile industry (where its membership included many women), with a benevolent eye. The union was run by a 'confederal bureau', but had a 'conseil théologique' to which any matters that impinged upon religion were referred. It believed in social partnership, and was moderate in its strike policy. This did not redeem it in Pétain's eyes, for whom all trade unions regardless of their allegiance fed the class struggle; furthermore, he believed that by encouraging sloth in their members, unions had helped to lose the war and deserved to be punished. To even the most loyal of the bishops, Mgr Liénart, this view was unacceptable, as the cardinal's past record demonstrated. Backed by Pius XI, in 1929 he had supported the CFTC strikes at Halluin against the industrial 'barons' of the Roubaix-Tourcoing-Lille textile consortium. In 1936 he had likewise defended the right of the CFTC to exist when its much larger rival, the CGT, by then reunited with the CGTU, had sought to swallow up the Christian union. Vichy's proposal to abolish it — it had half a million members in 1939 — came therefore as a shock both to its leaders and to the cardinal, in whose diocese it was particularly strong.[22]

How did these conflicting viewpoints clash, and what part did the Church play? The opening shot was fired even before the Third

Republic had formally ceased to exist. On 8 July 1940 Zirnheld, the CFTC chairman, wrote in conciliatory terms to Pétain requesting that, in any new constitution, trade union rights should be respected. (Incidentally, he also asked for measures to promote the family, and for the reinstatement of the pre-war social legislation.) The Marshal's response was cordial but non-committal. Meanwhile the CGT was already aware of rumours of a revised status for the unions. Jouhaux, its leader, contacted Tessier, the Secretary-General of the CFTC, urging joint action, and at the same time instructed his departmental sections to liaise with their Christian counterparts in defence of unionism. Once the new regime was in being, other elements in the CFTC were to prove less amenable than Zirnheld: in the Lyons area the CFTC had links with the PDP; in Toulouse, through Canon Jaize, it was in contact with Mgr Saliège. Both the political party and the bishop supported the continuance of the union.

Thus the law of 16 August 1940 on 'the provisional organisation of industrial production' came as a bolt from the blue. It dissolved all national organisations of employers and employees, thereby abrogating a right of association guaranteed workers since 1884. At national level not only the Confédération Générale du Patronat français (CGPF), the employers' organisation, and the Comité des Forges, the organisation of ironmasters and steel barons, but also the CGT and CFTC formally ceased to exist as country-wide organisations. The Labour minister, René Belin, the former CGT leader, declared that at local level the unions could continue. In practice this robbed them of almost all power. In their stead were set up 312 'Comités d'organisation', representing each branch of industry. Their task was to compile lists of firms, assess the means of production and stocks available, draw up future output levels, allocate raw materials, and fix production rules and prices. Committee members would be official appointees — inevitably these would be largely drawn from the employers. The committees would exercise a general oversight of any departmental or local trade unions. Eventually there would be only one occupational association for each industrial sector.

Zirnheld promptly indicated to Vichy that the CFTC could not co-operate in this new scheme. With Gaston Tessier, the union's Secretary-General, and Jouhaux, for the CGT, a statement was issued regretting that the union '[was] being crushed under the weight of old hostilities, old mistakes... [and] the ceaseless repetitions of present-day politicians, the same ones as before'.[23]

A joint CFTC/CGT delegation met with Colonel Cèbe, of Pétain's staff, on 28 August 1940. Cèbe was charged with setting up a committee to work out a 'Labour Charter' ('Charte du Travail'). The delegation pressed for a plurality of unions and the right to appoint members to all such committees, but the official reaction was wholly negative.

The Armistice division of the country into zones, with the added complication of a 'zone interdite' in the industrial North, made communication between the various CFTC sections difficult. Tessier, the Secretary-General, located in the North, managed however to liaise with union leaders such as Poimbœuf in the south. Both were opposed to the Vichy proposals, whereas Perès, the CFTC representative in Paris, was more inclined to co-operate. The decrees of 9 November 1940 formally dissolving the unions were to crystallise this difference in views. Three days later the CFTC appealed unsuccessfully to the Conseil d'Etat as to the legality of the decrees. The measures provoked what became known as the 'Manifeste des Douze', signed by nine CGT and three CFTC members (Zirnheld, Tessier and Bouladoux), which set out a 'natural right' (for Christians, as affirmed in *Rerum Novarum*), of freedom of association and from government interference. In 1945 this document was seen as having been a veritable act of Resistance. It insisted on the worker's right to unionise, to choose his union, and to be represented on any government committees concerned with labour matters. It also seized the opportunity to reject the 'mentality of defeat' as well as to repudiate any union responsibility for the collapse in 1940, and to condemn anti-Semitism and any form of religious persecution, or punishment for 'crimes of opinion' ('délits d'opinion') — the right of free speech, for example.[24]

In spite of grave misgivings, the instinctive reaction of the Hierarchy was to support the regime, provided certain safeguards were given. Meeting in January 1941, the ACA stated that it regretted the abandonment of trade union freedom, asked for assurances that any putative 'syndicat unique' should not engage in politics, and demanded respect for religion. 'If this is so, Christian workers can agree to it.'[25] But this was only a half-hearted and provisional endorsement of the new dispensation.

The CFTC did in fact win representation on the 'Comité d'organisation professionnelle', which first met on 27 March 1941 to plan the new Labour Charter. Poimbœuf — and not Perès — was appointed to the committee. Pétain was fully aware of the hostility his proposals had created, and responded in the spring of 1941 by making no less than three public 'social' pronouncements, the gist of which was that he agreed that the mentality of the class struggle could be imputed to employers no less than to the work-force,[26] but otherwise he made no concessions. Meanwhile, the CFTC in the Nord department decided to approach the Marshal directly. Their pleas for survival were accompanied by a letter of support from Cardinal Liénart. They asserted they had always opposed the trade union 'monopolism' of marxism. They favoured a formula that encapsulated 'la liberté syndicale dans la profession organisée'. They welcomed the abandonment of the class struggle and inter-party strife and the abolition of the right to strike or to impose a 'lock-out'. But they could not agree to the compulsory enrolment of workers in a 'syndicat unique', since this was contrary not only to the 1890 encyclical, but to later papal pronouncements such as *Quadragesimo Anno* and *Divini Redemptoris,* not to mention the letter of support regarding the textile strikes in the North, sent to Cardinal Liénart before the war by the Sacred Congregation, by which they placed much store.

Indeed in *Rerum Novarum* some Catholic trade unionists found a moral justification for passing from rejection of the regime's measures to joining the Resistance. The encyclical had affirmed: 'A law does not merit obedience unless it conforms to correct reason and to the eternal law of God.' About this time Catholics unconnected with trade unions also began to reflect upon the general implications of this statement.

At their summer meeting the ACA reiterated its views. It still thought desirable the continuance of Catholic trade unions, but if this were refused Catholics should not persist in boycotting the new institutions.[27] Meanwhile the union representations had not been dismissed out of hand by Pétain, and another CFTC leader, Charlemagne Broutin, on 22 August 1941, informed Liénart, with whom the union remained in close contact, that there was some hope of winning over the Marshal. However, union sentiment was bitter: a revival of paternalism was feared, and what the workers desired was being denied them; 'Instead of the fair wage that allows them to live "independently" [...] they [the government] would rather offer them the charity of workers' soup kitchens or the Secours National, [provided by] those who retain the prejudices of a past era and live in an ivory tower.'[28]

The Charte du Travail, published on 26 October 1941, confirmed the CFTC's worst fears.[29] It divided industry and commerce into twenty-nine occupational branches, each comprising six categories: employers, engineers, managerial and commercial cadres, foremen, white-collar workers, and blue- collar workers. Within each category would function a single, national, obligatory union. Strikes and lock-outs, as anticipated, were outlawed. At local level a 'comité social professionnel' drawn from each category would take all the major decisions affecting an occupation. These local committees would choose representatives for a regional committee, which in turn would appoint members of a national committee, over whose membership the government had the right of veto. In addition every undertaking with over 100 employees had to set up local 'social committees' ('comités sociaux d'entreprise'), drawn in equal number from each of the six categories Their main task would be to resolve disputes, and establish charitable funds. Although blue-collar workers were by far the most numerous group, parity in the number of representatives in each category meant they could easily be overruled on these committees, so that power would continue to rest with the employers. At departmental and local level the old unions would be allowed to continue, as would their federations, but would clearly be unable to influence events.[30]

The CFTC, although approving of some features of the Charte, was divided as to whether it should participate in these committees. At a delegate meeting on 16 November 1941 Tessier reported on further consultations he had had with the 'conseil théologique' of the union, which had been in close touch with the Hierarchy. It appeared most bishops disliked the neutral stance of the Charte and would have preferred it to come out firmly in favour of the Church's social doctrines. However, they would not dissuade the unions from joining in the Charte. A motion was passed regretting the turn of events but allowed each federation and regional branch within the confederation to make up its own mind whether to participate or not. A few decided to do so. Some observers long associated with the CFTC, such as Abbé Tellier de Poncheville, who published an approving article in December 1941 in *La Croix*, welcomed participation. However, this provoked others to a hostile reaction, among them a former Vice-President of the CFTC, Alfred Michelin, who had a long-standing connection with the newspaper.

After the November meeting Torcq, another prominent CFTC leader in the North, wrote to Liénart (17 November 1941) reiterating that the Charte was incompatible with the Christian tradition. He attacked the principle of 'unicité'. Radio and propaganda were already a monopoly: had one to look forward to, he asked, 'sport unique', 'école unique', 'jeunesse unique' (which the ACA had already set its face against) and 'formation civique et morale unique'? This touched a sensitive nerve with Liénart who wrote back (26 November 1941) deploring the letter's tone and admonishing Torcq to observe the law, which he should try to change from within. Nevertheless the cardinal probably gave his blessing to yet another letter to Pétain (19 November 1941), this time from another union leader, Charlemagne Broutin. This argued that to abolish the CFTC was to dismantle the sole force capable of standing up to marxism. For some union leaders its disappearance would mean the annihilation of their life's work. Before the enabling decrees regarding the Charte were promulgated Broutin asked that amendments be made allowing pluralism and representativity.

On 23 December 1941 the ACA at last formally approved the Charte, but expressed the vague hope that the CFTC could continue still to function in some form or another. Liénart continued to interest himself in the matter. On New Year's Day, 1942, he addressed to the CFTC his 'fraternels encouragements'. Tessier wrote back (8 January 1942) enclosing a copy of a circular letter that, with the permission of Mgr Courbe, of Action Catholique, he had sent to the bishops of the occupied zone asking for their comments on the Charte. The results of this enquiry are not known, although by then it was evident that within the ACA, at least, two camps had formed. Mgr Feltin of Bordeaux urged total compliance with the law; Mgr Liénart, Mgr Saliège, and Mgr Fillion, Archbishop of Bourges, backed by Mgr Hoguet, Vicar-General of Arras, continued to support the official CFTC view. The matter was clearly not definitively settled. An ACA motion dated 14 February 1942 again regretted the disappearance of specifically Christian trade unionism but did not discourage participation (to what extent was not specified) in the institutions of the Charte. An unofficial adviser to the CFTC, Abbé Lesage, of the Missionaires du Travail, wrote to Feltin, with a copy to Liénart, at about the same time, complaining that the syndicalism propounded in the Charte was a pale shadow of the real thing. He was aware that Cardinal Liénart had advised against precipitate action, but he (Lesage) was saddened to see how little the bishops prized Christian unionism. In spite of the letter's sharp reproach, this time Liénart did not rebuke its author. Indeed it may well have determined him to make his one and only journey to Vichy on 10 April 1942, where, (so he asserted after the war) he had pleaded for workers' rights, and union freedom, 'même celle des cégétistes' ('even that of members of the CGT'). Later (8 June 1942) the cardinal wrote to Laval hinting that a plurality of unions with diverse beliefs was no bad thing, that working-class co-operation was essential, and warning against the new law's enabling decrees merely being imposed mandatorily. Meanwhile Eugène Duthoit, for the Catholic Secrétariat Social du Nord, joined Abbé Lesage in another memorandum to Pétain urging the abandonment of the 'syndicat unique'.

On 6 July 1942 Lagardelle, now Labour minister, announced to union representatives that, according to Mgr Chappoulie, the bishops favoured the Charte in its present form and did not insist on a separate Christian trade union.[31] Acting as Lagardelle's intermediary, Père Villain warned Liénart (25 July 1942) that a plea for unreserved support of the 'syndicat unique' would be made directly to the ACA. Liénart gave a robust reply. On 1 August 1942 he wrote: 'I do not admit... that the very clear directives of the Holy See that for fifty years have recommended Christian employers and workers to incorporate themselves in unions permeated with Christian social doctrine, were of a transitory nature, dependent on circumstances, and today have lapsed.'[32]

The cardinal wrote off to Vichy, this time to Lagardelle, but received only a vague hint of slight modifications to the enabling decrees. The Minister flatly rejected Liénart's contention that the 'syndicat unique' would be 'a remedy worse than the evil itself'.Indeed Mgr Chappoulie had assured him, he stated, that the bishops as a whole did not consider the concept of a 'syndicat unique' contrary to Church social doctrine.[33] Vichy's stand was backed by the collaborationist press, which ascribed the desire to preserve union pluralism to wishing to add a confessional or political dimension to syndicalism.[34]

In the other camp, on 2 October 1942, Mgr Feltin, in a pastoral letter, publicly endorsed the principle of a single union, provided that Christian morality were respected and, outside the union framework, workers could meet for moral and religious education; for him, the single union was a powerful means of combating communism.[35] At the ACA meeting later in the same month matters came to a head. Notes made by Liénart at the time reveal how greatly the problem still perplexed him, as it called into question, as never before, his absolute loyalty to the regime. He acknowledged that a plurality of trade unions had never been seen as essential by the Vatican, as the examples of Italy and Portugal demonstrated. On the other hand, the papacy had always encouraged Christian trade unions. He took the opposing view from Feltin: it was Christian trade unions that were an effective bulwark against both marxism and liberal capitalism. He pleaded for a transition period for phasing-in the Charte, with workers able directly to elect representatives to the 'comités d'entreprise' and the 'comités sociaux'.[36]

The ACA eventually came out publicly in favour of complete participation in the new institutions, but refrained from formally endorsing the 'syndicat unique'. The ACA declaration of 22 October 1942 ran:

> Faced with the fact of one single union, the Assembly, without however giving up the thesis of union pluralism, but above all concerned to ensure the maintenance of Christian influence in working life, wishes all Catholics, both employers and employees, individually and each in the position that Providence has assigned to them, to contribute to the organising of occupations at present in progress.[37]

This represented a partial victory for the minority in the CFTC, since the majority wanted nothing to do with the Charte until the question of the 'syndicat unique' was reconsidered. However, according to one source, Liénart maintained that the ACA had expressed no preference for the participationist camp.[38] Other prelates continued to take an active interest. Tessier, the CFTC's Secretary-General, met frequently with Cardinal Gerlier, who was persuaded — unsuccessfully — to intervene with de Canisy, Pétain's adviser on social matters. The other cardinal, Mgr Suhard, however, invited a theologian to study the Charte; his recommendation was that the Church, whilst preferring a confessional union, should accept the 'syndicat unique'. It was plain that Church leaders continued to be deeply divided, as a letter from Liénart to Saliège demonstrates: 'Some of us have been less [unanimous than on the question of youth] as regards the single union.'[39]

Nevertheless the matter dragged on. In early April 1943 Tessier had another interview with Pétain, who told him that plans for the 'syndicat unique' were evolving and that Suhard was on the verge of agreeing to it. Tessier immediately asked Liénart (5 April 1943) to make one last appeal to the Marshal. Radio Moscow must have had wind of this, because in a broadcast on 21 April 1943 it praised the cardinal warmly, promising that the Communists would help him to defend the Christian unions 'presently under attack by the Germans and Vichy'.[40] For the union the crunch came at a general meeting of the whole Confédération in Paris on 27 June 1943. It was asked to vote for or against participation (whether wholly or in part). The final resolution presented ran: Christian trade unionism as such, no matter what the position or tactics adopted previously, will refrain from any participation in the installation of unified unions and in their working.[41]

Representatives were informed that the bishops had allowed them a free choice, and that not only Cardinal Liénart but also Radio Vatican had warned against 'unicité', which might presage other monolithic movements. The resolution, with thirty-four departments, representing 85 per cent of CFTC members, voting for it, was carried; only sixteen departments voted against. These defied the majority and resolved to participate in the new institutions. They were expelled from the movement, an action disapproved of, however, by Mgrs Gerlier, Liénart, Guerry, and Marmottin (Rheims).[42] A reason for expulsion was the action of Paul Hibout, one of their leaders, who wrote a tendentious article for the collaborationist journal, *Voix Françaises*, 'Destin du syndicalisme chrétien'.The bishops, so jealous of any attempt to regiment their youth movements, thus seemed to concur in the sacrifice of the CFTC.

The Jesuits of Action Populaire, headed by Père Desbuquois, also reluctantly swallowed the Charte du Travail. Even Père Villain, who sympathised with the views of Archbishop Feltin, had been highly critical of some of its clauses, but maintained that in the exceptional circumstances prevailing the State could legitimately curtail all manner of freedoms.[43] Eugène Duthoit, President of the Semaines Sociales, was reported in mid-1943 as then backing the new legislation fully.[44] A Radio Paris report that even Liénart eventually rallied to the Charte is probably unreliable,[45] for at the CFTC's Ecole Normale Ouvrière on 19 July 1943, the cardinal, speaking, he said, as Bishop of Lille and not for the ACA, voiced his continued disapproval of the 'syndicat unique'. Other Catholics thought it wisest to accept the new dispensation. Charles Soyez, the Director of the Secrétariat Social, reported from Lille in 1944 that over a thousand 'comités sociaux' had already been set up; for him, the Charte although not 'perfect', was 'perfectible', and Christians, as workers and Frenchmen, should play their part in improving it. Moreover, it did not preclude Catholics from meeting separately to discuss matters relating to their work.[46]

Another Catholic organisation, the Ligue Ouvrière Chrétienne, consisting of young adults, many of whom were former members of the JOC, the Catholic young workers' movement, was undecided. Its governing body, meeting in 1942, supported those provisions of the Charte that were aimed against the class struggle and promoted justice and fraternity, but demanded that the dignity and freedom of the workers should not be undermined or subordinated to economic and political ends.[47] This was a brave but vague declaration that had no tomorrow.

The CFTC majority, for its part, did not budge from the uncompromising stand it had taken. Tessier, its foremost leader, perhaps taking to heart the doctrine of the 'just law', had already joined the Resistance movement Liberation-Nord in 1941 and eventually became Vice-President of the Conseil National de la Résistance. Poimbœuf, who had been active in the early negotiations, had left for London. As for the ACA, perhaps its conscience was not entirely clear, and it may have felt that it had let down Christian workers. Its Paris declaration of 17 February 1944 spoke of the continuing need for a fairer, more fraternal social order for the workers.

Meanwhile, what organisation was acceptable to the agricultural community? France as a nation of peasants was a rural idyll long cherished by certain sections of the clergy, although the war had wrought big changes. They felt more at home in a country parish, where the peasantry might be more amenable to religion, and family farming was the rule. Nevertheless, the wartime reality was often far from ideal. Conditions were hard. A typical village might consist of some thirty families living in insanitary conditions; most agricultural workers washed thoroughly only once a week — on Sundays before mass. Wartime diet was monotonous, consisting mainly of a potato-based soup, with bread, bacon, cheese, eggs and pork, the traditional staples of the countryman, in short supply, and with butcher's meat available only on Sundays, if at all. Work — hard manual labour — occupied between ten to thirteen hours a day. Alcoholism was a scourge: in winter the peasant reckoned to consume, if he could obtain it, one litre of wine a day; in summer this quantity was often more than doubled. Sundays was a day of rest, but even then the animals had to be looked after. In the absence of their men as prisoners of war, the women's lot had become particularly strenuous. Rearing animals required their rising at 5 a.m., and the morning was spent between the stable and the pasture; cultivating crops meant that from March to November the task was continually back-breaking; on an arable farm, apart from fetching and carrying, the women would farrow and even plough the fields.[48]

Pétain himself was proud of his peasant origins. In his rallying call to the French people of 25 June 1940 he had asserted: 'The soil does not lie. It remains your resource. It is our country itself.'[49] One of the tenets of the Révolution Nationale — although a singularly unsuccessful one when put into practice — was the 'retour à la terre', a formula which the Church could wholeheartedly endorse. It would stimulate the restoration of family life: the peasant and his family worked, ate and spent their scant leisure time together; it could prove a factor in the moral and physical regeneration of the nation, because rural workers provided a stable element in the social system. Thus how agriculture could be renewed became a major preoccupation of the new regime. How it could be organised was not so contentious as it was for industry: the Church was in favour of improving the peasant's lot; moreover, he was often owner, manager and (with his family) worker all in one. The same problems did not therefore arise.

Not surprisingly, the solution proposed was the same corporatist one. Corporatism in agriculture had been advocated before the war by Le Roy Ladurie, who was later to become Vichy's Agriculture minister, and backed by Louis Salleron, who was recognised as the expert in the field. Salleron, however, wanted an agricultural sector autonomous and independent of the State, a position favoured by the Church as not threatening its own interests.[50]

The law of 2 December 1940. proposed a 'Corporation Paysanne' functioning at three levels. At the base was a communal or intercommunal union, for farm labourers, farmers and landowners, headed by a 'syndic' (administrator) appointed by the region. A regional corporative union would act as an intermediate body linking all local unions. It would consist of regional delegates appointed by the Agriculture ministry. Finally, at national level there would function a corporative national council consisting of regional representatives and members of specialised associations such as those for wheat farmers and wine-growers. All other agricultural organisations — co-operatives, farmers' loan and state insurance funds, or agricultural friendly societies — would be subordinated to this organisation. Social legislation regarding agriculture was in future to be based on the family, since there were few paid workers in the industry. Although Salleron had wanted the corporations to be free-standing, Caziot, Vichy's first Agriculture minister, was anxious for the State to retain ultimate control. Moreover, in order to reinforce the family as the prime agricultural unit and promote greater efficiency the minister legislated to enlarge the size of parcels of land by rationalising the redistribution of small plots (law of 9 March 1941 on the 'remembrement des terres') and by limiting succession rights so that only the eldest son could inherit land (laws of 20 July 1940 and 19 November 1940).

The Church approved of these measures, particularly those relating to the family, but still wanted to avoid complete State control. Fortunately, many of those called upon to administer the new system had been members of the Catholic-inspired Union Nationale des Syndicats agricoles; some of the leaders were former members of JAC, the Church's Young Agricultural Workers, who came from the Ligue Agricole Chrétienne (LAC), a movement started at the instigation of the bishops, and one which also favoured a corporatist organisation of agriculture.[51] This time, after an agreement signed in July 1941, there was no direct clash of views. Indeed so close did co-operation become that bishops even attended meetings of the Corporation Paysanne.

Theirs was also a watching brief. Some Catholics still feared their own movements might be swallowed up by the new organisation. The JAC, in particular, felt itself threatened by the Jeunesses Paysannes, an authoritarian movement, the so-called 'Chemises vertes', set up by Henri Dorgères in 1935 for those aged between sixteen and thirty-five in order to promote his committees for 'la Défense Paysanne'. In the new Corporation Dorgères became the general delegate for propaganda,[52] and the regime allowed his semi-syndical, semi-political youth movement to continue. But a single organisation for young rural workers was opposed in principle by the Church. Eventually the rival movements concluded agreements (3 June 1942 and 24 January 1943),[53] in which they pledged mutual co-operation in education and the training of rural cadres, and in setting up rural youth centres, thus allaying ecclesiastical fears of a monopolistic youth movement.

The reforms in the industrial field were the only ones of the Révolution Nationale — apart from the Service du Travail obligatoire — to which there was considerable episcopal opposition. The Church had condemned the liberal Capitalist model for society as it had the Marxist paradigm, but with the exception of Mgr Saliège, its leaders had no specific alternative to put forward. On the other hand, despite some friction, it approved Vichy's agricultural reform, which incidentally was one of the few initiatives of the regime that survived the Liberation.

The measures the regime proposed regarding the family and social life in general were on the whole welcomed by the Church. It had become alarmed at the break-up of the family through drunkenness and adultery, leading to separation and divorce, with often tragic consequences for the woman left with the children. For both Church and State, the family was the natural community par excellence, a reality that merited its inclusion in the new national motto, and was also a bulwark against 'individualism'. Thus the policy was to encourage the family as a social unit in as many ways as possible.

In so doing, Vichy was only partially innovatory. The Third Republic had linked the shortcomings of the family with population decline. In 1939 a decree-law had introduced a Code de la Famille, and granted newly-weds a start-up loan, a debt which was progressively reduced as they had children. Pétain and his generals were deeply conscious that at the outbreak of war France had been able only to draw on a pool of under 19 million men for its armed forces, as compared with almost 34 million available to the Greater German Reich. The Church saw depopulation as a danger for religion. The 1939 Congress Jaciste (JAC) reported that in the one-fifth of rural France that could be still termed Christian births happily still exceeded deaths but that the villages in the other four-fifths constituted 'villages cercueils', where proselytising was difficult. In Connaux (Gard), for example, with a population of 800, in 1938 there were no births registered, but sixteen deaths. (Some communities had become 'villages des vieillards': in Plounazé (Finistère), a quarter of the population were over sixty.) For the whole of France, according to the Jesuit Père Doncœur, out of 12,804,877 families, 5,926,497 (46 per cent) had at least one child, but almost half had no more than one.[54]

Those who sought to 'rechristianise' France — the Catholic youth movements no less than the Mission de France started during the war by Cardinal Suhard — were convinced that this could only be accomplished through the family. When Zirnheld, the chairman of the CFTC, first approached Pétain in July 1940 regarding trade unions, he had also urged the Marshal, it will be recalled, to encourage the family.[55] A committed Christian, General de la Laurencie, Pétain's friend and adviser, was convinced that the 'dechristianising' of the family had led to its break-up, and had set children against their parents; the Church's task was to restore the Christian family as the basic social unit.[56] (Incidentally the General praised British resistance to the Germans and declared the war was 'la croisade des Peuples libres contre les Dictateurs'.) As to the cause of population decline, in 1942 a survey in the unoccupied zone revealed that some 50 per cent of those polled ascribed it to the 'insufficiency' or absence of religion.[57]

Thus steps to promote larger families taken in the law of 18 November 1940 met with Church support. The law extended the advantages accorded by the Code de la Famille. On the birth of the first child a lump sum was given. For further children a sliding scale of allowances applied. Parents with two children received an extra 10 per cent of the average wage in a department; for four or more children this rose to 50 per cent. Fathers with five children or more were given certain civic advantages. If the mother remained at home and did not seek employment, an extra allowance was payable, as was also the case if there was only one breadwinner in the family. On the other hand negative discrimination was also applied by the State: thus, for example childless state-employed lawyers could expect only limited promotion.

The abortion and divorce laws were tightened up. In 1940 one Catholic source reckoned that at least half a million pregnancies a year were terminated and some 20,000 marriages a year were dissolved.[58] The law of 2 April 1941 prohibited divorce in the first three years of marriage, and then only in very exceptional cases, for physical or moral cruelty; the judge, even after granting a divorce, could postpone the decree absolute for up to two years. Divorce purely on the grounds of adultery was not permitted. This may have been due to the special wartime circumstances, which encouraged sexual promiscuity.

As regards depopulation these policies seem to have met with some success. In 1940 deaths exceeded births by 4.4 per 1,000; by 1943 the deficit was only 0.3 per 1,000.[59]

Although many Catholic movements were concerned with the family,[60] but the largest and most active was the LOC, started in 1935 by nineteen former members of the male and female branches of the Jeunesse Ouvrière Chrétienne.[61] Leading lights in the movement, such as Paul Bacon and Robert Prigent, were to achieve governmental office in the Fourth Republic. In 1941 LOC comprised 722 sections established nationally, and was particularly strong in the industrial North, Lyons, Saint-Etienne and Marseilles. It saw itself not as a welfare organisation or charity, but one of self-help among workers. It had adopted a slogan of its parent movement, JOC: 'entre eux, par eux, pour eux', and provided services ranging from food co-operatives, rehousing and assistance to bombed-out families, children's holiday camps ('colonies de vacances'), food parcels to war and political prisoners, and help with rationing and health matters.

In 1941–42 LOC broadened its clientele and added MPF (Mouvement populaire des Familles) to its acronym. The new LOC-MPF was thrown open to all working-class families, not so much in order to shake off its Catholic image as in the belief that charity might induce conversion of the poor.[62] At its 1942 National Council MPF, as it eventually became known, set out its aims not only in terms of need, but also to 'organise the conquest of the workers to Christianity', as well as to promote social justice and develop a fraternal spirit among the workers. According to Prigent, this broadening of its scope made the organisation 'la CGT des familles'. It certainly had widespread ramifications. Its periodical, *Monde Ouvrier*, raised its circulation from 12,000 in 1939 to 74,000 in 1944. In 1939 members of the movement comprised 10,000 families and at its wartime peak 200,000 wives of prisoners of war were involved in its activities.

Although LOC-MPF was a distinctly class (although Catholic) organisation, which went against Vichy's policy of 'unicité' of movements, it was allowed to continue. Other, non-Catholic family organisations had existed before the war, and the government decided to set up a co-ordinating centre for all such bodies. Catholics were much involved in this centre: Georges Hourdin, a member of the PDP both before and after the war, became its director, and was assisted by Charles Flory, a past ACJF leader.[63] Catholics were also associated with a national Comité Consultatif de la Famille, set up on 5 June 1941, which on 23 June 1943 developed into the Conseil Supérieur de la Famille. Among them were Georges Pernot, who had played a part in drawing up the Code la Famille in 1939, and Père Viollet, a well-known charity worker.

The so-called Loi Gounot of 29 December 1940, which, with modifications, survived the Liberation, instituted a Fédération Nationale de familles françaises, with branches planned for every department and commune. This was to make representations to local councils on family matters and to manage related services. Existing Catholic family institutions would continue, and members of other Catholic organisations such as the Ligue féminine d'Action Catholique were encouraged to join the new local associations.[64] The enabling decree for the law did not appear till 9 December 1943, with the result that by the Liberation only four departmental associations had been created. The Church was gratified that the new legislation sanctioned a plurality of family associations and the question of a State monopoly did not arise.

Since family associations carried on essentially daytime activities, in towns women inevitably assumed a prominent role. (Indeed, after LOC broadened its scope in 1942, although its leaders remained men, there was a real intermingling of the sexes, rare even in adult movements associated with the Church.)

Nevertheless the Vichy regime fostered the ideal of domesticity for women, a policy that coincided with Catholic views on the home. For the bourgeoisie the typical female role was as 'la maîtresse de la maison' and for all women the watchword was 'la femme au foyer'. This policy of women in the home meant that in school girls were discouraged from embarking on an academic course because it would divert them from their 'true' vocation as mothers and housewives: domestic science and family education lessons were compulsory. In view of the population decline, propaganda extolled the joys of motherhood. Domesticity, fostered by Church and State, was an aspiration that was even continued after the war by the MRP, despite women's being given the vote.

Initially, after the collapse the policy could be justified on grounds of expediency. There was a spell of urban unemployment — in 1940 the unemployed numbered 961,000 (not counting the 1.5 million prisoners of war). Various ministries, particularly the Education ministry, even took steps to force married women out of their employ. The law of 11 October 1940 prohibited them from working in the public service if their husbands were also civil servants; women over fifty were to be pensioned off. This measure, ostensibly taken to reduce male unemployment, was undoubtedly acceptable to the Church. However, as the industrial economy began to serve the German war machine female machine-minders were needed in the factories. By 1941 the number of unemployed had dropped to 395,000 (and by 1944 to 23,000),[65] so that discriminatory measures were dropped. Later the threat of calling up women for work in Germany evoked a sharp negative reaction from the ACA. In the countryside the gap left by absent prisoners of war was keenly felt. A majority of them had worked in agriculture — many industrial workers had escaped mobilisation as being in essential employment. It was the women who were left to exploit the farm or smallholding. Since women had traditionally worked in the fields alongside the men this did not draw down Church disapproval. In any case it relied on movements such as the Union féminine civique et sociale to look after female interests. But as regards other forms of female labour, the bishops eventually had to compromise.

Sunday work, for both men and women, was opposed by Communists and Catholics alike. Already putting in long hours, miners in particular opposed seven-day working or working on traditional holidays. In late 1941 a German edict decreeing Sunday shifts sparked off a long strike at Montceau-les-Mines; on 28 December 1940 40 per cent of workers in the northern coal basin failed to report back for work after the Christmas break. They received tacit support from the rank and file clergy. However, this was also a battle the Church eventually lost, although sporadic refusals to work occurred up to September 1943.[66]

Despite virtually full employment, the Allied blockade and the German pillage of France directly condemned many urban low wage earners and their families to poverty and misery. The wealthy patronised extensively the black market, which had quickly arisen because of the shortage of foodstuffs. In November 1941 Cardinal Gerlier warned that such illegal trafficking, which had reached 'deplorable' proportions, was a matter of conscience and morally wrong.[67] The *Semaine religieuse* of Rodez was even more categoric: 'The following sin: those who sell at a price above the normal maximum; those who buy below the common minimum price; those who sell or buy above the controlled price; those who offer or accept for controlled goods a sum considerably above the set price.'[68] Nevertheless the ACA may not have held quite such a rigorous view. An archive document notes that, although to observe official prices was a matter of conscience, in mitigating circumstances a 'fair price' might legitimately be asked.[69] This was because official prices did not rise in line with wages, so the producer who acted honestly was penalised. The parish priest realised that the farmer would not sell, but hoard, unless prices reflected a reasonable return.

The urban poor were forced therefore to rely on official rations, what they could grow for themselves, obtain on forays to the countryside, or receive from more fortunate relatives. Prices rose astronomically: bread, for example, cost four times more than in 1939, butter twelve times, potatoes fifteen times. On average prices by the end of the war were nine times more than when it started, whereas wages had risen by less than five times.[70] The misery of the industrial worker worsened as time wore on, so much so that Mgr Pinson, Bishop of Saint-Fleur (Cantal), protested that some were even dying of hunger.[71] Religious bodies such as the Society of Friends tried to alleviate the plight of the children. In February 1941 the Quakers were supplying a midday meal and half a litre of milk a day to 30,000 children in eight towns, as well as running sixteen camps where children could recuperate.[72] Official relief agencies such as the Secours National and the Red Cross were kept busy. Garric's work as head of the Secours National was sneered at by collaborationists as being 'clerical', and he, despite his close connection with the Church, was labelled 'attentiste', if not 'gaulliste'.Likewise they dubbed the Red Cross, in which Catholics also played a leading role, 'the aristocracy of Gaullism'.[73]

Intermingling of the sexes occurred in France less frequently before the war. In the village church men sat on the right, women on the left. Coeducation was rare, even in the State system: parallel primary schools were the rule. On trains there were 'Ladies' compartments for those who wished to travel alone. The bishops highly approved of this state of affairs. Social mixing of the sexes, was frowned upon, and segregation was particularly rigorously enforced in the Catholic youth movements, so as to avoid the temptation to illicit sexual behaviour. It was for this reason that a reconstituted mixed youth hostel movement, with its former Ajiste leaders, was opposed by the episcopacy.[74] In most spheres of public and social life France remained a male-dominated world.

In such an ambience wartime promiscuity flourished. First the Allies in 1939, and then the Germans from 1940 onwards: men far from home sought sexual gratification. Prostitution posed a problem for Vichy, as it had done for the Third Republic. In 1935 the number of prostitutes was estimated at between 300,000 and 500,000, but there were only 1,235 brothels, worked in by a few thousand prostitutes. In Paris alone, in 1940 the number of 'street women' was reckoned to be about 100,000, and only about 2,000 prostitutes worked in 'maisons closes'.

Vichy's solution was to attempt to drive all such women into brothels. On 24 December 1940 Peyrouton, then minister of the Interior had circulated to the prefects in the occupied zone a 'model regulation' ('arrêté-type') and had enjoined them to publish a similar regulation for their department. Its effect was to give brothel-keepers a monopoly. It meant that any woman forced through poverty into occasional prostitution could be arrested by the police as a 'vagabond' ('femme sans aveu') and dealt with harshly.

Peyrouton's solution to a perennial question was seen as sweeping the problem under the carpet, and aroused great indignation among Christians. The Ligue française pour le Relèvement de la Moralité publique,[75] backed by the ACA, protested, as did the Fédération Protestante de France.[76] The ACA duly discussed the regulation and concluded that it would 'tend more to provoke vice than to contain it'.[77] Although the system was progressively introduced, it proved remarkably ineffective.

For ordinary people, life in wartime France was dreary. The Révolution Nationale had proclaimed a new moral order based on spiritual values. Thus the Church supported controls on drink, a ban on dancing, and censorship of films. Alcohol consumption was excessive. The shortage brought about a diminution in the amount of wine consumed, which on high days and holidays had been supplemented by spirits and liqueurs. The Church had welcomed the laws of 24 August 1940 and 7 October 1940 that prohibited the unlicensed distillation of spirits and the sale of alcohol on certain days, and limited the strength of the 'pastis' to 16 degrees — in any case a ban was imposed on the aperitif for the under-twenties. The anti-alcohol campaign was led in rural areas by the JAC. Dancing — 'le bal' — was likewise frowned upon, and even forbidden in the unoccupied zone: it was deemed scandalous to dance when so many Frenchmen were languishing in German prison camps. The ban pleased the bishops, who continued to see the local dance hall as a source of immorality. The popularity of the cinema induced the Catholic Centrale du cinéma et de la radio to ask permission to run its own film shows in parish halls. It complained bitterly that the COIC (Comité d'Organisation de l'Industrie cinématographique), the new state regulatory body for the film industry set up under the Charte du Travail to license films, was dilatory in responding to its requests for licenses.[78] On 8 September 1943 L. Jacquemin, Administrator of the Centrale Catholique du Cinéma, wrote to Laval complaining that out of the 495 applications for permits submitted between 20 May 1941 and 13 Novmber 1941, 267 had still not been dealt with. Catholic cinema associations aimed at putting on moral films in a family atmosphere under the supervision of the parish priest. In March 1943, however, COIC even forbade them to arrange their own programmes without consultation.[79] Another source of entertainment about which the Church frequently complained was jazz. One Carcassonne priest wrote to Pétain: 'It [the radio programme's jazz bands] — Jo Bouillon and his orchestra — takes us back to the worst days of the irreligious and immoral propaganda of the Front Populaire.' He considered this one aspect of the shameless immorality that was rife.[80]

Even the Frenchman's weekly flutter on the Loterie Nationale was called into question. Ménétrel, Pétain's private secretary, convinced that gambling was immoral, invited Père Doncœur to suggest what action should be taken on the lottery. The Jesuit duly came up with two solutions. The most radical was purely and simply abolition, for 'The National Lottery [...] is one of those rotten institutions of the former regime that the Marshal has done away with.' The other solution was that it should no longer be run by the State. After all, Pétain had declared that money should be earned. Writing in August 1942, Doncœur added: 'You know that many Frenchmen think and say that the Révolution Nationale is a farce. I am among those Frenchmen who do not accept that serious matters should be mocked at.'[81]

Whereas the Church's active participation in worthy causes was appreciated, what was perceived as its killjoy attitude to what was pleasurable, did not make it popular with the not inconsiderable number of Frenchmen who remained indifferent to religion.

Notes

Unless otherwise stated the place of publication is Paris

1. J.-M. Mayeur, *Catholicisme social et démocratie chrétienne*, 1986, p. 55.
2. See article by Louis Bertrand, Catholic convert and Maurrassian, in the *Revue des deux Mondes*, 15 December 1939.
3. P. Droulers, *Le Père Desbuquois et l'Action Populaire*, vol. 2, *1919–1946*, 1981, p. 352, n. 4.
4. Quoted in P. Droulers, 'Catholiques sociaux et Révolution Nationale (été 1940–avril 1942)', *Actes*: Lyons, p. 214.
5. See A Dio, Lille, 2 B 1, ACA 1944; E. Poulat, *Une Eglise ébranlée*, 1980, p. 86; also, P. Lebret, *La France en transition. Etapes d'une recherche*, 1957.
6. See collective work, *Les événements et la foi*, 1951.
7. P. Soupiron, 'Un discours du Cardinal Gerlier sur l'Eglise et le problème social', *Le Temps*, 17 June 1941.
8. 'Une lettre de Mgr Delay aux Catholiques de Marseille', *Marseille-Soir*, 16 May 1941.
9. 'Discours prononcé le 26 octobre 1941 à Epinal par Mgr Blanchet, évêque de Saint-Dié', *Revue diocésaine*, no. 22, Saint-Dié, 15 November 1941.
10. AN 2 AG 493. Reported in *La Semaine catholique*, 7 February 1943: 'La propriété a d'abord une destination communautaire. Le caractère proprement privé de la propriété est considéré comme une nécessité morale, un pis-aller, bref, comme la conséquence du péché originel.'
11. AN 2 AG 493. 'Note (Secret)', 8 March 1943.
12. See *Témoignage Chrétien, Courrier*, no, 5, November 1943, 1980, p. 244; *France* (London), 9 December 1943, quoting an (undated) report from the *Berner Tagewacht*, gives a slightly different version of Mgr Saliège's address.
13. See R. Irving, *Christian Democracy in France*, London, 1973, *passim*.
14. R.F. Kuisel, *Capitalism and the Rise of the Modern State in France*, Cambridge, 1981, p. 130.
15. For a discussion of Vichy's professed anticapitalism, see L. Liebmann, 'Entre le mythe et la légende: l'anticapitalisme de Vichy', *Revue de l'Institut de Sociologie* (Brussels), 1964, I, pp. 109–48.
16. AN 2 AG 80.
17. P. Ory, *Les Collaborateurs, 1939–1945*, 1976, p. 14.
18. Mgr Gabriel Garrone (ed.), *Le secret d'une vie engagée. Mgr Guerry d'après ses carnets intimes*, 1971, p. 91.
19. See M. Déat, *Perspectives socialistes*, 1930; A. Bergounioux, 'Le néo-socialisme. Marcel Déat: réformisme traditionnel ou esprit des années '30?' *Revue Historique*, no. 528, October–December 1978, p. 400.
20. See the works of La Tour du Pin, such as *Jalons de Route* and *Vers un ordre social chrétien*.
21. Duc de Lévis Mirepoix, *Grandeur et Misère de l'individualisme français*, 1962, pp. 234 ff.
22. The most complete account of the CFTC under the Vichy regime is given in two papers by M. Launay: 'Les syndicats chrétiens du Nord de la France', *Actes*: Lille, pp. 475–93; and, 'Le syndicalisme chrétien et la Charte du Travail', *Actes*: Lyons, pp. 189–212. The present writer wishes to acknowledge his debt to them. Chapter I of G. Adam, *La CFTC, 1940–1958. Histoire politique et idéologique*, 1964, also gives a good account of unionism during the period.
23. J. Duquesne, *Les Catholiques français sous l'Occupation*, 1966, p. 225.
24. G. Cholvy and Y.-M. Hilaire, *Histoire religieuse de la France contemporaine, 1930–1988*, 1988.
25. A Dio, Lille ACA 2 B: 'procès-verbal', January 1941.
26. Pétain's 'message' at Saint-Etienne, 1 March 1941, stated baldly: 'Employers, some of you have a share in responsibility for the class struggle.'
27. A Dio, Lille ACA 2 B 1. ACA, 24 July 1941.

28. A Dio, Lille ACA 2 B 1. Documentation: 'Questions sociales'. Letter from Maurice Duhamel to Cardinal Liénart, Lille, 15 July 1941.

29. For a description of the law see J-P. Le Crom, 'Syndicat ouvrier et Charte du Travail', in: J.-P. Azéma and R. Bédarida (eds), *Vichy et les Français*, 1992, pp. 433–43.

30. Note, however, that this organisational framework was never completely realised. After Laval's return to power, when Lagardelle had supplanted Belin at the Labour ministry, in practice the principle of 'dirigisme' rather than corporatism prevailed.

31. Tessier wrote to Cardinal Suhard on 13 July 1942 expressing astonishment and regret at an official letter dated 11 July 1942 from Vichy, according to which Mgr Chappoulie had declared that the bishops wished the Charte to be applied, and disavowed those trade unionists seeking to oppose it. See A Dio, Lille, 2 B 1, ACA 1942–1945.

32. Launay, *Actes*: Lille, p. 489.

33. AN 2 AG 609. Letter of Liénart to Lagardelle, 30 July 1942; Lagardelle's reply is dated 13 August 1942.

34. See 'Opposition au syndicat unique', *La France socialiste*, 3–4 October 1942.

35. Feltin's views were eventually published in a brochure by the Information ministry. Writing in *Action Française* on 4 March 1943, Maurras interpreted them to mean that France was 'tending towards the corporative system, which is in accordance with Christian thought'. See AN F60.1674. Quoted in English in *News Digest* No. 1099, 30 March 1943.

36. A Dio, Lille, 2 B 1, ACA, 1942–1945: 'Sur les syndicats chrétiens', and 'Motion de l'ACA sur l'organisation professionnelle', both in Liénart's handwriting.

37. G. Adam, *La CFTC, 1940–1958 .Histoire politique et idéologique,* 1964, p.30: 'Mise en présence du fait du syndicat unique, l'Assemblée, sans renoncer pour autant à la thèse de la pluralité syndicale, mais soucieuse avant tout d'assurer le maintien de l'influence chrétienne dans la vie professionnelle, souhaite que tous les catholiques, employeurs et employés, apportent leur concours individuel, chacun à leur place providentielle, dans l'organisation professionnelle en cours'.

38. Ibid., p. 31.

39. A Dio, Lille, 2 B 1, ACA 1942–1945. Letter dated Lille, 24 October 1942.

40. A Dio, Lille, Dossier Pétain 8 M 1. Letter from the Commissaire aux Renseignements Généraux, Lille, to Carles, Préfet du Nord, dated 3 May 1943, reporting a Radio Moscow broadcast at 22.30, 21 April 1943.

41. Quoted in *Courrier* , no. 4, October 1943, vol. 2, p. 239.

42. Duquesne, *Les Catholiques français*, pp. 235f.

43. See Père Villain, *La Charte du Travail et l'organisation économique et sociale de la profession*, Vanves, December 1941.

44. AD du Nord, Lille, 1 W 2301. Letter of Commissaire aux Renseignements Généraux, Lille, 15 July 1943, to Interior ministry, Vichy.

45. AN F60.1674. Broadcast from Radio Paris, 08.00, 20 May 1944. 'Informations et revue de presse'.

46. C. Soyez, *La mise en place de la Charte du Travail*, Lille, 1944.

47. M. Chauvière, 'Structures de sociabilité et travail de la socialité: des Associations familiales sous Vichy', in *Sociabilité, Pouvoirs et Société* (Actes du Colloque de Rouen, 1983), 1987, p. 564.

48. See H. Mendras, *Etudes de sociologie rurale. Novis et Virgin*, with a preface by Gabriel Le Bras, 1953; idem, *La fin des paysans*, 1967; Report of the *Congrès Jaciste*, Jeunesse Agricole Chrétienne, 1939.

49. Pétain, 'Appel', 25 June 1940.

50. In the event, the Charte Paysanne represented a compromise between the autonomist ideas of Salleron, the views of Caziot, the Agriculture minister, and the constraints imposed by food shortages. Both wanted a 'peasants' charter' in order to modernise and increase productivity in the industry.

51. Chauvière, 'Structures de sociabilité', p. 358; see also Elisabeth Morfin, 'Les rapports

entre l'Eglise catholique et la Corporation paysanne de 1940–1944', *Actes::* Grenoble, pp. 120ff. The LAC eventually merged into the Mouvement Familial Rural.

52. Eventually Dorgères fell out with Pétain and joined the Resistance.
53. Duquesne, *Les Catholiques français*, pp. 240–46.
54. P. Doncoeur, *Produire d'abord des Français*, Saint-Etienne, n.d. [1943?].
55. Launay, 'Le syndicalisme chrétien'. Letter to Pétain dated 8 July 1940, cited on p. 129.
56. AN AJ 429. Report of a speech by General de la Laurencie at a Colours ceremony, Saint-Didier-en-Rollat, Allier, n.d. [1941?]
57. Duquesne, *Les Catholiques*, pp. 85ff.
58. AN 2 AG 654. Memorandum to Pétain from Canon Gouget, 8 July 1940, headed 'Quelques notes sur la famille'.
59. B.R. Mitchell (ed.), *European Historical Statistics, 1750–1975*, London, 1981, vol. 6, p. 125. gives the figures for France as follows:

Vital Statistics

Year	Births	Deaths	Increase (decrease) in total population
(per thousand of population)			(in thouands)
1940	13.6	8.0	(179)
1941	13.1	17.0	(153)
1942	14.5	16.6	(81)
1943	15.7	16.0	(11)

60. Among them: Association du Mariage chrétien, La Plus Grande Famille, Association Catholique des Chefs de Famille, Ligue des Droits de la Famille, Ligue pour la Vie, Alliance nationale pour l'accroissement de la Natalité.
61. For the information that follows I am much indebted to the paper by Chauvière, 'Structures de sociabilité'.
62. E. Poulat, *Une Eglise ébranlée*, 1980, p. 83.
63. See M. Chauvière, 'Le baptême républicain de l'UNAF', *Les Cahiers de l'Animation*, 1986, IV and V., nos. 57 and 58, pp. 187–94.
64. A Dio, Lille, ACA 2 B 1, ACA 1942–1945.
65. See Mitchell, *European Historical Statistics*, vol. 3, pp. 174–7.
66. R. Bourderon and Y. Avakoumovitch, *Détruire le PCF. Archives de l'Etat Français et de l'occupant hitlérien, 1940–1944*, 1988, p. 113.
67. 'La pratique du marché noir et ses conséquences morales. Un mandement du Cardinal Gerlier', *La Croix Meusienne*, 8 November 1941.
68. *Semaine religieuse* (Rodez), quoted in *La Croix*, 5 November 1941.
69. A Dio, Lille. Guerre 1939-1945. Annales 8 M 1: Document: 'Taxes et marché noir'.
70. *Le Monde Ouvrier*, 16 October 1946, gives price rises as follows:

Prices in 1946
(Index: 1939 = 100)

Bread	400
Meat	535
Shoes	700
Coal	925
Butter	1225
Milk	1350
Potatoes	1500
Clothing	1500
Wine	1600
Eggs	1750

71. *La Croix*, 5 October 1943, quoting *La Croix de Cantal*.
72. AN 2 AG 75. Communiqué de presse, 7 February 1941.
73. M. Déat, 'Les Jeunes dans les ruines', *Le National–Populaire*, 11 September 1943.
74. B. Cacérès, *Histoire de l'Education populaire*, 1964, pp. 129–30.
75. Pamphlet: 'Le système de la réglementation de la Prostitution au service des Tenanciers: un arrêté-type scandaleux', Ligue française pour le Relèvement de la moralité publique, n.d. [1941?].
76. Letter from Georges Marty, Président de la Commission d'Action morale et sociale de la Fédération Protestante de France, to Dr Huard, Secrétaire Général de la Santé publique.
77. A Dio, Lille, 2 B 1. ACA meeting of 23 April 1941.
78. AN 2 AG 609.
79. AN 2 AG 487.
80. Ibid. Letter of Canon Astruc, vicar of Saint-Vincent, Carcassonne, dated 2 January 1942 to Pétain's Private Office: 'Jamais je n'avais vu, autour de mon clocher, s'étaler tant d'impudeur et d'immoralité'. Of the radio, he added, 'Ces jazz... Jo Bouillon et son orchestre, nous ramènent aux plus mauvais jours de la propagande irreligieuse et immorale du Front Populaire'.
81. AN 2 AG 75. Letter of Père Doncœur to Pétain's Private Office.

–16–

Youth Policy and the Church

The Révolution Nationale sought to mobilise the energies of young people. Requiring from them a 'moral reformation', a sense of civic duty, patriotism and political conformity, it nevertheless assigned to them a subordinate position in society. They had therefore to be disciplined and regimented. This was the task given to the newly-created Secrétariat Général à la Jeunesse (SGJ). Christians at first reacted positively to the demands made upon them. But circumstances enlarged the role of youth in unexpected ways not always agreeable. Students, young workers, and the young middle-class, Christian or non-Christian, eventually questioned Vichy's 'doctrines' and even more its practice. They rejected the breast-beating penitential approach to the country's plight no less than the government's increasing compliance with German wishes. Deportation for work in Germany was the last straw. Some joined the Resistance, either escaping to London or joining the Maquis. A few steered an opposing course and collaborated. However, the majority reluctantly and unwillingly obeyed. All in all, the history of Vichy's youth policy, like so much else, is a chronicle of failure.

What therefore was the background to the options proposed by the Vichy government, and how did young people, particularly Christians, arrive at the choices they made? How could youth be mobilised for the task of national 'regeneration'? Henri Massis, Pétain's Maurrassian youth adviser, saw the problem as primarily one of civic education. It was argued that young people had not only been unpatriotic but lacked a sense of social responsibility and morality. Physically unfit, they shunned sport, and overindulged in tobacco and alcohol. The charge might equally have been levelled against their elders — after all, it was they, and not the young, who had lost the Battle of France — or indeed against all the belligerents. In any case its truth was questionable. But in 1940 the regime required scapegoats: youth was yet another convenient victim.

Against this backdrop a policy had to be hammered out. One solution was to create a monolithic youth movement, a 'jeunesse unique' on

Nazi lines. This expedient, as will be seen, at one stage almost carried the day. Alternatively existing movements and new ones established *ad hoc* could be used. This course ultimately prevailed. To follow it, the SGJ, in effect a full-blown Youth ministry, was set up, whose task was to help train young people, approve compulsory programmes for citizenship, and to control, inspect and grant subsidies to youth movements.

Immediate action was urgent, but partially paralysed because the Germans formally banned all youth organisations in their zone. Meanwhile, in unoccupied France many youngsters aged between sixteen and nineteen, whether refugees, unemployed or destitute, were banded together in a new, voluntary movement, the Compagnons de France, and set to perform manual tasks to help get the country on its feet. There was also the problem of young soldiers of twenty-one, the 'class of 1940', only recently called up. Under the Armistice conscription was banned. It was decided to enrol them compulsorily in a new civil organisation — but run on military and Scouting lines — the Chantiers de la Jeunesse, in which they also would be pressed into useful tasks. Eventually it was decided that all young men would serve an eight-month stint, as a substitute for military service. Discipline, physical and civic education, and hard physical labour were prescribed for both these new state movements. A prominent leadership role in them was played by Christians, especially Catholics, as will be seen. Some were clerics, more were lay persons, and many were army officers. In 1940, Vichy considered these to be the sole reliable sources of leadership cadres.

Meanwhile use had to be made of existing youth movements. To understand later developments some consideration of their pre-war history is necessary.

Pre-war voluntary youth movements, whether political, social or religious, had never appealed to more than 15 per cent of the age range. Christian ones, mainly Catholic, preponderated. These epitomised ideas that the new regime now found chimed closely with its own. It was therefore with religious movements that at first it worked most closely.

Indeed it had no alternative. The youth organisations of the now banned political parties, from the Jeunesses Communistes to the Jeunesses Patriotes, were automatically ruled out. It is true that a few other political or crypto-political youth groupings, such as Bucard's Francistes, or those set up with German support, such as the Jeunes de l'Europe nouvelle, were tolerated, but their numbers were small. Young Catholics had not been very attracted to the Jeunesses Démocrates Populaires of the Christian PDP, itself now suspect. Some had enthused for the Camelots du Roi, the youth movement of Action Française. But the 'king's hawkers' (a title that advertised their monarchism and their

Prefecture licence to sell their newspaper on the streets), had been mainly patronised by the aristocratic and upper class scions of the Catholic 'bien-pensants'. Moreover, Action Française, formally banned by the Pope in 1926, had not been rehabilitated until 1939.[1] Young Catholics, like young Protestants, were therefore thrown back upon their own Church movements. The Catholic movements now saw a large increase in numbers.

Christians between the wars had been much exercised by the problems of youth. Social Catholic circles recognised that class conflict was inimical to the re-Christianisation of France, which the Church saw as the supreme task for the rising generation. Young people were urged to look beyond both Capitalist and Marxist materialism, because 'le matérialisme béat a fait son temps'.[2] Both ideologies lacked humane and spiritual content, a view incidentally not shared by some more worldly Catholic families, who rather perceived their sons' interest as lying in a regime of economic liberalism, and were opposed to any betterment of the working class.[3] Nevertheless the search for a third way, neither Liberal nor Communist, was put forward as an ideal for young Christians by men such as Archbishop Saliège and Emmanuel Mounier.

The Equipes Sociales, a youth organisation that grew out of social catholicism, also influenced Vichy youth institutions. It had been founded in 1919 by an ex-officer, Robert Garric.[4] A fervent, impressive Catholic, he appealed to such diverse personalities as Simone de Beauvoir,[5] as well as Catholics such as Lamirand, Pétain's first Secretary-General for Youth, and Edmond Michelet, who was among the first to denounce the Armistice. This Christian, nonconfessional, movement sought to break down barriers between students and young workers. Through joint study groups social mixing ('le brassage') would, it was hoped, reduce class differences. In addition, the chances of young workers would be improved by giving them extra part-time education.

Garric, assisted by Père Forestier, the Dominican priest always very active in youth affairs, in 1932 took over the movement's periodical, the *Revue des Jeunes*. Apolitical, although condemning both totalitarian ideologies, and neutral as regards democracy, its readership consisted of young Catholic academics, students and executives, considered to be the future leaders in society. The focus was on moral and social questions. It treated, for example, themes taken up later by the Révolution Nationale such as depopulation, alcoholism, and civic responsibility. Thus after the abortive general strike of 1938 it published an article by Lamirand urging co-operation between moderate trade unionists and 'fair-minded employers'.[6] Clerics of widely differing views were also contributors: Père Doncœur, later a very ardent Pétainist, and Père de Lubac, whose clandestine writings condemning Vichy were to circulate widely.

Garric had been influenced by Marshal Lyautey, the great colonial soldier and administrator, who had urged him: 'Faites du social.' Lyautey himself had presided over a pre-war 'bureau interfédéral du scoutisme' seeking to foster contact between the Catholic, Protestant and non-denominational Scouts. This bore fruit under Vichy, when the Catholic Chief Scout, General Lafont, became the head of a new, federal movement, 'Le Scoutisme français'.

Lyautey, following up the ideas of Albert de Mun, a pioneer of social catholicism, had written a work that was seminal among Catholics concerned with young people at the time. *Le Rôle social de l'officier* had particularly impressed Garric's friend Lamirand, himself also a disciple of Lyautey. Lamirand a veteran of both wars, an engineer by profession and a onetime director of Renault, had attracted Pétain's attention through his imitative work, *Le Rôle social de l'ingénieur* (1926), to which Lyautey had written a preface. The industrialist wanted to apply to the young worker the military leader's ideas on character-formation through discipline, constructive action, and obedience to a hierarchical social order. Pétain had a similar aspiration, viewing conscription, for example, as a continuation of the educative role of the school. Thus the Marshal, in appointing Lamirand as Secretary-General for Youth, considered him well qualified for the post.

A group of army officers, mainly Catholic, inspired by Lyautey, had formed clubs before the war to debate social questions. Prominent among them was General De la Porte du Theil, now called upon to head the Chantiers de la Jeunesse, and de Segonzac, the Catholic cavalry officer who later founded the 'école des cadres' for training leaders at Uriage. Another such officer was Commandant La Chapelle, assigned in 1940 to Paul Baudouin's staff to deal with youth matters, and then transferred to the SGJ, where he worked until December 1940. He too had served under Lyautey, and was a friend of Père Forestier.

In fact Forestier, and his elder and mentor, Père Doncœur, the founder of the Rover Scouts (in French, 'les Routiers', signifying mature Scouts setting out on the path of adult life), became influential figures at Vichy in youth affairs. Forestier, a Scout commissioner since 1936, like his friend du Theil, now became Chaplain-General to the Chantiers de la Jeunesse. The two priests, it has been said, 'Frenchified and Catholicised' the ideas of Baden-Powell.[7]

In 1940 the importance of youth concerns was underlined by appointing Ybarnégary, closely linked to Borotra (the ex-Wimbledon tennis champion who was to become Vichy's Commissioner for Sport), as minister for the Family and Youth. However, the pivotal person in youth matters at the time was undoubtedly Baudouin, who since 16 June had been Pétain's Foreign minister. In February 1938 Baudouin had written an article for the *Revue de Paris* calling for national revival.[8] A liberal conservative, neither Maurrassian nor enamoured of democracy, he argued for a Christian but authoritarian and technocratic approach to the problems of youth. The article's conclusions were subsequently reproduced in the *Revue des Jeunes*,[9] which in January 1939 published a further article by Baudouin, a 'manifesto' in which he called for a leader to save France from anarchy and totalitarianism and — this time the approach was not technocratic but romantically medieval — exhorted Christian youth to constitute a new 'chivalry' to defend Western values and the Christian heritage.[10] In June 1940 Baudouin was not only in close touch with Pétain on youth matters but, also with Weygand, who, incidentally, sent him a note on 28 June 1940 advocating — prophetically — 'Dieu, Patrie, Famille, Travail' as watchwords for the future.

Baudouin quit the Foreign ministry after the 'handshake' of Montoire, but retained an interest in youth matters after his appointment as a secretary of state with responsibility for the LFC and a watching brief on youth, finally resigning from the government in January 1941, upon the nomination of Flandin to succeed Laval. As for the *Revue des Jeunes*, it remained influential until 1942.[11]

Close ties therefore linked Catholics concerned with youth in 1940, whether they came from the priesthood, the Army, Scouting, or the Equipes Sociales. Yet the perspective of each was slightly different. The clergy's influence upon the Scouts was reactionary, *stricto sensu*: antisecularist, antimaterialist, and antiliberal. The army officers were intent on avoiding a German stranglehold upon French youth, and some undoubtedly were determined on a war of revenge. Garric and his associates were more concerned with the eradication of social problems affecting young people. The common strand uniting them all was their Christian faith, although in Vichy and Paris others did not share their beliefs. Henri Massis, as Pétain's personal adviser on youth matters, was a Maurrassian journalist of traditionalist and hierarchical views. By 1941 those in Paris who rallied round Pucheu, then an official concerned with propaganda but a future Interior minister, favoured a totalitarian, elitist society; in it youth must know its place and, if this was as subject to a victorious Germany, so be it.

On 6 September 1940 the SGJ was placed under the Education ministry, emphasising its educative role. Lamirand appointed to the key Youth Directorate Pierre Goutet, another Catholic Rover Scout and National Commissioner, and then, from February 1941, the Catholic Garrone, a former teacher at the Ecole des Roches, a private institution modelled on the English public school. Other Catholics were drawn in, either directly or as regional youth delegates. Thus Dupouey, a friend of

Goutet, who had run a 'patronage' (parish youth club) before the war, headed the key Bureau des Mouvements, dealing with all youth organisations. Pierre Schaeffer, a Catholic engineer like Lamirand, and founder of a Rover Scout troop in the 'grandes écoles', was placed for a while in charge of a daily radio programme entitled 'Radio Jeunesse'.

Bishops had misgivings at this Catholic monopoly of key posts in the new state apparatus for youth. Some feared that the Church's own movements would be deprived of good leaders — or even members. The Bishop of Montpellier, in his pastoral letter of spring 1942, instructed his flock to enrol their children solely in Church organisations. Other bishops wanted it made plain that in the state youth movements churchmen did not act in their function as Catholics ('en tant que catholiques') but only in a Catholic spirit ('en catholiques'). Jealous of its own individuality, the Church was always careful to avoid overidentification with secular organisations. It was a position appreciated by some of the laity. Mounier, the editor of *Esprit*, as a Catholic with a deep interest in youth, disliked the 'inflation' of Catholic cadres in the new organisation and movements, although his personalist philosophy greatly influenced the 'doctrine' of the new Compagnons movement and the Ecole des Cadres at Uriage. By 1941 he had fears that the Compagnons might succumb to totalitarian doctrines. In his diary he noted that 'X' (not named), one of the 'chefs compagnons', possessed 'unlimited ambition', and some of its leaders favoured the movement developing into a 'jeunesse unique'.[12]

Despite some episcopal reservations, the choice of personnel and the organisation of the SGJ was generally gratifying to other Catholics. *La Croix* (28 January 1941) described (in English) Lamirand as 'the right man in the right place'. However, the new head of French youth, who assigned to himself principally the task of propagandist among young people·for the regime, sometimes did not impress all Christians. In February 1941, on a tour of Languedoc, he exhorted his youthful audience to have 'no thought of revenge'.[13] In Bordeaux he spoke of France's place in what was then perceived as being a German 'New Order': 'A new world is being organised. France has its place in it, its rightful place. We must participate in this new construction'.[14]

Lamirand, mainly based in Paris, delegated most other tasks to his Vichy office, which Garrone took charge of in 1941. His brief was not only the civic and occupational training of young people, but also their moral education. As regards the latter, the Church deemed his role superfluous. It considered, as did, incidentally, the non-believer Maurras, that the moral question was above all a religious one. Indeed the veteran political writer even went so far as to recommend the teaching of the Ten Commandments for moral education, because 'Voilà la grande vérité'.

The Church was grateful, however, to Lamirand for opposing the idea of a compulsory national youth movement, whether monopolistic or not.[15] He withstood the efforts of a caucus in Paris associated with the Information and Propaganda ministry to wrest control of youth from the SGJ — politicians such as Pucheu and Marion, Gaston Bergery, who had the ear of Pétain, and Jean Maze, his friend — and, even within the SGJ itself, Pelorson, Lamirand's deputy for propaganda in the occupied zone — all of whom wanted a totalitarian youth organisation.

In March 1942 the Youth Commission of the Conseil National, the body established by Pétain to draft a new constitution, met to review achievements to date. Although its twenty-strong membership included prominent Christians such as Mgr Beaussart, Pastor Boegner, Generals De la Porte du Theil and Lafont, and Jean Le Cour Grandmaison, Lamirand and his colleagues came in for severe criticism. The attack was mounted by those critical of Christian involvement. Replying to criticism that the condition of youth remained deplorable, Beaussart retorted that it was because since 1940 it had been dinned into young people that France was a lost cause.[16] Boegner, when the accusation was made that France was turning again to anticlericalism, took up the cudgels on the bishops' behalf, adding, somewhat ingenuously that they themselves were anticlerical. Bergery reminded the commission that in the occupied zone, of 535 centres established for the young unemployed, 450 were run by parish 'patronages', which he thought could only stoke the fires of anticlericalism. Massis attacked Mounier's doctrine of Christian Personalism as being pernicious for the new State institutions. For Pétain's youth adviser, this was an 'intolerable scandal'.[17] The class basis of the constituent movements of the Action Catholique de la Jeunesse Française (ACJF) came under fire. Mgr Beaussart, as the ACA's representative, retorted that this was inevitable: social divisions were an undeniable reality.[18] Marcel Roy, a trade union member of the commission who had thrown in his lot with Pétain, claimed that 95 per cent of youth in the occupied zone considered youth movements 'clérico-réactionnaires'. The indefatigable Mgr Beaussart again spoke up, although perhaps with tongue in cheek: the Church would even be prepared to give up its own movements if the interests of the Révolution Nationale were thereby better served.

Although Lamirand survived this avalanche of criticism and continued in office until March 1943, long after Laval's return to power and Bonnard's appointment as Education minister, his room for manœuvre was increasingly circumscribed. His initial entourage of Catholics, loyal, patriotic, hostile to collaborationism, and more socially than politically oriented, had by then mostly left the SGJ. Many of their successors, like Pelorson, held extremist views.[19]

Thus from spring 1943 onwards the SGJ became more subservient to what had become effectively a collaborationist government. Laval, however, was ever mindful of the delicacy of his relationship to the Church, and of its views on youth. Appointing Félix Olivier-Martin to succeed Lamirand, he warned him: 'Be careful: above all, don't get me into awkward situations with the priests'. Olivier-Martin, much later commented wryly, 'That was to be the chief point of my work'.[20] By then, however, Church influence on youth was much diminished, and the shortcomings in Vichy's initially idealistic policies were patent.

Policies were designed to protect young people, such as antialcohol measures: a ban on the siting of cafes near schools and on the consumption of strong liquor. The regime could not, however, stem the rise in juvenile delinquency: the number of minors aged between eight and eighteen sentenced for various offences trebled between 1938 and 1942.[21] It was powerless to halt the prostitution of minors: nine times as many girls were arrested in 1945 for soliciting as in 1939. The Church, for its part did what little it could. It condemned dance-halls as a breeding ground for promiscuity, deplored the pornographic literature that circulated, and what it called the 'cinéma vulgaire',[22] even publishing in each parish guidelines for young people on the films being screened locally. But to campaign against cinema-going, the most popular leisure pastime in wartime, was a thankless task: 4,000 cinemas flourished during the Occupation, attracting a weekly audience of over one and a half million minors, out of five million cinema-goers in all. In fact neither the regime nor the Church could remedy the underlying causes of juvenile crime and immorality: the father's absence as a prisoner of war or deportee; school truancy; undernourishment, which led to the black market; and the general climate of unrest, even civil war, that prevailed, at least in 1943–44.[23]

On minor matters the bishops fell out with the authorities. They set great store by their parish youth clubs, and particularly their associated sports sections, recognising their value in binding young Catholics more closely to their local church. They wanted to preserve the independence of the Catholic national sports federation, the Fédération Gymnastique et Sportive des Patronages de France. This ran counter to the ambitions of Jean Borotra, who as the 'Commissaire à l'Education générale et aux sports' (CEGS), wanted a national, monolithic organisation. 'L'union entre tous les sportifs' on the playing fields would, he believed, promote harmony, ironing out class and ideological differences.

The ACA refused point blank to give way[24] and informed Borotra accordingly. Its refusal stirred up hostility, even in very Catholic areas: the Prefect of Loire-Inférieure reported that the decision had given rise to a resurgence of anticlericalism.[25] A dispute also arose over the use of the new sports facilities that were being provided. The bishops demanded that such facilities should be as freely available to Catholic schools as to state schools.[26] Another cause of friction arose from the national drive to train all physical education teachers. The bishops wanted to continue training their own. The introduction of PE in Catholic schools, which the bishops agreed to, also presented problems. Borotra was informed that teachers in religious orders would not be allowed to take girls' classes, but special 'monitrices' should be appointed. Girls would not be allowed to wear shorts nor would mixed sports meetings be permitted.[27] Apparently all these stipulations were eventually accepted, and the Church retained control of all its outdoor activities.

Sections of the Catholic youth press also proved a thorn in the authorities' side. Perhaps the fate of the monthly *Cahiers de notre Jeunesse*, the organ of the ACJF, which began publication in June 1941 and was forced to close down two years later, was the most cogent example of this. In its first issue an editorial by Albert Gortais, then the leader of the movement, exhorted youth to stop repining: France had had its ups and downs before and had survived. In November 1941 he defended the rightness of the declaration of war: as for the defeat, the nation could be reproached for its failure, but not for the cause it had sought to defend. The Révolution Nationale should not be a parade of uniforms and slogans, but encompass a change in individuals. The periodical mocked the 'frais disciples de Péguy', who quoted the Catholic writer for wrong ends. Invoking its own title, it cited allusively such watchwords of the Catholic writer as 'mieux souffrir que trahir'.[28] The anti-Vichy intention was clear.

In March 1943 it crossed swords more openly with the regime. Its issue of 17 March 1943, replete with quotations from Maritain and Bernanos — not exactly Vichy's favourite authors — reminded readers that in March 1937 communism was not the only ideology condemned by Pius XII. For this taunt at the Nazis it was suspended for two months. But its number of June 1943 was the last straw for the regime, and the periodical's swansong. Obliquely condemning forced labour in Germany, it asserted it would not undertake 'the devil's work' ('des besognes démoniaques'). After its definitive closure, the editorial team linked up with the Resistance: Gortais fought with the Maquis in Brittany, Jean Domenach ended up with Segonzac and the FFI in Tarn, and Gilbert Dru was finally shot for Resistance activities by the Germans in July 1944.

The most bitter struggle, however, was between the Church and influential pro-Nazi groups, some in power, which ensued over the latter's attempt to impose a single national youth organisation. In 1940

Christians feared a totalitarian youth movement on the German or Italian model. In July Déat had canvassed support at Vichy for his proposal for a 'parti unique' but had been sent packing. Retiring to Paris, this rebuff sharpened his hostility to the regime and all its works. The Church, for its part, was relieved to see his mission fail, but the setback did not kill the idea of a 'jeunesse unique'.

Catholic and Protestant youth organisations alike were bent on preserving their independence. An autonomous ACJF was strongly backed by the bishops, who saw its constituent movements as essential active proselytisers for the re-conversion of France, carrying the Church's message into the world of working life and education, and acting as a recruiting agency for the priesthood.

The question of a 'jeunesse unique', stimulated by ideas of a one-party state, had surfaced early. In late July 1940 when representatives of many pre-war youth movements met at Randan to consider what should be done, Dhavernas, the future first Chef Compagnon, then on Baudouin's staff, thought it necessary to state explicitly that there would be no one single youth organisation. On 13 August Pétain made a speech in which he pledged himself to respect the existing plurality of movements. Despite the Marshal's assurances, however, the argument continued.

From his position as Secretary of State with special responsibilities for young people, Baudouin moved swiftly to reassure Cardinal Gerlier that he too was against a 'jeunesse unique'. At Lyons in November 1940 he declared to an audience of young people: 'I never neglect an opportunity of protesting publicly against the youth movement so strongly demanded by Doriot and Déat'.[29] He followed this up with a meeting at the SGJ in Paris where he repeated to 20 representatives of youth groups that there was no question of amalgamating them into a single body.[30] Nevertheless, in December 1940 a new collaborationist publication, *Jeunesse*,[31] urged youth to unite; in its second issue it again called for unity 'above all divisions', and in its third declared aggressively 'French youth must be one'.[32]

After Darlan took over the reins of government, surrounding himself with a number of thrusting young men eager for radical solutions to problems, the debate had been revived in earnest. An article by Edouard Lavergne in January 1941, published in the Maurrassian *Revue Universelle*, whose director, incidentally, was Henri Massis, fuelled the argument.[33] Lavergne, advocating a single, compulsory movement, attacked pre-war confessional youth organisations for having failed to turn out strong, virile young Frenchmen. For its part, the ACA, meeting a few days later, seemed to be more accommodating than previously. Whilst Catholic youth movements should continue, it conceded, surprisingly, that young people should not 'be forbidden to enter any future national single youth movement'.[34] It was of course assumed that this would not preclude membership in their own movements, which would continue. On 6 February 1941 the ACA members in the unoccupied zone thought it prudent to remind the Church of Pétain's words, 'Tous les mouvements de jeunesse existants seront maintenus'. Co-operation with the State was accepted, but in return the independence of Church movements should be guaranteed, because they were not concerned solely with temporal matters. The ACA was alarmed because a single movement necessarily implied a single civic 'doctrine', whereas it wanted the SGJ merely to outline a minimum citizenship programme for all movements. The Catholic movements would then supplement this with Christian instruction; they could not teach merely from a standpoint of secular 'neutrality'.

With SGJ approval the Ecole des Cadres at Uriage convened a meeting in February 1941 of some twenty-five different youth movements. The assembly comprised representatives of the six Scouting organisations, seven from the various movements of the ACJF, five from the different Protestant youth organisations grouped under the Conseil Protestant de la Jeunesse, three from other Catholic organisations, including Catholic students, one from the Compagnons de France, one from the national students' organisation, two from new movements concerned with civic action, Equipes et Cadres de la France nouvelle (made up of former Jeunes DRAC) and Jeunesse de France et d'Outre-mer), and two from political movements with distinctly Fascist leanings (Dorgères's Jeunesses Paysannes and Doriot's Union populaire de la Jeunesse française). At this, the most representative meeting of youth called since one at Randan, immediately after the defeat, somewhat surprisingly all accepted that a plurality of movements was desirable, provided these were effective. Uriage now entered the lists in support of the status quo: its journal *Jeunesse... France,* in its April issue, delivered a powerful response to Lavergne's January article.

This conclave of interested parties inspired Lamirand to set up a Conseil National de la Jeunesse, which held its first meeting on 7 April 1941. General Lafont represented the Scouts de France; Jeanne Aubert, its president, the JOCF; Albert Gortais, the ACJF; and Charles Nicot the Jeunesses Paysannes. Together with three distinguished outsiders, Garrone, then new to the SGJ, and Segonzac, head of the 'leadership school he had created at Uriage, these constituted a powerful lobby on which the Church's interests were well safeguarded. The impact of this new body is not known, but most probably Garrone used it as a sounding-board for his innovatory ideas.

Meanwhile circles close to Darlan — Pucheu and Marion, and Bergery and Maze — had begun manoeuvring to take over the

Compagnons de France in order to turn it into the single youth movement that the extreme Right wanted. It was apparent that this could take at least two forms. It could be a state movement exercising a monopoly, compulsory for all youngsters aged between sixteen and nineteen; or it could be one, perhaps compulsory, standing side by side with existing movements. In any case in the Church alarm bells continued to ring. At its April meeting the ACA reaffirmed that national co-operation in implementing a minimum programme was feasible: 'One single grouping, no; but a youth united at top level through a prescribed programme'. Cardinal Liénart wrote to Cardinal Suhard in May 1941 reiterating his fears: '[I have] the very definite impression that [...] we are witnessing the first systematic acts of gradually snatching young people away from the Church's influence, and of preparing for the advent of a "single youth movement" as it has been conceived and realised elsewhere'.[35]

The cardinal clearly feared a French movement on the lines of the Hitlerjugend, which in Germany had supplanted all other movements.

The occasion for this letter was the threat of seizure of assets of Catholic youth movements by the Germans in the occupied zone, despite the fact that the Church had made plain that an attack upon the movements of Action Catholique would be considered an attack on itself. Liénart suggested that it be made widely known that when the Germans had proposed the winding-up in the occupied zone of two ACJF movements, the JOC and the JAC, it had been made crystal-clear that these were essentially religious organisations. At a time when the French government was partly responding to their demands for active collaboration, the renewed German hostility to youth organisations was puzzling.

By the summer, however, the Church deemed the immediate crisis over. Its final statement, confirmed at the ACA meeting in Paris on 24 July 1941, ran: 'A united youth in the service of the nation, yes! A single youth organisation, no!' It had clearly clarified its position since the April meeting. The decision was communicated to all the movements of the ACJF.[36] Garrone, a Catholic of a mystical turn of mind, in a lecture at Uriage in July had reassuringly affirmed his vague belief in 'pluralism in order and control [...] with no temporal domination of consciences'.[37] At the SGJ Lamirand, and other officials such as Dupouey, together with the group at Uriage that included Segonzac, Chombart de Lauwe, and Beuve-Méry, the future founder and editor of *Le Monde*, backed this conviction. The ACA meeting noted with relief that 'authority accepts pluralism' and that the civic 'doctrine' proposed for youth was being elaborated to take account of this. However, in December 1941 Cardinal Gerlier was still being harassed by Cherrier, on the staff of

Pucheu, now Interior minister, to accept a compromise on a 'jeunesse unique'.[38]

Dissentient voices were raised in the collaborationist press. In *L'Œuvre* (12 August 1941) René Chateau asked, since confessional youth movements were allowed to continue, why not all political youth movements? A further article (10 August 1941) accused the Church of Ultramontanism.

The nature of the 'doctrine' for youth and of the programmes of civic education was considered very important. The anticlerical 'young Turks' round Darlan wanted it to reflect an authoritarian, anti-Marxist revolution of a National Socialist kind. Within the SGJ itself there was division. Pelorson, still hankering after a single monopolistic movement, postulated a civic education that was racist, Fascist and 'European' (i.e. favouring the new European order of the Germans). He advocated 'strong-arm tactics'. Lamirand, moderating the spirit of some of his earlier declarations, wanted a programme limited to serving the ends of the Révolution Nationale. His vision of a new order was one of youth showing qualities of loyalty, obedience and discipline, industriousness and helping others; selfishness and the alleged 'laisser-aller' of the inter-war years would be banished. Garrone wanted emphasis placed on the 'natural communities', with particular attention to the rights and duties of the family, the Church and the school.[39] Clearly there were two broadly differing conceptions of civic education that were irreconcilable. In fact, the Church never formally accepted for its movements the programmes for civic education eventually put forward.

Protestants were just as opposed as Catholics to a single youth movement. Pastor Boegner, who liaised closely with Cardinal Gerlier on this matter,[40] had set up a Protestant Conseil de la Jeunesse to deal with the SGJ. In October 1941 in an interview with Pucheu, who as Interior minister theoretically had general oversight over both education and youth, he made plain his view that religious movements should continue intact. Pucheu did not disagree but warned that he intended to set up other, rival organisations, whose task would be to train the politicians of the future.[41]

In a patent allusion to those whose ideas tended towards a totalitarian youth movement Mgr Saliège commented in November 1941: 'One cannot train leaders with show and verbal patriotism. Leaders are trained through their lifestyle, by life, as well as a patriotism that is loyal, sincere, effective, opposing the black market, disgraceful denunciations, the idolising of the State, and empty cradles'. For him totalitarian movements were a violation of natural law: the Church could only make its contribution to national revival in a condition of freedom.[42]

The year ended stormily with a special number of the Doriotist periodical *Jeunesse* (21 December 1941) entitled 'Un an de lutte pour l'unité'.[43] Twenty-three writers gave their views on a unified youth movement. The more radical contributors, such as the poet Paul Bazan and the Catholic collaborationist writer Chateaubriant, again held up the German and Italian youth movements as models. Sicard, the editor of the collaborationist *Emancipation Nationale*, proclaimed Nazi ideals for French youth, who must, by coercion, if necessary, acknowledge the primitive forces that form a nation: soil, blood and race. Maurice Bardèche, then a young lecturer at the Sorbonne, advocated heroism — and brutality; for him a unified youth movement was the prelude to a one-party State, a hope shared by two other contributors, Drieu la Rochelle and P. Cousteau of *Je Suis Partout*. The debate continued into 1942, when, it was alleged, the Germans would only approve SGJ appointments to posts as local youth delegates those supporting a 'jeunesse unique'. A meeting was organised in Paris by the pro-German Groupe Collaboration, which had its own youth movement, Les Jeunes de l'Europe nouvelle. Present were representatives of the Hitlerjugend, of other French youth movements, and even of the SGJ. Guy Crouzet, the leader writer of *Les Nouveaux Temps,* seized the occasion to canvass once more for a single youth movement.[44]

Meanwhile the *Semaine religieuse* of the Paris diocese[45] still deemed it imperative to make the Church's position plain. The bishops, it said, rejected any political programme for its youth. What they did want was one that promoted the development of conscience, a moral code, and principles of order and discipline, respect for authority, sobriety, and a sense of family, because these were the values Catholic parents would wish for their children. The partisans of a 'jeunesse unique', on the other hand, flatly repudiated a programme with any moral purpose. For Catholics some of their leaders were tainted — former firebrands of the young radicals or socialists, whose roots lay in Freemasonry or marxism. Catholics wanted neither statism nor clericalism. but a fair agreement 'on a single aim: the education of a youth that is healthy, devoted, energetic, and enthusiastic, united in service to the country'.[46] The argument was between the choice of a moral or a political programme.

In such a situation the Church felt itself insecure. It was only too aware that in the occupied zone the Germans still merely tolerated the existence of its movements. Since secular movements that flourished in the southern zone, such as the Compagnons de France, were forbidden in the North, a vacuum was there waiting to be filled. Thus in late 1941 Pelorson set up a new youth organisation, the Equipes Nationales, which was seen as yet another attempt to create a 'jeunesse unique'. Although it did valuable work helping in air raids and welfare services, the organisation, spurned by the main youth movements, never really took off.

In March 1942 at the youth commission of Pétain's Conseil National, the Marshal, in an opening address (after which he withdrew from the deliberations) had stated categorically: 'There can be no question of creating a state youth movement [because] youth belongs to nobody [and] the bulk of the educational task falls by right upon the natural communities — the family, and the spiritual and occupational communities'.[47] The State's role should be to exercise overall control, to stimulate, and to lay down a 'doctrine' for youth. He wanted, he said — and the Church had accepted this — a programme of civic and patriotic education of which a part would be common to all movements. This should have been the last word on the matter. It demonstrates how little real respect the Marshal enjoyed among some of those present that, despite this, in the proceedings that followed they — Bonnard, his future Education minister, and Gaston Bergerey, both collaborationists — nevertheless continued to advocate a 'jeunesse unique' as an aspiration, if not for now, for the future. In the final report drawn up by Georges Pernot, a former minister for the Family and a good Catholic, the latter thought it necessary to underline the need for plurality.

After the Commission had dispersed Déat commented in *L'Œuvre* (23 March 1942) that deadlock had been reached, because 'in the Marshal's entourage there are officials that pay too much attention to the higher clergy' He reiterated that without a 'jeunesse unique' and a 'parti unique' no genuine modern State could exist. A little later Laval's appointment of Bonnard as Education minister with overall charge of youth affairs, fanned the hope, according to *La France socialiste* (23 April 1942), that 'fanatics' not truly representative of Catholic opinion would no longer be able to oppose a unitary youth movement. Meanwhile Pelorson expected that Bonnard, the new Education minister, would promote the newly-formed Equipes Nationales to fill that role.

Indeed the Catholic youth movements had to be on their guard until the very end of the regime. A letter from Cardinal Liénart to Mgr Saliège in October 1942 drew attention to a Radio Vatican programme in French, 'Jeunesse et Travail', citing the unification of youth as still a 'frightening danger'.[48] Another broadcast, in May 1943, set out once more the Christian ideal: 'The Church claims that where Christians are concerned, she has the right to deal with their youth. This is her duty, and she has long repeated that she will cede this right to nobody'.[49] After Lamirand's resignation, the question of a 'jeunesse unique' flared up officially for the third and last time. Lamirand's successor, Olivier-Martin, backed Pelorson, his deputy, and at last the Equipes Nationales theoretically became the nucleus of a single youth movement: its members were put into uniform and underwent a specially designed civic education programme. The collaborationist press supported these moves. Pierre Vitrac, in *Les Nouveaux Temps* (25 April 1943) wrote: 'We demand [such] a national, energetic organisation'.[50] Georges Simond, in *L'Effort* (11 May 1943), dubbed all other youth movements a failure, a charge emphatically repudiated in *La Croix* (21 May 1943). As late as October 1943 the *Semaine religieuse* of Arras thought it necessary to inveigh against 'Messieurs les unificateurs présomptifs' — 'these escapees from, and ghosts of marxism and Freemasonry, partisans of co-education, promiscuity, naturism and the permanent wearing of shorts',[51] reminiscent of the Front Populaire.

In the end, the Church won. It was of course a struggle of much wider significance. A national youth movement would have been another move towards Fascism, and acquiescence in a German-dominated Europe, in which youth would have been indoctrinated with the Nazi creed. The ever-weakening forces of moderation at Vichy would have been overwhelmed. If the Church was intent on preserving its own narrow sectarian interests, it also stood, as leaders of its movements within it, and of many of those of the Compagnons de France outside it, well realised, for Christian ideals that would have been irrevocably compromised. The fate of Christian youth movements in Germany, a first step along the road to a 'Nazi Christianity' or paganism, was a salutary example of what could happen in France. As Pastor Boegner testified at Pétain's trial, 'We wished to have complete freedom to continue our task of education protected from the evil-sounding theories that purported to be covered by the term "Révolution Nationale", and our complete freedom to continue to see trained [...] a resisting youth that [...] showed what it was capable of on the eve of the Liberation'.[52]

'Resisting youth' as an aim for the Church may well be a hyperbole.

Notes

Unless otherwise stated the place of publication is Paris

1. Cardinal Baudrillart, as head of the Paris Institut Catholique, noted that his students paid little heed to this ecclesiastical condemnation. See E. Weber, *Action Française. Royalism and Reaction in Twentieth Century France*, Stanford, 1962, p. 242.
2. R. Alix, *La nouvelle jeunesse*, 1930, p. 86.
3. G. Hoog, *Histoire du catholicisme social en France, 1891–1931*, 1942, pp. 326–38.
4. Garric, appointed by Daladier to head the national relief organisation, the Secours

National, occupied the post throughout the Occupation and later even under de Gaulle.

5. Simone de Beauvoir, *Mémoires d'une jeune fille rangée*, 1958, p. 182.

6. G. Lamirand, 'Après la grève l'indispensable collaboration', *Revue des Jeunes*, 10 March 1938, pp. 314–35.

7. For much of the information above (and elsewhere) I am deeply indebted to B. Comte's brilliant and monumental doctoral thesis, 'L'Ecole nationale des cadres d'Uriage', in two volumes, published by the Atelier National de Réproduction des thèses, Lille, 1988. Henceforth: Comte, *Thesis*. This has appeared abridged in book form: *Une Utopie combattante. L'Ecole des cadres d'Uriage, 1940–1942*, 1991. See also: H. Rollet, *Sur le Chantier social. L'action sociale des catholiques en France, 1870–1940*, 1955.

8. P. Baudouin, 'Les données du problème français', *Revue de Paris*, 1 February 1938, pp. 571–95. For a more general account of young people and youth movements (excluding the confessional movements) see W.D. Halls, *The Youth of Vichy France*, Oxford, 1981.

9. *Revue des Jeunes*, 10 March 1938, pp. 314–315.

10. P. Baudouin, 'Témoignage. Discours à des jeunes qui entrent dans la vie', *Revue des Jeunes*, January 1939.

11. Comte, *Une Utopie combattante*, p. 35.

12. E. Mounier, *Œuvres*, vol. IV, *Recueils posthumes. Correspondance*, 1963. For references to the Compagnons see p. 682. Entretiens X, 19 October 1940; p. 685, Entretiens XI, 14.January 1941.

13. *La Croix*, 5 February 1941.

14. *La Croix*, 24 April 1941.

15. G. Marcel and G. Fessard, *Correspondance*, 1985, p. 203, n. 2: 'Il menait. un combat acharné contre l'emprise totalitaire'.

16. AN 2 AG 650. Conseil National. 5ᵉ séance, commission de la Jeunesse, 7 March 1942: 'Depuis deux ans on rabâche à la jeunesse que la France est un pays perdu'.

17. AN 2 AG 650. Conseil National. 7ᵉ séance, commission de la Jeunesse: 'Il y a là un scandale qui ne saurait être toléré plus longtemps.'

18. AN 2 AG 650. Conseil National. 9ᵉ séance, commission de la Jeunesse, 9 March 1942.

19. See B. Comte, 'Encadrer la jeunesse?' in D. Peschanski *et al.* (eds), *La propagande sous Vichy, 1940–1944*, Paris, 1990, pp. 40–58.

20. Hoover Institution, *France during the German Occupation,*, vol. 2. *Testimony of Olivier-Martin*, quoted in English, Stanford, 1958.

21. H. and F. Joubrel, *L'Enfance du Coupable*, 1946, p. 23; H. Gaillac, *Les Maisons de Correction, 1830–1945*, 1971, p. 361.

22. The expressions used are those of Mgr Beaussart at the fifth session of the Youth Commission of the Conseil National, 7 March 1942.

23. Gaillac, *Les Maisons de Correction,* p. 361.

24. A Dio, Lille, ACA 2 B 1. 'Assemblée , 24 juillet 1941'.

25. AN F17.13376. 'Rapport du préfet de Loire-Inférieure au Ministère de l'Intérieur, 2 octobre 1941'.

26. J. Gay-Lescot, 'la politique sportive de Vichy', *Cahiers de l'Institut d'Histoire du Temps Présent*, no. 8, IHTP, June 1988, p. 64.

27. A Dio, Lille, 2 B 1 ACA, 1942–1945. Minutes of meeting of 14–15 January 1942.

28. C. Bellanger *et al.*, *Histoire générale de la Presse française*, vol. IV, *De 1940 à 1958*, p. 79.

29. P. Baudouin, *The Private Diaries of Paul Baudouin*, London, 1948, p. 277. Diary entry for November 17–19, 1940.

30. Baudouin, *Private Diaries*, p. 279, entry for 28 November 1940.

31. Not to be confused with *Jeunesse... France*, published by the Ecole des Cadres at Uriage.

32. Mgr Guerry, *L'Eglise catholique en France sous l'Occupation*, 1947, p. 147.

33. E. Lavergne, 'Pour une jeunesse nationale', *Revue Universelle*, 15 January 1941.

34. A Dio, Lille, Dossier ACA 2 B 1. Minutes of meeting of January 1941: 'on ne devrait pas interdire aux jeunes l'entrée dans un mouvement éventuel de jeunesse unique'.

35. A Dio, Lille 2 B 1. Minutes of ACA of 23 April 1941: 'Groupement unique, non; mais jeunesse unie par les sommets sur un programme déterminé'; A Dio, Lille, ACA 2 B 1. Letter from Liénart to Suhard dated Lille, 18 May 1941.

36. Guerry, *L'Eglise catholique*, p. 157: 'Jeunesse unie au service du pays, oui! Jeunesse unique, non!'

37. Comte, *Utopie*, p. 247 and n. 3.

38. A Dio, Lille, ACA 2 B 1, 'Compte-rendu', ACA of 24 July 1941; Comte, *Thesis*, vol. 2, p. 827, n. 31.

39. Comte, 'Encadrer la jeunesse?'

40. See *Les Eglises protestantes pendant la guerre et l'Occupation*, Actes de l'Assemblée générale du protestantisme français, Nîmes, 22-26 October 1945, 1946.

41. R. Mehl, *Le pasteur Marc Boegner. Une humble grandeur*, 1987, pp. 152f.

42. *Semaine Catholique* (Toulouse), 23 November 1941.

43. For the contents of this issue see Mgr Guerry, *L'Eglise catholique*, pp.147f..

44. G. Crouzet, 'La morale d'une rencontre—Jeunesse unique', *Les Nouveaux Temps*, 4 February 1942.

45. 'Action catholique: jeunesse unie ou jeunesse unique?' quoted in *La Croix des Côtes du Nord*, 22 February 1942.

46. Ibid.

47. Quoted in Comte, *Utopie*, p. 405

48. A Dio, Lille, 2 B 1 ACA 1942–1945. Letter of Liénart to Saliège, Lille, 24 October 1942.

49. AN F60.1758. English transcript of Radio Vatican broadcast, in French, 21.00 , 28 May 1943.

50. Cutting in AN F60.1676.

51. Quoted in H. Claude, 'La hiérarchie catholique, le gouvernement de Vichy et l'occupant', *Actes*: Lille, p. 265.

52. Pétain, *Le Procès du Maréchal Pétain*, 1946, vol. 1, p. 365.

-17-

Youth Movements

The pressures on youth to conform were strong. How did the Catholic and Protestant youth movements react, and to what extent was Christian influence apparent in the secular movements? The original organisation for the Catholic movements was the Action Catholique de la Jeunesse Française (ACJF), which had been started in 1886 by Albert de Mun for young people between fifteen and thirty. It eventually served as the overarching body for the more specialised Catholic youth movements considered later.[1] In the 1920s it already comprised 140,000 members, constituting, according to its membership booklet, 'an elite of young Frenchmen openly Catholic, determined to restore Christian principles in morality and institutions — "instaurare omnia in Christo" '[2]

In the 1930s its motto of 'Piété' (by frequent attendance at the Sacraments), 'Etude', (through hard work), 'Action' (through fulfilment of an apostolic mission), and its Maltese cross badge, were widely known. Its aims foreshadowed those of Vichy; it sought the restoration of the 'communautés naturelles' — nation, occupational grouping and family — and was pledged to combat individualism, 'introduced into our moral behaviour and our laws by the Revolution'.[3] Civic education and regional life were to be encouraged. The movement was subject absolutely, it declared, to Church authority, and its chaplains — some, such as Mgr Guerry, became bishops — were very influential. Former presidents included Bazire, (whose slogan, 'Sociaux parce que catholiques', proclaimed its social orientation, to which after 1918 was added, 'Civiques parce que sociaux'), and Cardinal Gerlier (president 1909–13, when he was still a layman). It comprised some working-class members, which caused its Marxist enemies to accuse it of being 'an attempt by clericalism to put a stranglehold on the labouring classes'.[4]

Branches worked through study groups, congresses and 'conférences' (lecture groups). The movement was intensely patriotic. In the First World War 15,000 of its members had been killed. It was also a militant organisation: in 1904–05, and again in the 1920s, it had demonstrated against the secularisation laws. It had natural affinities with other Catholic organisations concerned with social questions, sport and workers' rights.

During the 1930s a network of Catholic youth organisations developed under the aegis of ACJF: JOC, JAC, JEC, JMC, JIC — respectively for young workers, rural Catholics, students, those with a seafaring background and those coming from families of the self-employed or of independent means, together with corresponding female organisations.[5]

In 1940 in the occupied zone the various movements had to act circumspectly because of a German ban. In unoccupied France they sought to avoid political entanglements, but the size of their membership, increased by a kind of religious revival, made them a tempting target for unscrupulous extremist politicians. Already in October 1940 the constituent movements totalled 116,000, with some 5,000 sections.[6] Estimates of the numbers eventually involved vary considerably, from, in 1942, 380,000 — a figure given at the time — to 600,000–700,000 [7]

The ACJF was said to be the apple of Cardinal Gerlier's eye.[8] But, despite its very orthodox past, its allegiance to Vichy was qualified. At the four national Councils it held during the Occupation it did not hesitate to discuss Nazi propaganda and totalitarianism, opposition to Maurrassianism and anti-Semitism , and to a 'jeunesse unique'.[9] Notably, at a meeting in May 1943 it refused to recommend compliance with the STO. Yet a certain ambivalence remained. Thus, on the third anniversary of the founding of the LFC on 29 August 1943, in practically every department in the southern zone Catholic youth organisations attended the celebration ceremonies, whereas few bishops did so.[10] Maurras was not impressed. Castigating the continued hostility to the regime, as he saw it, of these organisations, he deplored the 'insidious anarchy' rife among young Catholics and quoted the judgement of one of his young supporters: for young Catholics, 'The Tricolour, nationalism, these are the enemy. As for the Marshal, there are whisperings.'[11]

In northern France sentiment was particularly anti-Vichy. In the mining basins of the North and the industrial complex of the Lille-Roubaix-Tourcoing triangle, where the JOC flourished, in rural Flanders, where JAC was strong, and along the coast with the smaller JMC, the prevailing mood was one of opposition.

In Lille itself, Hovaere, Vichy's Youth Delegate, regretted that he was persistently obstructed in his work. The writer Daniel-Rops took leave to wonder whether the new secular youth movements, rather than Christian ones, might be better builders of a new France.[12]

At the Youth Commission of the Conseil National the segregative social nature of the ACJF movements had been criticised. This 'spécialisation par milieu', as the Church preferred to call it, did not find favour in some Vichy circles. How far it existed, however, is open to question. The bishops had previously commissioned a sample analysis of the social composition of one of the more recent movements, the female branch of the JIC (Jeunes Indépendantes Catholiques, as its members were called), which had flourished since 1939 and might be considered to be the most class-oriented of all. A sample of 203 sections (out of 700 in all) undertaken in 1941 revealed that 24 per cent came from the petty bourgeoisie, 38 per cent from the middle bourgeoisie, 33 per cent from the upper bourgeoisie, and 7 per cent from the aristocracy.[13]

Since the working class would hardly be greatly represented in this particular movement, the results show a wider social mix than might be expected. Even the JOC, however, was not exempt from the criticism that its working-class converts tended to distance themselves from their humble origins.[14] The Church was clearly sensitive to the charge that it perpetuated class distinctions. However, 'social specialisation' within the ACJF had arisen because by the early 1920s the movement had lost impetus. Because of the considerable social differences in its membership it had responded by creating separate movements based on class and occupational differences.

The first, and under Vichy, the most significant of these, was the Jeunesse Ouvrière Chrétienne (JOC), which had originated in Belgium in 1919. The first French group was set up in Clichy by Abbé Guérin, but flourished particularly in the industrial North. Sometimes dubbed 'l'infanterie de Marie', JOC might be considered the Church's riposte to the Jeunesses Communistes — in fact the two movements before the war had a similar industrial agenda: the well-being of the young worker, although their main aims were of course poles apart.. In the Nord department JOC had supported the textile strikes of the early 1930s and the factory sit-ins of 1936. But its overriding purpose remained the re-Christianisation of France, as it proclaimed: 'Nous referons Chrétiens nos frères,/ Par Jésus-Christ nous le jurons'.

At first it played a positive role in Vichy plans. It set up centres for the young unemployed[15] and was also active in the Secours National, distributing food supplied by JAC, its agricultural counterpart, to the needy. In 1940 it founded an Institut de Culture ouvrière, which ran youth training courses on social and trade union matters, the family, and civics, as well as dispensing general education.[16] Other activities were not so helpful to the regime, as when it undertook wage comparisons which showed the economy up in a bad light. Examples were:

Food industry employee	Fr 750 a month.
Bank employee	Fr 872 a month
Post and Telegraph employee	Fr 750 a month
Foundry worker	Fr 40 a day
Errand boy	Fr 15–40 a day.

Comments of individual Jocistes on these pitiful earnings ranged from: 'it's as if I earned 6 kg of dried apricots a month', to 'Me, [I earn] a bar of nougat a day'.[17] Such expressions of disaffection were not liable to please the powers that be.

By 1942 things had indeed turned sour. Jocistes began to look to the Allies for salvation. Measures such as the abolition of Christian trade unions were particularly resented. In the Lille area, whenever a section met, ostensibly as a 'study group' in order to satisfy German restrictions, their first action was to hide the ubiquitous portrait of the Marshal. Some members even carried de Gaulle's picture in their inside pocket. In 1943 Brun, the regional Prefect at Clermont-Ferrand, was so exasperated by JOC rebelliousness that he summoned the leaders, and warned them to cease their anti-Vichy and anti-German propaganda forthwith, threatening condign punishment otherwise.[18]

The Germans were especially incensed when the JOC opposed Sunday working in the mines, and when JOC chaplains, following Cardinal Liénart's advice regarding the STO, interpreted as 'accept working in Germany if you feel it an apostolic mission, otherwise act according to your conscience', nevertheless tended to counsel refusal. Jocistes were even rumoured to commit acts of 'terrorism' in cahoots with young Communists. Liénart was accused of connivance. When the police, on German instructions, informed the cardinal that Jocistes hid arms in his palace, where they had their headquarters, he summoned their leaders, who naturally pleaded ignorance. The police did not dare search the bishop's residence, although the cardinal must have known what was going on.

JOC opposition became ever more blatant. A Jociste, Jean Clair, wrote in *Le Monde Ouvrier*: 'Calm, clear-headed, and firm, let us hold on tenaciously, in the storms and difficulties that may come up... We'll get them'.[19] The last phrase — 'On les aura!' — was a veiled reference to the slogan of the First World War, 'On les aura, les Boches'. In 1943 Laval canvassed for support of collaborationist organisations, whereupon JOC expressly forbade its members to join them.[20] Meanwhile the movement's own political activity was growing, particularly in the North: in April 1943 it was reported to be distributing anti-Vichy propaganda in factories, aided and abetted by employers, and even infiltrating clandestine young Communist groups.[21] In 1944 it was circulating tracts openly in Douai deploring the misery of young female workers:

> Every morning long lines of workers make their way to the coal tip, 400–500 every day. 200 to 300 of them youngsters! It's not for the pleasure of it: it's dark, it's cold; wind and rain bring tears to the eyes. Our fingers bleed... We stagger under the weight of the sacks. Our young bodies, exhausted by excessive hard work, are worn out, old before their time. Young working class women, we are forced to dress like men, and our dignity suffers. Every day boys and girls are stripped, abused and perverted... Thieves are arrested, but those who are stealing the wives of their comrades who are prisoners of war get off scot-free. Scenes that would disgrace the brothel take place before the eyes of the young.[22]

By the spring of 1944 Jocistes were flocking to the Resistance — in the Nord department, to join not only the Voix du Nord network but also the Communist-led Francs-Tireurs et Partisans (FTP). Three hundred Jocistes died in the subsequent struggle. By contrast the collaborationist Légion des Voluntaires Français (LVF) recruited only two Jocistes in the Pas-de-Calais area.[23] A Gaullist source summed up the JOC: 'It is among its members that the Catholic Church finds the best elements in its resistance to totalitarianism'.[24] If bishops such as Mgr Girbeau, of Gard, preached youth's duty to obey their superiors, the JOC movement stuck out as a notable example of disobedience.

The Jeunesse Agricole Chrétienne (JAC), founded in 1929 to revive rural life and improve harsh conditions for young workers, was less confrontational than JOC, partly because 97 per cent of those working the land were owner, farm manager and manual worker all in one.[25] Pétain's call for a 'retour à la terre' was well received, although without much practical effect. JAC's popularity rapidly increased, as was demonstrated by the annual sales of its calendars, which rose from 125,000 in 1939 to 950,000 in 1944. Each year JAC selected a theme for its study groups; it is perhaps symptomatic of its comparatively softer line that during the war all had Pétainist overtones, ranging in 1940–41 from 'work in the fields' to 'being a man' in 1943–44.

JAC loyalty to Vichy endured, even to the extent of reporting in mid-1943 unauthorised dances ('bals clandestins') in rural areas. Relations did not always proceed so smoothly with the Germans: in June 1941 it was fined Fr 200,000 for allowing its members to organise games; the Prefect of Tours was even ordered to forbid it to organise excursions.[26] On the whole, however, JAC was less harassed than the other movements.

The Jeunesse Etudiante Chrétienne (JEC), and JECF, its sister organisation, consisted of young people in higher and secondary education, including those in the 'écoles primaires supérieures' (EPS), which Vichy had upgraded to the status of 'collèges'. The last group were by far the most numerous: whereas in 1941 JECF had 60,000 members in the traditional secondary schools (and far fewer in the universities), there were more than double that number in the EPS. The EPS contingent was important because, whereas others in the JEC belonged mainly to the bourgeoisie and the upper classes, its links were with industrial and white-collar workers. There was of course some overlap with JOC, but whereas the latter concentrated on employment conditions, JEC dealt with other aspects of working-class life.[27] Although JEC was not able to start up again in schools and universities until the new academic year began in 1941, by 1942 it had already re-established 200 centres.

JEC attitudes had been coloured by their pre-war knowledge of nazism. Thanks to some excellent chaplains — men such as Père Drujon, its chaplain-general, Père Dillard and Père de Montcheuil, chaplain to JEC students at the Sorbonne — they were well informed as to conditions in Germany. Jécistes had even in the past had contacts with the Hitlerjugend, but had not been deceived by what one author popular with them, Robert d'Harcourt, termed 'the gospel of force'.[28] *Messages*, the movement's periodical, continued the defiant note it had adopted before the war, until it was eventually closed down by Vichy.[29] Up to late 1941 a few of its leaders did indeed contribute articles to Lesourd's *Voix Françaises*, until they realised that this so-called Christian periodical was tarred with the collaborationist brush. Politically JEC condemned the old order and assented to the idea of a spiritual revival, although it continued to be wary of Vichy's plans.

In particular, it made known its opposition to Vichy's anti-Jewish policy. The 1941 issue of its highly popular yearly diary, was interlarded with quotations from Bergson, the Jewish-born philosopher. Its 1942 edition, which ran to 67,000 copies, quoted St Paul: 'There is neither Jew nor Greek, there is neither male nor female, for you are all one in Jesus Christ'.[30] Perhaps because it recruited from educational institutions, in which, by June 1942 Jewish youngsters in the occupied zone were forced by the Germans to wear the rowel, the Star of David, JEC was more sensitive to the treatment of the Jews than other ACJF organisations.

In the occupied zone some Jécistes were upset by the overtly pro-Pétain stance of the bishops; Jean Badelle led a delegation to express their concern to Cardinal Suhard. Already in March 1942 *Messages* was referring to 'the common good' as the sole yardstick whereby a regime's legitimacy could be measured, implying that Vichy fell short on this score. Although by then JEC had adopted the 'salute to the Colours' and other Vichy ceremonies, it was perhaps more as an anti-German gesture than obeisance to the status quo. Maurras, again, was not deceived. In the article entitled 'Catechism of covert anarchy'[31] he cited a JEC circular dated 20 November 1942, sent out after the North African invasion. The circular stated. in terms reminiscent of Père Fessard's tract, 'le Prince esclave', that Vichy being no longer a free agent, any duty of loyalty had lapsed.

Within the movement, however, there were conflicting voices. A local JEC leader in the Haute-Garonne as late as June 1943 could write that allegiance to 'established authority' was still required, although he admitted to being at a loss to see how such obedience could be given in what was for Christians so divisive a situation.[32] Later still, in March 1944 Père Doncœur addressed 500 Jécistes in terms that give one pause: 'Conscious of its duties, youth will have the joy of working for the renewal of France and the new Europe.'[33] What his audience made of this is not recorded. But by then many Jécistes had already joined the Maquis.

Apart from the ACJF, the Scouts were undoubtedly the other most potent influence at Vichy. Since Catholic former Scouts occupied many key posts in the SGJ and in the new secular youth movements, Vichy youth policy incorporated many scouting ideas.

Rivalry existed between the ACJF and the Scouting movement, in which the Catholic Scouts de France formed the largest contingent. The bishops had long been lukewarm towards Scouting, partly because of its Protestant and British origins, partly because the non-Catholic Scouting organisations were suspected of links with Freemasonry. However, after the Pope had officially sanctioned Catholic Scouts in 1929, their doubts lessened. They still feared the Scouts would 'poach' from the ACJF or the local 'patronages', and that junior Church organisations such as 'Cœurs Vaillants' (for younger boys) and 'Ames Vaillantes' (for younger girls) would lose their members to the Wolf Cubs and Brownies. Nevertheless enthusiastic priests such as Doncœur and Forestier saw the Catholic scouts, somewhat romantically, as a quasi-elite order of chivalry, functioning in a feudal-type organisation. Their call, like that of Vichy, was to duty in social and private life. Sporting, enthusiastic for the great outdoors, the ideal Scout would have 'a virile and upright bearing, the frank gaze, a discipline of body and soul'. Since it penetrated even into the 'grandes écoles', the movement would produce the leaders in society. Semi-military in character, the Catholic Scout movement, under Vichy, became more conservative and antimodernist. Its pledge of obedience meant that it supported Pétain to the end, and thus was more willing than the ACJF to accept such exactions as forced labour in Germany.

Scouting became immensely popular in the southern zone, where it could recruit freely. In 1941 members of the various branches of the Catholic Scouting movement numbered 46,138; by 1942 the figure had risen to 57,000 (comprising some 20,000 Wolf Cubs, 23,000 Scouts, 5,000 Rovers, and 8,000 Scoutmasters and commissioners, including 900 chaplains).[34] By 1944 numbers had risen in the southern zone to some 85,000.[35]

Nominally forbidden in the occupied zone, and lacking the protection the bishops could give the ACJF, Scout troops nevertheless continued to meet, but had to tread warily. The Germans had not forgotten that in the First World War, even before French Catholic Scouts officially existed, Père Savin had illegally formed a troop at Mouscron, on the Belgian frontier, under the very noses of the occupying forces. In 1940, meeting clandestinely, they were intensely patriotic. Some troops paraded in the form of a hexagon, the geographical configuration of France in its 1939 borders, and grouped around a home-made mast, would solemnly hoist the colours, in an act that symbolised the unity of France.[36] As a sign of patriotism and devotion, Arras Scouts walked barefoot to Notre-Dame-de Lorette (Pas-de-Calais), the site of violent battles in the First World War.[37] Nor did they confine themselves to symbolic gestures. Forbidden to undertake direct social action, they set up a cover organisation, the Comité Sully, to run fifty centres for unemployed youth.[38]

In the South links with the Church were considerably strengthened. Camp masses, Stations of the Cross, and religious campfires became features of Scouting life. One momentous event was the massive pilgrimage organised in 1942 by Rover Scouts to the statue of the Black Virgin ('la vierge noire') at Le Puy. All Catholic youth movements participated. Groups set out from every part of France on 5 August, converging together round the statue ten days later, on the feast of the Assumption. The Nuncio and Cardinal Gerlier presided over the religious ceremonies, assisted by a bevy of archbishops and bishops. Pontifical mass was sung in the cathedral; a huge open-air service, celebrated by Mgr Choquet of Lourdes, also took place. Messages were read from the Pope, from Pétain, represented by Commandant Féat, and the two absent cardinals. Lamirand, the local Prefect and the Mayor also attended.[39] It was the last great act of union of Church, Catholic youth and the State before the gathering storm.

Girl Guides played a more restricted role. 'The Scout is above all for the world outdoors [...] and the life of the city; the Guide is above all for the indoor life [...] the home'.[40] The task of the Catholic Guides de

France was seen as to prepare for marriage and motherhood. The Church's vision of 'la femme au foyer' chimed with Vichy's — and the Nazis's — view of a woman's place in society.

Special mention must be made of the Jewish scouts, the Eclaireurs israélites de France (EIF). To his credit, Lamirand never sought to discriminate against Jewish Scouts or Jewish youngsters in other movements. Indeed, on a visit to Toulouse, he made a point of meeting the local Jewish Scout troop.[41] Even Vallat permitted their activities.[42] When, however, Darquier de Pellepoix took over the EIF came under attack, but was shielded by General Lafont, the Chief Scout. When Bonnard became Education minister in April 1942 he ordered Jews to be expelled from all youth movements. Catholic and Protestant Scout troops, some of which had deliberately enrolled Jewish converts to protect them, ignored the directive.[43] The EIF was nevertheless forcibly disbanded. Many of its members joined the Maquis, led by Captain Gamzon, and fought in Savoy side by side with Segonzac, the former leader of the Uriage 'école des cadres'.

The most active Protestant youth movements were the two Unions Chrétiennes de jeunes Filles et de jeunes Gens (UCJG: the equivalents of the YWCA and the YMCA), and the Protestant Scouts, the Eclaireurs Unionistes, presided over by Marc Beigbeder, the former contributor to *Esprit*. Also important was the very active Fédération française des associations chrétiennes d'étudiants (FFACE), known as 'la Fédé' (the equivalent of the Student Christian Movement). Former members of the 'Fédé', it will be recalled, were involved in drawing up the 'thèses de Pomeyrol', which set limits to Christian obedience to state authority. On a practical plane its members were associated with CIMADE, the organisation which assisted refugees and Jews. If Catholic movements had their influential chaplains, the 'Fédé' had clerics of the calibre of Pastors Maury, Westphal and Casalis, who moulded the anti-Nazi attitudes of young Protestants.

Protestant youth movements numbered no more than 20,000 in all — less than half of all young Protestants. Unlike the ACJF movements, initially their link with their Church was looser. However, from July 1941 the Conseil Protestant de la Jeunesse brought them more under the Church's wing. To become eligible for subsidies, they accepted the principle of civic education, although not favouring the idea of training national elites as such.44 Under Karl Barth's influence, they openly rejected totalitarianism as being incompatible with the transcendence of God. In fact, in April 1942 the Conseil Protestant de la Jeunesse issued a statement that read like a challenge to Vichy: 'Service to the state finds its limits in the faith that governs it... Christian obedience cannot be blind... It is absolutely certain that the spiritual has primacy over the political'.[45] They were also very internationally-oriented: the UCJG was linked to the international YMCA and YWCA, the 'Fédé' to the international Federation, whose president in 1940 was Pastor Visser 't Hooft, then leading the embryo ecumenical movement located in Geneva. Links with Switzerland — the Swiss Pastor de Pury and Boegner himself were occasionally allowed to cross the frontier without too much difficulty — gave them a window on a world outside occupied Europe.

The Gard department, being in the unoccupied zone, was a focal point for Protestant youth, since the traditional Protestant centre was at Nîmes. Mgr Girbeau, Bishop of Nîmes, did not look too favourably upon them: for him they lacked discipline, were too 'ecumenical', and not sufficiently faithful to the regime. Yet Pastor Boegner, despite personal reservations on Vichy policies, continually exhorted his movements to remain loyal. The Protestant Scouts, like their Catholic counterparts, were more likely to comply with this injunction than the other movements. Nevertheless, matters boiled over in November 1942, just before the North African landings. At the national Protestant Scout congress in Nîmes, attended by Boegner and Gastambide, the Protestant national Scouting Commissioner, De la Porte du Theil, Segonzac, and Chiappe, the local Prefect, the atmosphere was distinctly rebellious. Complaints were voiced over food shortages, and about the German occupation (which had not yet swept south). To cap this, hopes for an Allied victory were openly expressed. Chiappe was incensed, and as a reprisal forbade the broadcast of a Protestant service.[46] Without the restraining influence of an episcopal hierarchy and with a greater tradition of freedom, Protestant youth was less inclined to knuckle under.

In the founding and functioning — but only in the southern zone — of the two state youth movements, the voluntary Compagnons de France for adolescent boys and the compulsory Chantiers de la Jeunesse for young men, Christians were prominent.

The Compagnons movement was the brain-child of Henri Dhavernas. A practising Catholic, a Scout commissioner, and a young Finance inspector, he persuaded Baudouin to advance Fr 50 million to start up this new secular movement, intended initially for the young unemployed. Through hard physical labour, such as forestry and road-repairing, and by the imposition of a paramilitary discipline, their character would be strengthened. The movement was launched at a meeting at Randan, near Vichy, in 1940, of all pre-war youth leaders, including the Jeunesses Socialistes and Action Française as well as the confessional movements, many of whose leaders had been associated with Scouting. Dhavernas chose as his deputy Cruiziat, another Catholic

Scout. Other future leaders were drawn from the ACJF: Jean Barraud was an ex-Jéciste; Paul Noddings, Francis Lemarque, and Paul Delouvrier were ex-Jocistes. The initial 300–400 cadres, moreover, included many former Scouts.[47] Pierre Schaeffer, a Catholic Rover Scout, after a stint at Vichy's Radio Jeunesse, founded Jeune France, a theatrical company attached to the Compagnons, with the assistance of ex-Scout artistes of the Comédiens Routiers. Representing Protestantism in the Compagnons were Emmanuel Niedrist, Marc Beigbeder, and above all Jean Gastambide, not only a national Scout commissioner but a former leader in the (Protestant) Fédération des Etudiants Chrétiens.

Indeed Protestantism was perhaps overrepresented. Yet it brought to the movement a sense of openness and a dislike of the personality cult. It was Gastambide who, although he did not remain long in the movement, drew up its Code of Honour. This combined Christian and Scouting virtues: service to others, patriotism, loyalty, diligence, boldness, perseverance, helpfulness, sobriety, chivalry, frankness, cheerfulness, respect for the family, implacableness in opposing the corruption of money, softness and cowardice.[48] Such a catalogue of all the virtues may appear today to be naive, but was taken in deadly earnest by the young idealists of 1940.

The movement had a hard row to furrow. Its enemies accused it of being too Christian Democratic. Catholic Scout leaders distrusted it because its loyalty to the regime — but not to Pétain — became suspect, and were resentful because it had usurped their methods. The ACJF and its associated Catholic movements, although less warm towards the regime than the Scouts de France, saw it as a potential rival and maintained a certain distance. The JEC particularly distrusted the movement's political leanings. After the resignation of Dhavernas, the movement's first Chef Compagnon, who eventually escaped to North Africa to join the Allied forces, in 1941 the Compagnons underwent a leadership crisis only resolved by the appointment of Commandant Tournemire, who had later to flee from Laval and the Germans. A bid by Pucheu when Interior minister to take control of the movement and use it as the nucleus of a 'jeunesse unique' failed miserably.[49] Pucheu even accused Garrone, at the SGJ, of plotting with Cardinal Gerlier for the movement to be taken over by the Church. Incidentally, the Compagnons' leaders were lukewarm towards de Gaulle, preferring Giraud, although the Gaullists themselves were by no means unsympathetic to the movement.[50] Thus the Compagnons seemed to be subject to attack from all sides. Perhaps because of its independent attitude the movement did not find favour with the Church — it did not even have chaplains — despite its Catholic leaders.

Indeed the Church kept it at arm's length. Mgr Couderc, Bishop of Viviers, exhorted Catholics to co-operate where necessary, but not at the expense of the Church's own youth movements.[51] From Annecy Canon Dufournet issued a warning: 'The Compagnon movement, however excellent it may be, could never offer youth an ideal and training as complete as our Christian movements'.[52] This reflected the considered judgement of the Church on the movement.

The Church may have had greater expectations from the compulsory Chantiers de la Jeunesse, seen as a substitute for conscription. Although a secular organisation, its head, General De La Porte du Theil, as a former Catholic Scout commissioner, intended a direct Christian influence to be exerted. His friend, Père Forestier, appointed Chaplain-General, was assisted by a team of priests fully integrated into the Chantiers cadres. The general, a military leader of note — in 1940 he had fought to the bitter end — intensely loyal to Pétain and the ideals of the Révolution Nationale, firmly believed that moral conduct depended on Christian belief — 'On ne fait pas une société sans religion', he was wont to declare.[53] He added that without his experience of Scouting the idea of the movement would not have occurred to him. Indeed, the first 'groupements' (entities of 2,400 men) were commanded by ex-army captains known for their scouting prowess, and the smaller 'équipes' (twelve men) were often led by former Scouts. A healthy outdoor life for recruits, together with civic education, was supplemented by counselling from the large number of chaplains. (There was even provision for fifty Protestant chaplains, although only ten posts were ever filled.) The ambitious aim was the social, physical and moral transformation of young men. Some 384,000 of them passed through the Chantiers during the Occupation.[54] Thus the effect of Christianity on them could have been significant.

That it was not was due to circumstances. Distrusted by Laval, his movement viewed by the Germans as a breeding-ground for Resisters — a not unfounded accusation — Du Theil saw his organisation progressively undermined. In January 1944 he himself was summarily arrested and deported to Germany. His departure was immediately followed by the resignation of Père Forestier, who regarded his mission as 'terminated'.[55] Its ranks depleted by compulsory transfer to the STO, eventually the Chantiers were converted into a Service National du Travail, for which, as late as April 1944, Déat, by then Labour minister, was requesting a new Chaplain-General.[56] But the time was then well past when idealistic young men of the Chantiers would plant huge crosses on the mountain tops and march kilometres in the snow to attend Sunday mass. If the Chantiers were a not unsuccessful school for patriotism, as even de Gaulle conceded, there is scant evidence that the

Church, despite the privileged position it occupied in the movement, succeeded in converting it into a school for Christianity.

The same Christian influence, but more indirect, was exerted at the Ecole des Cadres of Uriage, founded by Segonzac, another practising Catholic. Although intended for all ages, inevitably its courses were mainly attended by the younger generation. Uriage, as an attempt to develop 'un humanisme révolutionnaire d'inspiration chrétienne ou personnaliste',[57] was nominally 'neutral', but its instructors were mostly Christians. The chief instructor, Eric d'Alençon, has been characterised as a 'moine-soldat', because of the asceticism of his intense Christian personal life. Many of Segonzac's team were former Scouts. The spiritual aspects of the Uriage 'doctrine' were reinforced first by Abbé Naurois, a fierce opponent of nazism, and then his successor, Père Maydieu, a personal friend of Segonzac. Notable Christians were invited to lecture to the students: Mgr Bruno de Solages, Père de Lubac, Mounier and Jean Lacroix (the last two being the joint architects of personalism), and even Mgr Guerry. A young Protestant, Lochard, was on the permanent staff; Père Fraisse, a Jesuit, joined him on a temporary appointment in 1942. An atmosphere of liberty and ecumenism prevailed. In 1942 a short course was even mounted for Catholic priests. Yet, despite the predominance of Christian instructors, secularists and rationalists were welcomed on the courses. There was, it was held, a set of higher values to which those of all creeds or of none could subscribe.[58]

The 'leadership school' was not without its critics. The regime grew suspicious of it — the Germans even more so. The bishops blew hot and cold. They disliked the somewhat Christian Democratic political analyses the staff allegedly expounded to their students. Uriage's relations with the Chantiers were cool: for Père Forestier, the Chantiers' Chaplain-General, the nominal neutrality in leadership schools — and Uriage was not the only one — was dangerous. Had not the Marshal stated that 'life was not neutral'?[59]

The ACJF was also initially critical, but on practical grounds: cadres, it held, could not be trained on a cursory three-week course. Nevertheless, politically and ideologically the views of the ACJF, and particularly of the Jocistes, eventually began to coincide with those of Uriage. Catholic Scout leaders were less favourably inclined. They could only approve of the methods used, since many were borrowed from them, but remained deeply suspicious of Uriage's intellectual and political tendencies.

After Laval's return to power, Uriage survived only until December 1942. It then decamped from its castle fastness, and became a clandestine organisation, with strong links to the Resistance. With its ethos of honour and its cult of the heroic perhaps this was its inevitable destiny. It was, it has been said, the dream of a Vichy that might have been.

For the first time the state had positively encouraged Christian involvement in nominally secular youth movements. The attempt was patently unsuccessful, perhaps flawed by the very nature of the regime.

The appointment in February 1941 of a Catholic, Garrone, as Directeur de la Formation des Jeunes in the SGJ came just as the arguments about a 'jeunesse unique' were boiling up. To counter the charge that the SGJ's supervision of youth movements was perfunctory some mechanism of control had to be devised. A procedure for granting official recognition ('agrément') and financial aid was thought up by Garrone as a means of exercising indirect control over the movements without their losing their autonomy.[60] To receive a State subsidy a movement had to be 'recognised' ('agréé').

In June 1941 Garrone expounded at Uriage his plan for 'agrément' to representatives of the various movements. Initially recognition would be granted to ten movements on condition that their leaders attended a course at one of the State 'leadership schools'. Each movement had to submit its activities to the SGJ's 'moral' and financial control. If this was satisfactory, it would receive a regular quarterly subsidy. The SGJ interpreted 'moral' control in terms of 'civic education'. Movements had to pledge themselves to national unity; socially, they should seek to eradicate class divisions; and spiritually, promote the restoration of the 'natural communities'.[61]

The ACA found subjection to such 'control' difficult to swallow, in view of the ACJF's non-political nature. Mgr Chollet, its Secretary-General, was instructed to negotiate on its behalf, so as to safeguard the religious character of its constituent movements and prevent the imposition of any political 'doctrine'. The bishops even demanded the right to have an oversight ('un droit de regard') of other, non-religious movements. Whereas the SGJ quickly signed an agreement with the Scouts, now federated into one national organisation, and the Compagnons de France, negotiations with the ACA were protracted.

The negotiations were reviewed at a meeting of ACA members in the unoccupied zone on 4 and 5 September 1941 and by those in the occupied zone on 16 October 1941. Finally, on 25 October 1941 Mgr Chollet was authorised to sign an agreement.[62] It covered not only the ACJF movements, but also the male and female student federations, and the two movements for younger boys and girls, Cœurs Vaillants and Ames Vaillantes. (The 'patronages' for boys [parish youth clubs], which the ACA wished to include in the agreement, were excluded.) Liaison with individual bishops would be in the hands of departmental youth delegates of the SGJ. Catholic programmes for civic and physical education, and for vocational guidance would be submitted for nominal approval. It was accepted that Catholic youth leaders would undergo a short training course at an 'école des cadres'. (However, after the Church insisted that all its leaders were religious leaders, this was modified to include only full-time workers, who would 'occasionally' spend a short time at Uriage and could be accompanied by Catholic chaplains, a facet of the 'droit de regard' the Church demanded.)

Before signing an agreement, in a further letter of clarification to Garrone Mgr Chollet[63] had insisted that the bishops wanted a clear distinction maintained between temporal and spiritual matters. He added that any religious questions that arose should be a matter for talks between the Vatican and the government, and eventually for a Concordat. On 10 December 1941 Garrone replied avoiding mentioning any such high-level talks;[64] he gave an assurance that the State had no wish to diminish the Church's influence over youth but sought merely to ensure that young Christians were properly integrated into national life. He noted that although the bishops had pledged themselves, 'Certain leaders, clergy and laity, have recently departed from such a loyal attitude and too often the instructions given to militants of Action Catholique have been so reticent regarding State initiatives that they could have been taken as implied reproaches'.[65] So much therefore in practice for the distinction drawn between the spiritual and the temporal. Garrone feared that the ACJF, as part of the Action Catholique, wanted to remain too independent, shutting itself off from the rest of French youth. This reproach, perhaps aimed at the JOC, nevertheless did not prevent the final signing of the agreement on 20 December 1941. There, for the time being, the matter rested.

Meanwhile Pastor Boegner negotiated for the movements in the Conseil Protestant de la Jeunesse. This body had joined to its request for 'agrément' a strongly worded note in which it declared its loyalty but, taking its stand on the Gospel, seized the opportunity to reiterate its opposition to racism, totalitarian nationalism and the cult of force. It nevertheless secured 'agrément' by the end of the summer.

With the re-emergence of Laval the SGJ began to change. Lamirand, although soldiering on for another year, yielded more power to the authoritarian Pelorson. Garrone and his associates were reluctant to remain in the SGJ after April 1942. Dupouey, in charge of youth movements, affirms that he left his deputy, Moreau, to carry on, perhaps as a kind of 'spy in the camp'. Thus in April 1942, under pressure from Pelorson, when the 'agréments' were renewed more stringent conditions were threatened.

By then subsidies had begun to work on a systematic basis. Pelorson in allocating them for the autumn quarter of 1942, commented upon the recipients (figures for membership given in the document appear somewhat arbitrary.):[66]

Scouts: The five associations were very active: from only 42,000 members in 1941 they had risen to 150,000. The Catholic Scouts de France (50,000 members) received Fr 1.6 million. According to Pelorson, they showed 'discipline civique et vitalité' and were in the vanguard of Catholic movements. The Protestant Eclaireurs de France (19,000 members in the unoccupied zone) received Fr 900,000 and, surprisingly, were characterised as 'deserving more'.

Of the movements of the ACJF: JAC (120,000 members) received the 'somme infime' of Fr 100,000; JACF (mainly concerned with family and housecraft among young countrywomen), Fr 40,000; JEC, Fr 80,000, and JECF, its female counterpart, Fr 50,000; JIC, with few members — it was considered to act only as a link between the bourgeoisie and the other specialised movements — Fr 20,000; JOC, 'the most representative of the Catholic youth movements', Fr 180,000.

Among other Catholic movements: The Fédération française des Etudiants catholiques received Fr 80,000; the Fédération des Patronages catholiques de Jeunes Filles de France, 'very numerous', and busy elaborating programmes of civic and physical education, Fr 40,000 to assist this development.

Protestant youth movements: Since the main Protestant youth movements were seemingly not increasing in number, they received only Fr 25,000; but the Unions Chrétiennes de Jeunes Gens, the oldest French movement of all, which had grown from 6,000 to 15,000, received Fr 70,000; the parallel feminine movement, L'Alliance française des Unions Chrétiennes de Jeunes Filles, Fr 50,000; the Protestant student movement, the Fédération française des Associations Chrétiennes d'Etudiants, much smaller than its Catholic counterpart, Fr 15,000.

Clearly, as compared with the Scouts as a whole, the movements most closely associated with the Church, both Protestant and Catholic, did not fare so well, perhaps a sign of official displeasure at their lukewarm attitude to the regime.

That summer the new directives tightening up controls were made known, the most significant of which was that government representatives were to be attached to all movements — more 'spies in the camp'. They were also pressed to provide leaders for the new movement, the Equipes Nationales, that Pelorson had founded in his bid to establish a 'jeunesse unique'.[67] The Churches contrived largely to circumvent these directives

Lamirand's successor at the SGJ in February 1943, Félix Olivier-Martin, was more in tune with the new ruthlessness of the regime's overall youth policy, as expressed in the conscription of young men for work in Germany and the establishment of the Milice to suppress the Resistance. On 2 June Olivier-Martin gave notice, duly reported to the ACA by Mgr Chollet on 28 July, that he intended to end the 'agrément' system[68] on the pretext that the total occupation of France rendered it impossible to administer two different modes of control over youth movements, some of which were still theoretically not allowed to function in the former occupied zone. This was seen as a ruse to promote the Equipes Nationales. The bishops became alarmed. Mgr Girbeau, Bishop of Gard, for example, although in his diocese the Equipes Nationales were headed by a Catholic scout leader and a Protestant female Cubmaster, forbade Catholics to participate in their activities.[69] The fear was that the SGJ was now aiming at a take-over of the Christian youth movements. Some bishops responded by confining their activities to purely religious exercises.

Thus the 'agrément' system and the concept of a 'jeunesse unique' were closely linked. The minimum civic programme imposed on all movements may also be seen as a sign of renewed authoritarianism. The bishops, for their part, resisted these steps towards a totalitarian state, despite an outcry by the collaborationists.[70]

The Occupation authorities, not unreasonably, viewed all young people as potential Resisters. The ban they had imposed on 28 August 1940 in their zone applied to all youth organisations. Meetings, the wearing of uniforms and badges, and the flying of flags were forbidden. Despite this general prohibition, the Germans were prepared to tolerate parish youth institutions whose activities were wholly religious. They did not even allow sporting activities. In the Nord-Pas-de-Calais region, which was at first governed from Brussels, the Scouts might also meet, provided they complied with the ordinance in other respects. Thus the Fifth Lille Scout Troop and the Third and Fourth Tourcoing Troops functioned throughout the war. But the position remained unclear. The bishops promptly interpreted the ban as not applying to the main Catholic youth organisations — the JOC, the JAC and the JEC — which they maintained were an integral part of the Church. The Germans took a different view and on 18 December 1940 the Commandant of Gross-Paris issued a further order, which resolved nothing.

The Hierarchy thereupon decided the organisations should continue to meet unobtrusively. Mgr Chollet of Cambrai instructed those in his diocese to assemble in church and confine their activities to a homily, a hymn and a prayer.[71] The Occupation authorities redoubled their vigilance. Prefects were asked to bring pressure to bear upon the bishops, and Lamirand issued a circular urging compliance with the German prohibition.

All was to no avail: the bishops remained obdurate. On 9 May 1941 the Gestapo struck. They raided JAC headquarters in Rennes and sealed its Paris offices. Funds and documents were seized and employees arrested. Cardinal Suhard requested government intervention to allow the movements to function unimpeded and to release those arrested, including three Paris priests also imprisoned for the 'crime' of having accompanied some Catholic youths to a sports field. Brinon, Vichy's 'ambassador' to the Germans in Paris, was asked to appeal to the Occupation authorities, emphasising that, although the youth movements were registered under the law as associations, they were an integral part of Church life. Their sole aim was to spread Christian doctrine and provide mutual assistance and charity. They were the flower of French youth and France would suffer if the movements were suppressed, because its 'restoration' ('revalorisation') depended upon them. This was hardly an argument likely to appeal to the Germans, who had no interest in France or its young people prospering unduly. The German ban, it was argued, 'endangered the spirit of understanding and collaboration in the country', an argument perhaps more relevant at a time when the Germans were asking for transit facilities in Syria for their warplanes.[72]

The appeal had some success. Cardinal Suhard, backed by Mgr Roques of Rennes, procured the release of all the imprisoned personnel save one, Pierre Lucas, who was sentenced to one year in prison for smuggling a letter across the demarcation line. Suhard obtained the agreement of Abetz and Schleier, of the German Embassy, that Catholic youth movements could continue, provided they indulged in no political activity and held no meetings of over 300 persons.[73] In its turn the ACA formally declared in July that its youth organisations had been 'mandated' to carry out 'purposes that were exclusively religious, apostolic and social, beyond any partisan politics'.[74]

For two years an uneasy truce reigned. The JAC and the JEC were left comparatively unmolested. With the JOC it was a different story. Jocistes in the industrial North came increasingly under surveillance.[75] Prefects were detailed to enquire whether the movement was active in their areas. The bishops replied affirmatively, but refused to provide the names of local leaders. Thereupon at least one, Abbé Masse, of Dijon, was arrested, and in early 1943 the Germans moved against the Catholic youth movements once more. Abbés Pihan and Maussion, two chaplains of the junior youth organisations, were arrested for running an illegal movement[76] and imprisoned for three months. The SS, which had now taken over the policing of France, and Kuntze, the SS officer most concerned, claimed they knew nothing of any understanding reached by Suhard with the German Embassy in 1941. In any case, since 1 June

1942 the Embassy lacked jurisdiction in such matters. There was plainly a power struggle going on between the diplomats and the SS. Kuntze was prepared to consider applications from movements to operate in the occupied zone, although his blunt view was that all priests were anti-German Resisters who should be 'broken'.[77] Meanwhile he threatened further action.[78] Cardinal Suhard asked Bonnard, the Education minister, to intervene. The matter was urgent because the Cœurs Vaillants were engaged in organising summer camps for thousands of youngsters. Kuntze magnanimously agreed to consider what could be done, perhaps by placing the holidays under a kind of 'union de colonies de vacances'. Suhard appealed to Schleier at the German Embassy on 11 June 1943. Schleier replied that he would get the chaplains freed, but could not himself grant permission for the youth movements to function. At the same time he implied that the true motive for this renewal of German activity was that the ACA had failed fully to endorse the call-up of young Frenchmen for work in Germany, a refusal he considered almost as bad as the activities of 'dissidents'.

On 3 August 1943 Abbé Guérin, the JOC national chaplain, was arrested. Cardinal Suhard protested, and sheltered in his own villa at Bagneux other JOC officials. He claimed Guérin worked under his orders.[79] Oberg, the SS police chief, retorted (30 August 1943) that he was sceptical that the JOC role was purely religious: the clergy had been instrumental in persuading Jocistes to shirk their duty to work in Germany. He wrote:

.

> It will not have escaped you that the majority of the French bishops and a large number of priests [...] have done everything in their power during recent months to prevent French youth entrusted to their pastoral care from going to work in Germany. Consequently I can easily imagine that the members of JOC have to a very large extent been subjected to this influence.[80]

This was undoubtedly partly true. By now, in the Nord department Jocistes were linked to the Resistance network and to the young Communists. After Guérin's arrest, in a gesture of solidarity, the latter had even produced a leaflet: 'Jeunes Français, sauvons L'abbé Guérin... Il faut nous unir pour sauver la JOC'. Cardinal Suhard replied that no bishop had directly counselled young men to avoid the STO and 'on pourrait même citer des exemples contraires'.

In fact Guérin may have been arrested for a specific reason. He had produced a devotional work entitled, *Prières du Travailleur*, which the Germans forbade distribution of because it was 'un missel jociste'. A preface had been written by Abbé Rodhain, Chaplain-General for prisoners of war, and the volume was to be handed out by POW chaplains who might have contact with young French workers in Germany. Suhard claimed the Germans had already authorised publication and complained that an atmosphere of religious persecution was developing. But by now German suspicions about the activity of the JOC in Germany were acute. The bishops, denied permission to provide chaplains to minister to French workers, were beginning to despatch priests clandestinely.[81]

Others intervened. Mgr Chappoulie, the Church's representative at Vichy, wrote to Brinon that the Germans disliked the volume because 'it gave to work [in Germany] a character of sadness, whereas it should appear to be a joy'.[82] Abbé Rodhain informed Oberg's lieutenant, Wohlfahrt, that responsibility for the book was his alone, and his publishers, Editions Ouvrières, had 5,000 copies ready, for distribution. The Germans, he declared, had asked him a score of times to enlighten them upon the Catholic attitude towards the STO; this book would help. Moreover, what, he asked, would be the effect on young Catholics of Guérin's arrest?

Nevertheless the priest stayed in prison. At its meeting of 20–21 October 1943 the ACA discussed the situation.[83] It was agreed that Suhard should make one last approach to the Germans to resolve all outstanding differences. A memorandum was drawn up promising no mass meetings of youth organisations, as well as renewing the pledge that no activities other than religious and social ones[84] would be undertaken. In return Abbé Guérin should be released, and the seals placed on the Paris offices of JOC and on the Union des Œuvres should be removed. Suhard wrote communicating these proposals to the Germans but had to wait until March 1944 for a formal reply, although Guérin had already been freed on 23 December 1943. The Germans then stipulated that for meetings of over 600 people their permission would be needed; for meetings of 200–600 they merely required to be notified. No JOC groups should be formed from STO workers in Germany. The stipulation regarding the STO was, however, not agreeable to the Church, although it was aware that French government representatives in Germany had banned JOC. The position was therefore deadlock, despite the fact that by then the question was almost academic and the Germans had other fish to fry.

Plainly the Church adopted a strong line when the existence of its youth movements was at stake, and Cardinal Suhard went to some lengths to express his opposition to German demands, which were initially made to restrain young people but later served as a lever to induce the Church to toe the line. As the above three incidents show, on the matter of the youth movements, the bishops — even Suhard, who on other issues was prepared to compromise with the Germans — were not prepared to yield.

Vichy's attempt to mobilise Christian youth in the service of the State had proved a failure. The Church missed a golden opportunity for 're-Christianisation' among the estimated million young people[85] in its youth movements and the further three-quarters of a million that through the Compagnons de France, the Chantiers de la Jeunesse, Uriage and similar institutions came indirectly under Christian influence. Christian youth leaders who had been fired with enthusiasm in 1940 were now dispersed: they had been dismissed, had resigned, had been deported, had defected to de Gaulle or Giraud, or joined the Maquis. Young people, Christian or no, had rejected the regime, and chosen to disobey the Church if they thought fit. So long as the Germans occupied France, the course of events was ineluctable. In their battle for the hearts and minds of the young Vichy, the Church and the Germans had suffered a defeat.

On the question of forced labour in Germany, to which we now turn, the Hierarchy did not show itself so resolute.

Notes

Unless otherwise stated the place of publication is Paris.

1. For a detailed study of the ACJF see J. Ageorges, *Une histoire et une épopée: l'ACJF de sa fondation à nos jours*, 1942.
2. ACJF, *Mon carnet de l'ACJF*, (édition générale), 1926 p. 5 and p. 9.
3. Ibid. p. 10.
4. Ageorges, *Une histoire*, p. 47.
5. JOC: Jeunesse Ouvrière Catholique; JAC: Jeunesse Agricole Catholique; JEC: Jeunesse Etudiante Chrétienne; JMC: Jeunesse Maritime Catholique; JIC: Jeunesse Indépendante Catholique.
6. AN 2 AG 654. File: A308. Jeunesse. The numbers were as follows:

	Sections	Members
JOC	1,900	40,000
JAC	2,700	35,000
JEC	n/a	35,000★
JIC	150	2,500
JMC	80	3,500

★ Including 20,000 'sympathisants' (associate members).

7. Y-M. Hilaire, 'L'Association catholique de la Jeunesse française: les étapes d'une histoire (1886–1956)', *Revue du Nord*, (Lille), vol. LXVI, April–September 1984, p. 913. Hilaire estimates that with the Catholic Scouts the total might reach one million. Others put the numbers even higher.

8. Pucheu's allegation that Gerlier had ambitions to enlarge it by taking over the Compagnons de France and turning it into a Church movement seems however exaggerated. Pucheu accused Garrone of conniving in 'une absurde et étonnante tentative cléricale de s'emparer de la direction de la jeunesse française'. (See P. Pucheu, *Ma Vie*, 1948, pp. 292f).

9. Councils were held at Avignon in January 1941 and January 1942, at Avignon in March 1943, and at Montmartre in November 1943. See *Actes*: Biviers, 1987, p. 279.

10. AN 72 AJ 249. *Le Bilan de l'Action Légionnaire de la Quinzaine*, nos. 13–14, 1943.

11. C. Maurras, 'Toujours le catéchisme de l'anarchie larvée', *Action Française*, 12 July 1943.

12. Unidentified quotation from Daniel-Rops (Henri Petiot) in: AN F60.1676. Scoutisme, Jeunesse Chrétienne et Jeunesse. File B2770.

13. A Dio, Lille, 2 B 1. Assemblée, 24 juillet 1941. Document: 'La JICF doit-elle réformer sa structure?'

14. M. Montlucard, 'L'Eglise et le mouvement ouvrier', in *Des événements et la foi, 1940–1952, Jeunesse de l'Eglise*, 1951, p. 45.

15. J. Serge Morel, 'Une lueur d'espoir: les centres de Jeunesse', *Les Cahiers Français*, 1942, pp. 84–8; see also *La Croix*, 8 August, 14–15. September, 12 December 1941.

16. Mgr Guerry, *L'Eglise Catholique sous l'Occupation*, 1947, p. 225.

17. 'Jeunes ruraux, rendez-vous compte', *L'Eveil du Gard*, no. 63, November–December 1942.

18. AN F60.1676. Fighting French file. Orientation de presse. No. 2982, CNI (Commissariat National à l'Intérieur).

19. Quoted in *La Croix*, 27 October 1942.

20. AN 2 AG 492. 'Note de police. (Secret)', 2 March 1943.

21. AD du Nord, Lille, R. 2410. Report of Commissaire aux Renseignements Généraux to Prefect, 28 April 1943.

22. AD du Nord, Lille, 1W 1262. 'Propagande catholique, sous-préfecture de Douai, mars 1944'. Tract of JOC.

23. L. Berthe, 'La JOC du Pas-de-Calais pendant la guerre', *Actes*: Lille.

24. AN F60.1676. Scoutisme, Jeunesse Chrétienne et Jeunesse.

25. G. Hoog, *Histoire du catholicisme social en France, 1918–1931*, 1942, pp. 252–258.

26. AN F 60. 1676. 'La JOC', *Le Volontaire*, (London), 15 September 1942.

27. A Dio, Lille, ACA 2 B 1. 'Assemblée, 24 juillet 1941'. Letter to Canon Tiberghien, Lille, for onward transmission to Cardinal Liénart.

28. See R. d'Harcourt, *Le visage de la jeunesse du III^{e}Reich: l'Evangile de la Force*, 1938.

29. A. Michel, 'Mouvements de jeunesse et Nazisme avant 1939', *Actes*: Biviers, pp. 62–71. See also Michel's study, *La JEC 1938–1944. Face au Nazisme et à Vichy*, 1988, to which I am much indebted.

30. Translation from New American Standard Bible, Gal. 3:.28; see Michel, *La JEC*, pp. 148f.

31. C. Maurras, 'Catéchisme d'une anarchie larvée', *Action Française*, 25 June 1943.

32. AN 2 AG 609. Intercept entitled: 'JEC: recommendations en matière de politique. Loyalisme de principe avec certaines latitudes de fait'. Letter from Massard, Secrétaire Général de la Haute Garonne, Toulouse, to B. Montagnes, Revel, Haute-Garonne, dated 4 June 1943.

33. AN F1a.3784. Ref. XCG/5/36801.

34. AN 2 AG 492.

35. AN F60.1676. Scoutisme, Jeunesse Chrétienne et Jeunesse.

36. AN 2 AG 440.CCIIIN. Note: 'Le patriotisme chez les scouts de la zone occupée'.

37. S. Laury, 'Aspects de la vie religieuse pendant la seconde guerre mondiale', *Actes*: Lille.

38. AN 2 AG 609. 'Position'.

39. AN 72 AJ 1863, and *Cahiers de Notre Jeunesse*, no. 11, July–August 1942.

40. Extract from the pre-war *Règlement des Guides de France*.

41. Centre de Documentation Juive, Paris, Archives, Carton LXXVIII - Etat major allemand., Hotel. Majestic, Paris, p. 108.

42. AN F17.13348. 'Note sur les scouts israélites'. See also: Centre de Documentation Juive, Paris, Series, *Etudes et monographes*, No. 4, *L'activité des organisations juives en France*, Chapter VI, Paris, 1947.

43. Centre de Documentation Juive, Archives, Carton LXXVII - Etat major allemand.. Hotel. Majestic, Paris, p. 25. See also M. Boegner, *The Long Road to Unity. Memories and Anticipations* (translated by R. Hague), London, 1970, pp. 168f.

44. A. Dumas, 'Une nouvelle donne pour l'Eglise. Les mouvements de jeunesse protestants avant, pendant et après la guerre', *Actes*: Biviers, 1987.

45. AN F60.1676. File B2770.

46. A. Cosson, 'Les mouvements de Jeunesse dans le Gard', in J.-P. Azéma and F. Bédarida, *Vichy et les Français*, 1992, p. 429.

47. AN 2 AG 609. Position du scoutisme français [Document marked in pencil: 'Received 13 September 1941'.]

48. R. Hervet, *Les Compagnons de France*, 1965, p. 40.

49. W.D. Halls, 'Les Compagnons de France et la politique', in (presented by) M. Vaisse, *Les Compagnons de France*, Club Compagnons, Paris, 1994.

50. AN F60.1676. 'Rapport LTE sur la jeunesse',1942, Forces Françaises Libres, London.

51. *La Croix*, 16 April 1941. The bishopric of Marseilles issued a similar statement. See *La Croix*, 27 February 1942.

52. H. Baud (ed.), *Histoire des Diocèses de France: (Genève)*, Annecy, 1985.

53. *Bulletin des Chantiers de la Jeunesse*, BPO 26, 13 February 1941.

54. Obituary notice of General De la Porte du Theil, *Le Monde*, 7–8 November 1986.

55. A Dio, Lille, 2 B 1, ACA 1944. Letter (copy) of Forestier to Colonel Bernon, acting Director-General of the Chantiers, Châtel-Guyon, 7 January 1944.

56. A Dio, Lille, 2 B 1 ACA, Minutes of meeting of July 1944.

57. Comte, *Thesis*, vol. 1, p. 2. For a stringent criticism of Uriage see J. Hellman, *The Knight-Monks of Vichy France. Uriage, 1940–1945*, Montreal, 1993.

58. B. Comte, 'L'expérience d'Uriage', *Actes*: Grenoble, pp. 251ff.

59. R.-P. Forestier, 'Note sur l'organisation des écoles des cadres', *Revue des Jeunes*, 15 December 1940.

60. P. Gallaud, 'Le Bureau des Mouvements de Jeunesse au SGJ. Entretiens avec MM. Dupouey et Moreau', *Les Cahiers de l'Animation*, 1985, nos. I and II, 49–50, pp. 33–6.

61. B. Comte, *Une Utopie combattante. L'Ecole des Cadres d'Uriage, 1940–1942*, 1991, p. 318.

62. A Dio, Lille, ACA 2 B 1. 'Convention entre le SGJ et l'épiscopat français'.

63. A Dio, Lille, ACA 2 B 1. Letter from Mgr Chollet, Vénissieux, 25 October 1941.

64. A Dio,, Lille, ACA 2 B 1, Document, Vichy, 10 December 1941.

65. Ibid.

66. AN F17.13367. 'Analyse par Pelorson des notes d'études établies par le Bureau des Mouvements, SGJ, au sujet des subventions accordées aux Associations de Jeunesse'.

67. A. Coutrot, 'Quelques aspects de la politique de la Jeunesse', in *Le Gouvernement de Vichy, 1940–1942*, 1972, pp. 276ff.

68. A Dio, Lille, 2 B 1, ACA 1944–1945.

69. A. Cosson, 'Etude départementale: les mouvements de jeunesse dans le Gard', in J.-P. Azéma and F. Bédarida, *Vichy et les Français*, 1992, p. 429.

70. See *Je Suis Partout*, 25 June 1943, quoted in Mgr Guerry, *Le rôle de l'épiscopat français sous l'Occupation allemande*, Lille, n.d. It accused the bishops 'd'exciter la jeunesse contre l'Etat, contre le Maréchal, contre la loi'.

71. H. Claude, 'La hiérarchie catholique, le gouvernement de Vichy et l'occupant', *Actes*: Lille, p. 265.

72. AN 2 AG 492. The incident is dealt with in a letter of Lavagne, as Pétain's official for religious affairs, to Suhard, Vichy, 26 June 1941, and in an *aide-mémoire* prepared for Brinon by another official, M. Canisy.

73. AN F17.13346.

74. Quoted in Michel, *La JEC*, p. 191.

75. Guerry, *L'Eglise catholique*, p. 178.
76. AN F17.13346; see also G. Cholvy and Y.-M. Hilaire, *Histoire religieuse de la France contemporaine, 1930–1988*, 1988, p. 89.
77. AN F17.13346. Note to Bonnard, Education minister, by Abbé Courtois, Secretary-General of the Union des Œuvres catholiques and head chaplain of the Cœurs Vaillants, dated 8 May 1943,
78. AN F17.13346. Note to Bonnard by Emile Moreau, 8 May 1943.
79. Cardinal Suhard, *Vers une Eglise en état de mission*, 1968, p. 103.
80. The version of events given here is largely taken from AN F1a. 3784. Note received in London 20 December 1943, ref: XCG/1/35/701. The extract from Oberg's letter is quoted in French.
81. AN 2 AG 493. Secrétaire Général du Chef de l'Etat, Vichy, 19 August 1943, to Brinon, Paris. Suhard, he wrote, was 'protesting vehemently' ('s'élève avec force') against German measures, which were taking on 'an air of veritable religious persecution' ('l'aspect d'une véritable persécution religieuse').
82. AN 2 AG 493. Letter from Mgr Chappoulie to Brinon, Paris, 5 August 1943
83. A Dio, Lille 2 B 1 ACA 1942–1945.
84. Ibid. 'Note sur les activities catholiques en France', 25 October 1943.
85. Y.-M. Hilaire, 'La Jeunesse dans l'Eglise', *Actes*:: Biviers, 1987, p. 277.

–18–

Christians and Deportation to Germany

Of all the burdens placed upon young Frenchmen the one that hit hardest was the obligation imposed upon them to work in Germany. The introduction of the Service du Travail Obligatoire (STO) was a direct result of the increasing need by 1942 to conscript more Germans into the Wehrmacht. Germans working in the war factories were required for army service on the eastern front. Nazi propaganda argued that, since Germany was fighting the 'Bolsheviks' to save European civilisation, the occupied countries should make sacrifices by working in the Reich and elsewhere, in relative safety, for the German war machine, whilst its soldiers bore the brunt of the fighting.

In June 1942 Sauckel, a former Gauleiter placed in charge of the recruitment of foreign labour, demanded 350,000 French workers, of whom 150,000 should be skilled. He agreed with Laval to release one prisoner of war for every three such workers recruited. This one-for-three deal constituted the so-called 'Relève', but only 17,000 skilled workers had volunteered. In August therefore Sauckel issued an ordinance, applicable throughout occupied Europe, decreeing liability to call-up of all men and women aged between eighteen and fifty-five. Laval obtained an exemption for France, which was granted on condition that Vichy took other steps to supply the necessary manpower. Hence the law of 4 September 1942, applicable to men aged between eighteen and fifty and single women aged between twenty-one and thirty-five, authorised the government to direct them to employment where, as, and when required. This direction of labour was only gradually enforced.

The final battle for Stalingrad was imminent, and Hitler was on the point of proclaiming total war when Sauckel arrived in Paris on 11 January 1943 with the now more limited objective of recruiting 250,000 men, but still demanding that 150,000 of them should be skilled workers. On 16 February the Vichy government instituted the STO, calling up for two years three groups of young men aged between twenty-one and twenty-two. Agricultural workers and students were at first exempt. This obligatory forced labour, it is estimated, was performed eventually by 625,000 to 700,000 young men, mainly in Germany, but also in strengthening the Atlantic coastal defences in France against an Allied invasion.

The law aroused an avalanche of protests. The Church was taken unawares: in the occupied zone the ACA had met in January, just before the passage of the law. It had then discussed the possibility of despatching chaplains to Germany to minister to volunteer French workers already there. With the introduction of the STO this was to become a high priority.[1] The members of the ACA located in the former unoccupied zone met on 5 and 6 February, still before the law was promulgated.[2] However, a statement by Cardinal Gerlier to be read in his churches on 21 February 'without comment' already spoke of family rights being under attack as 'the painful consequence of the war' and asked members of Action Catholique to support those called up and their families.[3]

The first Protestant reaction came on 27 February when the Consistory of Lyons met and sent a message to Pastor Boegner expressing 'reservations' about the law. The Protestant leader saw Laval on 11 March and registered formal disapproval. Further Catholic reaction came from the National Council of the ACJF, meeting at Avignon on 6 March. Although within some of its constituent movements there were divided views — some of the JEC, for example, criticised the unwillingness to compromise of leading lights such as Jean-Marie Domenach and André Mandouze — the general reaction was hostile. An episcopal reaction came on the following day from the archbishop of Besançon and his four provincial bishops. However, it dealt not with the principle of the law, but with the manner of its execution: those called up were being treated almost like criminals deported en masse. Some had not even been able to bid farewell to their families.[4] The censorship forbade publication of their statement. Nevertheless, on 14 March a letter from the ACA was read at mass announcing the dedication of France to the Virgin Mary but which also alluded obliquely to the STO, asserting that people had rights as well as duties, rights that no temporal power could undermine.[5]

It fell to Cardinal Liénart, from whose industrial diocese many workers would be requisitioned, to crystallise the thoughts of the Church on the subject. His first effort failed to impress. On March 15 he spoke to a large audience of young people at Roubaix. His theme was the problem of conscience related to obedience to the civil power. The collaborationist press and Vichy radio interpreted his remarks as an instruction to accept the STO. He had, claimed the *Grand Echo du Nord*, exploded[6] Allied propaganda seeking to persuade Christians that the Pope wished the Russians to win and had intentionally cited Joan of Arc in order to stir up anti-British sentiment. They could therefore no longer hesitate between 'the strange homilies of the astonishing Protestant Bishop [*sic*] of Canterbury and the voice of authority of their diocesan pastor' *Le Petit Parisien* (19 March) displayed the bold headline: 'Un appel du cardinal Liénart aux jeunes en faveur du service du travail obligatoire'. Even *La Croix* (20 March) was misled; the cardinal was quoted as saying: 'It is France that is suffering today. The duty of each one of us is therefore to assume our share of the burden that weighs her down'. Regarding the STO: 'Let us accept the task. It would be cowardly to evade it. We want no privilege. No one can escape the common burden'.

The cardinal expected neither accolades nor recriminations, but got both. He seemed to be saying to young Christians: 'If you are forced to go, do so in a spirit of sacrifice, sharing it with non-Christians and using the opportunity to convert them'. No doubt the bulk of his audience consisted of the bourgeoisie, and not the young workers immediately at risk. His advice for his seminarists was categoric: as future priests they should accept the STO and be prepared to leave for Germany.[7] Local Jocistes sought an audience with the cardinal. The sentiment in the factories, according to one of their leaders, Roger Bailleul, was that he was acting as the pro-German Cardinal Baudrillart might have done. Liénart realised that his meaning had been distorted and some clarification of his position was necessary.[8]

He therefore spoke again, on Sunday March 21, in the St Maurice church at Lille, before an audience of 6,000–7,000 young people, at the end of a 'journée de prières'. He shared their anguish, he declared, at the threat of leaving for Germany that hung over some of them. He posed the question: What, in the circumstances, should be a Christian's attitude? He regretted that what he had said elsewhere had been misinterpreted, even by many Christians. The Church, for instance, refused to be drawn into any 'war against bolshevism'. He did not accept anti-German propaganda that it was wrong to go and work in Germany, but neither did he accept anti-Bolshevik propaganda that it was right to do so in order to destroy bolshevism. Although bolshevism threatened Christian civilisation, the Russians could not be condemned for defending their homeland. Nor should young Christians hate the Germans, although they had imposed heavy burdens upon families and had no regard for human liberty. The Church should be neither resigned nor opportunist. There followed the nub of the Cardinal's message:

I do not say that it is a duty of conscience to accept compulsory labour service. No, because what is in question are demands that go beyond the limits of our just obligations. One can therefore evade it without sinning. Nor have I to advise you to leave. We are up against constraint, and so I say: if you are obliged to go, you will do so in a truly social and national spirit, adopting the attitude that I shall describe...

Personal interest should not come into the decision. The working class had already had to make sacrifices. Others should not shrink now from doing so, because 'if the one who is called upon to go fails to do so, he forces another to go in his place'. All Christians should accept the common burden, whether required to bear it in France or elsewhere. He had seen young Catholics who, having left for Germany, devoted themselves there to the service of their fellow-workers. This was a truly Christian attitude.

The substance of this message was repeated by the cardinal elsewhere in his diocese: on 22 March in the St Christopher's church at Tourcoing to about 5,000 young people; on March 24 to about 4,000, including many Jocistes, at Armentières; on the following day at Wattrelos to about 1,500. In addition his message appeared in tracts circulating in the area.[9]

The novelty of Cardinal Liénart's stance was two-fold. First, and by far the more important, for the first time the Church conceded openly to the individual what, in the final analysis, it had sometimes implicitly acknowledged: ultimately the human conscience must be the overriding arbiter of action, and not even ecclesial prescripts could prevail over this supremacy. Second, the traditional obedience of the Church to the civil power (although historically perhaps more honoured in the breach than in the observance) was obliquely questioned: the most loyal of all the bishops to Marshal Pétain had declared it was no sin to disobey a Vichy law. The repercussions of these innovatory principles were to be felt in France long after the Vichy regime had disappeared.

Nevertheless, a certain ambiguity remained. One cannot help feeling by reading the mere words, that, at this stage, the cardinal inclined more to compliance than rejection. Perhaps he was mindful of his audience and felt young Christians, particularly the better off, had less right than others to refuse. Otherwise, however, the balance was finely drawn. Both Russians and Germans, for example, were treated even-handedly, although it was undoubtedly a brave act to stigmatise the Nazis so openly.

As a result of Liénart's attempts at clarification, government attention focused on the Church's reaction. One police document that came into the hands of Ménétrel, Pétain's private secretary, was positively alarmist.

It noted that Gerlier had already used the word 'deportations', that the bishops in eastern France were also up in arms, and concluded that if further severe demands were made, 'the Church [...] will not hesitate to free the faithful from their obligations to the State'.[10]

However, it did not come to that. On 6 and 7 April, for the first time since the occupation, the ACA met as a plenary body. It adopted Cardinal Liénart's line, although Mgr Suhard and Mgr Chappoulie were opposed to making their view public.[11] The statement issued under the authority of the three cardinals caused another stir in government circles.[12] It was reckoned that, although the general public would take it as approving the STO, 'those more in the know' ('les personnes plus averties') — the government, the Germans and 'dissidents' — would be alert to certain phrases that were hostile. It appeared that Pétain had approved the text, which was originally to be read on Easter Sunday (25 April) at pontifical high mass and precribed that 'the bishops, wearing the mitre and crozier in hand, will mount the pulpit solemnly to read their declaration'. Laval's first reaction, 'in a moment of abandonment and resignation'('dans un moment d'abandon et de résignation'), had been not to oppose the demonstration. Jardel, of Pétain's entourage, had signified to the cardinals the government's acceptance of the statement, although it insisted that an allusion to the possible deportation of women be removed, and that the occasion should not be marked by undue solemnity; parish priests should be asked to read the declaration on Low Sunday (1 May),[13] when congregations would be small. In the event the reading of the statement was delayed, and general publication of the statement, given to the press on 9 May, was forbidden. Nevertheless copies of it were widely circulated. It was read finally on 9 May, the feast-day of Joan of Arc, in some churches and cathedrals. In Notre Dame it was read by Cardinal Suhard himself. Elsewhere its content was still unknown. On Sunday, 16 May many parish priests were awoken early by gendarmes and informed that, on Laval's orders, they were neither to read it from the pulpit nor comment on its content. They had to sign a statement acknowledging they had taken note of this prohibition. Some disobeyed, others informed their congregation and promised to read it later.[14]

The message, however, was more innocuous than that of Cardinal Liénart. It acknowledged the prerogatives of the civil power, although asserting that the Church had a right to consider the religious and moral viewpoint. It shared the distress of families and the sometimes inhumane way in which departures (it did not use the word 'deportations') had been effected. It deplored the fact that as yet permission had not been given for French chaplains to minister in Germany. Compliance with the order to leave was not an obligation of conscience. The STO was one more suffering imposed upon their country, but those who accepted it would be preparing for the 'resurrection' of France.[15] The tone was one of resignation in the face of stark reality.

Theologically, however, the statement was attacked by 'théologiens sans mandat' whose writings were circulating clandestinely more freely than ever before: no mention was made, they declared, of the injustice of the law that imposed this new hardship. *Témoignage Chrétien* (no. XVII. Déportation, July 1943, pp. 9–11, pp. 19–21) put the arguments for and against compliance with the STO. Was there a political argument for acceptance? Was the so-called struggle against bolshevism based on irrational fear or realisation of a danger? Was the patriotic argument valid? Was loyalty to Pétain and to one's country at stake, or did it signify mere passive conformity? What was the social argument? Should the bourgeoisie accept out of a sense of solidarity with the working class, or would this be merely overweening paternalism? In any case the kind of solidarity the workers hoped for was a refusal to leave for Germany. Spiritually, much play had been made of the apostolate mission — 'Nous referons chrétiens nos frères'. That mission could not be carried out. In any case did such a desire to proselytise spring from a genuine generosity of spirit or was it mere pharisaism? For those who argued, out of despair and from a practical viewpoint, for acceptance, was this to have a sense of realism or mere submission to the law of numbers?[16] The declarations of the Belgian and Dutch bishops, whose flocks were subject to the same constraint, were quoted. The Dutch bishops, in a message to the authorities (17 February 1943), had characterised the arrest and deportation of young men as resembling hunting after slaves. The Belgian bishops (21 March 1943) had condemned from the pulpit such iniquitous measures that went against the Christian conscience, and had even threatened with excommunication those that complied voluntarily with the German demands. Moreover, such demands broke international law. The state of war between France and Germany still existed, and therefore the government had no right to compel young people to collaborate with the enemy. The more popular publication to *Témoignage Chrétien,* its *Courrier Français* (no. 1, vol. 2, May 1943, Lyons), concluded that young men should refuse to accept this 'unjust deportation' or leave only under compulsion. The Christian's duty was to help those who refused, as well as their families. In a subsequent issue (no. 3, vol 2, September 1943, Lyons) it condemned those bishops who saw acceptance of the STO as an obligation. It asserted that there was no duty to follow a leader who had erred, and added, significantly, that even a sworn oath of loyalty was also subject to the imperative of conscience.

Without waiting for any formal declaration by the ACA, Archbishop Saliège, addressing a group of Toulouse Scouts about to leave for Germany, made plain his views:

> You are leaving for Germany. Is it under constraint, or is it voluntarily? I do not have to know. One can submit to a law without giving it inner compliance... However humiliated France is at the present time, go on proudly hoping. Our cause was just, you can never be told this enough [...] the German people thinks itself the chosen people, the race of the elect that has a mission, because of its blood, the mission to rule the world. To that mission everything is sacrificed: individual and family. Whoever cannot serve that mission must disappear. He is worthless... Faced with this collective arrogance, you will represent the French conception of life, the human conception, in which the person counts, in which peoples have rights, in which men are brothers.[17]

A close watch was kept on Saliège. A police report[18] alluding to the archbishop's poor physical state claimed that some Catholics who favoured the STO thought he was not fully *compos mentis*. But it also noted with a slight satisfaction that in a message read at a recent prayer vigil he had first intended to use the term 'deportations', but had subsequently modified it.

Nevertheless the archbishop continued to make his views forcibly known. On 18 April he spoke of the 'constraint' and 'forced labour' of young men in Germany. Mgr Théas (Montauban), later delivered a sermon in similarly vigorous terms.

As we have seen, one Protestant group had registered its protest early on. On 11 March Pastor Boegner lodged an official complaint with Laval at the severity of the law; he promised to tone it down. The Conseil de la Fédération Protestante authorised Boegner to make a concerted approach with Cardinal Suhard. This Suhard refused to do. On 14 April came a considered response from the Conseil, to be read in Protestant churches from the pulpit. Although it did not take its stand upon freedom of conscience, its purport was plain: There is an irreconcilable clash between the Gospel whose repository is the Church and any conception of mankind or society that tends to envisage work as a good that one is justified in buying or requisitioning at will, without taking into consideration the person of the worker, his conscience, or his most sacred feelings.[19]

Pastor Boegner had already informed Pétain of the distress the measures had caused. Protestants were worried about those who had already left for Germany, not least because their churches were not allowed to send pastors to minister to them.

Although young Protestants were probably not so affected by the call-up as others, their refusal to accept the STO was widespread, and caused many to join the Maquis. The Union Chrétienne des jeunes Gens protested against 'the character of deportation and veritable slavery of the STO'.[20] On the other hand, one or two pastors urged compliance. Pastor Noel Vesper, the right-wing monarchist, writing in *Action Française* (12 June 1943), accused the Union of countering government decisions. Pastor Lengereau, in Toulouse, even threatened to excommunicate any young Protestant 'réfractaires': 'No Protestant can opt out from the harsh Christian duty of the "Relève" if he wishes to be and remain a Christian'.[21]

Cardinal Gerlier came as near as he dared to disavowing the STO law. On 14 March, at the Fourvière scholasticate (Lyons), he spoke of a violation of the rights of man. On 2 April, just before the ACA Declaration, he sent a message to some 5,000 relatives of those already deported to Germany and of prisoners of war assembled in the churches of his diocese. He referred to the 'harsh requisitioning' of workers as an 'assault on natural law and the rights of the human person'.[22] Cardinal Suhard, having refused to join Pastor Boegner in making a protest to Vichy, mildly pointed out to Pétain the moral danger that the deportees ran, and renewed the Church's demand for chaplains to be sent.[23]

Among the bishops one early advocate of compliance was Mgr Dutoit (Arras). His emphasis was on what he saw as a double duty: obedience to orders and not rejecting the sacrifice demanded of the nation.[24]

Nevertheless, a certain ambiguity characterised the Church's position, at least until the formal declaration by the ACA, as can be deduced from the differing attitudes adopted by other bishops. Mgr Martin (Le Puy), for example, blew hot and cold. Before the ACA's declaration, at the St Joseph Basilica in Clermont-Ferrand on March 28, accompanied by Abbé Laporte, who had just been repatriated from Germany, he referred three times to the 'deportation' of young men, and asserted that all the bishops disapproved. Radio-Révolution, a collaborationist enterprise, reporting his sermon, commented, 'Il est bien connu que Mgr Martin est gaulliste.'[25] By June, however, the bishop had changed his mind: 'The finest Christian attitude is not to grumble or to escape from [the STO] but to attempt to overcome the ordeal, to gain as much benefit from it as possible, to share the fate of one's brethren and in the end to make the cross we bear an instrument of sanctification, of an apostolate, and of redemption'.[26]

At the same time he attacked the 'anonymous theologians' who were giving contrary advice: the bishops were more qualified in theology than they were, and had been chosen by God to teach the true doctrine.

Mgr Caillot (Grenoble) urged acceptance of the STO in almost similar terms. On 15 March the first train of labour conscripts left Grenoble for Germany. On 21 March he asserted that this was necessary on patriotic and Christian grounds. On the other hand, his Vicar-General, Père Henri Groués, published a tract under the *nom de plume* of 'Abbé Pierre' in which he condemned the 'chasse aux esclaves', and in the secret of the confessional it transpired that he had urged young men to disobey the call-up.[27] On 1 August, in an address at La Salette Mgr Caillot again urged compliance and joined the attack on the anonymous theologians. One of his flock, signing himself 'un catholique de Saint-Bruno', circulated a tract saying this was no way for the Church to behave: the Pope had never counselled submission to forced labour.[28] Although the ageing prelate had proudly announced that thirty of his seminarists were ready to leave, in the event only two reached Germany.

Mgr Piguet (Clermont-Ferrand) followed a similar tack: preaching in his cathedral on 27 July, he made compliance an act of loyalty to Pétain. Already on 3 July, he had asserted that any dissent was equivalent to promoting disorder and anarchy.[29] It was deplorable that young Frenchmen listened more to foreign bishops than to their own, and accepted the arguments of 'theologians' not competent to advise them. But he did mention that constraint did not impose any duty upon a Christian conscience and regretted that the laws of war no longer applied.[30] Likewise Mgr Auvity (Mende) advocated acceptance: 'Your interest and wisdom require you to go; [this is based] on the facts and good sense'.[31]

A few bishops spoke in a mood of resignation. Mgr Pic (Valence) asserted that the 'fresh misfortunes' the country was suffering were a 'painful consequence of the war and defeat'.[32] He nonetheless threw open the monastery of Aiguebelle as a refuge for 'réfractaires'. Some prelates, however, took a more aggressive line. Mgr Théas (Montauban) castigated the STO as an attack on natural law (8 March). From Bayonne Mgr Vansteenberghe's use of the word 'deportations' provoked a protest to Laval by Schleier, of the German embassy in March.[33] Mgr Rémond (Nice) was even more forthright. Speaking on 28 March in his cathedral, during a ceremony of dedication to the Virgin Mary, he declared: 'Although unwell, I owed it to myself to preside over this ceremony and mount the pulpit to protest against the deportation to Germany of our young men, snatched away from their work, their family, and their country. *Such exactions are called crimes'*.[34]

It is difficult to form an overall view of what the bishops advised. By 1943 seventy-eight diocesan bulletins were still being published, but only nineteen gave the clear-cut views of the local bishop on the STO. Five of these advocated complete acceptance; most contented themselves with quoting the pastoral instructions of the Chaplaincy-General for prisoners of war and French workers abroad.[35]

Laval, fearing for his collaborationist policy, and alarmed at German protests at the Church's stance, quickly abandoned his former resigned attitude. In May 1943 a German Embassy warning prompted him to inform Mgr Chappoulie that the State would brook no interference in its policy. At a meeting of the Conseil des Ministres on 15 May Cathala, the Finance minister, proposed the Church be punished; it was, he claimed, being led astray by Cardinal Gerlier and the Nuncio; subsidies to Catholic schools should be blocked.[36] The Germans were furious at the Church's reaction to the law, which belied their assertion that its activity was confined only to the religious sphere.[37]

The head of the SS in France, Oberg, bitterly asserted that 'the majority' of bishops were against the STO and 'a large number' had done all they could to prevent departures. Such a stance was incomprehensible when through working in Germany young men would be helping 'the essential struggle for the very existence of the Catholic Church that Germany and its allies were carrying out against bolshevism'.

Meanwhile, what was the Vatican's view? On the general question of any workers at all being forced to leave for Germany, the Nuncio had allegedly seen Pétain and reminded him that in 1914–18 the then Pope had categorically condemned forced labour by French and Belgians deported from the German-occupied areas.[38] In March the rumour circulated that Valerio Valeri was to make further representations to Pétain, and since the Marshal had not personally signed the STO law, this fact should be made widely known.[39] Later in the year *Témoignage Chrétien* quoted an earlier broadcast by Radio Vatican, made on 19 February: 'The Church does not accept regimes based on forced labour or on the uprooting of populations'.[40] It would appear that the statement referred to slavery by the Romans, but the allusion was plain.[41] Radio Vatican also broadcast on 26 April the full text of Liénart's speech at Roubaix, after collaborationists had distorted it to favour the STO.[42]

Following the line of Laval and the Germans, the collaborationist press waxed indignant at the Church. Armand Petitjean, a former member of the Compagnons de France and onetime candidate for its leadership, accused the Hierarchy of 'sliding towards Christian democracy'.[43] *Le Petit Parisien* (19 March 1943) and *Paris-Soir* (20 March 1943) gave biased extracts from Liénart's address at Roubaix, interpreting it as advocating acceptance. *Au Pilori* (27 May 1943) reported that on 21 April Liénart had received an accolade ('un bouquet') from Radio Moscow for his advice, which had interpreted it as rejecting the STO law. Under the headline 'The Anti-National Cardinal' the collaborationist newspaper alleged that he had always been for the PDP, was anti-national, had protected high-ranking Freemasons, and had ridiculed fellow ecclesiastics such as Cardinal Baudrillart — in short he was sabotaging a French revival, and was a 1000 [*sic*] per cent Anglophile.[44] Georges Suarez, writing in *Aujourd'hui* (19 May 1943), chose Cardinal Suhard as his target, characterising him as one of the upper clergy who had become instruments of Stalinist and Gaullist propaganda. They showed a decided taste for conspiracy. Under Léon Blum no archbishop would have dared to get up in the pulpit and say a quarter of what was being said. He finished with a veiled threat: 'Fear is a good counsellor.'

Déat, in *L'Œuvre*, was in his element. He noted with satisfaction (28 April 1943) that the call-up also applied to seminarists and religious. On 13 May 1943 he linked the STO to a recent meeting between Laval and Hitler. Henceforth the die was cast: it was either acceptance or dissidence. He criticised Liénart's speech in Lille as a specious attempt at impartiality. But 'what was not a sin for the Cardinal's casuistry is desertion in the eyes of the law and this offence will be punished as such'. When the sons of workers left for Germany the upper clergy kept quiet, but, he asked ironically, 'How could they tolerate that the offspring of the bourgeoisie should in their turn be invited to perform their European [compulsory labour] service?'[45] There was some force in this argument, although not only loyal Catholics but bourgeois collaborationists were alarmed when their own sons were called up.[46] More heavyweight publications also added grist to the mill. *Je Suis Partout* declared that the rot had set in with Cardinal Verdier before the war. Now, the lower clergy, controlling the services set up to assist the 'requis' — an allusion to the welfare organisations — had stuffed their heads full of British, Communist and Gaullist nonsense.[47] In another article it characterised Liénart's address in Lille as inspired by the British Intelligence Service and the OGPU! The STO was none of the Church's business. Its intervention jeopardised the subsidies to Catholic schools. With a final flourish it wrote: 'After generals and admirals [Giraud and Darlan], now it is the cardinals who are turning traitor'.[48]

Among Catholic periodicals a few openly favoured acceptance of the STO. This was the case of the collaborationist-tainted *Voix Françaises* and *La Croix du Rhône*, as well as the Lyons publication *L'Echo de Fourvière*. By far the most influential journal, however, was *La Croix*, which, having now revised its initial view, let its opposition be known in subtle ways. Among the secular press, the director of *La République du Sud-Ouest*, Irénée Brochier, was so impressed by Liénart's message that he [*sic*] sent a copy to all of his 350 correspondents in five departments. Vichy enquired into his motive, but he replied he was merely doing his duty.[49]

The Resistance within France could not publicise its views on the STO so easily. On the other hand, those who evaded service, the 'réfractaires', comprised its largest pool of recruitment. The clandestine *La Voix du Nord et du Pas de Calais* had already alleged that on 29 November 1942, a day the Church dedicated to remembering the prisoners of war, Cardinal Liénart, speaking in his cathedral, had declared that the prisoners were not only in camps in Germany, but that France itself was a prison camp, guarded on all its frontiers.[50] The Resistance now interpreted his message on the STO as countering enemy propaganda aiming to get the Church to accept the deportations.[51]

Most of the rank and file clergy, as was predictable, were hostile to the STO.[52] Some priests even saw it as a challenge to open warfare for the Church. At Lons-le-Saunier one preacher, speaking against forced labour, declared, 'Les Français ne sont plus seulement vaincus, mais asservis'.[53] Many connived in hiding those affected by the call-up. However, some who held semi-official positions refused to take sides. Thus Père Desbuquois, the Director of Action Populaire, whilst conceding that youth had a free choice, out of loyalty did not oppose Vichy policy.[54]

How, in fact, did young Catholics react? The National Student Council, which included the religious student movements, met in Lyons on 15 April. Among the Christian representatives present were Lecerf, Secretary-General of the Fédération Française d'Etudiants catholiques, Cazalis, President of the (Protestant) Fédération française des Associations chrétiennes d'Etudiants, Gautier, Secretary-General of the JEC, and a representative of the Rover Scouts. Pierre Brunereau, the government delegate in charge of university propaganda, attended and submitted a report on the meeting to Creyssel, with a copy to Bonnard, the Education minister. He did not mince his words: the report, perhaps with a certain relish, spoke of the revulsion Catholic and Protestant students felt at the STO law. They considered it a cowardly measure tantamount almost to treason. Why do the Germans' dirty work and organise 'deportation'? Christian leaders would instruct their members to obey their conscience. They refused to co-operate in work training courses organised before they left for Germany, and particularly in so-called 'political training': technically-trained personnel would simply save the Germans a job; 'political training' was superfluous: as Christians and Frenchmen they already knew how to comport themselves. Laval's arguments were unacceptable because he was 'lending himself to German manipulation and... delivering over his country to the enemy' Brunereau concluded, correctly, that many would end up in the Resistance.

He added that Christian student leaders had informed him in no uncertain terms that France had been right to wage war in 1939. It would be more honourable for it now to be in the state in which Belgium or Poland found themselves. As for national renewal, they considered 'there can be no question of a French revival before the crushing of Nazi Germany, and all our efforts must be directed towards its defeat'.[55]

Students initially had been exempt from the STO law for one year. Perhaps as a result of this violent reaction, in July 1943 Bonnard sent out a circular to universities extending postponement of their call-up further, and allowing ex- students to be requisitioned for work only in France. Meanwhile open opposition to the law continued. On 9 March, at Romans (Drôme), on the occasion of departures for Germany, demonstrators, including many members of the JOC and JAC, had protested. The Internationale had even been sung. The train was delayed, but left the following morning only after fifteen young men, mostly Catholics, had been arrested.[56] Hostile tracts were circulating. One, signed 'Un groupe de jeunes étudiants chrétiens', urged Lyons Christian students to refuse to leave. The argument that they should do so out of solidarity with young workers lacked force, because the latter also refused. Christian students had to lead, and not to follow: 'The moment has come to accomplish a political action which is firstly for us an act of unconquerable hope'. Refusal was imperative.[57]

But these were isolated outbursts. On March 6 the Conseil Fédéral of the ACJF met at Avignon and formally decided to oppose the STO. In June its secretariat sent out a 'note d'information' comprising four statements: Liénart's address at Lille on 23 March; the cardinals' letter of 9 May; the Dutch bishops' letter of 17 February; and the Belgian bishops' letter of 15 March. Also included were a statement of principle and a reasoned criticism of arguments urging compliance:

> Before altruism, the apostolate, social and national solidarity, there is justice: where lies the good, where the evil? Where are what is just and what is unjust? It is only after having resolved this question — and if we in conscience esteem ourselves to be free to choose between several solutions — that we can, for example, ask ourselves: 'Where does it appear to me that my apostolate will be most fruitful?' For a question of conscience must not be resolved by questions of supernatural usefulness.[58]

Various arguments therefore followed. The argument that young working-class men should not go to Germany alone was invalid. They had done everything, including striking, in order not to go; and they expected others to do likewise. To the reasoning that says if you do not go, another one will have to take your place one should respond by refusing, and helping one's neighbour also to refuse. 'Apostles' might be needed in Germany, but some were there already and others would doubtless follow. Those who counselled compliance were unaware of the dangers for those who agreed to leave: 'They leave as conquerors, will they not return as renegades?' ('Ils partent en conquérants, ne reviendront-ils pas en rénégats?'). The argument that a German defeat would mean the installation of bolshevism and the ruin of European civilisation had not cut much ice with Cardinal Liénart, nor indeed with the Belgian bishops. The conclusion was clear: Christians must refuse the STO. The position was neatly summarised in *Cahiers de notre Jeunesse*: We shall not be resigned, and if we are not allowed to do more, we can at least have the courage to say *NO*.[59] Within Christian youth organisations the debate sometimes became heated. The Rover Scouts, perhaps more 'Vichyssois' than the rest, urged compliance, 'faced with the inevitable... Such will be the service you render, one for which you have neither chosen the place nor the conditions'.[60] This had initially been the stance taken by the Catholic students' federation before the national meeting at Avignon. On 10 March Etudiants had published a communiqué from its leadership: 'It is not a matter of hiding away, but one of bearing witness' ('Il ne s'agit pas de se planquer, il s'agit de témoigner').

Heart-searching was particularly strong in the JAC, JEC, and JOC. For JAC members working on the land, particularly in mountainous areas, escape to a nearby Maquis group was easy. Elsewhere agricultural workers also quickly found refuge. The clandestine Communist leaflet, 'La Terre', in October 1943, allegedly quoting prefectoral sources, claimed that in rural Finistère and Côtes du Nord over 90 percent had evaded the call-up.[61] The JEC, recruiting in the upper classes of schools as well as in higher education, found itself in some difficulty. It published the proceedings of the Avignon meeting of the Conseil National of the ACJF in its periodical *Messages* (June 1943), defying the censorship, which earned the periodical an immediate ban. It seems, however, that the Jécistes were divided as to whether to accept the STO, but some, particularly in the northern zone, were perhaps inclined more to refusal.[62] The JOC was likewise divided, although, being an organisation of young workers, it felt more need for solidarity with its non-Christian fellows. In northern France the number of 'réfractaires' grew as the months passed. Local JOC chaplains often spoke out. One, for example, preaching in Rheims on Good Friday, dwelt on the fate of STO Jocistes, linking it to the 'Calvary' from which France seemed unable to free itself.[63] Once in Germany, moreover, the Jocistes were to prove a perpetual thorn in the Nazi side. All three movements — JAC, JEC and JOC — from which were drawn the bulk of some 10,000 practising and militant Catholics (3,000 of the total were seminarists), out of the

700,000 French workers who eventually found themselves in Germany, reacted by mounting massive support for their deported members. But doubtless many young Catholics were also numbered among the half million 'réfractaires'.[64]

Vichy viewed these developments with mounting unease. In its publications the Church continued occasionally to speak of young men 'deported' to Germany — the term was employed in at least one pastoral letter. The authorities felt there was a real danger that if still more stringent demands were made, or if the policy of collaboration was extended to military matters, 'The Church will not hesitate to release the Faithful from their obligations to the State.'[65] In the event, things never came to this pass, as Mgr Chappoulie attested in a letter to Bérard, the French Ambassador to the Vatican. Bérard had reported rumours on the 'Gaullist radio' (London) of the bishops' dissatisfaction and the various divergent opinions among Catholics. Chappoulie, writing with Suhard's approval, made light of it: all the bishops maintained their 'most respectful and affectionate attachment' to Pétain, and remained loyal to the government (that is, Laval). They had no desire to intervene in temporal matters. They rejected the views of clandestine 'theologians' as expressed in tracts circulating surreptitiously, such as 'Consultations sur quelques cas de conscience posés aux catholiques'. But the STO measures had forced them to speak out, when confronted by 'the deep emotion that is shattering almost the whole of the French masses'. In their April statement they had alluded to the legitimate authority of the government. He (Chappoulie) had been requested by Suhard to inform Bérard that the declaration 'in no way constituted a declaration of war, neither against the government nor the occupation authorities'. But the Hierarchy persisted in protesting against abuses that had come to light; these were due in part to the Todt Organisation, responsible for building the so-called 'Atlantic Wall' as a defence against an Allied invasion, as well as to the refusal to allow French chaplains to minister to the workers in Germany. It was true that the STO was not an obligation of conscience but 'this reservation did not mean that the French episcopacy had the intention to incite workers to disobedience — far from it... This eventuality is not even envisaged'.[66]

There, for the moment, the matter rested. After their meeting in October 1943 the ACA deemed it necessary to disavow yet again tracts circulated by the clandestine theologians 'whose conclusions are usually opposed to the authority and the legitimacy of the regime' ('dont d'ordinaire les conclusions sont opposées à l'autorité et à la légitimité du régime'). The authorities, however, remained nervous. They attempted to ensure that a day of prayers for 'the absent' (in Germany) on 17 October, particularly for the STO conscripts, should not provoke an 'apitoiement démesuré'. A letter from the three cardinals announcing the occasion was not allowed to be made generally known. But at least one parish priest, in Carmaux, announced previously that prayers would be said for all those away from home, including those in prison or concentration camps.[67] Much was now being spread by word of mouth.

How did young Catholics fare in Germany? The most influential group were the Jocistes. They established some 1,000 cells — their use of Communist terminology is significant — in 400 German towns, grouped in seventy federations.[68] Before any chaplains arrived JOC had dispatched to Germany their own clandestine lay missionaries in the guise of workers. But JOC had also a political aim.

The Vichy organisation in Germany, the Délégation générale des Travailleurs français en Allemagne, established in Berlin since March 1942, worked with the Deutsche Arbeitsfront (DAF), the monolithic Nazi labour movement that had supplanted the German trade unions. The head of the French Delegation was Bruneton; many of his subordinates had been appointed by Bonnard, the Education minister, and were as anticlerical as their minister. Key posts were in fact occupied by members of the collaborationist PPF, Bucard's Francistes and the Jeunes du Maréchal, a movement supporting Pétain but later banned by the Marshal himself for its Nazi tendencies. JOC's objective was to oust these collaborationists and replace them with its own nominees. This policy was to be carried out down to factory level, and to include the so-called 'Vertrauensmänner' ('shop stewards') the Germans used as their contacts.

It is not known how far the ban on JOC activity in Germany was enforced. The movement was closely watched. A worker-priest, Père de Porcaro, wrote from Leipzig on 23 October 1943: 'The [French] youth delegate from Berlin has here, in the presence of the delegates of the camps, banned the JOC, which is, he says, an antisocial movement! And our regional delegate has announced that he would break up all existing movements (the JOC being particularly the target). But "non possumus non loqui".'[69]

For its part the DAF, in a circular on 15 December 1943 to all the (German) camp commandants ('Lagerführer'), warned them against the Jocistes, who were accused of dabbling in politics and having frequent contacts with the German clergy.[70] On the very same day the JOC regional delegate in Würzburg launched a survey in the local camps with the aim of 'a possible extension of the role of JOC', including the establishment of a chaplaincy for French workers.[71]

The JOC continued its active apostolate role as well as seeking to make itself useful in as many ways as possible, organising leisure activities, mutual self-help groups, etc., and even creating escape routes for French prisoners of war and others. The Germans, aware of the hostile attitude of the organisation, reflected this in their repressive measures against it in France.

In France priests received adverse reports of what was happening to their former young parishioners. One, Père Jean Godbert, wrote to Commandant Féat, of Pétain's staff, citing extracts from letters he had received: 'We have to put in a great effort without much in our stomach' ('Il faut fournir un grand rendement avec pas grand chose dans l'estomac'); 'For grub, it's the same old story: spuds and sauerkraut' ('La bectance, c'est le même refrain: patates choucroûte'); 'At the moment, I am hunting lice' ('Pour le moment je fais la chasse aux punaises'). They did, however, go to a church where the priest spoke a little French.[72] According to *Témoignage Chrétien*, their religious and moral condition remained pitiable. Sunday was a working day. Although theoretically at liberty, in reality their plight was worse than that of prisoners of war.[73]

Vichy naturally tried to put the best gloss on conditions. Press instructions were issued on 19 May 1943 ordering newspapers to display prominently the news that the first mass had been said in Germany for French workers. Under the heading, 'Abbé Rodhain, Aumônier Général des prisonniers', they were instructed to report that Rodhain had 'invited the faithful to practise the principles of Christian fraternity towards their German and European comrades'.[74] But a German ordinance still forbade any French priest as such entry to Germany. Cardinal Suhard continued also to be badgered about the anti-German stance of the JOC.

Suhard remained concerned at the lack of chaplains to minister to the STO workers. Already in January 1942 he had requested in vain that French chaplains should be allowed into Germany. Nothing daunted, he drew up a new plan under which twenty clergy who were prisoners of war would function as chaplains, under his control and subject to Abbé Rodhain, as Chaplain-General to French prisoners. The project was submitted to the Germans and to Bichelonne, the Production minister.[75] The service would include those STO working for the Organisation Todt on coastal defences, who worked a twelve-hour day, including Sundays, and were often isolated. The Germans rejected the project outright. Suhard nevertheless persisted and eventually the ACA decided to act on its own initiative. Abbé Rodhain was secretly informed that Père Hadrien Bousquet, a priest from Rodez, had volunteered to go as a worker and exercise his ministry clandestinely. On New Year's Day 1943 he received Suhard's blessing and on 15 January arrived in Berlin. The cardinal, ever a stickler for correctness, was concerned about the priest's status under canon law. He consulted Père Le Blond, a professor at the Gregorian University in Rome, who had just been repatriated after two years' captivity, as to the position under canon law. Le Blond advised that ecclesiastical status required a cleric not to exercise any other inappropriate occupation, but manual work, as already being freely undertaken by the religious orders, did not fall in this category. Even payment for work done did not infringe Church law. Armed with this ruling, Suhard had a wider proposal for clandestine priests endorsed by the ACA.[76]

In February the cardinal wrote to Laval asking him to intervene with the Germans, pointing out that Frenchmen working in 1,300 factories in Germany were asking for a chaplain. The danger was surely that the Communists would spread their own propaganda. Either POW priests or others sent specially from France should be allowed to function.[77] Laval passed on the request to the German Embassy, where it was not unfavourably received, although it did stipulate that any clerics sent should be politically reliable. Ribbentrop and Sauckel adopted the same position, in the hope that such a concession would encourage more workers to go to Germany. Meanwhile, receiving no definite reply, Suhard went ahead with the commissioning of more clandestine worker-priests. On 2–3 March he gathered together a score of volunteers and outlined their task. Theirs was 'a mission of salvation'; they represented the Church; they also had to ensure respect for France and safeguard Catholic Action.[78] In all twenty-two more priests finally left for Germany. (Of the total, eight eluded being ferreted out by the Gestapo; fourteen were arrested, and of these six were expelled to France, six were sent to Dachau, where two, including Père Dillard, died, and one to Belsen, who also died; the fate of the last one is unknown.)

The declaration of the cardinals on 9 May, taken by the Germans as a condemnation of the STO, blighted all hopes of sending chaplains officially. The SS, upheld by Martin Bormann, by now aware that worker-priests were being infiltrated as well, and perturbed at the activities of the Jocistes already in Germany, put its foot down.

Nevertheless Suhard continued to press for the establishment legally of chaplains. On 24 June he appealed to Pétain: young men in Germany, he argued, were being exposed to all kinds of physical and moral dangers; government intervention was necessary, so that their spiritual welfare, particularly that of seminarists, could be protected.[79] The Marshal was sufficiently impressed to ask Laval to approach the Germans again, to whom he pointed out that there was increasing immorality in the camps and factories, and venereal disease was rife. Families were justifiably worried. Such conditions favoured recruitment to the Resistance. Permission should be sought to appoint 'supervisors' ('moniteurs') to oversee conditions, to allow doctors to be sent, and priests already on the spot to exercise their ministry.[80] But when the

ACA met on 20 and 21 October Rodhain could report no progress.[81] On 25 November Bruneton reported from Germany that permission to appoint chaplains had been definitively refused.[82] Rodhain put the number of French workers (including ex-POWs) in Germany at 350,000 in January 1943, but at one million by the end of the year. This is perhaps an over-estimate, but the sheer number of young Frenchmen in their country, not readily controllable, and backed by leaders sent by the French Church may have prompted the German refusal, as well as other reasons.

The overall situation exasperated some bishops. Even Mgr du Parc, Bishop of Quimper, not noted for his liberal views, now upheld the right of young Catholics to obey their conscience. The very Catholic Commandant Féat, of Pétain's staff, wrote to him indignantly regarding his nephew, a seminarist at Quimper, who had evaded call-up on grounds of conscience. Féat alleged that the bishop, through the Superior of the seminary, Père Louvière, who was also Vicar-General for the diocese, had advised that this was a proper course to adopt. He reproached the bishop for proffering such anticivic advice. Louvière, on the bishop's behalf, sent a vitriolic reply. Féat's nephew bore sole responsibility for the decision. Féat's letter '[would] remain a document illustrating the meddling of the navy in every field'. For him, the Commandant was obviously trying to ' get a foot in' ('une mise à pied') regarding matters that were not his business.[83] To forestall Féat, at the same time the Vicar-General wrote to Pétain reaffirming that whether young Catholics should accept or refuse the STO was a matter for them and their parents; Féat's nephew had acted with the bishop's formal approval.[84] Clearly Catholic attitudes were evolving rapidly.

The liability of the clergy and seminarists to the call-up was a thorny question. Whether particular priests should be subject to the STO was, like that of civil servants and teachers in Catholic schools, a matter for a governmental decision.[85] One clandestine worker-priest described how at Dijon, on the point of departure for Germany, one young man had harangued his comrades: 'Where are the priests among you? There aren't any. You are deported. Them? They've found a bolt-hole'.[86] He himself had acted off his own bat and was unaware that other worker-priests had already preceded him. He had the approval of his bishop, Mgr Delay (Marseilles), who had granted him a 'celebret' (permission to celebrate mass anywhere). Moreover, he had ascertained that Cardinal Faulhaber of Munich was aware of and tolerated the presence of clandestine priests.[87] By February 1944 Vichy's position was clarified. All priests and seminarists previously exempt could now be called up.[88] However, on 21 February 1944 the effect of this was largely nullified when Himmler signed a decree expelling all seminarists and members of religious orders.

This was the signal for the Gestapo to round up as many clandestine priests as possible. Some had been already sent packing. Thus Père Perrin, who had left to work as a turner in June 1943, had been caught three months later, spent five months in prison and was finally expelled in April 1944.[89]

It would seem that several hundred priests eventually functioned illegally in Germany, although not all at the one time. These consisted not only of the first wave of those sent clandestinely, but also seminarists who had been hurriedly ordained before leaving for STO, a few who had left 'unofficially', former clerical POWs who had been freed on condition that they worked in German factories, and those deported for other reasons. One source puts the total at some 300 in all.[90] Abbé Rodhain, at Pétain's trial, spoke of 'hundreds' ministering to a 'Church of the catacombs'.[91] Fears had been expressed by the Mgr Auvity of Mende as to how they would sustain their religious faith in such circumstances, but Cardinal Suhard flatly rejected such misgivings.

The call-up of women and girls had been rumoured even in early 1943, but the Church had at first dismissed this as inconceivable. One case, however, put it on its guard. In February Liénart wrote to the General Commanding OFK 670 (the Lille area) protesting that some fifty women working in the two military hospitals of Calmette and Saint-André had been warned that they were to be moved to Germany. He spoke of the bad memories of the 1914–18 occupation that such a step would revive, when female workers had been forced to work away from home. If female workers had to leave measures should be taken to safeguard their moral situation. The general promptly replied that there was a misunderstanding. A score of female workers had been made redundant and sent off to the Werbestelle (the German Employment Office) for placing elsewhere. Of the twenty, only two had volunteered for work in Germany. He waxed indignant at the implication in the cardinal's letter: 'There is no reason to suppose that the dangers of a moral nature indicated by you are greater for those workers employed in the Reich than those in their own country, and particularly in the city of Lille'.[92]

It is perhaps no coincidence that in the same file appears the abortive intervention of Cardinal Liénart on 27 February 1943 in order to save the life of Abbé Bonpain, the curate of Rosendael found guilty of Resistance activities. From early 1943 onwards, particularly after the Church's protests against the STO, the Lille Feldkommandantur became increasingly hostile to Liénart. Liénart thought it prudent to raise the matter of female deportation with the regional Prefect, Carles. He stated that one girl, after a radiography examination, had been told that she was to work in Halle, and had been scared into signing a contract to do so.

Carles took up the case. It transpired the girl had agreed to go as a chambermaid, and her mother had thereupon volunteered to accompany her.[93] Bichelonne, the Production minister, later intervened to cancel the contract. Liénart also protested on principle to Laval, who replied on 27 February that he had taken steps 'for this measure not to be applied', but whether he referred to the particular case raised or to the principle is unclear. Catholic families were clearly alarmed. Hermant, head of Vichy's Bureau de Documentation in Lille, received a protest complaining that, if such an eventuality occurred, 'guarantees of a moral and religious kind demanded by the religious authorities have been refused'.[94] Other Christians were also worried: on 19 April Pastor Boegner saw Pétain, at the request of Protestant female youth organisations, and obtained his assurance that girls would not be conscripted. Misgivings remained, however, because it was realised that the Marshal now had little control over events. A priest of Sable-sur-Sarthe unsuccessfully raised the question with Commandant Féat, of Pétain's Cabinet Civil, asking for confirmation that work for the Germans by girls outside his own village was illegal: they went off every day to work in an ammunition factory ten kilometres away.[95] On All Souls Day, preaching in his cathedral at Limoges, Mgr Rastouil, whilst affirming his complete loyalty to the government, protested against any conscription of young women for work in Germany.[96] The Germans registered a black mark against him.

The direct cause of concern was a further law of 1 February 1944 that made all females aged between eighteen and forty-five eligible for 'requisitioning' for work, without specifying whether this meant only locally. This was an immediate cause for the intervention of the ACA.

At the ACA meeting on 16–18 February 1944, the STO was in fact high on the agenda. Some such as Cardinal Gerlier, Théas, Bishop of Montauban, representing Archbishop Saliège, and Moussaron and Petit de Julleville, Archbishops respectively of Albi and Rouen, were for adopting a firm line, and asked for a general review of all the STO measures; on the other hand Cardinals Suhard and Liénart urged prudence. In the end Suhard and Mgr Chappoulie were authorised to make representations to the authorities. The final statement issued spoke of the call-up of young men as having 'affected hundreds of thousands of families and caused anguish in the hearts of mothers' ('atteint des centaines de milliers de familles et jeté l'angoisse dans le cœur des mères'). It went on not only to condemn total war and the 'terrorist' bombings, but also the threat of a female call-up: 'The very idea of such a call-up [...] strikes severely at family life and the future of our country, at the dignity and moral delicacy of women and girls, at the vocation assigned them by Providence.'[97]

The mildness of the document aroused a fierce response from Saliège, whose poor health had prevented his attendance at the meeting. In a letter to Liénart he attacked on all fronts. The declaration did not affirm the right in conscience, conceded to men, of women to refuse the call-up. There was indeed no mention of rights, although duties carried with them corresponding rights. About this, as for the other matters raised in the declaration, it would be said that the Church only spoke out when its own interests were in jeopardy. Thus the question of total war had been dwelt on too much since 1940. Concern for the workers was limited to a timid paternalism. There was nothing about profiteering and the black market. 'To read the declaration one would say that the Church of France is borne along by material and political forces'. It was being said that it was a manifesto of fear, one at which the Communists would rejoice as fuelling anticlericalism, a fresh concession to state totalitarianism. He supposed matters had not been put to the vote.[98] Cardinal Liénart sent off a weak reply.[99] He admitted that the text lacked clarity, so that it could be misinterpreted. But it did represent fairly the views of the Assembly.

Saliège continued to voice his opinions. In a letter addressed to his diocesan priests, to be read from the pulpit on 23 April, he declared: 'Women as slaves, women as machines that one moves around, women as merchandise to be shipped hither and thither, never, never... History will one day execrate [...] what might be termed without exaggeration "the traffic in girls and women".'[100] Women had to be defended by the State; their place was in the home, and at home.

The collaborationist press, led by Déat, who on 16 March was to become Labour minister, roared its disapproval of the Church's attitude in general. On 9 March, in *L'Œuvre,* he deplored the fact that the ACA, by temporising over the STO, had provided the pretext for young men to take off to join the maquis. He claimed the rumour was unfounded that women would be packed off to Germany, although there had been a census of females in the Vichy area. In any case there was no excuse for not putting them to work in France in defence occupations. Working-class women were already doing so. Why not therefore 'young ladies of good family, the daughters of our French bourgeoisie, the progeny of the "my dears" so assiduous in the sacristy?' ('jeunes filles de bonne famille, les filles de notre bourgeoisie, les rejetons des "Madame-ma-chère", si assidues aux sacristies?'). When a stronger (Fascist?) state came into existence such extravagant outbursts by cardinals and archbishops would no longer be tolerated. *Les Nouveaux Temps* went one further: the cardinals were 'in the camp of Jewry, plutocracy and communism'.[101]

What were the effects of the STO law upon Christians? For the first time the Church had explicitly recognised the right of Catholics to obey their conscience, even if in defiance of their appointed leaders. This mistrust of, and even challenge to ecclesiastical discipline subsisted after the war. In 1958 a pastoral letter published in the *Semaine religieuse* of the Paris diocese (1 January 1958) entitled 'Obéissance et liberté' regretted this:

> The sorrowful war years have deeply marked our era. In France and elsewhere a whole generation has grown up in an atmosphere of contesting the established order, in a climate of resistance to constituted authority. Events having justified these concrete positions, the fact is forgotten that they then had a motive which today has dropped out of sight and, in spite of changed circumstances, something of the mentality adopted has been retained.

Archbishop Feltin of Bordeaux expressed himself in similar terms, as did Guerry in his defence of the Church immediately after the war.

For those young Christians that accepted their fate life in Germany was hard. According to Poulat[102] it was a heroic kind of Christianity they practised, without benefit of clergy or the sacraments. On the other hand, young Catholics and Protestants realised, perhaps for the first time, that what they had in common as Christians together, as well as with non-Christians, was greater than what divided them. They mingled with young workers, for whom Christianity was often an empty word; they encountered Russians and Germans, and discovered that not all were Communists or Nazis: their common humanity was greater than any ideology. But the 'apostolate' that many, particularly the Jocistes, thought to exercise by accepting the STO, was on the whole a failure. They did not come back 'better', nor was their number greatly increased: 'revenir meilleur, revenir plus nombreux' had turned out to be a false slogan. Yet the hardships they endured enabled them to envision, and for a few post-war years to realise, a different future for the Church, and for the role of the priesthood.

As for those Christians who disobeyed the call-up, became 'réfractaires' and fled to join the Maquis, they rendered signal service to the Church at the Liberation. By then the two largest groups in the Resistance consisted of Christians and Communists. The services rendered in the Resistance by Christians weighed favourably in the balance when it came to judging the conduct of the bishops during the Occupation.

The judgement on the bishops must be that they were overscrupulous (with a few notable exceptions) in their respect for the law, principally because they felt the STO had Pétain's backing. Although the advice they tendered to young Christians was — perhaps not deliberately — somewhat ambiguous, on the whole they favoured compliance, making a virtue out of necessity. They resented the challenge to their authority by 'anonymous theologians' who counselled refusal of the STO, and claimed they alone had the right to act as spiritual directors of conscience. On the positive side, the despatch clandestinely of priests in the guise of workers to Germany marked the beginnings of the worker-priest movement, which, though it ultimately collapsed, did bring the Church and the working-class somewhat closer together.

By now the moment had come to judge the record of Christians, bishops, priests, pastors and laity alike. Would they at the Liberation be weighed in the balance and found wanting?

Notes

Unless otherwise stated the place of publication is Paris

1. A Dio, Lille, 2 B 1, ACA 1942–1945. ACA 20–22 January 1943.
2. E. Poulat, *Naissance des prêtres-ouvriers*, Tournai, 1965, p. 250.
3. AN 2 AG 492.
4. AN 2 AG 493. Extract from a pastoral letter (n.d), reported in *Libération*, (London), 30 March 1943; AN F60.1674 (Fighting French file). *News Digest,* no. 1245, 18 September 1943.
5. Quoted in Poulat, *Naisssance*, pp. 250ff.
6. C. Tardieu, 'Les baudruches crevées', *Grand Echo du Nord*, 16 March 1943,
7. Mgr Georges Leclercq, then the head of the Grand Séminaire, Lille, said that Cardinal Liénart made several visits to the seminary to urge the seminarists to go to Germany.
8. *Actes*: Lyons, p. 316.
9. AD du Nord, Lille, R 2457. File: Cardinal Liénart. Letter enclosing tract from Commissaire Central de Police, Lille, 26 March 1943, to Carles, Prefect of Nord.
10. AN 2 AG 75. 'Note (secret)', 26 March 1943.
11. AN 2 AG 492. 'Note', ref: 4/SA, Vichy 20 April 1943.
12. AN 2 AG 492. 'Note' by Lavagne, Vichy, 20 April 1943.
13. Ibid. The archive note links this, without clarification, to the many rumours of peace that were circulating in the spring of 1943, in which the Pope might act as mediator.
14. AN F60.1674. CNI (Fighting French file). Message received 26 June 1943.
15. The complete text of the declaration is printed in *Cahiers* no. XVII, 'Déportation'.
16. See J. Evrard, *La déportation des travailleurs français dans le IIIe Reich*, 1972.
17. *Semaine Catholique*, Toulouse, 25 March 1943, The full text of this message was produced in the clandestine *Courrier*, no. 3, Lyons, July 1943, pp..226f, and reprinted in part in the *Courrier de Genève*, 10 September 1943.
18. AN 2 AG 492, 'Note (Secret)', 8 April 1943.
19. *Actes*: Biviers, p. 180.
20. AN F60.1758. Quoted in *Pour la Liberté*, monthly bulletin in French of the British Information ministry, May–June 1943, under the title: 'Les Eglises françaises et les cercles d'étudiants résistent toujours'.

21. Quoted in *Actes*: Lyons, p. 324.
22. AN 2 AG 492 and AD du Nord, Lille, R 2457. File: Cardinal Liénart. 'Note (Secret)', 8 April 1943.
23. AN 2 AG 493. Letter from Suhard to Pétain dated 24 June 1943.
24. *Le Petit Parisien*, 1 April 1943, quoting the *Semaine religieuse* of Arras, n.d.
25. AN F60.1758. Report of broadcast by Radio-Révolution (France), 21.45, 7 April 1943; AN F60.1674 Report of broadcast by Radio Brazzaville I, 23.00, 12 April 1943.
26. A Dio, Lille, Dossier Pétain, 8 M 9. Leaflet: 'Lettre de Mgr l'Evêque à un jeune catholique de son diocèse', Le Puy, 19 June 1943.
27. P. Silvestre, 'STO, maquis et guérilla dans l'Isère', *RHDGM*, no. 130, April 1983.
28. E. Jarry and J.R. Palanque (eds), *Histoire des diocèses de France: Grenoble*, pp. 278f.
29. AN 2 AG 492. *Semaine religieuse*, Clermont-Ferrand, July 1943.
30. *L'Avenir du Plateau Central*, 28 July 1943.
31. AN 2 AG 493. Open letter published in *La Quinzaine catholique du Gevaudan*, no. 17, 2 July 1943. See also AN F60.1674.
32. AN 2 AG 493. Brochure on the STO.
33. *Actes*: Lyons, pp. 390ff.
34. Present writer's emphasis. AN F60.1674. Fighting French file: 'France — politique. Rapport sur Nice. OCM Bureau civil',
35. Poulat, *Naissance*, p. 249.
36. *Actes*: Lyons, pp.390 ff.
37. A Dio, Lille. 2 B 1. ACA 1944. Letter by head of the SS, Paris, 30 August 1943: 'Vous insistez sur le fait que l'activité de la JOC se limite exclusivement au domaine religieux. Je ne puis accueillir cette assertion qu'avec le plus grand scepticisme'.
38. AN F60.1758, *France*, London, 24 October 1942, quoting the *Daily Mail*.
39. AN 2 AG 492. 'Note (Secret)', 25 March 1943.
40. *Cahiers* , XVII, p. 213.
41. P. Duclos, *Le Vatican et la seconde guerre mondiale. Action doctrinale et diplomatique en faveur de la paix*, 1955, p. 161.
42. AN F60.1674. Information given at 13.00 on Algiers Radio, 27 April 1943.
43. *Idées*, March 1943.
44. AN F60.1674. Press cutting.
45. 'Politique et religion', *L'Œuvre*, 13 May 1943.
46. P. Limagne, *Ephémérides de quatre années tragiques*, vol. 2, 1987, p. 105. Diary note for 28 February 1943.
47. 'Le cardinal Verdier était-il franc-maçon?'*Je Suis Partout*, 2 July 1943.
48. Quoted in *Courrier* no. 3, September–October 1943.
49. A. Jobert, 'Le dossier "Nazisme" d'un aumônier des jeunes', *Actes*: Biviers, p. 96.
50. AN F60.1674. *La Voix du Nord*, no. 47 of 1 January 1943.
51. Idem, no. 53, 5 April 1943.
52. AN F1a.3784. Gaullist file. Information dated April 1944, ref: RIA/2/36200.
53. AN F60.1788. Lettre de Nouvelles Catholiques, 'L'Eglise nous convoque à la guerre', no. 73, London, 17 April 1943.
54. *Actes*: Lyons, pp. 219ff.
55. AN F17.13349. Report by Brunereau. See also AN 2 AG 609. Someone—probably Bonnard— had pencilled on the document in red, 'Gaullisme!'
56. AN 2 AG 492. 'Note'.
57. AD du Nord, Lille, R 2457. Tract: 'A mon camarade chrétien', dated 2 April 1943, distributed in the Lyons faculties.
58. Quoted in Poulat, *Naissance*, pp. 265ff.
59. *Cahiers de notre Jeunesse*, no. 18, June 1943.
60. *La Route*, 1 March 1943, quoted in Poulat, *Naissance*, p. 256.
61. Quoted in Gordon Wright, *Rural Revolution in France*, Stanford, 1964, p. 93. n.37.
62. See A. Michel, *La JEC face au nazisme et à Vichy*, 1988, p. 225; cf., however, *Actes*: Grenoble, p. 238.

63. F60.1674. 'Où est la vérité?' Cutting from *L'Appel*, 1 July 1943.
64. These figures are taken from Poulat, *Naissance*, pp. 55ff. but A. Cherrier, 'L'Eglise et le Service du Travail Obligatoire', *Actes*: Lille, quotes statistics of the Aumônerie Générale des Prisonniers for 1943, which give 2,500 priests as POWs, 960 seminarists and 240 priests working under the STO.
65. AD du Nord, Lille, 1 W 2241. Letter of Commissaire de police (Renseignements Généraux) to the Prefect, 22 March 1943.
66. 2 AG 492 CCB. Politique religieuse. Questions religieuses. Dossier Bérard: 'Cette réserve ne signifie pas que l'épiscopat français ait l'intention d'inciter les travailleurs à la désobéissance—loin de là—cette éventualité n'est même pas envisagée'.
67. AN F60.1674. 'Prières pour les absents'.
68. For much of what follows I am indebted to Poulat, *Naissance*, pp. 258ff.
69. Cardinal Suhard, *Vers une Eglise en état de mission*, 1965, p. 102.
70. A Dio, Lille 2 B 6, ACA 1944.
71. Ibid. 'Note du délégué régional de la JOC', Würzburg, 15 December 1943. The note ended: 'Vive Pétain'. Clearly the Head of State had not yet lost all credibility.
72. AN 2 AG 609. Letter of Abbé Jean Godbert to Féat, Sable, 22 October 1943.
73. *Cahiers*, vol. 2, no. XVII.
74. AN F60.1674. Communiqué du Bureau de presse de la France Combattante, 29 June 1943.
75. AN 2 AG 492. Note by Lavagne, Vichy, 26 January 1943, headed 'Projet de service d'aumônerie pour les Travailleurs français en Allemagne'.
76. Suhard, *Vers une Eglise*, p. 99.
77. Ibid.,p. 90.
78. Ibid.
79. AN 2 AG 493. Letter of Suhard to Pétain, Paris, 24 June 1943.
80. AN 2 AG 492. Letter of Pétain to Laval, Vichy, 30 June 1943.
81. A Dio, Lille, 2 B 1. ACA 1942–1945.
82. Suhard, *Vers une Eglise*, p. 90.
83. AN 2 AG 609. Letter of Féat to Mgr du Parc, Vichy, 23 August 1943. The reply to the letter stated that it would remain 'un document illustrant l'intrusion de la marine dans tous les domaines'. The role of the Navy in Vichy politics has often been commented upon.
84. AN 2 AG 609. Letter from Père Louvière to Pétain, Lesneven, 12 September 1943.
85. A Dio, Lille 2 B 1, ACA 1942–1945. ACA of 28–29 July 1943.
86. Père Jean Damascène de la Javie (with R. Hervet), *Prêtre ouvrier clandestin*, 1967, pp. 13f.
87. Ibid.,p. 49.
88. A Dio, Lille 2 B 1, ACA 1942–1945. Note of Mgr Chappoulie, 17 February 1944.
89. Jean Perrin, 'Apôtres clandestins. Journal d'un prêtre ouvrier', *Etudes*, January 1945, pp. 54–77.
90. Poulat, *Naissance*, pp. 54ff.
91. Pétain: *Le Procès du Maréchal Pétain*, vol. 2, 1945, p. 804. Testimony of Abbé Rodhain.
92. A Dio, Lille. Guerre 1939–1945, 8 M 7. 'Interventions 1943'. Letter of Liénart dated 12 February 1943.
93. AD du Nord, Lille. W 4576.
94. AN 2 AG 609. Letter (writer unknown) to A. Hermant, Bureau de Documentation, 34, rue des Fosses, Lille, 16 February 1943.
95. AN 2 AG 609. 'Lettres adressées au Commandant Féat'. Letter from Abbé Jean Godbert, 11 rue St Nicholas, Sable-sur-Sarthe, 22 October 1943.
96. AN 2 AG 493 'Note (Secret)', 3 November 1943.
97. AD du Nord, Lille, R 1361. See also A Dio, Lille, 2 B 1. ACA 1944
98. A Dio, Lille, 2 B 1 ACA, 1942–1945. Letter of Saliège to Cardinal Liénart. Toulouse, 26 February 1944.
99. AD du Nord, Lille, R 1361. Letter of Liénart, Lille, 21 March 1944.

100. AN F60.1674. Letter of Saliège to his parish priests, Toulouse, 22 April 1944, entitled 'La mission de la femme dans un pays civilisé'. According to another source (AN F1a.3784, ref: OJQ/2/36800. Fighting French file), the message was rammed home even further: 'La femme n'est pas un instrument de production. La femme n'est pas une ouvrière économique qu'on peut déplacer. dépayser, déraciner à loisir'.

101. *Les Nouveaux Temps* entitled its editorial of 3 March 1944, 'Casuistique. Pardonnez-leur, Seigneur'.

102. Poulat, *Naissance*, pp. 57ff.

PART VI

SETTLING THE ACCOUNTS

Christians and the Collaborationists

For many Frenchmen, Christians or not, some contact with the Germans was unavoidable. Cardinals Liénart and Suhard, apart from the irritating obligation to obtain travel or curfew passes from the Occupation authorities, had often to deal directly with them when their priests were arrested. Such collaboration, should be distinguished from 'collaborationism'. (Recently the term 'collaborationiste' has come to designate those who had embraced Nazi doctrines and staked everything on a German victory.) Collaborationists were the most critical of Catholic and Protestant attitudes. Some, including others who were themselves Christians, tried to win over the Church. In this chapter an analysis is made of collaborationist institutions, in some of which Christians were active participants, and their attitude to the Church; finally a few individual cases of clerics and Christian laity are considered.

In Paris the chief criticism of the Church, as will be seen, came from the collaborationist journals. Their strictures intensified from mid-1942 onwards, when it was apparent that Vichy was losing credibility, and German demands on the French, including Christians, were increasing. Meanwhile the regime was condemned for its clericalism. In *Révolution* Combelle wrote: 'Official France seems to wish to find once more its beauty by swallowing the youth potion of Abbé Soury [a popular 'rejuvenating' remedy at the time] and by caring for its wounds with holy water. *Post mortem*, 'Abbé Bethléhem' is gradually becoming its spiritual director. Here, hair to be shaven, there sex to be cut down'.[1]

The political parties tolerated by the Germans operated from Paris. Failing to promote their totalitarian ideas at Vichy, Déat and Doriot, the heads of the two main collaborationist parties, had installed themselves in the capital. Whereas Déat's Rassemblement National Populaire (RNP) was hostile to the Church, but prepared to tolerate it if it co-operated in the new 'European order', Doriot's Parti Populaire Français (PPF), after 1942 actively courted bishops and clergy in an effort to win them over. Doriot, who had enlisted in the LVF, returned on leave from the Eastern Front convinced of the need to enlist religious co-operation. The PPF leader was seconded by Alain Janvier, the party delegate for religious and cultural affairs, who believed, as he put it, that 'the destiny of most Frenchmen is enclosed within the baptistery of our churches and the cross on our tombs'.[2] For him national unity could only be achieved with the help of the Church. Cultural delegates of the PPF were ordered to approach local religious leaders to ascertain their views on collaborationism. They found young priests, seminarists and the religious orders on the whole very hostile, some declaring outright 'for their friends the English', others were 'tainted' with 'extreme Gaullism'.[3] Some of the more senior clergy were not so unanimously opposed. In the Agen diocese, of thirty-one contacted, four were against the PPF's policies — the figure included one royalist and one Gaullist — eleven were favourably disposed, and the rest held no firm opinion. But Mgr Rodié, the Bishop, although favouring the PPF's social doctrine, wanted nothing to do with collaborationism. But this, according to the survey, was because he was a 'bon vivant, ami de la tranquillité', who sought a quiet life.[4]

On 1 October 1943 Janvier submitted to the party the results of a national enquiry made among forty-three bishops. The survey had been supported by a number of Christians, including the late Cardinal Baudrillart, Mgr Beaussart, Dom Lambert Beaudouin, a Benedictine monk, and Le Fur, a professor of international law. Its purpose was to identify the 'correct' relationship between Church and State, within the framework of collaborationism and under a totalitarian regime. Janvier classified the attitudes of the archbishops, bishops, and auxiliary bishops he had canvassed as being either 'cordial', 'courteous', or 'reserved'.[5] Significantly, among those who gave the enquirers a 'cordial' reception were some whose conduct was criticised at the Liberation, although it fell far short of collaborationism: Mgrs Beaussart, Courbe, Merguen, Feltin, Caillot, Marmottin, Serrand and Du Bois de la Villerabel; among those classed as 'reserved' was Mgr Théas of Montauban, who was later commended by de Gaulle. One remarks the absence from the list of Cardinals Liénart and Gerlier, as well as Archbishop Saliège. Two religious orders were also questioned: the Jesuits, it would seem, were 'courteous and interested' (but this may have been no more than casuistry); the Dominicans were 'very reticent'. Indeed R-P. Gillet, of the Dominicans, whose attitude was nevertheless later blamed by the de Gaulle government, allegedly believed Doriot was the devil incarnate! However, the list, more than anything else, is perhaps merely further proof of some bishops' political naiveté.

Cardinal Liénart, at least, was well aware of the PPF's machinations. He had studied carefully, but without accepting its premises, a four-page brochure by Janvier[6] (a reprint of an article appearing in the PPF publication, *L'Assaut*, 25 July 1942) entitled, 'Vers une politique religieuse'. In it the PPF leader was at one with the bishops in ascribing France's downfall to de-Christianisation, individualism and materialism — the bitter fruits of the Third Republic's secularising policy. Yet, he argued, Church and State needed each other: democracy had only brought about the Separation; in the present circumstances a Concordat would be the 'logical' solution. It would comprise: educational freedom ('la liberté d'enseignement') — had not Doriot in 1939 already blamed the secular education system for France's misfortunes?; protection of priests in the exercise of their duties; legal recognition of religious marriages and ecclesiastical courts; State payment of clerical salaries; and the Church to have the right to own buildings and other property. The problem of aid to Catholic schools and the training of young people should be pursued further. In exchange the State would be consulted on episcopal appointments and clergy would pledge their loyalty to the constitution, whilst forswearing active participation in politics.

Apparently the brochure was sent to priests in certain selected dioceses. In Lot-et-Garonne, according to Pétain's Private Office, it met with a cool reception. Its recipients were in the main against collaboration.[7] However, from another PPF enquiry carried out as late as February 1944 in Nîmes, although it showed the cathedral canons as belonging to the 'wait and see' school, only a minority were classed as anticollaborationist.[8]

These PPF surveys, however, in the main reinforce the view that the Church remained unfavourable to co-operation with the Germans, despite inducements held out to it. It may well have realised — at least by 1943 — that any promised advantages would turn out to be illusory.

However, the most implacable and formidable adversary of the Church was Marcel Déat, the leader of the RNP. His newspaper, *L'Œuvre*, had been anticlerical before the war; it remained so. In a series of three articles (20, 21 and 22 October 1942) Déat exhorted Christians to collaborate in the 'European Revolution' unfolding before their eyes. Faced with the Church's condemnation of Jewish persecution, the ambiguous note it struck regarding economic co-operation with Germany, and what was seen as lukewarm support of the 'anti-Bolshevik' war, he discussed Church–State relationships. In the first article, on 'Christianisme et démocratie' (20 October 1942), he accused both of identifying with each other. Hence the Church's lack of comprehension of the new European order. Christianity should be in harmony with the new religion of nazism, with its appeal to 'la Race, le Sang et le Sol'. The next article, on 'L'Eglise et la Révolution' declared there was no antinomy between the revolution and religion, using the latter term in its broadest sense. The final article, 'Europe et Chrétiené'

(22 October 1942), even asserted that the 'new order' and catholicism were seeking the same goals: the ending of the abuse of wealth, and the regulation of profit, but allowing individual ownership of property, and upholding the doctrine of the 'fair price', pride in one's family and occupation, and the development of a community spirit. Catholics were wrong to object to the 'syndicat unique', an 'école unique', a 'jeunesse unique' or a 'parti unique'. The Church had to work out a different form of Christianity; if it failed to do so, the new Europe would take shape without it.

Déat was willing to concede substantial freedom to the Church, in particular the right to evangelise. If the 'Lyons dilemma' (a reference to Cardinal Gerlier's allegedly hostile attitude) were to continue, however, in its opposition to the new Europe, then it would be war to the knife. The Church would lose, and a new Reformation would bring about its downfall because National Socialist ideology possessed 'the conquering and converting drive of a new Islam'; 'Through the thunder and lightning we would witness a new twilight of the gods.' The Church had to opt: 'The choice is as urgent, as decisive as at Dakar. And moreover, it is the same choice'.

Le Cour Grandmaison, of the FNC, in *La France Catholique* (3 March 1943), took up the challenge: it was not, he declared, the Church's role to take sides. If Déat thought the 'new gods' would prevail, the answer was that the Church, over two millennia, had buried many such false gods of more recent origin than itself. Déat later returned to the attack:[9] the Church might be attracted by universalism, but, established on the national territory and being a totalitarian institution, it tended to encroach illegitimately upon State power. He reiterated that in the present uncertain times the choice was between the old order and a new one which was 'communautaire'. By opting for the latter it could thrive in the new revolutionary atmosphere, and reinvigorate its own totalitarian doctrine through contact with new, young states. In any case, its sphere of activity should be confined to the individual; only the state had the right to look to the collectivity as a whole.

Déat in fact lost no opportunity to attack the Church. He even accused the Vatican, through Cardinal Tisserant, of seeking reconciliation with the Orthodox churches, a move that would benefit Stalin. As has been seen, he regarded the ACA's attitude regarding the STO in 1944 as providing arguments for the Maquis and 'réfractaires'.[10] When he became Labour minister he claimed to have agreed with Cardinal Suhard regarding the sending of chaplains to the Frenchmen working in Germany, provided that each emissary 'confined himself to his own field and his own viewpoint'.[11] He clearly saw that field as a limited one. It is perhaps ironical that at the end of the war, this onetime secularising neo-Socialist escaped to Turin, took refuge in a convent, and before his death in 1955 turned to catholicism. Although a more formidable propagandist than Doriot, who was an ex-Communist, Déat, whose past record had been also not unblemished, had less success in favourably disposing Catholics to collaborationism.

Less political, and more cultural and literary, the Groupe Collaboration was instituted by the Catholic writer Alphonse de Chateaubriant on 24 September 1940 and from January 1941 was allowed also to function in the unoccupied zone. Chateaubriant was a Romantic in his beliefs: for him God could be found in nature just as well as in a church; his values harked back to those of the Middle Ages and of the Restoration writers de Maistre and Bonald. In 1936, already almost sixty years old, he had visited Germany and upon his return, in *La Gerbe des Forces*, had extolled the Nazi ideal type and lauded Hitler to the skies. He saw no difficulty in reconciling nazism with Christianity. In 1940 he had been invited by Abetz to start a weekly, *La Gerbe*. The founding of the Groupe Collaboration, whose aim was the development of cultural ties and of which Cardinal Baudrillart was a member, was a natural consequence. The movement had some success: it comprised some 30,000 members in 1942, but at the peak of its activities in 1943 had probably treble this number.[12] Local groups were penetrated by the PPF, which gave the movement a more political tone. Chateaubriant, however, remained true to his own formulation of the Catholic faith. At the Liberation he fled to the Austrian Tyrol, where he died in 1951.

Among the collaborationists other prominent writers, in contrast, kept up the onslaught upon Christianity. In November 1941 Montherlant published his reflections on the defeat. For him the time had come to cast aside an outdated religion in favour of the 'roue solaire' (the swastika): 'the Galilean' had finally been defeated. (A lesser writer, Armand Petitjean, likewise proclaimed in the *Nouvelle Revue Française* that the time had come to abandon the Christian ideal for nazism.)[13] Meanwhile Brasillach inveighed against the Church, which he accused of being an 'Internationale catholique'. His charges ranged widely, from its official silence on the war against the Soviet Union to accusations that convents were no more than staging posts for those seeking to join de Gaulle.[14] Another writer, Paul Shack, the ex-naval officer and prolific novelist, in the last of his three 'Lettres à un Prélat' written for *Aujourd'hui* (31 August 1943), also played the 'European' card: why did the Church not wake up to the fact that 'certain European governments' were the sole bulwark against its demise? It could only be shielded, according to Louis Rebatet,[15] by the two leaders whom God favoured, Franco and Hitler.

Other collaborationist periodicals, this time in the southern zone, joined in the polemics. Some spoke from within the Catholic camp itself: the Lyons daily *Le Nouvelliste*, had called Montoire 'une journée historique'; *La Croix du Rhône*, which *Témoignage Chrétien* dubbed 'la croix gammée du Rhône', published an article that the clandestine journal termed nothing less than 'un éloge catholique et français d'Adolf Hitler'.[16] *La Croix de Savoie*, the Savoyard paper with the largest circulation, went as far in justifying collaboration from the religious viewpoint: the young packed off to work in Germany were indirectly defending Christianity against bolshevism.[17]

Some collaborationists had the episcopacy particularly in their sights. Georges Suarez, in *Aujourd'hui* (19 May 1943), threatened to turn 'dissident bishops' into 'disciplined and law-abiding Frenchmen'. A tract circulating in 1943 in the Lyons area accused Cardinal Gerlier of hobnobbing with Third Republic politicians before the war, and of coveting the papacy — Britain had promised him the pontifical tiara if it won the war.[18] But then, insinuated an editorial in *Je Suis Partout* (2 July 1943) arrestingly entitled: 'Le cardinal Verdier était-il franc-maçon?' Catholicism had always been betrayed by its upper clergy. Numerous collaborationist pamphlets against Jews and Freemasons circulated, whose purpose was to win over the Catholic laity. Thus on station bookstalls could be bought such edifying works as *Les Papes ont toujours été contre le communisme,* a tract backed by quotations from encyclicals from the eighteenth century onwards.[19] In fact, no section of the Church was spared propaganda efforts by pro-German Frenchmen either to discredit it or to convert its members to collaborationism.

Among collaborationist institutions there was sometimes a distinctly Catholic element. This was particularly true in the Milice, created in the southern zone to stamp out the Maquis and round up 'réfractaires', which attracted many young men from the Catholic bourgeoisie before it became also the resort of the dregs of society. Leaders such as Bassompierre, a friend of Darnand, and the founder of the LVF's Service de l'Ordre, from which sprang the Milice, came from old Catholic families. Well-to-do parents allowed their sons to enlist: what could be more respectable than an organisation run by the very patriotic Darnand, a hero of both wars and unswervingly loyal to the Marshal?[20] Did not one of the 'Twenty-one Points' of the Milice credo run: 'Contre la franc-maçonnerie païenne, pour la civilisation chrétienne'? One young Milicien wrote to Pétain declaring that he and 90 per cent of his comrades were practising Catholics.[21] The Milice periodical *Combats* symbolically bore the picture of a crusader. In August 1944, out of ninety-seven Miliciens who gave themselves up to the Resistance in Haute-Savoie, some sixty were members of organisations connected with Action Catholique. After the Liberation Miliciens shot at Annecy went to their death crying 'Vive le Christ-Roi'.[22] They justified even their vilest actions by asserting that theirs was a crusade for Christianity against bolshevism, and for delivering France from Jewish clutches. The same Milicien who wrote to Pétain reported how he had attended a lecture given by 'un grand catholique', M. Delpont de Vaux, who had demonstrated that Israel, the instrument of the devil, already held the world in its clutches.[23]

Since the Milice, however, found the Church far from sympathetic to its activities, the organisation contemplated action against those bishops it found most hostile. Prominent among these was Mgr Rémond, Bishop of Nice, whose see was in the very heartland of the Milice. When he refused to officiate at mass if it was present they characterised his conduct as 'intolerable and scandalous'. Mgr Giraud, one of his canons, who was even 'more dangerous' than the bishop, had not hesitated to preach an 'antinational' sermon. The diocesan clergy had allegedly spread a rumour that Maurras had been the victim of an unsuccessful attack in Lyons, thereby escaping what these bloodthirsty clerics termed 'la mort qu'il mérite mille fois'.[24] Mgr Rémond also became the centre of another controversy. By mid-1944 the Milice was requesting the Church to appoint chaplains. On behalf of the Milice Darnand, by then Interior minister, wrote to Cardinal Suhard suggesting the appointment as the Milice's Chaplain-General of Abbé Bouillon, a personal friend. Bouillon, a notorious extremist, had already appeared at Milice ceremonies in uniform. Rémond, to whose diocese Bouillon was attached, reprimanded him for allowing his name to go forward without permission. In the event, Suhard rebuffed Darnand, replying that he had no authority to make such an appointment; in his view local parish priests could equally well minister to the Milice.[25]

A more serious incident involving the Milice concerned Mgr Rastouil, of Limoges. On 10 June 1944 the terrible massacre at Oradour-sur-Glane had occurred. On 13 June the Bishop, accompanied by the regional Prefect, Freund-Valade, went to the scene of the slaughter. On June 15, on the feast of the Sacred Heart, he used the occasion to speak out against the atrocity, after having received the excuses of the German commander, General Kleiniger. On 22 June a memorial service for the victims was to be held in Limoges Cathedral. The Germans had tried to put off would-be attenders by ostentatiously making searches in the neighbourhood for bombs. The Bishop had thereupon alerted the police. Two small bombs had in fact been placed by the Milice inside the church, one under the pulpit. Although these had been discovered, the mass had had to be broken off. On 7 July the Bishop was arrested, and taken to Chateauroux, where he was detained. It was alleged that in his sermon he sought yet again to condemn the death of the victims of the massacre. In any case, it was said, he was notorious for speaking out against collaborationism, and favoured Gaullism. He had later compounded these offences by refusing the Milice's demand, after the assassination of Henriot, for a commemorative mass, allegedly replying: 'You have prevented me from officiating at a commemoration in honour of good Frenchmen [those of Oradour]. Well, I refuse to say a mass for an enemy of France'.[26] The Milice reported this to de Vaugelas, head of the forces for the 'Maintenance of Order' for the Limoges region. Rastouil, detained at Chateauroux after his arrest, was only released after the personal intervention of Laval.[27]

The Milice also took it upon itself to demand that a score of priests, including Père Glasberg and Père Girard, the Vice-Rector of the Catholic faculties, and others from the Lyons area, should be forcibly stopped from involvement in clandestine political action, for, they declared, 'quiconque usera du glaive, périra par le glaive'.[28]

How this paramilitary body, an offshoot of an organisation intensely patriotic and loyal, often commanded by young officers with a strongly religious upbringing, came to become an instrument of Nazi brutality and often hostile to the Church, is one of the more incomprehensible phenomena of the Occupation.

The other institution, and the most glaring example of collaboration, with which the Church willy-nilly had dealings, was the Légion des Volontaires Français (LVF), set up to fight on the Eastern Front. From the very beginning Catholics were involved. On the two 'comités d'honneur' set up — one for each zone — served, together with non-Catholics, Cardinal Baudrillart and Canon Tricot, his colleague at the Institut Catholique in Paris, Chateaubriant, the Catholic writer, and Gabriel Cognacq, chairman of the charitable organisation Entr'aide d'Hiver.[29] Since the LVF was tolerated by the Vichy regime the Church had no option but to hide the reservations it held about it.

The history of the LVF can be briefly told. The creation of all the collaborationist parties — although only Doriot of the PPF actually went to fight in the USSR — the Légion drew many of its volunteers from Catholic families. They were fired with the idea of a war to defend Christianity. Bassompierre, for example, transferred from the Milice to the LVF. A few were inspired by a 'European' or Nazi idealism. Others saw in it adventure or gain. Later, after the Allied invasion in the West, some of the Milice volunteered for it, because, having burnt their boats, they saw no other way out. Yet others enlisted to avoid the STO. A first contingent was despatched to the Eastern Front in September 1941, where it remained till mid-February 1942. In December 1941 it saw a fortnight of action, but with only mediocre results, largely because of the incompetence of its commander, Colonel Labonne. By then it had become a hotbed of political argument. Mgr Mayol de Luppé, its Chaplain-General, wrote to the German High Command on 7 March 1942 pointing out the poor quality of the officers, and urged it to assume direct command. The Germans duly did so, purging the cadres and stamping out the political bickering which was rife.[30] Henceforth the force was employed mainly behind the German lines hunting down partisans. However, in July 1944 it was involved in an offensive, and suffered heavy losses. It was then incorporated into the SS Division Charlemagne, which was caught up in the great German retreat — some of the former Milice were even fighting in the streets of Berlin immediately before the surrender.

The cleric most immediately embroiled in LVF affairs because its headquarters were in Paris was Cardinal Suhard, who adopted a temporising attitude. He protested in vain (28 November 1941) when one recruiting office opened in Paris using the name 'Etat-major des chasseurs de Jeanne d'Arc', presumably to entice Catholics to enlist.[31] At a ceremony commemorating the first anniversary of the LVF Admiral Platon represented Pétain, Cardinal Suhard pronounced the absolution for those who had been killed, and Cardinal Baudrillart gave the blessing. *L'Œuvre* (29–30 August 1942) saw this as a political gesture that should give Catholics pause: 'Perhaps it will contribute to putting a brake on the wave of Gaullism sweeping unceasingly through the rectories and [the Church's] charitable organisations'.[32]

In Lyons, Cardinal Gerlier was made of sterner stuff. In September 1942 he refused to celebrate a funeral mass in honour of a Legionary, François Sabiani, who had been killed on the Eastern Front and decorated with the Legion of Honour — an award that caused Herriot to resign from the Order. According to the Fighting French newspaper *France* (22 September 1942), Gerlier may even have instructed his priests to refuse the sacraments to members of the LVF.[33]

The LVF had been supplied with a chaplain-general from the very beginning.[34] The colourful figure of Mgr Mayol de Luppé, who occupied the post throughout, dominates the history of the Legion, and indeed of its successor, the SS Division Charlemagne. Born in 1873 and ordained in 1900, he served as a chaplain in the First World War, was captured, released and returned to the front, where in 1918 he was seriously wounded. He remained in the army until 1927, when he retired. He became chaplain to the Bourbons and was sent by the royal house to Germany, where in 1938 he met Abetz. He accepted the appointment as Chaplain to the LVF with the agreement of Cardinal Suhard, who first consulted in Paris Canon Jourdain, of Notre-Dame des Victoires, as to its canonical propriety. Luppé was personally a convinced 'crusader against bolshevism'.

In the field his bravery won him the Iron Cross, which he wore along with sixteen other French decorations, including the Legion of Honour. A commanding figure, he would ride round visiting the troops on horseback. When in June 1942 a detachment was surrounded by Russian partisans, despite his age, he immediately seized a machine gun and succeeded in beating off the attack.[35] Immensely popular with the rank and file, after celebrating Sunday mass he would end with, 'Heil Hitler! Et pieux dimanche, mes fils!' Indeed his faith in a German victory never left him. Even in January 1945 he declared that he had never been so convinced of a successful outcome to the war.[36] When defeat eventually came he sought sanctuary with the Archbishop of Munich, but was extradited to France. On 14 May 1947 he was sentenced to twenty years' hard labour, but was freed in 1951, dying five years later. His rather naive beliefs had led to his undoing.[37]

Cardinal Suhard's tacit sanctioning of the LVF by allowing Mayol de Luppé to minister to it was later held against him. There was indeed enthusiasm for the Légion among a few rare lower clergy: one parish priest informed Doriot that he offered up a mass for it every week.[38] On the other hand, an (anonymous) bishop wrote to one volunteer, 'Quelle erreur vous commettez!' Plainly a small minority of Christians did not entirely disapprove of fighting side by side with the Germans for what they considered a legitimate cause.

There was a similar minority of Protestants who believed in collaborationism. Perhaps the most eminent among them was Admiral Platon, the defender of Dunkirk in 1940. Austere in his religious beliefs, 'd'une droiture inquiétante',[39] in 1941 he served under Darlan as secretary of State for the Colonies. From 1942 onwards, when he accepted a junior portfolio in the Prime Minister's Office until resigning in December 1943, he became convinced that Laval's policies of commitment to a German victory were right. He was a notorious anti-Semite. At the Liberation he was summarily executed by the Maquis. Anti-Semitism, no less than collaboration, also characterised the small group of Protestants known as the 'groupe Sully', led by Pastor Noel Nougat of Nîmes.

On the whole, the Church did pay heed to the cautious and patriotic voices raised against throwing in France's lot with the Germans. One such was that of Radio Vatican, which gave its opinion early on: 'One hears it said that we must collaborate and be integrated into the new order... it is extremely disturbing to hear these words insistently repeated at the present time, words that can cover everything... One must know in what one is becoming involved, with the necessary guarantees having been given'.[40]

All in all, the clergy were revolted by any idea of collaborationism.[41]

By October 1943 it would seem many a parish priest was speaking out almost openly against having any truck with the Germans. The church, it was said, was the one place where the truth could still be heard from the pulpit, so much so that sermons were popular even among the young, as well as many older men not known for their attendance at Sunday mass.[42]

To this general attitude of rejection by the clergy, there were, however, individual exceptions — one German official wildly exaggerated their number when in 1941 he estimated that 25 per cent of those in the occupied zone favoured collaboration.[43] The occasional crank would voice extreme views. One such priest, for example, wrote to Cardinal Liénart advocating Franco-German co-operation because of Britain, which he said, had interfered in French affairs since the eighteenth century, robbing France of its Empire just as it was doing then. It was even 'le grand responsable de notre déchristianisation et de nos ruines'. Germany, by contrast, could re-Christianise Europe. Even its racial doctrine accorded with catholicism, which, like nazism, did not encourage mixed marriages or the intermingling of peoples; in such cases sterilisation could be justified. Religious persecution in Germany was a myth. There was, in fact, no ideological obstacle to collaboration.[44] Such sentiments were very uncommon in northern France.

Those clergy, mainly based in the occupied zone, who expressed such views were either theologically or politically motivated. The support given to the views of Père Lesaunier, Director of the Carmelite seminary in Paris, by the Archbishop of Rheims has already been mentioned. The former believed it was a Catholic duty to knuckle under to the Occupation authorities, no less than to the Vichy regime.[45] Lesaunier's attitude eventually infuriated other Catholics, for whom Vichy was a mere German tool,[46] and they made plain their views to London.

Among clerics politically committed to collaboration one of the most eminent was Canon Polimann, friend of the collaborationist propagandist Philippe Henriot and Deputy for the Meuse since 1933. On Bastille Day 1940 it was he who had celebrated the solemn mass attended by Pétain and his government in the Church of Saint-Louis at Vichy.[47] At Vichy in 1940 his stock was high. Pétain appointed him to the Conseil National set up to elaborate a new constitution. He had ambitions for a mitre, but was clearly not so highly esteemed by the bishops, who failed to back his candidacy. He strongly supported the LVF and consequently was *persona grata* with the Germans. His influence, however, waned over time. Thus in June 1944 he intervened with the Gestapo to attempt to secure the release of three bishops recently arrested, Mgr Rodié (Agen), Mgr Piguet (Clermont-Ferrand), and Mgr Théas (Montauban). The Germans, smarting under the gesture of Mgr Picot, Bishop of liberated Bayeux, who had received de Gaulle in his cathedral, and angry at the continuing hostile activities of the Jocistes (which the good canon 'feared' were true) were prepared to release only Mgr Rodié.[48] In December 1945, after the Liberation, Polimann was sentenced to five years' imprisonment. Released in 1948, he retired to the obscurity of a country living.

Another 'political' collaborationist cleric, but one who did not live to see the Liberation, was Abbé Sorel, dying in 1943, also appointed to the Conseil National. Sorel believed collaboration would allow France to take its rightful place in the new Europe. A popular speaker at meetings of the Groupe Collaboration, he favoured ever stricter measures against the Jews.[49] He was also involved with Bucard's Franciste movement, which prided itself upon its Christian piety.[50]

Other clerical 'political' collaborationists had links to the Paris press. One such was Père Gorce, of the Frères Prêcheurs, who ran his own newspaper, *L'Emancipation nationale*. He received the accolade of having an article reproduced, with an introduction by Doriot, in *Le Cri du Peuple* (3 April 1941), under the title, 'La Révolution Nationale: l'avis d'un prêtre'. 'Le grand Jacques' himself wrote of it: 'C'est avec une grande joie que nous publions cette page hardie d'un prêtre averti des choses de la politique et du social'. In it Gorce set out his reflections on current affairs.

Religion, he wrote, was not solely 'un culte rendu aux divinités', but also a set of doctrines that raised the individual above his own selfish interest. For Germany and Japan religion had become 'le foyer du dynamisme national'. The contrast with Daladier's France in 1939 was striking, where what prevailed was 'le culte de l'apéritif, la religion du triangle maçonnique, chacun cherchant à se caser'. Those that wanted revenge for the defeat of 1940 should be shot as traitors because it would mean a return to the Third Republic. On race, again the comparison with Germany was made. The Nazi ideal of race produced favourable political results. By contrast French politics had been a prey to a 'funeste parlementarisme', which, he extravagantly claimed, was linked to tuberculosis, alcoholism and syphilis. Nevertheless, some hope remained, because a French race did exist, more or less pure, more or less healthy. But race should be improved like the breeding of dogs: 'A French bourgeois, who would not let his Pekinese bitch be covered by a hare, will nevertheless willingly marry his daughter off to a Levantine, the son of a Syrian Jew and a Burmese', if there is a prospect of financial gain. In his view France badly needed a sound racial policy.

He held strong views also on the young: the various youth movements should be merged and put into uniform.[51] After General De La Porte du Theil had been dismissed in January 1944 from his post as head of the

Chantiers de la Jeunesse and deported to Germany, Gorce saw his opportunity. He put himself forward to Bonnard, the minister of Education, for the vacant post, now that its leader had, as he put it, been 'dumped' ('débarqué'). He envisaged the Chantiers as the nucleus of that 'jeunesse unique' which the bishops had always opposed. He was the right man for the task, because, he declared, in a stab against the hapless general, 'un curé collaborationiste vaut bien un militaire revanchard'.[52] He even wanted to create a junior movement of the Chantiers in which the fourteen- to sixteen-year-olds would be enrolled for the school holidays.

Other Parisian clergy accused of collaboration after the Liberation were: Père Bruno, who ran the review *Etudes carmélitaines*, and also wrote for Chateaubriant's paper, *La Gerbe*; and Canon Renaud, of Saint-Louis en l'Ile (de la Cité), 'un prêtre acquis à la collaboration'.[53]

Of particular notoriety, however, were the journalistic activities of a nucleus of clergy from the Bordeaux area. Mgr Feltin, at the Liberation, was blamed, as their ecclesiastical superior, for not having forbidden them to publish. The situation arose in part because of the lack of a Catholic press in the occupied zone. *La Croix*, installed at Limoges during the battle of France, had refused to return to Paris in 1940. It was this gap that *Voix françaises*, published from Bordeaux, traditionally a centre for French publishing, set out to fill. Its founder, Paul Lesourd, a former teacher at the Paris Institut Catholique and a friend of Baudrillart, enlisted the services of Canon Peuch, a member of the archiepiscopal council and diocesan director of Catholic schools. The paper used the presses of a Catholic regional newspaper.[54] The other Catholic periodical, *Soutanes de France*, which also resumed publication from Bordeaux about the same time, under the direction of Abbé Bergey, had similar ties. The links that both journals tried adroitly to establish with Archbishop Feltin took on, with the passage of time, a distinctly collaborationist tint.

Lesourd had written occasionally for *La Croix* and *Le Figaro* before the war.[55] Already in 1940 his thoughts were turning towards collaboration: he declared that there was 'certainly nobility in accepting the situation of the defeated party'.[56] But the first issue of *Voix françaises* gave no hint of being pro-German. The 'Programme' set out was one that envisaged the rebuilding of France on a Christian basis, backing Pétain and the Révolution Nationale. Archbishop Feltin was enthusiastic: he took copies of the new weekly to a meeting of the ACA and hoped for many subscribers.[57] However, within six months Lesourd had got into hot water for publishing an article by Serge Jeanneret attacking Chevalier, who when Education minister had given aid to Catholic education and tried to promote religious education in state schools.[58] Moreover, as time went by, and contributions were published from collaborationists such as Abel Hermant, the friend of Bonnard, a distinctly extremist note crept in.

In 1943 what particularly infuriated Parisian Catholics in touch with Jean Marin, who broadcast their views in French from London, was that so distinguished a theologian as Père Sertillanges contributed a weekly article to *Voix Françaises*. That he should associate himself with Lesourd, 'ce commerçant de la basse pensée', who favoured the Relève and deified Pétain, was an outrage. They believed that Lesourd's encomiums of the Marshal served to bolster up the position of the bishops, 'a fair number of whom have incurred the accusation of indirect collaboration with the enemy: trembling with fear and thirsting for power [...] they have sucked up to the Vichy government'.[59]

Lesourd's fate after the Liberation is obscure, but in the 1950s he was running *L'Observateur catholique*, which was then caught up in the incipient debate on 'progressivism' and 'integralism' in the Church.

The other limb of the Bordeaux near-collaborationists was a more formidable figure, Canon Bergey, parish priest of Saint-Emilion and twice Deputy for the Gironde before passing on his constituency to his friend, Philippe Henriot. Already before the war Bergey had a reputation for extremism — as early as 1926 a police report had branded him as the departmental head of the Fascist movement Le Faisceau .[60] In November 1940 Bergey had relaunched his small pre-war publication, *Soutanes de France*, the organ for ex-servicemen clergy of the Ligue nationale des Prêtres Anciens Combattants (PAC). According to its founder, from 6,000 subscribers in 1940 it had risen to 34,000 in January 1944, a figure that included 7,000 of the laity. Given the number of priests who actually served during the First World War, these figures demonstrate that he enjoyed a wide audience for his opinions.

Bergey professed his views to be those of a realist who opposed the 'attentisme' of certain Catholics, and representing those of a Europeanist mindful of France's future role, one wishing to avoid the massacre that occurred 'every twenty years' as well as to prevent a Bolshevik takeover.[61] But Bergey's Pétainism gradually cooled: 'Le Maréchal est un homme. Il peut se tromper. Il s'est trompé quelquefois'.[62] As his ardour grew cold, his pro-German leanings increased. By January 1944, probably in response to complaints about his views, he wrote to Archbishop Feltin explaining his position. He knew that nazism, bolshevism, Freemasonry and secularism had all been condemned by Rome, yet France could only choose between these options. What he hoped for was a German victory, although he knew it would bring difficulties. The alternative, the triumph of the 'Anglo-Saxons', would mean the return of the Third Republic politicians, 'an upsurge of

Anglicanism' (*sic*: 'une poussée anglicane') and economic dictatorship; as for a Communist victory, that was unthinkable.[63] He knew many bishops opposed his views, but it was not he (did he imply that it was the bishops?) who had commended spying for the Allies and forging identity cards, or persuaded young men to join the Maquis, 'ce maquis devenu une école de banditisme, sous la dictature de bandits professionnels'.[64] But by then Bergey's justifications were superfluous: in 1944 his time was rapidly running out.

The machinations of this collaborationist journalism carried on by Catholics in Paris and Bordeaux had two purposes. The first was to drive the Church into the arms of the Germans; the second was to counteract the effect of the largely secularising collaborationist press. At Bordeaux the bond that linked them together was Philippe Henriot.

One cannot indict the whole Church because a few notorious Catholic laymen turned to collaboration. Yet Henriot, whose Catholic credentials were impeccable and whose broadcasts were listened to by everyone, friend or foe,[65] wielded great influence over Catholic opinion. His mission, he declared, was 'to reconcile national socialism and the Church, and to unite the two nations of the Rhine'.[66] For him the natural corollary to this ambition was the fight against bolshevism, as the enemy of Christianity. Another target was the Christian Democrats, whom he accused of betrayal — he condemned defectors such as Valentin, the former head of the LFC, whom Giraud had appointed as Justice Commissioner in Algiers.[67] At first he spoke weekly on Radio Vichy, but after his appointment as Secretary-General for Information and Propaganda (6 January 1944) he gave two broadcasts a day. His eloquence and power to convince were recognised even by the Catholic Resistance, who were puzzled at his silence regarding Nazi doctrines.[68] His stock with some prelates was not high: Cardinal Liénart disliked him and turned down an invitation to attend a lecture given by him in Lille on 29 January 1944. Eventually his exhortations to hunt down 'terroristes' persuaded the Maquis that he was too great a propaganda success. On 28 June 1944 he was assassinated.

Some clue is given to the bishops' attitudes a few weeks from the Liberation by their different reactions to the ceremonies that marked his funeral. Cardinal Liénart, whose withdrawal from any posture that smacked of politics was absolute, declined to attend a commemorative mass in Lille on 7 July 1944, but authorised the parish priest to conduct the service. In his letter of refusal, whilst paying tribute to 'one of the most distinguished orators at our Catholic meetings' — a reference to his pre-war oratory on behalf of the FNC — for his talent, he wrote: 'J'estime que cette cérémonie [...] aura, qu'on le veuille ou non, une signification politique'.[69] Cardinal Gerlier did attend a service at Lyons on 15 July 1944 but was warned beforehand that at the service he should make no adverse comments on government policy; if he did so, said Boutémy, the regional Prefect, he himself would rectify any statement by addressing the crowd outside the church immediately afterwards. To mark his displeasure, Gerlier left the service ten minutes before the end. After the incident had been reported to Laval, Mgr Moncelle, a counsellor at the French Embassy to the Vatican, thought the Head of Government should formally rebuke the cardinal.[70] In Paris Cardinal Suhard, attended by Mgr Chappoulie and Mgr Beaussart, presided over the funeral mass itself in Notre Dame, in the presence of the German commanding officer for Gross-Paris.[71] He refused, however, to pronounce a funeral oration. Gerlier privately criticised Suhard's participation, but the latter argued that as a Catholic and as a minister in office Henriot had a right to a state ceremony. However, at Vichy a mass had been celebrated on 5 July 1944, which Pétain had attended in civilian clothes to denote that he came in his private capacity.

Elsewhere various ceremonies were held. In Marseilles Mgr Dulay, going against the advice of his Resistance clergy, did actually give an address. In Bordeaux Archbishop Feltin attended a ceremony. In Rouen Archbishop Petit de Julleville used the occasion to speak out against the perpetrators of the assassination.[72] Ceremonies were held in Nice, Cannes, Menton and Grasse: the Riviera was a stronghold of the Milice, of which Henriot had nominally been a member. It was probably this commemoration, coming so close to the Liberation, of one who had attacked them so relentlessly that triggered off the bitterly hostile reaction of the Resistance, including many Catholics, to the bishops a few weeks later. As late as May Henriot had attacked some of the clergy for encouraging 'rebellion'.[73] Even in his death the eloquent Catholic orator, once a leading light among the Catholic laity, did not fail to make an impact.

What, however, of the bishops, who, rightly or wrongly, came under suspicion at the Liberation?

Notes

Unless otherwise stated the place of publication is Paris

1. L. Combelle, 'Avec ou sans prières', *Révolution*, 22 August 1942.
2. Quoted in AN 2 AG 492. 'Note de Police (Secret)'. 'Politique religieuse du PPF', 20 February 1943.

3. Ibid.
4. AN 2 AG 492. 'Note de Police (Secret)', 11 February 1943. Report drawn up by the Toulouse branch of the PPF.
5. M. Sicard (Saint-Paulien), *Histoire de la collaboration*, 1964, pp. 338f. Sicard gives the year of the enquiry as 1942. From other sources it would appear more likely to be 1943. The list of prelates falling into each category was:

Cordial: Beaussart (Paris), Courbe (Paris), Cazaux (Luçon), Merguen (Poitiers), Mathieu (Dax), Martin (Amiens), Béguin (Auch), Feltin (Bordeaux), Sembel (Dijon), Caillot (Grenoble), Terrier (Tarentaise), Vittoz (Grenoble), Grente (Le Mans), Marmottin (Rheims), Serrand (Saint-Brieuc), Grumel (Saint-Jean-de-Maurienne), Choquet (Tarbes), Du Bois de la Villerabel (Aix);

Courteous: Suhard (Paris), Costes (Angers), Megnin (Angoulême), Cesbron (Annecy), Lebrun (Autun), Roeder (Beauvais), Tissier (Châlons), Durieux (Chambéry), Gaudel (Fréjus), Bonnabel (Gap), Liagre (La Rochelle), Rastouil (Limoges), Courcoux (Orléans), Marceillac (Pamiers), Rodié (Agen), Lefèvre (Troyes);

Reserved: Richaud (Laval), Fillon (Bourges), Harcouët (Chartres), Chassaigne (Tulle), Delay (Marseilles), Villeplet (Nantes), Pic (Tulle).

6. A Dio, Lille, Guerre 1939–1945. 1939–1942, Annales 8 M 1.
7. AN 2 AG 492. 'Note (Secret)', of Lavagne, 10 February 1943.
8. See AN F1a.3784. Document ref: XCG/5/35315. Information received 19 March 1944; and F60.1674. Document CNI. no. 5483, received 12 April 1944 (Fighting French files).
9. 'L'Eglise catholique et le bolchévisme', *L'Œuvre*, 1 June 1943 ; and 13 December 1943.
10. 'Inutiles réticences',*L'Œuvre*, 9 March 1944.
11. M. Déat, *Mémoires politiques*, 1989, pp. 815f.
12. B. Gordon, *Collaborationism in France during the Second World War*, Ithaca and London, 1980, chapter 8.
13. *Nouvelle Revue Française*, 'Huit mois de défaite', May 1941.
14. 'Les sept Internationales contre la patrie', *Je Suis Partout*, 25 September 1942,
15. L. Rebatet, *Les Décombres*, 1942, p. 559.
16. L. Donnas, 'Jouons le jeu français', *La Croix du Rhône*, 23 November 1941.
17. *La Croix de Savoie*, 24 March 1943, quoted in *Actes*: Lyons, p. 81, n. 6.
18. AN 2 AG 82 'Note (Secret)', 16 March 1943, with copy of the tract, 'Lyonnais, voici ton Maître'.
19. F60.1674. 'Note'.
20. In the Isère department in 1943 28 per cent of the Milice came from the professional, industrial and managerial classes—the least numerous group in the population—i.e. usually from practising Catholic families. See M. Chanal, 'La Milice française dans l'Isère (février 1943–août 1944)', *RHDGM*, no. 127, July 1982, Document XIV, p. 39.
21. AN 2 AG 609. Letter of Jean Mulson to Pétain, Béziers, 16 July 1943.
22. G. Cholvy and Y.-M. Hilaire, *Histoire religieuse de la France contemporaine, 1930–1988*, 1988, p. 113. See also H. Amouroux, *Joies et douleurs du peuple libéré*, 1988, p. 517.
23. AN 2 AG 609 Letter of Jean Mulson, Franc-Garde, to Pétain, Béziers, 16 July 1943.
24. AN F1a..3784. Fighting French file. Document ref: PJR/1/35304. Information received 13 April 1944.
25. A Dio, Lille, 2 B 1 ACA, 1942–1945. Minutes of ACA meeting, July 1944. Darnand's letter to Suhard was sent from Vichy on 19 June 1944, and Suhard's refusal is dated 28 June. See also J. Duquesne, *Les Catholiques sous l'Occupation*, 1966, p. 358.
26. AN F1a.3784. Fighting French file. Document ref: PAK/2/35300, dated 8 August 1944. It would seem that M. Chaudier, the local Protestant pastor, also protested against the Oradour massacre.

27. To Kessler, the German ultimately responsible for the arrest, Laval declared that it was bad luck to imprison a bishop. A few days later Kessler was killed in a skirmish with the Maquis. See A. Mallet, *Pierre Laval*, vol. 2, 1955, pp. 166ff.

28. AN F60.1674. 'Appel de la Milice et de l'Action Française à certains prêtres abusés'. Document no. 4445 received by the Commissariat National de l'Intérieur, Algiers, 9 February 1944.

29. Sicard, *Histoire*, p. 242.

30. AN 72 AJ 258. Study by General A. Merglen, rue de la Libération, 06520 Magagnos, n.d.[post-war document?].

31. P. Ory, *Les Collaborateurs, 1939–1945*, 1986, p. 241; see also H. Michel, *Paris allemand*, 1981, p. 119.

32. AN F60.1674.

33. Cutting in AN F60.1674.

34. The LVF was keen for its religious needs to be met: General Lavigne Delville complained that in their camp at Kruzina (Poland) there was no Christian presence to greet reinforcements when they arrived. See AN 72 AJ 258, letter from General Lavigne Delville to Brinon, Paris, 18 September 1942.

35. H. Amouroux, *Les beaux jours des collabos*, 1978, p. 275 and n. 53.

36. Reported in *La Gerbe*, 1 July 1943.

37. R. Tournoux, *le Royaume d'Otto. France, 1939–1945*, 1982, p. 353.

38. Quoted in Amouroux, *Les beaux jours*, p. 252.

39. M. Martin du Gard, *La Chronique de Vichy 1940–1944*, 1948, p. 136.

40. Quoted in R. Bédarida, 'La Voix du Vatican (1940–1942). Bataille des ondes et Résistance spirituelle', *Revue d'Histoire de l'Eglise*, vol. 64, 1978, p. 224.

41. E. Fouilloux, 'Le Clergé', in J-P. Azéma and F. Bédarida (eds), *Vichy et les Français*, 1992, p. 464f.

42. AN F60.1674. Report CNI No. 3426, received October 1943.

43. AN AJ 40.563. Gestapo report, Paris, 13 May 1941.

44. A Dio, Lille. ACA 2 B 1. 'La conscience catholique devant l'Allemagne', by 'Jacques Benoit'. Liénart had written on the document: 'Note anonyme émanant sans doute d'un prêtre. Inadmissible'.

45. P. Ory, *La France Allemande*, 1977, p. 116, quotes an article by Lesaunier in *Nouvelles Continentales*, 9 November 1941: 'Ce sera notre devoir non seulement de Français mais aussi de catholiques, de nous soumettre à toute cette réglementation.'

46. AN F60.1674. Fighting French file. NM/182: 'Lettre des inconnus catholiques à l'attention de Monsieur Jean Marin', 24 March 1943.

47. C. Paillat, *L'Occupation. Le pillage de la France, juin 1940–novembre 1942*, 1987, p. 159.

48. AN 2 AG 76, SP 3. Letter from Polimann, 28 Boulevard Poincaré, Bar-le-Duc, 26 June 1944, to Ménétrel, Pétain's private secretary, whom he addressed as 'Bernard'.

49. *Aujourd'hui* [Paris], 26 October 1942. 'Il faut mettre un frein à leurs activités.'

50. Bucard went to his execution singing one of the Franciste songs: 'Je suis chrétien, voilà ma gloire/ Mon espérance et mon soutien/ Mon chant d'amour et de victoire/ Je suis chrétien, je suis chrétien.' Quoted in Y. Lambert, *Dieu change en Bretagne. La religion à Limerzel de 1900 à nos jours*, 1985.

51. *Jeunesse. Organe de la Génération 40.* [A Doriotist weekly], no. 17, 20 April 1941, p. 1.

52. AN F17.13347. Letter to Bonnard, Paris, 5 May 1944.

53. L. Rebatet, *Les Mémoires d'un fasciste*, vol. 2, *1941–1947*, 1976, p. 62. A. Latreille, *De Gaulle, la Libération et l'Eglise* catholique, 1978, p. 30, also mentions Père George, another Parisian cleric of lesser notoriety.

54. C. Lévy, 'La presse collaborationniste de Paris et de Bordeaux et l'Eglise de France', *Actes*: Lyons, 1978, pp. 443–50, gives the general background.

55. G. and J. Ragache, *La vie quotidienne des écrivains et des artistes sous l'occupation, 1940–1944*, 1988, p. 116.

56. J. Duquesne, *Les catholiques français sous l'occupation*, 1966, quoting an article in *Le Mémorial de Saint-Etienne*, 12 September 1940

57. A Dio, Lille, ACA, 2 B 1, 15–17 January 1941.
58. A Dio, Lille, ACA, 2 B 1, 24 July 1941. A letter of 11 July 1941 to Cardinal Liénart from Joseph Toulemonde, a northern industrialist, who was later to attempt to negotiate further aid for Catholic schools on the cardinal's behalf, and who asked: 'Va-t-on continuer, comme par le passé, attaquer les catholiques qui mettent... leurs actes en concordance avec leur foi?'
59. AN F60.1674. Doc. NM182 4718/CHR/10/1 (PNF), 24 March 1943.
60. AN F7.13208. Document A. 494. Police report, Bordeaux, 2 January 1926.
61. A Dio, Lille, ACA 1942–1945. Minutes of the ACA meeting of 16–18 February 1944.
62. AN 72 AJ 1863. Dossier: France 1940–1942, report of OFI–Havas, 16 October 1942, quoting from *Soutanes de France*.
63. AN 2 AG 494. Bergey, 'Au delà des frontières', *Soutanes de France*, January 1943.
64. A Dio, Lille, 2 B 1 ACA 1942–1945. Minutes of the meeting of the ACA, 16–18 February 1944. Letter from Bergey to the one whom he termed his 'chef hiérarchique', Archbishop Feltin, Saint-Emilion, 27 January 1944.
65. Martin du Gard, *La Chronique de Vichy,* 1948, p. 433.
66. A. Mallet, *Pierre Laval*, vol. 2, 1955, p. 47.
67. P. Henriot, 'Les bons élèves de la démocratie chrétienne', *Combats*, 2 October 1943.
68. 'A Philippe Henriot. Lettre d'un militant chrétien',*Témoignage Chrétien*, no. 8, March 1944.
69. A Dio, Lille, Dossier Pétain, 8 M 1. Letter from Liénart to Ghys, the local representative of the Information ministry, 4 July 1944.
70. AN F1a. 3784. Document ref: ACB/112/36800. Service courrier, 25 August 1944 [*sic*].
71. AN 72 AJ 258. Various press cuttings.
72. AN 72 AJ 258.
73. *France*, London, 10 May 1944, quoting a Reuters report.

-20-

'Epuration' and the Higher Clergy

At the Liberation many Frenchman, particularly those in the Resistance, hardly distinguished collaboration with the Germans from co-operation with the regime. This was because what might be termed the 'second Vichy' under Laval had increasingly subordinated policy to Nazi demands. However, although the bishops had, up to a certain point, fallen in with the wishes of the government, it would be patently untrue to assert they were manifestly guilty of advocating or practising collaborationism.

There were two principal exceptions: Cardinal Baudrillart and Mgr Dutoit, Bishop of Arras.

Baudrillart, who had died in 1942, had been Rector of the Paris Institut Catholique since 1907. At first he was treated by the Germans with justifiable reserve. In 1940 they searched his quarters, as they had done those of his confrères. They recalled how, during the First World War, he had campaigned against them.[1] It was not until the 1930s that his attitudes changed. He began to consider atheistic communism, because it was a global creed, as more dangerous than nazism, which initially was restricted to Deutschtum, those considered to be German . Despite a friendship with Poincaré the cardinal was no lover of parliamentary democracy; his sympathies were more with Action Française. In 1939 he had dubbed Hitler 'un monstre', and after war broke out declared the time had come to 'se mesurer avec une barbarie renouvelée du paganisme'.[2] Up to the defeat his patriotism was unquestionable, but in the aftermath he feared a Communist coup and civil war. By the autumn of 1940 he had made a complete volte-face and predicted that the Führer would go down as one of the greatest men in history. He was reported in *Le Cri du Peuple* in December as not forgiving the British for defeating Napoleon and for supporting 'le traître de Gaulle'. About this time he suffered a decline in his mental and physical faculties — he was then already in his eighties. Almost blind, he relied heavily on 'le très énigmatique chanoine Tricot',[3] Vice-Rector *pro tempore belli* of the Institut Catholique. After the handshake of Montoire he had seconded a motion by Bonnard to send a congratulatory message to Pétain, supported at a sparsely attended meeting by only Bellesort, the Académie's Permanent Secretary and Abel Hermant,[4] but opposed by Duhamel, Valéry and three others. Baudrillart described the defeat of the motion as scandalous, motivated by hypocrisy and fear.[5] About this time his pro-German sentiments became widely known. On 21 November the Agence Interpresse published a statement under the title 'Ce que pense un prince de l'Eglise de la collaboration franco-allemande'. Reproduced in full in *La Gerbe*, it exhorted Frenchmen to follow Pétain (he had written a book, *La Voix du Chef*, about the Marshal) and pleaded for Franco-German entente: 'Le Maréchal, homme d'action et bien informé, a prononcé le mot de collaboration qui déplaît aux imaginations intoxiquées.'[6] The attempt to secure a lasting peace between the two nations must be made.

His views found a faint echo with prelates such as Mgr Marmottin (Rheims) and Mgr Duparc (Quimper). They were backed by Mgr Vincent, Rector of the Angers Institut Catholique and a few other Catholic academics, as well as some Army officers. Marshal Pétain thought fit to send him a letter of thanks.[7]

Baudrillart had lived through three wars between the two countries. This experience and a generation gap explain the adverse reaction his views provoked among younger Frenchmen.[8] One, contrasting the cardinal's stance in 1915 with that of 1940, asked incredulously if he had a 'look-alike' ('un sosie'). A number of clandestine publications in the occupied zone, estimated by the ACA to have an audience of 50,000, published a 'Réponse au cardinal Baudrillart' emphasising the unfavourable impact of his support of nazism.[9]

Baudrillart joined the Groupe Collaboration, as did Hermant and Bonnard, his two fellow-members of the Académie Française. His wholehearted approval of the Nazi attack on the Soviet Union drew a broadside from an anonymous theologian belonging to a religious order: 'C'est une dérision de placer Hitler et le nazisme en tête d'une croisade de chrétienté', as the cardinal had claimed.[10] He also gave his patronage to the LVF, calling it, with geographical inexactitude, 'a chivalry that will deliver the tomb of Christ'. He promised help in recruiting for the LVF when Doriot, the PPF leader, came on leave from the Eastern Front in January 1942. In August he and Cardinal Suhard presided over a mass to commemorate the first anniversary of the LVF; the collaborationist press saw their joint presence as one of political significance over which Catholics should ponder deeply (*L'Œuvre*, 29–30 August 1942). By the end of the year the cardinal was dead. In a last message he reaffirmed his collaborationist views: 'I am about to face God... the only road to salvation for France consists in an alliance and general definitive reconciliation with Germany, i.e the Greater Germany of tomorrow'.[11] Canon Tricot defended his superior's views, pointing out that his advocacy of collaborationism had never been condemned by Rome.[12] His funeral was the occasion for an extraordinary show of solidarity by the episcopacy, some thirty bishops attending the requiem mass in Notre Dame on 25 November 1942.

Dutoit, the only diocesan bishop that could really have been said to have 'collaborated' — and then in words only — although very anti-Nazi in 1939, had also been won over by Pétain's Montoire statement. His pastoral letter of 22 December 1940 regretted that the Marshal's policy had been misunderstood. The defeat had administered a lesson to France, but providentially Pétain had assumed power. Dissidents who attacked the new regime should be punished.[13] There followed a very tortuous argument to justify collaborationism, one not at all typical of Catholic thinking at the time.[14] Honour would not be sacrificed. 'Collaboration merely assumes a free, loyal will to seek an understanding. I collaborate; therefore I am no longer a slave to whom is forbidden every initiative of speech and action, one only good enough to receive and carry out orders. I collaborate: thus I have the right to contribute my personal thinking and original effort to the common task... Collaboration is the sign under which, in order to last, the peace of tomorrow must be concluded'. Pétain's gesture 'may well count one day in history as an effective and laudable contribution to the peace and happiness of the whole world'.

Such a thesis betrays a naiveté sometimes apparent in other episcopal pronouncements. Dutoit's definition of collaboration was too sanguine, and certainly unacceptable to the Nazis. The French people had not been consulted. Hitler had certainly not abandoned the idea of revenge: he was determined that France should pay dearly for having declared war. There was the huge presumption that a Franco–German alliance would promote universal peace. So long as the Allies continued the fight, and the Americans continued to back them, this was a remote contingency, and even in December 1940 German hopes of an early victory were receding.

The Germans made capital out of the statement. French POWs were informed that the bishop had come out in favour of Franco–German collaboration.[15] But a number of priests in the diocese refused to read out the pastoral letter in church. (Mgr Sauvage, the Archdeacon of Boulogne, was accustomed to read out the British war communiqué in his basilica.) Mgr Chiappe, Archdeacon of Arras, issued a New Year message which he concluded by wishing pointedly 'that those who don't feel at home with us should find their own home again as quickly as possible'. ('que ceux qui ne se sentent pas chez eux chez nous se retrouvent chez eux au plus vite').

In his Lenten letter the good Bishop re-emphasised the duty of obedience to Pétain's exhortation to collaborate.[16] Some of the staff of the Lille Institut Catholique wrote supporting him; in others such sentiments aroused astonishment and resentment. Six law faculty lecturers set out a systematic refutation of the Bishop's arguments. The sovereignty of the Marshal's government, because of German pressure, was, to say the least, questionable. They questioned the Bishop's definition of collaboration as not in accordance with the facts. There was no 'libre et loyale volonté d'entente'. In fact, on the very day that Brinon had declared that French policy was set fair for collaboration Goebbels had proclaimed that Germany and Italy alone had the right to rule Europe.[17] Regarding the regime their message to the Bishop was clear: 'We do not dissent from the view that in the face of this domination we must close ranks. But this can only be a provisional grouping around a *de facto* government imposed by circumstances'.[18]

They raised wider issues. The Bishop had implied that Pétain had accepted defeat in order to bring about internal change in France; this was hurtful to French patriotism. It pained them to see the Church apparently wishing to restrict the little liberty that remained to their compatriots. It had exhorted the faithful to respect 'established authority', but Catholics could only accept this if those that governed were worthy of esteem. A face-to-face meeting with the Bishop produced no meeting of minds. One of the six summed up the discussion: 'We set ourselves up as a jury and have condemned the guilty party'. The affair is significant because it represents the first open rejection by laity of a bishop's pronouncement upon the actions of the regime. They were not willing to accept a complete abdication of conscience.

Mgr Dutoit was perhaps unduly under the influence of one of his vicars-general, Canon Edouard Maréchal, an overt collaborationist who contributed virulent Germanophile and Anglophobe articles to the Pas-de-Calais *Courier*. To Pétain the worthy canon wrote declaring that he was surrounded by Gaullists who were convinced that in his heart of hearts the Marshal was of the same mind as the 'ex-general'; it would be salutary if Pétain could rid them of this 'aberration' and set them both back on 'the right path'.[19]

Meanwhile Dutoit continued to voice extreme views. He castigated the unremitting bombing of the area as 'une catastrophe dont l'horreur et la cruauté ont été rarement égalées'. This aroused the indignation of the Resistance. The clandestine *Voix du Nord* predicted (correctly) that one day the Vatican would cease to impose upon a victorious France 'un évêque pro-Boche'.[20] As late as 1944, in his New Year message the Bishop characterised the Resistance as 'partisans qui s'érigent en arbitres et vengeurs du patriotisme', whereas in reality they were 'bandits de profession'.[21] It was perhaps for these statements rather than his appeal for collaborationism that the Bishop was condemned.

At the Liberation he left his diocese in haste, but was detained for twenty-four hours before taking refuge with Cardinal Liénart in Lille, where he had formerly been a vicar-general. The new Pas-de-Calais prefect had formally placed him under adminstrative internment for his various injudicious statements — three others had appeared in the *Semaines religieuses* in 1942–43.[22] Bishop Théas of Montauban, who had stood up to the Germans, on a visit to the Pope in November 1944 asked the Vatican to secure his release, but the effort was in vain. The Prefect, backed by several prominent local Catholics, advised that any return of Dutoit to his diocese would be 'inopportune'.[23] However, from his exile in Lille in 1945 the Bishop issued a New Year message to his diocesans in which he declared 'our souls are torn between joy and sadness', which was rather a tepid rallying to the new dispensation, compared with his enthusiastic acceptance of Pétain in 1940. Plans were laid to indict him before the special courts set up to deal with collaborators. These were dropped, but it was suggested he appear before a 'chambre civique', and indicted on the lesser charge of 'indignité nationale', a course favoured by the Interior ministry.[24] This was also not proceeded with. Supporters even petitioned that he should be able to resume his see at Arras, which was the Vatican's initial reaction. However, on 19 July 1945 he formally resigned. Until his death in 1953 at the age of seventy-nine, he continued to reside in Lille.

Apart from these two cases, charges of direct collaboration against other bishops were not sustainable. However, a number were reproached for not protesting against the treatment of the Jews and positively recommending the acceptance of the STO. In the climate of the Liberation those who had condemned the Resistance and Gaullism, had labelled the Maquis as terrorists, or who had characterised the Allied bombings as 'barbaric' were particularly stigmatised. Thus, for example, the Maquisards, many of them escapees from the STO, particularly resented Mgr Auvity, Bishop of Mende. He was arrested on 19 August 1944 and forced to quit his diocese for Bonnecombe (Aveyron), whence he was destined never to return. The same fate overtook Mgr Dubois de la Villerabel, Archbishop of Aix, a notorious 'maréchaliste' who was generally disliked: it was said that when he asked some Christian workmen, 'Que dit-on de moi?' the answer came back, 'Monseigneur, on dit qu'il faut vous pendre.' [25] He fled to Solesmes. These were the only other two bishops forced to resign, although others, as will be seen, were in jeopardy.

Demands for action against prelates arose from local sources — the greater the grass-roots insistence the more likely central government was to move. Other cases than those of the three eventually deposed from their sees were just as serious, but local pressure was not so effective and thus they escaped.

The general charge against the Hierarchy was an accusation of compromise, 'attentisme' and 'mutisme'. The reproach was that it had not spoken out and given Christians a clear lead. Yet even before the Germans had been driven from French soil the ACA issued a declaration in October 1944 claiming that the bishops had fulfilled their prime duty of sustaining the Church and its religious life. If they had remained silent on other matters, they had followed the Vatican's example. In so doing they had protected the faithful, particularly the young. To some extent this was true. Some bishops had demonstrated their independence from the State in various ways. Others no longer recalled such statements as that of Bishop Fleury of Nancy, 'From the moment when a government refrains from interfering in faith and morals, recognises God and the human person, the Church remains silent.'[26] However, does not silence give consent, and even approval?

The adherence of the bishops to Pétain to the bitter end, the passive acquiescence of a few in Hitler's plans for a 'New Order', and the active collaboration of a few priests had already alarmed those Catholics who had joined the Resistance early on. As early as December 1941 the clandestine *Défense de la France* had voiced doubts about the post-war future of the Church. Clergy who had thrown in their lot with the Maquis addressed an open letter to the cardinals and bishops on 15 May 1944, in which they were exhorted to switch sides before it was too late. Their call went unheeded. Another cleric, Père Carrière, by then Vice-President of the Algiers Consultative Assembly, put the position more brutally: Resistance Catholics considered this was no time for forgiveness; their fellow believers would have to submit to 'God's justice', albeit administered by men.

Thus other indictments of bishops continued to flow in. Mgr Serrand, of St-Brieuc, decorated and severely wounded in the First World War, came under fire for his anti-Resistance stance. However, the local Liberation Committee considered that a public acknowledgement of his error would suffice. He could then officiate at services once more, but, since he was over seventy, it would be appropriate for an auxiliary bishop to assist him — a delicate way of easing him out.[27] The case of Mgr Marmottin, Archbishop of Rheims, was more complicated. In 1942 he had publicly supported the pamphlet by Lesaunier, a Carmelite, entitled, 'La conscience catholique en face du devoir civique actuel', in which was stated: 'So long as the Armistice is in force the duty of every

Frenchman as also of every Catholic is one of submission to [...] the established order. Consequently for us Catholics any violence towards the occupying power, any manifestation of hostility towards it, is ruled out'.

The Germans had made great play of this statement, and it had been published in thirty-two newspapers.[28] Mgr Marmottin's support for it seemed, as one correspondent put it, to be a plea for 'une loyale et franche collaboration franco-allemande'.[29] At the time Marmottin had received the backing of some bishops in the occupied zone. An inspector of the Milice asserted that he had also shown 'sa sympathie pour la LVF'.[30] Another bishop, Mgr Béguin of Auch, was reproached for warning his flock after the North African landings that 'the occupying forces have also a right to respect', and to expect correct behaviour towards them.[31] Mgr Brunhes, Bishop of Montpellier, at the same juncture, had urged absolute compliance with instructions, with no provocation of the occupying forces.[32] Mgr Courcoux, Bishop of Orléans, was accused of belonging to the Groupe Collaboration.[33] Later, at the municipal elections in November 1945, the Bishop of Nancy, was charged with supporting the candidacy of Dr Schmitt, the pro-German Mayor under the Occupation.[34] On the other hand, many accusations could be easily rebutted. Mgr Pic, of Valence, branded as a collaborator, had employed a Jew, wearing a cassock, as his secretary, and had not hesitated on occasion to criticise Germans to their face.[35] Many denunciations were bandied about at the time, but allegations often represented only half-truths or even downright lies.

The desire for justice, even revenge, was strong, and even rebounded on smaller fry. A Resistance priest, Abbé X, of Savoy, suggested regional committees of patriotic priests to judge their peers — a new kind of ecclesiastical court — with the decisions they arrived at to be submitted to the Justice ministry through the Nuncio.[36] No such bodies were established; if they had been, a few excesses might have been avoided. In Brittany, the Cévennes and Languedoc suspect collaborationist clergy — lesser lights ('des lampistes') — were summarily executed. In Pyrénées Orientales two priests, Père Favre, of Sournia, and Père Niort, of Totavel, were tortured to death. Abbé Mandroux, of Saint-Privat (Ardèche) was despatched by a pistol shot in the neck.[37] At Baud (Morbihan) the clergy had to take flight because they were branded as Breton autonomists.[38] These were, however, exceptions. The bulk of the clergy had been anticollaborationist, if not Resistentialist, as Paul Reynaud judged: 'As a whole, the French clergy, whether regular or secular, had an extremely patriotic attitude'. And, he added, Catholics also 'had their apostles and martyrs under the yoke of the Gestapo'.[39]

The fact remained that over the bishops as a whole in 1944 there hung a political question mark. The cases described above were the most flagrant, but even these were only resolved after long delays. De Gaulle, received by the Pope on 9 July 1944, had raised the desire for an 'épuration' of the episcopacy, but the Pope had pretended not to hear him.[40]

At the Liberation the mood became more extreme. The scene was set by what occurred on 26 August 1944 in Paris. Before the service of thanksgiving at Notre Dame Cardinal Suhard was informed that his presence was unwelcome, because of his general comportment during the Occupation. In fact, two nights previously Beaussart, his auxiliary bishop, accompanied by the local parish priest, had turned up at the Hôtel de Ville just as the great bell of the cathedral was pealing forth in jubilation. He met with an icy reception. Through Abbé Bruckberger, the Resistance hero and FFI chaplain, de Gaulle's decision was communicated to him.[41] The ACA considered the rebuff unjustified, and later, at Cardinal Liénart's suggestion, offered its sympathy to the unfortunate cardinal and made a formal protest.[42]

Cardinal Suhard's actions demonstrated that sometimes co-operation had indeed sailed close to collaboration. Had he not allowed masses, claimed his accusers, to be said for members of the LVF fallen on the Eastern Front?[43] Only a few weeks before the Liberation had he not welcomed Pétain to his cathedral and in July presided over the funeral service for Philippe Henriot? According to Umbreit, the German military historian, the archbishop had certainly made remarks favourable to collaboration.[44] But he had probably felt obliged to put out temporising statements such as his declaration of 12 December 1940, that 'his dearest wish was for an understanding between the two peoples' of France and Germany. German opinion of him demonstrates a certain ambiguity about his real attitude. The military inclined to believe that he wished for a fair relationship based on reciprocity; the Sicherheitsdienst could not make up its mind; Abetz, the Ambassador, assessed him as favouring, for tactical reasons, some forms of collaborationism. All such evaluations, including the fact that he wished above all the good of France, are probably correct over time. A statement the cardinal made as late as 7 February 1944, when German defeat was almost inevitable, that the war in the East remained a 'European crusade', seems as puzzling as it was gratuitous.[45] Nevertheless, indiscretions cannot be construed directly as collaborationism, although at the Liberation Suhard had to suffer for them.

This is therefore why in August 1944 de Gaulle dispensed with the official welcome of the Church at the portico of Notre Dame. (The events that followed were unexpected. Shots fired at the congregation by persons unknown rang out. Unperturbed, the general took his place in the chancel — on the archiepiscopal throne. In a side chapel a group of children, led by a nun, sang, 'Sauvez, sauvez la France, au nom du Sacré Cœur'. In the chancel were two solitary religious, the Dominican monk, Bruckberger, and a Franciscan. The choir waited expectantly. However, instead of the traditional canticle of thanksgiving, the *Te Deum*, reserved for a Head of State, the Franciscan burst into the *Magnificat* — a delicate touch — which was taken up by the choir. Bruckberger remarks: 'Thus, instead of a prince of the Church and the higher clergy of Paris, it was a son of St Francis of Assisi and a son of St Dominic who welcomed General de Gaulle and the new government of liberated France'.)

Tractations regarding what should be done about the bishops were long drawn out. Even before the Liberation of Paris Georges Bidault, as head of the Conseil National de la Résistance and de Gaulle's future Foreign Minister, himself a lifelong Catholic, had drawn up a detailed note dated 27 June 1944 demanding severe sanctions, possibly more stringent than those sought by the General. His memorandum reflected also those of other Catholic Resistance hard-liners.

Bidault's indictment nevertheless began by affirming categorically that there were no collaborationists among the bishops. Instead, in effect he accused them of a blinding lack of commonsense, as demonstrated in their overenthusiasm for the Vichy regime, in making utterances useful to German propaganda, and promoting a new Moral Order partly to give advantages to the Church. The traditional requirement of obedience by the faithful to the government of the day, as decreed by the bishops, had been carried to excess, leading politically to total submission to Pétain. Bidault singled out particularly Cardinal Gerlier and the Archbishop of Rheims, as well as the Bishops of Marseilles and Nancy. Others were reproached for their prohibition against Catholics reading clandestine Resistance literature, especially *Témoignage Chrétien* — here the Bishop of Montpellier was named. The Archbishop of Aix and the Bishops of Clermont-Ferrand and Le Puy were accused of condemning the anonymous 'théologiens sans mandat' who had questioned obedience to Vichy. Other accusations were also levelled: the silence maintained regarding the Pope's pre-war condemnation of nazism, whereas his declaration against communism had been praised at the time of the attack on the Soviet Union. A whole list of bishops who had exhorted young men to accept as a duty of conscience forced labour in Germany was cited: the Bishops of Clermont-Ferrand, Le Puy, Viviers, Mende, Rodez, Montpellier, Lille, and the Auxiliary Bishop of Cambrai. And there were other accusations: the list was long, and the net cast widely.

For Bidault, although any mass resignation of the episcopacy was excluded, examples should be made of those whose actions and attitudes had caused offence. Black lists A and A *bis* appended to the document comprised the names of those whose resignation could be justified. All three cardinals appeared on the lists, although it was conceded that Rome was unlikely to allow any of these to be dismissed. The fact that German propaganda had used the ACA declarations for its own purposes meant special blame attached to Cardinal Suhard, as well as Mgr Courbe, his auxiliary bishop and Secretary of Action Catholique, and to Mgr Chappoulie, the ACA's representative at Vichy. Four archbishops, including Mgr Feltin (Bordeaux) and Mgr Du Bois de la Villerabel (Aix), and sixteen bishops were named. The continued publication of the diocesan *Semaines religieuses* after they came under censorship was condemned, as were also the pro-German journalistic activities by priests in the Bordeaux diocese. Feltin was accused of tolerating this Catholic collaborationist press in his diocese. That he had intervened strongly in favour of the Jews and even instigated the ACA letter of protest to Pétain on 22 August 1942 was forgotten.[46] Mgr Ruch, Bishop of Strasbourg, also named in the document, was a special case. His patriotism was beyond question, but his pre-war attitudes might make his removal prudent. (He had opposed the secularisation of schools in Alsace and in 1929 had occurred Daladier's displeasure when he had supported claims for the teaching of German in the province.) A possible replacement might be Canon Flory, Archdeacon of Montbéliard. All in all, a quarter of the Hierarchy was therefore indicted.

Cynics remarked that such a purge was probably unnecessary. The Church, having adopted a subservient attitude to Vichy, would knuckle under to the new government in the same way. Had not this already proved to be the case with the North African bishops?

The Bidault document also comprised a 'white list', List B. If Cardinal Suhard could be persuaded to retire, Mgr Chevrot, priest of St François Xavier in Paris, should replace him. A cardinal's hat was proposed for Mgr Saliège of Toulouse. Six bishops should be promoted to archbishoprics, including Mgr Heintz (Metz) and Mgr Théas (Montauban). Twenty-two priests were recommended for bishoprics, including Mgr Bruno de Solages, who should also be appointed head of the Paris Institut Catholique, and Abbé Rodhain, the chaplain to French POWs.

This somewhat curious document gave no detailed justification for the removal of the bishops indicted. Failing to mention any episcopal opposition to Vichy policies, it was hardly fair. Later it was also criticised for omitting from the indictment Mgr Mesguen (Poitiers), whose anti-Gaullism was such that some of the local Maquis wanted to attack his palace with grenades, and Mgr Girbaud (Nîmes), whose conduct, it was maintained, had been far more reprehensible than others who figured on the list. In any case, such a lengthy black list, drawn up by a Catholic layman, was a humiliation for the Church.

It was to these proposals that André Latreille, the Catholic historian, had to react shortly after his appointment in 1944 as the new Sous-Directeur des Cultes — the post of director was in abeyance — in the Interior ministry.

A memorandum he drew up on relationships between the Provisional Government and the Church[47] showed that the overall situation was very fluid. The Commissaire de la République at Lille was quoted (20 November 1944) as reporting that catholicism still retained a firm hold in his area, even among the workers, because the lower clergy had opted to support the Resistance and de Gaulle. Latreille noted that the bishops were 'plainly embarrassed by the memory of their general submission [...] to the Marshal and the orders of Vichy'.[48] His view was that the government should treat the bishops just like any other group in society: if they had made wrong decisions they should be made to pay for them.

However, there were certain difficulties in the way ahead. Catholics were fully aware that the advantages the defunct regime had conferred upon them were now at risk and were prepared to fight. Moreover, nothing could be resolved, as Mauriac reported in *Le Figaro,* until the Provisional Government had renewed ties with the Vatican. Here there was deadlock. Despite de Gaulle's audience with Pius XII, Bérard having resigned, France was represented at the Holy See only by a chargé d'affaires. Valerio Valeri remained in Paris as Nuncio, but now had no official standing, since the Vatican had not yet recognised the new government. By December 1944 this recognition was a matter of urgency. If Valeri were to depart for Rome without officially taking leave, the position would be worsened.[49]

Meanwhile Latreille continued with his analysis of the political situation. A not inconsiderable part of rural France, particularly in the West and in an arc south of the Massif Central, habitually followed the lead of the parish priest, voting anti-Communist and for the Right — a factor that could weigh in future elections. However, the reconstituted Algiers administration contained only two Communists, out of twenty-two in all; its general tendency was to the Left, but not extremely so. Catholics could therefore support it. There was even the possibility that more 'progressive' Catholics would ally themselves with the Communists, who had said they would look upon them with a benevolent eye. For the first time women would have the suffrage — and many of these were Catholics. Their vote was an unknown factor. Big business, alarmed by the structural reforms and nationalisations promised, might sway the 'bien pensants' of the bourgeoisie to register a protest vote. Thus a positive government policy towards the Church was vital.

There was, however, 'un passé à liquider'. There might be a resurgence of anticlericalism if the question of the bishops was not dealt with. Latreille accepted Bidault's view that a clean sweep of the episcopacy was ruled out, if only because a few of its number had played a distinguished role in opposition to Vichy and the Germans; Mgr Piguet had even been deported. Rome would not accept a wholesale purge, nor did the people demand it. An effort should therefore be made to replace a limited number, but the deposition of a bishop was a matter for the Pope alone. Moreover, most bishops, as persons, were, Latreille generously asserted, 'extremely venerable, commendable for the saintliness of their lives, their desire for spirituality, and their wholly Gospel-like charity'.[50]

In Brittany, in the Côtes du Nord, and in towns such as Vannes, a counter-reaction to attacks on the local bishops had already occurred. Clergy and their flocks had closed ranks behind their diocesan. Resistance priests in Paris had warned of a backlash if measures were taken against Cardinal Suhard. However, Latreille had taken soundings, and thought the pope might not object if 'three or four' bishops were persuaded to resign; the cardinals, 'princes of the Church', remained inviolable. Papal standards were different: the pronouncements of Bishop Dutoit would be judged less severely than, for example, a refusal to appoint chaplains to the Maquis, that is, to men in mortal danger.

Latreille believed the question of the Nuncio was not insoluble. After all, the office was not that of an ambassador, but of the Pope's spokesman to the bishops of the national Church. Although Valerio Valeri had remained at Pétain's side to the very end, this should not prevent his staying on under de Gaulle's government. Pius XII himself, as Cardinal Pacelli, had seen four administrations come and go during his term as Legate in Germany. But here Latreille was not supported by his political masters.

Indeed, by now the 'épuration' of the bishops had turned into a matter of high politics. Tixier, the Socialist Interior minister in the Provisional Government, was being pressed by his party to act, and was strongly supported by Bidault as Foreign Minister. Attention was focused upon 'the silence of the bishops of France concerning the attacks by occupation authorities and Vichy on the most sacred rights of the human conscience'.[51] This was to refuse to differentiate between the two. The difference had been pointed out by the ACA when, meeting in October 1944, they protested in private against moves to depose bishops as being unjustified.[52] Public opinion was also unclear as to the distinction to be drawn between the occupying forces and the regime. Nevertheless a poll conducted in November 1944 had shown that 82 per cent wanted bishops alleged to have 'collaborated' to be punished, with only 10 per cent disagreeing; 8 percent had no opinion. Of the 82 per cent in favour of punitive action, 57 per cent thought the government should take the initiative, and 32 per cent the Church.[53] The legal basis for action was shaky. Article 75 of the Penal Code stated that 'any Frenchman who in time of war maintains communication with a foreign power or its agents, in order to further the undertakings of that power against France [...] is guilty of treason and should suffer death'.[54] On the other hand, how could the bishops, or indeed any institution, have functioned without some contact with the Germans? Moreover, had Vichy been an agent of Germany — was it not, in 1940 at least, the legitimate government of France itself? It is true that the lesser charge of 'national unworthiness' ('indignité nationale') created by the Algiers government, might be brought and bishops, if found guilty, reported to Rome.

A Catholic plan to send an emissary to discuss the problem privately with the Vatican had already been devised. Cardinal Suhard, in agreement with the Nuncio, had alerted the Pope to the proposed mission through the American Cardinal Spellman, but the project fell through.[55]

Manifestly there was hesitation as to how to proceed. It was decided to sound opinion further. Thus in late 1944 the Interior ministry asked the Commissaires de la République to report on what the general attitude of the clergy had been towards the Germans, the Vichy regime, the Resistance, and was now, to the provisional government. The investigation confirmed what was now becoming apparent: the Church's comportment towards the Germans had been 'froide et digne'. Regarding the regime the report was also confirmatory: the bishops, vicars-general and canons had maintained a personal devotion and loyalty to Pétain, but the lower clergy had shown a 'réserve sensible'. The religious orders, particularly the Jesuits, Dominicans and Franciscans, had shown a spirit of resistance, especially in Lyons, Le Puy and Montpellier. In Brittany the parish priests had fought particularly fiercely against the STO. Two bishops, Mgr Beaussart and Mgr Pinson, were accused of having leanings to Doriot's PPF and the LVF.[56] Towards the Resistance the higher clergy had been condemnatory. On the other hand the new regime established at the Liberation had commanded clerical support from the outset — perhaps demonstrating a certain opportunism on the part of the bishops. Latreille summed up: on the whole the reports were 'extremely favourable'. The people acknowledged what some Christians had done to assist those whom the law had persecuted, although the Church has also lost some credibility.[57]

The report of the Commissaire de la République at Châlons-sur-Marne is worth closer examination for its detailed analysis of the situation in the ecclesiastical province of Rheims during the

Occupation.[58] The attitude of the few Protestants in the area was characterised as 'parfait'; the case of Pastor Casalis at Rheims, a Resister who came out publicly against the STO, was cited. The Commissaire then quoted the evaluation of the pro-German Regional Inspector of the Milice, de Rose, made on 9 August 1944, a few weeks before the Liberation. The clergy of the Rheims diocese, in the eyes of this collaborationist witness, were 'generally resistant to National Socialist ideas' but were 'faithful to the Marshal'. The Milice inspector approved of Mgr Marmottin, the Archbishop, who was 'very moderate in his judgement' and 'very troubled' about the question of Resistance groups, but refused to shake hands with Germans. He had agreed to celebrate a mass for the LVF, but on condition that no other ecclesiastical dignitary was present. He was severe regarding the Allied bombings. A few days after Rheims had been bombed for the third time on 30 May 1944 he had declared he had thought twice was more than enough, but 'We were mistaken; the fatal task they had already accomplished had not satisfied the murderers'. He had nevertheless declared, 'these immolations hasten [...] the hour of our deliverance'. However, like Mgr Gayet, his Archdeacon — 'homme compréhensif et bon', according to the Milice Inspector — he had shown 'his sympathy for the LVF'. Likewise, this collaborationist further commented, the bishop of Châlons 'was not against us', and had a reputation of neutrality. In the Aube department the clergy favoured the Resistance and, although in Haute-Marne they were more neutral, the balance 'pencherait plutôt pour nos adversaires'.

The Commissaire de la République appended his own observations to this collaborationist report. For him the bulk of the Rheims clergy had resisted nazism — 'leur germanophobie était certaine', — and their patriotism was not open to criticism. In the Langres diocese, whose bishop had been 'parfaitement correct', the lower clergy had been particularly anti-German and had aided Allied airmen, STO defaulters, and the Resistance. The patriotic behaviour of the Christian Brothers merited special praise. Not accepting the evaluation of de Rose, the Milice Inspector, the Commissaire considered that the Bishop of Châlons, old and venerable, was 'un excellent homme'; the Bishop of Troyes also made a very good impression. On the other hand the collaborationist's judgement of Mgr Marmottin was correct; it was to cost the Archbishop any future promotion to the purple. This report from one area was typical of many.

Latreille generally endorsed the accusations against certain bishops made by Bidault. He noted that Du Bois de la Villerabel, the Archbishop of Aix, had even forbade listening to the foreign radio[59] Many years later, in 1978, Latreille gave his own personal black list. Its value lies in the fact that it is the considered judgement of an eminent Catholic historian rather than that of the temporary civil servant caught up in the hurly-burly of the immediate post-Liberation period. It comprised: Archbishop Feltin of Bordeaux, and Mgr Guerry of Cambrai; bishops Dutoit (Arras), Sembel (Dijon), Choquet (Lourdes), Delay (Marseilles), Auvity (Mende), Serrand (St-Brieuc); Beaussart and Courbe (auxiliary bishops of Paris); and Vielle, the 'vicaire apostolique' of Rabat.

None of these was accused of out-and-out collaboration. Their error or offence was to have clung too much to Vichy, as did many others. Rendering unto Caesar what was Caesar's, they had, perhaps unwittingly, shifted from a religious to a political position. They thought, as Archbishop Feltin expressed it as late as September 1942, a harmony existed between the 'principes chrétiens' of the Church and the 'idées maîtresses' of the Révolution Nationale, and went beyond the ACA policy of 'loyalisme sans inféodation'.[60] When their political stance became untenable, as it did with the STO, they fell back on the traditional religious position of the duty of obedience to the civil power. Because that duty was questioned, they then somewhat belatedly half-revived the doctrine of the personal conscience, which allowed legitimate authority to be questioned in certain cases. Not all bishops conceded this last position, and even where they did, it was hedged in with many qualifications. Hence some pastoral letters continued to characterise Resisters as 'rebels' and 'traitors'.[61]

It was this obduracy that infuriated many Gaullists. Catholic Resisters, according to one noted religious historian, 'considered the bishops had been too lukewarm towards them... However, it may be said that on the whole the Church of France and its episcopacy had been able to resist the temptation of Vichy'. He declares that the bishops found themselves in a situation that limited 'the spontaneity of their action'. This seems indulgent.[62]

In the autumn of 1944 the situation regarding the bishops thus appeared insoluble. A British view at the time casts an interesting sidelight on the question. Duff Cooper, the British Ambassador to Paris, reported (20 October 1944) that de Menthon, the Catholic Resister now Justice minister, had been asked (it was presumed by the Vatican) to draw up a list of bishops for 'épuration'. Upon enquiring at the Vatican, Sir David Osborne, the British emissary to the Holy See had been told that the suggestion was 'preposterous' (report of 23 November 1944). Indeed, 'On the general question, I was given to understand that the Vatican was unlikely to take any initiative since the Pope was satisfied that no French bishop would allow his actions to be dictated by political motives'. This was in accordance with 'the established policy of the political neutrality and abstentionism of the Church'. The Holy See was particularly surprised at the accusations against Mgr Dutoit, whose reputation at Rome was one of 'holding extreme democratic views'.[63] If the Vatican has been correctly reported, this evaluation shows how much it was out of touch with events.

However, in late December 1944 Valerio Valeri was replaced as Nuncio by Cardinal Roncalli (the future Pope John XXIII). Jacques Maritain was proposed as the new Ambassador to the Vatican. Theoretically matters could now move forward once more. Bidault drew up yet another list of some thirty bishops that he still wished removed from their sees.[64] Roncalli clearly held that double figures were impossible — even two or three resignations would be difficult. Rome still sought to temporise, and a settlement remained remote.

By the spring of 1945 the uncertainties of policy were having an effect within France. Laffon, an Interior minisry official concerned with local administration, expressed disquiet to his minister: if things dragged on the clergy might regain some of its lost prestige, the government would lose some of its own, and any further intervention would be impossible.[65] The Commissaire de la République at Angers, a centre of catholicism, reported on 1 February 1945 episcopal disquiet at the lack of progress.towards a resolution of the affair.[66] Latreille noted that, as events began to fade, the episcopacy, backed by the new Nuncio, was now reluctant to countenance any sanctions at all. A fresh list was required, and in possibly only three sees could sufficient evidence be assembled to justify action. Moreover, he noted the question had now become linked to that of subsidies for Catholic education, which would clearly mobilise Catholic electors round the Church. (Incidentally, he urged that, since subsidies were temporarily to be continued, they should be a quarter of that given in the previous year. Unless this happened the bishops would be unable to pay their teachers.)

On 10 April 1945 Tixier, the Interior minister, received Maritain, at last about to take up his appointment, who wished to know what his instructions were regarding the bishops. The minister also commented, after perusing three dossiers on the Bishops of Arras, St Brieuc and Mende, that, judging from the reports of the Commissaires de la République, he might have expected other adverse reports.[67]

Latreille tried another tack in an effort to force a political decision. On 12 December 1945 he declared that a vote in the Assembly on 28 March 1945 against the continuance of subsidies to Catholic schools beyond the end of the school year was likely to mean 'the reappearance of religious struggles in our political life'.[68] Formal negotiations regarding the bishops would now begin in a poisoned atmosphere and would be seen by some as a malevolent attack upon Church rights. Apart from the 'schools question', other religious matters required resolution: the status of the religious orders and their overseas missions; the question of the ownership of Church property; and a fresh religious settlement in Alsace-Lorraine, now restored to France. Tixier responded to the promptings of his two officials.[69] He now wished cases to be pursued only against bishops who had patently collaborated, who had condemned the Resistance, or had treated de Gaulle publicly as 'rebel' or 'traitor'. He named specifically Mgrs Dutoit, Serrand, Auvity, Delay and Marmottin. The Vatican, he hinted, would be wise not to be too negative in its attitude. Subsidies to schools might be abruptly stopped and action taken against unauthorised religious orders. Although nuns of cloistered orders had been massively registered on the new electoral rolls, so much so that their vote could be the determining factor in certain areas, their eligibility to vote could always be questioned.

It was then that de Gaulle decided to intervene; his Private Office took over negotiations with the Nuncio, who had asked the head of government what were the final demands for a 'purge'. De Gaulle submitted the names of five bishops and requested also that neither Mgr Feltin (Bordeaux) nor Mgr Marmottin (Rheims) should be promoted cardinal. (Ironically Feltin nevertheless became Archbishop of Paris in 1949 and received the purple in 1953.)[70] Roncalli agreed to investigate these cases but would not accept that of Mgr Serrand, although he did agree that he should remain out of his diocese for a year, and that an auxiliary bishop should be appointed to assist him.[71]

On 30 May Latreille learnt that the Pope had now agreed to some resignations; names would be communicated to the Foreign Affairs ministry. The question arose as to how the changes could best be effected. The bishops concerned could simply be replaced, or a co-bishop be appointed to carry out their duties, whilst they still retained their title. In this case they would keep their stipend and other emoluments. The Vatican preferred the second solution as being less hurtful to the bishops and more in accordance with public opinion. Latreille favoured replacement as being politically more acceptable, and had already anticipated that the State might be asked to provide pensions.[72] Tixier also plumped for simple replacement[73] but for him there could be no question of any financial payment. Such a proposal would stir up further debate in the Assembly on religious matters: 'Le résultat serait certainement négatif et le dommage moral et politique serait grand'.

Finally, and with the minimum of publicity, on 27 July 1945 the resignations of Dutoit, Auvity and de la Villerabel were made known. Mgr Beaussart gave up his appointment as Auxiliary Bishop of Paris (although later, on the death of Cardinal Suhard, the chapter appointed him *ad interim* Archbishop until a successor was named). Three Apostolic

Vicars overseas also resigned: Vielle (Rabat), Poisson (St Pierre et Miquelon) and Grimaud (Dakar). By then the situation had relaxed considerably and initial demands for a total purge had been toned down.

The reverse of the medal was a fresh list of recommendations for promotion, a definitive 'white list' that again included Mgrs Saliège, Bruno de Solages, Chevrot,[74] Heintz and Théas, as well as, for promotion to archbishoprics, Mgr Blanchet (St Dié), whose attitude was described as having been 'firm and dignified',[75] Mgrs Debray (Meaux), Mathieu (Aire et Dax), and Mgr Terrier (Tarentaise). In the event Saliège was made a cardinal in October 1945, as were later two others not on the list: Mgr Petit de Julleville (Rouen) and Mgr Roques (Rennes).

Thus ended what had been a very uncomfortable period for the French bishops, one that their colleagues in the other occupied countries of Western Europe had not had to undergo, and which stemmed in part because France, unlike those other nations, had enjoyed a theoretical sovereignty throughout the Occupation.

The moral authority of the bishops had suffered because of their attitudes and their incapacity to react. Their *magisterium* had been, to say the least, defective.[76] Extremists, particularly anticlericals, characterised it as pernicious. Christians in the Resistance felt bitter about the way their Christian superiors had treated them. Perhaps for the first time, they had been in contact with Socialists and Communists, and this had modified their view of these traditional bogeymen of the Church. If prelates such as Cardinal Gerlier retained a modest popularity, Mgr Saliège was of course lauded to the skies. The posture adopted by the bulk of the bishops was almost one of injured innocence: they could not see how they had done wrong. In an interview with Jean Verlhac in November 1944[77] Gerlier even accused the Resistance of persecution. They regarded the new regime almost with apprehension, even whilst accepting and even welcoming it. They felt their probity was questioned and noted with alarm the summary justice dispensed at the Liberation. The fate of their fellows who had literally been hounded out of their episcopal palaces — even the very old Mgr Caillot (Grenoble) had only been saved by the intervention of Resister priests — was almost incomprehensible to them.

The Resistance did not accept gladly the outcome of the settlement. Some Catholics were particularly enraged. André Mandouze wrote to Mgr Delay (Marseilles) exhorting him to acknowledge his past errors and admit that, if certain Catholics, priests and laity, had not disobeyed him during the Occupation, few bishops would still be in their posts.[78]

De Gaulle, 'au grand dam de Bidault',[79] was inclined to greater indulgence, realising that the establishment of a peaceable atmosphere was of paramount importance. Thus, in September 1944, in his efforts to reassert the power of the central authority, he had toured the provinces, making a point of meeting not only Salière and Gerlier, but even Feltin; in his native city of Lille he had attended a mass at which Cardinal Liénart officiated, despite the visible coolness between them. In May 1945, at a service to mark the end of the war in Europe, he had been received at the portico of Notre Dame by Cardinal Suhard, whom he had spurned a few months previously. There was thus a partial reconciliation.

Notes

Unless otherwise stated the place of publication is Paris.)

1. See Baudrillart's Preface to (Collective work): *L'Allemagne et les Alliés devant la conscience chrétienne*, 1915.
2. For Baudrillart the present writer is much indebted to P. Christophe, *1939–1940, Les Catholiques devant la guerre*, 1989, pp. 60–90, which is based on a study of the archives.
3. AN F60.1674.
4. At the monthly meeting of the *Académie* on 13 June 1940 Baudrillart was the only member who turned up. See G. and J. Ragache, *La vie quotidienne des écrivains et des artistes sous l'Occupation, 1940–1944*, 1988, p. 21.
5. See Archives de l'Institut Catholique de Paris, MS 6673, 31 October 1940, pp. 207–10, quoted in Christophe, *1939–1940, Les Catholiques*, pp. 159f.
6. 'Choisir, vouloir, obéir', *La Gerbe*, 21 November 1940. Reprinted as a sixteen-page pamphlet and published at Vanves.
7. Christophe, *1939–1940. Les Catholiques*, pp. 80ff.
8. Y. Marchasson, 'Autour du Cardinal Baudrillart', *Actes*: Lyons, pp. 227–36, reports a sampling of Baudrillart's correspondence that substantiates this assertion.
9. A Dio, Lille, Guerre 1939–1945. Annales 8M1.
10. 'Lettre d'un religieux théologien', August 1941, quoted in Christophe, *1939–1940. Les Catholiques*, p. 61.
11. AN F60.1674. Broadcast from Radio Hilversum, quoted in English in [Allied] *News Digest*, 4 November 1942.,
12. AN F60.1674. *News Digest*, 13 August 1942., quoting a report in *Le Nouveau Journal* (Brussels), 8 June 1942.
13. H. Claude, 'L'Evêque, le Maréchal, la Collaboration, 1940–1945', *RHDGM*, [a special issue on 'Collaboration et Résistance dans le Nord et le Pas-de-Calais'], no. 1135, July 1984, pp. 58–61.
14. The text is given in the important contribution by H. Claude, 'La hiérarchie catholique, le gouvernement de Vichy et l'occupant', *Actes*: Lille, pp. 271f.
15. *Le trait d'union*, a German-controlled newsletter, no. 48, 12 January 1941, p. 3, quoted in Claude, 'La hiérarchie catholique'.
16. *Semaine religieuse*, 'Le mot de Monseigneur', (Arras), April 1941, pp. 106f.
17. AD du Nord, Lille, 1W 2279. Report of Commissaire Spécial, Lille, to Prefect, 25 June 1941.

18. Claude, 'La hiérarchie catholique', p. 272.
19. AN 2 AG 74. Letter from Canon Maréchal to Pétain, Arras, 6 April 1941.
20. AN F60.1674, *La Voix du Nord*, no. 27, 18 March 1942.
21. A. Latreille, *De Gaulle, la Libération et l'Eglise catholique*, 1978, p. 50, n.1.
22. A Dio, Lille, Dossier 8 M 1. Document dated 26 October 1944. The issues of the *Semaines religieuses* in question were: no. 35, 22 October 1942; no. 12, 1 April 1943; and no.13, 8 April 1943, relating to the STO and attitudes towards the Germans.
23. AN F1a.3351. Dossier XVI-C-1.
24. AN F1a.3354.
25. J. Duquesne, *Les Catholiques français sous l'occupation*, 1966, p. 439.
26. *Semaine religieuse* (Nancy), 28 September 1941.
27. AN F1a.3351. Letter from Interior ministry to Foreign ministry, Paris, 23 June 1945.
28. AN 72 AJ 1863. 'Note pour M. Hermes', 3 March 1945.
29. Mgr Marmottin declared his support in *Notre Journal*, the periodical of Action Catholique in his diocese. See AN 72 AJ 1863. Report of Agence Paris-Centre, 14 March 1942. Support for the bishop was widespread. The letter quoted was from L— L—, St Gilles par Fismes (Marne), to an unknown correspondent. It passed through the German censorship at Rheims on 16 March 1942. It was typical of many.
30. AN F1a.3355. Report of the Commissaire de la République for the Marne, 18 December 1944.
31. *Semaine religieuse* (Auch), 21 November 1942.
32. AN 2 AG 494. Articles et documents réservés à la presse catholique. Information de l'Etat Français, 27 November 1942.
33. AN F1a.3351. Note from Tixier, Interior minister, to Laffon (ref: 5929/45) and Latreille (ref: 5836/45), 23 April 1945.
34. AN F1a.3351. Extract from a report of the Commissaire de la République, Nancy, 2 November 1945.
35. *Actes*: Grenoble. Intervention of Abbé Loche, pp. 332ff.
36. H. Michel, *Les Courants de pensée de la Résistance*, 1962, p. 345.
37. M. Sicard (Saint-Paulien), *Histoire de la Collaboration*, 1964, p. 535.
38. Robert Aron, *Histoire de la Libération de la France. Juin 1944–Mai 1945*, 1959, pp. 216–19.
39. P. Reynaud, *La France a sauvé l'Europe*, vol. 2, Aix, 1947, p. 541.
40. The visit was the subject of much sarcastic comment by Xavier Vallat on Vichy Radio. See AN F60. 1674. Radio Vichy, 19.30, 9 July 1944. The broadcast was made at a time when de Gaulle was still being treated as of little account by the Americans.
41. Latreille, *De Gaulle*, p. 21, and de Gaulle, *Mémoires de Guerre: Le Salut 1944–1946*, 1959. For a detailed account of the scene see R.L. Bruckberger, *Tu finiras sur l'échafaud*, 1981, pp. 382–91.
42. See A Dio, Lille, 2B1 ACA, 1942–1945. Procès-verbal de l'Assemblée, 18–19 October 1944. 'Pièce annexe A'.
43. Suhard sent a message via Mgr Beaussart to the LVF declaring that mass would be said just as much for the Russians as the French. See R. Tournoux, *Le Royaume d'Otto. France 1939–1945*, 1982, p. 282.
44. H. Umbreit 'Les services d'occupation allemands et les églises chrétiennes en France', *Actes*:: Lille, p. 304.
45. Umbreit, 'Les services d'occupation', p. 307.
46. J. Palomque and B. Plogeon (eds), *Histoire des diocèses de France: Le diocèse de Bordeaux*, by B. Guillemain *et al.*, 1973, p. 253. Feltin is alleged to have hidden from the Germans in June 1940 the flag presented by Napoleon to the Ecole Polytechnique, which he handed back to General de Charme, the school's commanding officer, on 22 June 1945.
47. AN F1a.3351. 'Note', November 1944.
48. 'Se trouve manifestement gênée par le souvenir de la soumission générale [...] maintenue jusqu'au bout, au Maréchal et aux consignes de Vichy.'

49. AN F1a.3351.
50. '[Ce] sont des prêtres extrêmement vénérables, recommandables par la sainteté de leur vie, de leur souci de spiritualité et d'une charité toute évangélique.'
51. H. Lottman, *The People's Anger. Justice and Revenge in post-Liberation France*, London, 1986, pp. 201ff.
52. A Dio, Lille, 2B1, ACA, 1942–1945. Procès-verbal de l'Assemblée, 18–19 October 1944.
53. Lottman, *The People's Anger*, pp. 201ff.
54. Quoted in Ragache and Ragache, *La vie quotidienne*, p. 274.
55. AN F1a.3351. 'Additif' [undated, probably September–October 1944].
56. Latreille, *De Gaulle*, p. 56.
57. A. Latreille, 'Directions de recherche', *Actes*: Grenoble, pp. 361f.
58. AN F1a.3351. Report to Interior minister, 18 December 1944. Reply to telegram of 4 December 1944.
59. Latreille, *De Gaulle*, p. 27.
60. See Archbishop Feltin's Introduction to P. Coulet, *Les Catholiques et la Révolution Nationale*, Toulouse, 1942, pp. 5–6.
61. See Latreille, *Actes*: Grenoble, p. 360.
62. The quotations are from V. Conzemius, *Eglises chrétiennes et totalitarisme national-socialiste*, Louvain, 1969, p. 134.
63. PRO FO. 37142102. Conduct of French ecclesiastical hierarchy during occupation.
64. This is the figure given by P. Novick, *The Resistance versus Vichy. The Purge of Collaboration in Liberated France*, London, 1968, p. 131. See also A. Latreille, 'Les débuts de Mgr Roncalli à la nonciature de Paris. Souvenirs d'un témoin, décembre 1944–août 1945', *Revue de Paris*, August 1963, pp. 66–74. Mgr Lustiger, the present Archbishop of Paris, in *Le Choix de Dieu*, 1987, p. 106, puts the number of bishops at twenty-four, and adds, 'Les évêques français n'ont certes pas collaboré', hinting that de Gaulle was inclined to take a more charitable attitude than his Foreign Minister. A. Mallet, *Pierre Laval*, 1945, vol. 2, p. 166, gives the number as eighteen.
65. AN F1a.3351. 'Note à l'attention de Monsieur le Ministre', Paris, 5 March 1945.
66. AN F1a.3351. 'Note' of Latreille for Tixier, Interior minister, 6 March 1945.
67. AN F1a.3351. Note: 'Epuration des évêques', 10 April 1945.
68. AN F1a. 3351. 'Note d'information: politique religieuse du gouvernement', addressed to the Interior ministry, 12 April 1945.
69. AN F1a.3351. 'Note à M. Laffon (5774/4V) et à M. Latreille (5775/AV)', 23 April 1945..
70. De Gaulle, *Lettres, Notes et Carnets, 8 mai 1945–18 juin 1951*, 1984, pp. 19ff.
71. Lottman, *The People's Anger*, p. 202.
72. AN F1a.3351. Dossier XVIB. Rapports entre le Gouvernement et le Saint-Siège. Document AL/JMB. 'Personnel et confidentiel', Paris, 31 March 1945, entitled, 'Note d'Information pour Monsieur le Ministre'. In the margin of this document someone has written, 'L'Assemblée ne le voterait pas.'
73. AN F1a.3351. Note to M. Laffon (ref: 6976/45) and M. Latreille.
74. Latreille, *De Gaulle*, pp. 29ff.
75. Ibid., p. 61 note.
76. F. Delpech, *Actes*: Grenoble, p. 340.
77. Cited by P. Bolle, *Actes*: Lyons, p. 464.
78. Ibid.
79. E. Fouilloux, 'Eglise catholique et pouvoir(s) à la Libération', reported in *Bulletin*, no. 31, March 1988, of IHTP, Paris, pp. 11f.

-21-

Concluding Remarks

Was Simone Weill correct when, from London in 1942, she declared 'Cette guerre est une guerre des religions?' For her the clash of the Allies and the Germans was 'un drame religieux'.[1] It was certainly a conflict of ideologies: democracy, communism and nazism. The Church saw it in a particular light. Largely disdainful of democracy after its experience under the Third Republic, on both the warring sides it saw elements of a new paganism that might jeopardise its very existence. Faced with the two heathen creeds that threatened to dominate Europe, and abhorring both, Church leaders, Catholic and Protestant, had to set priorities. Only slowly did they realise, as did some of the politicians — not all at Vichy were collaborationist — that the evil on their doorstep was more menacing than that which might sweep down upon them from the Russian steppes and overrun Western Europe.

Spurning both ideologies, the bishops had nevertheless to make choices. Leading Churchmen held no love for the British, who had immediately made common cause with the Russians when the Nazis launched their attack on the USSR; they could not forget what they saw as the Allied betrayal of France in 1940 after the prudent but, as they saw it, ignominious retreat from Dunkirk, and the refusal of Churchill to commit warplanes to help stem the German advance. For them de Gaulle, particularly in view of his previous close connections with Marshal Pétain, having allied himself with the British and, as Dakar and Syria proved, not hesitating to fire on his fellow countrymen, had put himself beyond the pale. The terrible Allied bombings, which brought suffering to innocent civilians, and the onslaughts of the Maquis, which the bishops characterised as terrorism, made them close ranks round Pétain even more. The Resistance they felt to be misguided, or even antipatriotic. Christians that joined it were branded as disloyal to their Church.

On the other hand they felt threatened by extremists at Vichy and out-and-out collaborationists in Paris. In Vichy Maurrassians (who had conveniently forgotten their previous anti-German stance) hobnobbed with former Left-wingers who saw a French form of national socialism as the road to salvation. In Paris Nazi converts, whether formerly of the Right or the Left, flourished, and many were fiercely anticlerical. Again, Church leaders felt themselves under attack. Again they fell back on Pétain.

The reverse of the coin was that the Church was a perpetual thorn in the side of the Germans and their collaborationist allies. Although its leaders certainly preferred an authoritarian regime to the alternative of parliamentary democracy, they undoubtedly detested nazism and rejected fascism.[2] From 1940–1942, during the first phase of the regime, in some respects the Church could be held to have acted as a bulwark against a totalitarian state. It had stood out against certain typical characteristics of any Fascist regime. It was against a State monopoly on a number of issues: the creation of a 'jeunesse unique'; the teaching of a single State-imposed moral and civic programme in the youth movements; the placing of all sports organisations, attempting to include those of the Church, under one organisation; even the implementstion of the principle of corporatism (the imposition of a 'syndicat unique', was only reluctantly accepted by Cardinal Liénart). To those extremists at Vichy who wanted an 'école unique' it had reacted by strengthening the position of its own Catholic school.

The 'second Vichy', as it has been called, was inaugurated in 1942. At what point did Christians begin to feel unease at the course of events? Symptomatic of the belief that it had committed the Church to an overpolitical position was the ACA's injunction already in late 1941 for the clergy not to identify itself too closely with the LFC, which Laval wanted later to use as substitute for a 'parti unique' in order to impose his policies. By March, when the Conseil National met, they became fully aware of the many discordant voices that were now being raised, and realised that the much vaunted Révolution Nationale — the attempt at a counter-revolution which at first had commanded wide support — was in its death throes. The philosophy it embodied, which the Church had shared so enthusiastically in 1940, they now saw as destined never to be implemented. The return of Laval to power the following month strengthened Christian suspicions that the aged Marshal was no longer in absolute charge. Gradually it dawned among the more perceptive that the regime was inexorably on the downward slope to fascism.

Their misgivings were confirmed that summer when the most ferocious phase of the persecution of the Jews was unleashed. The lower clergy and laity saw the attack in humanitarian terms. Such sentiments swayed also Church leaders, although they continued to believe the State faced a 'political problem' as to how to deal with foreign or recently naturalised Jews. The deportation of Jews who had been French for generations may have convinced them otherwise. It certainly stretched loyalty to the utmost. Indeed the mistreatment of the Jews was the hinge on which Christians' duty to the Etat Français turned. The incompatibility between such persecution and Christian doctrine was patent. Thus when Laval in 1943 threatened a further round of denaturalisations principally affecting Jews it was the ACA that deterred him.

External events strengthened their scepticism as to the effectiveness of the regime in preventing France from being swallowed up by Germany. The November invasion of North Africa convinced many that, now the USA had begun to participate actively in the land war, Germany could not win. At best, it could only hope for a compromise peace. Assurances from the Americans that communism would not be allowed to overrun Western Europe were only half-believed, but seemed the better option.

Conscience, according to Cardinal Newman, is the first of all the Vicars of Christ. For many Christians it began to take precedence over all ecclesiastical authority. The ambiguities in the positions of the Church leaders, and disagreements among them, meant that Catholics and Protestants alike were forced to make decisions according to the dictates of their own conscience. For Protestants, with their tradition of independence, this was easier than for Catholics, who had for many years submitted to the *magisterium* of the Church. Yet, as Domenach, of the 'école des cadres' at Uriage, noted, *Quidquid fit contra conscientiam aedificat ad Gehennam* ('Whatever goes against one's conscience helps the building of Hell'). Faced with conflicting advice from their spiritual leaders, or sometimes no guidance at all, or counsel from those 'anonymous theologians' the bishops abhorred, seeing the example set by Christians whom they respected and who had either joined de Gaulle or become part of the internal Resistance, the rank and file, both clergy and laity, had to work out their own salvation.

On this, as on many other matters, it was apparent that there was a generation gap between the more elderly of the higher clergy and the younger parish priests. The latter, more vigorous, and less inclined to knuckle under and accept defeat, largely carried their congregations with them. Their audience was swollen in numbers by the war.

Certainly from 1939 to 1945 religious practice underwent a revival, which was sustained for a few years afterwards, but Cardinal Suhard was well aware of the missionary task that remained to be accomplished. The Mission de France, which he created, marked the beginning of the worker-priest movement which flourished in the immediate post-war years. Younger priests regarded it as a particular challenge to get closer to the everyday life of the working class. At the same time many of the more rigorous practices of the Catholic church, which were irksome to the laity, such as the obligation to fast before Communion, or to 'manger maigre' on Fridays, were set aside because of the circumstances of war.[3] There was an atmosphere of greater religious freedom.

This was reflected in closer contacts between the denominations. The ecumenical movement launched in 1909 only began to take formal shape just before the war. In 1937 Bishop Bell, who attempted to act as an intermediary in peace negotiations during the war, had presided over an ecumenical conference in Oxford that led to the formation of an embryonic World Council of Churches whose President was Archbishop Temple of Canterbury and Vice-President Pastor Boegner. In 1939 a Dutchman, Visser 't Hooft, became its Secretary-General and on the outbreak of war had established a skeleton World Council in Geneva. Pastor Boegner was in touch constantly with 't Hooft throughout the Occupation. The movement included the Eastern Orthodox Church, but not the Uniate Catholic Church. The repercussions of the movement were nevertheless felt among French Roman Catholics.

Adversity is a great unifier, as those in the German prison camps discovered. Amongst POWs of all nationalities there was much denominational mixing. In the concentration camps possibilities for the practice of religion, let alone ecumenicism. were fewer. However, Catholics, Protestants and Communists, men of all creeds and of none, were thrown together, and in many cases found that the differences that divided them were less important than what they shared in common. Dachau, where offending French priests were invariably despatched, also housed Protestant pastors and even Orthodox popes. It became a place of ecumenical brotherhood. It was there that Mgr Piguet, of Clermont-Ferrand, carried out the clandestine ordination of a seminarist, with Protestants actively involved in the preparations for the ceremony.[4]

In the armed Resistance co-operation between Catholics and Protestants was strong. In the Vercors Maquis Pastor Atger and Père de Montcheuil worked in harmony; in the Tarn maquisard Catholics and Protestants fought side by side. In less spectacular activities such as saving the Jews, CIMADE, the Protestant relief organisation collaborated in Amitié Chrétienne, as we have seen, with Père Glasberg. Père Chaillet, the leading light behind the clandestine *Témoignage Chrétien*, had intended to call it *Témoignage Catholique*, but decided to change it at the last moment in order to reflect the ecumenical nature of the periodical — a sticker had even to be placed over the original title. On a national scale Pastor Boegner worked very closely with Cardinal Gerlier, although in Paris Protestant-Catholic relationships were not so warm. Mounier's review *Esprit* had had as contributors notable Catholics such as Lacroix and well known Protestants such as Denis de Rougemont. It was on foundations such as these that Père Yves Congar, a prisoner of war for six years, was to work indefatigably for Christian unity later. The bishops, however, remained largely untouched by ecumenical thinking. Some, in areas where Protestantism was strong, still saw the Reformed church as a rival.

What did the Church gain from the Vichy regime? The answer must be: very little of any lasting consequence. Most of the laws that were passed in its favour were declared null and void at the Liberation (although religious were allowed to continue to teach and the subsidies given Catholic schools set a precedent, so that the Debré Law of 1959, granting aid to Catholic education, was facilitated.) The fiction that the Church could stand outside politics was dispelled. The MRP, which dominated French politics in the immediate post-war years, and which had emerged from the Resistance, was evidence of this. It also showed that the doctrines of social catholicism could have practical political consequences. But the Church did not emerge unscathed. The battle between clericalism and anticlericalism continued, and there was no lasting peace between the parties. (The 'schools question', that political football of the Third Republic, can still excite great passion.) The authority of the Church, particularly its leaders, had been undermined. Measures of even greater severity, however unjustified, would have been taken against the bishops had their comportment not been redeemed by the outstanding part that Christians had played in the Resistance.

Despite those activities, French Catholics and Protestants alike were not fully aware of the influence they could have wielded during the Occupation. Dutch and Danish Christians were much firmer in their opposition to the Germans. It is true that in Poland Catholics had been hunted down mercilessly, but the French Church was better organised and potentially more formidable. The cardinals, and in particular Cardinal Liénart, were men of great stature — as indeed was Pastor Boegner. As the sole surviving national institution after the collapse in 1940, the Church could have asserted itself more vigorously. Why it did not do so is puzzling, but part of the answer may lie in the silence of the Vatican.

Notes

Unless otherwise stated the place of publication is Paris.

1. Simone Weill, *Ecrits de Londres et dernières lettres*, 1957, p. 98 and p. 105.
2. See M. Cointet, *Vichy et le fascisme*, 1987.
3. R. Rémond, 'Le catholicisme français pendant la Seconde Guerre Mondiale', *Revue d'histoire de l'Eglise de France*, vol. 64, 1978, pp. 203–13.
4. Mgr G. Piguet, *Prison et Déportation. Témoignage d'un évêque français*, 1947, pp. 103f.

Appendix I

Before the War: *L'Aube* and the Catholic Intellectual Press

In 1924 Francisque Gay founded the weekly *La Vie catholique*. This left-wing Christian, who before the First World War had been linked to Marc Sangier's *Sillon* movement, sought to unite all shades of Catholic opinion, but encountered resistance from right-wing Catholics sympathetic to *Action Française* and General Castelnau's FNC. He decided therefore in 1932 to publish a political daily, *L'Aube*, and invited Georges Bidault to direct it. Until it closed down after the defeat of 1940, the number of subscribers hardly exceeded 10,000, yet through the movement that grew up around it, the Nouvelles Equipes Françaises (NEF), which lasted barely a year, it exerted a disproportionate influence on public life. This new grouping sought complete independence for the press, the defence of the family and other Christian values — hence in particular an abhorrence of totalitarian extremes — a reform of the parliamentary system, and a rejection by politicians of the Munich mentality. A note of defiance, of Resistance 'avant la lettre', characterised it. Study groups were set up in the provinces. In Rennes under Henri Fréville, as well as in Paris, they were particularly active. Lectures were given by men later active in the Resistance inside and outside France, such as Bidault, Charles d'Aragon and Maurice Schumann (who wrote under the name of André Sidobre). Edmond Michelet, who has some claim to be the first Resister of all, ran the group at Brive.[1]

In the same year as *L'Aube* Mounier began publishing *Esprit*, which, though it professed not to be a Catholic review, was undoubtedly largely the fief of Catholic intellectuals, whilst welcoming outside contributors.

Mounier's Utopian vision is summed up in his 'adaptation' of Maurras's '3 Rs': *Renaissance*, to be conceived of as the assault upon individualism; *Reformation*, to be effected from within a Church thrown open to the world; and *Revolution*, envisaged as an attack on a capitalist system dating back to the Renaissance.[2] Asserting the 'primacy of the spiritual', as opposed to Maurras's 'politique d'abord', Mounier nevertheless found, as the years progressed, that he had to descend into the political arena. From 1934 onwards his political 'engagement', still expressed in terms of 'ni droite ni gauche', became transparent. The attacks he made on nationalism and militarism — while eschewing pacifism — aroused the wrath of the FNC. By the Right he was accused of communism and of anti-Italian sentiment: he had come out against the Ethiopian campaign in 1935. Nor did his repeated assaults on parliamentary government endear him to the Left. On the Spanish Civil War *Esprit*, which first inclined to abstain from taking sides, eventually came down in favour of the Republicans, on the grounds that the Communist danger was less apparent than the threat of fascism.

Other journals of Catholic tendency intended for an elite had also appeared in the pre-war years. In 1926 the condemnation of *Action Française*, much read by many clergy, left a vacuum, which was filled by the launching by a Dominican in 1928 of a new review, *La Vie Intellectuelle*, whose purpose was to remove Catholics from the clutches of the political Right by reminding them that their ultimate vocation was not political at all.

In 1934 another Dominican publication, *Sept*, appeared, the work of a group of Dominican priests operting from the La Tour-Maubourg centre in Paris. It was resolutely anti-Fascist. By 1937 it already printed 50,000 copies and boasted 25,000 subscribers. Yet in August 1937, allegedly because of financial difficulties, it abruptly ceased publication. For the higher clergy, who did not countenance another leftist Catholic journal, it was decidedly overpolitical; hence the edict came from Rome that it should cease publication. The immediate cause was the fact that on 19 January 1937 it had printed an interview given by Léon Blum to Maurice Schumann, and this was deemed inadmissible. Writing shortly after the ban *Esprit* commented: '*Sept*, a Christian journal has been strangled by Christian hatred.'[3] Nothing daunted, a number of distinguished contributors, including Bernanos, Gabriel Marcel, Jacques Maritain, Mauriac and Mounier, gathered round Stanislas Fumet and, making sure that it would not slip into the episcopal net, founded yet another periodical, *Temps Présent*, which, however, in its turn was forbidden in 1943.

Pre-war Catholic periodicals manifested mainly an antitotalitarian bias, with an intelellectual disregard for the views of the Catholic establishment. It is therefore not surprising to find many of the leading lights of this section of the press under Vichy either profoundly hostile to the regime or participating in the Resistance.

Notes

Unless otherwise stated the place of publication is Paris.

1. See F. Mayeur, 'Une Résistance avant la lettre: les Nouvelles Equipes Françaises (NEF)', *Actes:* Lyons, pp. 43–50.
2. M. Winock, *Histoire Politique de la Revue 'Esprit', 1930–1950*, 1975, p. 103.
3. H. Noguères, *Front Populaire, 1935-1938*, 1977, pp. 202–3.

Appendix II

Bishops and Archbishops by Province

As at 1 November 1942

Province of Aix

Aix	Du Bois de la Villerabel (Archbishop)
Ajaccio	Llosa
Digne	Jorcin
Fréjus	Gaudel
Gap	Bonnabel
Marseilles	Delay
Nice	Rémond

Province of Albi

Albi	Moussaron (Archbishop)
Cahors	Chevrier
Mende	Auvity
Perpignan	Bernard
Rodez	Challiol

Province of Algiers

Algiers, Carthage, Constantine, Oran
.

Province of Auch

Auch	Béguin (Archbishop)
Aire	Mathieu
Bayonne	Vansteenberghe
Tarbes and Lourdes	Choquet

Province of Avignon

Avignon	de Llobet (Archbishop)
Montpellier	Brunhes
Nîmes	Girbeau
Valence	Pic
Vivier	Couderc

Province of Besançon

Besançon	Dubourg (Archbishop)
Belley	Maisonobe
Nancy	Fleury
St-Dié	Blanchet
Verdun	Ginisty
Leuce (titular)	Petit (Co-adjutor)

Province of Bordeaux

Bordeaux	Feltin (Archbishop)
Agen	Rodié
Angoulême	Megnin
La Rochelle	Liagre
Luçon	Cazaux
Phaena (titular)	Massé (Auxiliary)
Périgueux	Louis
Poitiers	Mesguen

Province of Bourges

Bourges	Lefebvre (Archbishop)
Clermont	Piguet
Le Puy	Martin
Limoges	Rastouil
St-Flour	Pinson
Tulle	Chassaigne

Province of Cambrai

Cambrai	Chollet (Archbishop)
Acrida (titular)	Guerry (Co-adjutor, Archbishop)
Arras	Dutoit
Lille	Liénart

Province of Chambéry

Chambéry	Durieux (Archbishop)
Annecy	Cesbron
St-Jean de Maurienne	Grumel
Tarentaise	Terrier

Province of Lyons

Lyon	Gerlier (Archbishop)
Ténédos (titular)	Bornet (Auxiliary for St-Etienne)
Autun	Lebrun
Dijon	Sembel
Bilylinis (titular)	Vittoz (Auxiliary)
Langres	Chiron
St-Claude	Faure
Grenoble	Caillot

Province of Paris

Paris	Suhard (Archbishop)
Elitea (titular)	Beaussart (Auxiliry)
Castoria (titular)	Courbe (Auxiliary)
Blois	Audollent
Chartres	Harscouët
Meaux	Debray
Orléans	Courcoux
Versailles	Roland-Gosselin

Province of Rheims

Rheims	Marmottin (Archbishop)
Amiens	Martin
Beauvais	Roeder
Châlons	Tissier
Soissons	Mennechet

Province of Rennes

Rennes	Roques (Archbishop)
Quimper	Duparc Auxiliary: Cogneau, titular bishop of Thabraca
St-Brieuc	Serrand
Vannes	Le Bellec

Province of Rouen

Rouen	Petit de Jullevile (Archbishop)
Bayeux	Picaud
Evreux	Gaudron
Séez	Pasquet

Province of Sens

Sens	Lamy (Archbishop)
Moulins	Jacquin
Nevers	Flynn
Troyes	Le Coudic

Province of Toulouse

Toulouse	Saliège (Archbishop)
Chrysopolis (titular)	de Courrèges d'Uston (Auxiliary)
Carcassonne	Pays
Montauban	Théas
Pamiers	Marceillac

Province of Tours

Tours	Gaillard (Archbishop)
Angers	Costes
Laval	Richaud
Le Mans (Archbishop)	Grente
Jonopolis (titular)	Fouin

No province mentioned [Alsace-Lorraine]

Strasbourg	Ruch
Metz	Heintz

Four bishops.	Antilles and Réunion:

The list, which appears to be incomplete, was published in the *Bulletin du Secrétariat d'Etat à l'Intérieur,* no. 115, 10 November 1942, a copy of which is to be found in AN 2 AG 492, CC72 BC.

Of the eighty-two bishops diocesan of metropolitan France proper that are named, it is striking how few — perhaps some thirty only — appear to have played any noteworthy role during the Vichy period, and perhaps only a score any significant part, despite the large degree of autonomy the bishops enjoyed.

Interestingly, for Alsace-Lorraine, the names of the bishops driven out by the Germans are given in the document, rather than their acting replacements.

Bibliographical Note

The bibliography on the Vichy period is prolific, so much so that it would be otiose to list all the volumes to which reference could be made in writing a history of politics and society in relation to Christianity in France from 1938–45. For the archives that were consulted the reader is referred to the Preface.

For the general history of France between 1938–45 the best overview is by J.-P. Azéma, *De Munich à la Libération, 1938–1944,* Paris, 1979. On the Vichy period R.O. Paxton's *Vichy France. Old Guard and New Order, 1940–1944,* London, 1972, remains a seminal work. Recent outstanding collective works include J.-P. Azéma and F. Bédarida (eds), *Vichy et les Français,* Paris, 1992, and J.-P. Azéma and F. Bédarida (eds), *La France des années noires,* 2 vols., Paris, 1993.

On the part played by Christians — mainly Catholics — during the period the sole work to date that gives a general overview is: J. Duquesne, *Les Catholiques français pendant l'Occupation,* Paris, 1966, slightly revised edition, 1986. On the other hand, there are a number of volumes, extremely rich in material, reporting the proceedings of various colloquia, to which both historians and eyewitnesses contributed. The confrontation between the two protagonists was of singular importance. Details are as follows:

X. de Montclos *et al.*,(eds), *Eglises et chrétiens dans la IIe Guerre mondiale. La région Rhône-Alpes.* (Colloque de Grenoble), Lyon, 1978

[Sous la direction de] Y.-M. Hilaire, *Revue du Nord,* Lille, nos. 237 and 238, April–June, and July–September 1978. (Report of: Colloque de Lille, relating to northern France)

X. de Montclos *et al.*, (eds), *Eglises et chrétiens dans la IIe Guerre mondiale. La France.* (Colloque de Lyon), Lyon, 1982

P. Bolle and J. Godel, (eds), *Spiritualité, théologie et résistance. Yves de Montcheuil, théologien au maquis du Vercors.*(Colloque de Biviers), Grenoble, 1987

For a significant study of one comparatively small locality, relating almost exclusively to Protestants , the reader is referred to:

P. Bolle (ed.), *Le Plateau Vivarais-Lignon. Accueil et Résistance 1939–1944,* (Colloque du Chambon-sur-Lignon), Le Chambon-sur-Lignon, 1992

Select Bibliography

Unless otherwise stated the place of publication is Paris.

Abetz, O., *Pétain et les Allemands*, 1948

Adam, G., *La CFTC, 1940-1958. Histoire politique et idéologique*, 1964

Ageorges, J., *Une histoire et une épopée: l'ACJF de sa fondation à nos jours*, 1942

Alix, R., *La nouvelle jeunesse*, 1930

Amouroux, H., *La grande Histoire des Français sous et après l'Occupation*, 10 vols. 1976–1992

Aron, Robert, *Histoire de la Libération de la France. Juin 1944 – Mai 1945*, 1959

Assemblée générale du protestantisme français, *Les Eglises protestantes pendant la guerre et l'Occupation: Actes, 1945*, Nîmes, 1946

Azéma, J.-P., *1940: L'année terrible*, 1992

—— *De Munich à la Libération, 1939–1944*, 1979

Azéma J.-P.,and Bédarida, F., (eds) *Vichy et les Français*, 1992

Azéma, J.-P., Prost, A., Rioux, J.-P.(eds)., *Le parti communiste français des années sombres, 1938–1941*, 1986

Barthélémy, J., *Ministre de la Justice, Vichy 1941–1943. Mémoires*, 1989

Baud, H.(ed.), *Histoire des Diocèses de France: (Genève), Annecy*, 1985

Baudouin, P., *Neuf mois au gouvernement, avril–décembre 1940*, 1948 (cf *The Private Diaries of Paul Baudouin*, translated by Sir Charles Petrie, London, 1948)

Beauvoir, S. de, *Mémoires d'une jeune fille rangée*, 1958

Bédarida , R. (ed.), [Facsmiles of] *Témoignage Chrétien , 1941–1944*, 2 vols., 1980

Benoit-Guyon, G., *L'Invasion de Paris (1940–1944). Choses vues sous l'Occupation*, 1962

Berstein, S., *Edouard Herriot ou la République en personne*, 1985

Bertin,J.-P., *Le cinéma français sous Vichy: les films français de 1940 à 1944*, 1980

Bidault, G., *D'une Résistance à l'autre*, 1975

Blond, G., *Pétain, 1856–1951*, 1966

Boegner, M., *L'Exigence œcuménique. Souvenirs et perspectives*, 1968

Boegner M., Siegfried A., (eds), *Le Protestantisme français*, 1945

Boegner, P., *Ici on a aimé les Juifs*, 1982

Boulard, F., Achard, A., Emérard, H., *Problèmes missionaires de la France rurale*, 1945

Boulard, F., *Premiers itinéraires en sociologie religieuse*, 1954

Bourderon, R., Avakoumovitch, Y., *Détruire le PCF. Archives de l'Etat Français et de l'occupant hitlérien, 1940–1944*, 1988

Bourdrel, P., *Histoire des Juifs de France*, 1974

Brès, E. and Y., *Un maquis d'antifascistes allemands en France (1942–1944)*, Montpellier, 1987

Bruckberger, R., *Tu finiras sur l'échafaud*, 1981

Cacérès, B., *Histoire de l'Education populaire*, 1964

Chalas, Y., *Vichy et l'imaginaire totaliitaire*, Arles, n.d.

Chambon, A., *Quand la France était occupée 1940–1945*, 1987

Chapsal, J., *La Vie politique en France depuis 1940*, second edition, 1969

Charles-Roux, *Huit Ans au Vatican, 1932–1940*, 1949

Chaudier, A., *Paris-Limoges*, 1980

Chelini, J., *La Ville et L'Eglise*, 1958

Cholvy, G., Hilaire, Y.-M., *Histoire religieuse de la France contemporaine, 1930–1988*, 1988

Christophe, P., *Les Catholiques et le Front Populaire*, 1986

——, *1939–1940: Les Catholiques devant la guerre*, 1989

Cianfarra, C., *La guerre et le Vatican*, 1947

Clavier, H., *The Duty and the Right of Resistance*, Oxford, 1946

Closon, F.L., *Le Temps des Passions. De Jean Moulin à la Libération, 1943–1944*, 1974

Closset, R. *L'Aumônier de l'Enfer. Franz Stock, aumônier de Fresnes, du Cherche-Midi et de la Santé, 1940–1944,* Mulhouse, 1965

Cointet, J.-P., *La Légion française des Combattants: vers le parti unique*, 1991

Cointet, M., *Le Conseil National de Vichy: Vie politique et réforme de l'Etat en régime autoritaire*, 1989

Comte, B., *Une Utopie combattante. L'Ecole des cadres d'Uriage, 1940–1942*, 1991

Conzemius, V., *Eglises chrétiennes et totalitarisme national-socialiste*, Louvain, 1969

Cornec, J., *Laïcité*, 1965

Cottereau J., *L'Eglise et Pétain*, 1946

Crémieux-Brilhac, J.-L., *Les Français de l'An 40. I: La Guerre, Oui ou Non?* 1990

Déat, M., *Mémoires politiques*, 1989

——, *Perspectives socialistes*, 1930

Debré, R., *L'honneur de vivre*, 1974

Délégation française auprès de la Commission allemande d'Armistice en France, Recueil de documents, 1948

Delperrié de Bayac, J., *Histoire du Front Populaire*, 1972

Detrez, L., *Du Sang sur les parvis lillois (1940–1945)*, Lille, 1947

——, *Quand Lille avait faim (1940–1944)*, Lille, 1945

Devailly, G. (ed.), *Histoire des Diocèses de France: Bourges*, 1973

Droulers, P., *Le Père Desbuqois et l'Action Populaire*, 2 vols., 1981

Duclos, P., *Le Vatican et la seconde guerre mondiale. Action doctrinale et diplomatique en faveur de la paix*, 1955

Duquesne, J., *Les Catholiques français sous l'Occupation*, 1966 (new, slightly enlarged, edition,1986)

Durand Y. (ed.), *Histoire des diocèses de France: Nantes*, 1985

Evrard, J., *La déportation des travailleurs français dans le III ᵉReich*, 1972

Fabre-Luce, A., *Journal de la France, 1939–1944*, 2 vols., 1946

Falconi, C., *The Silence of Pius XII*, translated by B. Wall, London, 1970

Faure, C., *Le projet culturel de Vichy. Folklore et Révolution Nationale*, Lyon, 1989

Fessard, G., *Epreuve de Force*, 1939

Gaillac, H., *Les Maisons de Correction, 1830–1945*, 1971

Gard, M, du, *La Chronique de Vichy, 1940-1944*, 1948

Garrone, G.,(ed.), *Le secret d'une vie engagée. Mgr Guerry d'après ses carnets intimes*, 1971

Gaulle, C. de, *War Memoirs, The Call to Honour*, vol. I, 1940–1942, London, 1955

Godin H., Daniel, Y., *La France: Pays de mission*, 1943

Gordon, B., *Collaborationism in France during the Second World War*, Ithaca and London, 1980

Granet, M., *Histoire du réseau de Résistance Cohors-Asturies*, 1971

Griffiths, R., *Marshal Pétain.*, London, 1970

Guerry, Mgr, *L'Eglise catholique en France sous l'Occupation*, 1946

Halls, W.D., *The Youth of Vichy France*, Oxford, 1981

Harcourt, R. d', *Le visage de la jeunesse du IIIᵉReich: l'Evangile de la Force*, 1938

Hellman, J., *The Knight-Monks of Vichy France. Uriage, 1940–1945*, Montreal, 1993

——, *Emmanuel Mounier and the New Catholic Left, 1930–1950*, Toronto, 1981

Hervet, R., *Les Compagnons de France*, 1965

Hildesheimer, F. (ed.), *Histoire des diocèses de France: Nice et Monaco*, 1984

Hoog, G., *Histoire du catholicisme social en France, 1891–1931*, 1942

Hoover Institution, *France during the German Occupation, 1940–1944*, Stanford, 1958

Irving, R., *Christian Democracy in France*, London, 1973

Jäckel, E., *Frankreich in Hitlers Europa*, Stuttgart, 1966

Jarry, E., Palanque J.R. (eds.),*Histoire des diocèses de France:: Grenoble*, 1981

Joubrel, H. and F., *L'Enfance du Coupable*, 1946

Joutard, P., Poujol J., Cabanel, P., *Cévennes, Terre de refuge, 1940–1944*, Montpellier, 1987

Kedward, H.R., *Resistance in Vichy France*, 1978

Kuisel, R., *Capitalism and the Rise of the Modern State in France*, Cambridge,1981

Labarthète, H. Du Moulin de, *Le temps des illusions*, Geneva, 1946

Laloum, J., *La France antisémite de Darquier de Pellepoix*, 1979

Lambert, R.-R., *Carnet d'un Témoin, 1940-1943*, 1985

Lambert, Y., *Dieu change en Bretagne. La religion à Limerzel de 1900 à nos jours*, 1985

Latreille, A., *De Gaulle, la Libération et l'Eglise catholique*, 1978

Latreille, A., et al., *Histoire du catholicisme en France*, vol. 3. *La période contemporaine*, Book VII, edited by R. Rémond

Laubier, P. de, *La Pensée sociale de l'Eglise catholique*, Fribourg, 1984

Launay, J. de, *La France de Pétain*, 1972

Le Bras, G., *L'Eglise et le Village*, 1976

——, *Introduction à l'histoire de la pratique religieuse en France*, 1942

Lebrun, F., *Histoire des Catholiques en France du XVe siècle à nos jours*, Toulouse, 1980

Léonard, E., *Le Protestant français*, 1953

Lestringant, P.,*Visage du Protestantisme français*, Tournon (Ardèche), 1959

Limagne, P.,*Ephémérides de quatre années tragiques,* 2 vols., 1987

——, *Journaliste sous trois Républiques*, 1983

Lottman, H.,*The People's Anger. Justice and Revenge in post-Liberation France*, London, 1986

——,*Pétain. Hero or Traitor?*, London, 1985

——,*The Left Bank: Writers in Paris from Popular Front to Cold War*, London, 1982

Lubac, H. de, *Résistance chrétienne à l'antisémitisme. Souvenirs 1940–1944*, 1988

Lustiger, Mgr, *Le Choix de Dieu*, 1987

Mallet, A., *Pierre Laval*, 2 vols., 1955

Marcel G., Fessard, G., *Correspondance*, 1985

Marrus M., Paxton, R., *Vichy France and the Jews*, New York, 1981

Martin du Gard, M., *La Chronique de Vichy, 1940–1944*, 1948

Mayeur, F.,*L'Aube (1932–1940). Etude d'un journal d'opinion*, 1966

Mayeur, J.-M., *Catholicisme social et démocratie chrétienne*, 1986

——, *Lenten Letters of the French Bishops (Repertory, 1861–1959)*, Strasbourg, 1981

Mehl, R., *Le pasteur Marc Boegner. Une humble grandeur*, 1987

Mendras, H., *Etudes de sociologie rurale.Novis et Virgin*, 1953

——, *La fin des paysans*, 1967

Michel, A.R., *La JEC face au nazisme et à Vichy*, Lille, 1988

Michel, H., *Paris Allemand*, 1981

——, *Les Courants de pensée de la Résistance*, 1962

Michelet, E., *De la fidélité en politique*, 1949

Miller, G.,*Les pousse-au-jouir du Maréchal Pétain*, 1975

Mitchell, B.R.,(ed.), *European Historical Statistics, 1750–1975*, London, 1981

Mours, S., *Les Eglises réformées en France (tableaux et cartes)*, Strasbourg, 1958

Nicolle, P., *Cinquante mois d'armistice. Vichy, 2 juillet 1940–26 août 1944. Journal d'un témoin.*, 1947

Noguères, H., *Front Populaire, 1935–1938*, 1977

Novick, P.,*The Resistance versus Vichy. The Purge of Collaboration in Liberated France*, London, 1968

Ory, P., *Les Collaborateurs, 1939-1945*, 1976

Paillat, C., *L'Occupation. Le pillage de la France, juin 1940–novembre 1942*, 1987

Palanque, R.,(ed.), *Histoire des diocèses de France* , 1971

Pérouas, L., *Refus d'une religion, Religion d'un refus en Limousin rural, 1880–1940*, 1985

Pertinax, *Les Fossoyeurs*, New York, 1953

Pétain, P., *Le procès du Maréchal Pétain*, 1945

Pierrard, P., *Juifs et Catholiques français. De Drumont à Jules Isaac*, 1970

Piguet, Mgr G., *Prison et Déportation. Témoignage d'un évêque français*, 1947

Poulat, E.,*Une Eglise ébranlée* ,1980

——,*Naissance des prêtres-ouvriers*, Tournai, 1965

Pucheu, P., *Ma Vie*, 1948

Pury, R. de, *Journal from my cell (Journal de cellule)*, translated by B. Mussey, London, 1948

Ragache, G. and J.,*La vie quotidienne des écrivains et des artistes sous l'Occupation 1940–1944*, 1988

Rauch, R., *Politics and belief in contemporary France. Emmanuel Mounier and Christian democracy*, The Hague, 1972

Raymond-Laurent, R., *Le parti démocrate populaire,1924–1944.*, 1986

Rebatet, L.,*Les Mémoires d'un fasciste*, vol. 2, *1941–1947,* 1976

——, *Les Décombres*, 1942

Reynaud, P., *La France a sauvé l'Europe*, Aix, 1947

Riquet, M., *Chrétiens de France dans l'Europe enchaînée*, 1972

Rollet, H., *Sur le Chantier social. L'action sociale des catholiques en France, 1870–1940*, 1955

Schmid, C., *Erinnerungen*, Frankfurt, 1979

Schoenbrun, D., *Maquis. Soldiers of the Night. The Story of the French Resistance*, London, 1981

Schor, R., *Mgr Rémond, 1873–1963,* Nice, 1984

Sernaclens, P. de., *Le mouvement* Esprit, *1932–1943,* Lausanne, 1974

Sicard M., (Saint-Paulien), *Histoire de la collaboration,* 1964

Simonnot, P., *Le Secret de l'Armistice 1940,* 1989

Suhard, Cardinal, *Vers une Eglise en état de mission,* 1968

Sweets, J.F., *Choices in Vichy France. The French under Nazi Occupation,* New York, 1986

Thorez, J., *Mémoires. Dans la bataille clandestine.* Part I, *1940–1942,* 1970

Tournoux, R., *Le Royaume d'Otto. France 1939–1945,* 1982

Umbreit, H., *Der Militärbefehlshaber in Frankreich, 1940–1944,* Boppard, 1968

Vallat, X., *Le Grain de Sable de Cromwell. Souvenirs d'un homme de droite,* 1972

Vanino, J., *De Réthondes à l'Ile d'Yeu,* 1952

Vigneron, P., *Histoire des crises du clergé français contemporain,* 1976

Weber, E., *Action Française. Royalism and Reaction in Twentieth Century France,* Stanford, 1962

Weill, S., *Ecrits de Londres et dernières lettres,* 1957

Wellers, G., *L'étoile jaune à l'heure de Vichy,* 1979

Winock, M., *Histoire politique de la revue 'Esprit', 1930–1950,* 1975

Index